THE PATH TO EUROPEAN ECONOMIC AND MONETARY UNION

THE PATH TO EUROPEAN ECONOMIC AND MONETARY UNION

by

Scheherazade S. Rehman
The George Washington University

SPRINGER SCIENCE+BUSINESS MEDIA, LLC

Library of Congress Cataloging-in-Publication Data
Rehman, Scheherazade S.
The path to European economic and monetary union / by Scheherazade S. Rehman.
p. cm.
Includes bibliographical references and index.
ISBN 978-0-7923-9951-3 ISBN 978-94-011-5358-4 (eBook)
DOI 10.1007/978-94-011-5358-4
1. European Monetary System (Organization) 2. European currency unit. 3. Monetary policy--European Union countries. I. Title.
HG925.R44 1997
337.1'42--dc21 97-17513
CIP

Originally published by Kluwer Academic Publishers in 1997

Printed on acid-free paper.

TABLE OF CONTENTS

ACKNOWLEDGEMENTS

I dedicate this book to my parents, Zarina and Khalil, whose ever-present love and support made this possible.

I would like to thank Sir Alan Walters for his continuous support, humour and patience over the last seven years.

I owe a tremendous debt of gratitude to Professor Geza P. Lauter whose support has been indispensable over the last eight years and whose advice was invaluable over the course of this project.

The following individuals' editing assistance, research and technical support was extremely helpful in putting this book together: Bulent Ozbilgin (World Bank); Levent Ozbilgin (MBA candidate, George Washington University); Gokhan Akinci (PhD candidate, George Washington University) who researched and wrote part of Chapter V, particularly the sections on the structure and management of the ECB and the EMI; Mehmet Özkaya (PhD candidate, George Washington University) who researched and wrote part of Chapter IV, in particular, the section on the costs and benefits of a single currency; Milana Wojna and Rakibe Musal (both MBA candidates, George Washington University).

I would also like to thank the George Washington University, the School of Business and Public Management and the International Business Department for the support that I have received over the years. In particular, I am indebted to Professor Hossein Askari for his advice and Dean David Fowler for his support and encouragement.

I also want to express my gratitude to members of the EU Commission, OECD, EBRD, EU central bank and finance ministry officials, particularly in Germany, the U.K., France and Belgium, who assisted my research in a number of different ways.

Lastly, but not least, I would like to thank my friends who constantly asked "is it done yet?"

ACRONYMS

BENELUX	- Belgium, Netherlands and Luxembourg (customs union)
CAP	- Common Agricultural Policy
CDU	- Christian Democratic Union (FRG)
CEE	- Central and East European (nations)
CFSP	- Common Foreign and Security Policy
CIS	- Commonwealth of Independent States (former-USSR)
DM	- German mark
EAEC	- European Atomic Energy Community (EURATOM)
EBRD	- European Bank for Reconstruction and Development (World Bank)
EC	- European Community (ECSC, EEC AND EURATOM after fusion);
ECB	- European Central Bank
ECSC	- European Coal and Steel Community
ECU (Ecu)	- European Currency Unit
EEA	- European Economic Area (formerly European Economic Space, EC and EFTA)
EEC	- European Economic Community
EFTA	- European Free Trade Association
EIB	- European Investment Bank
EMA	- European Monetary Agreement
EMCF	- European Monetary Cooperation Fund
EMI	- European Monetary Institute
EMS	- European Monetary System
EMU	- Economic and Monetary Union
EPU	- European Payments Union (OEEC)

ERDF	- European Regional Development Fund (FEDER in French)
ESCB	- European System of Central Banks (EC)
EU	- European Union (EC, CFSP and Home Affairs and Justice Policy)
FFR	- French franc
FTA	- Free Trade Area
FSU	- Former-Soviet Union
G-7	- Seven most industrialized nations (Canada, France, Federal Republic of Germany, Italy, Japan, United Kingdom, United States of America)
GATT	- General Agreement on Tariffs and Trade
GDP	- Gross domestic product
GDR	- German Democratic Republic
GNP	- Gross national product
IGC	- EU Intergovernmental Conferences
IMF	- International Monetary Fund
NAFTA	- North Atlantic Free Trade Area
NATO	- North Atlantic Treaty Organization (Atlantic Alliance)
OECD	- Organization or Economic Cooperation and Development (formerly OEEC)
OEEC	- Organization for European Economic Cooperation
p.a.	- Per annum, yearly
SDP	- Social Democratic Party
SDR	- Special Drawing Rights
SEA	- Single European Act
TARGET	- Trans-European Automated Real-Time Gross Settlement Express Transfer System
TEU	- Treaty of European Union (Maastricht Treaty)
TRIPS	- Trade-Related Intellectual Property rights (GATT)
UK	- United Kingdom
Union	- Several connotations, especially "European Union" (as of November 1993)
US	- United States
USSR	- Union of Soviet Socialist Republics (Soviet Union)
VAT	- Value-added tax
WTO	- World Trade Organization
WW1	- First World War
WW2	- Second World War

FOREWORD

Sir Alan Walters

ex-chief economic advisor to PM Margaret Thatcher

Whether it succeeds or fails, Europe is everyone's concern. The idea of a united Europe has been entertained, even partially at least, achieved, inter alia, Charlemagne, Napoleon, Hitler, and in our day by Spaak, Monet and Chancellor Kohl: the first three by military conquest, the last three by "negotiation" and the creation of integrating institutional arrangements. The motives varied from the twisted paranoia of the Nazis to the idealism of Spaak/Monet/Kohl in avoiding conflicts and wars.

Under the protection of NATO the European Coal and Steel Community soon was transformed into the EEC by the 1957 Treaty of Rome. The massive reduction of trade barriers, particularly between France and Germany, was rewarded by vigorous growth over the next 15 years. Even as late as 1972, when Britain acceeded to the Treaty of Rome, the EEC was thought to be largely a customs union: in de Gaulle eyes the EEC was simply a collection of sovereign states who cooperated primarily on trade. Each state however enjoyed a veto; decisions had to be unanimous.

But in the decade of the 1980s, a profound change began. The Rome treaty was interpreted as a license for the considerable surrender of sovereignty - over economic and social and even security policy - to the central government of what became the European Union. The directives and regulations of the European Union overrode national law and the supreme court of all the states was the European Court of Justice.

The integration of the once sovereign states of Europe into one United States of Europe has been pursued most successfully in the sphere of economic policy. The ultimate aim is to have first a monetary union and then a single currency, the euro.

This is a complex and, to the uninitiated, a confusing story. Only the insider will be able to appreciate the prodigious efforts of Dr. Rehman in not merely telling the story in an accessible way but also analysing the play of political and economic power that determined the outcome.

There are many books on this subject. Yet I suggest that none have the comprehensive and detailed analytical content of Dr. Rehman's text. It is encyclopeadic in its coverage, sophisticated in dealing with the political power-plays, and lucid in its explanations. One can be content with it as the best source book ever issued on this subject. She has managed to bring it right up to date, and with hints of prophesy she almost takes us into the future.

This will not be the last word on this subject; but it is certainly the last word for now.

I OVERVIEW OF EUROPEAN MONETARY INTEGRATION

THE EVOLUTION OF THE EUROPEAN UNION (EU)

Post-World War II events provided the motivation for European integration: America offered hope and support while the Soviet Union exerted pressure and generated fear. In the end, hope conquered fear.

The idea of a community of Western European nations is an old humanist-pacifist dream that was repeatedly destroyed by the conflicts that brought so much pain and suffering to the European Continent during the last two centuries. It took an almost total collapse of the warring nations at the end of World War II to give new impetus to this dream, at least on the Western side of the political divide. Today the European Union (EU) is comprised of 15 member states about to fully integrate.

To understand the process of integration, it is important to recognize the relationship of economic cycles to the integration process as this relationship influences the depth and speed of integration. This is particularly important in the EU economic and monetary union (EMU) integration process. Figure 1.1 illustrates this relationship over a period of 36 years.

The idea of integration goes back 50 years to Winston Churchill's speech on the "United States of Europe" in 1946. Churchill was followed by U.S. Secretary of State George Marshall, who, through the Marshall Plan, extended a helping hand to the

Figure 1.1
The Relationship Between EU Economic Cycles and the Integration Process
(EU's real GDP percentage change from a year earlier)

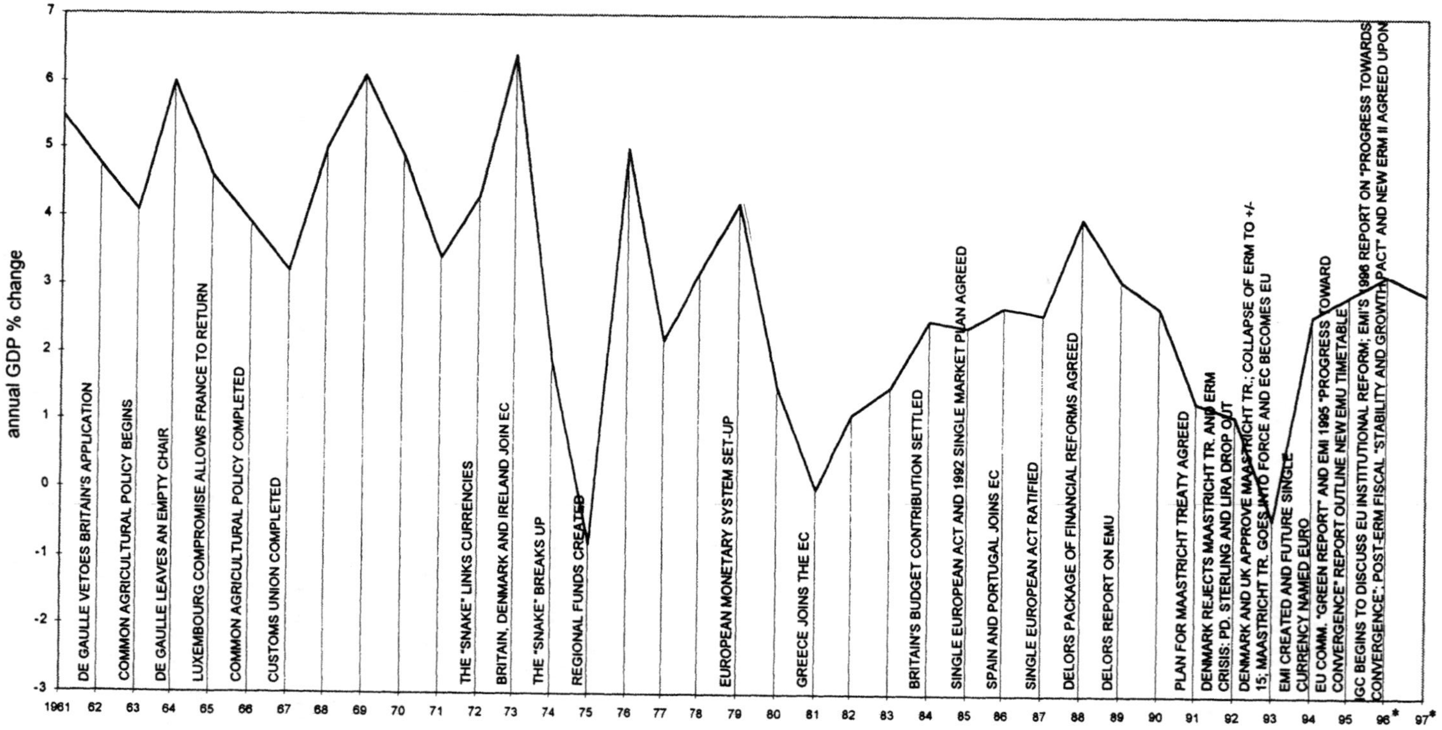

* = estimates.

Source: Data collected from the OECD, Financial Times, The Economist and the EU Commission European Economy, Annual Report, 1995.

war torn European nations to rebuild their economies. Through these two speeches the idea of European economic and political cooperation and eventual integration began to take shape. The institutional foundations were established by Jean Monnet and Robert Schuman, two visionary French statesman, together with other such notable Europeans as Altiero Spinelli, the Italian federalist, and Konrad Adenauer, the German Chancellor.

In April 1948 the Organization for European Economic Cooperation (OEEC) was formed by 16 European states. In May 1950 the French Foreign Minister Robert Schuman, inspired by Jean Monnet, announced that France, together with the Federal Republic of Germany and any other Western European country wishing to do so, was pooling its coal and steel resources under a joint authority--the European Coal and Steel Community (ECSC). The ECSC Treaty of 1951 integrated the coal and steel resources of Belgium, the Netherlands, Luxembourg, Italy and, most important, of the age-old adversaries France and Germany. Thus, Germany's political and economic reintegration into Europe became institutionalized. This trend was reinforced by the October 1954 Treaty on the Western European Union (WEU) which was an attempt to create common defense policies.

In June 1955 the foreign ministers of the ECSC member states met in Messina, Italy, and agreed to extend integration to all branches of their economies. Thus, the ECSC was followed by the European Economic Community (EEC) and the Atomic Energy Community (EURATOM), established in Rome in March 1957. The Treaties of Rome, along with the ECSC Treaty of Paris, thus established three communities: the ECSC, the EEC and EURATOM. The EEC and the EURATOM institutions were set up in Brussels and began work in January 1958. The first step towards integration was the gradual elimination of customs duties among member states and the establishment of common external tariffs in January 1959. In 1979, the European Monetary System (EMS) with its semi-pegged Exchange Rate Mechanism (ERM) was founded. This was followed by the establishment of the integrated "Single Market" on January 1, 1993.

In December 1991 at Maastricht, member nations agreed on the Treaty on the European Union (EU), which became informally known as the "Maastricht Treaty". After a lengthy ratification process, the Treaty came into force on November 1, 1993. It officially adopted the name the European Community (EC) (consisting of the EEC, EURATOM and ECSC) which became the first pillar of the newly created European Union (EU). It also established a Common Foreign and Security Policy (CFSP) and a Home Affairs and Justice Policy which serve as the other two pillars. Moreover, as part of the first pillar the Maastricht Treaty also called for an European Economic and Monetary Union (EMU) which entails the creation of the European Central Bank (ECB) and the European single currency, the Euro, by 1999. It also formalized a set of monetary and fiscal convergence criteria that serve as a precondition of joining the EMU.

Appendix A provides a detailed chronological summary of the events leading to the formation of the EU. Also see Annex I-1 for a summary of the EU institutional structure.

THE HISTORY OF EUROPEAN MONETARY INTEGRATION

The European Payments Union (EPU)

The post-World War I era was marked by international financial policy errors such as the 1920s floating exchange rate system and the subsequent competitive devaluations of the 1930s. To avoid similar problems following World War II, under the 1944 Bretton Woods Agreements a fixed exchange rate system was created with the International Monetary Fund (IMF) as the primary caretaker of the global financial system. The signatories agreed to make their currencies convertible so as to promote a multilateral trade regime. For the first 15 years, however, parts of the agreements remained dormant owing to the post-war economic reconstruction efforts, the dominance of domestic transactions and the use of controls on trade and payments, together with limited coordination of macroeconomic policies.

The absence of a working international financial system constrained the development of trade during the late 1940s. Thus, it was primarily conducted through bilateral arrangements supported by credit lines which, when exceeded, were settled in gold. This created problems, particularly in Europe where more than 200 bilateral trade agreements impeded the management of bilateral balances because of a lack of formal compensation schemes or foreign exchange markets. European currencies were not convertible; as a consequence, nations could not offset deficits and surpluses through multilateral clearing operations.

The problem was compounded by the "dollar gap." The European countries were experiencing serious difficulties with their balance of payments because demand for imports, especially from America, far exceeded exports. Most governments tried to preserve their depleted gold stocks by using quotas and tariffs to avoid payment settlements. This problem proved difficult to correct. Nations attempted to achieve unilateral currency convertibility by making their currency tantamount to the U.S. dollar, but this compelled others to earn bilateral surpluses, thereby further aggravating balance of payments difficulties. The ensuing dilemma was illustrated by the U.K.'s failed 1947-attempt to reestablish convertibility. Despite an extraordinarily large credit of US$5 billion, the pound sterling maintained its convertibility for seven weeks only.

A devaluation of the European currencies to manage the "dollar gap" was not possible for two reasons. First, the problem was structural, caused by the low elasticity of import demand and export supply during the post-war years. Thus, currency depreciations did not significantly affect the trade balances. Second, major currency devaluations resulted in a significant J-curve[1] effect.

---

[1] The J-curve effect describes the time lag involved in a real currency depreciation improving the current account balance. If export and import demand adjust gradually to real exchange-rate changes, the current account may follow a J-curve pattern after a real currency depreciation, first worsening and then improving. If such a J-curve exists, currency depreciation may have a

It was difficult for European countries to establish unilateral convertibility against the U.S. dollar and thus it soon became clear that the restoration of convertibility required a joint effort. Under U.S. leadership, the seeds of the first monetary cooperation efforts were sown through the creation of the Organization for European Economic Cooperation (OEEC) in 1948, later renamed the OECD.[2] However, despite the 1948-52 Marshall Plan, which provided a brief reprieve for the intra-European payments system by easing the "dollar gap," the OEEC failed to correct the growing problem which by the late 1940s had resulted in payment bottlenecks. To deal with the difficulties, the 15-member European Payments Union (EPU) was established by the OEEC member countries in the fall of 1950.[3]

Owing in part to the size of the pound sterling and French franc trade zones, the EPU covered an area that accounted for approximately 70 percent of world trade. Under its rules, bilateral deficits and surpluses of member central banks were offset on a monthly basis to determine overall net positions in the EPU.[4] Nations had only a single EPU settlement at the end of the month; they did not have to clear with their trading partners. However, the positions had to be settled in a complex manner, combining convertible currency, dollars, gold, credits and loans. Credit quotas varied from country to country with the largest, slightly over US$1 billion, assigned to the U.K. and the sterling area,[5] followed by France, with a US$520 million quota.

Of the many problems the EPU faced, the German crisis of 1950-51 was the most important. The Federal Republic of Germany was experiencing large current account deficits which were in excess of its quota, and this, coupled with low reserves, meant that the government could not settle its deficits in gold. The nation's quota was relatively small (US$320 million) compared with that of the other member nations and thus it soon became clear that unless some action was taken the country would have to drop out of the system. Through a coordinated EPU effort prescribing tight domestic monetary policy, the granting of a special credit of US$120 million and the reduction of imports, the crisis was avoided. This was an important event because from this point onward EPU member countries readily accepted interference by their partners in domestic economic policies. Other developments reinforced this trend. For example, France, the U.K. and the Netherlands, because of increasing inflation caused by the Korean War and a deterioration of their terms of trade, generated trade deficits that exceeded their quotas, had to apply the prescribed corrective policy measures to receive

---

contractionary initial effect on output.

[2] The OEEC was expanded and renamed the Organization for Economic Cooperation and Development (OECD) in 1960.

[3] The EPU agreement was signed on September 19, 1950 and implemented retroactively as of July 1, 1950.

[4] The Bank of International Settlements (BIS) - 21st Annual Report, Basle: BIS, June 11, 1951, p.226.

[5] The sterling bloc extended beyond the British Empire and encompassed Scandinavia, Egypt, Argentina and a number of Middle Eastern countries such as Persia (Iran) and Iraq.

assistance from the EPU. The acceptance of such measures was significant, as it laid the foundation for future monetary cooperation and integration.

But the EPU proved unable to apply corrective pressure to the emerging surplus countries such as Germany.[6] This asymmetrical feature not only reappeared in the EMS established 30 years later but continues to plague the current EU and global monetary system. However, it should be noted that this asymmetry was an important factor in the success of the EMS. While the countries affected by higher inflation had to take corrective action, the Bundesbank was able to continue its stability-oriented policies. During the second half of the 1950s, owing to EPU policies, a significant increase in international official borrowing, lending and the liberalization of trade, the "dollar gap" was eventually reduced. The European nations made their currencies convertible and removed foreign exchange controls to achieve a more flexible economic policy formulation process. The successful eight-year EPU arrangement was ended by mutual agreement in 1958.[7]

The importance of the EPU cannot be overstated. It not only furnished the post-World War II world with a system that allowed trade to continue unhampered but it also served as a model for the establishment and functioning of an international monetary system and regional institutions. More specifically, the EPU contributed to European monetary integration through the effective first-time application of a system of multilateral surveillance of national economies. As has been mentioned, this eventually developed into monetary policy coordination.

The EPU was replaced by the European Monetary Arrangement (EMA) which had been negotiated as a successor as early as 1955. The EMA provided US$600 million for economic reconstruction projects and called for close monetary cooperation among all OEEC countries. However, unlike the EPU, the EMA had no influence over policy adjustments because this task was handed over to the IMF's Executive Board.

The dissolution of the EPU set the tone for the 1960s. Despite the signing of the Treaties of Rome in 1957, which established the EEC,[8] no major steps were taken to enhance European economic and monetary cooperation. The (EEC) Treaty contained only two rather brief sections on economic policy and balance of payments coordination, and two relatively indefinite and weak Articles (104/105) with regard to monetary policy coordination. The following excerpt from Article 104 illustrates the treatment of monetary issues: "...each member state shall pursue the economic policies

[6] After the 1950-51 crisis, Germany, except for 1979-81, had an almost uninterrupted series of current account surpluses until 1990.

[7] Over a period of eight years, the EPU's net aggregate balances amounted to approximately US$15.5 billion.

[8] The six member nations had signed the Treaty of Paris, establishing the ECSC in April 1951 (ratified in 1952). The Treaties of Rome were signed by Belgium, France, the Federal Republic of Germany, Italy, Luxembourg and the Netherlands. It not only established the EEC but also created the EIB and the European Atomic Energy Community (EURATOM).

necessary to maintain an equilibrium in the overall balance of payments position and confidence in its currency, while at the same time maintaining a high level of employment and stable prices...." And although the Treaty was explicit[9] in emphasizing that policy coordination and exchange rate policies by member nations were of "common European concern," the IMF's de facto dominance in these two areas made this provision irrelevant.

While the EEC Treaty did not further monetary integration, it called for the establishment of a Monetary Committee comprised of 14 representatives: two from each member nation (one each from the central banks and ministries of finance) and two from the EEC Commission. The Committee eventually developed into the Council of Economic and Finance Ministers (ECOFIN).

The Bretton Woods Agreements

Although the Bretton Woods Agreements were signed in July 1944, they became fully operational only in 1958-59, following the reestablishment of currency convertibility in the major industrialized nations. The agreements created a fixed exchange rate system in which all currencies were pegged to the U.S. dollar and, in turn, through the U.S. dollar at $35 an ounce, to gold. Managed by the IMF, the system allowed currencies to fluctuate only +/-1 percent against their central dollar parities. Nations could change these parities only if their balance of payments was in fundamental disequilibrium. Intra-European exchange rates could fluctuate up to 4 percent. Eventually, however, the European governments decided to restrict movements against the dollar to +/-0.75 percent so as to limit fluctuations among their currencies to a maximum of 3 percent.

In retrospect, the Bretton Woods Agreements had a detrimental effect on the furthering of European monetary integration as they called for monetary sovereignty to be partially handed over to the IMF. Thus, uncoordinated national monetary policies prevailed during the 1960s which delayed the European monetary integration process. Nonetheless, during the same decade steps were taken to promote integration through, for example, the Customs Union and the establishment of the Common Agricultural Policy (CAP) within the EEC.

The early 1960s were marked by the formation of numerous EEC committees, such as the Committee for Conjunctural Policy in 1960, the Committees for Medium-term Economic Policy and Budgetary Policy in 1964,[10] and the Committee of

---

[9] Paragraphs 103 and 107 of the EEC Treaty of Rome, 1957.

[10] As part of the 1974 drive toward better coordination, the Committees for Conjunctural Policy, Medium-term Economic Policy and Budgetary Policy were consolidated into the Economic Policy Committee.

Governors of EEC Central Banks, also in 1964.[11] Yet macroeconomic cooperation[12] was not successful. But this was not a major issue because Europe was enjoying a period of low unemployment and relatively stable prices. Moreover, when compared with the 1990s, the level of economic integration was relatively limited. For example, the ratio of intra-EEC trade to the common GDP was approximately 6 percent in 1960, 12 percent in 1975 and 15 percent in 1992. Hence, there was little need for strong intervention. But had unemployment and/or inflation increased, the need for intervention would have quickly arisen.

The dominant monetary issue during the 1960s was the impact of exchange rate adjustments on the EEC Customs Union in general and on the CAP[13] in particular.

European Monetary Integration Plans

The second half of the 1960s was a period of change for the EC[14] as the economies of the member nations were beginning to diverge. French economic conditions forced a franc devaluation while the continued German balance of payments surplus called for a Deutsche mark revaluation. Moreover, the six-member Community was on the verge of expanding; the admission of new members became a policy priority. Thus, it became necessary to increase efforts at "deepening" both monetary and non-monetary coordination. Such moves were politically sensitive because they included the transfer of some national sovereignty to the common institutions in Brussels. Nonetheless, the transfers became feasible. The six member nations had achieved the Customs Union in 1968 as stipulated under the Treaty of Rome. Their economies were well integrated, as approximately half of their trade was conducted with each other. The CAP created an atmosphere conducive to monetary integration because it relied upon stable (i.e., semi-pegged) exchange rates. Moreover, the EC had become one of the world's most important trading areas and held significant gold and convertible currency reserves. As a result, France argued that the EC should obtain a "common international monetary personality" in the form of an economic and monetary union with a single currency.

By 1968 the industrialized world had experienced a full decade of relatively

---

[11] Although the Committee of Central Bankers gained influence in the 1970s, it was not until the 1980s that it began to play a major role in policy formulation.

[12] The calm 1960s were disturbed by the 1967 pound sterling crisis which had resulted in an approximately 15 percent devaluation of that currency. In 1969, the French franc was devalued by 11.1 percent and the Deutsche mark was revalued.

[13] The CAP was influenced by exchange rate adjustments through the pegging of agricultural product prices to the common monetary unit called the European Currency Account (ECA), and later through the system of Monetary Compensatory Accounts (MCAs). The ECA was linked to the U.S. dollar as well as to gold and later was transformed into the European currency unit (Ecu).

[14] By the late 1960s the EEC together with the other two communities was informally renamed the European Community (EC). The new name was officially adopted by the Maastricht Treaty signed in 1992.

stable exchange rates, and thus a European economic and monetary union was no longer considered an impossibility. The idea was formally accepted at the end of 1969 when, at the December 1-2 European Council Summit at The Hague, the six founding members of the EEC[15] agreed to move toward an economic and monetary union. It should be noted that The Hague Summit also planned the admission of new members while calling for the establishment of such an economic and monetary union -- an early illustration of the "widening" and "deepening" dilemma of the 1990s. By 1969 several proposals, such as the Schiller Plan, the First and Second Barre Reports and the First and Second Werner Reports were under consideration.

The Schiller Plan

The 1969 Schiller Plan, named after the German Minister of Economics Karl Schiller, called for the coordination of national monetary (interest rate) and fiscal policies, with an emphasis on the latter. The Plan was based on the proposition that before embarking on the road to a monetary union, there must be economic convergence. This became known as the "economist" view of the EMU.[16] Schiller proposed supranational controls over budgetary policies, the introduction of a federal reserve system based on the U.S. model, the use of limiting margins to reduce fluctuations among currencies, a qualified majority vote requirement to adjust exchange rates and the creation of a European Reserve Fund to assist in dealing with balance of payments problems. The final stages of his plan called for "supranationality" under which economic and monetary authority would be transferred to common institutions such as a new European Central Council of Banks (the former Committee of the Governors of Central Banks) which would reach decisions through majority voting and oversee the eventual introduction of a single currency. The Schiller Plan could not be accepted for political reasons.

The First and Second Barre Reports

The First Barre Report was issued in 1969. Named after French Prime Minister Raymond Barre, it called for the coordination of economic and monetary policies. It emphasized the need for compatible medium-term policies and proposed the establishment of a short-term monetary support and medium-term financial assistance mechanism for EC member nations.

The more important Second Barre Report, which was adopted during the December 1-2, 1969, European Council Summit at The Hague, called for the establishment of the EMU in stages. The Report opposed the "economist" view of the

---

[15] Federal Republic of Germany, France, Italy, Belgium, the Netherlands, and Luxembourg.
[16] Karl Schiller was the main architect of the "economist" viewpoint of the EMU.

Schiller Plan. It promoted the "monetarist" view of the EMU[17] by calling for monetary integration prior to economic convergence; this was supported by the Commission. It also favored fixed exchange rates and called for an EMU by 1978 at the latest. But, the Report resembled the Schiller Plan in that it called for the transfer of economic and monetary authority to common institutions, the introduction of a European Reserve Fund, the harmonization of taxes, the creation of a common banking system to be overseen by a Council of Governors of the Central Banks, and the introduction of a single currency following a period of irrevocably fixed exchange rates. The reports recommendations could not be implemented due to political considerations. Nonetheless, the Barre Plan provided the foundation for subsequent EMU proposals included in both Werner Reports and had a major influence on the eventually approved Second Werner Report.

The First and Second Werner Reports

The First Werner Report, based on the Second Barre Report[18] and named after Pierre Werner, Prime Minister of Luxembourg, was reviewed by the finance ministers at Venice in May 1970 and, subsequently, at Luxembourg in June 1970. The report received little support. Ministers accepted only the recommendation to reduce the fluctuation margins around the currency parities.

The Second Werner Report on the "Realization by Stages of Economic and Monetary Union",[19] outlined a three-stage process. It was initiated by German Chancellor Willy Brandt and was published in October 1970. The report called for the EMU process to begin in 1971 and to be completed by 1980. The objectives were defined as follows: "...[to] realize an area in which goods and services, people and capital will circulate freely and without competitive distortions, without thereby giving rise to structural or regional, disequilibrium."[20] Such equilibrium would be achieved by factor mobility, including financial transfers. The report defined the monetary union as: "...the total irreversible convertibility of currencies, the elimination of margins of fluctuation in exchange rates, the irrevocable fixing of parity rates and the complete liberalization of movements for capital."[21] After national governments endorsed the idea,[22] the ECOFIN Council called for an EMU to be established in three stages.

---

[17] The principal architects of the "monetarist" view were Raymond Barre and Valéry Giscard d'Estaing.

[18] A committee had been formed under the chairmanship of Pierre Werner in March 1970 to design an EMU plan.

[19] Werner, Pierre, Baron Hubert Ansiaux, Georg Brouwers, Bernard Clappier, Ugo Mosca, Jean-Baptiste Schöllhorn, and Giorgio Stammati. "Report to the Council and the Commission on the Realization by Stages of Economic and Monetary Union in the Community," Commission of the European Communities, Luxembourg, 1970.

[20] Werner Report, 1970, p.7.

[21] Werner Report, 1970, p.7.

[22] In addition to being endorsed by the six original EC member governments, the Werner Report was subsequently also endorsed by the three new entrants, Denmark, Ireland and the U.K. in

Stage I, set for 1971-74, called for greater coordination, the harmonization of budget and fiscal policies and the elimination of barriers to capital mobility. Central banks were expected to narrow currency fluctuation margins against the U.S. dollar. Furthermore, during this stage, the Report called for drawing up "...broad lines of economic policy at the Community level and quantitative guidelines for the principal elements of the whole of the public budgets."[23]

Stage II involved: "...the laying down of global economic guidelines, the coordination of short term economic policies by monetary and credit measures, and budget and fiscal measures, the adoption of Community policies in the matter of structures, the integration of financial markets, and the progressive elimination of exchange rate fluctuations between Community currencies."[24]

In general, the first two stages involved an integration of national decision-making through common guidelines, as follows:

> The creation of liquidity throughout the area and monetary and credit policy will be centralized; monetary policy in relation to the outside world will be within the jurisdiction of the Community; and policies as regards capital markets would have to be unified...the essentials [six] futures of the whole of the public budgets, and in particular variations in their volume, the size of balances and the methods of financing or utilizing them, will be decided at the Community level. Regional and structural policies will no longer be exclusively within the jurisdiction of the member countries; and a systematic and continuous consultation between the social partners will be ensured at the Community level.[25]

The report further suggested that there will be a need for "...the creation or the transformation of a certain number of Community organs to which powers, until then exercised by the national authorities, will have to be transferred."[26]

Stage III involved the creation of a "Community System of Central Banks" structured similarly to the Federal Reserve model. The system will "...conduct the principal elements of internal monetary policy and be responsible for intervention on the foreign exchange markets."[27] In addition, the report called for the establishment of a European Fund[28] as the precursor of the System of Central Banks. The Fund would take

---

October 1972.

[23] Werner Report, 1970, p.27.

[24] Werner Report, 1970, p.28.

[25] Werner Report, 1970, p.28.

[26] Werner Report, 1970, p.28.

[27] Werner Report, 1970, pp.13, 26 and 29.

[28] Later, in 1973, founded as the European Monetary Cooperation Fund (EMCF).

over the short- and medium-term support mechanisms and would irreversibly manage the common reserves during the second stage.

It was during the discussions of the two Werner Reports that the differences between the "economist" and "monetarist" views of the EMU first became clear. The "economist" or "coronation" theory, first evident in the Schiller Plan and supported in 1970 mainly by Germany and the Netherlands, called for the irrevocable fixing of exchange rates and the centralization of monetary policy as the final stage. This stage could be implemented only after member nations have achieved economic convergence through voluntary policy coordination and relinquished budgetary control to a centralized common authority. In contrast, the "monetarist" point of view (first evident in the Second Barre Report), supported by France, Italy and Belgium, proposed expedient monetary integration and assumed that economic convergence and policy coordination would follow.

The Second Werner Report, although a compromise between the "monetarists" and the "economists," inclined more toward the "monetarist" view as it called for the narrowing of the fluctuation margins around the central parities. This was in effect a call for the first stage of the EMU, otherwise known as the "Snake." The report relied heavily on the Bretton Woods system of fixed exchange rates based on the U.S. dollar but did not provide for credit to member nations with balance of payments problems. But, it called for the full convertibility of currencies, the elimination of exchange rate fluctuations, the irrevocable fixing of parity rates and the liberalization of capital movements. While the authors were not committed to a single currency, they expressed a preference for it. In retrospect, the relative ease with which the report was ratified by national governments can be attributed not only to the unavoidable compromises necessary for such an agreement but also to the restrictions placed on the coordination of national economic policies in the first two stages. Any transfer of national sovereignty to common institutions was delayed until the final stage.

With hindsight, it is apparent that the key compromises necessary to achieve the goals of the Werner Report were essentially the same as those needed 20 years later to achieve the EMU, as called for in the 1989 "Report on Economic and Monetary Union in the EC," otherwise known as the Delors Report. This report, also affected by the "economist versus monetarist" debate, was later amended and ratified as part of the Maastricht Treaty signed in 1992. The Werner Report and the Delors Report were accepted because both called for simultaneous efforts to pursue monetary and non-monetary integration.

On a number of points, however, the Werner Report differed from the Delors Report. Although the former called for parallel progress in monetary integration and economic convergence toward the EMU, it focused more on exchange rate management and monetary policy coordination. It also emphasized the need to establish a centralized common authority overseeing national budgetary policies. There was even a discussion of a joint incomes policy. During the 1950s to the mid-1970s, Keynesian economics prevailed and thus price levels were seen as a function of wage negotiations and costs. External imbalances were ascribed primarily to disparities in national demand management or fiscal policies, in particular to government budgets. The authors of the Werner Report had the foresight to be more concerned about the long-term risk of diverging economic policies and performances and, consequently, designated responsible budget policies as the cornerstone of monetary integration. In line with this concern, the report laid the foundation for non-monetary cooperation within the EC through its proposed Center of Decision for Common Policy, which was to report to the European Parliament and coordinate economic policies, including national budgetary policies. But the report did not stress as much as the EMU proposal of the 1990s the importance of economic convergence and, in particular, of low inflation. The 1990s emphasis was the result of expanding EU membership and the diverging economic conditions among member nations, conditions which were not present in the 1970s.

The Werner Report also differed from the Delors Report in that it did not address the creation of new, or the reform of existing common institutions to support monetary integration. The Werner Report only alluded to a new management structure through a proposed "Community System of Central Banks"[29], fashioned after the U.S. Federal Reserve system, which would implement monetary and exchange rate policies in relation to third currencies. However, this was not surprising as there was no need for a European Central Bank. The Bretton Woods Agreements provided Europe with a stable fixed exchange rate system during the 1960s without the need for a central monetary authority other than the IMF. It should be borne in mind that the European exchange rate stability of the 1960s was largely due to low levels of inflation and unemployment in an environment of low capital mobility. There was no need to make major adjustments in either fiscal or monetary policies and therefore, relatively few sacrifices were needed to pursue a policy of stable exchange rates which were still under the jurisdiction of the IMF. The ambiguity of the Werner Report on these issues can, in part, be attributed to the political complexities surrounding such an endeavor, as evidenced by the EMU debates of the 1990s.

The Werner Report was conscious of the importance of fiscal convergence and thus made it its central theme. However, because of the prevailing political problems this idea could not be followed through. Ultimately, the proposals calling for monetary convergence and exchange rate policies gained the upper hand. In contrast, the political atmosphere surrounding the Delors Report, despite the compromise reached on a parallel monetary and fiscal approach to the EMU, began with an emphasis on monetary convergence underpinned by a common monetary authority and a single currency. It was only in the later stages of the Maastricht Treaty debates that the fiscal issues surfaced. It should be noted that the political complexities surrounding the EU in the 1990s are much more intricate than the complexities that had affected the EC in the 1970s. This was due in part to the growing membership and increasing

---

[29] Under the Delors Report this is known as the "European System of Central Banks" (ESCB).

economic divergence. But it can also be argued that the architects of the Delors Report first focused on monetary integration because of the controversial and political nature of fiscal coordination.

In summary, the Second Werner Report called for national budget deficits and regional policies to be jointly managed under a centralized common authority. It is interesting to note that 20 years later the EMU discussions also emphasized that economic convergence and budgetary discipline were the basis for responsible monetary policy and, thus, the cornerstone of successful monetary integration. The ECOFIN Council unanimously accepted the Werner Plan in March 1971. It should be noted, however, that the plan was amended prior to ratification. The "Center of Decision for Common Policy" was deleted by the ECOFIN Council. This was a revealing decision. Just as the architects of the Second Werner Report discovered the political problems involved in proposing binding common fiscal constraints, the architects of the EMU plan have faced similar difficulties in the 1990s.

The Werner Plan was never really implemented. Ironically, its reliance on the Bretton Woods system was one of the reasons that the Plan failed as it attempted to complete Stage I by the end of 1973 -- the year that the system collapsed.[30]

The "Snake"

The Second Werner Plan yielded an intra-EC exchange rate mechanism and the European Monetary Cooperation Fund (EMCF),[31] which survived the collapse of the Bretton Woods system and laid the foundation for economic policy convergence.

The authors were concerned with the fluctuation margins of the bilateral European currency rates and called for the narrowing of the intra-European fluctuation margin of +/-1.5 percent (3 percent) which was twice the fluctuation margin of +/-0.75 percent (1.5 percent) established against the U.S. dollar. They believed that the system created a disadvantage for the European currencies because the dollar was still more predictable and hence was more sought after by the business and financial communities. Thus, the authors proposed a bilateral fluctuation margin of +/-0.3 percent (0.6 percent) which was to be gradually eliminated.

The reductions of EC bilateral fluctuation margin was important when the U.S. dollar's initial parity level with third country currencies had a fluctuation margin of 0.75 percent. Such a move, however, became imperative when the Smithsonian Agreement was signed in 1971. This Agreement was a rather timid attempt to save the Bretton Woods system of fixed exchange rates. It tripled the U.S. dollar's fluctuation margins against third country currencies to +/-2.25 percent (4.5 percent), thus enlarging the EC

[30] The Bretton Woods system collapsed in March 1973.

[31] Also known by the French acronym FECOM.

currencies' bilateral fluctuation margins to +/-4.5 percent (9 percent). The EC could not accept this Agreement, and four months later it signed the Basle Agreement[32] which reduced the bilateral fluctuation margins of its member nations' currencies to +/-2.25 percent (4.5 percent). This became known as the "Snake" in the "dollar tunnel." However, the "dollar tunnel" disappeared a year later as the U.S. currency was floated in March 1973, leaving the "Snake" as a joint float. Box 1.1 provides a summary overview of the evolution of the "Snake."

The "Snake" represented a concrete step toward the EMU. But the Second Werner Report also generated lessons that the architects of the Delors Report did not heed. For example, initially the Delors Report opted for the complete elimination of fluctuations in one step during Stage II of the EMU. This idea was eventually abandoned because a special committee chaired by the Governor of the Belgian Central Bank recommended against an "overnight" approach. Such a drastic step was deemed feasible only during the more advanced stages of monetary and economic integration -- a condition not present during Stage II. These concerns were only gradually recognized during the EMU debates of the early 1990s.

Because of the volatility in the foreign exchange markets, currencies frequently dropped in and out of the "Snake." There was also a tendency for the participants to cluster into weak and strong currency groups, as illustrated by the 1978 ERM structure. Spiraling inflation, volatile exchange rates and rising oil prices in 1973 set the tone and as a result the 1974-78 period was turbulent, marked by frequent realignments and interventions. For example, between 1976-78 there were five realignments.

[32] The Basle Agreement became effective on April 24, 1972.

Box 1.1
The History of the "Snake"

1972	
24 April	The Basle Agreement enters into force: Belgium, France, Germany, Italy, Luxembourg, the Netherlands.
1 May	The United Kingdom and Denmark join.
23 May	Norway becomes associated.
23 June	The United Kingdom withdraws.
27 June	Denmark withdraws.
10 Oct.	Denmark returns.
1973	
13 Feb.	Italy withdraws.
19 March	Transition to the joint float: interventions to maintain fixed margins against the dollar ("tunnel") are discontinued.
19 March	Sweden becomes associated.
19 March	The Deutsche mark is revalued by 3 percent.
1 April	Establishment of the European Monetary Cooperation Fund is approved.
29 June	The Deutsche mark is revalued by 5.5 percent.
17 Sept.	The Dutch guilder is revalued by 5 percent.
16 Nov.	The Norwegian krone is revalued by 5 percent.
1974	
19 Jan.	France withdraws.
1975	
10 July	France returns.
1976	
15 March	France withdraws.
17 Oct.	Agreement on exchange rate adjustment ("Frankfurt realignment"): The Danish krone is devalued by 6 percent, the Dutch guilder and Belgian franc by 2 percent, and the Norwegian krone and Swedish krona by 3 percent.
1977	
1 April	The Swedish krona is devalued by 6 percent, and the Danish and Norwegian krone are devalued by 3 percent.
28 Aug.	Sweden withdraws; the Danish and Norwegian krone are devalued by 5 percent.
1978	
13 Feb.	The Norwegian krone is devalued by 8 percent.
17 Oct.	The Deutsche mark is revalued by 4 percent, the Dutch guilder and Belgian franc by 2 percent.
12 Dec.	Norway announces decision to withdraw.
1979	
13 March	The European Monetary System (EMS) becomes operational.

Source: Gross, Daniel and Niels Thygesen. European Monetary Integration: From the European Monetary System to European Monetary Union, London: St. Martin's Press, 1992, p.17.

The EMCF was established in April 1973 as a monitor of the exchange rate system. It was subject to the directives of the ECOFIN Council, but the Council's role was minimal because members of the Committee of Central Bank Governors objected to national governments exercising political influence through the ECOFIN over "Snake" interventions. As was expected, the Bundesbank objected to the EMCF because it was a common monetary authority. Thus, the EMCF activities were limited to the management of the very-short and short-term credit facilities of the 1979 EMS.

The European Monetary System (EMS)

Origins

During the late 1970s, the nine EC nations were divided into two groups with differing economic performances and exchange rate systems. The first group, comprised of Germany, the three Benelux countries and Denmark, with Norway as an associate member, followed Stage I of the Second Werner EMU plan (i.e., the "Snake"). This group had managed to restrain inflationary pressures. The second group included France, the U.K., Ireland[33] and Italy. They had floated their currencies and experienced strong inflationary pressures, large current account deficits and currency depreciations.

Thus, a compromise had to be found between the "Snake" and the floating currency approach. Germany and the other "Snake" participants asserted the need to uphold the arrangement, basing their arguments on the successful operation of the six-year-old system. They wanted the floating currencies to be brought in so as to complete Stage I of the Werner Plan. In contrast, France, and to some extent the U.K. and Italy, claimed that the "Snake" mechanism, albeit technically sound, was inherently flawed, owing to its asymmetrical nature which resulted in German domination. Not only was the Deutsche mark the only internationally strong currency within the system, but also the German economy represented two-thirds of the combined GDP of member nations. It should be noted, however, that Germany's influence was rather modest as most of the time it accepted other views on realignments and/or domestic adjustments.

To achieve a compromise between the "Snake" and the floating currency approach and to modify the former, several proposals were discussed. Of these, four were seriously considered. They included the Fourcade Plan of 1974, the Duisenberg Plan of 1976, the EC Commission initiative of late 1977 and the 1978 Schmidt-Giscard initiative, which was eventually approved. This was the brainchild of the German Federal Chancellor Helmut Schmidt and President Valéry Giscard d'Estaing of France.

[33] Ireland and the U.K. were in a monetary union from 1800 to 1979 in which the Irish punt was pegged to the pound sterling. The last 56 years represented a "voluntary" linkage as Irish independence was achieved in 1922.

Their move to replace the "Snake" with the EMS was not only based on the proposals of the first three plans but also on the lessons learned over time.

The Fourcade Plan

In September 1974[34] the French government submitted the Fourcade Plan to the ECOFIN Council. The Plan, named after Finance Minister Jean-Pierre Fourcade, called for a four-stage approach, comprising (i) an increased use of intramarginal interventions; (ii) the endorsement of larger credit lines; (iii) the use of the European Unit of Account (EUA) based on a fixed basket of EC currencies as the nucleus (i.e., indicator of divergence) in the revised exchange rate system; and (iv) the adoption of a common policy in relation to the U.S. dollar. The Plan met with resistance, especially from Italy and the U.K., which were experiencing inflationary pressures. But an element of the Plan, the EUA, was incorporated in the EMS as the European Currency Unit (Ecu), launched in 1978. It should be noted that the Fourcade Plan contained one of the first candid criticisms of the "Snake's" asymmetrical nature and in this way influenced the EMS by stressing the necessity of an equal sharing of the adjustment burden. It was also the basis for the 1987-88 revision of the EMS.

The Duisenberg Plan

The Duisenberg Plan, developed by the Dutch Finance Minister Wilhelm Duisenberg, was introduced in July 1976 following a sharp depreciation of the pound sterling and the lira. It called for the establishment of a target zone which did not require any intervention. Owing to strong German opposition, it was set aside.

The EC Commission Initiative

The EC Commission Initiative was launched by EC President Roy Jenkins at the European University Institute in Florence in 1977. It was a revised version of the Duisenberg Plan and included fiscal federalism through the enlargement of the common budget's allocative and redistributive functions argued for in the McDougall Report of 1977.[35] Jenkins' ideas were also influenced and supported by Robert Triffin, the principal architect of the 1950 EPU, Jacques van Ypersele, the Belgian Chairman of the Monetary Committee and Michael Emerson, a member of Jenkins' Cabinet and of the McDougall Committee. However, lack of support by the governments and the public

---

[34] Although the French franc had dropped out of the "Snake" in January 1974 owing to rising inflation, oil prices and exchange rate volatility, its reentry into a revised "Snake" looked feasible in September 1974. The franc eventually returned to the system in July 1975 at its previous central parity.

[35] McDougall, Sir Donald et al. "Report of the Study Group on the Role of Public Finance in European Integration," Vol. I-II, Brussels: Commission of the European Communities, 1977.

and the depreciation of the dollar, as well as a slowdown in economic growth in late 1977, made the initiative unacceptable.

The Schmidt-Giscard Plan

The first three proposals sought to coordinate monetary policy by attempting to achieve stabilization against the U.S. dollar -- either bilaterally through individual currency target zones or by implementing a version of the Duisenberg Plan (the adoption by four major countries of a target zone for their effective exchange rates). However, by 1977 it became economically and politically difficult to achieve monetary stability in relation to the dollar. This made it politically feasible to revisit the discussion of the EMS which rather than attempting to achieve monetary coordination through stabilization against the dollar, furthered intra-EC monetary i.e. exchange rate stability.

The Schmidt-Giscard Plan was introduced at the Copenhagen European Council Summit in April 1978. There were several reasons why monetary integration beyond the "Snake" had become desirable and, more important, feasible, aside from the objective of curtailing the economic divergence between the two groups of nations with different exchange rate regimes and of providing for a more stable framework for common economic policies. There were also three political reasons promoting a common system with minimum prerequisites that would embrace both groups of nations. The first was the strengthening of the political positions of Schmidt and Giscard in 1977-78 not only within their own political parties but also nationally. This provided the needed leverage to pursue common policies. The second reason was the enhancement of the political authority of Schmidt and Giscard through the growing tensions with the United States and the growing concerns about developments in Italy where the Communist Party gained political clout. The third reason came from a change in the overall mood, in particular in Germany, which became ripe for the pursuit of greater independence from the United States. America was in the midst of a domestic economic expansionary effort resulting in stagflation, which placed pressure on surplus countries such as Germany and Japan to stimulate their economies and to act as global "locomotives." This was accompanied by the United States' "talking down" of the dollar which placed upward pressure on the Deutsche mark and the yen, thus impairing the international competitiveness of German and Japanese industries.

Schmidt's response to the external pressures was twofold. First, he wanted to spread the impact of the weakening dollar over a wider area by linking the Deutsche mark to other floating EC currencies, with the idea that this would reduce the pressures on German trade, curtail international and OECD pressure to pursue expansionary policies and, at the same time, leverage common international economic policy formulation. This last goal, however, required an influential common institutional framework, which was wanting. Schmidt also sought to pursue domestic expansionary policies through budgetary measures such as higher expenditures and tax cuts. At the

Bonn Economic Summit of July 1979 he announced a stimulation package to increase domestic demand by approximately 1 percent during the same year.

While coping with international pressures, Schmidt wanted to ensure that anxiety over German inflation would not increase. His response to international pressure exerted by the United States at the World Economic Summits and through the OECD was to call for more global economic growth in general, and for the narrowing of current account imbalances among the Triad nations in particular. This appealed to the other EC nations, particularly France, because such moves not only promoted cohesion in policy formulation but also lessened international pressures. Nonetheless, there was disagreement among Germany's partners as to how to achieve these objectives. For example, the U.K. wanted the German economy to assume the role of "global locomotive"[36] while France was keen on the development of a new common monetary cooperation framework.[37]

In early 1978 the French and German interests finally converged, not only in a common challenge against the U.S. policy agenda but also in the creation of a common monetary cooperation framework. This called for tighter policy coordination and stringent national intervention in defense of intra-EC exchange rates. Moreover, it required the establishment, after a two-year period, of a successor to the "Snake's" EMCF in the form of the European Monetary Fund (EMF). The new organization was expected to implement joint exchange-rate policies through a managed pool of foreign exchange reserves and to provide balance of payments assistance. The EMF was also expected to be less influenced by the ECOFIN Council, to exercise more power than the EMCF and to finance external imbalances. The EMF idea, however, was shelved in December 1980 owing to a lack of agreement concerning its responsibilities and accountability. In particular, the Bundesbank objected to the mixing of central banking and political functions such as interventions and very-short-term to medium-term balance of payments assistance. The need to amend the Treaties of Rome, and the possibility of creating additional international liquidity which could have led to monetary laxity within the ERM member nations, were additional problems. Thus, the EMCF continued to function.

Schmidt and Giscard extended an invitation to U.K. Prime Minister James Callaghan to join the EMS Initiative. However, Callaghan wanted to promote global

---

[36] At the 1977 London Economic Summit, the U.K., in cooperation with the United States, attempted to pressure Germany to become the principal engine of increased global economic growth and of the reduction of current account imbalances within the Triad (United States, EC, Japan).

[37] France had long been involved in plans to develop a more stable international monetary system. It participated in the Committee of Twenty (1972-74) which studied the possibility of fixed-but-adjustable exchange rates for the global monetary system and also took part in the IMF effort to develop a multilateral surveillance of economic policies (Second Amendment to the IMF Articles of Agreement of 1976). During most of the 1970s, France played an active role in modifying the global monetary system and the European integration process.

economic coordination rather than a new international currency exchange rate mechanism. Moreover, in May 1979 general elections were held in the U.K. and galvanizing support for the EMS during the pre-election period was not feasible. Other considerations included the usual resistance to the loss of exchange rate sovereignty, problems of maintaining the international competitiveness of U.K. exports if the pound sterling were linked to the Deutsche mark and worries about domestic inflationary pressures on the pound sterling. U.K. citizens also believed that the pound sterling had certain distinctive features not characteristic of the other EMS currencies. In their view, the pound played an important role in trade and financial relations with non-EC countries and was sensitive to oil price movements.

The Schmidt-Giscard Plan follow-up was rather unusual. Initial negotiations were conducted outside the established common framework. The Monetary Committee, the ECOFIN Council, and the Committee of Central Bankers were bypassed and were rarely informed of the Plan's progress.[38] Not surprisingly, in May 1978 objections were voiced by Bundesbank President Otmar Emminger who stated that he knew nothing of the Schmidt-Giscard proposal. Schmidt purposely alienated the Bundesbank and the Committee of Central Bankers so as to free the plan of the gradualists and cautious tendencies of these institutions. In the same vein, the preparations for the forthcoming European Council Summit meeting in Bremen in July 1978 were delegated to the Office of the Federal Chancellor and the Governor of the Banque de France, who was acting as the French President's personal representative.

Nonetheless, the European Council Summit discussions in Bremen were conducted by the usual committees and the Schmidt-Giscard EMS Plan began to take shape. It called for a zone of monetary stability underpinned by a new money, the Ecu. The Ecu, based on a basket of the "Snake" currencies,[39] was the center of the Exchange Rate Mechanism (ERM) which entailed a bilateral parity grid of the participating currencies. Each currency was pegged at a central rate against the Ecu and this rate could be changed only through agreed realignments. The central rates were used to formulate the bilateral currency grid as, for example, the Deutsche mark against the French franc. The Ecu was also used for settlements by EC authorities, and the monetary authorities were required to conduct interventions to maintain the bilateral parities. Subsequent European Council meetings refined the EMS by bringing to light potential inconsistencies. The resulting compromises led to the final approval of the system at the December 1978 European Council meeting in Brussels. It became operational on March 13, 1979.[40]

---

[38] They continued to discuss the 1977 EC Commission Plan.

[39] The Ecu was not "real money," as it fulfilled only two of the three requirements of money; it was a store of value and a unit of account, but not a medium of exchange.

[40] The original date of January 1, 1979 was changed owing to unresolved issues in relation to the Monetary Compensatory Accounts (MCAs) which linked the newly created Ecu to the price system of the CAP.

The EMS agreement was based on some of the lessons learned during the discussion of the 1970 Second Werner Report in that it paid more attention to national sovereignty and thus was less controversial than previous proposals aimed at monetary integration. Moreover, the agreement also provided lessons for future integration plans just as the discussion of the proposed EMF did for the 1988 Delors-EMU Plan.

Structure of the EMS

The EMS came into existence on March 13, 1979. Its aims were (i) to promote greater macroeconomic convergence among participating nations and thus to promote the adoption of common macroeconomic policies; (ii) to control levels of inflation; (iii) to promote exchange rate stability; (iv) to foster the role of the Ecu in the EC; and (v) to further overall integration.

The system was periodically modified. The present-day EMS is comprised of three key elements: (i) the Ecu, based on a currency basket; (ii) the ERM, based on a semi-pegged exchange rate system; and (iii) the EMCF, providing a pool of reserve assets and credits to member nation central banks for intervention.[41]

The European Currency Unit (Ecu)

The initial step taken by the Council of Ministers in crafting the EMS was the creation of a new monetary unit, the Ecu. The origins of the Ecu can be traced back to the European Unit of Account (EUA) established in 1974. The EUA, a basket of currencies of the nine EC members, was officially adopted in 1975 as an accounting unit by the European Development Fund and later by the EIB and the common budgeting authorities. With the creation of the EMS, the EUA was renamed the Ecu[42] in 1978 and soon thereafter Ecu bonds were issued in the financial markets.

The Ecu is based on a basket of currencies defined by fixed quantities of national currencies according to the relative economic size of nations. In 1974, the official economic criteria for determining a currency's weight in the basket were the share of a national economy in the combined EU GDP, its share in intra-EC trade and its share in the EMS financial support system. However, since 1979 these criteria serve only as broad indicators[43] and market exchange rates play a determining role. The Ecu performs four functions: (i) it is a reserve asset; (ii) it is a means of settlement for intra-

---

[41] The ERM requires participating central banks to manage their currency within the set bands. They can use a range of tools as, for example, interest rate adjustments and/or central bank market interventions, which are the most common and most effective.

[42] Ecu is also the name of a medieval coin used in France and England.

[43] It should be noted that since 1979 the shares of the Deutsche mark and the Dutch guilder in the Ecu basket have always exceeded their economic weight, while the weaker currencies have always been underrepresented.

EU transactions among the central banks; (iii) it is a numeraire of the ERM; and (iv) it serves as a foundation for the divergence indicator as well as a unit of account for EMS interventions. For a theoretical definition of the Ecu, see Box 1.2.

The number of units of each national currency in the basket is fixed. However, the weights of the various currencies vary over time depending on intra-system exchange rate fluctuations. This is particularly true for currencies that are part of the Ecu but not of the ERM. Adjustments take place every five years, or upon request if and when the weight of any participating currency has changed more than 25 percent.

Box 1.2
Definition of the European Currency Unit (Ecu)

Ecu = the European Currency Unit is composed of the 12 EU member nations' currencies.

Equation 1= "defines the value of the Ecu in terms of a currency **i**, **Ecui**, based on the quantities of the individual currencies **qj** and the exchange rates between currency **i** and the remaining currencies **Sij**, defined as units of currency **i** per unit of currency **j**:"

$$\textbf{(1)} \qquad Ecu_i = \sum_{j=1}^{n} q_j s_{ij}$$

"The relative weight of currency **j** in the value of the Ecu, **wj**, is the ratio"

$$\textbf{(2)} \qquad w_j = s_{ij} q_j / Ecu_i$$

"Central parities in the ERM are stated in two equivalent ways: either as a parity grid of all member currencies, or by relating each currency to its Ecu central parity, from which bilateral central parities can be derived."

Source: Fratianni, Michele and Jürgen von Hagen. The European Monetary System and the European Monetary Union, Oxford: Westview Press, Inc., 1992, p.40.

Table 1.1 shows the Ecu weight shares defined in terms of individual national currencies and their ERM central parities while Table 1.2 illustrates the Ecu basket revisions over time. Not surprisingly, the Deutsche mark has dominated the Ecu basket since its inception in 1979. This, coupled with its regional strength, makes the Deutsche mark the unofficial anchor currency. Thus, Germany has played a dominant economic and monetary role in the EMS over time.

Table 1.1
Composition of the Ecu, 1990

	Amount of each currency in the Ecu basket	Weight in Ecu (percentage)	Central rates in the ERM (fixed value of 1 Ecu in each currency)*
Deutsche mark	0.6242	30.61	2.05586
French franc	1.332	19.23	6.89509
Pound sterling	0.08784	12.14	0.696904
Italian lira	151.8	10.01	1538.24
Dutch guilder	0.2198	9.58	2.31643
Belgian franc	3.301	7.74	42.4032
Spanish peseta	3.885	5.23	133.631**
Danish krone	0.1976	2.50	7.84195
Irish pound	0.008552	1.12	0.767417
Greek drachma	1.44	0.76	205.311***
Portuguese escudo	1.393	0.78	178.735**
Luxembourg franc	0.13	0.30	42.4032

* = These central rates are used to form a parity grid in which bilateral central exchange rates of each currency against each other currency and the fluctuation margins of 2.25%+/- and 6%+/- are established. A central rate change expressed in Ecus implies a simultaneous change in the other Ecu central rates, since the Ecu is comprised of a basket of currencies.

** = The Ecu basket was revised on September 21, 1989 to include the Portuguese escudo and the Spanish peseta.

***= This is hypothetical as the Greek drachma is not a formal participant of the ERM.

Note: The Austrian schilling, Swedish krona and Finnish markka have, to date, not been incorporated into the Ecu basket.

Source: EU Commission data, October 8, 1990.

Table 1.2
Revisions of the Ecu Basket (1979-89)

Currency	Basket March 13, 1979 Currency Amount	Revision (1)* Sept. 17, 1984 Currency Amount	Change (%)	Revision (2)** Sept. 21, 1989 Currency Amount	Change (%)
Deutsche mark	0.828	0.719	-13.16	0.6242	-13.18
Pound sterling	0.0885	0.0878	-0.79	0.08784	+0.05
French franc	1.15	1.31	+13.91	1.332	+1.67
Italian lira	109.00	140.00	+28.44	151.8	+8.43
Dutch guilder	0.286	0.256	-10.49	0.2198	-14.14
Belgian franc	3.66	3.71	+1.37	3.301	-11.02
Lux. Franc	0.14	0.14	-	0.130	-7.14
Danish krone	0.217	0.219	+0.92	0.1976	-0.98
Irish pound	0.00759	0.00871	+14.76	0.008552	-1.81
Greek drachma	-	1.15	-	1.440	+25.22
Spanish peseta	-	-	-	6.885	-
Portuguese escudo	-	-	-	1.393	-

* = Revision (1) of the Ecu basket on September 17, 1984 was due to the inclusion of the Greek drachma and accordingly adjusts the weights of the other currencies in the basket.

**= Revision (2) of the Ecu basket on September 21, 1989 was due to the inclusion of the Portuguese escudo and the Spanish peseta and accordingly adjusts the weights of the other currencies in the basket.

Source: EC Commission data, 1989.

The Exchange Rate Mechanism (ERM)

Within the ERM each national currency has a central rate in relation to the Ecu expressed as the price of one Ecu in the national currencies. These central rates are fixed and can be altered only through an official realignment. Based on the central rates, bilateral rates are developed as, for example, the Deutsche mark against the French franc. These bilateral central rates form the ERM parity grid or currency band. Member nations must maintain their market exchange rates in relation to the other participating currencies within assigned margins based on the bilateral central parity. Until August 1993 the bilateral margins were +/-2.25 percent[44] or +/-6 percent of the central parity, thus the width of the fluctuation band for any bilateral rate was 4.5 percent or 12 percent, respectively. The various currencies could not exceed the upper and lower limits of the band. The larger +/-6 percent bilateral fluctuation bands were given to new ERM entrants such as the lira,[45] the pound sterling,[46] and the Spanish peseta[47] for a

[44] The bilateral fluctuation bands of the ERM were not exactly +/-2.25 percent, as they were computed by multiplying (dividing) the central rate by 1.022753 in order to bring consistency to the grid. Thus, the exact percentages were +2.275 and -2.225 percent.

[45] The lira moved to the narrow +/-2.25 percent band in January 1990, but dropped out of the

specified transitional period to provide governments with flexibility and time to adjust domestic economic policies. Thus the Ecu serves as a numeraire and it is the parity grid that represents the nucleus of the ERM. Such an arrangement not only stabilizes exchange rates but also promotes low inflation growth, as the Deutsche mark dominated the Ecu basket since its beginning in 1979. Thus, transferring the credibility of the Bundesbank and the Deutsche mark to the other currencies.

A series of unforeseen economic and political shocks forced the U.K. and Italy to drop out of the ERM in September 1992 and caused Spain to realign and devalue its currency in September and November 1992, and again in May 1993. These shocks also caused the Portuguese escudo to be devalued in November 1992 and again in May 1993, while the Irish pound was devalued in February 1993. These moves culminated in the August 1993 crisis, resulting in the widening of the currency bands from +/-2.25 to +/-15 percent. As a result, except for the Deutsche Mark and the Dutch guilder,[48] all currencies are within the wider bands, albeit temporarily.[49] On October 14, 1996 the Finish markka joined the ERM and on November 25, 1996 the Italian lira rejoined the ERM, albeit amidst some controversy. Box 1.3 shows EMS/ERM membership between 1979 and 1996, the dates at which the various nations joined, the initial bands to which the different currencies adhered, and the changes in membership over time.

The central rates shown previously in Table 1.1 are used to form a parity grid in which the bilateral central exchange rates of each currency against the others and the fluctuation margins of +/-15 percent (previously +/-2.25 percent and +/-6 percent) are established. The grid is used to determine whether members must intervene. Table 1.3 shows the central parity grid and the upper and lower limits of the currency bands (i.e., the exchange rates in Ecu of any two ERM currencies). The parity grid is shown as of November 25, 1996, the date when the Italian lira rejoined the ERM.

ERM during the September 1992 crisis only to rejoin again in November 1996 under the new +/-15 percent band.

[46] The pound sterling joined the ERM in 1990 and left it during the September 1992 ERM crisis.

[47] The Spanish peseta joined the ERM in 1989.

[48] Germany and the Netherlands continue to adhere to the narrow +/- 2.25 percent bands on a voluntary basis under a bilateral agreement.

[49] For more detail, see the section on "Performance of the EMS (1979-95)" in this chapter.

Box 1.3
Membership of the EMS and ERM (1979-1996)

EMS Membership	**ERM Membership**
March 1979 EMS begins	**March 1979** ERM begins with bilateral fluctuation margins at +/- 2.25% normally and +/-6% in special cases.
March 1979 Belgian franc	March 1979 Belgian franc +/-2.25%
March 1979 Danish krone	March 1979 Danish krone +/-2.25%
March 1979 Deutsche mark	March 1979 Deutsche Mark +/-2.25%
March 1979 French franc	March 1979 French franc +/-2.25%
March 1979 Irish pound	March 1979 Irish pound +/-2.25%
March 1979 Luxembourg franc	March 1979 Luxembourg franc +/-2.25%
March 1979 Dutch guilder	March 1979 Dutch guilder +/-2.25%
March 1979 Italian lira	March 1979 Italian lira +/-6% Jan. 1990 lira moves to +/-2.25% Sept. 1992 lira drops out of ERM Nov. 1996 lira rejoins ERM +/-15%
March 1979 pound sterling	Oct. 1990 pound sterling +/-6% Sept. 1992 pound drops out of ERM
Jan. 1981 Greek drachma	The drachma has not joined the ERM
Jan. 1986 Spanish peseta	June 1989 Spanish peseta +/-6%
Jan. 1986 Portuguese escudo	April 1992 Portuguese escudo +/-6%
	***August 1993 all ERM bilateral fluctuation margins are broadened to +/-15% ***
Jan 1995 Austrian schilling	Jan 1995 Austrian schilling +/-2.25%
Jan 1995 Swedish krona	The krona has not joined the ERM
Jan 1995 Finnish markka	Oct. 1996 Finish markka +/-15%

Source: EU Commission data, 1997.

Table 1.3
ERM Parity Grid - Bilateral Central Parity and Upper (selling) /Lower (buying) Limits of Currencies
(November 25, 1996)

		BFr/LFr 100=	DKr 100=	FFr 100=	DM 100=	I£ 1=	DFl 100=	P Esc 100=	S Pta 100=	A Sch 100=	FM 100=	L 1,000=
Belgium/Lux	S	-	627.880	714.030	2395.20	57.7445	2125.60	23.3645	28.1525	340.420	787.830	24.1920
	C	-	540.723	614.977	2062.55	49.7289	1830.54	20.1214	24.2447	293.163	678.468	20.8337
BFr/LFr	B	-	465.665	529.660	1776.20	42.8260	1576.45	17.3285	20.8795	252.470	584.290	17.9417
Denmark	S	21.4747	-	132.066	442.968	10.6792	393.105	4.32100	5.20640	62.9561	145.699	4.47400
	C	18.4938	-	113.732	381.443	9.19676	338.537	3.72119	4.48376	54.2170	125.474	3.85294
DKr	B	15.9266	-	97.9430	328.461	7.92014	291.544	3.20460	3.86140	46.6910	108.057	3.31810
France	S	18.8800	102.100	-	389.480	9.38950	345.650	3.79920	4.55780	55.3545	128.107	3.93379
	C	16.2608	87.9257	-	335.386	8.08631	297.661	3.27188	3.94237	47.6706	110.324	3.38773
FFr	B	14.0050	75.7200	-	288.810	6.96400	256.350	2.81770	3.39510	41.0533	95.0096	2.91750
Germany	S	5.63000	30.4450	34.6250	-	2.80000	(103.058)*	1.13280	1.36500	16.5050	38.1970	1.17290
	C	4.84837	26.2162	29.8164	-	2.41105	88.7526	0.975561	1.17548	14.2136	32.8948	1.01010
DM	B	4.17500	22.5750	25.6750	-	2.07600	(76.4326)*	0.840140	1.01230	12.2410	28.3280	0.86990
Ireland	S	2.33503	12.6261	14.3599	48.1696	-	42.7439	0.469841	0.566120	6.84544	15.8424	0.486472
	C	2.01090	10.8734	12.3666	41.4757	-	36.8105	0.404620	0.487537	5.89521	13.6433	0.418944
I£	B	1.73176	9.36403	10.6500	35.7143	-	31.7007	0.348453	0.419859	5.07688	11.7494	0.360789
Netherlands	S	6.34340	34.3002	39.0091	(130.834)*	3.15450	-	1.27637	1.53793	18.5963	43.0378	1.321560
	C	5.46286	29.5389	33.5953	112.6730	2.71662	-	1.09920	1.32445	16.0149	37.0636	1.138110
Fl	B	4.70454	25.4385	28.9381	(97.0325)*	2.33952	-	0.946611	1.14060	13.7918	31.9187	0.980132
Portugal	S	577.090	3120.50	3549.00	11903.30	286.983	10564.0	-	139.920	1691.80	3915.40	120.2400
	C	496.984	2687.31	3056.35	10250.50	247.145	9097.55	-	120.493	1456.97	3371.88	103.5410
Esc	B	428.000	2314.30	2632.10	8827.70	212.838	7834.70	-	103.770	1254.70	2903.80	89.17000

continued...

Table 1.3 (...continued)
ERM Parity Grid - Bilateral Central Parity and Upper (selling) /Lower (buying) Limits of Currencies
(November 25, 1996)

		BFr/LFr 100=	DKr 100=	FFr 100=	DM 100=	I£ 1=	DFl 100=	P Esc 100=	S Pta 100=	A Sch 100=	FM 100=	L 1,000=
Spain	S	478.944	2589.80	2945.40	9878.50	238.175	8767.30	96.3670	-	1404.10	3249.50	99.7800
	C	412.461	2230.27	2536.54	8507.18	205.113	7550.30	82.9927	-	1209.18	2798.41	85.9311
Pta	B	355.206	1920.70	2184.40	7326.00	176.641	6502.20	71.4690	-	1041.30	2410.00	74.0000
Austria	S	39.6809	214.174	243.586	816.927	19.6971	725.065	7.97000	9.60338	-	268.735	8.25219
	C	34.1107	184.444	209.773	703.550	16.9629	624.417	6.86356	8.27008	-	231.431	7.10655
Sch	B	29.3757	158.841	180.654	605.877	14.6082	537.740	5.91086	7.12200	-	199.305	6.12032
Finland	S	17.1148	92.5438	105.253	353.008	8.51107	313.295	3.44376	4.14938	50.1744	-	3.56570
	C	14.7391	79.6976	90.6422	304.000	7.32960	269.806	2.96570	3.57345	43.2094	-	3.07071
FM	B	12.6931	68.6347	78.0597	261.1801	6.31217	232.353	2.55402	3.07740	37.2114	-	2.64438
Italy	S	5573.60	30138.0	34276.0	114956.0	2771.70	102027.0	1121.50	1351.30	16339.0	37816.0	-
	C	4799.91	25954.2	29518.3	99000.4	2386.95	87864.7	965.805	1163.72	14071.5	32565.8	-
L	B	4133.60	22351.0	25421.0	85259.0	2055.61	75668.0	831.700	1002.20	12118.0	28045.0	-

S = Exchange rate at which the central bank of the country in the left hand column will sell currency identified in the row at the top of the table.
C= Bilateral central rate.
B = Exchange rate at which the central bank of the country in the left hand column will buy the currency identified in the row at the top of the table.
***** = These buying and selling rates are not operational. Reflecting a bilateral agreement between the German and Dutch monetary authorities, the following rates apply: Netherlands (100DM: selling 115.2350, buying 110.1675), Germany (100Fl: selling 90.7700, buying 86.78). National Ecu Central rates for the DRA and GBP are 295.269 DRA and 0.793103 GBP respectively, for 1 Ecu.
Source: Financial Times, November 26, 1996.

The EMS in Action

The original EMS plan called for central rates and intervention limits set by the Ecu. It did not include bilateral intervention grid limits. This was due to the French demand that the Ecu maintain a central role in the ERM mechanism so as to force Germany to the front line of interventions. The French expected that this would require Germany to revalue the Deutsche mark or ease monetary policy toward the EC average. However, the Germans objected to this arrangement, and at the 1978 German-French bilateral summit in Aachen the French agreed that mandatory interventions could only be triggered when two ERM currencies tested their bilateral margins.

Nonetheless, the French managed to give the Ecu a major role in the ERM through the Belgian Compromise of 1979. According to this compromise, bilateral margins are the trigger for mandatory interventions, but divergence has to be calculated in terms of the Ecu so as to improve policy coordination. The divergence indicator, albeit vague, represented an important innovation within the context of international monetary policy coordination. If member nations exceed the maximum divergence of 75 percent they have to reverse it by (i) trying other means of intervention; and/or (ii) applying appropriate domestic economic policies; and/or (iii) altering their central rates. This arrangement was the first example of the use of a specific multilateral indicator as a trigger mechanism for policy coordination.

When intervening, each central bank must ensure that its currency does not exceed the prescribed central parity margin when engaging in foreign exchange market operations. Thus, central banks are obliged to intervene when bilateral parities reach the upper or lower limits. Marginal intervention must be carried out by both central banks involved, and there is no limit to the financing of such intervention. Central banks may buy and sell each other's currencies before the outer limits of the bilateral band have been reached, thereby permitting intra-marginal intervention. However, such intervention is subject to the approval of the central bank whose currency is being sold or bought. It should be noted that there were few provisions for intra-marginal intervention until the Basle-Nyborg Agreements of 1987. Intervention in other currencies -- usually in dollars -- is always permitted and is not subject to mutual authorization.

Not surprisingly, the Bundesbank obtained an assurance from the German government that if a conflict arises between the external and internal affects of monetary policy, domestic price stability would be given priority over exchange rate stability. In other words, the Bundesbank gained permission to suspend interventions if they threaten domestic price stability. It should be noted that the Bundesbank was well aware that if its pursuit of domestic price stability was in conflict with the ERM, it would come under heavy international pressure to compromise its domestic concerns. This was well illustrated by the 1992 and 1993 ERM crises.

The ERM's system of semi-pegged exchange rates provides the benefits of fixed exchange rates, yet retains the flexibility of the intermittent realignments of central parities. To create a more symmetrical system than the "Snake", ERM realignments are subject to mutual consent. While some consider such realignments critical for member economies undergoing changes, others see realignments as a systemic failure. As usual, the truth lies somewhere in between, thus periodic realignments occur. Although there are many views as to the efficiency of regional coordination of monetary policies in general and that of the ERM in particular, it is likely that regional coordination improved the ability of the participating nations to respond to external shocks such as changes in U.S. monetary policies or global oil price movements.

Ideally, the ERM should have started out as a symmetrical system without an anchor currency; thus the burden of adjustment would have been a joint responsibility of all central banks. If, for example, the French franc/Deutsche mark cross-rates reached the upper or lower limit, there would be an onus on both the Banque de France and the Bundesbank to defend the band, regardless of which would be the weaker currency. However, in reality the system quickly developed into an asymmetric one -- with the Deutsche mark as the anchor currency and the Bundesbank as the anchor central bank. Yet while the Bundesbank provided a stable, non-inflationary base, the adjustment pressure is on the central banks defending the weaker currencies. The central bank of the stronger currency although obliged to intervene could opt to do so with only a token amount. It should be noted that the asymmetry of the ERM can be justified in that member central banks with unsatisfactory inflation records could use the ERM to borrow the credibility of the anchor (i.e., the Bundesbank). Of course, in return, they have surrendered a portion of their monetary policy authority.

Monetary integration theory is concerned with the costs and benefits of "symmetric" versus an "asymmetric" system. The symmetric system, in which the burden of exchange rate adjustments is equally allocated among the participating countries, is more about overall monetary coordination and cooperation. In contrast, the asymmetric system highlights sustainable low inflation levels, assuming that the anchor central bank conducts a stable monetary policy which, in fact, the Bundesbank does. Thus, the functioning of the ERM is to some extent dependent on asymmetry.

The European Monetary Cooperation Fund (EMCF)

Under the ERM, participating central banks are required to intervene in the foreign exchange markets to preserve upper and lower currency band limits (i.e., they must buy their currency at the lower end and sell it at the higher end). To facilitate official ERM interventions, the 1979 Belgian Compromise provided the EMCF with 20 percent of the ERM member nations' gold[50] and dollar reserves in return for an equivalent claim denominated in Ecu, based on a revolving three-month swap

[50] These gold reserves were revalued semi-annually to reflect market value.

arrangement. The provision of gold and dollar reserves was mandatory for ERM participants but voluntary for other nations. Thus, albeit modestly, the Ecu became a reserve asset and a means of official settlement for the EMCF. But the EMCF has never become influential, because on its behalf central banks have continued to hold and manage gold and dollar reserves and to receive interest on them.

Other tools that can be used to achieve the same outcomes include the monetary authorities' "talking" currencies up or down, discrete signals to traders, foreign currency borrowings, market interventions, interest rate changes, capital controls and other economic policy changes. However, such measures are resorted to only under extreme conditions, mostly to control speculation. Of all of these measures, interest rate adjustments and sustained, coordinated market interventions are the most effective. But it should be noted that central banks are finding it increasingly more difficult to influence the markets, owing to their approximately US$1 trillion and US$7 trillion daily turnover in foreign exchange and capital transactions, respectively.

To provide for official ERM interventions when cross-rates reach their bilateral limits, three types of EMS financing facilities are provided through the EMCF: (i) the Very Short-Term Financing Facility (VSTF); (ii) the Short-Term Monetary Support (STMS); and (iii) the Medium-Term Financial Assistance (MTFA). The VSTF and the STMS are under the jurisdiction of national central banks, while the MTFA is administered by the ECOFIN Council. The STMS provides short-term financing for temporary balance of payments problems while the MTFA provides medium-term financing in the form of two-to-five-year conditional loans.

Such credit provisions represent a commitment and an obligation to the ERM. Thus, the participating central banks are required to provide unlimited credit financing for marginal interventions through the VSTF, which is designed to support the credibility of the bilateral ERM parities. No central bank within the ERM system is ever allowed to run out of reserves in the short run. Banks defending the weak currency are able to borrow unlimited "hard" currency, that is, they can receive credit from other central banks which they must pay back within three months with a possible partial payment delay for six months. Any further extensions are subject to individual arrangements. Inter-central bank credits to finance "intra-marginal" interventions to move before cross-rates reach their upper or lower limits are also provided.

Prior to the 1987 Basle-Nyborg Agreements, up to 50 percent of the VSTF credit claims were repayable in Ecu, with additional amounts payable only with the consent of the debtor country. Nations with net deficit positions in the EMCF could pay interest on the Ecu debt based on the weighted average of all the discount rates of the participating countries, thereby promoting the use of the Ecu by debtors. The rates on net surplus positions were based on market rates, thereby encouraging positive net positions. Under this system, central banks had the ability to "sterilize" foreign exchange interventions through the use of domestic interest rates or open market operations. Market confidence in the ERM was reflected by the interest rate differentials between the stronger currencies of the system, such as the Deutsche mark and the other currencies. Confidence in long-term currency stability was represented by the differences in long-term bond yields.

The EMCF was modified through the Basle-Nyborg Agreements in September 1987.[51] As a result of the major 1986-87 ERM realignments, caused by external circumstances as opposed to internal disequilibria, borrowing arrangements were changed by extending the roles of both the MTFA and the VSTF. These changes facilitated intra-marginal interventions which improved the capability of the systems to weather external shocks by requiring more of a symmetric intervention by all central banks -- not just by those of the nations whose currency tested the lower bands of the ERM. The Agreements sought to provide a better balance among intra-marginal interventions, changes in interest rate differentials and compulsory interventions -- the three operational instruments of the EMS. Before 1987, interventions were used in almost all cases.

More specifically, the Basle-Nyborg Agreements extended the life of the EMCF credits arising from mandatory interventions from 45 to 75 days, starting with the month of intervention. Additionally, the STMS was doubled and member nations obtained more flexibility in using the VSTF for intra-marginal interventions. Consent of the issuing banks was assumed and not required and the creditor banks could seek reimbursement in their own currencies. Moreover, the Agreements raised the Ecu settlement limit from 50 to 100 percent for the VSTF for a period of two years; this was later extended for another two years. Shortly after they were signed, the Agreements were put to the test by the October 1987 stock market crash. They survived.

The EMS/ERM represents a delicate balance between the intricate rules of intervention and settlements on the one hand and coordinated discretionary realignments on the other hand. The EMS may have been possible because it did not call for budget policy coordination.

Performance of the EMS and ERM: 1979-96 and Beyond

The performance of the EMS and its ERM during 1979-96 can be divided into four phases; Phase I: March 1979-March 1983, Phase II: March 1983-January 1987, Phase III: January 1987-August 1993, and Phase IV: August 1993-?. The 1979-96 ERM bilateral central realignment changes are shown in Table 1.4 in percentages.

---

[51] The Basle-Nyborg Agreements received their name from the Meeting of the EC Central Bank Governors in Basle, and from their ratification at the ECOFIN Council meeting in Nyborg.

Table 1.4
ERM Realignments: Percentage Changes in Bilateral Central Rates (1979-96)

	Belgian & Luxembourg francs	Danish krone	Deutsche mark	Finnish markka	French franc	Italian lira	Irish pound
Sept.24,1979		-2.9	2.0				
Nov.30,1979		-4.8					
Mar.23,1981						-6.0	
Oct.5,1981			5.5		-3.0	-3.0	
Feb.22,1982	-8.5	-3.0					
June 14,1982			43.25		-5.75	-2.75	
Mar.21,1983	1.5	2.5	5.5		-2.5	-2.5	-3.5
July 22,1985	2.0	2.0	2.0		2.0	-6.0	2.0
Apr.7,1986	1.0	1.0	3.0		-3.0		
Aug.4,1986							-8.0
Jan.12,1987	2.0		3.0				
June19,1989							
Jan.8,1990						-3.7	
Oct.8,1990							
April 6,1992							
Sept.8,1992				F			
Sept.13,1992						-7.0	
Sept 14,1992	3.5	3.5	3.5		3.5		-3.5
Sept.16,1992							
Sept.17,1992						Drops Out (F)	
Nov.19,1992							
Nov.22,1992							
Dec.10,1992							
Feb.1,1993							-10.0
May 13,1993							
Mar.5,1995							
Oct. 14,1996							
Nov. 25, 1996						Rejoins ERM	

continued...

Table 1.4 (...continued)
ERM Realignments: Percentage Changes in Bilateral Central Rates (1979-96)

	Dutch guilder	Norwegian krone	Portuguese escudo	Spanish peseta	Swedish krona	Austrian schilling	Pound sterling
Sept.24,1979							
Nov.30,1979							
Mar.23,1981							
Oct.5,1981	5.5						
Feb.22,1982							
June 14,1982	4.25						
Mar.21,1983	3.5						
July 22,1985	2.0						
Apr.7,1986	3.0						
Aug.4,1986							
Jan.12,1987	3.0						
June.19,1989				Joins ERM			
Jan.8,1990							
Oct.8,1990							Joins ERM
April 6,1992			Joins ERM				
Sept.8,1992							
Sept.13,1992							
Sept.14,1992	3.5		3.5	-3.5			-3.5
Sept.16,1992							Drops Out (F)
Sept.17,1992				-5.0			
Nov.19,1992					F		
Nov.22,1992			-6.0	-6.0			
Dec.10,1992		F					
Feb.1,1993							
May 13,1993			-6.5	-8.0			
Jan 1, 1995						Joins ERM	
Mar.5,1995			-3.5	-7.0			
Oct. 14,1996					Joins ERM		
Nov. 25,1996							

KEY: Drops Out = Dropped out of the ERM.
F = Floating.

Source: Data from Financial Times, Oct. and Nov. 1995; and Ungerer, Horst, Jouko J. Hauvonen, August Lopez-Clatos, and Thomas Mayer. European Monetary System: Developments and Perspectives, Occasional Paper no. 73, Washington D.C.: IMF, November 1990, p.55 and Barnes, Ian and Pamela Barnes. The Enlarged European Union, New York: Longman Group UK Ltd., 1995, p.129.

Phase I: March 1979 - March 1983

Phase I proved to be a trial period for the EMS. Frequently, it resembled the preceding "Snake" system (i.e., it was characterized by high rates of inflation, differing economic policies, and various economic conditions). In the absence of a common economic policy strategy to deal with exogenous disturbances, member nations tried to familiarize themselves with the system. The period was also marked by oil shocks, sizable current account and budget deficits, falling output and rising unemployment. During the early part of this period the weak dollar forced the ERM into realignments. Consequently, as member countries responded to these pressures through diverging national policies, there were seven realignments.[52] Of these, at least four were precipitated by speculative attacks on the bilateral currency exchange rate parities. Although there was no standard formula to determine the magnitude of the realignments, interest rate differentials were accommodated.

The election of French President Mitterand in May 1981 and of German Chancellor Kohl in 1982 underscored the lack of national policy convergence as the new French government's response to the recessionary pressures was budgetary expansion while the new German government emphasized its rejection of inflation and public deficits.[53] With hindsight, many consider it fortunate that the ERM was signed in 1978 as the subsequent atmosphere was not conducive to policy coordination, especially between France and Germany, the backbone of the EMS system. However, the U.S. exchange rate policy turnaround, which resulted in a stronger dollar during the early 1980s reduced some of the speculative pressures on the ERM as the international competitiveness of European exports increased. By 1983 France had abandoned its expansionary fiscal policies and had begun to re-establish competitiveness through exchange rate adjustments.

---

[52] For a detailed chronology of the ERM strains and subsequent realignments, see Ungerer, Horst and Jouko J. Hauvonen, August Lopez-Clatos, Thomas Mayer. European Monetary System: Developments and Perspectives, Occasional Paper no. 73, Washington D.C.: IMF, November 1990.

[53] In 1982-83, French, Belgian and Danish economic policies converged to some extent. However, the impact of this convergence was experienced only after considerable delay.

Phase II: March 1983 - January 1987

Phase II was a period of relative stability characterized by disciplined convergence policies, a focus on disinflation and some minor ERM adjustments in 1985. Such measures were effective because national inflation rates began to converge, as did nominal costs, wages and other monetary aggregates, and realignments became less necessary. The dollar appreciation and eventual overvaluation aided the stability of the EMS. As a matter of fact, following the end of Phase I (March 1983), it took 28 months (to July 1985) until the next realignment. The Bundesbank's increased use of intra-marginal interventions induced a very stable domestic monetary policy, which led to the Deutsche mark's emergence as the nominal anchor of the ERM. This enhanced the role of the Deutsche mark as an alternative reserve currency, which increased the influence of the Bundesbank in determining the exchange rate between the ERM currencies and the dollar.

The need for exchange rate stability was underscored by the 1985 SEA, which liberalized capital movements, and by the 1986-87 turmoil in the currency markets that was due largely to the dollar's volatility -- which peaked in 1985 and then continued on a two-year downward trend. The ERM nations began to rely on intra-marginal interventions using the Deutsche mark rather than the dollar, which not only reinforced German regional monetary leadership but also increased the Deutsche mark's role as an international means of payment and reserve asset. However, this situation increased the discord between Germany and its regional neighbors, in particular France. Such an outcome was not unexpected: indeed, the Bundesbank had always feared that German domestic monetary stability would at some point conflict with the economic policies of neighboring countries. It should be noted that the EMS nations agreed to a concerted effort to make speculation unrewarding by keeping future realignments infrequent and small, within the bilateral parities.

Phase III: January 1987 - August 1993

The early part of Phase III saw a renewed commitment to exchange rate stability, as manifested by the narrowing of interest rate differentials resulting from the 1987 Basle-Nyborg Agreements, as well as growing capital movement liberalization. This was a period of symmetry for the EMS. However, a series of unforeseen economic and political shocks proved unsettling, and eventually the bilateral currency bands had to be expanded because of two subsequent crises in 1992 and 1993.

The September 1992 crisis forced the U.K. and Italy (and Finland) to float their currencies and was followed by a Spanish devaluation that touched off additional flotations and devaluations. These events culminated in the August/September 1993 crisis, which resulted in the widening of the currency bands from +/-2.25 to +/-15 percent -- a de facto suspension of the mechanism. As a result, except for the Deutsche mark and the Dutch guilder,[54] all currencies started to achieve the wider bands, albeit temporarily. This is akin to a floating exchange rate system because open market floats do not fluctuate much over +/-15 percent. With such a widening of the ERM currency bands, policymakers are enjoying freedoms that allow monetary policy flexibility. This is always appealing during hard economic times.

It is generally agreed that the two chronologically separate but interrelated crises were, essentially, a crisis of the EMU's credibility. The financial markets doubted the ability of the governments to keep their currencies within the narrow ERM bands during the long Stage II transition period to EMU. Although there is disagreement about the specific causes of these crises, the following are possible factors that may have triggered the same: (1) problems involved with ratifying the Maastricht Treaty; (2) fundamental misalignments within the ERM; (3) the prolonged and deep European recessions; (4) inherent design flaws in the ERM (the "Walters Critique")[55]; (5) the "Emminger Letter"[56]; (6) the effects of German reunification; (7) an increase in the number of countries linking their currencies directly or indirectly to the Deutsche Mark and/or the Ecu; (8) the general unwillingness to adjust central parities; (9) the Maastricht Treaty deadline pressures; (10) increasing frictions between ERM policies and domestic economic concerns; and (11) the actions and reactions of the financial markets. See Chapter II for more details on the ERM crises.

Phase IV: August 1993 - ?

Phase IV is best characterized by a question mark, concerning not only the future of the ERM but perhaps even that of the EMU. The 1992 and 1993 ERM crises left behind an aura of uncertainty.[57] In October 1993, following the widening of the ERM bands to +/-15 percent, all the currencies of the former narrow band (+/-2.25 percent), except for the Deutsche mark and the Dutch guilder,[58] moved outside their former narrow band vis-à-vis the strongest currencies. Once these currencies were outside the ERM, the pound sterling and the Italian lira regained the ground they had lost during the summer of 1993, as did the Greek drachma, the Finnish markka and the Swedish krona. The Austrian schilling was tightly pegged to the Deutsche mark. From May 1994 onward, the Italian lira began to depreciate significantly, and the Greek

---

[54] Germany and the Netherlands continue to adhere to the narrow +/- 2.25 percent bands on a voluntary basis.

[55] This refers to Sir Alan Walters' (ex-chief economic advisor to Prime Minister Margaret Thatcher) critique of the ERM. See Chapter II for details.

[56] This refers to Otmar Emminger's (ex-Bundesbank president) letter to the German government with respect to the Bundesbank's role in the EMS. See Chapter II for details.

[57] See Chapter II for a detailed discussion of this crisis.

[58] As agreed upon by a bilateral agreement, the Dutch guilder stayed in the +/-2.25 percent band with the Deutsche mark.

drachma came under pressure during May and June of the same year.[59]

On January 9, 1995 the Austrian schilling joined the EMS and entered the ERM while the Swedish krona and the Finnish markka only joined in the EMS. However, during the first quarter of 1995, the ERM again began to experience significant pressures. Currencies that were under strain included the Spanish peseta, the Irish pound, the French franc and the Danish krona, particularly in March of that year. The non-ERM currencies, the Swedish krona, Italian lira and pound sterling also came under strain during the early part of 1995. Following the Spanish government's request for a realignment, on March 5, 1995 the ECOFIN Council responded by reducing the peseta's central rate by -7 percent and that of the Portuguese escudo by 3.5 percent. Tension eased over the summer, but the French franc and the Irish pound remained weak.

In general, the volatility during 1993-95 was "higher than in the years preceding the 1992 ERM crisis."[60] The exchange rate variability of some currencies in 1995 was as high and, in some cases higher than during the second half of 1993, immediately preceding the second ERM crisis of August 1993. However, it should be pointed out that, by contrast, interest rate levels and differentials were less volatile in the 1993-95 period, as monetary authorities had greater exchange rate flexibility and did not have to rely on interest rates to maintain the old ERM's narrow parities. Moreover, the size of the foreign exchange intervention was smaller in 1995 than during the second half of 1993.

On October 14, 1996 the Finish markka joined the ERM. The Italian lira soon followed suit by rejoining on November 25, 1996, albeit amidst controversy over its central parity. Both nations rushed in before the end of 1996 in order to join the first wave of EMU membership in 1999.

Since the widening of the ERM currency bands to +/-15 percent several proposals to restructure the ERM (and thus provide a basis for transition to a single currency) have been discussed. They included (1) an early return to the old ERM; (2) a delayed return to the old ERM; (3) the introduction of a reformed ERM; (4) the combination of options 2 and 3 with capital and foreign exchange controls and taxes; (5) the combination of options 2 and 3 with coordinated interventions and changes in short-term interest rates; and (6) the continuation of the present wide bands for an extended period of time. Eventually, at the December 13-14, 1996 Dublin European Council Summit, participants agreed to adopt Option 3 -- the "introduction of a reformed ERM", the "ERM II". The ERM II is based on the single currency, the Euro, and is set to begin January 1, 1999. It is based on a "hub and spokes" concept with the Euro as the anchor of the exchange rate mechanism. Non-EMU member nations will

---

[59] The market exerted pressure just prior to the lifting of Greece's remaining capital controls.

[60] "Progress Towards Convergence," European Monetary Institute (EMI), Frankfurt am Main, November 1995, p.40.

target their currencies against the Euro only. Although the fluctuation band was not specified, it is likely that it will be relatively wide like the original ERM's +/-15 percent band. Non-EMU member currencies will be allowed to target narrower bands if they so choose. Membership in the new ERM II is not compulsory, although non-EMU EU nations are "expected" to join. Moreover, the ECB's obligation to support weaker currencies under speculative attack is limited.[61] However, what is still not clear is whether the ERM II structure can accommodate the needs of its members together with the needs of those nations that cannot qualify or choose not to join. See Chapter VI for more details on the ERM II.

It should be noted that some of the pressures that led to the expanded ERM bands (+/-15 percent) are still affecting the EU currency markets. These pressures will greatly influence the performance of the ERM II, and, ultimately, the single currency, the Euro.

The Evolution of the European Economic and Monetary Union (EMU)

The 1987 Basle-Nyborg Agreements were reached following the January 1987 ERM realignment to strengthen the EMS. In early 1988, amid dissatisfaction with the ERM, the discussion of the EMU and of the creation of a common central bank started all over again. The initiative came from three nations -- France, Italy and, surprisingly, Germany.

The French have always been active in the ECOFIN Council. In a January 8, 1988 memorandum to the Council, French Minister of Finance Edouard Balladur insisted on an institutional reform of the EMS/ERM rather than on the use of the measures contained in the 1987 Basle-Nyborg Agreements. The strongly worded memorandum criticized the ERM's asymmetry for not spreading the costs of interventions and claimed that the ERM's credit provisions created only temporary symmetry and, thus, gave the anchor currency, the Deutsche mark, too much influence. This memorandum emphasized that the only solution was to strive for a more comprehensive and symmetric common monetary arrangement as soon as possible. Balladur argued that

> ....ultimately it is the central bank whose currency is at the lower end of the permitted range which has to bear the cost. However, it is not necessarily the currency at the lower end of the range which is the source of the tension. The discipline imposed by the exchange-rate mechanism may, for its part, have good effects when it serves to put a constraint on economic and monetary policies which are insufficiently rigorous. It produces an abnormal situation when its effect is to exempt any countries whose policies are too restrictive

---

[61] "Pact sets rules for ins and outs of ERM". Financial Times, December 17, 1996, p.2.

> from the necessary adjustment. Thus the fact that some countries have piled up current account surpluses for several years equal to between 2 and 3 percent of their GDPs constitutes a grave anomaly. This asymmetry is one of the reasons for the present tendency of European currencies to rise against the dollar and the currencies tied to it. This rise is contrary to the fundamental interest of Europe and of its constituent economies. We must therefore find a new system under which this problem cannot rise.[62]

The Italians had similar but more candid views concerning asymmetry. They were expressed by the Italian Minister of the Treasury, Giuliano Amato, in a memorandum to the ECOFIN Council, dated February 23, 1988. Amato argued that the Deutsche mark was undervalued, that the German current account surplus had become structural and that this reduced the growth potential of other nations. He also emphasized that Italy had still assumed the risk of reducing exchange controls and thus needed exemptions not only with regard to the proposed Single Market directive on the liberalization of capital movements, but also with respect to taxation, supervision and the convergence process. He proposed an EMCF recycling mechanism "which could borrow funds on the market and reallocate them in such a way as to compensate the inflow and outflow of capital."[63] Amato also favored expanding the ERM's +/-2.25 percent band to establish uniform conditions of ERM membership and to facilitate the entrance of the pound sterling. Like the French, he wanted to identify diverging countries which should be required to adjust, regardless of the direction of their imbalances. In other words, the French and the Italians were proposing fundamental reforms of the EMS/ERM arrangements.

The 1988 relaunching of the EMU proposal had received unexpected German support. The French proposal had been deliberately vague about the structure and nature of the institutional changes, and the Italian plan had intentionally highlighted the need for economic policy coordination. This reaction had provided an opportunity for the German Minister of Foreign Affairs, Hans-Dietrich Genscher, to point out the dual nature of policy formulation in Germany and to propose a structure for the common central bank as well as alternatives for a single currency area. His institutional proposal[64] was based on the Bundesbank Act of 1957 and the German Stability Act of 1967. The former calls for an autonomous central bank with a clear mandate to maintain price stability and a distinct separation of money creation and the financing of public debt. The 1967 Stability Act requires the Federal government to promote price stability, high employment, external equilibrium and economic growth through

[62] January 8, 1988 memorandum by Edouard Balladur to the ECOFIN Council as translated for the EC Monetary Committee (April 29, 1988).

[63] February 23, 1988 memorandum by Giuliano Amato to the ECOFIN Council, published as "Un motore per lo SME" in the Italian newspaper *Il Sole*.

[64] Memorandum of 1988 by Hans-Dietrich Genscher, "A European Currency Area and a European Central Bank."

budgetary and other economic policies. Genscher's proposition was influenced by the desire to reduce the dollar's influence in Europe, to improve exchange rate management in relation to third country currencies and to pass the proposed directive on capital liberalization under the German presidency of the Council of Ministers during the first half of 1988. The Committee of Central Bankers was not enthusiastic about the propositions, as they had recently instituted the 1987 Basle-Nyborg Agreements, which strengthened the EMS/ERM. The Committee wanted even more attention devoted to these Agreements and was concerned about differences in national economic policy objectives which did not have to be addressed under the EMS. However, when the time for the 1988 Hanover European Council Summit arrived, the Committee was anxious not to be left out of the process.

The German, French and Italian support behind the institutional changes and the economic convergence process was sufficient to relaunch the EMU. During the 1988 Hanover Summit, the European Commission was authorized to form a committee to study the issue and to propose concrete steps towards achieving this goal. In addition to Jacques Delors and other Commission members, 12 national central bank governors and 3 independent economists[65] were included. On April 17, 1989 the Committee published its "Report on Economic and Monetary Union in the European Community," also known as the Delors Report proposing not only an operational definition of the EMU but also a step-by-step process of achieving it. The Report was discussed at the European Council Meeting in Madrid in June 1989.[66]

The Delors Report on the Economic and Monetary Union

The Delors Report defined the principal features of a monetary union as a currency area in which joint policy management would be used to realize common macroeconomic objectives. The three necessary conditions were identified as "(i) the total and irreversible convertibility of currencies; (ii) the complete liberalization of capital transactions and full integration of banking and other financial markets; and (iii) the elimination of currency fluctuations and the irrevocable locking of exchange rates."[67]

---

[65] Alexander Lamfalussy, the General Manager of the Bank of International Settlements (later President of the EMI); Niels Thygesen, Professor of Economics, Copenhagen University; and Miguel Boyer, President of Banco Exterior de España.

[66] At the June 26-27, 1989 Madrid Summit, the European Council decided that Stage I of the Delors Report, should begin on July 1, 1990, and requested that the "competent bodies" implement the necessary provisions and to organize an IGC to begin the preparatory work required to "lay down the subsequent stages."

[67] Report on Economic and Monetary Union in the European Community, Article 22. Committee for the Study of EMU, Luxembourg: Office for Official Publications of the European Communities, 1989, pp.18-19. These features were originally identified by the Werner Reports of the early 1970s.

According to the authors of the report, the principal features of an economic union in conjunction with a monetary union include an unrestricted common market based on a set of rules such as (i) the free movement of people, goods, services and capital; (ii) competition policy and other measures aimed at strengthening market mechanisms; (iii) common policies aimed at structural changes and regional development; and (iv) macroeconomic policy coordination, including binding budgetary policy rules.

The Delors Report proposed a step-by-step approach in three stages. Stage I consisted of increased voluntary coordination in the monetary and budgetary areas and required full capital movement liberalization. To this end, the deregulation of financial systems, including the establishment and coordination of necessary institutional and legal frameworks, is required. Although costly, such deregulation is basic to the movement of foreign direct and portfolio investments, which promote growth and in the long run reduce structural economic differences, as required for effective integration. The first stage was set to begin July 1, 1990.

Stage II, without specific dates, called for the establishment of the European Monetary Institute (EMI), the forerunner of the European Central Bank (ECB). Although the EMI is independent, it is structured so as to be representative of the central banks of all member nations. It coordinates monetary policies and undertakes all technical preparations for an eventual common monetary policy. But until the ECB becomes a reality, monetary policy continues to be set by national central banks. The EMI also monitors the smooth functioning of the ERM and can thus intervene in the markets. The extent to which it can do so depends on the bilateral agreements governing the transfer of foreign exchange reserves among central banks. The EMI may also act as an agent for the member states as long as it does not undermine national monetary policies. As a final step, Stage II requires the irrevocable locking of exchange rates. This represents the first move toward the introduction of a single currency, a revised Ecu[68], in Stage III. At the same time, the ECB and common monetary policies also have to be established, as locked exchange rates require such arrangements.

The Delors Report defined the functions and responsibilities of the European System of Central Banks (ESCB) as the formulation and implementation of monetary policy, foreign exchange market interventions against third currencies within the framework of the common exchange rate policy guidelines and the management of official reserves.[69] The report places the ECB within the structure of the ESCB in charge of monetary policies because "the establishment of a monetary union would have far reaching implications for the formulation and execution of monetary policy in the Community... there would be a need for a common monetary policy, which would

---

[68] The single currency's name (the "Euro") was decided at the Madrid European Council Summit in December 1995. Sections of this book that discuss 1989 Delors Report and 1992 Maastricht Treaty events in a historical context continue to refer to the single currency as the Ecu.

[69] Delors Report, Article 60, 1989, p.40.

be carried out through new operating procedures."[70] The new institution is necessary because

> ...a single [common] monetary policy cannot result from independent decisions and actions by different central banks. Moreover, day-to-day monetary policy operations cannot respond quickly to changing market conditions unless they are decided centrally...the domestic and international monetary policy-making of the Community should be organized in a federal form, in what might be called a European System of Central Banks (ESCB). This new system would have to be given the full status of an autonomous Community institution... and could consist of a central institution [the European Central Bank (ECB)] ...and the national central banks....[71]

The ESCB's specific objective is price stability.[72] Thus, it supports common economic policies and is responsible for the implementation and formulation of monetary policy, exchange rate management, and oversight of the payments system. The ESCB is not responsible for prudential supervision, but it is in charge of the coordination of supervisory policies.

The policy instruments available to the ESCB are not clearly spelled out. They are stated only in general terms as "... to conduct central banking operations in financial and foreign exchange markets as well as to exercise regulatory powers; while complying with the provision not to lend to public sector authorities, the System could buy and sell government securities on the market as a means of conducting monetary policy."[73]

The Delors Report follows the recommendations of the Werner Reports and specifies the structure of the proposed system of central banks as a federal structure similar to that of the U.S. Federal Reserve System and the structure and independence of the Bundesbank. It calls for the creation of,

> - an ESCB Council compiled of the governors of the central banks and the members of the Board, the latter appointed by the European Council, which is responsible for the formulation of monetary policies;

---

[70] Delors Report, Article 24, 1989, p.19.

[71] Delors Report, Article 32, 1989, p.25.

[72] This is one of the major differences between the Delors Report and the Werner Reports. While the Werner Reports considered sustained growth and other macroeconomic aims as the major objective of the new common institution, the Delors Report identified price stability as the primary objective.

[73] Delors Report, Article 32, 1989, p.26.

- a Board with supporting staff that monitors monetary developments and oversees the implementation of common monetary policies;

- national central banks, which execute operations in accordance with the decisions taken by the ESCB Council.[74]

The report stresses that "the ESCB Council should be independent of instructions from national governments and common institutions."[75] Its accountability is assured through the submission of a required annual report to the Parliament and the European Council. The President of the ESCB may also be invited to report to these institutions.

The 1992 Maastricht Treaty on Economic and Monetary Union

When the European Council reviewed the Delors Report at the Madrid European Council Summit on June 26-27, 1989, it concluded that revisions would have to be made to the Treaties of Rome to achieve the EMU.[76] As a result, at the European Council Summit in Dublin in June 1990 the heads of state/governments agreed to convene a summit to amend the Treaties.

The agreement reached at the Maastricht Intergovernmental Conference (IGC) in December, 1991 was heavily influenced by the Delors Report. This agreement had two distinct features: (i) provisions for the transition to economic and monetary union through the use of convergence criteria, and (ii) institutional arrangements and regulations to govern macroeconomic policy in the EMU through common decision-making structures such as the ECB. The agreement also laid down a three-stage timetable for the creation of a single currency and the transfer of economic and monetary policy formulation authority to the common institutions. More specifically, the Maastricht Treaty, officially known as the Treaty on European Union and signed in February 1992, calls for a number of major amendments to the basic treaties. The most striking of these amendments involves the creation of the EU, the establishment of an EMU by 1999, institutional reforms that increase the power of the European Parliament, extension of the qualified majority voting system to certain areas of social policy and agreements for coordinating defense and foreign policies. Box 1.4 describes the key features of the Maastricht Treaty in more detail.

---

[74] Delors Report, Article 32,1989, p.26.
[75] Delors Report, Article 32,1989, p.26.
[76] The decision to proceed with the revisions of the Treaties of Rome was also augmented by German re-unification.

Box 1.4
Key Features of the Maastricht Treaty

The Maastricht Treaty on European Union is essentially a treaty within a treaty, that is, an entity like European Union is created and given a general outline. In fact, the entity has no legal personality nor institutions of its own and lacks legal powers. The Maastricht Treaty generally addresses the entity of the European Community (EC), which replaces the EEC. Other features include:

- The establishment of an Economic and Monetary Union (EMU) and of a single European currency by 1999

- Institutional reforms to increase the power of the European Parliament (involvement in the enactment of legislation, right of approval prior to appointment of the Commission, power of assent for all major international agreements)

- Extension of qualified majority voting to certain areas of social policy and further progress on social policy, without the participation of the U.K.

- Introduction of a common foreign and security policy (agreements for coordinating defense and foreign policies)

- Rights for European citizens and Union citizenship.

- New powers for the EC such as a more active role in consumer protection, visa policies, public health; the creation of trans-European transport, telecommunications and energy networks; provisions for development cooperation, industrial policy, education, culture; increased emphasis on environmental protection; augmentation of research and development; cooperation in the fields of justice and home affairs.

Source: Adopted from Nicoll, William and Trevor C. Salmon. Understanding the New European Community, Hertfordshire: Harvester Wheatsheaf, 1994, p.281.

The Maastricht Treaty was hailed as a landmark on the road to European integration. Since then, however, it has become controversial. Thus, its fate will either unite or divide the EU, as is illustrated by the rather precarious ratification process involving a Danish "No" and the subsequent request for a revision of the Treaty, followed by a much too narrow "Yes" from the Treaty's main supporter, France, and a delayed approval by the U.K. Parliament. This was followed by an obscure Danish "Yes" in a second referendum, an eventual "go-ahead" from the U.K., and, finally, a much-worried-about "Yes" from the German Federal Constitutional Court. At best, these events, coupled with an eventual German parliamentary review near the end of the decade raise questions about the future of economic and monetary integration. Moreover, since its ratification the Maastricht Treaty has been plagued by problems such as the long-term impact of the September 1992 and August/September 1993 ERM crises. The political and economic controversies surrounding the Treaty raise concerns about, among others, the objectives and timetable of the EMU. Nonetheless, according to the Treaty (and the Delors Report), integration must take place at the latest by 1999, in three stages.[77]

Stage I. There is no explicit mention of Stage I in the Maastricht Treaty. However, the Treaty embodies provisions governing the first steps, which establish the stage for the eventual establishment of the EMU. Thus, Stage I involves the removal of all restrictions on payments and movements of capital within the EU and between member nations and third countries in line with the provisions contained in Article 73.b of the Maastricht Treaty.[78] Stage I also prohibits overdrafts or other types of central bank credit facilities, as well as privileged access by governments or other public institutions to financial institutions.[79] This includes direct purchases of government securities by the ECB or national central banks.

In addition, member nations are expected to adopt annual programs to promote economic convergence toward the EMU, paying particular attention to the maintenance of price stability and sound public finances.[80] Nations are also required to manage their EMS exchange rate policies as a matter of common concern.[81]

Stage II. The second stage, which, unlike Stage I, is explicitly mentioned in the Treaty, began on January 1, 1994 with the creation of the EMI[82] and the gradual reform of the existing common institutions. During this stage, nations are expected to intensify preparations for the EMU including the eventual irrevocable locking of currency exchange rates. Once Stage I and most of the Stage II requirements are fulfilled, determination of membership will start. The selection is based on the EMU convergence criteria which are designed to achieve low levels of inflation, limit budget deficits (i.e., promote growth) and identify economic concerns that could potentially weaken the EMU, once established.

---

[77] Stage I was announced to begin on July 1, 1990 at the June 26-27, 1989 European Council Meeting in Madrid. This stage is not controversial.

[78] Article 109.e.2 of the Maastricht Treaty, 1992.

[79] Articles 104-104.a of the Maastricht Treaty, 1992.

[80] Article 109.e.2.a of the Maastricht Treaty, 1992.

[81] Article 109.m.1 of the Maastricht Treaty, 1992.

[82] The EMI, located in Frankfurt, is the forerunner of the European Central Bank (ECB). As specified by the Treaty, its functions are the coordination of monetary policies and the preparation of all technical requirements for a common monetary policy. Although such policy will continue to be set by the national central banks, the Treaty requires that the central banks be independent of government control by the end of Stage II. In essence, the EMI will take the place of the EC Committee of Central Bank Governors and will assume the functions of the European Monetary Co-operation Fund (EMCF), currently administered by the Bank of International Settlements (BIS). Moreover, the EMI will monitor the smooth functioning of the ERM and thus can intervene in the market. However, the extent to which it can do so depends on the bilateral agreements it will have with member state central banks with respect to the transfer of foreign exchange reserves. The EMI can act as an agent for the member states as long as it does not undermine national monetary policies.

The convergence criteria address German concerns about the economic performance of EMU member nations, although the concept of the criteria was developed by the Delors Committee. The debate about the criteria divided the Committee into the "monetarist" and the "economist" groups. The monetarists included Delors himself, France, Italy, and some of the other, weaker, economies such as Greece, Ireland, Spain and Portugal. The monetarists took the position that monetary union would automatically bring about economic convergence. Germany, the Netherlands, Denmark, Benelux and the U.K. believed that before a process toward monetary union could begin economic convergence should take place. Ironically, for a while in the early 1990s Germany itself did not meet the inflation and budget deficit criteria. It should be noted that this minimized the pressures on Chancellor Kohl to call for a fast-track mini-EMU with France in the event that the ERM or the Maastricht Treaty fell by the wayside.

According to the Treaty, nations can become EMU members only if they meet the following four specific convergence criteria, which require that:

> 1. A country's inflation rate in the year before its performance is examined does not exceed the average of the three best-performing economies by more than 1.5 percentage points. Inflation is measured by the consumer price index.
>
> 2. The annual general government budget deficit (including social insurance) does not exceed 3 percent of GDP while the government debt ratio remains below 60 percent of GDP. Nor can the annual general government budget deficits exceed public investment expenditures.
>
> 3. The nation's currency is part of the EMS exchange rate mechanism (ERM) and has remained within the "normal" fluctuation margins[83] for at least two years prior to examination. Currencies cannot be unilaterally devalued during this period.
>
> 4. In the year before performance is assessed, long-term market interest rates (taking government bonds as a benchmark) are not more than 2 percentage points higher than the average comparable interest rates in the three countries with the lowest inflation.

According to the Treaty, the European Council had to decide by a qualified majority vote, no later than December 31, 1996, whether at least seven member states

---

[83] "Normal" fluctuation margins originally pertained to the +/- 2.25 percent currency bands of the ERM. It should be noted that in the aftermath of the ERM crisis and the subsequent widening of the currency bands to +/-15 percent, what was "normal" was debatable (among EU member nations) for a long time. However, to date, the EU's official position is that the +/- 15 percent currency band is "normal."

had met the economic convergence criteria[84] by the end of 1995,[85] and whether it is advisable to enter Stage III. If the answer was affirmative, Stage III was to commence on January 1, 1997. However, if this was not feasible, Stage III would automatically begin on January 1, 1999, following another review of the convergence performance of member states. As the January 1, 1997 EMU starting date was not feasible, it was decided that the review of the convergence performance for the first wave of EMU members would take place in 1997 using 1996 performance data, with final decisions on membership to be made in early 1998. (This date was later changed again.)

Member nations are required to gradually grant national central banks full independence and to amend national legislation so that it complies with the relevant provisions of the Maastricht Treaty and with the statutes of the ESCB (Articles 108 and 109.e.5). Following the establishment of the EMU membership, Stage III will begin with the formation of an ECB followed by the introduction of a single currency and a common monetary policy.

Stage III. According to the Treaty, Stage III could begin in 1997 but must begin no later than January 1, 1999.

> If by the end of 1997 the date for the beginning of the Third Stage has not been set, the Third Stage will start on 1 January 1999. Before 1 July 1998, the Council, meeting in the composition of Heads of State or of Government...taking into account the reports...and the opinion of the European Parliament, shall, acting by a qualified majority and on the basis of the recommendations of the Council referred to in paragraph 2, confirm which Member States fulfill the necessary conditions for the adoption of a single currency...the Governments of the Member States without a derogation shall appoint...the President, the Vice-President and the other members of the Executive Board of the ECB. If there are Member States with a derogation, the number of members of the Executive Board may be smaller...but in no circumstances shall it be less than four.[86]

---

[84] It should be noted that the wording of the Maastricht Treaty text allows a great deal of political and economic flexibility in determining if and when member states have met the convergence criteria.

[85] On February 17 1993, the deadline was extended to the end of 1996. Doubts about meeting the convergence requirements have grown because of their deflationary impact in times of rising unemployment (about 17 million people). On May 31, 1995, the EU Commission's Green Paper further delayed the deadline to meet the convergence criteria to 1997 (and possibly to 1998). In the November 1995 EMI Report "Progress Towards Convergence," the deadline was again revised and it was recommended that the participation decision deadline be set for in early 1998. This new deadline was officially adopted during the December 16-17, 1995 European Council Summit in Madrid with the understanding that actual 1997 performance data would be used to make the selection.

[86] Article 109.l and 109.j.4 of the Maastricht Treaty, 1992.

This stage will be marked by the following:

- the irrevocable locking of exchange rates leading to the adoption of a single currency, the Ecu[87];
- common economic and fiscal policies;
- an exchange rate policy determined by the Council of Ministers and the ECB;
- and the transfer of monetary policy to the European System of Central Banks.

The May 1995 EU Commission Green Paper

In its May 1995 "Green Paper: On the Practical Arrangements for the Introduction of the Single Currency"[88] the EU Commission spelled out a more detailed timetable for the introduction of the single currency. However, it also introduced the possibility of a further delay in the timetable. The three-phase timetable includes Phases A, B and C over a four-year period. Phase A involves the launch of the EMU. In Phase B the EMU will be implemented together with the emergence of a critical mass of Ecu activities. Phase C represents the final changeover to the single currency.[89] These phases are discussed and illustrated in greater detail below. Table 1.5 shows the planned sequence of events in the three phases involving the introduction of the single currency while Figure 1.2 presents the timetable for the introduction of the single currency in 1999.

Phase A. This phase lasts one year and begins with the Council of Ministers' decision to move forward.[90] During this phase, all the decisions and measures required in Phase B must be made and developed. Of these, the establishment of the ESCB and the ECB and the appointment of its Executive Board are the most significant. In conjunction with banks and financial institutions, the ECB also introduces the operational instruments required for applying monetary and exchange rate measures in the Ecu.

---

[87] Later renamed the "Euro" at the Madrid European Council Summit in December 1995.

[88] "Green Paper: On the Practical Arrangements for the Introduction of the Single Currency". EU Commission: Brussels, May 31, 1995.

[89] As before, the following section will continue to refer to the single currency as the Ecu because it is a historical recapitulation of the May 1995 Green Paper.

[90] Article 109.j and 109.l of the Maastricht Treaty, 1992.

Table 1.5
The May 1995-EU Commission Green Paper Sequence of Events for the Introduction of the Single Currency

Phase A The Launch of EMU	**Phase B** The Start of EMU	**Phase C** The Full Introduction of the Single Currency
Start of the phase: • List of participating Member States; • Date of start of the EMU announced (or confirmed); • Deadline for the final changeover to the single currency set; • Creation of the ESCB and the ECB; • Start of production of notes and coins; ***Throughout the phase:*** Stepping-up of preparations and implementation of measures that will, if possible, have been adopted beforehand: • Legal framework; • National steering structure; • Banking and financial community changeover.	***Start of the phase:*** • Fixing of conversion rates; • Ecu becomes a currency in its own right;* • Monetary and exchange-rate policy denominated in Ecu; • Inter bank, monetary, capital, and exchange markets in Ecu; • New government debt issued in Ecu; • Corresponding wholesale payment system denominated in Ecu; ***Throughout the phase:*** • Banks and financial institutions continue the changeover; • Public and private operators other than banks proceed with the changeover circumstances permitting.	***Start of the phase:*** • Ecu notes and coins introduced; • Banks complete the changeover (retail business payment systems); • Notes and coins denominated in national currency are withdrawn; • Public and private operators complete the changeover; • Only the Ecu is used.
1 year maximum	***3 years maximum***	***Several weeks***

* = Later renamed the "Euro" at the Madrid European Council Summit in December 1995.

Source: "Green Paper: On the Practical Arrangements for the Introduction of the Single Currency." Brussels: EU Commission, May 31, 1995, p.22.

Figure 1.2
The May 1995-EU Commission Green Paper's Timetable for the Introduction of the Single Currency

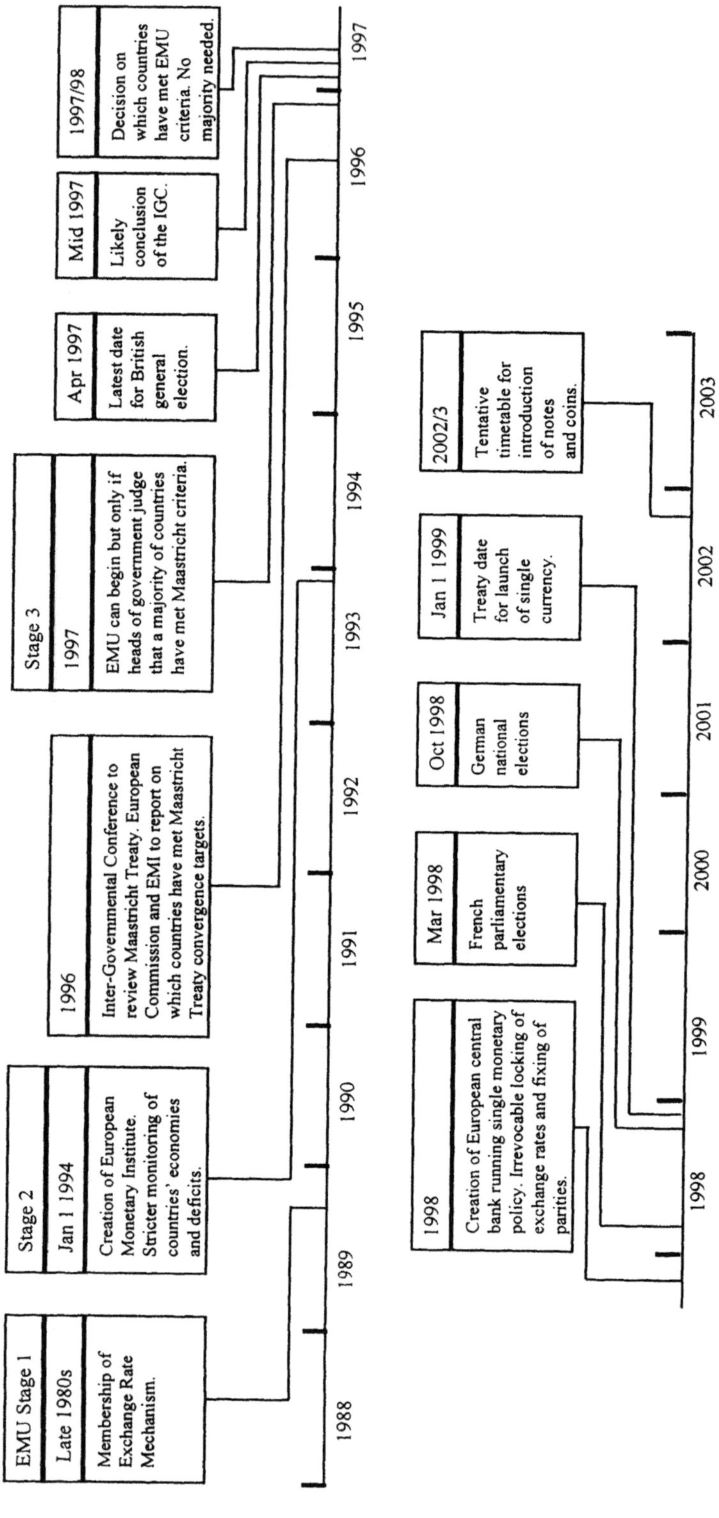

Source: Financial Times, September 29, 1995, p.2.

> In addition, Phase A involves the establishment of:
>
> - the legal framework allowing the single currency to be introduced at the start of Phase B. Inter alia, this would include conditions for using the new currency in the different sectors and in relations with national currencies, continuity of contracts and legal obligations; legislation enabling financial and tax authorities to collect some payments in Ecu at the start of Phase B;
>
> - the characteristics and technical specifications of notes and coins such that cash handling machines and information systems can be adapted...
>
> - [the] establishment of a national steering structure for supervising the move to the single currency, involving all the currency users concerned (government, central bank, private sector, consumers)...
>
> - [the] definition of a changeover plan in each country by the banking and financial community which would specify the speed and scope of the technical adaptation of its members.[91]

According to the Green Paper, "in order to generate irreversible momentum," the Council of Ministers also announces the final date for the full introduction of the single currency, four years after the start of Phase A, at the latest.

Phase B. This phase marks the irrevocable fixing of exchange rates and requires the ECB to assume the responsibility for the management of common monetary policy. It also calls for the emergence of a critical mass of activities conducted in the Ecu which ceases to be defined as a basket of currencies and becomes a currency in its own right for which the national currencies are perfect substitutes. As a result, national foreign exchange markets cease to exist. The report defines critical mass to include (i) monetary and exchange rate policy activities; (ii) inter-bank, monetary, capital and exchange markets; (iii) new government debt; and (iv) wholesale payment systems. All steps must be taken in consultation with the banking sector and the ECB, which is responsible for preparing the monetary policy framework.

Thus, Phase B marks the beginning of Stage III of the EMU. The Green Paper mandates that the changeover of all operations and systems be completed within three years so as to reinforce the credibility and irreversibility of the EMU.

- Monetary and exchange rate policy in Ecu: the Commission takes

---

[91] Green Paper, para.29, May 1995, p.17.

the view that the single monetary policy should be defined and implemented in terms of the single currency from the start of this phase. The ESCB would conduct Ecu transactions with all operators involved in monetary policy (national central banks, banks). This would affect the whole range of instruments associated with monetary policy: refinancing, open-market operations and, more generally, short-term transactions. In addition, and following the same logic, the ESCB would deal exclusively in Ecu vis-à-vis third currencies (dollar, yen). Settlement of monetary policy transactions would be made through the real-time wholesale TARGET system[92] that the EMI has undertaken to render operational by the end of 1996;

- New issues of public debt: new debt issues by the public sector would be denominated in Ecu as from the start of Phase B to the extent that it is technically possible. The issues which would be most appropriately denominated in Ecu would be those addressed to institutional investors and those maturing after the start of Phase C. Private issuers could decide to follow a similar path.

- Inter-bank, monetary and capital markets: globalization implies that markets affected by the conduct of the single [common] monetary policy would have to be able to work in Ecu simultaneously from the start of Phase B. This changeover concerns primarily Treasury bills, bonds and their derivatives. All operators on these markets (banks, investment funds, insurance companies, institutional investors, intermediaries) would operate in Ecu, as would the associated market systems (quotation, settlement, delivery, registration);

- The wholesale settlement systems, TARGET and the private systems of the Ecu Banking Association would be available to process large-value payments in Ecu.[93]

In addition, this phase involves the use of national currencies by banks and most of their customers; the payment of some taxes in Ecu and the denomination of

[92] In May 1995, the EMI Council released a report describing the TARGET (Trans-European Automated Real-time Gross settlement Express Transfer) system. This is a unified EMU-wide payment mechanism provided by the ESCB at the beginning of Stage III of the EMU. The TARGET system is necessary to secure implementation of the common monetary policy and to facilitate the settlement of large-value cross-border payments among member nations. TARGET is based on the existing national Real-Time Gross Settlement (RTGS) systems and their interlinkages. The RTGS is in operation in four member states and is currently being implemented in all of the other EU member nations. It is expected that by the end of 1997 all national RTGS system will be operational.

[93] Green Paper, para.32, May 1995, p.18-19.

public expenditures, whenever possible, in Ecu; the use of the Ecu by non-bank private businesses; and the continuing use of national currencies by individuals owing to the limited availability of Ecu as a means of payment.

Phase C. In this phase the final changeover to the single currency takes place. Although its starting date is announced at the beginning of Phase A, it could begin before the announced date if the European Council so decides. National notes and coins will be replaced by the Ecu and the same will become the only legal tender. Thus, all payments will be converted into Ecu and all transactions by the private non-banking sector will also be denominated in Ecu. During a statutory time period laid down in each country, the national currencies will be exchanged free of charge at national central banks. The actual changeover is expected to take only a few weeks in order to avoid complications caused by a prolonged period of dual currency circulation.[94] Thus, this phase completes the introduction of the single currency.

The November 1995 EMI Report on the EMU: "Progress Towards Convergence"

The EMI released its first progress report on the EMU in November 1995 in accordance with Article 7 of its statute.[95] This report, titled "Progress Towards Convergence,"[96] addressed the critical issues of Stage III of the EMU: (i) it laid out a revised timetable for the achievement of the single currency (this was a modification of the EU Commission's May 1995 Green Paper), and (ii) assessed EU member nations' ability to meet the Maastricht convergence criteria. Most of the report was devoted to the latter issue.

Timetable for Stage III of the EMU: The EMI Report laid out a three-phase timetable for the completion of the EMU as follows:

- ***Phase I*** *(January 1, 1989 - December 31, 1998)* marks the end of the transitory Stage II when EMU participants are selected and move to permanently fixed exchange rates.

[94] Green Paper, May 1995, pp.20-21,38.

[95] Article 7 of the EMI statute requires that once a year, it provides the European Council information on the readiness of EU member nations for Stage II of the EMU. "These reports shall include an assessment of the progress towards convergence in the Community, and cover in particular the adaptation of monetary policy instruments and the preparation of the procedures necessary for carrying out a single [common] monetary policy in the third stage, as well as the statutory requirements to be fulfilled for national central banks to become an integral part of the ESCB."

[96] "Progress Towards Convergence," European Monetary Institute (EMI), Frankfurt am Main, November 1995.

- ***Phase II*** *(January 1, 1999 - December 31, 2001)* marks the beginning of Stage III when the single currency is introduced on a non-cash basis.
- ***Phase III*** *(January 1, 2002 - July 1, 2002)* marks the last phase of the EMU when the single currency is physically introduced and becomes the sole legal tender in the EMU participant nations.

Figure 1.3 shows the revised EMI timetable for Stage III of the EMU, published in November 1995.

The EMI Report recommended that the decision to choose the EMU member nations should take place in early 1998, one year prior to the move toward permanently fixed exchange rates. Thus, January 1, 1999 will mark the end of Stage II and the beginning of Stage III. The EMI emphasized that the selection decision should be made prior to 1999, as new legislation would be needed to place the single currency on a "sound legal footing."[97] Legislative measures would be required, for example, concerning the conversion rates at which the EMU participants' national currencies will be irrevocably fixed, the manner in which the national currencies will be phased out in favor of the single currency, and the legal status of the new currency. The EMI Report maintained that legislation was also necessary to ensure that "economic agents should not be compelled to use the European monetary unit[98] before the completion of the changeover." On January 1, 1999, although all national currencies will remain in place, the exchange rates of the selected EMU participants should turn into "conversion rates" so that "national currencies will become different expressions of what is economically the same currency."[99]

---

97 "EU central bank maps road to Euro-currency." Financial Times, November 15, 1995, p.3.

98 The Report uses the term European monetary unit for the single currency.

99 "Progress Towards Convergence," EMI, November 1995.

Figure 1.3
The EMI's Revised Timetable for Stage III of the EMU
(November 1995)

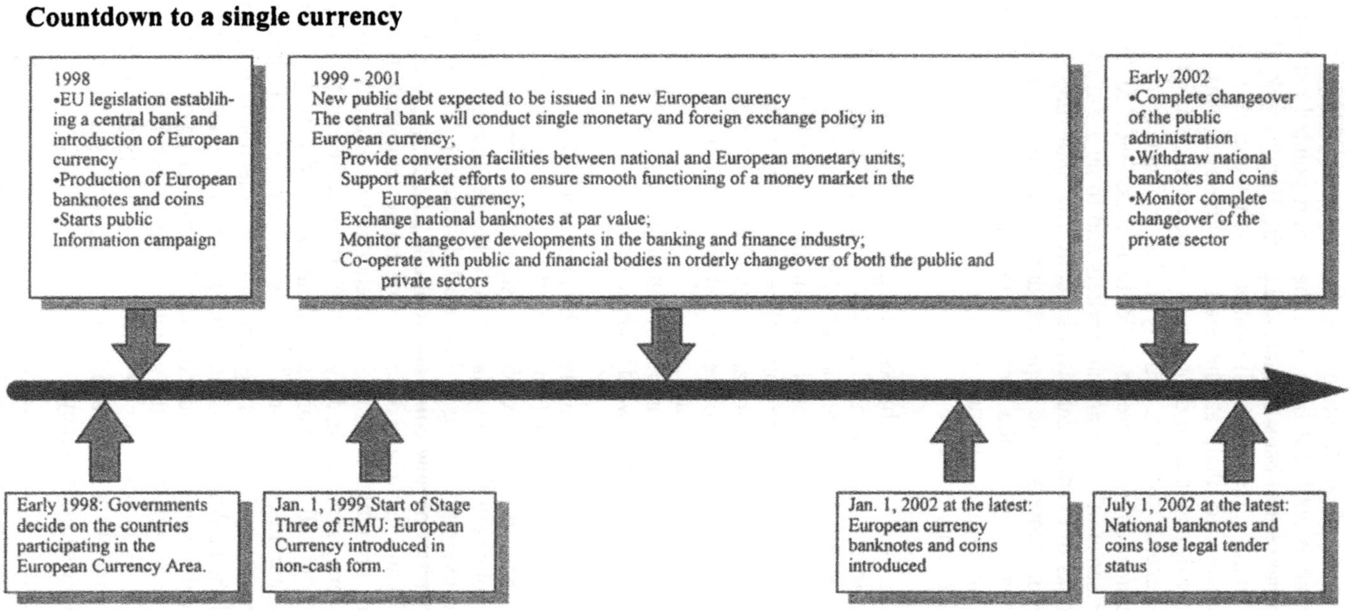

Source: Financial Times, November 15, 1995, p.3

The report proposes the introduction of the single currency on a non-cash basis at the start of Phase II (or Stage III) of the EMU, on January 1, 1999. Private economic agents will be free to use the single currency but would not be required to do so prior to the final deadline of the changeover. They could continue to use national currencies until that time. But the report pointed out that the ECB and its member national central bank affiliates (e.g., the Bundesbank) should be required to use only the single currency for all monetary policy and exchange rate operations. It further recommended that, at the start of Phase II when exchange rates are irrevocably fixed, new public debt issues be denominated in the single currency, in particular as regards securities actively traded in financial markets. The purpose of this recommendation is to create a "critical mass" i.e., to foster the new single currency's presence in the financial markets and to augment its liquidity and depth. When the stocks of existing debt will be converted into single currency is not clear. The EMI Report expressed the hope that during this interim stage "financial markets will largely change over to the European monetary unit at an early stage....However, most private individuals and most enterprises are expected to continue to operate in the national monetary units."[100]

To aid the smaller banks during the transition period, the EMI Report recommends that "conversion facilities" should be established which will be terminated when national currencies are discontinued as legal tender. The facilities should be provided by the national banks of the participating nations "to enable those counter-parties to deal with the national central banks in the national monetary units for all payments, in particular for all monetary policy operations. These facilities will allow them to send payment orders or other information to national central banks expressed in national monetary units."[101] Potential EMU participants such as Germany that have a large number of small banks, are very concerned about the conversion costs of moving toward a single currency.

Phase II should be completed by December 31, 2001 and will be succeeded by the six-month-long Phase III, in which the new currency, for the first time, will be physically introduced. This third phase is scheduled to begin on January 1, 2002. The EMI Report points out that the phasing in of the new banknotes and coins cannot be accomplished overnight owing to logistical difficulties i.e. the time needed to mint sufficient quantities of new coins and to modify existing automated teller machines. But the EMI considers the six-month time frame long enough to ensure a smooth transition (i.e., no bottlenecks) and short enough to avoid any prolonged side affects of a dual currency system. On July 1, 2002 the changeover to a single currency will be completed "for all operations and all agents" and national banknotes and coins "will disappear from circulation"[102]. The single currency will become the sole legal tender. All monetary liabilities de jure will be redeemable only in the new single currency and the banking and finance industry will no longer be permitted to use the extinct national currencies. Thus, on July 1, 2002, the process of implementing the EMU comes to an end. Given the gravity of this undertaking, it is not surprising that the November 1995-EMI Report changed the timetable of the EU Commission published in its 1995 "Green Paper" concerning the actual switch-over from national currencies to the single currency.

---

[100] "Progress Towards Convergence," EMI, November 1995.
[101] "Progress Towards Convergence," EMI, November 1995.
[102] "Progress Towards Convergence," EMI, November 1995.

Meeting the Maastricht Convergence Criteria (Reference Values)

In addition to setting a new timetable for Stage III of the EMU, the EMI Report also assessed the EU member nations' ability to meet the Maastricht convergence criteria or reference values comprised of limits on inflation, debt, deficit, interest rates and exchange rates. It should be noted that although the tone of the report is optimistic, its conclusions are realistic with respect to the various nations' ability to meet the criteria.

Just like the financial markets, the EMU has concluded that meeting the criteria will be an arduous task. The report pointed out that progress towards convergence is "insufficient....at present, there does not exist a majority of EU member states which satisfy all the criteria."[103] This, the report emphasized, is specially true in the area of public finances, where member nations have to significantly improve their performances. The criteria mandates that budget deficit and public debt ratios stay below 3 percent and 60 percent of GDP, respectively. Yet, according to the report, the observed results are disappointing. As of June 1995, 12 of the 15 member nations had an excessive deficit. "Either the deficit ratio was too high (France and the U.K.), or both the deficit and debt ratios were excessive to varying degrees (Belgium, Denmark, Greece, Spain, Italy, the Netherlands, Austria, Portugal, Finland and Sweden)."[104] The report identified only Germany, Luxembourg and Ireland as having met both fiscal criteria. It should be noted that a "soft" approach was used in the case of Ireland as it technically did not meet the 60 percent of debt to GDP ratio because its 1994 ratio was over 90 percent. The hazards of setting a precedent in using the "soft" approach are discussed in Chapters III and IV.

The EMI found much better performance concerning the maintenance of price stability and the level of interest rates. Over the 12-month period from October 1994 to the end of September 1995, 11 nations (Belgium, Denmark, Germany, France, Ireland, Luxembourg, the Netherlands, Austria, Finland, Sweden and the U.K.) met the inflation criterion. The three best-performing nations were Finland, Belgium and France, with inflation between 1.3 and 1.7 percent. But four countries, Greece, Spain, Italy and Portugal did not meet the criterion. As regards to long-term interest rates, ten countries met the requirement between October 1994 and September 1995. The five nations that failed to do so were Spain, Greece, Italy, Portugal and Sweden.

The EMI Report did not include an exchange rate criterion analysis, as there was still a controversy with respect to whether the Treaty's "normal" ERM band designation referred to the old +/-2.25 percent or new +/-15 percent band. Instead the report reviewed the stability of the member nations' currencies between October 1993 and September 1995. It found that the Deutsche mark, the Dutch Guilder and the Austrian schilling[105] were the most stable currencies over the required two-year period. Beginning with 1994, the Belgian and Luxembourg[106] francs were also classified as stable. The Danish krone, French franc and Irish pound were erratic and drifted away from their central parities. The Spanish peseta began to weaken in late

---

[103] "Progress Towards Convergence," EMI, November 1995, p.ix.
[104] "Progress Towards Convergence," EMI, November 1995, p.x.
[105] The Austrian schilling joined the ERM on January 9, 1995.
[106] The Belgium and Luxembourg francs are in a monetary association.

1994 and was adjusted downward in March 1995. This was followed by an official downward adjustment of the Portuguese escudo. The non-ERM currencies, such as the Finnish markka, appreciated while the pound sterling and the Swedish krona experienced weaknesses in early 1995 but recovered some ground in mid-to-late 1995. The Italian lira experienced substantial downward pressures beginning in the spring of 1994 but also recovered somewhat in mid-to-late 1995. The Greek drachma's performance was the worst, even though it appreciated in real terms, it actually depreciated nominally at an accelerating pace.

All in all, the EMI Report indicated that as of mid-1995 only Germany, Luxembourg and Ireland have met the Maastricht convergence criteria and were thus eligible for EMU membership. On strict technical grounds, Ireland should not be able to join as it exceeded the upper limit of the 60 percent debt to GDP ratio. However, by applying the “soft approach”, it could be considered as a candidate for admission. Table 1.6 shows a summary of the EMI findings.

The 1995 EMI Report implied a very small initial EMU membership. The likely participants were identified as Germany, France, Luxembourg, the Netherlands, Belgium and Austria. France's participation was uncertain because of its deficit. However, French participation is mandatory for a credible EMU. If Germany insists on a strict adherence to the convergence criteria, then the EMU would in all probability have to be delayed until the French can fulfill all the requirements. Italy's inflation, debt and deficit performance makes it difficult to include it in the EMU, regardless of the political implications. Although the Maastricht Treaty allows some liberal interpretation of the criteria, political and central bank circles, particularly in Germany, have stressed the strict interpretation of the criteria in order to reinforce and preserve the EMU's credibility. Theo Waigel, German Finance Minister, even proposed penalizing EMU members if they breach the deficit criteria, once they have become EMU members. This has been endorsed by France. Chapter VI provides a more detailed discussion of the politics of EMU membership.

Table 1.6
Assessing National Performance with Regards to the EMU Convergence Criteria (or reference values) (excluding the exchange rate criterion)

		Inflation[(a)]	Long-term interest rate[(b)]	General government lending(+) or borrowing(-)[(c)]	General government gross debt[(c)]
Belgium	1994	2.4	7.8	-5.3	135.0
	1995[(d)]	**1.6	**7.9	-4.5	134.4
Denmark	1994	***2.0	***7.8	-3.8	75.6
	1995[(d)]	2.1	8.6	# -2.0	73.6
Germany	1994	2.7	6.9	# -2.6	# 50.2
	1995[(d)]	2.1	7.1	# -2.9	# 58.8
Greece	1994	10.9	20.8	-11.4	113.0
	1995[(d)]	9.9	18.8	-9.3	114.4
Spain	1994	4.7	10.0	-6.6	63.0
	1995[(d)]	4.7	11.5	-5.9	64.8
France	1994	**1.7	**7.2	-6.0	# 48.4
	1995[(d)]	***1.7	***7.8	-5.0	# 51.5
Ireland	1994	2.4	7.9	# -2.1	[(e)]91.1
	1995[(d)]	2.5	8.5	# -2.7	[(e)]85.9
Italy	1994	3.9	10.6	-9.0	125.4
	1995[(d)]	4.9	12.3	-7.4	124.9
Luxembourg	1994	2.2	6.4	# 2.2	# 5.9
	1995[(d)]	2.1	6.2	# 0.4	# 6.3
Netherlands	1994	2.8	6.9	-3.2	78.0
	1995[(d)]	2.2	7.2	-3.1	78.4
Austria	1994	3.0	7.0	-4.4	65.2
	1995[(d)]	2.5	7.4	-5.5	68.0
Portugal	1994	5.2	10.4	-5.8	69.4
	1995[(d)]	4.2	11.7	-5.4	70.5
Finland	1994	*1.1	*9.1	-5.8	# 59.8
	1995[(d)]	*1.3	*9.4	-5.4	63.2
Sweden	1994	2.3	9.7	-10.4	79.7
	1995[(d)]	2.8	10.8	-7.0	81.4
United Kingdom	1994	2.4	8.0	-6.8	# 50.1
	1995[(d)]	2.7	8.4	-5.1	# 52.5

*,**,*** = first, second and third best performer in terms of price stability.
= public deficit not exceeding 3% of GDP; public debt not exceeding 60% of GDP.
(a) = Annual rates
(b) = In percentages, annual average
(c) = As a percentage of GDP
(d) = Twelve-month period ending September 1995 for inflation and long-term interest rate; general government lending/borrowing and general government gross debt for 1995 are European Commission estimates.
(e) = In 1994 and 1995 Ireland was not the subject of an EU Council decision under Article 104c(6) of the Treaty that an excessive deficit exists.
Source: Adopted from "Progress Towards Convergence." European Monetary Institute (EMI), Frankfurt am Main: November 1995, p.62.

The report also addressed monetary policy options.[107] However, they were vague, for example, it stated that reserve requirements[108] "could figure" among the chosen monetary policy instruments of the ECB. Although in line with the Bundesbank's policy, this violates the Bank of England's philosophy.

The December 1995 Madrid European Council Summit

The December 16-17, 1995 Madrid European Council Summit meeting reaffirmed the previously informally agreed upon revision of the EMU timetable published by the EMI in its November 1995 Report.[109] The summit also dealt with issues related to EU enlargement and institutional reforms, which are on the 1996-97 Intergovernmental Conference (IGC) agenda.[110]

On the first day of the summit, the EU heads of state unanimously agreed to name the single currency the "Euro." They also approved the EMI's proposed timetable, including January 1, 1999 as the launching date of Stage III, the introduction of the Euro, initially for non-cash purposes only. It was decided that the European Council would select the EMU participants on the basis of 1997 economic performance rather than forecasts.

According to the agreement reached, the eventually chosen EMU member governments will have to issue tradable debt in Euros once exchange rates are irrevocably locked and a single monetary policy is in place by 1999. This, as has been mentioned previously, involves the creation of a "critical mass" for the new currency well before the actual physical issue of Euro-notes and coins in 2002. At Germany's request, nontradable debt may be denominated in national currencies during the transition phase of Stage III (January 1, 1999- December 31, 2001). However, the conversion date of debt into Euros continues to be uncertain. Commercial banks are given the option to take deposits and open accounts in Euros ahead of the mandatory changeover deadline in 2002.

It should be noted that the German proposal to use the name Euro as a prefix to existing national currencies as, for example, Euro-mark, Euro-franc or Euro-guilder was rejected, thus, the name Euro will stand in its own right. French President Jacques Chirac's appeal for a delay in using the name Euro until it is widely accepted by the public, was also rejected. The heads of state/governments committed themselves to a three-year advertising and sales campaign to win support for the single currency. This campaign was launched at a conference hosted by the European Commission in Brussels, on January 22, 1996, and was attended by businessmen, financiers, the media and politicians.

Among the issues that were not resolved at Madrid was the sensitive question of the relationship between the "inner core" of the EMU member nations

---

[107] The EMI has evaluated the monetary policy options during 1996.

[108] Reserve requirements require banks to deposit funds with central banks.

[109] "Progress Towards Convergence," EMI, 1995.

[110] The IGCs are high-level meetings (i.e., European Council, ECOFIN Council, etc) added to the European Council's bi-annual summits to discuss and negotiate common EU concerns and agreements based on previously agreed agendas.

and those countries that either fail to qualify for membership or wish to "opt out" of the EMU.[111]

The November 1996 EMI Report on the EMU: "Progress Towards Convergence"

The EMI released its second progress report on the EMU in November 1996 in accordance with Article 7 of its statue. The report titled "Progress Towards Convergence 1996"[112] is a follow-up to a similar 1995 report.

The November 1996 report was not encouraging as its findings, although softly voiced, "...conclude[d] that at present a majority of member states [did] not fulfill the necessary conditions for the adoption of a single currency." In spite of the fact that the report found the "environment of low costs and price pressures" favorable, it emphasized that progress towards the reduction of budget deficits was too slow despite some positive signs during 1996[113] and cautioned that nations should not try to meet the Maastricht convergence criteria through short-term fixes. It called on the governments to address the fundamental economic issues such as high unemployment, the funding of pensions and the needs of aging populations, because the resolution of these problems will eventually determine the individual national currencies' irrevocably locked exchange rate against the Euro, long-term interest rates and competitiveness against the dollar. The EMI emphasized that no EU nation is effectively addressing these problems and concluded that most countries have not yet reached a sustainable medium-term fiscal position. Without using France Télécom as an example, it stated that "that the improvement of the deficit by measures with a one-off effect does not ensure sustainable consolidation, and great attention will have to be paid to the substance and not only to the accounting methods used in measuring both deficits and debt."

The report also pointed out that earlier improvements in Germany's deficit position have been reversed while Austria's deficit has been declining in recent years. Most other nations have managed to reduce their deficits since 1993, but the current levels are still above the Maastricht Treaty criterion of 3 percent. The EMI expects that the deficits of Spain, France, Portugal and Sweden will remain somewhat higher than 3 percent while those of Greece and Italy will stay well above the required maximum level. The report also pointed out that the EU nations' public debt reduction performance was mixed. For example, Italy's debt is too high and has not significantly declined since 1994. But Belgium's debt, while also too high, has shown improvements over the past three years. Germany, Spain and Austria had continually rising debt levels up to 1995 (Germany up to 1996), while the Netherlands, Portugal, Finland and Sweden have shown varying results in recent years. The report predicted that in 1996, four nations, Denmark, Ireland, the Netherlands and Luxembourg would meet the 3 percent deficit criterion while Luxembourg, France and the U.K. would meet the 60

---

[111] This issue is discussed in Chapter 6 under the section titled the "New ERM II".

[112] "Progress Towards Convergence 1996." European Monetary Institute (EMI), Frankfurt am Main, November 1996.

[113] The November 1996 EMI "Progress Towards Convergence" report was in sharp contrast to the European Commission's bi-annual report on economic prospects which painted a much more glowing picture of progress towards the EMU. It claimed that 12 nations, except Greece, Italy and the U.K., would meet the deficit criteria by 1997. This overly optimistic report matched the government budget and expected growth rate projections.

percent debt limit requirement.

In contrast to its fiscal performance findings, the EMI report found that most member nations were enjoying relatively low inflation and price stability. Over the 12-month period from October 1995 to September 1996, the best performing nations, in terms of lowest inflation rates, were Finland (0.9 percent), the Netherlands (1.2 percent) and Germany (1.3 percent). As many as ten nations (Belgium, Denmark, Germany, France, Ireland, Luxembourg, the Netherlands, Austria, Finland and Sweden) met the inflation criterion of 2.6 percent. The remaining five nations, Greece, Spain, Italy, Portugal and the United Kingdom did not meet the criterion.

As regards to the long-term interest rate criterion, member nations performed even better than on the inflation criterion. Eleven nations met the long-term interest criterion of 8.7 percent over the reference period between October 1995 and September 1996. The three best performing nations' ten-year government bonds yields in terms of price stability ranged between 6.3 percent to 7.4 percent. The four nations that failed to do so were Spain, Italy, Portugal and Greece[114]. The EMI suggested that although convergence in long-term interest rates has accelerated among all member nations, differentials among some nations remains high.

The 1996 EMI report did not include an exchange rate criterion analysis. Rather the report reviewed the developments over the two-year period beginning in October 1994 and ending in September 1996. It found that the Belgian/Luxembourg franc, Deutsche mark, Dutch guilder and Austrian schilling were the most stable currencies over this period. The Danish Krone, the French franc and the Irish Pound occasionally drifted away from their central parities. However, by the end of the two-year period, market rates of these currencies were close to their central rates. After the downward alignments of the Spanish peseta and the Portuguese escudo in early 1995, both currencies recovered ground to their previous 1994 levels and to their new central parities. The non-ERM currencies such as the Finnish markka[115] and the Greek drachma remained stable, while the Italian lira[116] and the pound sterling were erratic followed by some recovery. Although the Swedish krona also experienced a period of turbulence in early 1995, it appreciated significantly over the two-year period.

See Table 1.7 for the EMI's 1996 assessment of how individual EU member nations performed with regards to the Maastricht Treaty EMU convergence criteria (or reference values).

---

[114] Long-term interest rates in Greece are indexed to the twelve-month Treasury bill rate. Therefore, they should not be used for comparisons with other nations, rather they serve as a rough guidepost for inter-temporal comparisons.

[115] The Finnish markka joined the ERM on October 14, 1996.

[116] The Italian lira re-joined the ERM on November 25, 1996.

Table 1.7
Assessing National Performance with Regards to the EMU Convergence Criteria (or reference values) (excluding the exchange rate criterion)

		Inflation[(a)]	Long-tern interest rate[(b)]	General government lending (+) or Borrowing (-)[(c)]	General government gross debt[(c)]
Belgium	1995	***1.4	***7.5	-4.1	133.7
	1996[(d)]	1.6	6.7	-3.3	130.6
Denmark	1995	2.3	8.3	#-1.6	71.9
	1996[(d)]	2.2	7.4	#-1.4	[(e)]70.2
Germany	1995	1.5	6.9	-3.5	#58.1
	1996[(d)]	***1.3	***6.3	-4.0	60.8
Greece	1995	9.0	17.4	-9.1	111.8
	1996[(d)]	8.4	15.1	-7.9	110.6
Spain	1995	4.7	11.3	-6.6	65.7
	1996[(d)]	3.8	9.5	-4.4	67.8
France	1995	1.7	7.5	-4.8	#52.8
	1996[(d)]	2.1	6.6	-4.0	#56.4
Ireland	1995	2.4	8.3	#-2.0	[(e)]81.6
	1996[(d)]	2.1	7.5	#-1.6	[(e)]74.7
Italy	1995	5.4	12.2	-7.1	124.9
	1996[(d)]	4.7	10.3	-6.6	123.4
Luxembourg	1995	1.9	7.6	#1.5	#6.0
	1996[(d)]	1.3	7.0	#0.9	#7.8
Netherlands	1995	**1.1	**6.9	-4.0	79.7
	1996[(d)]	**1.2	**6.3	#-2.6	78.7
Austria	1995	2.0	7.1	-5.9	69.0
	1996[(d)]	1.7	6.5	-4.3	71.7
Portugal	1995	3.8	11.5	-5.1	71.7
	1996[(d)]	3.0	9.4	-4.0	71.7
Finland	1995	*1.0	*8.8	-5.2	#59.2
	1996[(d)]	*0.9	*7.4	-3.3	61.3
Sweden	1995	2.9	10.2	-8.1	78.7
	1996[(d)]	1.6	8.5	-3.9	78.1
United Kingdom	1995	3.1	8.3	-5.8	#54.1
	1996[(d)]	3.0	8.0	-4.6	#56.3

*,**,*** = first, second and third best performer in terms of price stability.
= public deficit not exceeding 3% of GDP; public debt not exceeding 60% of GDP.
(a) = Annual rates.
(b) = In percentages, annual average.
(c) = As a percentage of GDP.
(d) = Twelve-month period ending September 1996 for inflation and long-term interest rate; general government lending/borrowing and general government gross debt for 1996 are European Commission autumn 1996 estimates.
(e) = In 1994, 1995 and 1996 Ireland was not the subject of an EU Council decision under Article 104c(6) of the Treaty that an excessive deficit exists. In 1996 this was also the case for Denmark.

Source: "Progress Towards Convergence 1996," EMI, 1996, p.IV.

The December 1996 Dublin European Council Summit

The December 13-14, 1996 European Council Summit meeting held in Dublin managed to keep the two largest and politically most sensitive projects – the EMU and EU enlargement to the East, on course. However, the timetable of the latter appears to depend more and more on the realization of the EMU on schedule – by 1999.

At this meeting, the EU governments reached an agreement on a post-EMU fiscal "stability" pact which, at the insistence of the French, they renamed the "Stability and Growth Pact." It includes a system of penalties and trigger points to restrain members from undermining EMU's stability by running deficits over 3 percent of GDP. The acceptance of near but not fully automatic penalties for running such deficits represents a combination of the German position of triggering fines and the French view that maximum political discretion should be used in deciding the magnitude of penalties.

The pact narrows the Maastricht Treaty's definition of "exceptional and temporary circumstances" under which EMU nations can escape the penalties related to running excessive deficits. Yet it manages to uphold the Treaty's commitment to retaining the discretionary powers of the ECOFIN Council. EMU members running deficits over 3 percent of GDP will be exempt from near automatic fines if either of the following two conditions exist: (i) a natural disaster, or (ii) a decline in GDP of at least 2 percent over a period of one year.[117] In the case of nations that have excessive deficits and have experienced a decline between 0.75 percent and 2 percent in their GDP, the ECOFIN Council, including the affected country, will have discretionary authority concerning the imposition of fines. In doing so, the Council may take into account mitigating circumstances such as the abruptness of the downturn. Although not specifically mentioned, it is assumed that automatic fines will also be imposed on nations that have excessive deficits and have experienced a decline of less than 0.75 percent in their annual GDP. The fines can be as large as double-check percent of GDP.

If these rules had been enforced in 1996, only Denmark, Ireland, the Netherlands and Luxembourg would have escaped fines for excessive deficits. Germany could have been fined up to DM10 billion (US$7 billion). Yet the German's were not pleased when they were forced to give up their original demand of automatic fines as illustrated by a statement of the Bundesbank's chief economist and board member, Otmar Issing following the Dublin Summit: "Unrestrained automaticty would not have been possible but one cannot be satisfied with a decision mechanism in which potential sinners pass judgment on actual sinners."[118] Thus, the disagreements over which nations could join the Euro club and who controls that decision are far from over.

Little progress was made on the issue of enlargement of the EU to the East, asides from a draft treaty which summarized national views on the issue but did not contain any proposed measures. In connection with this, Germany and France insisted

---

[117] In all of the 15 nations, the latter condition i.e. a recession of severe magnitudes has occurred 9 times over the last 25 years.

[118] "EU warned over policing EMU." Financial Times, December 17, 1996, p.1.

not only on more majority voting but also on the re-weighting of the votes so that the large nations could exert more influence. They also demanded a smaller EU Commission. What was not spelled-out but implied was that enlargement will move forward only if the EMU and Euro timetable are adhered to.

Other significant issues discussed at the Summit included currency discipline and the legal status of the Euro. Governments agreed to enforce currency discipline through the ERM II. This new mechanism is based on the "hub and spokes" concept according to which the Euro will act as the anchor of the exchange rate mechanism and non-EMU members will target their currencies at the Euro only, so as to extend the Euro's zone of stability to such currencies. The ERM II is a modification of the original ERM of 1979 which was created to minimize currency fluctuation. It will come into force on January 1, 1999, and involve the following three principles (i) flexibility, (ii) non-coercion, and (iii) reinforced convergence. The ERM II plan also includes ways of regulating the relationship between the EMU "ins" and "outs."

According to the flexibility principle, the EMU "outs" (also known as the "pre-ins") will select a central rate for their currency vis-à-vis the Euro in consultation with the EMU member nations (referred to as the "Euro bloc"), and the European Central Bank (ECB). Although the fluctuation band was not specified, it will probably be relatively wide just like the present +/-15 percent band of the original ERM. Non-EMU currencies will be allowed to target narrower bands.

The principle of non-coercion was adopted on the insistence of the U.K. and Sweden. It insures that membership in the ERM II is not compulsory, although non-EMU EU nations are "expected" to join. As a result of the Bundesbank's demand, this principle also implies that the ECB's obligation to support weaker currencies under speculative attacks is limited. While future intervention is described as "automatic and unlimited," according to the final agreement the "ECB and central banks of other countries can suspend intervention if this were to be in conflict with the primary goal of maintaining price stability."[119]

The last and final principle of the ERM II is "reinforced convergence," Brussel's terms for all member nations submitting their economic plans for ministerial surveillance at the EU level, regardless of EMU or ERM II membership. The U.K., however, insisted that nations whose plans are not in line with those of the majority not be penalized, and that the ECOFIN Council issue "non-binding recommendations only when necessary" to avoid misalignments and excessive nominal exchange rate fluctuations.

The ERM II incorporates some of the lessons of the 1992-93 currency crises when the U.K., Italy, Spain and France held out against a realignment for political reasons. To avoid major misalignments in the future, the adjustment of ERM II central rates is undertaken in a "timely fashion." To this end, all parties, including the ECB, have the right to initiate confidential talks. See Chapter VI for more details on the ERM II.

---

[119] "Pact Sets Rules for Ins and Outs of ERM." Financial Times, December 17, 1996, p.2.

Annex I-1:
THE EU INSTITUTIONAL STRUCTURE

The supranational structure of the EU is made up of the Commission; the European Parliament with its directly elected members; the Council of Ministers (renamed the Council of the European Union), comprised of national ministers; the Committee of Permanent Representatives (COREPER); the European Council, representing the heads of state/governments; and the European Court of Justice. Additional institutions include the Court of First Instance, the Court of Appeals, the Court of Auditors, the European Investment Bank (EIB), the Economic and Social Committee and the latest additions, the European Monetary Institute (EMI) and the Committee of the Regions. Figure 1.4 shows the EU decision-making structure.

Figure 1.4
The EU Decision-Making Structure

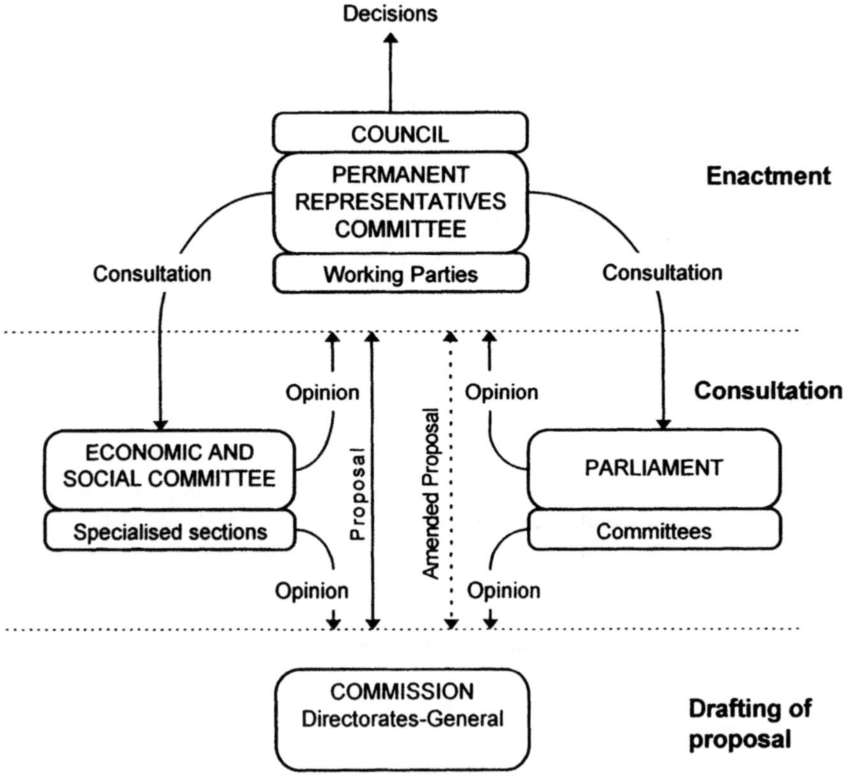

Source: Barnes, Ian and Pamela Barnes. The Enlarged European Union, New York: Longman Group UK Ltd., 1995, p.15.

The Commission

The 20-member Commission is the executive body of the EU and as such is supported by 23 Directorates-General which plan and manage the common day-to-day activities. France, Germany, Spain, Italy and UK each have two seats while the remaining member nations are limited to one seat. Commissioners act independently of their national governments and other interest groups. Their term of office is five years. Table 1.8 provides a list of the European Commission's 23 Directorates-General; Table 1.9 shows the past and present Presidents of the Commission and Table 1.10 lists the Commissioners appointed in 1995.

The Commission resides in Brussels, although it sometimes meets in Luxembourg. Its primary responsibility is the formulation of policy initiatives. Its tasks also include; (i) ensuring that the founding treaties and their amendments are carried out; (ii) drawing up the budget; (iii) exercising sole power to initiate legislation (directives and regulations) and to amend legislation at any stage; and (iv) implementing decisions reached by the Council of Ministers.

The Secretariat General of the Commission coordinates the work of the Commissioners. It is comprised of a Statistical Office and other functional departments providing supporting services. The Secretariat General also coordinates activities among the Commission offices in member countries, 85 foreign nations and in four international organizations.

Table 1.8
The European Commission's 23 Directorates-General

DG-1	External Relations and Trade Negotiations
DG-2	Macroeconomic and Monetary Affairs
DG-3	Internal Market and Industrial Affairs
DG-4	Competition, Cartels, and State Aids
DG-5	Employment, Education, and Social Affairs
DG-6	Agriculture
DG-7	Transport
DG-8	Aid to Developing Countries
DG-9	Personnel and Administration
DG-10	Information and Communication
DG-11	Environment, Consumer Protection, and Nuclear Safety
DG-12	Research and Development
DG-13	Telecommunications
DG-14	Fisheries
DG-15	Financial Services, Company Law, and Tax
DG-16	Regional Development
DG-17	Energy
DG-18	EC Borrowing and Lending
DG-19	EC Budget
DG-20	Internal Financial Control
DG-21	Customs Union and Indirect Tax
DG-22	Coordination of Structural Instruments
DG-23	Small and Medium-sized Enterprises

Source: The European Commission, 1996.

Table 1.9
The Past and Present Presidents of the Commission

1958-1967	Walter Hallstein (Germany)
1967-1970	Jean Ray (Belgium)
1970-1972	Franco Maria Malfatti (Italy)
1972-1973	Sicco Mansholt (Netherlands)
1973-1977	Francois-Xavier Ortoli (France)
1977-1981	Roy Jenkins (U.K.)
1981-1985	Gaston Thorn (Luxembourg)
1985-1994	Jacques Delors (France)
1995-	Jacques Santer (Luxembourg)

Source: European Commission, 1996.

Table 1.10
Commissioners Appointed in 1995

	Portfolio
Jacques Santer, President (Lux)	CFSP, monetary matters, institutional questions, ICGs
Manuel Marin (Spain)	External relations - Mediterranean, Middle and Near East, Latin America
Martin Bangemann (Germany)	Industrial affairs, information technologies, telecommunications
Sir Leon Brittan (UK)	External relations, common commercial policy
Karel van Miert (Belgium)	Competition
Hans van den Broek (Netherlands)	External affairs CE states, CFSP
Joao de Deus Pinheiro (Portugal)	External affairs ACP states
Padraig Flynn (Ireland)	Employment and social affairs
Marcelino Oreja (Spain)	Relations with EP, communications, audio-visual policy, publications office, institutional questions, IGC preparations
Edith Cresson (France)	Science, RTD, JRC, education
Ritt Bjerrgaard (Denmark)	Environment, nuclear safety
Monica Wulf-Mathies (Germany)	Regional policy, CoR, Cohesion Fund
Neil Kinnock (UK)	Transport including TENS
Mario Monti (Italy)	Internal market, taxation
Emma Bonino (Italy)	Consumer Policy, Fisheries
Yves-Thibault de Silguy (France)	Economic and financial affairs, monetary matters
Christos Papoutsis (Greece)	Energy, EURATOM, SMEs, tourism
Anita Gradin (Sweden)	Immigration, JHA
Franz Fischler (Austria)	Agriculture and rural development
Erkki Liikanen (Finland)	Budget

Source: European Commission, 1995.

The Parliament

The Parliament resides in Strasbourg where its monthly plenary meetings are held. Its Secretariat, however, is located in Luxembourg. It also has offices in Brussels, where it meets on occasion to facilitate cooperation with the Commission.

The Parliament is made up of 626 members directly elected by the citizens of the 15 countries on the basis of population size. Germany has 99 seats, France, Italy and the U.K. 87 each, Spain 64, the Netherlands 31, Belgium, Portugal and Greece 25 each, Sweden 22, Austria 21, Denmark and Finland 16 each, Ireland 15 and Luxembourg 6 seats. The various parliamentary political groups represent 370 million people and are organized into 20 committees that prepare the plenary meetings. Table 1.11 shows the number of seats allocated to member nations; Table 1.12 lists the past and present presidents; Table 1.13 shows the political parties; while Table 1.14 shows the permanent committees.

The Parliament has supervisory responsibilities, it approves the budget and the appointment of the President of the Commission. The 1987 SEA increased cooperation among the various common institutions and allowed the Parliament two interventions in the legislative process. This Act also conferred the right to approve EU membership through a majority vote. The Parliament received additional powers under the Maastricht Treaty, for example, it was empowered to select an Ombudsman to investigate malpractices by common institutions. The Treaty also gave the Parliament additional powers i.e. co-decision with the Council of Ministers to oversee regulations and directives in the areas of consumer protection, research and technological development, culture, social and economic cohesion, health, social policy, the environment and education. Figure 1.5 and Figure 1.6 illustrate the new powers of the Parliament.

Table 1.11
Number of Seats Allocated to Member Nations

	1989	1994	1999
Belgium	24	25	25
Denmark	16	16	16
Germany	81	99	99
Greece	24	25	25
Spain	60	64	64
France	81	87	87
Ireland	15	15	15
Italy	81	87	87
Luxembourg	6	6	6
Netherlands	25	31	31
Portugal	24	25	25
U.K.	81	87	87
Sweden*			22
Austria*			21
Finland*			16
Total MEPs	518	567	626

* = Members as of 1995.

Source: European Parliament data, 1996.

Table 1.12
The Past and Present Presidents of the EU Parliament

1979	Simon Veil (French MEP)
1982	Piet Dankert (Dutch MEP)
1984	Pierre Pflimlin (French MEP)
1987	Sir Henry Plumb (UK MEP)
1989	Enrique Baron Crespo (Spanish MEP)
1992	Egon Klepsch (German MEP)
1994	Klaus Hansch (German MEP)

Source: European Parliament data, 1995.

Table 1.13
The Political Parties of the EU Parliament

	1994	1989
Group of the Party of European Socialists (SPE)	200	197
European People's Party (EEP)	148	162
Liberal and Democratic Reformist Group (ELD)	44	44
Green Parties (Green)	22	27
European Democratic Alliance (EDA)	24	20
Rainbow Group (ARC)	8	16
Technical Group of the European Right (ER)	13	12
Left Unity (LU)	12	13
Independents (IND)	96	27
Total	567	518

Note: Direct elections of the EU Parliament began in 1979.
Source: European Parliament data, 1996.

Table 1.14
The Permanent Committees of the EU Parliament

Foreign Affairs and Security
Agriculture, Fisheries and Rural Development
Transport and Tourism
Environment, Public Health and Consumer Protection
Budgets
Economic and Monetary Affairs and Industrial Policy
Culture, Youth and the Media
Energy, Research and Technology
Development and Co-operation
External Economic Relations
Civil Liberties and Internal Affairs
Legal Affairs and Citizens' Rights
Budgetary Affairs
Social Affairs, Employment and the Working Environment
Regional Policy and relations with regional and local authorities
Institutional Affairs
Women's Rights
Petitions

Source: European Parliament data, 1995.

Figure 1.5
New Powers of the EU Parliament: Co-operation and Consultation Procedures

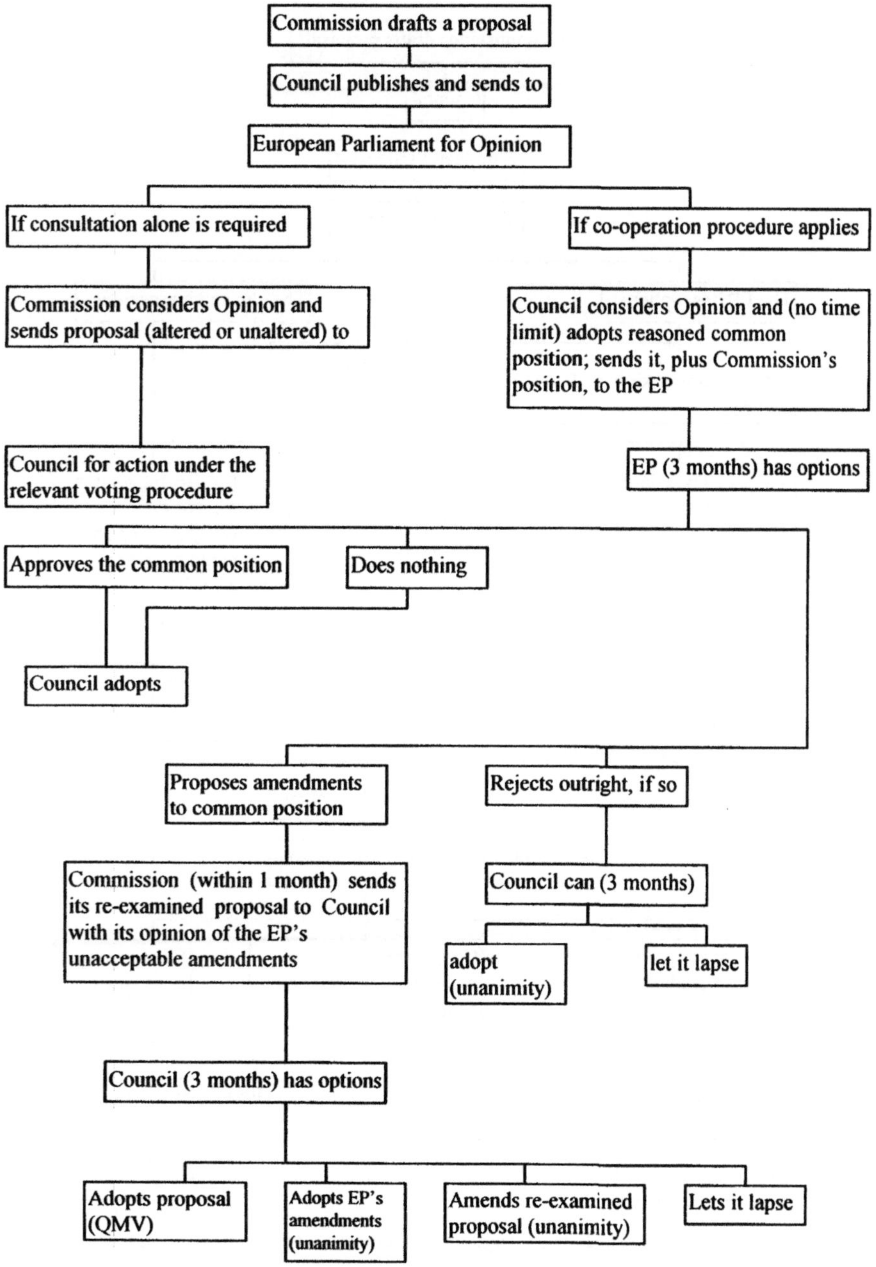

Source: Barnes, Ian and Pamela Barnes. The Enlarged European Union, New York: Longman Group UK Ltd., 1995, p.39.

Figure 1.6
New Powers of the EU Parliament: Co-decision Procedures

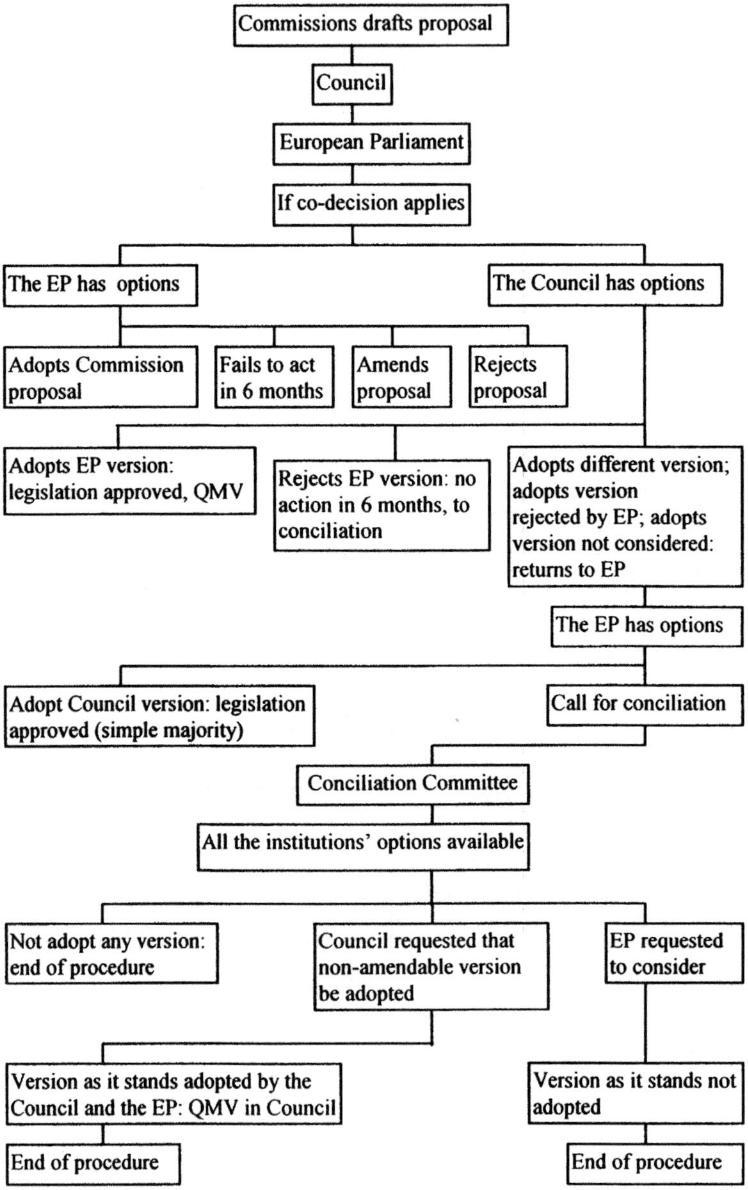

Source: Barnes, Ian and Pamela Barnes. The Enlarged European Union, New York: Longman Group UK Ltd., 1995, p.40.

The Council of Ministers[120]

The Council of Ministers is the basic decision-making body. At any particular time, it is made up of the 15 relevant ministers (to the issue at hand) of the member states. The presidency of the Council is rotated every six-month. The different ministerial groups meet about 100 times a year.

In addition to making decision, the Council of Ministers coordinates policies among the member states in close cooperation with the Parliament. In regard to common foreign and security policies, the Council coordinates member state activities, defines common positions and implements measures to achieve the set objectives. It also makes recommendations with respect to justice and home affairs.

Recent procedural changes provide for a wider use of the qualified majority voting process, under which 62 votes out of a total of 87 constitute a qualified majority. However, the Council must reach unanimous decisions in the areas of common foreign and security policy, justice and home affairs, taxation, agricultural policies, and the movement of people. A rejection of a Commission proposal or an amendment of the same by the Parliament also requires unanimity. Unanimity is not required when the Maastricht Treaty explicitly allows the Council to do without it.

The allocation of votes is based on the size of the member nations. Germany, France, Italy and the UK each have ten Council votes; Spain has eight; Greece, the Netherlands, Portugal and Belgium have five votes each; Austria and Sweden have four votes each; Denmark, Finland and Ireland have three votes each; and Luxembourg has two votes. Table 1.15 provides an overview of the allocation of votes in the Council of Ministers.

Table 1.15
Allocation of Votes

	Population (millions)	Votes
Germany	80.6	10
France	57.5	10
Italy	56.9	10
U.K.	57.9	10
Spain	39.1	8
Belgium	10.0	5
Greece	10.3	5
Netherlands	15.2	5
Portugal	9.8	5
Austria*	7.9	4
Sweden*	8.6	4
Denmark	5.2	3
Ireland	3.5	3
Finland*	5.0	3
Luxembourg	0.4	2

Note: population data as of 1 January 1993.
* = Members as of 1995.
Source: European Commission, 1994.

[120] Under the The Maastricht Treaty the Council of Ministers was renamed, the "Council of the European Union". However, to avoid confusion, the original designation will be used throughout this book.

The Committee of Permanent Representatives (COREPER)

The Council of Ministers is supported by COREPER, which is made up of the member states' permanent ambassadors to Brussels. COREPER is responsible for preparing the various issues submitted by the Commission to the Council of Ministers for decision-making. It also assists the Council by preparing special studies and serving as a link of the governments to the Commission.

The European Council

The European Council was established informally in 1974 and was formalized through the SEA in 1987. It is comprised of the heads of state/governments, the President of the European Commission, a member of the Commission and the 15 Foreign Ministers. It is considered the principal institution of the EU as it is common to all three pillars of activities.

The European Council in general has the responsibility of guiding the EU's activities, overseeing policy measures and approving the admission of new members. Its decisions are reached behind closed doors. The Maastricht Treaty requires that the economic and finance ministers attend its meetings whenever economic and financial matters are discussed.

The Court of Justice

The Court of Justice is comprised of 15 judges and 9 advocates-general appointed for six-year terms by agreement of the member nations. The Court interprets the Treaties of Rome and other legislation, through cases brought to it by the Commission, member states, private parties and national courts. Its judgments are binding on member states.

Cases submitted to the Court usually involve the annulment of binding legal acts, failures to act, infringements of the various treaties, preliminary hearings, and illegal activities or actions. Preliminary rulings on the validity of common laws are also issued. The Court may impose lump-sum penalties on member states that do not comply with its decisions.

The Court of First Instance and the Court of Appeals

The Court of First Instance was created in 1989 to hear competition cases, ECSC matters and other actions brought to it by firms and individuals. Its decisions may be appealed on legal grounds to the Court of Appeals, which deals exclusively with cases brought to it by individuals and businesses that are appealing points of law.

The Court of Auditors

The Court of Auditors was established in 1975. It consists of 15 members appointed by the Council of Ministers in consultation with Parliament. The President, the first among equals, is elected for a renewable three-year term by the other members. The Court monitors the implementation of common expenditures through an annual report provided to the Council of Ministers and the European Parliament. It undertakes investigations on its own and delivers opinions and reports on other institutions as requested.

The Court of Auditors received additional responsibilities under the Maastricht Treaty. It is now also expected to evaluate the effectiveness, reliability, regularity and legality of all EU transactions.

***The European Investment Bank* (EIB)**

The EIB was set up by the 1957 EEC Treaty to contribute to balanced economic development. The 1987 SEA realigned its activities by calling for more investments in less developed nations.

The EIB's primary focus is on regional development involving small and medium-size businesses. But it also finances projects to develop telecommunication and trans-European transport networks, to secure the availability of energy, to enhance competition and to protect the environment. The EIB operates as a non-profit lender worldwide; it finances development projects in the Lomé Convention countries, in the Mediterranean region and in the Eastern and Central European nations.

Its staff is made up of officials of the finance ministries and includes a representative of the Commission. It is managed by a President and six Vice-Presidents appointed by the member states.

The Economic and Social Committee

The Economic and Social Committee, also called the consultative assembly, is made up of representatives of various interest groups. It gives advisory opinions on Commission proposals.

The Committee's 222 members include employers (public or private), workers (trade union reps) and representatives of other interest groups such as the scientific and teaching communities, members of cooperatives, small and medium-size manufacturers, ecological movements, and consumer representatives. Its Committees on Transport, Agriculture, Economic Affairs, Social Affairs, Environment, Industry, Regional Development, Energy and External Relations provide non-binding opinions to the Council of Ministers. Members are appointed by the Council of Ministers upon nomination by member states.

The European Monetary Institute (EMI)

The EMI was established on January 1, 1994 in Frankfurt. It is in charge of coordinating the activities of the "European System of Central Banks" (ESCB) and is the forerunner of the European Central Bank (ECB). The EMI has no executive power and can only develop proposals and form opinions. All central bank governors sit on its governing board known as the Governing Council which serves as the decision-making body and is headed by the EMI President. The institute is managed by a Director-General and is organized into four departments that report to the Director-General. The four departments include the General-Secretariat, the Monetary, Economic and Statistics Department, the Administration Department, and the Information and Communications Systems Department. Additionally, EMI maintains various sub-committees and working groups to help carry out its tasks and functions.

The Committee of the Regions

The Committee of the Regions was established by the Maastricht Treaty in 1991; it held its first meeting in March 1994. Its 222 members represent local and regional bodies and are appointed by the Council of Ministers. The Committee is assisted by the staff of the Economic and Social Committee. The Committee must be consulted by the Council of Ministers and the Commission on matters of youth, culture, social cohesion, trans-European transport, education, public health, energy networks and telecommunications. It may issue opinions on its own initiatives.

II POLITICAL AND ECONOMIC DILEMMAS OF THE EMU

Numerous political and economic dilemmas have confronted the European Economic and Monetary Union (EMU) since 1989, when it was resurrected by the Delors Report. Some of these dilemmas have eventually faded away as, for example, the ratification difficulties of the Maastricht Treaty (the Treaty on the European Union), while others continue such as the political challenges facing the Maastricht Treaty, the impact of the Exchange Rate Mechanism (ERM) crises, as well as the implications of the admission of new members. Still other problems loom on the horizon as, for example, the institutional and decision-making reforms needed to provide for the efficient functioning of the EMU, the implications of a multi-speed EMU and the effects of the opt-out and of the non-EMU member nations on monetary integration. These past and continuing dilemmas are the subject of this chapter.

THE MAASTRICHT TREATY RATIFICATION PROCESS

The ratification of the Maastricht Treaty was an arduous and uncertain process until the very end. The major problems included the potential German opt-out and the democratic accountability issues; the Danish rejection; the dilemmas facing the United Kingdom (U.K.); the French elections and the ERM crises.

The Potential German Opt-out and the Issue of Democratic Accountability

Although the Bundestag and the Bundesrat, representing the 16 federal Länder (states), have approved the Maastricht Treaty, they did so with certain conditions.[1] Both houses have retained the right to review the EMU plans before the final stage of introducing the single currency and the European Central Bank (ECB) in 1999. In other words, the conditions that the Bundestag and the Bundesrat attached to the ratification of the Treaty (although they are not likely to be exercised) are tantamount to the opt-out right of the U.K.

Owing to the German constitutional requirements concerning democracy and a law-based social-market-oriented federal state, the ECB would have to be answerable to the members of democratically elected common institutions. Currently, only the Parliament is such an institution while all other bodies, whose members are appreciated, serve as an example of the "democratic deficit" within the EU's institutional framework. Moreover, although under Article 189b of the Maastricht Treaty, the Parliament gained the right of co-decision with the Council of Ministers,[2] this right does not apply to certain critical areas such as foreign policy, defense, judicial cooperation or economic policy formulation. Thus, unless the Parliament is additionally strengthened, or a new democratically elected body is created, further integration does not seem compatible with the German Constitution despite the Federal Constitutional Court's approval of the Treaty on October 12, 1993. This approval was conditional in that the Court found that the meeting of the EMU convergence criteria supersedes Article 109j of the Maastricht Treaty, which states that the EMU is to be set up by January 1999 at the latest. Germany retains the right to withdraw from the EMU if the convergence criteria are not consistently fulfilled by the other nations. It should be noted that the EU Commission's 1993 draft document "Restoring Growth and Employment: Strengthening Convergence,"[3] intended as a "macroeconomic blueprint" to the end of this century, and, more recently, the November 1995 and 1996 European Monetary Institute (EMI) Report on "Progress Towards Convergence"[4] have also called for significantly "more credible convergence programmes for member states"[5] if the EMU is to be realized by 1999.

The Danish "No"

Although the signing of the Maastricht Treaty was an achievement of historic proportions, with hindsight it seems to be the least difficult hurdle facing

---

[1] Measures affecting sovereignty require a two-thirds majority in both the Bundestag and the Bundesrat.

[2] As mentioned in Chapter 1, under the Maastricht Treaty the Council of Ministers was renamed the Council of the European Union as of November 1, 1993. To avoid confusion, the term Council of Ministers will be used throughout this book.

[3] This draft paper was submitted for approval to the European Council at the December 1993 Summit in Brussels.

[4] "Progress Towards Convergence," European Monetary Institute (EMI), Frankfurt am Main, November 1995 and "Progress Towards Convergence 1996," European Monetary Institute (EMI), Frankfurt am Main, November 1996.

[5] "Brussels Says EU Must Act on Jobs of Risk Social Unrest." Financial Times, November 16, 1993. p.1.

economic and monetary integration. The Treaty should have been ratified by all national parliaments by December 31, 1992. However, the Danish rejection by a 51.4 percent majority at the June 2, 1992 referendum, halted the Treaty "locomotive" on its tracks. This result focused attention on the loss of sovereignty associated with the plan which led to a much-needed realization that unless the citizens of all the member nations understood the Treaty and were convinced that the economic benefits of the EMU would outweigh its costs, approval by most nations might be difficult. This has been a problem since the inception of the Treaty because its clauses require member nations to give up control not only over monetary policies but, to a large extent also, over fiscal policies, to meet the convergence criteria requirements. Moreover, 11 of the 15 member nations currently do not have independent central banks like the Bundesbank, thus they will have to undergo a major restructuring of financial systems. Most important, the Danish "No" allowed major doubts about the EMU to surface in all EU member nations. It even became acceptable for the Germans to publicly voice concerns about abandoning the Deutsche mark.

It was this realization that caused Commission President Jacques Delors to give in to the notion of "subsidiarity" and "transparency." According to subsidiarity, "the EU acts -- with the Commission proposing and the member nations deciding through the Council of Ministers, subject to review by the Parliament only when national and/or local actions would be demonstrably less effective."[6] Transparency requires that the meetings of the Council of Ministers and of the Commission be open to the public and/or be televised and that the voting patterns be published. These issues were discussed at the much anticipated but ultimately rather unproductive emergency Birmingham European Council Summit and at the equally unproductive Edinburgh European Council Summit in November and December 1992, respectively.

Denmark eventually approved the Treaty through another referendum in May 1993 and soon thereafter the U.K.'s House of Commons gave its "go-ahead." Although the Danish government had attempted to dilute the Treaty by a series of amendments, none came to pass, but Denmark's right, among others, to opt out of the EMU was reconfirmed.[7] Yet, the argument that the Treaty could not have survived another Danish "No" is not convincing, given the EU's propensity to circumvent legal difficulties[8] through complicated amendments.[9] Chancellor Kohl, on February 22, 1993, reemphasized this point, albeit more subtly, when he said that if Denmark and the U.K. did not ratify the Treaty soon, then the EU would have to proceed without them.[10]

---

[6] "EC Must Regain Its Street Credibility." Financial Times, September 22, 1992, p.2.

[7] Denmark has had the right to opt out of the Treaty since its acceptance on February 7, 1992. This, however, was not well known to the Danish citizens prior to the June 1992 referendum.

[8] The Treaty needs unanimous approval by all national parliaments, otherwise it cannot serve as an amendment to the Treaties of Rome.

[9] As in the case of the U.K. with respect to the Social Charter.

[10] The economically weaker member nations such as Greece, Portugal, Spain, Ireland and Italy have ratified the Treaty without delay as they will be the primary beneficiaries of the single currency and of the ECB.

Ironically, Germany was the last to ratify the Treaty, which was under review by the Federal Constitutional Court until its approval on October 12, 1993.

The Dilemma of the United Kingdom

Prime Minister John Major used up much of his political capital to obtain a majority in the House of Commons during the second attempt to pass the Treaty in 1993,[11] as was illustrated by the more than 300 amendments that had been proposed. One of the problems he faced was the linking of the single currency and of the ECB to many other issues such as the equally, if not more, politically sensitive Social Charter. Consequently, to improve the chances of ratification, Major divided the Treaty by separating the Social Charter from the EMU. However, the EMU ratification in the House of Commons does not automatically solve the U.K.'s 1999 dilemma of whether to opt out of or join the EMU.

Major does not want a more federal EU, hence, he shows little enthusiasm for "handing over" the pound sterling or the Bank of England to Brussels via the EMI and eventually the ECB. Moreover, he is only mildly interested in an idea of an independent Bank of England. Yet as President of the European Council during the fall of 1992 he was obliged not only to endorse the Treaty at the Edinburgh Summit in December 1992 but also to deliver a "Yes" vote in the House of Commons in July 1993. His remark that "Great Britain would be at the heart of the Community is more or less an acknowledgment that since the U.K. did not want to be left out of the EU, its only choice was to be "at the core" of it. Major faced a dilemma in that only through parliamentary approval could he assure that his nation would remain an active and influential participant in the integration process. On many occasions he has stated that "the essential question is simply: are we or are we not in this country to play a central role in Europe's development?"[12] Nonetheless, there are numerous examples of quiet attempts by Major to slow the progress toward an enlarged and more powerful bureaucracy in Brussels. A case in point is his repeated call for a "widening" (i.e., the admission of new members), which could postpone the "deepening" (i.e., increased integration), at least for a while.

The French Elections and the ERM

It was anticipated, before the September 20, 1992 French referendum that a "Yes" to the Treaty would not be sufficient to put the EU back on its track toward

[11] In early November 1992 Major had achieved a very narrow majority in the House of Commons (319 to 316) in support of restarting the Treaty ratification process and also in order to have another vote in early 1993. Although the government had a majority of 21 votes over all other parties, it could not convince 30 Conservative Euroskeptics and had to rely on the support of 19 out of the 20 Liberal MPs.

[12] "Major Survives Maastricht Vote." Financial Times, November 5, 1992, p.1.

further integration. However, a French "No" would have made it extremely difficult to even attempt this. Nonetheless, the narrow 51 percent margin of approval dampened the idea of integration. The French domestic election results of March 1993,cast an additional shadow over the future.

When the European Monetary System (EMS) and the ERM were created in 1979, there was an implied commitment by the Bundesbank to support the franc's parity against the Deutsche Mark as long as the French government followed an inflation-free monetary policy (i.e., shadowed the Bundesbank). Through a play on words concerning the location of the Bundesbank which serves as the supporting arch of the ERM, this became known as the "franc-fort" policy. This policy is the backbone of the ERM, as it symbolizes the 40-year-old Paris-Bonn axis on which integration has to be achieved.

Prior to the March 1993 French national elections, the winning right-of-center politicians had tried to calm the financial markets by stating that they would continue the "franc-fort" policy and make the Bank of France independent. However, their campaign argument aiming at lower unemployment contradicted such claims. For some time, France faced persistently high short-term interest rates,[13] slow growth, rising unemployment and political discontent. Not surprisingly, there were speculative attacks on the French franc during the summer of 1993. The financial markets erroneously assumed that the government would bow to domestic political pressures and devalue the franc, as not all of the newly elected politicians supported the "franc-fort" policy. Although through the support of the Bundesbank the franc has managed to stay out of trouble, in early September 1993 it was the target of an all out assault which jeopardized its position within the ERM narrow band. Because a devaluation would have signaled that the German-French alliance was weakening and that the ERM was on its last legs, the attack was countered by the Bundesbank's intervention using approximately US$80 billion, joined by the Bank of France with a US$40 billion war-chest. In spite of these interventions, the speculators were not deterred. Consequently, in an effort to reduce the pressure on the franc, a special weekend meeting of the ERM member nations was convened on August 1-2, 1993, to merge and widen the ERM bands to +/- 15 percent. Once the more relaxed ERM was in place, the currency speculators again wrongly assumed that the French government would instantly take advantage of this and lower short-term interest rates. But, the government didn't oblige. Thus, the financial markets learned yet another costly lesson about the degree of French political commitment to EMU. It should be noted that any success on the part of the speculators could have interfered with the planned independence of the Bank of France.

The stability of the ERM, which is essential to progress toward the EMU, has been reduced by events that began in September 1992. The U.K. and Italy removed their currencies from the +/- 2.25 percent narrow band; Spain, Ireland and Portugal devalued. These ongoing crises precipitated yet another special meeting of the Finance

---

[13] These rates remained high as long as the Bundesbank kept the Lombard and discount rate high because of worries about inflation.

Ministers on October 9-10, 1993. The Ministers agreed not to return to the old ERM in the foreseeable future because of general low growth and high unemployment rates. In the end, this translated into a de facto suspension of the ERM and possibly a delay in the EMU timetable, as the expanded bands removed the disciplinary framework which promotes monetary convergence. The U.K.'s call for a slower EMU, a longer Stage II and a shift to a new and more flexible ERM generated additional pressures. The British were not alone in their call for a "new ERM" which was approved during the December 13-14, 1996 Dublin European Council Summit and is due to start on January 1, 1999. The "ERM II" is discussed in greater detail in Chapter VI.

THE POLITICS OF THE MAASTRICHT TREATY

The manner in which the EMU is envisioned in the Maastricht Treaty, raises many questions. Some are technical-economic in nature but the most important are political such as the question on which the success of the integration process depends. They concern the willingness of the Germans to change their economic and monetary policies, or, to put it another way, their readiness to "Europeanize" such policies. The same question can be posed from the point of view of the other member nations by asking whether they are willing to accept a German-style economic and monetary policy. Although the latter point of view is more plausible than the former, if the answer to either is "Yes" then there is hope for the EMU. The question is critical, because without Germany there can be no EMU.

Although the Bundesbank is known for its insistence on "price stability," the Deutsche mark has lost more than two-thirds of its value since 1948. In other words, what the Bundesbank is really doing is holding down the rate of price changes. This calls for a considerable amount of judgment, which the Bundesbank exercises whenever it finds it useful. But on many occasions its judgment has been based on the notion that the end justifies the means. An example of this was its refusal to lower short-term interest rates during 1993, despite the looming Europe-wide recession. The Bundesbank can act in this manner because it enjoys the confidence of the citizens to a degree not enjoyed by other post-War German institution or chancellors.[14]

---

[14] A minor, yet telling, example is that the head of the Bundesbank is paid approximately one-third more than the Federal Chancellor. A more somber example is the Bundesbank's record in standing up to the various chancellors over the years. Tight monetary policy precipitated the first German post-World War II recession, contributing to Chancellor Ludwig Erhard's downfall. In 1969, although the Deutsche Mark was eventually revalued according to the Bundesbank's proposal, the row between the central bank and the government prior to the decision helped reduce Chancellor Kurt George Kiesinger's re-election chances. In 1981-82, high interest rates expedited Chancellor Helmut Schmidt's resignation.

The continued monetary and social burdens of reunification are still underestimated by many Germans. Thus, it is unlikely that the head of the Bundesbank will give up the Deutsche mark for an untested and, by German standards, possibly inflationary, single currency. This is understandable if one considers that five years after the signing of the Maastricht Treaty it is still unclear what, if any, economic benefits Germany would realize from the EMU. It should also be noted that if the "Monnet spirit" (i.e., the desire to keep the EU together on the road to full integration) is to be preserved in the course of trying to achieve monetary integration, the weaker economies must achieve and sustain a higher level of monetary and fiscal discipline. Although the time for such ideas has passed, there is evidence indicating that, on the whole, the EMU would have been more easily achieved if the weaker and less disciplined nations had initially been required to improve their economic performance – that is, had the weaker and less disciplined nations been required to join a "pre-EMU" club first. It would have been sounder economically and more realistic politically to have aimed for an initial pre-EMU, which applied the Maastricht Treaty's convergence requirements first only to the weaker economies. This would have provided them with the needed monetary and fiscal discipline. Conversely, better performing economies with internationally strong currencies could have stayed out of the EMU until the weaker economies had arrived at an "acceptable" monetary and fiscal performance through meeting the convergence criteria. Only then should the EU have embarked on the more ambitious full-membership EMU which governments are currently considering and struggling to attain. This might have lessened the economic (i.e., Cohesion Fund) and political costs of the EMU.

However, if the stronger economies had not tried to influence the convergence criteria, this could have raised the acceptable levels of inflation and interest rates -- that is, it could have reduced standards, as the monetary convergence criteria are based on the average of the three best-performing economies. Despite this problem, a "pre-EMU" club would have ensured fiscal discipline and would have been able to set more realistic targets for monetary discipline currently absent in the planned multi-speed EMU. A full economic and monetary union with Portugal, Greece, Ireland, Spain, and Italy on a more equal footing with the stronger economies, would stand a better chance not only of succeeding but also of preserving the "Monnet spirit." Again, although the time for such discussion has passed, such an approach may have been more acceptable to the Bundesbank and to the U.K. which would still prefer a slower more stable "EMU train," given the German economic[15] and the British political concerns.

[15] Under Chancellor Kohl's leadership the German government is doing everything possible to meet the 1999 EMU deadline.

Treaty Hurdles

Problems of Creating a German-Style Common Monetary Regime

The Maastricht Treaty endeavors, among other things, to establish a central bank that is free of political interference and that can prescribe common price stability requirements regardless of the cost in terms of unemployment, at least in the short run. In fact, the Treaty attempts to build a German-style monetary regime, including common institutions and macroeconomic policies, without the same strong German influence that existed in the original ERM. Not only are the Treaty's rigorous stipulations similar to those of the German Central Bank, but its specific convergence criteria restrict admission to only those nations that shadow German economic policies. However, what is often overlooked is that simply creating a "super-EU-Bundesbank"[16] does not guarantee German economic performance. This is dependent on more than just the charter and the structure of the central bank. The economic history of the last four or five decades has demonstrated that the German politicians, central bankers, trade unions and voters – have accepted the price-stability goal much more readily than any other EU nation. Nor do the other member nations have the German type of labor-management relations which, to date, have contained major wage-price spirals.

The ECB can maintain a Bundesbank-like grip on price stability only if: (i) EMU membership is confined to nations that have shown a convincing commitment to price stability; (ii) price stability is the primary objective of all common institutions involved in macroeconomic decisions; (iii) the ECB decision-making structure gives more weight to the votes of those central bankers as opposed to national representatives who pay more attention to price stability; and/or (iv) the Bundesbank itself is the dominant force in setting common macroeconomic policies, as it did in the original ERM.

The loosely worded Maastricht Treaty has not ensured that the ECB can have a Bundesbank-like dominance over monetary policy. The Treaty has also failed to guarantee that macroeconomic policy decision-makers would be adverse to inflation and that the voting would be done by way of a simple majority. Not only does the Treaty refer to the convergence criteria as "reference points," it also calls for a qualified majority vote by member nations to determine whether the criteria have been met. Thus, EMU membership is not entirely contingent upon price stability performance. Through the ECOFIN Council, member nations also retain control over common exchange rate management which is independent of the ECB's monetary policies. Finally, the Treaty has neither automatic nor binding sanctions on the "free-riding" EMU member nations that incur large budget deficits. Even the 1996 post-EMU fiscal

---

[16] Eichengreen, Barry and Jeffry Frieden, eds. The Political Economy of European Monetary Unification. San Francisco: Westview Press, Inc., 1994, p.52.

"Stability and Growth Pact"[17] is awash with political discretion concerning the use of near automatic fines.

From an economic point of view, it is difficult to understand why the German government, which wields one of the strongest currencies and boasts one of the most credible central banks in the world, wants to participate in the EMU. However, this is much more obvious from a political viewpoint. World War II, German reunification, and the collapse of the Soviet Union put Germany at the forefront of European integration. The timing of the EMU proposal and the subsequent Maastricht Summit meeting were conducive to German leadership. But the economic realities of the EMU Treaty have only just begun to raise domestic political controversies in the EU nations, including Germany.[18] The Bundesbank has sounded the alarm as diplomatically as possible and is arguing for a multi-speed EMU. But its own behavior shows that it has not yet fully appreciated the significance of giving up the Deutsche mark and its own existence. Given German concerns, it is difficult to envision the final stage of the EMU as laid down by the Maastricht Treaty. Instead, it is possible that some type of fixed exchange rate regime involving a few selected member nations with a high degree of macroeconomic coordination could evolve -- a sort of a Group of Seven (G-7), at least initially.

The Convergence Criteria and the ESCB/ECB Protocol

The Maastricht Treaty has two distinct features: (i) provisions for the transition to monetary union through the application of the convergence criteria and arrangements; and (ii) regulations that will govern macroeconomic policy formulation by institutions like the ECB. However, the loose wording of the Treaty does not specify the convergence criteria as "hard-and-fast" requirements for admission; membership will be decided by a qualified majority vote.

For example, Article 109j, para.1 stipulates that eligibility is contingent upon "the achievement of a high degree of sustainable convergence" which would "...be apparent from a rate of inflation which is close to that of at most the three best performing Member States." Another example of such loose wording is Article 104c, para.2a, which states that the deficit has to decline "substantially and continuously and has to ... reach a level that comes close to the reference value." Accordingly, the Treaty calls on decision-makers to consider not only the meeting of the convergence criteria but also the "good faith" efforts of nation's in trying to meet the same.

---

[17] A post-EMU fiscal "Stability and Growth Pact" was singed at the December 1996 Dublin European Council Summit. See Chapter VI for more details.

[18] For example, the student and union strikes in France during 1995 and 1996 over austere budget cuts and high rates of unemployment. In Germany, Oscar LaFontaine, the leader of the German Social Democratic Party, challenged Chancellor Kohl on the EMU numerous times. See Chapter VI for more details.

Barring any major asymmetric shocks, countries such as Germany, the U.K., France, Luxembourg, Denmark and the Netherlands are likely to either fully meet the convergence criteria or be close to doing so by the end of the century.[19] Belgium, Italy, Spain, Portugal, Ireland and Greece, however, may be facing very austere conditions if their governments attempt to meet the convergence criteria, given growth and unemployment rates. The dilemma of "economic prudence versus political expediency" may be most apparent with regard to Belgium and Italy, as the former's public debt and the latter's debt and budget deficits may be too difficult to reduce in the short to medium term. Despite German insistence on meeting the criteria,[20] it is not clear whether the founding members, in the case of Italy, a key member of the EU, could be excluded from the EMU.

Article 7 of the "Protocol on the Statute of the European System of Central Banks (ESCB) and of the European Central Bank (ECB)" protects the EU central banking apparatus from political intervention. Monetary policy will be directed by the ECB Governing Council which will be comprised of the six-member ECB Executive Board and the EMU central bank governors (up to 15 members).[21] As is stated in article 105, para. 1, the ECB's primary policy objective will be price stability, even at the expense of other economic objectives such as growth and employment. Article 104 prohibits the monetization of national deficits through credits provided by the ECB. The Treaty also augments the institution's independence by specifying the terms of appointment not only for the six-member Executive Board but also for the national central bank governors who sit on the Governing Council. Under Article 14, all EMU member nations must modify their domestic central banking structures. This includes the extension of the central bank governors' term of office to at least five years so that tenure terms are not shorter than the political election cycles. To this end, the President and Vice-President of the ECB are appointed to eight-year and five-year terms, respectively, while the other four members are appointed to terms ranging from five to eight years. The appointments of the six-member Executive Board are not renewable.

Notwithstanding the efforts to turn the ECB into a "super-EU-Bundesbank", the ECB may find it difficult to maintain low inflation levels. There are ambiguities in the Treaty concerning the management of exchange rates. Article 105 authorizes the ECB to conduct foreign exchange operations in consistency with Article 109, paras.1 and 2, which state that the ECOFIN Council, can with a unanimous vote "conclude

---

[19] It should be noted that asymmetric shocks will in all probability continue and may even increase as the nations strive to meet the Maastricht convergence, in particular the fiscal criteria. The French strikes during December 1995 were a good example of this possibility.

[20] As a condition to its acquiescence in the Maastricht Treaty, the German Constitutional Court has insisted that the "letter " rather than the "spirit of the law" be observed in applying the convergence criteria.

[21] Only EMU central bank governors can belong to the ECB Governing Council, which is a voting body. All 15 EU central bank governors, however, are members of the ECB General Council, which is a non-voting policy discussion forum.

formal arrangements for an exchange rate system for the single currency, the Euro, with respect to non-Union currencies" and with a qualified majority vote, may "formulate general guidelines for exchange rate management vis-à-vis these currencies." According to the Treaty, these guidelines must be "without prejudice to the primary objective of the ECB to maintain price stability." However, no corrective mechanism is provided if political pressures prevent the realization of this requirement.

The ECB Governing Council's simple majority decision-making process does not guarantee sound monetary policies. Its Governing Council could have as many as 21 members. This includes the 6 ECB Executive Board members and the 15 central bank governors. Each member nation participating in the EMU has one vote. If seven or more nations participate in the EMU through a simple majority vote, the national representatives could outvote the Executive Board. The General Council could then disagree concerning strong anti-inflationary policies because not all central bank governors can live up to the Bundesbank's expectations. Another factor to keep in mind is that as EMU membership expands, the definition of price stability also expands. Moreover, the weaker the economic performance of a member nation is, the more it is motivated to follow loose macroeconomic policies.

It is conceivable that with the loss of control over monetary and exchange rate policies the constraints on the fiscal policies of nations' might be relaxed. This could eventually allow member nations to "free-ride" by pursuing such expansionary fiscal policies as running large budget deficits, in which case they might consider themselves "too big to fail" and might believe that the EU would not let them become insolvent. Spending by such nations could be limited only by restricting their ability to raise capital in the international markets. However, even higher interest rates might not deter such countries, as real interest rate differences among member nations amount to only a few percentage points. For example, in Italy during the late 1980s real interest rates were only two percentage points higher than those in Germany, despite the differences in national debt and the possibility of a lira devaluation. Although Article 104c of the Treaty stipulates that member nations following "excessively" loose fiscal policies could be fined or would be required to maintain non-interest-bearing bonds with the ECB, these sanctions are ambiguous and could be difficult to rigorously enforce. As mentioned before, even the 1996 fiscal "Stability and Growth Pact" is riddled with political discretion. Moreover, the authority to take action against high debt or deficit nations resides not in the ECB but in the ECOFIN Council, where through the qualified majority voting process a minority could block sanctions.

Although the Maastricht Treaty includes safeguards to maintain price stability, it would be a mistake to consider their effectiveness a foregone conclusion. The only way German-style price stability can be achieved is by shadowing Bundesbank policies.

Intergovernmental Politics

The economic efficiency arguments in favor of the EMU, such as the optimal currency area, the elimination of transaction costs, increased commitment to price and exchange rate stability and the independence of central banks, are convincing. But an EMU also has certain costs as, for example, increased difficulties in managing asymmetric economic shocks and uncertainty concerning acceptance by the markets of the single currency and of the ECB. Whether the benefits outweigh the costs is debatable. The absence of compelling economic justifications for the EMU implies that the Maastricht Treaty was signed for political reasons and that nations have different views concerning the Treaty's nature, structure, composition and timetable. These differences are represented by the following two country groups: (i) Germany, the Benelux[22] and Denmark; (ii) France, Italy, Spain, Portugal, Greece and Ireland; the U.K stands alone.

The Treaty's most important signatory was the German government headed by Chancellor Helmut Kohl, an enthusiastic supporter of the EMU. This is quite interesting as Germany was quite comfortable with the original ERM in which the Deutsche mark is the anchor currency and which provides for considerable German macroeconomic and central bank autonomy in comparison with that of the other ERM nations.

Chancellor Kohl's enthusiasm for the Treaty is not only rooted in his own political philosophies but also in his government's belief that the eventual removal of capital controls could compromise the stability of the ERM and would thus negatively affect German trade, 60 percent of which is with other EU nations. The Germans also expect that the single currency, influenced by the Deutsche mark, could rival the U.S. dollar and the Japanese yen, which would lessen the impact of U.S. and Japanese macroeconomic policies on the German economy. They have a very clear concept of the structure and timetable of the EMU and are supported by the Benelux nations and Denmark, whose economic ties to Germany are strong.

But the Germans wants to limit EMU membership to those nations that demonstrate their belief in German macroeconomic policy through the acceptance of the convergence criteria and the acceptance of the "economist" view of achieving the EMU i.e. convergence first, integration second. The original German EMU blueprint called for unanimity in determining eligibility as opposed to the current qualified majority rule, because this would have allowed Germany to veto the admission of any country. The blueprint also envisioned complete control by an independent ECB over monetary and exchange rate policies without the influence of national representatives -- i.e., the ECOFIN Council -- but with the objective of price stability. The plan contained

---

[22] The Be-ne-lux an economic union includes Belgium, the Netherlands and Luxembourg. It was formed in 1948.

large automatic fines on EMU nations exceeding previously set budget deficit and/or public debt levels.

Although coveting Germany's monetary credibility and international economic reputation,[23] France, Italy, and the four less industrialized economies of Spain, Portugal, Ireland and Greece by the end of the 1980s found the political and economic costs of ERM participation too high.[24] Despite recessions and rising unemployment, the Bundesbank insisted on high interest rates. The problem was compounded by German reunification which resulted in even higher interest rates during the early 1990s. Consequently, under French President François Mitterand's leadership the EMU turned into a vehicle of softening the ERM while attempting to retain German-type economic credibility.

The above mentioned nations support the "monetarist" view of the EMU because with the exception of France, they need to rapidly refurbish their international monetary credibility through association with an independent and anti-inflationary ECB that is modeled after the Bundesbank. Although the same could be achieved by following sustained economic policies and by keeping their currencies within the narrow ERM band, these countries are willing to accept the high costs of acquiring the Bundesbank's reputation. But France and Italy find the proposition attractive only as long as it allows for policy flexibility during asymmetric shocks or regional recessions, while Spain, Portugal, Ireland and Greece expect compensation for adhering to the dictates of the required macroeconomic policies. Thus, they insisted on the establishment of the Cohesion Fund.

Under the leadership of the Conservative government of John Major, the U.K. is the only country that did not join the Deutsche mark core group or the counter-core group. Although not as anti-integration as Baroness Thatcher, Major is still preoccupied with the loss of sovereignty. The British support the German concept of price stability and the slow transition to the EMU, but still insisted on an opt-out clause that allows the U.K. to delay the final decision on whether to join the EMU until its membership is known.

---

[23] This was also the motivation, for the creation of the "Snake" and the EMS/ERM, following the collapse of the Bretton Woods system.

[24] French President François Mitterand shouldered the cost of ERM participation in the early 1980s when his experimentation with socialism was undermined by the Bundesbank's resistance to French fiscal expansion within the ERM. Mitterand again bore the costs in the early 1990s when in the midst of a French recession and rising double-digit unemployment the Bundesbank raised interest rates that eventually led to the ERM crisis, its semi-collapse and the widening of the bands to +/-15 percent. This was a partial reason for the Socialist loss of the 1993 parliamentary and 1995 presidential elections. The economic costs to Italy were very large despite its late entrance into the narrow +/-2.25 percent ERM band. Ireland also experienced difficult times owing to the ERM constraints in the 1980s. Spain and Portugal realized that they would have to join the narrow ERM band while Greece wanted to join the ERM soon. All knew that the economic costs would be high.

The main division at Maastricht was between Germany, the Benelux nations and the U.K. on the one hand and France, Italy and the four less developed countries on the other hand. The latter group wanted an EMU that leads to a union before convergence and thus to a rapid transition and looser operating rules.

The EMU Bargaining Process

Despite Germany's strong bargaining power, the final EMU Treaty and the subsequent agreements differ from the earlier German vision of the same. Ever since the discussions began in the late 1980s, the Germans wanted to achieve two main objectives: (i) the creation of an "economist" version of the EMU that involves strict convergence prior to full integration, and (ii) the establishment of an uncompromising, powerful and independent central bank. Not only did the wording of the Maastricht Treaty imply loose convergence criteria, but the U.K. obtained an opt-out clause. The less developed nations such as Spain, Portugal, Ireland and Greece received commitments for the establishment of a Cohesion Fund[25] in the amount of Ecu 15 billion (US$18 billion) as part of the Delors II budget package at the 1992 Edinburgh European Council Summit. It is apparent that the intergovernmental bargaining on the EMU was carried out in a broad political-economic context.

The most convincing explanation of Germany's acceptance of a sub-optimal EMU Treaty is the country's desire to promote a federalist EU driven by its wish not to repeat history. However, even such a strong foreign policy underpinning is not enough to explain the ready acceptance of the Treaty and of the subsequent EMU-related agreements. It is possible that Chancellor Kohl's desire to win the December 1990 elections through rapid reunification also played a role. Other nations could have slowed re-unification through a variety of measures and, thus, upset Kohl's election timetable. This convinced the Chancellor to accept a rapid move toward the EMU and a political union with loose economic convergence requirements. He accommodated those nations which, for political and/or economic reasons, wanted a loose EMU, such as Italy and the southern nations led by France. The resulting Kohl-Mitterand "bargain" was struck in 1990. It was a decisive pro-EMU and pro-political union stance, regardless of the eventual replacement of the Bundesbank and the Deutsche Mark.

Although the Maastricht Treaty was signed a little over a year after reunification, Chancellor Kohl could not push for a more German-style EMU because

---

[25] The Cohesion Fund, aimed at reducing economic disparities between member states, provides Ecu 15 billion (US$18.585 billion) over the 1993-99 period. The regulation establishing the Fund requires an indicative allocation of the resources among the four beneficiary countries: Spain: 52 to 58 percent; Greece: 16 to 20 percent; Portugal: 16 to 20 percent; and Ireland 7 to 10 percent. See Chapter III for (a) more details on the Cohesion Fund, (b) a summary of the differences between the Cohesion and Structural Funds, (c) actual disbursements among member nations, and (d) the assistance function of the Cohesion Fund in 1993.

in the wake of the 1989 collapse of the Soviet empire the early 1990s brought about a change in foreign policy orientation. German interests took on a long-term dimension as opposed to the short-term objective of the international acceptance of reunification. New emphasis was placed on creating irrevocable institutional ties to the EU so as to reaffirm commitment to integration. In addition to strategic concerns about geographic spheres of influence, through the ties of the former German Democratic Republic (GDR) to the former Soviet Union (FSU) economy, the Kohl government found itself involved in the economic events of the FSU in general and of Central and Eastern Europe in particular. This required generous amounts of economic aid which was also necessary to obtain Soviet approval of German reunification and the eventual mass immigration by ethnic Germans.[26]

The socioeconomic costs and the duration of the reunification process were grossly underestimated.[27] Not only is the integration of the former GDR economy taking more time than the originally projected five years, but it has also resulted in a significant increase in unemployment benefit payments, welfare provisions and in direct aid, which has raised the German budget deficit from 0.5 percent in 1989 to 3.3 percent in 1991 and 3.9 percent in 1996.[28] The public debt rose from 43.8 percent of GDP in 1990 to 60.8 percent in 1996. Moreover, as a result of reunification the number of elderly citizens has increased and this has precipitated an increase in early retirements. Other costs, albeit indirect, have included the breakdown of the ERM caused by the need to counter the threat of inflation generated by the reunification through an increase of short-term interest rates. Thus, increased EU social and economic integration became desirable to spread the adjustment burden over the member states.[29]

The need for intra-EU export markets played an even more critical role. Any progress toward integration aided German exports, whereas any slowdown or stagnation could have had an adverse impact on the same. Thus while pressing strongly for a German-style EMU, the Kohl government signed the sub-optimal Maastricht Treaty and the subsequent EMU agreements. Other member nations are cognizant of the mood of compromise that prevails in Bonn and have taken advantage of it. This

---

[26] Germany was favored by immigrants because of the liberal asylum laws and the cultural ties of the ethnic Germans who lived in the former Soviet Union. By October 1992, approximately 50,000 refugees were entering Germany every month - a 71 percent increase over 1991 and more than the number that entered the rest of Europe combined. Thus, in December 1992 the major political parties agreed to a modification of the laws, which went into effect in July 1993.

[27] German officials revised their 1989 reunification cost estimates to DM150 billion (US$98 billion) in late 1992. "Germany: A Survey," Financial Times, October 26, 1992.

[28] Germany's budget deficit in 1992 was 2.8 percent, in 1993, 3.5 percent, in 1994, 2.4 percent, and in 1995, 3.5. "Progress Towards Convergence 1996". European Monetary Institute (EMI), Frankfurt am Main, November 1996, p.20.

[29] Although some reunification aid was received through the EU structural fund for the economic transformation of the eastern region of Germany, the Bonn government still continues to pay for most of the financial cost. Moreover, Germany also shoulders the largest financial responsibility, among the EU nations, associated with aiding the transformation of the Central and Eastern European economies.

prevented the foundation of a strong price stability agreement and has led to other EMU-related concessions such as the Cohesion Fund, the loose wording of the Maastricht Treaty and a softer post-EMU fiscal "Stability and Growth Pact".

Post-Treaty Politics

If the politics surrounding the signing of the Maastricht Treaty were complicated and somewhat unpredictable, the ratification of the Treaty by national legislations was an eye-opener. The Treaty's strongest opponent should have been Germany -- in particular the Bundesbank and Minister of Finance, Theo Waigel. Instead, ratification and implementation concerns were raised by Denmark, France, and the U.K. and subsequently by the financial markets, which showed some instability. This was prompted by the Bundesbank's refusal to lower interest rates.

In retrospect, the signing of the Maastricht Treaty was relatively simple as like-minded governments were involved. Ratification, however, meant convincing citizens that giving up national currencies and the authority of central banks is not only safe but also beneficial in that it helps to reduce the Bundesbank's influence.[30] But in the midst of a Europe-wide recession in 1992, the public had a difficult time understanding how further integration and the replacement of national currencies would create more economic independence, particularly since they believed that integration was a major reason for the economic slowdowns in the first place. Thus, nationalism was the dominant force in most EU countries during the time that governments were attempting to ratify the Maastricht Treaty.

The problems of ratification not only illustrated the political nature of the Treaty but also hampered its timetable by making the rocky transition period to the EMU even more difficult. The negative public reaction, especially in those countries that were seen as the Treaty's main supporters, at first had an adverse impact on the ERM only. Later it created a critical problem. With the removal of capital controls in 1991, the ERM's stability hinged on the financial markets' belief that the mechanism serves as a stepping-stone to EMU. The weaker ERM currencies received artificial short-term support, as the mechanism's credibility depended on the market's belief that, irrespective of domestic economic and political conditions, member nations would defend their currency parities. The Treaty appeared to justify this belief. However, when it became clear that ratification was in trouble, commitments to the ERM quickly waned and the weaker currencies such as the pound sterling and the lira and those whose economic fundamentals were not sound as, for example, the French franc, were hit by speculative attacks. The ERM no longer seemed like a stepping-stone to the EMU. This precipitated the September 1992 and August 1993 ERM crises, despite

[30] The Constitutions of Denmark and Ireland required a referendum, while French President Mitterand wanted to use the referendum to capitalize on the mistaken notion that the Treaty had strong popular support.

attempts by the affected governments to reiterate their commitment to the ERM by raising interest rates and intervening in the foreign exchange markets.

In 1992 the Bundesbank was under domestic and international pressure to lower interest rates. Although the German central bank maintained its commitment to the ERM by intervening against the Deutsche mark's bilateral parities, it was not prepared to violate its mandate by lowering interest rates to ease the speculative pressures on other currencies. There are two views as to the motives of the Bundesbank. One is that the bank conducted itself as any other central bank would, focusing primarily on the domestic economy. In other words, the Bundesbank did not deliberately weaken the ERM in order to slow down the EMU. The second view points to statements made by the three highest officials of the Bundesbank, President Helmut Schlesinger, Vice-President Hans Tietmeyer and Chief Economist Otmar Issing, who left no doubt as to their opposition to the Treaty. Their views were based on: (i) the Bundesbank's mandate to maintain price stability, which could not be endangered by the EMU; (ii) a Darwinian approach to EMU membership i.e. the survival of the fittest; (iii) the inability of the current rules and economic convergence guidelines of the Treaty to maintain strict price stability; and (iv) the need to protect the ECB against political influence.

Today it seems that these views were just another expression of the differences between the federal government and the Bundesbank. The government had the political incentive to compromise on the EMU and possessed the lawful authority to sign the Treaty, thereby committing the Bundesbank. But the autonomous Bundesbank with its domestic mandate has the authority to set and sustain high interest rates to maintain price stability. As a result, the Bundesbank is often accused of promoting a two-speed EMU. However, this is erroneous because regardless of the Bundesbank's actions, the Treaty's convergence criteria automatically establish a two-speed EMU. Some countries as, for example, Greece cannot meet either the prescribed criteria or the established timetable. What the Bundesbank's monetary policy did was to focus attention on those nations that do not have sustainable solutions to their long-standing economic problems. Nonetheless, the Bundesbank's position reinforced the possibility of a two-speed EMU, as the number of eligible nations has declined, in part because of the high German interest rates. It can be argued that at the time the independence of the Bundesbank provided Chancellor Kohl with a useful excuse to explain the difficulties associated with a speedy EMU while maintaining his government's original reservations. Yet, during 1996 and 1997 the Chancellor moved full speed towards the 1999 EMU deadline.

The future of EMU depends on politics, because any future integration hinges on intergovernmental bargaining. Six years ago it would have been difficult to foresee the signing, ratification and acceptance of the Treaty by the major nations. The Treaty not only does not rule out the admission of less disciplined and less well-performing economies, but also contains regulations that accept political control over common monetary policies. Moreover, it has no airtight commitment to price stability, while at the same time it places the primary burden for such stability on Germany, which may have to accept higher inflation rates and/or continue to provide substantial financial assistance to the weaker member nations following the establishment of the EMU. Needless to say, the Bonn government paid a high price for reunification. Perhaps this was a shrewd, calculated gamble by Chancellor Kohl, as he relied on the Bundesbank's inevitable disapproval and more so on its ability, unlike that of any other central bank, to have an enormous impact not only on other economies but also on monetary integration. The raising of interest rates was inevitable, but combined with a deep Europe-wide recession certain ERM currencies came under a great deal of strain which, if continued, could have led to the full collapse of the mechanism. This, coupled with popular opposition to monetary integration in general and to the Maastricht Treaty in particular, created a powerful catalyst for destabilizing and thus slowing down the EMU process during 1992 and 1993. Perhaps the Bundesbank also wanted to send a powerful message showing that it intended to control domestic monetary policy and that it wanted to be consulted on common monetary issues. It is not implausible that Chancellor Kohl and the Bundesbank were partners in this undertaking.

THE IMPACT OF THE ERM CRISES ON THE EMU

When it was signed in 1992, the Maastricht Treaty was hailed as a landmark on the road to integration. Since then, however, it has become a controversial issue that will either unite or divide the EU. The political and economic controversies surrounding the Treaty raise concerns about, among others, the objectives and the timetable of the EMU. Of particular concern is the question of the long-term impact of the September 1992 and August/September 1993 ERM crises.

The 1992 crisis forced the U.K., Italy and Finland to float their currencies and was followed by a Spanish devaluation that touched off further flotations and devaluations. This culminated in the 1993 crisis that led to the widening of the currency bands from +/-2.25 percent to +/-15 percent -- a de facto suspension of the mechanism. Since then, except for the Deutsche mark and the Dutch guilder, all currencies adhere to the wider bands, albeit temporarily. This is akin to a floating exchange rate system, because open market floats do not fluctuate much over +/-15 percent. It is clear that with the widening of the ERM currency bands, policymakers are enjoying freedoms that allow monetary policy flexibility. In hard economic times this is always appealing.

The Treaty calls for an EMU by narrowing the exchange rate linkages between the ERM currencies. Thus, perhaps the most important effect of the two major ERM crises was a slight mitigation of the EMU controversy. Governments appear to be politically committed to the EMU, although some of them have economic doubts.

The 1992 and 1993 ERM Crises

There is agreement that the two chronologically separate but interrelated crises were generated by doubts about EMU's credibility. The financial markets questioned the ability of the member states to keep their currencies within the narrow ERM bands during the long Stage II transition period. But there is no agreement concerning the specific causes of the crises. The following discussion proposes eleven reasons that may have triggered them.

1. Problems of Ratifying the Maastricht Treaty

The 1992 Danish and French Maastricht Treaty referenda results created doubts in the financial markets concerning the political ability of the member nations to meet the strict EMU convergence criteria. The markets did not believe that member states such as Italy, caught up in a recession, could or rather would have the political will to maintain a fixed exchange rate against the Deutsche mark -- that is, to shadow German monetary policy.

2. Misalignment Within the ERM

Since its inception, the ERM has reduced and converged EU inflation rates.[31] It achieved this by allowing member countries to "piggyback" on the credibility and low-inflation policies of the Bundesbank. But such policy "shadowing" is possible only if the countries' central currency parity rates are fundamentally in line with economic performance. However, currencies such as the U.K. pound sterling and the Spanish peseta entered the mechanism at the wrong parity. The pound sterling came in at DM2.95; as shown by studies,[32] a more appropriate rate would have been DM2.50. By 1993, the U.K. current account deficit reached £12 billion (2 percent of GDP) and the economy was in the midst of one of its worst post-WWII recessions. Thus, it was clear that the pound sterling was overvalued and that its parity rate could no longer be defended. By late 1990 the peseta was also overvalued.[33] Thus, with the passage of time it was becoming increasingly clear that these and other currencies needed to be realigned. Not surprisingly, the more apparent this became, the more the financial markets insisted on it.

---

[31] There are those who argue that attributing the convergence of interest and inflation rates to the success of the ERM is erroneous, as they were converging anyway.

[32] John Williamson argued that to pursue acceptable employment policies countries must achieve exchange rate equilibria, which occurs when the current account surplus or deficit becomes equivalent to the capital flow. (John Williamson. "Fundamental Equilibrium Exchange Rates," National Institute of Economic and Social Research Review, December 1991.)

[33] Dornbusch, Rudiger. Two-track EMU, Now! In Britain and EMU. Center for Economic Performance in Association with Financial Markets Group, London School of Economics, 1990.

3. *The Prolonged and Deep Recessions*

As the EU-wide recessions deepened and the Bundesbank failed to lower short-term interest rates during 1992-93, anxiety increased. This created an atmosphere in which past exchange-rate performance and/or supportive political statements could no longer ensure currency stability. Moreover, the deepening recession damaged two of the underpinnings of the ERM and of the monetary integration process. First, it weakened the medium-term commitment to the narrow +/-2.25 percent band. Second, it lessened the likelihood that member states would experience similar broad endogenous or exogenous economic disturbances. The recession generated unemployment pressures and, as a consequence, dissimilar medium-term economic agendas. Germany's short- to medium-term policy objectives were also influenced by the reunification process, which introduced large asymmetric shocks. Thus, short- to medium-term domestic economic policy dilemmas played a critical role in the crises, especially in 1993.

4. *Inherent Design Flaws of the ERM (the "Walters Critique")*

There are many who believe that the ERM crises were caused by its design flaws, particularly by the nature of the adjustment mechanism. From the late 1980s to mid-1992 countries such as Spain and the U.K. experienced high inflation and interest rates, yet they did not come under monetary pressures from the ERM and thus were considered to be in good standing. Due to high inflation and interest rates, the adjustment mechanism required the Bank of Spain to conduct foreign exchange interventions without sterilization to support the peseta. In principle, monetary growth should have contracted, and interest rates should have remained high and fiscal policy tight, constraining domestic demand and growth. Using the Spanish peseta as an example, Figure 2.1 presents a detailed illustration of how the ERM is supposed to work versus how it has actually worked.

For over a decade, Sir Alan Walters[34] has argued that the ERM does not function in this manner. In his view, pegged exchange rates generate capital flows from countries with low interest rates to countries with high interest rates. This, in turn, causes downward pressures on nominal and real interest rates in the recipient countries and forces governments to intervene during the resulting inflation to lower the value of their currencies. The outcome, easier money, is exactly the opposite of the required tightening of monetary policy. This is what happened in Spain. Under such conditions fiscal policy becomes the critical policy adjustment tool. The "Walters critique" thus implies that the ERM should, or rather cannot, be reformed. This is why Sir Alan referred to the mechanism as "half-baked" and called for its elimination.

---

[34] Sir Alan Walters was Chief Economic Advisor to Prime Minister Margaret Thatcher.

Figure 2.1
How the ERM is Supposed to Work Versus How It Has Worked in the Past
(using the Spanish peseta as an example)

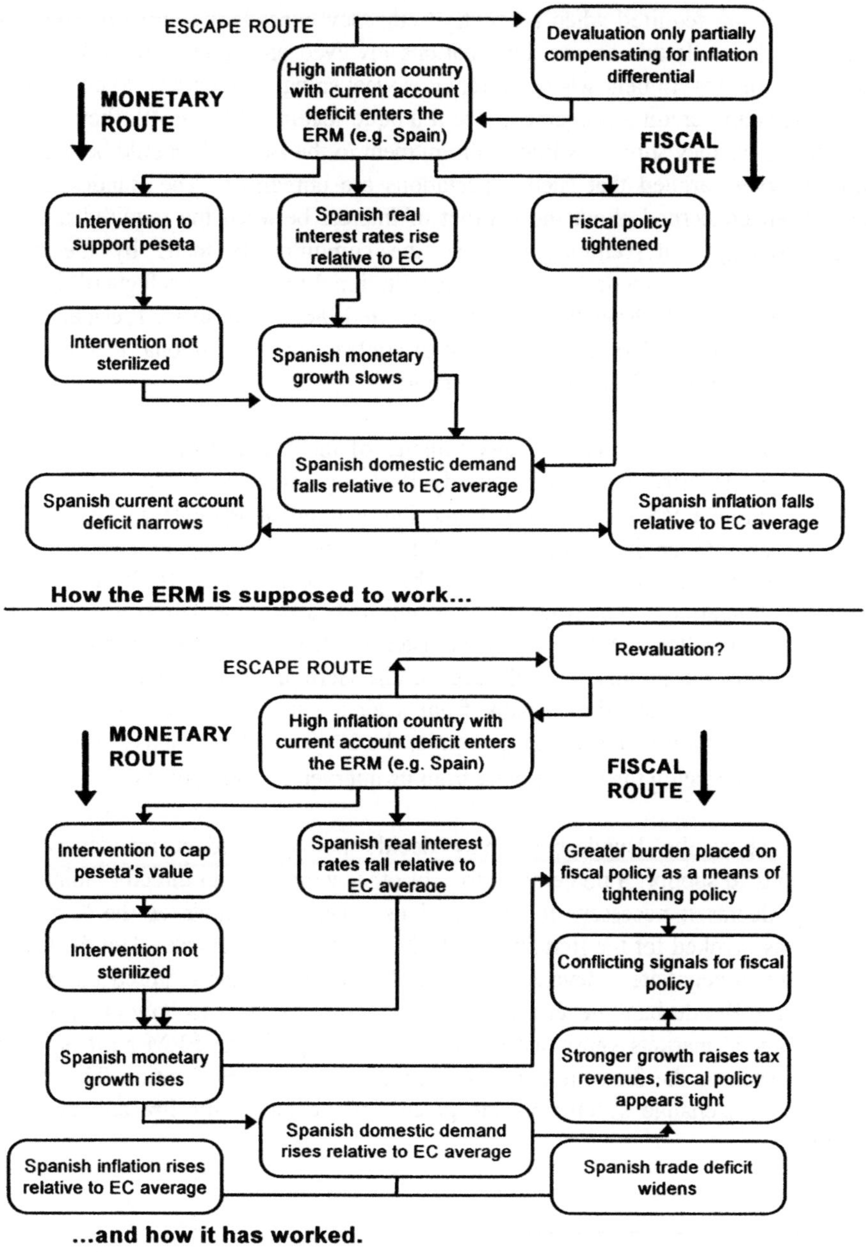

Source: Temperton, Paul, ed. The European Currency Crisis. Cambridge: Probus Publishing Co., 1993. p.22.

5. The Emminger Letter

The EMS intervention rules and credit arrangements are designed, to some extent, to protect the international reserves of the weaker currency countries. Interventions are required when a country's currency exceeds the limits of one of the bilateral parities. If this occurs, both nations involved are obliged to lend unlimited reserves to the government whose currency is weakening to intervene. Such unlimited interventions and credit arrangements are a unique feature of the EMS: they reinforce its credibility as they show a political commitment to the ERM. It should be noted that many observers argued that such expectations are unrealistic. The Bundesbank has always been concerned about the conflict of interest between the required unlimited foreign exchange interventions (that is, the commitments made by the federal government) and the Bundesbank's own constitutional mandate to safeguard the value of the Deutsche mark through price stability. In 1986, Bundesbank President Otmar Emminger asked the German government to confirm its constitutional mandate. The following is an excerpt from Emminger's letter:

> The autonomy in monetary policies of the Bundesbank would particularly be put in jeopardy if strong imbalances with the future EMS resulted in extreme intervention obligations which would then threaten the value of the currency. This would make it impossible for the Bundesbank to carry out its legal obligations. Referring to the repeated assurances from the Chancellor and the Finance Minister, the Bundesbank is starting from the premise that, if need be, the German government will safeguard the Bundesbank from such a situation, either by a correction of the exchange rate in the EMS or, if necessary, by discharging the Bundesbank from its intervention obligations.[35]

Thus, the Bundesbank may decide not to conduct mandatory ERM interventions to support a bilateral parity. In other words, it can directly violate EMS rules if it deems it necessary to do so. This exception, known as the "Emminger Letter," was invoked for the first time in 1992 when the Bundesbank asked the German government to negotiate a devaluation of the lira instead of the required intervention. Although the Bundesbank never refused intervention or credits to Italy or the U.K., it let the financial markets know that it preferred a change in the ERM parities. Such a move was seen by the financial markets as a sign of limited intervention. This, in turn, gave foreign exchange speculators the green light to attack the lira and the pound sterling.

---

[35] Otmar Emminger, 1986, translated by Peter Kenen, in "Capital Controls, The EMS and EMU," The Economic Journal, 105, Royal Economic Society, London: Blackwell Publishers, January 1995, pp.181-92.

In addition to the Emminger Letter, the 1993 reports[36] issued by the EC Monetary Committee and the Committee of Central Bank Governors in the aftermath of the 1992 ERM crisis also increased the ERM's vulnerability. For the most part the report focused on the need for more "timely" realignments, ahead of adjustments forced by the financial markets. However, there was no real discussion as to whether narrow bands coupled with more frequent realignments would increase the cost of speculation. Moreover, the reports failed to address the larger issue of finding a method to reinforce the ERM against speculative pressures. In fact, the findings fueled the markets' belief that the ERM is susceptible to speculation, because only through veiled references to the Emminger Letter did the reports acknowledge that the crises exposed a fatal flaw in the EMS; the obligation of unlimited intervention or credit provision. In addition, the reports reinforced the point that governments cannot guarantee an automatic response to market tensions involving symmetrical actions on the part of these countries whose currencies are involved.[37] The findings stressed that although voluntary action was possible, such action should not interfere with the management of domestic monetary conditions in the country with the intervention currency and that intervention must be consistent with the primary objective of achieving price stability in the EC.[38]

6. *The Effects of German Reunification*

German reunification had both obvious and subtle effects on the ERM and, consequently, on the EMU's future. The obvious effect was the major external shock that negatively affected the ERM. Although the ERM and the EMU were designed to absorb both external and internal shocks, they cannot accommodate major asymmetric shocks affecting primarily one nation, especially when that nation's currency is the anchor. Yet it should be noted that the ERM has experienced and survived major external shocks before, such as the 1979 oil price increase and the volatile 1979-83 period when exchange rates were realigned approximately every eight months.

While the ERM could have withstood the asymmetric German re-unification shock, it was strongly affected by the underestimation of its political, economic and social costs. In 1990, Chancellor Kohl and Finance Minister Waigel repeatedly asserted that the process was essentially self-financing[39] and that neither new taxes nor tax increases would be necessary. They also argued that the expected West German economic boom would not be inflationary.[40]

---

[36] The reports issued by the EC Monetary Committee and the Committee of Central Bank governors were released to the public by the EU finance ministers and central bank governors at their meeting in Kolding, Denmark on May 22, 1993.

[37] Kenen, Peter. "Capital Controls, The EMS and EMU," 1995, p.185. Abstract taken from the actual reports of the Monetary Committee and Committee of Central Banks.

[38] Kenen, Peter. "Capital Controls, The EMS and EMU," 1995, p.185.

[39] They predicted that reunification would be self-financing in the short run, as it would boost West German growth and thus raise government revenues.

[40] The boom in West Germany was not expected to be inflationary, as the East could provide

But this is not what happened. The politically conditioned[41] quick monetary union on July 1, 1990[42] based on a 1:1 exchange rate between the West and East German currencies created a wage-cost disadvantage in the East, as the real exchange rate was around 1:8. While wages in the East were approximately half of those in the West, productivity reached only 25 percent of the West German levels.[43] The resulting reduction in competitiveness could have been remedied if East German wages had fallen. But West German labor unions called for higher wages in the East. Chancellor Kohl's political maneuvers also fueled the wage increase as he promised that East Germans would quickly attain West German living standards. The result was a sharp increase in East German unemployment,[44] and the resulting benefit payments drained the West German budget. Deficits climbed to 3.5 percent of GDP, in 1993.[45] Inflation hit a high of 4.8 percent in March 1992 and stayed at over 4 percent for the remainder of 1993.

In response to increased economic growth, a surge in the government deficit and an increase in the money supply, the Bundesbank increased short-term interest rates. The Lombard rate went from less than 6 percent in 1988 to almost 10 percent in 1992 and settled around 9 percent in 1993. The discount rate, less than 3 percent in 1988, was more than 8 percent in 1992. It settled around 7 percent in 1993. In the context of the prolonged and deep EU-wide recession, this exerted strong pressures on the already misaligned ERM.[46]

---

low-cost labor which would increase output in the West and simultaneously exert downward pressure on West German wages.

[41] It should be noted that most officials, especially those of the Bundesbank, were aware of the potentially harmful fiscal and inflationary consequences of Chancellor Kohl's policies but recognized political necessity to proceed with reunification.

[42] The monetary union between the Ost-mark and the Deutsche mark took place three months prior to the official dissolution of East Germany on October 3, 1990, a date also known as "Unification Day."

[43] East German wages and aggregate productivity (GDP per employee) in the 3rd quarter of 1990 reached 39 and 26 percent of West German levels. However, by the first quarter of 1993, East German wages had risen to 70 percent while productivity reached only 42 percent of the West German levels. Temperton, Paul, ed. The European Currency Crisis. Cambridge: Probus Publishing Company, 1993, p.5.

[44] By 1991 approximately 8 million of the 16 million East Germans were either unemployed or employed part-time.

[45] Although West Germany did experience a short-lived economic boom, particularly in the construction sector, the tax revenue generated was not enough to cover the high transfer payments. Despite the 1991 tax increase, the 1993 government deficit rose to its highest level in ten years. During 1991 and 1992, East German subsidies cost West German taxpayers DM150 billion (approximately US$100 billion) annually.

[46] Initially, the 1992 crisis was surrounded by controversy, as there were calls for the temporary suspension of the Deutsche mark from the ERM parity grid until German monetary policy could get back on track. Although the Germans favored this option, others, especially the French, rejected it because they feared a loss of credibility of their own monetary policy during the German absence. The alternative option was a Deutsche mark revaluation within the ERM. However, even with a 1990 or 1992 revaluation in a low inflationary environment, the Bundesbank would probably still

7. Increased Currency Linkages to the Deutsche mark and/or the Ecu

The U.K. entered the ERM on October 5, 1990, two days after German "Unification Day," and Norway linked its krone to the Ecu during the same month. Seven other EU and non-EU nations also linked their currencies to either the Deutsche mark or the Ecu between June 1989 and mid-1992. Box 2.1 shows a list of the currencies that were linked to the Deutsche mark or the Ecu during this period.

Box 2.1
Currencies Linked to the Deutsche mark or the Ecu (June 1989 to mid-1992.)

IN...

- Spain joins the ERM in June 1989
- U.K. joins the ERM in October 1990
- Norway announces link to the Ecu in October 1990
- Sweden announces link to the Ecu in April 1991
- Finland announces link to the Ecu in June 1991
- Portugal joins the ERM in April 1992
- Cyprus announces link to the Ecu in June 1992

...OUT

- Finland devalues the markka in November 1991
- Finland floats the markka on September 8, 1992
- Italy devalues the lira on September 13, 1992
- U.K. withdraws from the ERM on September 16, 1992
- Italy suspends intervention agreement in the ERM on September 16, 1992
- Spain devalues the peseta by 5% on September 16, 1992
- Sweden floats the krona on November 19, 1992
- Spain and Portugal devalue by 6% on November 22, 1992
- Norway floats the krone on December 10, 1992
- Ireland devalues the punt by 10% on January 30, 1993
- Spain devalues the peseta by 8% on May 13, 1993
- Portugal devalues the escudo by 6.5% on May 13, 1993
- All ERM currencies move to fluctuation bands of +/-15% around unchanged central rates. Separate bilateral agreement between Germany and the Netherlands to maintain +/-2.25% bands on August 2, 1993.

Source: Temperton, Paul, ed. The European Currency Crisis. Cambridge: Probus Publishing Company, 1993, p.10.

---

have pursued a tight monetary policy to curtail money supply growth and to establish fiscal and wage restraints. This could have made it easier for the other EU member nations to tolerate high interest rates, but neither option was carried out.

It could be argued that these linkages may have been the result of underestimating the impact of German reunification. However, it is more likely that they were a manifestation of the increased use of exchange rates as symbols of economic strength, coupled with the desire to be a part of the EU by linking currencies either directly or indirectly to the Deutsche mark or the Ecu. This was particularly desirable because by the early 1990s the EMU "train" was at full speed.[47] It should be noted that the moves were in part also fueled by the benefits of linking up with a low-inflation country, albeit for most nations this was less important.

8. Unwillingness to Adjust Central Parities

There is a consensus that the crises had had a "therapeutic value" in that they corrected the ERM misalignments. During 1991 and the first half of 1992 there was no incentive to realign currencies. Most economies were growing and interest rate differentials with Germany were narrowing. The Maastricht Treaty was signed, the EMU plan was moving ahead, and the last ERM realignment was years back in 1987. Capital flows continued and increasing German inflation did not provide an incentive to realign, except to Italy.[48] In addition, countries hesitated to realign because establishing or maintaining monetary credibility had become a primary concern during the 1990s as opposed to the past emphasis on inflation differentials and trade performance. The 1993 use of the "franc-fort" policy,[49] which led to the dismantling of the ERM to save French monetary policy credibility, is a good illustration of the change in emphasis.

9. Maastricht Treaty Deadline Pressures

Of all the EMU deadlines, 1999, when exchange rates will be irrevocably locked and no future realignments will be possible has put the greatest pressure on the ERM bilateral parities. No matter how many times governments deny that there will be "one final realignment on the eve of EMU," the financial markets are skeptical, as there are numerous high-debt nations that would want to reduce their real debt by way of currency devaluations. Yet, there could be a need for one "last" realignment in order to restore "the competitive position of high inflation countries"[50] even if inflation convergence is achieved prior to the locking of exchange rates. The realignments of the early 1990s were not sufficient to offset the price-level divergences between 1995 and

---

[47] The Delors Report was published in April 1989. The October 1990 Rome European Council Summit meeting set the date of standing Stage II of the EMU for January 1, 1994. This called for the establishment of the EMI and for narrower ERM bilateral exchange rate parities. The Maastricht Treaty which set the timetable for Stage II and Stage III, was agreed upon in December 1991 and signed in February 1992.

[48] Italy needed to devalue the lira by approximately 17.4 percent against the ECU to be price competitive as measured by the ERM average.

[49] When the EMS and the ERM were created in 1979, there was an implied commitment by the Bundesbank to support the franc's parity against the Deutsche mark as long as the French government more or less followed an inflation-free monetary policy (i.e., shadowed the Bundesbank). Using a play on words concerning the location of the Bundesbank, which serves as the supporting arch of the ERM, this policy became known as the "franc-fort" policy. This policy is the backbone of the ERM, as it symbolizes the 40-year-old Paris-Bonn axis on which integration has to be achieved.

[50] Kenen, Peter. "Capital Controls, The EMS and EMU," 1995, p.185.

1999.

Other EMU-related deadlines may also have played a role. Considerable speculative pressure will be placed on the ERM currencies in 1998 when countries that have met the convergence criteria and countries that still have "excessive" budget deficits will be identified. Of all the reactions in the foreign exchange markets to EMU deadlines, none is likely to be stronger than the one that will occur when the final date of the introduction of the single currency is announced. It is difficult to predict whether the short- to medium-term impact of this date on the currencies will be positive or negative.

10. Increasing Frictions between the ERM and Domestic Economic Concerns

The success of the ERM in achieving low inflation and low interest rate convergence caused problems that eventually manifested themselves in the two crises.[51] In the autumn of 1991, amid worries about unemployment, the French government lowered its short-term interest rate, which generated fears of a franc devaluation. The currency took a nose-dive and dropped out of the narrow band. This forced the French government to quickly reverse its policy. As the specter of unemployment worsened, the French attempted another interest rate cut in July 1993. While the financial markets believed that the domestic fundamentals such as escalating unemployment would be the decisive factor, France managed to shock the world by choosing ERM stability and credibility over domestic concerns. Nonetheless, owing to political pressures the government eventually caved in and this resulted in the wider (+/-15 percent) bands.

11. The Actions and Reactions of the Financial Markets

Most of the ERM devaluations and flotations following September 1992 were caused primarily by large international capital flows. During the period 1987-91, such flows were placed into high-yield ERM currencies. This was primarily due to the growing perception by the international capital markets that the economies were converging toward the EMU. Thus, the financial markets favored higher interest rate yields for ERM currencies over the risk of exchange rate depreciation. The prevailing view argued that "Why settle for the yield on a Deutsche mark bond when you can get the higher yield on a peseta or lira bond without a compensating exchange rate risk."[52] Capital moved into peseta or lira and later pound sterling bonds, over Deutsche mark or dollar bonds.[53] The financial markets referred to this as the "convergence play."[54]

---

[51] During the early 1990s, (July 1990 in Denmark; June 1991 in France; July 1991 in Belgium; and the late 1980s - 1990s -- apart from 1991 -- in the Netherlands) interest rates fell below those of Germany. Although some of this could be attributed to the ERM's success, the effects of German reunification coupled with slow growth rates and the sharp fall in oil prices in 1986 also played a role.

[52] World Economic and Financial Surveys. "International Capital Markets: Part I: Exchange Rate Management and International Capital Flows," Washington, DC: International Monetary Fund (IMF) Publication, April 1993, p.8.

[53] For example, according to an April 1993 IMF Study, during 1987 - 1992, the average spread between the one-year lira yield over the corresponding Deutsche mark instrument was almost 5 percent. It was approximately the same for the dollar. ("International Capital Markets: Part I," IMF, April 1993).

[54] IMF estimates have set the cost of the convergence plays at US$300 billion.

However, it soon became apparent that the economies were not converging and that the locking of exchange rates was not forthcoming, owing to large fiscal deficits, financial sector weaknesses, cyclical economic differences, the resulting fiscal and monetary policy divergences and the subsequent loss of competitiveness. Such issues became even more pronounced in the aftermath of the Danish and French referenda as they raised questions not only about the ratification of the Treaty and the ability of member nations to achieve convergence, but also about the chance of sustaining the ERM parities. This is what led to large capital movements out of the pound sterling and the lira and the beginning of the crises.

Once a country appears to be unable to maintain its central ERM parity, the international capital and foreign exchange markets, with a daily turnover of over US$7 and US$1 trillion, respectively, go on the offensive. Central bank interventions, open market operations or supportive government statements cannot stop this process.[55] This became evident in early 1992 when prior to the first ERM crisis the central banks held only about US$275 billion in foreign exchange reserves. Not surprisingly, the resulting loss of confidence by the financial markets caused the pound sterling and the lira to "free-float" and the Nordic currencies to discontinue their link to the Ecu. It should be noted that the inability of governments to control the markets will probably be the single greatest challenge that central banks will face during the next decade.

ERM Policy Options and Their Impact on the EMU

The two ERM crises produced an aura of uncertainty. Since the widening of the ERM currency bands to +/-15 percent several proposals were presented to restructure the mechanism and thus to provide a basis for the Stage II transition process to the EMU. The following section explores the nature and feasibility of the discussed options[56].

Option 1: An Early Return to the Original ERM

The pressures that led to the expanded ERM bands are still affecting the currency markets. Thus, there is a consensus that an early return to the original ERM is not possible. With the widening of the bands national policy formulators have more monetary policy flexibility which they may not want to give up.

Option 2: A Delayed Return to the Original ERM

In today's financial markets, the original ERM adjustment mechanism is ineffective. This and the "Walters critique" shows that it would have been a mistake to revive this mechanism without modifications. A delayed return to the ERM would not

---

55 Other tactics for defending ERM parities include: official intervention; the use of existing stocks of international reserves; borrowing from private capital markets; borrowing from the official sector (i.e., the Very Short-Term Financing Facility (VSTF); defensive increases in interest rates; and capital controls.

56 The ERM II with its new anchor currency, the Euro, was officially proposed during the Verona, ECOFIN Council meeting in April 1996. It was approved during the 1996 Dublin European Council Summit. The ERM II is a transition mechanism to the final phase of Stage III of EMU

prevent the financial markets from pouncing on any country's currency whose government could not sustain the narrow bands and defend its central currency parities.

Option 3: A Reformed ERM

This option called for a return to the narrower bands after fixing the basic "fault lines" of the mechanism. But the nature of the "fault lines" is still under dispute. The disagreements concerning their nature range from the "Walters critique", according to which the ERM is beyond repair, through the argument that the system is faulty because it is asymmetrical, to the contention that the ERM does not have any fault lines at all. But, as argued previously and as pointed out by the IMF in 1993, central banks can no longer effectively intervene in the capital and foreign exchange markets whose total daily turnover is over US$8 trillion. Therefore, the banks could not maintain the central parities of a reformed ERM, regardless of the nature of the reforms.[57] An alternative would be to modify the ERM by having stable yet adjustable par values. However, this still would not resolve the credibility problem.

It is politically fashionable to call for a reformed ERM that is more symmetric. The lifting of capital controls requires close monetary coordination, particularly of interest rates, which in turn calls for shared monetary policy management. However, it is unrealistic to assume that the financial markets would simply go along with such a policy if they were told that the ERM's credibility remains the same when German influence in the system is lessened and Spanish and French influence is increasing.

Option 4: The Combination of Option 2 or Option 3 with Capital and Foreign Exchange Controls and Taxes

In addition to the eventual reintroduction of a modified or reformed ERM, this option calls for the application of the "Tobin Tax." Under this scheme it would be necessary, within the appropriate jurisdictions, to dampen short-term capital movements through a tax on all foreign exchange transactions or non-interest-bearing deposits held by central banks in order to control the open foreign exchange position of private banks. However, this option is unrealistic because it calls for global enforcement. Moreover, financial markets would quickly create new instruments to circumvent such constraints.

Option 5: The Combination of Option 2 or Option 3 with Coordinated Interventions and Changes in Short-Term Interest Rates

This option could improve the ERM through an early intervention and/or adjustment in short-term interest rates before a currency left its upper or lower bands. If applied on a monetary basis, such measures could also be used to maintain central parities. In addition, the intervention policy of "unlimited obligations" could be conditional on appropriate actions taken by governments. However, this could lead not

[57] These conclusions were reached by the Group of Ten and the IMF in their "International Capital Markets: Part 1," 1993.

only to politicized interpretations but also to other difficulties, because the balance between early and conditional interventions would have to be altered in such a manner that interest rates could be used more effectively. As has been mentioned, the influence of central banks in the financial markets is waning owing to the growing size of the markets, and this could weaken such an approach.

Other options for reforming the ERM were also offered. According to Peter Bofinger,[58] the internal Very Short-Term Facility (VSTF) and the Medium-Term Facility (MTF), under which debtor countries have three-and-a-half months to repurchase their own currencies acquired by the creditor banks for intervention, could be suspended. This would make the creditor central bank cautious about interventions, as it would increase reserves and generate inflationary pressures.

Graham Bishop, called for the loss of monetary autonomy for the country which loses a large amount of reserves through interventions while supporting its currency.[59] When liabilities -- that is, 15 percent of the M2 money supply -- accumulate in the form of reserves in other ERM member central banks, an international institution such as the IMF could oversee the necessary policy adjustments and increase interest rates so as to bring the debtor country's currency into alignment. Needless to say, political support for both of these options was limited.

Niels Thygesen argued that the majority of central banks quickly sterilized most of their past interventions.[60] He used the Bundesbank as an example by pointing out that it sterilized 90 percent of its interventions undertaken during the September 1992 crisis. However, large, combined sterilization of interventions causes instability in fixed exchange rate systems. Thus, if the ERM's repurchase obligations are suspended, thereby making sterilization difficult for the surplus countries, these countries would probably refrain from intervening, leaving the deficit countries to fend for themselves. There is also the danger that once they have used up their reserves, deficit countries might resort to devaluations. Therefore, if central banks are willing to abide by the Stage II specifications of the Treaty and hand over their foreign exchange reserves to the EMI, this forerunner of the ECB could oversee the day-to-day intervention and sterilization requirements of the ERM. This solution would be a bold step toward the EMU, but given the differences in reserves among the member states, it is politically unlikely. Moreover, the EMI is required to pursue common policies and not individual national policy targets.

Finally, Peter Kenen's plan[61] would allow the EMI to pursue price stability through the use of only one monetary policy instrument while allowing central banks to use all others to fine-tune their national economies. However, this would require institutional innovations such as the creation of an Ecu inter-bank market akin to the U.S. Federal Funds market. In light of the slow progress in getting the Frankfurt-based EMI off the ground, it is safe to conclude that common open-market operations or

---

58 Bofinger, Peter and Collighon, Stefan, Johnson Christopher and Bertrand de Maigret. The EMS in Transition. A study prepared for the EU Parliament. Paris: Association for the Monetary Union of Europe, July 1993.

59 Bishop, Graham. "Is There a Rapid Route to an EMU of the Few?" Economic and Market Analysis, London: Solomon Brothers, 1993.

60 Henning, Randall C., Eduard Hochreiter, and Gary Clyde Hufbauer. Reviving the European Union. Washington, DC: Institute of International Economics and the Austrian National Bank, 1994.

61 In Henning, Randall C. et al., Reviving the European Union, 1994.

credit measures would be politically difficult, at least in the near future. Furthermore, the partial pooling of member state reserves for intervention by the EMI would violate the Maastricht Treaty, which requires that the EMI and, eventually, the ECB forgo such activities because they continue to be the responsibility of the ECOFIN Council. The EMI/ECB is permitted only to "hold and manage reserves as an agent for and at the request of national central banks."[62] In fact, Article 6.4 of the EMI charter specifically states that during the transition the EMI "shall not interfere with the monetary policy and exchange rate policy of the competent monetary authority of any member state...."[63] In view of this, bilateral contracts to manage domestic money market operations would appear to be the best solution. But, this may be politically difficult to implement because of sovereignty concerns.

Option 6: Continuation of the Present Wide Bands for an Extended Period of Time

It seems that the move from the +/-2.25 percent to the +/-15 percent currency bands was made so that the ECOFIN Council would not have to meet too frequently to deal with ERM crises. However, the wider bands provide certain other advantages as well. For example, they preserve the central parities of the participating ERM currencies; they make it easier for the non-ERM currencies to reenter (as Italy did in 1996); they enable others to join the system and keep the existing members from experiencing domestic economic problems; they make the Maastricht convergence criteria easier to meet;[64] they sustain the EMU on its tracks and provide for a smoother transition from its Stage II to Stage III by mitigating or preventing currency shocks.

Maintaining the wider bands could also serve as a method to monitor the various countries' monetary performance, because the +/-15 percent bands allow a considerable degree of policy flexibility accommodating the EU nations' economic and political circumstances. However, after a period of time the ERM member nations could always choose to revert back to narrower bands. This could provide an opportunity to test the political will to achieve the EMU. Such a voluntary move would indicate a commitment to financial responsibility and readiness. But it must be pointed out that if the wider bands are ever tested through the competitive cutting of short-term interest rates and/or expansionary budgetary policies, internal trade and the integrated market would be adversely affected. Moreover, if they were used as a path to the EMU, wider bands would require considerable monetary coordination and budgetary consolidation.

Option 7: Rapid Moves toward EMU

This option is not politically feasible, given the objections and economic performance of some of the potential EMU participants.

---

[62] Article 6.4, EMI Protocal, Maastricht Treaty, 1992.

[63] Article 6.4, EMI Protocal, Maastricht Treaty, 1992.

[64] Article 109(j) of the Maastricht Treaty states that member nations' currencies must meet the "normal" fluctuation margins of the ERM for at least two years without devaluing against any other member currency. Initially, when the Treaty was approved "normal" fluctuation margins pertained to the +/-2.25 percent currency bands of the ERM. It should be noted that in the aftermath of the ERM crises and the subsequent widening of the currency bands to +/-15 percent, the EU regards +/-15 percent as "normal" during the EMU's 1997 membership review.

Additional Considerations

Other options included the simultaneous granting of greater independence to central banks and the increased coordination of not only monetary but fiscal policies at the common and the Group of Ten level. Also, a reexamination of the regulatory and the prudential frameworks of the financial markets in general and of the foreign exchange markets in particular could be undertaken, possibly under the auspices of the Basle Committee on Banking Supervision. All of these options are already used in some limited fashion.

The options of restructuring the ERM and using it as a base to transition from Stage II to Stage III of the EMU were limited. As the politically sensitive monetary integration moves forward, the resurrection of the original ERM would have recreated past crises. Leaving the ERM bands at +/-15 percent seems a simple solution as it not only makes meeting the ERM-related Maastricht convergence criteria an easier task but also offers some relief from the exchange rate rigidities that stifle economic growth. However, the wider bands could convince currency speculators that they have defeated the central banks, and this could mean problems for the EMU.

At the December 13-14, 1996 Dublin European Council Summit, the EU nations agreed that they would resort to Option 3 -- the "introduction of a reformed ERM" to be named the "ERM II". The ERM II is based on the European single currency, the Euro, and is set to begin January 1, 1999. It incorporates the "hub and spokes" concept i.e. the Euro will be the anchor of the exchange rate mechanism and non-EMU members will target their currencies against the Euro only. Although the fluctuation band was not specified, it will be relatively wide like the present +/-15 percent band. Non-EMU member currencies will be allowed to target narrower bands, if they so choose. Membership in the ERM II is voluntary, although non-EMU EU nations are "expected" to join. The ECB's obligation to support weaker currencies under speculative attack, is limited.[65] See Chapter VI for a detailed discussion of the "ERM II".

Regardless of which of the options discussed on the previous pages had been chosen, if the ERM is to play a supportive role on the road to the EMU, certain steps must be taken. For a start, the independence of the national central banks has to be increased. This could enhance the stability of the ERM II because monetary policy causes more independent of political agendas. Independence, however, must be combined with an agreement to pursue price stability as the single most important policy objective.

The two ERM crises have also raised some basic questions as to whether the mechanism should have more than one anchor currency, and whether monetary coordination could develop into a common policy. Moreover, the crises have focused attention on whether economic and monetary convergence could be achieved while the ERM is based on the +/-15 percent bands. But in considering these questions, certain realities must be accepted. To date, no other currency is strong enough to function side-by-side with the Deutsche mark; monetary cooperation may achieve price stability as effectively as common policies; and the wider bands make it easier to follow flexible

---

[65] "Pact sets rules for ins and outs of ERM". Financial Times, December 17, 1996, p.2.

policies during times of domestic political turmoil.

The two crises and the subsequent government actions not only highlighted specific EMU problems but also raised several general issues, including the following:

1. The changing relationship among central banks and the governments and financial markets in an increasingly deregulated global economy;
2. The increasing conflicts between national political priorities and economic realities;
3. The appropriateness of the fixed exchange rate structure (i.e., the irrevocable locking of exchange rates) followed by a single currency as the best possible approach to the EMU;
4. The extent to which the ERM-related economic policies have contributed to the persistently high levels of unemployment.[66]

The manner in which EU governments resolve these issues will determine the fate of both the EMU and further integration.

THE TRANSITIONAL DILEMMAS OF THE EMU

The key events of the early 1990s, such as the Maastricht Treaty ratification process, have created turmoil in the financial markets and have raised questions about the EMU. There are disagreements over the timetable and the wording of the Treaty both of which are open to broad interpretations. Nonetheless, nations will pursue some form of monetary integration. It is also very probable that no matter what form the EMU will take, there will be three constants involved in its establishment. The process will be multi-stage and multi-speed; it will be fragile and lengthy; and it will require, at first, a common central institution to manage transition and, near the end, an institution that controls and/or coordinates activities.

Policy Considerations

The basic objective of monetary policies under the EMU is to obtain the largest possible economic benefits. This is critical as it will not only affect the regulatory and welfare framework of the EU but will also influence the structure of the financial markets and other types of market integration processes. In particular, the following six issues are important: (i) the trade-off between increased financial market integration and increased harmonization of central bank instruments; (ii) the impact of the single currency on financial market credibility and stability as opposed to that of multiple currencies; (iii) the trade-off between centralized or decentralized monetary policies; (iv) the opportunity cost of the expected welfare costs/benefits versus the certitude of policy effects; (v) the efficiency and effectiveness of the decision-making structure of the transient EMI; and (vi) the impact of the "widening," that is, the 1995 admission of three new member nations on the EMU during the transitional stage.

---

[66] Temperton, Paul, ed. The European Currency Crisis, 1993.

Deep financial market integration runs contrary to the proposed EMU plan of increasing the harmonization of central bank instruments, which would augment regulations. Studies[67] have shown that both scenarios can produce compatible efficiency outcomes. The former is efficient if regulatory and prudential standards are harmonized in perfectly integrated capital markets. The latter is efficient if central bank reserve requirements and lending conditions are harmonized in disintegrated national capital markets.

The use of a single currency has a different impact on the credibility and stability of financial markets than the use of multiple currencies. Although in a credible monetary union a single currency is more efficient than multiple currencies, market efficiency could also be achieved by the latter. But a multi-currency monetary union is generally less credible than a single currency union because the financial markets perceive the cost of a member nation withdrawing from the union as not very high. Moreover, a multi-currency area could create more instability than a single currency and could thus frustrate integration. But, a single currency monetary union with less than full credibility might be more susceptible to the whims of the international foreign exchange markets than a multi-currency monetary union. The potential negative repercussions of a speculative run on a single currency in relation to the U.S. dollar or the yen could be disastrous for the member economies and for the EMU, especially in the early stages, whereas, a similar run on a multi-currency union might be more spread-out and thus less ruinous, as economic performance and political circumstances would differ.[68]

During the transition stage and beyond, the EU must choose between centralized and decentralized monetary policy designs. A centralized approach would employ common aggregate monetary targets, such as price and income variables. Alternatively, a decentralized approach would involve the adoption of a set of national targets to obtain an average outcome. If the EMU experiences real shocks which would require relative price adjustments, the trade-off between the two approaches could become important.

Under a decentralized approach, inflation levels differ among the various economies. Consequently, price adjustments responding to real shocks could be an explicit policy choice. For example, the Bundesbank's refusal to conduct a real appreciation of the Deutsche mark allowed prices to increase as a result of reunification, even though the ERM and moderate inflation in other nations already indicated an upward price adjustment. Alternatively, the U.K. and the Italian governments did not

---

[67] Fratianni, Michele and Jürgen von Hagen. "The Transition to European Monetary Union and the European Monetary Institute." In Eichengreen, Barry and Jeffry Frieden, eds. The Political Economy of European Monetary Unification. San Francisco: Westview Press, 1994, pp.129-48. The following section is based on the above-mentioned study.

[68] However, a multi-currency monetary union would require that the various central banks engage in more lender-of-last-resort activities and introduce more regulations than would be needed in a single currency union. The lack of credibility of such a monetary union would tend to hinder financial market integration.

deflate, even though such a move was necessitated by the ERM's bilateral parities and low German inflation rates. The two countries subsequently withdrew from the ERM. This illustrates that in a decentralized approach, the difficulties involved in reaching a consensus on EMU inflation targets may be substantial and could result in higher average inflation levels than those generated by a centralized monetary policy approach. In a decentralized scheme it would be problematic to convince central bankers to accept zero inflation levels. Moreover, it is quite conceivable that central bankers would attempt to conduct economic adjustments through identical price changes rather than relative price changes. Thus, overall economic performance would worsen.

A centralized approach calls for all monetary operations to be entrusted to a single institution -- the EMI or the ECB. However, in a decentralized design, national central banks manage their own monetary operations and have national monetary targets based on common goals such as short-term interest rates or reserve aggregates. This would require close coordination. However, such coordination would be less important if there is adequate market segmentation to ensure that national central banks can attain their national monetary targets and limit policy spill-over effects on other nations.

A centralized approach to monetary policy provides for either centralized or decentralized central bank operations. However, a decentralized monetary policy objective mandates decentralized central bank operations which would have a minimum amount of market segmentation. It should be noted that decentralized operations would be preferable in a multi-currency monetary union, although they require regulations with respect to the degree of currency substitution allowed. All in all, a centralized approach offers more choices than a decentralized design.

If the EU chooses a decentralized design, this would entail national as opposed to common policy objectives. Under such an arrangement, central banking operations would be decentralized and would be feasible only in a multi-currency monetary union with low market integration and coordination but with high regulatory standards to safeguard market stability. But if the EU chooses the centralized approach and a common monetary policy objective, this would provide more flexible alternatives for the achievement of objectives. Such an approach could be applied in either a multi or a single currency monetary union, offering a choice between centralized or decentralized central banking operations. This choice, however, requires a great deal of coordination and market integration. If the EMU plan is followed, common monetary policy objectives and common central banking operations are required. Such a task would be easier if central banks currently followed not only similar policy targets but also pursued parallel central banking operations. However, this is not the case. Table 2.1 shows the similarities and differences in the use of monetary policy instruments and central banking operations.

Central bank operations can be divided into two major categories as represented by the Bank of England's and the Bundesbank's activities. The former engages primarily in outright purchases and sales in the domestic open market and has minimal contact with the domestic banking sector. The latter deals chiefly with the domestic banking sector. The central banks of France, Denmark, Belgium, Spain and the Netherlands follow the Bundesbank model while the central banks of Italy, Portugal and Ireland emulate the Bank of England. Reserve requirements[69] and banking regulations vary[70] in both models. Table 2.2 illustrates these differences.

There is also a wide discrepancy in the role of central banks as lenders of last resort. In nations where there is a high degree of securitization, as in the U.K., the lender-of-last-resort role is important, whereas in Germany, where there is a comparatively low level of securitization, there is less need for this function.[71] Thus, it is the wide discrepancies in policy targets and in central banking operations that make it difficult to establish a centralized monetary policy based on common central banking operations.

Owing to political considerations, the EU targets a mixture of common policy objectives which have to be achieved in tandem with individual national monetary objectives through decentralized central banking operations. The choice of monetary policy design is critical, as it will determine the structure of the financial markets.

---

[69] The majority of central banks are shifting away from using reserve requirements as a monetary policy tool and are moving toward open market operations. In Belgium, Denmark, the Netherlands and the U.K., reserve requirements are still used as a monetary policy tool. In nations where reserve requirements are of sizable proportions, central banks pay interest on them. The costs and benefits of using reserve requirements are still debated. Although they are very effective, they are also far-reaching and powerful, and thus could be harmful to the banking systems' competitiveness.

[70] The central banks of Greece, Spain, Ireland, Italy and Portugal have broad-based regulatory authority in the banking sector, but the central bank of Denmark has no regulatory role at all.

[71] Under the Maastricht Treaty, the ECB performs only an executive and advisory role in relation to deposit protection.

Table 2.1
Use of Monetary Policy Instruments and Central Banking Operational Strategies

DEGREE OF USE OF MONETARY POLICY INSTRUMENTS	Belgium	Denmark	Germany	Greece	Spain	France	Ireland	Italy	Netherlands	Portugal	U.K.
Operations with individual intermediaries in domestic market	H	H	H	L	H	H	H	I	H	L	L
Central bank discretion over quantity	I	I	I	N	H	H	H	I	I	H	H
Central bank discretion over borrowing cost	H	H	H	N	H	H	H	I	I	H	H
Operations in domestic market	I	L	L	L	I	L	I	H	I	H	H
Central bank discretion over quantity	I	H	H	H	H	H	H	H	L	N	N
Central bank discretion over cost of liquidity	H	H	H	H	H	H	H	L	H	H	H
Forward foreign exchange operations	N	L	L	N	L	I	L	N	L	N	H
Degree of sterilization	L	L	H	L	I	I	H	I	L	I	I
Operations with treasury (volume)	L	N	L	H	I	L	L	H	L	I	N
Limits of treasury access to overdraft	I	H	H	L	L	I	H	L	I	I	H
Operations in government securities at issue	N	N	N	H	H	N	H	H	H	H	H
Open market operations in government securities	I	N	L	H	L	H	H	H	N	H	H
Reserve requirements	N	N	L	I	L	L	I	H	N	H	N

KEY: H=high; I=intermediate; L=low; and N=none

Source: Fratianni, Michele and Jürgen von Hagen. "The Transition to European Monetary Union and the European Monetary Institute." In Eichengreen, Barry and Jeffry Frieden, eds., The Political Economy of European Monetary Unification, Edited; San Francisco: Westview Press, Inc., 1994, p.138.

Table 2.2
The Supervisory and Regulatory Role of Central Banks

	CENTRAL BANK INVOLVEMENT IN BANKING SUPERVISION										
	Belgium	Denmark	Germany	Greece	Spain	France	Ireland	Italy	Netherlands	Portugal	U.K.
Regulation	L	N	I	E	E	I	E	E	E	E	E
Authorization	N	N	N	E	E	I	E	E	E	E	E
Prudential supervision	N	N	I	E	E	E	E	E	E	E	E
On-site control	L	N	L	E	E	E	E	E	E	E	I
Sanctions	N	N	N	E	E	E	E	E	E	E	E
Deposit protection	I	N	N	N	E	N	E	I	E	N	I
Memo: Nonbank supervision	N	N	I	I	E	E	E	E	E	E	N

Key: E=extensive; I=intermediate; L=low; N=none

Source: Fratianni, Michele and Jürgen Von Hagen. "The Transition to European Monetary Union and the European Monetary Institute." In Eichengreen, Barry and Jeffry Frieden, eds., The Political Economy of European Monetary Unification, Edited; San Francisco: Westview Press, Inc., 1994, p.140.

Different Types of EMUs and Their Welfare Implications

Table 2.3 outlines three possible EMU monetary policy scenarios.[72] The first, which largely preserves the current ERM structure but in a tighter form, calls for national monetary policy targets, decentralized central bank operations, multiple currencies and low capital market integration. The second, which is similar to the 1989 Delors Report proposals, requires common monetary policy targets but decentralized central bank operations, multiple currencies, low capital market integration and minimal coordination of national central banking operations or banking sector regulations. Scenario three is more or less the Maastricht Treaty plan under which central bank operations are centralized in the EMI and ECB, accompanied by common monetary policy targets with a single currency, deep capital market integration, and homogeneous regulatory standards which, however, could be low.

Scenario three generates maximum welfare gains because it maximizes capital market integration. However, this can occur only if there are credible linkages between the EMI's or ECB's monetary policy tools and the common monetary policy targets and goals. But little is known about the working of such linkages in an economic system as large as that of the EU. This creates a problem in that it could generate a great deal of uncertainty in the early stages of the EMU. Scenario two would yield lower welfare gains than scenario three, as it requires a lesser degree of market integration. However, because most of the linkages between the central bank instruments and the targets remain largely unchanged, there is much less uncertainty as to the outcome of such an arrangement. The remaining uncertainty is associated with the linkages between the national monetary targets and the common monetary policy objectives. Scenario one yields the lowest level of uncertainty but also the lowest level of expected welfare gains.

There are suggestions that the EU should begin the EMU with scenario one, followed by scenario two, and should then work its way up to the most efficient scenario three. This might, however, limit political support for the EMU during the crucial early stages, as scenario one yields the lowest welfare gains. More important, it does not eliminate one of the biggest problems -- the uncertainty surrounding the transition from scenario one to scenario three. It is scenario three, the introduction of a single currency and of the common monetary policy that represents the highest risk for monetary integration.

---

[72] The three scenarios were originally discussed in a 1994 study by Fratianni, Michele and Jürgen Von Hagen in "The Transition to European Monetary Union and the European Monetary Institute", in Eichengreen, Barry and Jeffry Frieden, eds., The Political Economy of European Monetary Unification, Edited; San Francisco: Westview Press, Inc., 1994. The following section is based on this study.

Table 2.3
Three Possible EMU Monetary Policy Scenarios

	Scenario 1	Scenario 2	Scenario 3
Definition of policy objective	National	Union	Union
Monetary policy operations	Decentralized	Decentralized	Centralized
Currency arrangement	Many	Many	One
Degree of money market integration	Low	Medium	High
Regulation	Heterogeneous, closely coordinated central bank instruments; heterogeneous, uncoordinated regulatory standards	Heterogeneous, closely coordinated central bank instruments; heterogeneous, high and coordinated regulatory standards	Uniform but low standards of regulation

Source: Adopted from Fratianni, Michele and Jürgen Von Hagen. "The Transition to European Monetary Union and the European Monetary Institute." In Eichengreen, Barry and Jeffry Frieden, eds., The Political Economy of European Monetary Unification, Edited; San Francisco: Westview Press, Inc., 1994, p.141.

Scenario three requires a very credible ECB, which has to be an independent, nonpartisan, and transparent central bank because monetary policy outcomes are uncertain. If the EMU is to succeed, any increase in inflation under the ECB, specially during the early stages, must be seen by the public as a temporary policy error while its commitment to price stability is unwavering. Under such conditions the role of the transitory EMI becomes pivotal as it is this institution that must lay the foundation for the ECB and must therefore play an important role in pre-EMU monetary policies to persuade and educate the financial markets of the ECB's future strategies and goals. More important, the EMI must convince the public of its belief in the importance of central bank independence and its firm commitment to price stability. If policy errors occur, such a stance would prevent an initial panic in the markets and would preclude any dwindling of political support for the EMU. For additional credibility, the EMI should introduce ECB-type operating procedures during the transitional stage so as to discover the flaws in the new common monetary policy prior to the creation of the institution itself.

Although the current path toward the EMU calls for a relatively inefficient transitional Stage II, from a political point of view no other option was available. Central bankers favored the more conservative scenario one approach, while their governments endorsed moving toward more integration. Given the influence of the Bundesbank, the Maastricht political compromise did not give the EMI any authority to establish a common monetary policy objective and requires it to conduct its coordinative function within the realm of national monetary targets. The Bundesbank insisted on a long transitional period without the transfer of any national monetary policy authority to a common institution prior to Stage III, when the ECB is established and the single currency is introduced.[73] The EMI Governing Council is structured in such a way that it is dominated by central bankers.

It should be noted that the management authority of the EMI (and subsequently of the ECB) is still uncertain and will remain so until such time as EMU eligibility and membership issues are resolved. The central banks of Germany, the Netherlands, Belgium and Luxembourg, and since the mid-1980s of France, are reluctant to relinquish their hard-earned price stability reputations in an EMU that embraces less credible central banks. Thus, until this threat is eliminated and the issue of membership is resolved, it is unlikely that the central banks will acquiesce in a loss of monetary authority. In all likelihood, they prefer an EMU that has a low cost of termination. In other words, they prefer an EMU with national monetary objectives, decentralized operations, multiple currencies and limited market integration. In terms of expected welfare gains, such an EMU would be inefficient and would have to restrict membership.

Restrictions on membership, such as a two-speed EMU, although a workable solution for the core group of nations with credible central banks (Germany, the Netherlands, Belgium, Luxembourg and France), is unacceptable to the peripheral group of nations with less credible central banks. These countries have trepidations about second-tier EU membership with diminishing bargaining power relative to the core group of nations. Moreover, the periphery nations maintain that a two-speed EMU would allow the core nations to pursue low-inflation policies without considering the consequences for the peripheral nations' economies, possibly even further delaying their entry into the EMU. Although the EMI statute mandates that all EU nations equally participate in its governing Council, this could be an inefficient arrangement as it may generate political conflicts between the potential EMU core and the peripheral nations.[74]

But the EMI's function is to promote low-inflation policies. Thus, the remaining question is what compromise would be politically feasible during the transitional Stage II. Since all 15 EU member nations are represented on the EMI Council, the only politically workable medium-term solution for Stage II is scenario

---

[73] Stage III is divided into two parts, Phase A and Phase B. During the former, the EU is still composed of 15 currencies and the EMU-eligible members "irrevocably" lock exchange rates, while during the latter phase a single currency, the Euro, is shared by the eligible EMU members. (Schlesinger, Helmut. "Auf dem Weg zur Europäischen Währungsunion: Die Rolle des Europäischen Währunginstituts," Aüszuge aus Presseartikeln 38, 1992, pp.1-4.)

[74] Although the ECB's General Council mandates the presence of all 15 central bank governors, this could also be the subject of political conflicts between the EMU core and the peripheral nations. The real power, however, lies with the ECB Governing Council which is the voting body of the ECB, while the 21-member ECB General Council comprised of all 15 member nations, is only a non-voting policy forum.

one, involving national monetary policy and decentralized monetary policy objectives. The EMU will remain an inefficient proposition as long as the EMI Council gives equal votes to all member nations. Stage III, however, mandates that the decision-making power of the ECB is shared by EMU participating nations and the six-member ECB Executive Board. Although a 15-member EMU under the third scenario would actually be the most desirable arrangement for Stage III, it is economically and politically inconceivable in the medium term.

The admission of Austria, Finland and Sweden on January 1, 1995 changed the EMU majority from 7 out of 12 to 8 out of 15 nations. As the core EMU group is represented by 5 nations and as the 3 new members are more or less guaranteed admittance to the core group[75], the credible central banks could possess the majority needed to move forward to a two-speed EMU. It is interesting to note that if the U.K. and/or Denmark opt out, the majority needed by the core nations would be even easier to obtain. Thus, it is not surprising that the peripheral nations have had a negative reaction to enlargement and demanded monetary compensation through the Cohesion Fund for a pro-enlargement vote.[76] However, it should also be noted that the three newly admitted members are net contributors to the common budget and that the major benefactors of this are Spain, Portugal, Italy, Ireland and Greece.[77]

The multi-speed approach is the only viable political and economic strategy through which the EMU can be achieved under scenario three, which is the most efficient in terms of welfare gains. If this is coupled with allowing the peripheral nations time and resources to achieve a higher degree of fiscal and monetary stability, scenario three becomes even more feasible in the long-term. By the time most of the peripheral nations are eligible to join the EMU, the core members would have already gained practical experience in managing common monetary policies. But, there is the danger that the core group would prolong the admission of the peripheral nations and thus leave the EMU incomplete for some time. To safeguard against such exclusionary behavior, the convergence criteria should be made more explicit and less subject to interpretations. The mandate of the ECB's General Council that all EU member nations must participate in the EMU can assist in this.

---

[75] All three new members are very close to fulfilling the Maastricht convergence criteria. Austria could become an immediate EMU member while Sweden and Finland are closer to joining the EMU than are some of the long-standing member nations. For now, Sweden has elected to remain outside of the ERM.

[76] This compromise was formalized at the December 1992 Edinburgh European Council Summit. The agreement also increased the ratio of the EU budget to the common GDP by 12 percent, beginning 1995.

[77] Austria, Finland and Sweden are net contributors to the common budget as they have above EU average per capita incomes, well-protected agricultural sectors and no serious regional problems.

The opponents of a multi-speed EMU[78] have misgivings because such an approach could develop into an "Europe à la carte" with varying obligations. The U.K. and Denmark are prime examples of a "Europe à la carte" as the former has retained the right to opt-out of the EMU at the last moment (and has opted-out of the Social Charter) and the latter has opt-outed of the EMU as well as the common defense and interior policies. Although these exceptions are caused by political concerns and as such may facilitate integration, they could also imperil the same if they result in inefficiencies.

EU ENLARGEMENT IMPLICATIONS

The 1995 enlargement of the EU through the admission of the former European Free Trade Association (EFTA) member nations of Austria, Finland and Sweden, increased EU membership from 12 to 15. The original 1958 EC had consisted of six nations: Germany, France, Italy, Belgium, Luxembourg and the Netherlands. Over the course of the last 28 years, membership has grown by 250 percent. The process began with the 1973 entry of the U.K., Ireland and Denmark, continued with the admission of Greece, Spain and Portugal in 1986 and concluded with the most recent admission of the three former EFTA nations.

The EEC, the EC and now the EU have always been open to all nations that are political democracies and are situated on the European Continent. However, enlargement has reduced the homogeneity of the original group of six nations, creating a less than optimal economic bloc. The growing membership has also created difficulties in the voting process and in relation to the use of additional official languages. It has also increased economic disparities. Average per capita income has decreased, national and regional variations have increased and agriculture has become more important.

If the past is an indication of the future, the EU will continue to enlarge, albeit at a slower pace. Future membership will be a function of a nation's ability to integrate with the "Single Market," to make contributions to the EMU, to the structural and economic convergence policies and to the other common activities such as defense. To achieve this and to maintain the EMU's credibility, some formal economic admission criteria will have to be established which will raise the political and economic price of entry.

---

[78] The convergence criteria requirements automatically create a two-speed EMU. Initially, the Germans took a hard line on these requirements as their preference was not for a multi-speed EMU but for an EMU that integrates only when all members are ready (i.e. when all EU nations meet the criteria). However, propelled by Chancellor Kohl's rush to meet the 1999 EMU timetable, most Germans recognize the necessity of a multi-speed arrangement. Nevertheless, they fundamentally disapprove of a "Europe à la carte."

Enlargement i.e., "widening", in many ways is contradictory to the notion of increased integration "deepening". For example, with the admission of the three former EFTA members not only has the likelihood of a multi-track EMU increased, but the meeting of the monetary convergence criteria by the less developed nations has become even more difficult. Thus, the weaker economies led by Spain are likely to try to block the admission of additional members and may also refuse any future compromise on "widening" unless the stronger economies make more generous contributions to the Cohesion Fund established by the Maastricht Treaty.

The Cohesion Fund, provides approximately US$18 billion to Greece, Spain, Portugal, Ireland, and Italy to enable these nations to meet the convergence criteria by 1999. This is the price the weaker economies have extracted for signing the Treaty. However, the convergence process requires much more resources than the stronger economies are willing to provide.[79] Thus, in line with appeasing the weaker economies, the Commission has over a period of seven years marginally increased the amount earmarked under The Structural Funds for regional development to US$116 billion. Under such circumstances there is no chance for the Central and Eastern European nations as, for example, Hungary, Poland and the Czech Republic to gain full EU membership during this decade. The weaker member nations are not willing to share Structural Development Funds and Cohesion Fund resources or the benefits of the Common Agriculture Policy, unless the wealthier nations are willing to substantially increase their contributions to the common budget. Thus, the admission of these countries could make a multi-speed EMU inevitable and very problematic.

The Institutional Impact

Any additional EU enlargement would also require changes in the Brussels institutions. The admission of the three new members on January 1, 1995 has already resulted in some restructuring of the common institutions. But it is not clear to what extent the present EU Parliament, Commission, Council of Ministers, European Council and Court of Justice, or of the ECB could efficiently support 18 or more member nations.

There are several options for improving the institutional structure. Membership in the Council of Ministers could be rotated like in the case of the United Nations Security Council, and representation could be based on districts or regions rather than on countries per se. Until recently, political and economic conditions provided little or no chance for the implementation of such plans.

---

[79] The Delors proposal's call for the financing of the Cohesion Fund through an increase in contributions to the common budget from 1.2 percent of GDP to 1.32 percent over a five year budget cycle (1994-99) was not approved by the heads of state during the Edinburgh Summit. Instead, the European Council established a one-time-only seven-year budget cycle (1992-99) and limited the increase to 1.27 percent of GDP, beginning in 1999.

However, in mid-1993 a concerted effort was launched to alter the decision-making process in favor of the large nations. France, Germany and the U.K. are investigating proposals to change the voting structure, as these larger nations worry about a paralyzed EU and about their own waning influence if additional small nations are admitted under the existing rules. Not surprisingly, changes in the decision-making structures are opposed not only by the smaller nations but also by the aspiring new applicants. Any institutional restructuring will also have to address the issue of the balance of power among the Council of Ministers, the Commission and the Parliament.

Table 2.4 shows the results of a strengths, weaknesses, opportunities and threats (SWOT) analysis of the current institutional structure.

Table 2.4

SWOT Analysis of the Current EU Institutional Structure

A SWOT (strengths, weaknesses, opportunities, threats) analysis of the current EU institutional system provides a conceptual framework for the challenges that policymakers face with regard to institutional changes in the context of EU enlargement
Strengths 1. Institutions provide a forum to unify and cooperate (vis-à-vis the common market and structural funds) 2. Institutions are stable and have a good record of responsibility and accountability
Weaknesses 1. Institutions are too bureaucratic 2. Democratic deficit (dominance by the Council) is pervasive 3. Lack of transparency (decision-making procedures overly complex, not close to EU citizens) 4. EU institutions do not have clearly defined roles in relation to national institutions (application of the subsidiarity principle) 5. Parliament has control only over executives 6. There is no focus on unemployment and poverty 7. There is no ability to prevent wars
Opportunities 1. Foundations of a political union exist 2. Creation of an institutional framework that is flexible to accommodating further enlargements is possible
Threats 1. Inertia and paralysis in common decision-making 2. Lack of credibility and limited acceptance by EU citizens 3. Regional development imbalances 4. Decreasing opportunities for a political union leading to a sophisticated EU free trade zone

Any structural change, apart from keeping institutions lean and efficient, must incorporate additional dimensions, such as more democratic and transparent decision-making processes and increased accountability.[80] With the admission of Austria, Sweden and Finland, the urgency for institutional reform has increased. Relevant reform proposals have been explored at the 1996-97 IGC meetings, with particular emphasis on problems caused by enlargement and the need to cope with decision-making inefficiencies. The meeting participants have addressed the problems raised by the increasing size of the executive committees and the recurring balance of power problems between current and new members. The impact of the potential institutional and decision-making changes on the evolution and credibility of the EMU is raising concerns.

Member nations are divided on what to do. One group, comprised of Germany, France and the Benelux countries, maintains that "widening" has to be accompanied by "deepening" so as to avoid a general slowdown of the integration process. The other group, consisting of the U.K., Denmark and Spain, takes the position that "widening" should not lead to a "deeper" EU. Fearing that Brussels could obtain too much power, they favor an EU that would be a sophisticated free trade zone. These differing positions could be brought together if "deepening" could be achieved without increasing the power of Brussels over national governments. However, the abandonment of the national veto is unacceptable to both groups of nations.

The U.K. supports a proposal that calls for enlargement without changes. Under such a plan, common institutions would not be "deepened" and new members, especially the Central and Eastern European (CEE) nations, would be integrated gradually.[81] But this could lead to a "soft EU" in which common policies may be difficult to agree on because of the exercise of the national veto. However, historically, EU "widening" has always been accompanied by "deepening." The agreement concerning Spain's and Portugal's admission, for example, coincided with the signing of the SEA in 1985.

Although Germany favors a multi-speed EU,[82] its concept differs from a "Europe à la carte". In the former all member nations essentially agree on the same common path but proceed at different speeds whereas under the latter approach countries are allowed to choose the type of common policies which they want to pursue.[83] The dangers of a multi-speed EU, however, are considerable. It could create different classes of nations and lead to considerably less convergence and

---

[80] Breadshaw, Jeremy. "Constitutional Reform after Maastricht," European Trends, First Quarter, 1994, pp.58-69.

[81] Meares, Richard. "Britain Vows to Opt to Veto EU Constitutional Changes." Reuter News, London, January 8, 1995.

[82] The initially German hard line on a multi-speed EMU has given way to Chancellor Kohl's rush to meet the 1999 EMU timetable. However, the Germans fundamentally disapprove of a "Europe à la carte."

[83] Murphy, Richard. "Britain Floats Proposal on European Integration." Reuter News, Bonn, February 20, 1995.

equality.[84] It should be noted that the Parliament is opposed to inequalities among member nations.[85] An "à la carte" membership is also rejected by most member countries, apart from the U.K. and Denmark.

Other proposals call for changes that could lead to enlargement through the admission of the CEE nations. They include the introduction of some type of qualified majority decision-making concerning all issues, that is, the elimination of the national veto.[86] Still others recommend enhanced clarification of EU objectives and further strengthening of the common institutions. Some proposals urge a clearer definition of "subsidiarity" and the prioritization of such issues as unemployment, poverty, international peace processes and human rights.

The 1996-97 Intergovernmental Conferences may fail to reach a consensus on institutional and decision-making changes. This would provide the core nations of Germany, France, Belgium, Luxembourg and the Netherlands with the opportunity to postpone any enlargement until such time as substantial institutional and procedural changes can be introduced. (See Chapter VI for a detailed discussion of the 1996-97 IGC).

Despite the widely divergent proposals for institutional and decision-making changes, there are four constants in the recommendations: (i) increased efficiency to maintain or improve the ability to act; (ii) adjustments in the balance of power, particularly in the voting structure; (iii) increased transparency; and (iv) more democracy. These recommendations have been reiterated many times by several parliamentary groups and by Brussels officials.[87]

Efficiency

The more nations participate in the decision-making process and the administration of the EU, the more difficult and sluggish the process becomes.[88] Not only would an increased number of votes and differing viewpoints lead to procedural inefficiencies, but decision-making could also be impeded by differences in income

[84] Adopted from a quote of a statement by former German Foreign Minister Hans Dietrich Genscher in "German CDU Pleased about Reform Controversy," Reuter Community Report, Bonn, September 8, 1994.

[85] "Multispeed Europe Inconceivable EP Says", Reuter Community Report, Strasbourg, September 28, 1994.

[86] "EU at Crossroads, Veto Should Go, EU Socialists Say," Lovell, Jeremy in Reuter News, Brussels, January 31, 1995. Former French minister Elisabeth Guigou, leader of the European Parliament Socialist group, proposed more qualified majority voting and an end to the national veto. She envisioned an EU of 27 members, and she proposed that any institutional change should consider a EU of that size.

[87] "European Union : European Christian Democrats Adopt Skin-Deep Consensus." European Information Service - European Report, April 4, 1995.

[88] Harrop, Jeffrey. The Political Economy of Integration in the European Community. London: Edward Elgar Publishing Limited, 1989, pp.185-93.

levels, particularly if the Mediterranean and CEE countries on the waiting list are admitted. Other differences that could create problems include differing economic growth cycles as in the case of Finland and Sweden; industry structures, as illustrated by industrialized Germany versus agricultural Greece; political instability such as in Italy; and welfare systems, as maintained in Scandinavia.

The potential problems are illustrated by the expansionary experiences of the original six EEC members. The founding nations were quite similar in terms of macroeconomic conditions and regulatory standards, while the Mediterranean nations of Greece, Portugal and Spain had and still have significantly lower income levels and less developed industry structures as well as regulatory requirements. Thus, the decision-making processes of the former EU 12 and of the current EU 15 were and are laborious.[89]

There is a very real danger that enlargement without institutional changes could stop the political and economic integration process and that the EU could be reduced to a mere free trade zone. Executive institutions such as the Commission, the Council of Ministers and the ECB's Governing Council could continue to function but would have to be reduced in size, and majority voting would have to be introduced to circumvent the bottlenecks created by national vetos.

There are numerous proposals for reducing the size of the executive committees of common institutions. They refer to the executive committee structures of large private corporations as examples to be followed and/or are based on academic organizational theories. They cite studies that show that the size of efficient executive committees rarely exceed 15 members and that in the German manufacturing, insurance and banking industries the boards of directors do not grow beyond seven to ten members.[90]

Limiting the size of executive committees and institutions would decrease direct national representation, affecting primarily the EU Parliament and the Council of Ministers. The German proposal for institutional and procedural restructuring calls for loss of representation,[91] but other nations such as the U.K., Denmark and Spain are reluctant to approve a reduction of their power in the common institutions. Most of the restructuring plans reduce the smaller countries' direct representation, consequently, it is not surprising that they object.

---

[89] There are numerous past examples, such as the difficulties of attaining consensus concerning the "Single Market" environmental and safety standards. The Southern members oppose standards that are too high because they see them as slowing down economic development and foreign investments. The Northern countries argue that too low standards place consumers and the environment at risk and would not only generate internal political pressures from consumer groups and opposition political parties, but would reduce the international competitiveness of industries.

[90] Is Bigger Better?- The Economics of Enlargement. Monitoring European Integration 3. A CEPR Annual Report, London: Center for Economic Policy Research (CEPR), 1992, p.96.

[91] Schaeuble, Wolfgang. "Kohl's Loyal Lieutenant," Financial Times, March 21, 1995, p.14.

From a political and legal point of view, it would be difficult to give up the principle of direct national representation in all decision-making bodies in exchange for an increase in efficiency. In the legislative institutions, for example, the Parliament, or in the decision-making bodies such as the Council of Ministers, the direct representation principle must be maintained because the legitimacy of these bodies rests on the direct representation of the citizens of the member nations. In the democratic political systems of the EU nations the authority to formulate laws is granted directly by the people. The appointed EU government representatives and elected EU parliamentarians have this legitimacy, and thus their decisions are binding. If the direct representation principle were surrendered, decisions would not be legally binding. But this is true only for those decisions that affect individual member nations only and not common interests. Institutions which deal with common policies that affect all member nations equally could be made up of a subset of European representatives. Thus, the size of these institutions could be determined by efficiency rather than by the requirement of full national representation.[92] Such institutions include the Commission, the Council of Ministers, the ECB and the Court of Justice.

At present, institutional membership is based on the national representation principle. The 1995 enlargement, for example, resulted in a 20-member Commission as each of the three new member nations received one seat. According to the same principle, the EMI Governing Council consists of 16 members,[93] while the European Council, the Council of Ministers, the Committee of Permanent Representatives (COREPER), the Court of Justice and the Court of Auditors have 15 members each. The Parliament now includes 626 members, and the Committee of the Regions and the Economic and Social Committee, 222 members each.

Empirical studies of the largest German firms have concluded that the size of their board of directors generally does not exceed 11, while the average board size of the largest firms is 7.[94] Organizational theory hypothesizes that the larger a committee becomes, the lower is its group cohesiveness and the less transparent its decision-making process. Consensus is less likely to emerge, and non-cooperative majority voting replaces the search for cooperative solutions. Increasing the size of committees beyond the optimal point also raises costs, increases the length of meetings, and reduces the quality of decisions. The recent EU enlargement has already increased the size of the decision-making committees and institutions beyond their optimal point.

If direct national representation cannot be abandoned without weakening the accountability of the executive institutions, integration fatigue could spread and the idea of the EMU and of the political union could be diluted. If member nations are unwilling to "deepen" by reducing direct control over institutions, political,

---

92 "Kohl's Re-election Bestows Added Clout in Setting the European's Course." The Wall Street Journal, October 18, 1994, Section A, p.14.
93 The 15 EU Central Bank Governors and the President of the EMI.
94 Is Bigger Better?- The Economics of Enlargement, CEPR, 1992, p.97.

economic and monetary integration will become more difficult and this could precipitate a move toward an EU free trade area without common policies.

It should be noted that Austria, Finland, Sweden and the EFTA nations which for the time being have declined to join (Norway and Switzerland), have frequently argued for a broader application of the "subsidiarity" principle. The U.K. and Denmark support such arguments. But their attempts to limit the power of the common institutions so as to not lose national sovereignty over fiscal, monetary and foreign policies slows integration in general, and the process of establishing the EMU, in particular. Therefore, to cope with the enlargement problem it is necessary to separate the issues of creating a political union from those promoting institutional changes.

If the national representation principle is abandoned and the Commission, the Governing Council of the ECB and the Court of Justice are no longer representative of countries, but rather are constituted of a limited number of members acting independently of their national base on issues that affect all members, there will be a political contest for these positions. Every nation will want to have its representative in these institutions because of their concern that commissioners, central bank governors or judges cannot withstand the influence of home governments.

Balance of Power

The entry of the three new member nations on January 1, 1995 called for a restructuring of the qualified majority voting process which determines relative influence on common legislation and policies. However, in this and any future enlargement, the problem is not only the determination of the number of new votes but the impact of the enlargement on the balance of power between the rich Northern and poor Southern nations. There are numerous proposals, mostly from the rich nations, to reform the decision-making process by shifting the balance of power toward themselves. Thus, the size of a blocking minority becomes critical. If it is made up of a few votes, bottlenecks could result, as decisions could easily be stopped, whereas more votes could infringe on national sovereignty because they would reduce the ability of nations to prevent unwanted legislation and policies. The rotation of the presidency of the Council of Ministers grants every nation six months during which it can, within certain limits, set the agenda and the pace of the decision-making process. However, after the 1995 enlargement and under the current alphabetical rotation system any additional enlargement could lead to a lengthy presidency by nations that represent a small fraction of the total EU population. Restructuring plans have attempted to deal with such issues by proposing, for example, to restrict or to abandon the veto, to apply qualified majority voting to issues involving not only the "Single Market," to increase the size of the blocking minority or to rotate the presidency only among certain nations. This is discussed in detail in the section "Institutional and Decision-Making Changes," later in this chapter.

Transparency

The current decision-making structure is a collection of 12 different procedures.[95] This hinders transparency and efficiency. To deal with the resulting concerns, several proposals have been put forward.

The French Socialist Parliamentary Group, for example, has recommended the reduction of the decision-making procedures from 12 to 3 as well as the establishment of three distinct decision-making categories: legislation, Treaty revisions and the Common Foreign and Security Policy (CFSP). In each category only one procedure could be used. For example, qualified majority voting could be applied in the Council of Ministers through co-decision-making with the EU Parliament for legislative decisions; this form of "reinforced" majority voting could also be resorted to for Treaty revisions, the CFSP, international agreements and the formulation of the EU budget. The French plan is based solely on majority voting and co-decision-making with the Parliament. In an effort to make the process easier and more transparent, the Socialist Group recommends that for legislative decisions affecting industry and the agricultural sector, procedures should not differ and national vetoes should be eliminated. The critical element of this plan is the number of votes each member nation receives and the number of votes needed to constitute a blocking minority.[96] But this "reinforced" majority voting could further delay decision-making.

Other proposals call for even greater decision-making transparency. Still others recommend institutional changes that are flexible and responsive to possible enlargement plans, with particular emphasis on the admission of the CEE nations.

The Democratic Deficit

The current institutional structure suffers from a "democratic deficit" in that of all the common institutions only members of the EU Parliament are directly elected by the citizens of the EU member nations. Yet members of the Parliament do not play a significant role in the decision-making process. Thus, the best way to reduce the democratic deficit would be to increase the authority of the Parliament.

As was previously pointed out, any decision-making reform in the Council of Ministers based on the increased use of majority voting would reduce the accountability of the ministers to their national governments. Such a loss of accountability could be redeemed by a Parliament with increased decision-making

---

[95] See Chapter I, Figure 1.4 (in Annex I-1), for a description of the EU decision-making structure.

[96] Reuters News (AL410reuec-rf). Brussels: EU Parliament-IGC. January 30, 1995.

powers such as the right to veto, as well as with closer ties to the national parliaments.

Institutional Changes in a Multi-Speed EMU

The creation of a multi-speed EMU, an arrangement under which members nations move at different speeds or participate only in a subset of common policies, would also require institutional changes. However, such changes would be extremely complicated and difficult to implement. Countries such as the U.K. that have opted out of certain common policies as, for example, the Social Charter and possibly the EMU, could create additional complications because nations exercising opt-out privileges cannot have the same decision-making powers as fully participating members.

Institutional changes could be further complicated if some countries apply common policies only at certain times due to their opt-out options or the multi-speed nature of the EMU. Moreover, institutions and decision-making processes cannot be restructured whenever new members are admitted. A flexible multi-speed decision-making process would be too complex and not transparent enough to be suitable.

A study conducted by the Centre for European Policy Studies (CEPS) identifies a set of policies that should be used as a guide in developing a multi-speed EMU in order to minimize some of the above-mentioned problems.[97] These recommendations include the following:

1. IGC treaties should be based on the ideas of those nations that are willing to integrate. Opting in should be the norm, opting out the exception;

2. those opting out of specific treaty obligations should still participate in the institutional frameworks; but

3. those opting out should have less than full rights in areas where they have opted out;

4. the majority of states should decide whether the actions of non-conforming member states are "destabilising or unacceptable"; and

[97] "Preparing for 1996 and a Larger European Union: Principles and Priorities." CEPS Report, Brussels. CEPS director Peter Ludlow and former Council Secretary General Niels Ersboell argue that in the 1996-97 the IGC have to deal with the post-Maastricht ratification crisis including the democratic deficit and the lack of transparency. This will start a parting of ways between those that want a deeper EU and those who do not.

5. the IGC treaties should have provisions for dealing with non-conforming states.[98]

The danger of agreeing to opt-out rights is that such rights dilute the idea of integration and could over time reduce the EU to little more than an association of states. But, as pointed out previously, multi-speed and opt-out options are necessary for political integration. Many observers and politicians as, for example, U.K. Prime Minister John Major, support such a "variable geometry" of integration as perhaps the only possible way toward a stronger political union. But, they caution that variability should be used only as a last resort and should not lead to a set of "à la carte" options.[99]

It is conceivable that the 1996-97 IGC discussions of institutional changes in general and of the decision-making process improvements in particular will continue into 1998. Even if enough nations meet the EMU convergence criteria, without a consensus on institutional and decision-making changes the EMU would probably be postponed.

Institutional and Decision-Making Changes

Until now, EU membership guaranteed the right of national representation on and in the common policy formulating committees and institutions. Consequently, any enlargement automatically increases the size of these bodies. As was pointed out, one of the key institutional implications of enlargement is the loss of the efficiency that results from increased size. As group cohesiveness diminishes, the efficiency of the decision-making process is reduced. This, in turn, induces the formation of informal subgroups, and makes for decreased transparency, higher costs and longer meetings. Thus, in an enlarged EU the principle of national representation should not be applied on efficiency grounds to institutions whose responsibility is to determine common policies involving autonomous regional or national interests, such as the ECB Governing Council or the EU Commission. Instead, under such circumstances institutional changes should be introduced according to one of the following approaches: (i) districting, (ii) alternating voting or (iii) the "denationalization" of appointed agents. Through such modification changes could be introduced in the qualified majority and/or unanimous voting systems.

The ECB Governing Council could be structured through a districting and/or alternating voting system. Districting involves the organization of member states into a smaller number of central bank districts, each of which is served by a

---

[98] "Preparing for 1996 and a Larger European Union: Principles and Priorities." CEPS Report, Brussels.

[99] This view is shared by European Socialist and the German CDU parliamentary groups.

joint district central bank whose governor sits on the ECB Governing Council. This is similar to the Bundesbank and the U.S. Federal Reserve System. Alternating voting does not change national representation by central bank governors, but prevents governors from holding a permanent seat on the Governing Council.

The 20-member Commission could to be changed through the "denationalization" of its appointed members in order to achieve an efficient size. The Council of Ministers, however, would have to retain national representation due to legal requirements reinforced by Article 126 of the Maastricht Treaty, which requires the empowerment of national representation. But it could use change in its qualified majority voting procedures. The European Council, COREPER, the Court of Justice and the Court of Auditors would also have to retain national representation owing to legal requirements, and it is likely that these institutions would not undergo any significant changes, if any. The size of the 626-member Parliament should be reduced through proportional representation. Other committees, such as the 222-member Committee of the Regions and the 222-member Economic and Social Committee also need streamlining, in all probability through proportional representation or districting. The following is a more detailed discussion of the possible institutional and decision-making changes to the ECB Governing Council, the Commission, the Council of Ministers and the Parliament.

1. The ECB Governing Council

As specified in the Maastricht Treaty, the ECB has two decision-making bodies: the six-member Executive Board and the Governing Council, consisting of the participating EMU member nation central bank governors and the six Executive Board members. While the main decision-making body is the Governing Council, the Executive Board is responsible for the execution of decisions and the day-to-day management of the ECB. The Governing Council uses a simple majority voting process, but only countries eligible for the EMU can vote on or participate in the formulation or implementation of common monetary policies. There is a third ECB body, the General Council, which is a non-voting policy forum in which all EU member nations are represented.

It should be noted that any potential enlargement of the EMU does not directly affect the decision-making structure unless the new member nations meet the EMU criteria. As it is unlikely that within the foreseeable future more than six or seven nations could meet the criteria, the Governing Council is not likely to exceed the reasonable size of 12 to 13 members. However, as the EMU membership increases, the ECB will face problems similar to those faced by the other common institutions such as the Council of Ministers and the EU Commission. For example, if the EMU has 12 participants, the ECB Governing Council grows to 18 members; if all 15 nations belong to the EMU, the Governing Council increases to 21.

The large nations, particularly Germany, would like to reform the ECB Governing Council because the simple majority decision-making process based on the one-nation, one-vote principle does not guarantee sound monetary policy. If seven or more member nations participate in the EMU and the Governing Council membership increases to over 13 (or goes up to 21), then a simple majority could outvote the six-member Executive Board. Thus, despite the Executive Board's commitment to sound monetary policy, it could not be guaranteed because not all central bank governors live up to the expectations of the Bundesbank. It should be noted that as EMU's membership changes so does the definition of price stability.

Even if the ECB does not require immediate institutional changes, it would in all probability need them in the future. Hence, it would be prudent to introduce the changes as early as possible, even if they are not required until the size of the Governing Council reaches the maximum number of 15. Both the districting and alternating voting membership systems could address the ECB's potential institutional and decision-making problems caused by enlargement of the EU. See **Annex 2.1** to this chapter for possible scenarios of districting and alternative voting for the ECB Governing Council and the impact of the scenarios on its ability to maintain Bundesbank-style anti-inflationary monetary policies.

The Districting System: In the districting system the voting structure is based on a defined district rather than on individual member nations. Under this arrangement, several nations comprise a district and share one vote. The assignment of nations to districts can be done according to GDP or population size or a combination thereof. This means that larger and/or wealthier nations would have a district of their own.

An example of such an arrangement is the U.S. Federal Reserve System under which 50 states are organized into 12 central banking districts, each with its own Federal Reserve Bank. This not only limits the size of the Federal Reserve monetary policy formulating body but also effectively organizes the regional distribution of central bank services, and thus capitalizes on the economies of scale. Another example of districting is provided by Germany. As the country expanded from 11 to 16 states through reunification, the Bundesbank system had to be changed. Prior to reunification the policy formulating body of the Bundesbank, the 17-member Central Bank Council, included 6 board members and the presidents of the 11 state central banks, the Landeszentralbanken (LZBs). As a result of reunification, without institutional reform the Central Bank Council would have increased to 22 members. But owing to political and efficiency considerations, the 16 states were reorganized into 9 district central banks whose governors now sit on the 15-member Central Bank Council.[100] The size of the districts ranges from 21.5 percent of the total population in Nordrhein-Westfalen to 6.3 percent in Sachsen.

---

[100] The Bundesbank Central Bank Council has a maximum of 16.

In the case of the ECB, districting would require smaller member nations to share a joint district central bank whose governor, selected by the governments of the member nations forming the district, would be a member of the ECB Governing Council. The advantage of such an arrangement is not only increased efficiency in decision-making but also the easier formulation of possible solutions to future problems caused by enlargement. Districts could be set up so as to include all potential future members. This could reduce political bargaining over shifting influence associated with enlargements. If the initial EMU membership is small, then the decision-making body of the ECB would be small as well. Other countries could join over time, thus delaying institutional problems if reforms are not carried out speedily. Since the CEE nations are likely to join the EU in small groups or as individual countries, it could be advantageous to integrate these nations without reorganizing the ECB Council every time a group or one of these nations is admitted. This could also define the position and the influence of new members in advance of their membership.

However, districting raises political concerns, particularly for the smaller nations which reject it because of their belief in national representation and national pride. Many of these nations see districting as a loss of influence over common monetary policy formulation. However, as the ECB is supposed to be independent of national governments, this argument is questionable. Nonetheless, the grouping of nations within districts would generate political problems.

Alternating Voting Memberships: If districting is rejected by the smaller nations, alternating voting is a backup solution to streamlining the ECB Governing Council. Again, the U.S. Federal Reserve System is a good example of this arrangement.[101] Its Federal Open Market Committee (FOMC) serves as the official monetary policy formulating body in charge of managing interest rates. The FOMC consists of an 11-member board with 6 permanent members and no more than 5 members from the 12 Federal Reserve Banks. Of the latter, one position permanently belongs to the New York Federal Reserve District Bank,[102] while the other four positions are rotated among the other Banks, with the Chicago and Cleveland Federal Reserve District Bank representatives serving every third year.

There are a number of possible variations in the alternating voting system as applied to the ECB Governing Council. For example, member nations could be assigned to four different groups with differing voting rights on the basis of either population size or real GDP, or a combination thereof.

---

[101] The U.S. Federal Reserve System is a combination of districting and of alternating voting membership.

[102] The New York Federal Reserve District Bank is a permanent member of the FOMC, owing to its importance as a commercial - investment banking and foreign exchange center, and to the fact that it is the bank that implements the FOMC's open market operations.

In an EU of 17 nations with 9 national central bank seats based on population size, the following system could be applied. The five largest countries, with over 10 percent of the total EU population, could be assigned to Group 1. Their central bank governors would receive permanent votes on the Council. The next four smaller nations with population sizes between 2.5 percent and 4 percent of the total, could be assigned to Group 2, with only two seats; thus, nations in this group would have their central bank governor represented on the ECB Council every other year. Group 3 could consist of three nations with a population size between 1.5 and 2.3 percent of the total and would receive only one seat, with the central bank governors of this group sitting on the ECB Council once every three years. Group 4 could represent the five smallest nations with less than 1.5 percent of the total EU population, and their central bank governors would be represented on the ECB Council every fifth year, as the group receives only one vote. Table 2.5 illustrates the details of such an arrangement.

One of the advantages of the alternating voting option is that it would not require any major changes in the existing central banking system. However, when new member nations are admitted, the arrangement would have to be redesigned and, thus, renegotiated to maintain the Council size. This could open a political Pandora's box. Not surprisingly, districting is favored over alternating voting because it would allow a permanent district assignment for all nations.

Like districting, alternating voting raises political concerns among the smaller nations. They view it as a loss of influence over common monetary policy formulation. As before, such concerns are erroneous because the ECB should be independent of national governments. Yet, such concerns exist and could create political problems.

Table 2.5
Annually Alternating Voting in an EU of 17 Nations with 9 Central Bank Governor Seats in the ECB Council

	% Of EU-17 Population
GROUP 1: *Permanent voting = 5 seats*	77%
1. Germany	21.0
2. Italy	15.4
3. U.K.	15.3
4. France	14.9
5. Spain	10.4
GROUP 2: *Voting every other year = 2 seats*	12%
1. Netherlands	3.9
2. Belgium	2.7
3. Greece	2.7
4. Portugal	2.7
GROUP 3: *Voting every third year = 1 seat*	6%
1. Sweden	2.3
2. Austria	2.0
3. Switzerland	1.7
GROUP 4: *Voting every fifth year = 1 seat*	5%
1. Denmark	1.4
2. Finland	1.3
3. Norway	1.1
4. Ireland	1.0
5. Luxembourg	0.1

Source: Is Bigger Better?- The Economics of Enlargement. Monitoring European Integration , no.3., A CEPR Annual Report, London: Center for Economic Policy Research (CERP), 1992, p.102.

2. *The EU Commission*

Of all the common institutions targeted for streamlining and increased efficiency following EU enlargement, the EU Commission would probably be the most affected. Under the prevailing system, apart from the president, the five largest countries have two commissioners each[103] while the other nations have one each. In 1995, with the admission of Austria, Sweden and Finland, the number of commissioners increased from 17 to 20. Ever since efforts are under way to streamline the Commission. The commissioners themselves have recommended a reduction of the size of both the Commission and its Directorate Generals.[104] Table 2.6 shows the structure of the enlarged Commission as of 1995.

Table 2.6
The Enlarged European Commission as of 1995

	Number Of Commissioners
Belgium, Denmark, Portugal, Ireland, the Netherlands, Luxembourg, Greece	1 each
Germany, Spain, France, Italy, the United Kingdom	2 each
EU-12 TOTAL:	17
NEW MEMBERS: Austria	1
Finland	1
Sweden	1
EU-15 TOTAL:	20

Source: EU Commission data, 1996.

"Denationalization" of the Appointed Representatives: "Denationalization" means that all decision-making body members would be appointed on the basis of qualifications rather than nationality. Such a move is inappropriate for policy formulating bodies that represent national interests as, for example, the Council of Ministers. But denationalization can be applied to bodies, such as the EU Commission, that manage common policies that affect all member states. Denationalization would promote integration, as the representatives appointed under this system would conduct policies on a professional and common basis and not according to national interests. This would shield Commission members from national pressures and could also help to streamline the Commission, as its size

[103] Germany, France, Italy, Spain and the U.K. have two commissioners each.

[104] Britto, Andrew and David Mayes. "Achieving Monetary Union in Europe," U.K.: National Institute of Economic and Social Research, 1992, pp.79-91.

would depend on the number of functions performed and not on national representation. Longer office terms would also be possible, and this could enhance institutional memory and efficiency, which are reduced by frequent rotations.

To some extent, the Commission has already been denationalized because it is "supposed to solve common policy problems affecting" all member nations in a similar way.[105] Moreover, its President is appointed through a consensus of national governments. Thus, the Commission is a good starting point for changes. The case for the denationalization of some of the other common decision-making bodies such as the Council of Ministers is less convincing and far more difficult. However, elements of denationalization are already present in the ECB Governing Council, whose six-member Executive Board is not based as much on national representation or districting as on professional qualifications.

The Commission, exclusive of the President, should consist of fewer than 10 commissioners instead of the current 20.[106] If its denationalization is not possible, the only alternative available would be districting or the maintenance of the status quo (national representation). It should be noted that districting could contain elements of denationalization, or rather of multinationalization, because the districts could be based on the ECB districting structure. If the structure of the Commission is not changed, the admission of additional members such as the CEE nations (Hungary, Poland and the Czech and the Slovak Republics) and of the smaller Mediterranean nations as, for example, Malta and Cyprus, could increase the Commission's size to 26 and, eventually, to more than 30. This would destroy its ability to perform its original functions.

3. *The Council of Ministers*

Despite the institutional changes discussed in 1996, it is unlikely that the 15-member Council of Ministers would be reduced in size or that it would lose its national representational structure. It is a body that represents national and not common interests, thus reorganizing the Council to increase its efficiency is not a convincing option. Yet there is a growing interest in reforming its decision-making process. Already in an EU of 12 nations, there was growing anxiety among the larger and richer nations concerning the disproportionate influence of smaller countries through the decision-making processes. With the admission of the three new members in 1995, this anxiety has increased. It is likely to grow with additional enlargements because potential future members, by any standard, are relatively small when compared with the large member nations such as Germany or France. Thus, there is a growing urgency among the larger nations not only to restructure the

---

[105] Is Bigger Better? The Economics of EC Enlargement, CEPR, pp.103-4.

[106] Article 126 of the Maastricht Treaty requires member state representation within the EU institutional structure, and any change of this article would require unanimous votes.

current voting system but also to limit voting weights, that is, to limit the influence of new members as much as possible.

Under the current system, all member states have direct representation on the Council of Ministers. This allows for the decision-making process to be conducted primarily on the basis of unanimity or, to a lesser extent, on the basis of qualified majority voting. However, in view of future enlargements, there are already numerous proposals calling for a revised system under which unanimous voting (that is, the possibility of using the national veto) would be eliminated and qualified majority voting would become the rule. In all likelihood such a voting system would entail a slight shift of power toward the richer and larger nations. It should be noted, however, that the larger nations would only agree to the abolishment of the national veto if the majority decision-making system is skewed in their favor.

Although the 1995 enlargement has made the decision-making process more laborious, it did not paralyze the Council of Ministers. But any subsequent enlargement involving the CEE nations or other smaller countries such as Cyprus or Malta, could do so. The decision-making process would be prone to more vetoes than currently. It is inevitable that in an expanded EU the significant differences in economic development, income levels, industrial structures, history and geography would generate conflicts concerning structural aid and the management of the common agricultural, monetary and foreign policies.

Qualified Majority Voting: The enlargement of the EU from 12 to 15 members in 1995 required the immediate restructuring of the qualified majority voting system. Prior to the admission of Austria, Sweden and Finland, 54 votes had constituted a qualified majority and the blocking minority required 23 out of 76 votes. In 1995, the admission of the three new members raised the total votes to 87 while the qualified majority grew to 62 votes and the blocking minority to 26. This has proportionally reduced the number of votes required by the blocking minority and has thus made it easier for groups of countries to obstruct proposals. For example, to determine whether and when to move to the EMU's Stage III as well as to decide which countries would be eligible under the convergence criteria, a qualified majority would require 62 votes while only 26 votes cast by the U.K., Spain, Greece and Portugal could block the decisions reached. It should be noted that in a compromise agreement related to the admission of the three new members in 1995, the 12 nations decided that in the event that any Council proposal is opposed by countries representing between 23 and 25 votes, the decision will be postponed and further discussion without a time limit will be allowed. Thus, it is entirely conceivable that the U.K., Spain and Greece could delay a move to Stage III.[107] Table 2.7 gives details of the 15-member qualified majority voting system in the Council of Ministers.

---

[107] There is an implied commitment in a special protocol attached to the Maastricht Treaty stating that all member states "shall...respect the will for the Community to enter swiftly into the third stage and therefore no member state shall prevent the entering into the third stage."

Table 2.7
The Council of Ministers' Qualified Majority Voting System in the EU of 15 Nations

	Weighted Majority Votes Of EU-12	Weighted Majority Votes Of EU-15
Belgium	5	5
Denmark	3	3
Germany	10	10
Greece	5	5
Spain	8	8
France	10	10
Ireland	3	3
Italy	10	10
Luxembourg	2	2
Netherlands	5	5
Portugal	5	5
United Kingdom	10	10
New Members Austria	-	4
Finland	-	3
Sweden	-	4
TOTAL NO. OF VOTES:	**76**	**87**
Qualified Majority	54	62
Blocking Minority	23	26

Source: EU Commission data, 1996.

As Table 2.7 shows, the changes also had to address the three new member nations' ability to create a blocking minority and/or to exercise their veto. They are relatively small and represent less than 10 percent of the combined GDP. Moreover, the three new member nations are likely to vote in the same way as the other small nations. Sweden and Finland are not EU enthusiasts and are burdened by high public debt which could make their EMU membership problematic. Moreover, like Denmark, these two nations have a history of independence and probably favor a less integrated EU.

Such considerations not only highlight the need for changes prior to the admission of additional member nations but also direct attention to the necessity of restructuring the decision-making bodies so as to accommodate future enlargements. The admission of new member nations will in all probability call for more qualified majority voting, as increased membership will render decision-making under the national veto system a laborious task. This trend is already apparent. Plans are under way to decide transportation and environmental issues through the qualified majority decision-making process. This could have far greater consequences than previous changes ever had.

The criteria used to determine voting weights and the representation of member nations involve controversial issues. The choice among GNP, GDP and population size as weight factors is significant because it could be either favorable to or unfavorable to smaller nations. The choice of other weighing factors such as per capita income could also negatively affect these countries. For example, Poland has a large population but a relatively small GNP or GDP, and a low per capita income.

The National Veto: As was discussed earlier, it is conceivable that future enlargements will diminish the role of the national veto, as more and more issues will need to be resolved through the qualified majority voting process.

If small countries such as Malta or Cyprus are admitted, it is questionable whether they should have veto rights at all. It is difficult to deny such rights but if the relative economic size and political importance of certain countries is only marginal, this becomes a practical consideration and not one of principle. Thus, it is conceivable that some future member nations may not be able to exercise the veto. In such a case, the EU would not only become a multi-speed union, but a union of unequals. Proposals along these lines are already under consideration. For example, the Hoensch Report which originated in the EU Parliament, calls for majority voting on all common issues and a rotation of Presidency of the Council of Ministers only among France, Germany, the U.K., Spain and Italy. However, the acceptance of such proposals is unlikely, because they require a unanimous vote.

***The Presidency of the Council of Ministers*:** The presidency is currently assigned to nations on an alphabetically rotating basis for six months. An EU of 12 member nations meant that a country held the presidency once every six years; with the addition of the three new members in 1995, the time span has increased to once every seven-and-a-half years. The admission of Hungary, Poland and the Czech Republic would result in a rotation that assigns the presidency to each country only once every nine years.

The large nations are likely to resist a system that would allow small countries or those that are in geographical proximity to claim the presidency for two or three years in a row and to set an agenda that would not necessarily represent the interests of the majority of EU citizens. Thus, the principle of districting or that of alternating voting could be applied to the Council of Ministers presidency rotation system. The Hoensch proposal, which calls for rotation of the presidency only among France, Germany, the U.K., Spain and Italy, could be modified with additional presidential tenures available for subsets of smaller nations that rotate the presidential function within their district. This could mitigate the effect of the political bottlenecks created by the smaller nations in response to the Hoensch Report and other similar proposals. Table 2.8 shows the rotation scheme of the presidency of the enlarged Council of Ministers up to the year 2007, while Table 2.9 shows the presidency rotation in an enlarged Council involving all potential 37 members sometime in the next century.

Table 2.8
The Enlarged EU Council of Ministers Presidency Rotation Schedule (1995)

Current Rotation	Next Rotation
JAN 1993 Denmark	JUL 2000 Belgium
JUL 1993 Belgium	JAN 2001 Denmark
JAN 1994 Greece	JUL 2001 Germany
JUL 1994 Germany	JAN 2002 Greece
JAN 1995 France	JUL 2002 Spain
JUL 1995 Spain	JAN 2003 France
JAN 1996 Italy	JUL 2003 Ireland
JUL 1996 Ireland	JAN 2004 Italy
JAN 1997 Netherlands	JUL 2004 Luxembourg
JUL 1997 Luxembourg	JAN 2005 Netherlands
JAN 1998 Austria	JUL 2005 Austria
JUL 1998 Finland	JAN 2006 Portugal
JAN 1999 Portugal	JUL 2006 Finland
JUL 1999 United Kingdom	JAN 2007 Sweden
JAN 2000 Sweden	JUL 2007 United Kingdom

Source: The Union of 16, Phoenix No.2, Association of Former Trainees of the European Union. Brussels: ADEK, Autumn 1994, p.16.

Table 2.9
Presidency Rotation in an Enlarged EU Council of Ministers Including All 37 Potential Members After The Year 2000

Rotation Would Occur Every 18½ Years		
Belgie (Belgium) Bosna E Hercegovia Bulgaria Ceska (Czech) Crna Gora (Montenegro) Danmark (Denmark) Deutschland (Germany) Eesti (Estonia) Ellas (Greece) Espana (Spain) France Helvetia (Switzerland) Hratska (Croatia)	Ireland (Eire) Island (Iceland) Italia (Italy) Kypron (Cyprus) Latvija (Latvia) Liechtenstein Lietuva (Lithuania) Luxembourg Magyarorszag (Hungary) Makedonija (Macedonia) Malta Nederland (Netherlands) Norge (Norway)	Österreich (Austria) Polska (Poland) Portugal Romania Slovenija (Slovenia) Slovenska (Slovakia) Srbija (Serbia) Suomi (Finland) Sverige (Sweden) Türkiye (Turkey) United Kingdom

Source: The Union of 16, Phoenix No.2, Association of Former Trainees of the European Union. Brussels: ADEK, Autumn 1994, p.15.

4. The EU Parliament

The EU Parliament has always been at the center of controversy because of the "democratic deficit." It is the only institution whose members are directly elected by the citizens of all member nations; all other decision-making common institutions are made up of appointees.[108]

Any change in the way the Council of Ministers functions, such as the increased use of majority voting, would reduce the accountability of the Council members to their national governments. This could be corrected by a more powerful Parliament with increased powers of decision-making -- that is, with a right to veto. Such a Parliament would eliminate the "democratic deficit." But if the Parliament gets more authority, this should be done in conjunction with providing for better coordination with national parliaments, as this would increase transparency.

Prior to the admission of the three new member nations in 1995, the number of parliamentary seats was 567. Following their admission, 59 seats were added through the next parliamentary election in 1999 for a new total of 626. Austria received 21 seats, Finland 16, and Sweden 22. Although it is not yet clear when additional new members will be admitted, their presence will significantly increase the size of the Parliament, which, in turn, would make it difficult for the institution to function effectively. Thus, in anticipation of future memberships the current size of the Parliament should be reduced. The parliaments of the larger EU nations, such as Germany, France, Italy and the U.K.,[109] have approximately the same number of seats as the current EU Parliament but the complexity of EU policy formulation renders the size of this institution cumbersome.[110] Table 2.10 shows the composition of the EU Parliament following the 1995 enlargement.

Even if only three or four CEE nations and a few other small countries such as Malta and Cyprus, are admitted early in the next century, the size of the Parliament could rise to well over 700. The politically most acceptable way of maintaining a reasonably sized Parliament would be to eliminate seats on a proportional basis across the board.

---

[108] Pinder, John. European Community: The Building of a Union. London: Oxford University Press, 1991, p.59.

[109] Germany has 662 representatives in the Bundestag (Federal Assembly - lower house) and 68 in the Bundesrat (Federal Council - upper house); Italy has 630 seats in the Chamber of Deputies and 315 in the Senate of the Republic; France has 577 seats in the National Assembly and 321 in the Senate; and the U.K. has 651 seats in the House of Commons and over 1,000 in the House of Lords.

[110] The average size of national parliaments (both upper and lower houses) of the EU-15 member nations is approximately 475 seats.

Table 2.10
The Enlarged European Parliament

	Number Of Seats		
	1989	**1994**	**1999**
Belgium	24	25	25
Denmark	16	16	16
Germany	81	99	99
Greece	24	25	25
Spain	60	64	64
France	81	87	87
Ireland	15	15	15
Italy	81	87	87
Luxembourg	6	6	6
Netherlands	25	31	31
Portugal	24	25	25
United Kingdom	81	87	87
12 Member EU TOTAL:	**518**	**567**	**567**
NEW MEMBERS: Austria	-	-	21
Finland	-	-	16
Sweden	-	-	22
15 Member EU TOTAL:			**626**

Source: EU Commission data, 1995.

THE IMPLICATIONS OF A MULTI-SPEED EMU

The Maastricht Treaty implies a multi-speed EMU as well as a two-tiered EU. A multi-speed EMU is possible because the Treaty mandates the meeting of monetary and fiscal convergence criteria prior to a move to Stage III of the EMU. Member nations unable to meet the criteria would be allowed a "derogation from the Treaty obligations" as they pertain to Stage III until such time as they can meet the convergence criteria. The Treaty also acquiesced in a two-tiered EU in that it allowed for the U.K. and Denmark to negotiate an opt-out of Stage III. There are those who argue that the EU has been a two-tiered entity since the creation of the ERM, as not all member nations belong to the semi-pegged exchange rate mechanism. Even today, three nations, the U.K., Sweden and Greece, are not obliged to conduct domestic policies in accordance with ERM requirements.

During the early 1990s the idea of a multi-speed EMU had a negative undertone. It was viewed by some of the more influential EU nations as a loss of tolerance for broad integration in favor of a faster "more exclusive monetary club for the wealthy few."[111] But by now it is clear that a multi-speed EMU and a two-tiered EU are the only politically realistic ways of maintaining the momentum toward

[111] Arrowsmith, John. "Economic and Monetary Union in a Multi-tier Europe." National Institute for Economic Review, No. 152, May 1995, p.76.

European monetary integration and also of "meeting the key Maastricht requirements of sustainable low inflation and sound public finances."[112] At the beginning of 1999 a number of, perhaps a majority of the EU member nations may be ready for Stage III of the EMU.

Although both the costs and benefits and the macroeconomic effects of EMU membership in Stage III have been extensively discussed, the impact of the EMU on the EU member nations that remain in Stage II as well as the impact of this "splitting" of the EU on further integration, remains unclear. The implications in terms of macroeconomic policies and political objectives for the "outer core" (i.e., non-EMU) member nations, however, are serious. Thus a better understanding of the impact of the "outer core" on the "inner core" is needed, as both will still share a significant number of decisions by way of either a qualified/simple majority or a unanimous vote on issues related not only to the EMU but also to labor, the social market, the environment, taxes and amendments to the Treaties of Rome.

To illustrate the point, in order to begin Stage III of the EMU on January 1, 1999, the European Council has to decide which nations have met the convergence criteria. It must then give its "go-ahead" to the integration process sometimes in 1998. But, if the U.K. and/or Denmark have exercised their opt-out rights in 1998, their role in the European Council's decision-making process is open to question.[113] The role of the opt-out countries in the unanimous, simple or qualified majority voting processes could be even more complicated. For example, in the case of a simple majority vote, the U.K. and/or Denmark would probably be excluded from the numerator, but not necessarily from the denominator when calculating the majority. In the case of a qualified majority vote in the Council of Ministers (62 out of 87 votes), it is not clear whether the U.K. and/or Denmark, again assuming that they have exercised their opt-out rights, will be permitted to vote, because together with other nations such as Sweden and Italy, they could constitute a blocking minority. As mentioned before, under the revised decision-making process and including the votes of the three new member nations, any qualified majority decision in the Council of Ministers that generates 23 to 25 opposing votes requires additional discussions without a time limit. Thus the opt-out U.K. together with Spain and Portugal could delay a required Council vote.

The effect would be even more pronounced in the case of the unanimity requirements concerning issues that include both future EMU and non-EMU member nations. These examples show that a multi-speed EMU and a two-tiered EU seriously change the dynamics of decision-making for all 15 countries. The 1996 and 1997 intergovernmental conference (IGC) talks, to some extent, have addressed but not resolved these problems.

---

[112] Arrowsmith, John. "Economic and Monetary Union in a Multi-tier Europe," 1995, p.76.

[113] For the U.K. and/or Denmark to prevent the other nations from proceeding to Stage III of EMU would mean to breach the commitment laid out in a special protocol attached to the Maastricht Treaty, according to which member nations "shall...respect the will for the Community to enter swiftly into the third stage and therefore no member state shall prevent the entering into the third stage."

In a multi-speed EMU and two-tiered EU, a common monetary policy is likely to have an asymmetric impact on member states. This could cause a shift in trading patterns not only between the EMU and non-EMU member states but also with non-EU nations. Two-thirds of EU trade takes place among member nations with less than 10 percent of the common GDP accounted for by trade with non-EU nations. Under these circumstances, there is a danger that the EMU could precipitate a more inward-looking EU. The EMU membership of the large and powerful economies in Stage III will not only create additional asymmetry between the "inner core" and the "outer core", but will also provide fewer incentives for the "inner core" to take into account the interests of the "outer core." Thus, one outcome of a multi-speed EMU will probably be a demand for more economic coordination and political cooperation than the EU has displayed to date.

It could be argued that the political and economic policy agendas of the "inner core" nations and those of the "outer core" differ less than the agendas of countries that have chosen to opt out of EMU altogether. This is especially true in relation to economic and budgetary policies. The

> procedures for the coordination and multi-lateral surveillance of economic polices (in accordance with broad guidelines laid down by the Council of Ministers) are in place. So too [also in place] are the prohibitions on central bank financing of public sector deficits, on privileged access for public sector borrowers to financial institutions and on the Community or its member states bailing out an over-indebted government.[114]

In Stage II, nations are discouraged to maintain excessive deficits or "stocks of debt," as they not only have to meet the Maastricht convergence criteria but are subject to scrutiny and pressure by other nations, and to the threat that any adverse economic data or unusual creative accounting may be officially published. The difference between Stages II and III is that in Stage III if they do not sustain the deficit and debt criteria, nations will be required to undertake specific corrective measures within a given time period. In addition to being fined for non-compliance, countries might be forced to publish an official warning when issuing debt, or may have their EIB investments suspended.

It is in monetary policy that the difference between the "inner core" and the "outer core" nations is marked. EMU nations i.e. Stage III participants will be required to share their monetary sovereignty with the Governing Council and to have their monetary policy implemented by the six-member Executive Board of the ECB "either directly or through instructions to the participating national central banks." Such nations will also have their exchange rates irrevocably fixed initially and around the middle of the year 2002, their currencies will be replaced by the single currency, the Euro. The "inner core's" foreign exchange reserves will be pooled as will any income generated by central banks resulting from seigniorage (i.e., the

---

[114] Arrowsmith, John. "Economic and Monetary Union in a Multi-tier Europe," 1995, p.76.

issuance of banknotes) and compulsory commercial bank reserves held. It should be noted that much of this income will revert back to the central banks in proportion to their capital contribution to the ECB.

The Council of Finance Ministers of the "inner core" nations will be responsible for the exchange rate between the single currency and non-EU currencies. Thus, the "inner core" nations will have the authority to determine the international role of the Euro. The Stage II, or "outer core," members will retain control over their national currencies and monetary policies. Although the outer core nations are not participants in the Governing Council of the ECB, they will be allowed to participate (just as the EMU opt-out nations) in the ECB's General Council[115] – a primarily advisory and reporting body. The General Council will negotiate and coordinate exchange rate relationships between the Euro and the currencies of the non-EMU members of the EU. A controversial, if vague, issue concerns the governance of the exchange rate policies of Stage II nations vis-à-vis that of non-EU nations.

It is clear that the move of the wealthy economies into Stage III will pose serious monetary and exchange rate problems for the nations remaining in Stage II. What is unclear is that it remains to be seen whether the current ERM or future ERM II, both with flexible +/-15 percent currency bands, can provide the discipline and credibility needed to pursue the convergence criteria. It is also still not clear whether the +/-15 percent band will be sufficient to deliver the "outer core" (Stage II) currencies to the point where they can eventually be irrevocably fixed as required by Stage III. In this respect the most important question is whether the "outer core" currencies can maintain the anti-inflationary policy credibility without the Deutsche mark as an anchor currency.[116] They need another anti-inflationary anchor and/or very effective monetary and fiscal policies to convince the international financial markets, it would take only the slightest policy miscalculation to create a speculative run on the currencies. The markets know the convergence criteria targets that must be met to enter Stage III.

The new single currency, the Euro, is the new anchor to the "ERM II" system and will dominate the mechanism even more than the Deutsche mark did in the original ERM. Moreover, under the ERM II, the burden of adjustment is officially on the "outer" members and not the EMU members. As such, the ERM II will be more asymmetrical than the original ERM. Thus, the "outer core" ERM II member nations left behind in Stage II will have a smaller say in the setting of EU-wide monetary and exchange rate policy than they will have under the proposed ECB General Council structure.

It is possible that after the 1996-97 and follow-up IGCs on institutional reform and decision-making, the Nordic bloc of the EU will have not only greater

---

[115] The Governing Council of the ECB is composed of the President and Vice-President of the ECB and the Governors of all the EU central banks. See Chapter V for more detail.

[116] It should be noted that with the dissolution of the Deutsche mark (and the Ecu), the current ERM automatically disintegrates.

economic weight but also a greater share of voting power in the Council of Ministers. It is also likely that, at least initially, most of the Stage III EMU nations will originate in this region. As the "inner core" nations work closer together, establishing common monetary and exchange rate policies as well as set common interest rates, they will be less receptive to the concerns of the "outer" or opt-out nations. There will be an inherent obligation on part of the Stage III member nations to pursue policies to assure the success of and to reject any policies that could threaten the credibility of the EMU, at least in the eyes of the international financial markets.

This problem will in all probability become even more pronounced as the EU enlarges and develops into a three-speed EMU and/or three-tiered EU, because most of the future EU members are relatively small economies. Further enlargement will probably embrace, apart from Norway and Switzerland, Malta, Cyprus, the Visegrad Group[117], Slovenia, the Baltic States and possibly Turkey. It is not realistic to assume that these countries could qualify for Stage II of the EMU. Thus, a three-speed EMU looms on the horizon. Some of these countries, for example, Malta and Cyprus, may not receive full voting privileges, (i.e., no veto power) and that could create a three-tiered EU. Given the marked disparities in living standards as well as the economic and systemic differences between the incoming group and the "inner core," it is very unlikely that the interests and concerns of the new member nations would be high on the policy agendas of the "inner core." Thus, countries that will not be in the first wave of EMU members, or close behind, will find it increasingly difficult to enter Stage III, with their chances diminishing rapidly as the number of EU-member countries increases.

Even though the ERM II provides a formal framework for exchange rate policy coordination between the "inner core" and the "outer core," dissension is inevitable. Therefore, some legal "code of conduct" may have to be devised.

It should be noted that the Maastricht Treaty is silent on how it will phase-out the Ecu basket during the transitional phase of Stage III (between the locking of exchange rates to the final abolishment of national currencies) as well as the possible impact of this on the exchange rate mechanism. Later plans call for a new ERM II anchored by the Euro and for all the Ecu financial instruments and accounts to be the translated into the Euro in 1999. However, in theory it is conceivable that the Ecu could coexist with the Euro during this transition stage. However, the nature of the Ecu basket's composition would change as some of it's currencies would lock their exchange rates and be fixed to the Euro.[118] As the currencies that are the most likely to lock their exchange rates are the ones with the largest weights in the Ecu, the Euro would function as the de facto new anchor. In that case, the Ecu's relationship to other international currencies would change.

A multi-speed EMU and a two-tiered EU will have consequences beyond the macroeconomic and monetary spheres. The "1992 Single Market" will be

---

[117] The Visegrad Group consists of Hungary, Poland and the Czech and Slovak Republics.

[118] Countries that meet the Maastricht convergence criteria are to irrevocably lock their exchange rates on January 1, 1999.

affected as the "inner core" will not face exchange rate risk. This could have an impact on trade patterns, probably to the detriment of the "outer group" nations which may influence the trade and foreign direct investment behavior of non-EU multinational companies.

The political and economic impact of a multi-speed EMU and of a two-tiered EU requires further study. The above discussion has assumed that the single currency, the Euro, would, after a transitional period, become a stable international currency. However, there is no guarantee that this will happen, as it is conceivable that even the best-matched "inner core" nations will undergo economic and political tensions as a result of common monetary policies. A policy aimed at EU-wide price stability may not consistently meet the short-term domestic needs of some "inner core" nations. The ECB's monetary policy might generate conditions under which German inflation could at some time be greater and longer-lasting than the Bundesbank would like; or EU monetary policy could require tightening prior to the completion of a cyclical recovery in France; the Irish economy could be drawn into recession by the U.K, which may opt out of the EMU. An ECB policy action could have more acute results in one particular country than in others. It is also possible that national governments could exploit the impartiality of common monetary policies to borrow for domestic budgetary purposes, knowing that the ECB's offsetting monetary tightening will be applied over the entire EU. There are some disciplinary actions associated with excessive deficit spending in Stage III, but they are untested and the trade-off between the disciplinary actions and domestic political concerns is difficult to estimate a priori. However, what is known is that the Euro's relationship to other international currencies in all probability is going to be quite different from that of the Deutsche mark.

A final possibility that has not received much attention is that a multi-speed EMU could lead not only to a two, but perhaps a three or four-tiered EU. For example, Germany and France are better off alone than with Italy and certainly better off than with Spain or Portugal. Spain and Portugal will not be part of the first wave, thus they could form their own group with fixed exchange rates and a shared monetary policy, while they are trying to qualify for Stage III.[119] For some countries, such as Italy, the choice is more difficult, because joining a Franco-German union could provide credibility but would generate economic, and thus political, instability.[120] Joining a Spanish-Portuguese group would allow Italy to continue its stable economic and exchange rate policies but would result in a loss of credibility.

Thus, the manner in which the EU moves toward the EMU is of vital importance to the future of integration. Under a multi-speed EMU different coalitions could form which increase the possibility of a multi-tiered EU. However, a multi-tiered EU not only violates the spirit of Jean Monnets's Europe but also may change the political and economic map of the continent.

---

[119] This could be done within the context of the "ERM II" in which, for example, Spain and Portugal would have a separate agreement to have tighter bi-lateral currency bands. This would be similar to the agreement Germany and the Netherlands had in the aftermath of the 1993 ERM crisis, which restricts their bilateral currency bands to +/-2.25 percent rather than to the +/-15 percent.

[120] This is assuming that Italy continues to have internal difficulties in reducing debt.

Annex II.1
COMBINATIONS OF DISTRICTING AND ALTERNATING VOTING FOR THE ECB GOVERNING COUNCIL AND THE ABILITY TO MAINTAIN A BUNDESBANK-STYLE ANTI-INFLATIONARY MONETARY POLICY

This section explores the different possible options of districting and alternating voting as well as the combinations thereof for the ECB Governing Council. Note that the Council (the voting body of the ECB) will be made up of a six-member Executive Board and participating EMU member nation central bank governors. The following options represent various possible scenarios for an EU of 15 member nations on districting and alternating voting. In most cases the deciding criterion is the size of population and GDP as a percentage of the total EU population and combined GDP. The population and GDP percentages are given equal weight (50-50). In addition to these demographic and economic considerations, political considerations are also taken into account when setting up the various districts. In all scenarios the ECB (six-member) Executive Board has six votes on the ECB Governing Council. The scenarios assume that the ECB Executive Board will, from the outset, follow Bundesbank-style anti-inflationary monetary policy. Thus, each scenario is evaluated on the basis of whether it provides an airtight guarantee of such policies i.e., if the Executive Board's six votes and the German vote can maintain a majority on the Governing Council.

Table 2.11 shows 1994 data concerning the population, GDP and GDP per capita of an EU of 15, 14 and 13 member nations, respectively.

As shown in Table 2.11, based on the proportional size of populations, the top five countries are Germany, the United Kingdom (U.K.), Italy, France and Spain. Germany stands far above the rest and Spain is well below the top four. Using a similar proportional approach to GDP data, the top five countries include Germany, France, Italy, the U.K. and Spain. Again, Germany is well ahead of the rest while Spain is still well below the top four. When both population and GDP are combined in a 50-50 proportion, the top five are Germany, France, Italy, the U.K. and Spain. Germany stands far above the others, while France, Italy and the U.K. are roughly equal, and Spain ranks below the top four. If the U.K. exercises its opt-out option, there is no substantial change in the ranking but no nation is close enough to take the U.K.'s place. Similarly, with both the U.K. and Denmark opting out, the top four nations are still so far ahead of the others that none could join their group.

Table 2.11
Population, GDP and GDP per Capita of the 15-member EU (1994)

		Population based shares				GDP based shares			Population + GDP			GDP per capita in thous. in 1994
	Population (Millions) 1994	EU(15) % of Total	EU(14) Opt-out Option 1	EU(13) Opt-out Option 2	GDP (bn $) 1994	EU(15) % of Total	EU(14) Opt-out Option 1	EU(13) Opt-out Option 2	EU(15) % of Total	EU(14) Opt-out Option 1	EU(13) Opt-out Option 2	
Austria	7,851	2.1%	2.5%	2.6%	186	2.7%	3.1%	3.2%	2.4%	2.8%	2.9%	23.7
Belgium	10,108	2.7%	3.2%	3.3%	222	3.2%	3.7%	3.8%	2.9%	3.5%	3.5%	22
Denmark	5,191	1.4%	1.7%		143	2.0%	2.4%		1.7%	2.0%		27.4
Finland	5,064	1.4%	1.6%	1.7%	102	1.5%	1.7%	1.7%	1.4%	1.7%	1.7%	20.1
France	57,847	15.6%	18.5%	18.9%	1,317	18.8%	21.9%	22.5%	17.2%	20.2%	20.7%	22.7
Germany	81,682	22.1%	26.2%	26.6%	1,817	25.9%	30.3%	31.0%	24.0%	28.2%	28.8%	22.2
Greece	10,417	2.8%	3.3%	3.4%	78	1.1%	1.3%	1.3%	2.0%	2.3%	2.4%	7.5
Ireland	3,564	1.0%	1.1%	1.2%	50	0.7%	0.8%	0.9%	0.8%	1.0%	1.0%	14.3
Italy	56,874	15.4%	18.2%	18.5%	993	14.2%	16.5%	16.9%	14.8%	17.4%	17.7%	17.4
Luxembourg	400	0.1%	0.1%	0.1%	12	0.2%	0.2%	0.2%	0.1%	0.2%	0.2%	31.5
Netherlands	15,346	4.1%	4.9%	5.0%	328	4.7%	5.5%	5.6%	4.4%	5.2%	5.3%	21.3
Portugal	9,776	2.6%	3.1%	3.2%	80	1.1%	1.3%	1.4%	1.9%	2.2%	2.3%	8.1
Spain	39,175	10.6%	12.6%	12.8%	478	6.8%	8.0%	8.2%	8.7%	10.3%	10.5%	12.6
Sweden	8,749	2.4%	2.8%	2.9%	196	2.8%	3.3%	3.3%	2.6%	3.0%	3.1%	22.4
United Kingdom	58,305	15.7%			1,013	14.4%			15.1%			17.5
Total	370,349	100.0%	100.0%	100.0%	7,015	100.0%	100.0%	100.0%	100.0%	100.0%	100.0%	19.38 (avg.)
Total (Opt-Out 1)	312,044				6,002							
Total (Opt-Out 2)	306,853				5,859							

KEY = Opt-out Option 1 (EU-14) assumes the U.K. would not participate in the EMU.
Opt-out Option 2 (EU-13) assumes the U.K. and Denmark would not participate in the EMU.

Source: Population: "European Marketing Data & Statistics," Euromonitor International, London, 1995, p.121; and GDP and GDP per capita: "Consumer Europe," Euromonitor International, London, 1995, p.30.

Scenario # 1: An EU-15 with 7 ECB Districts and 13 ECB Governing Council Votes

Each district=1 vote; ECB (6-member) Executive Board=6 votes; Total ECB Governing Council votes=13

District NO.	Member nations	Pop. in %	GDP in %	Pop + GDP in %	ECB Gov. Council Votes (% votes)
#1	Germany	22.1	25.9	24.0	1 (7.7%)
#2	France	15.6	18.8	17.2	1 (7.7%)
#3	Italy	15.4	14.2	14.8	1 (7.7%)
#4	U.K.	15.8	14.4	15.1	1 (7.7%)
#5	Spain, Portugal, Greece	16.0	9.0	12.5	1 (7.7%)
#6	Benelux, Austria, Ireland	10.0	11.5	10.8	1 (7.7%)
#7	Sweden, Denmark, Finland	5.1	6.3	5.7	1 (7.7%)
ECB (6-member) Exec Board	-	-	-	-	6 (46.2%)
TOTAL	-	100%	100%	100%	13

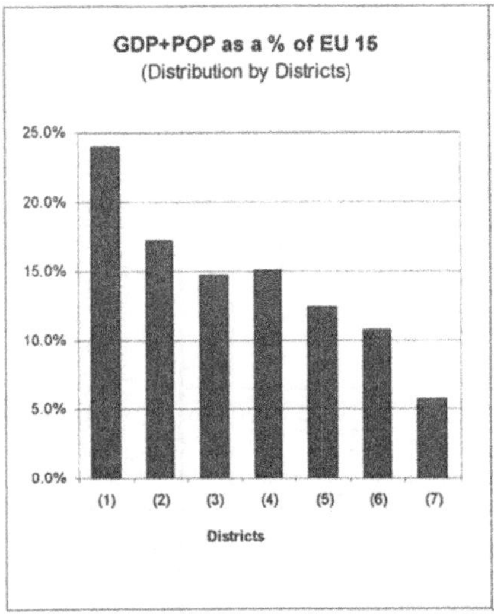

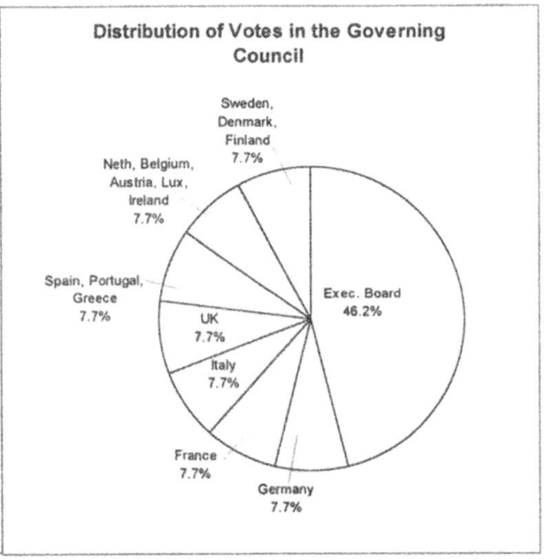

There would be seven districts with each receiving one vote. The four largest economies, Germany, France, the U.K. and Italy, receive their own districts. It should be noted that Germany's population and economic strength far outweigh its one vote. The other nations could either have one representative for their joint district or engage in annually alternating voting within their district. Although Spain is the fifth largest economy, its population is half that of Germany's and its GDP half that of Italy's, and thus it would have to share a district.

Overall, this is not an optimal arrangement, as the seven districts vary significantly in population and economic output. For example, District #1 (Germany) represents 22.1% and 25.9% of the total EU population and GDP, respectively, while District #7 (Sweden, Denmark and Finland) represent only 5.2% and 6.3%. Not only is Germany's population larger than the total of ten nations, but its GDP is roughly equivalent to that of three Districts (#5, #6 and #7) or 11 nations. Thus, if every district received one vote, certain smaller districts would be over-represented and Germany would probably object to this arrangement. The nations in District #7, #6 and #5, would have the most to gain.

ECB Governing Council: Despite the inequitable representation of the large nations on the Council, District #1 (Germany) plus the Executive Board achieve a majority of 53.9% in the Council and, thus, could pursue strict anti-inflationary monetary policies.

Scenario # 2: An EU-15 with 7 ECB Districts an 14 ECB Governing Council Votes

Each district=1 vote; except Germany=2 votes; ECB (6-member) Executive Board=6 votes; Total ECB Governing Council votes=14

District NO.	Member nations	Pop. in %	GDP in %	Pop + GDP in %	ECB Gov. Council Votes (% votes)
#1	Germany	22.1	25.9	24.0	2 (14.3%)
#2	France	15.6	18.8	17.2	1 (7.1%)
#3	Italy	15.4	14.2	14.8	1 (7.1%)
#4	U.K.	15.8	14.4	15.1	1 (7.1%)
#5	Spain, Portugal, Greece	16.0	9.0	12.5	1 (7.1%)
#6	Benelux, Austria, Ireland	10.0	11.5	10.8	1 (7.1%)
#7	Sweden, Denmark, Finland	5.1	6.3	5.7	1 (7.1%)
ECB (6-member) Exec Board	-	-	-	-	6 (42.9%)
TOTAL	-	100%	100%	100%	14

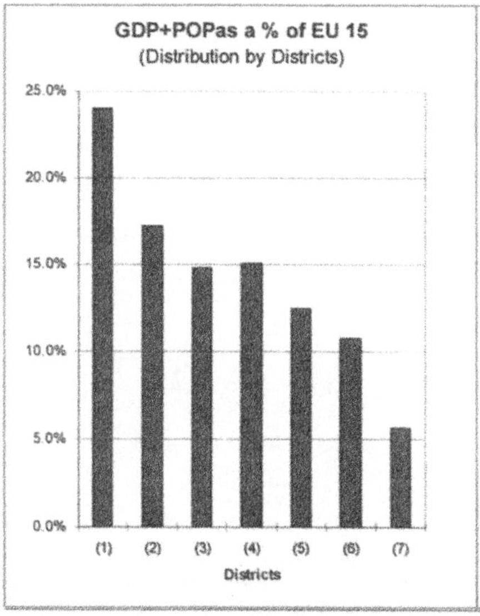

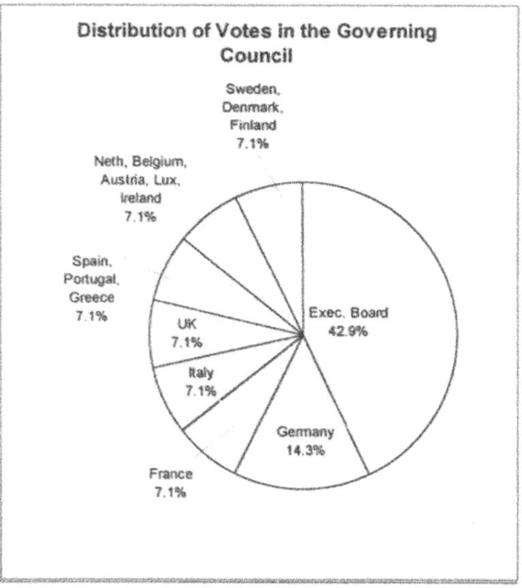

There would be seven districts with each district receiving one vote except for District #1 (Germany) which receives two. The four largest economies, Germany, France, the U.K. and Italy, receive their own districts. The other nations could either have one representative in their joint district or conduct annually alternating voting within the district. Under this arrangement, District #1 (Germany) would obtain a more equitable representation with two votes.

ECB Governing Council: District #1 (Germany) and the Executive Board achieve a clear majority of 57.2% within the Council. Thus, as in Option #1, strict anti-inflationary monetary policies could be enforced.

Scenario # 3: An EU-15 with 7 ECB Districts and 21 ECB Governing Council Votes

Each district=2 votes; except Germany=3 votes, Spain and Netherlands have permanent votes, others rotate; ECB (6-member) Executive Board=6 votes; Total ECB Governing Council votes=21

District NO.	Member nations	Pop. in %	GDP in %	Pop + GDP in %	ECB Gov. Council Votes (% votes)
#1	Germany	22.1	25.9	24.0	3 (14.3%)
#2	France	15.6	18.8	17.2	2 (9.5%)
#3	Italy	15.4	14.2	14.8	2 (9.5%)
#4	U.K.	15.8	14.4	15.1	2 (9.5%)
#5	Spain, Portugal, Greece	16.0	9.0	12.5	2 (9.5%)
#6	Benelux, Austria, Ireland	10.0	11.5	10.8	2 (9.5%)
#7	Sweden, Denmark, Finland	5.1	6.3	5.7	2 (9.5%)
ECB (6-member) Exec Board	-	-	-	-	6 (28.6%)
TOTAL	-	100%	100%	100%	21

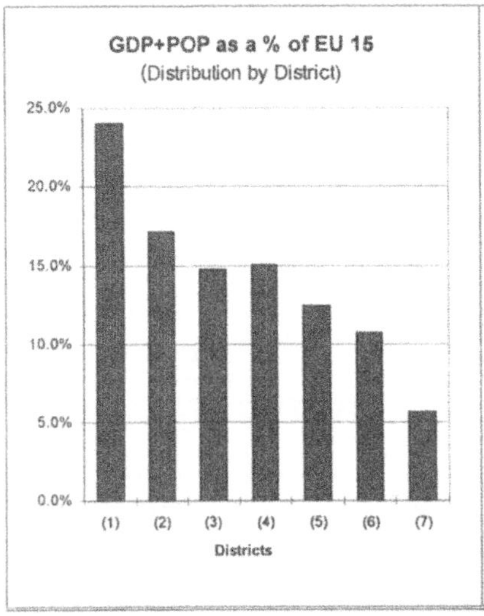

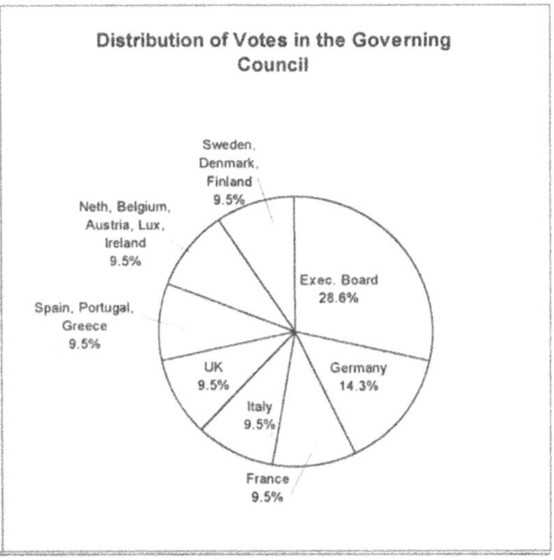

There would be seven districts with each district receiving two votes except District #1 (Germany) which receives three. The four largest economies, Germany, France, the U.K. and Italy obtain their own district. The other nations could either have one representative in their joint district or engage in annually alternating voting. Spain and the Netherlands would each receive one permanent vote in their respective Districts (#5 and #6, respectively).

ECB Governing Council: District #1 (Germany) and the Executive Board would not be able to achieve a majority in the Council and would have to enlist the help of at least one other district to ensure an anti-inflationary monetary policy stance.

Scenario # 4a: An EU-15 with 6 ECB Districts and 18 ECB Governing Council Votes

Each district=2 votes; Italy, Spain and Netherlands have permanent votes, others rotate; ECB (6- member) Executive Board=6 votes; Total ECB Governing Council votes=18

District NO.	Member nations	Pop. in %	GDP in %	Pop + GDP in %	ECB Gov. Council Votes (% votes)
#1	Germany	22.1	25.9	24.0	2 (11.1%)
#2	France	15.6	18.8	17.2	2 (11.1%)
#3	U.K.	15.8	14.4	15.1	2 (11.1%)
#4	Italy, Belgium, Austria	20.2	20.1	20.2	2 (11.1%)
#5	Netherlands, Sweden, Denmark, Finland, Luxembourg	9.3	11.2	10.3	2 (11.1%)
#6	Spain, Portugal, Greece, Ireland	17.0	9.7	13.4	2 (11.1%)
ECB (6-member) Exec Board	-	-	-	-	6 (33.3%)
TOTAL	-	100%	100%	100%	18

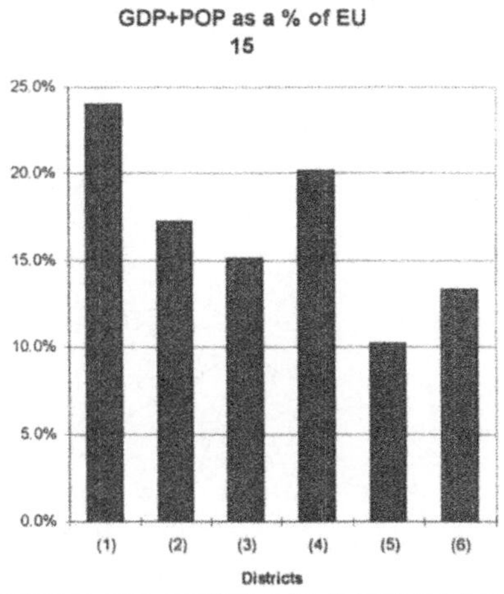

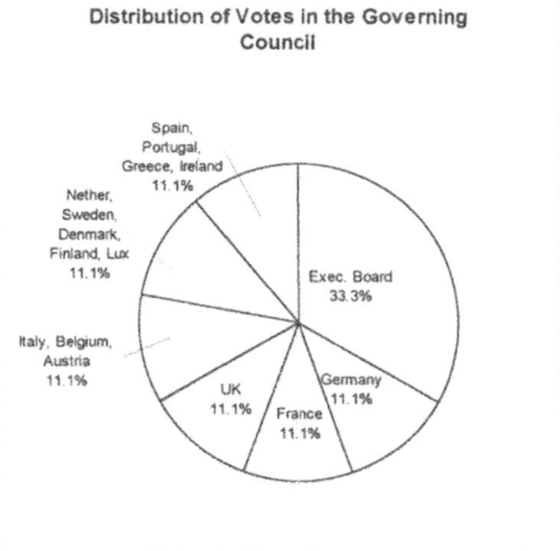

There would be six districts and each district would receive two votes. The three largest economies, Germany, France, and the U.K., obtain their own district. The other nations could either have one representative in their collective districts or conduct annually alternating voting. Italy, Spain and the Netherlands would each receive one permanent vote in their respective Districts (#4, #5 and #6, respectively).

ECB Governing Council: District #1 (Germany) and the Executive Board would not be able to achieve a majority in the Council and would have to enlist the help of at least one other district to ensure strict anti-inflationary monetary policies.

Scenario # 4b: An EU-15 with 6 ECB Districts and 18 ECB Governing Council Votes

Each district=2 votes; Spain and Netherlands have permanent vote, others rotate; ECB (6-member) Executive Board=6 votes; Total ECB Governing Council votes=18

District NO.	Member nations	Pop. in %	GDP in %	Pop + GDP in %	ECB Gov. Council Votes (% votes)
#1	Germany	22.1	25.9	24.0	2 (11.1%)
#2	France	15.6	18.8	17.2	2 (11.1%)
#3	U.K., Belgium	19.5	17.6	18.6	2 (11.1%)
#4	Italy, Austria	17.5	16.9	17.2	2 (11.1%)
#5	Netherlands, Sweden, Denmark, Finland, Luxembourg	9.3	11.2	10.3	2 (11.1%)
#6	Spain, Portugal, Greece, Ireland	17.0	9.7	13.4	2 (11.1%)
ECB (6-member) Exec Board	-	-	-	-	6 (33.3%)
TOTAL	-	100%	100%	100%	18

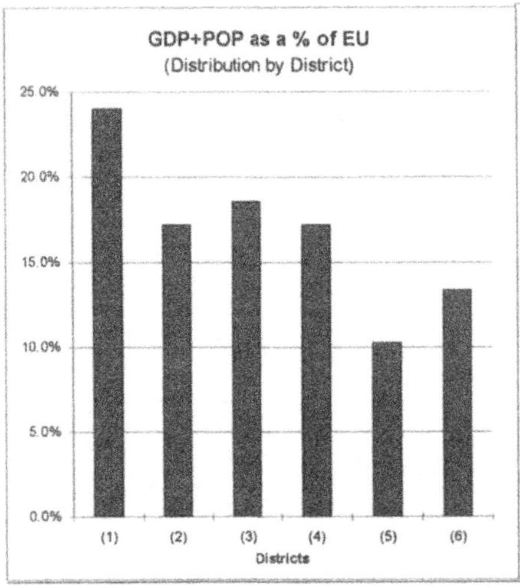

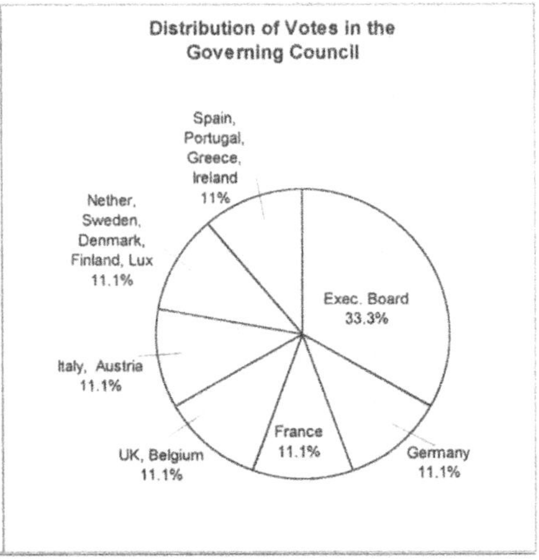

There would be six districts with each receiving two votes. The two largest economies, Germany and France, obtain their own districts. The other nations could either have one representative in their joint district or engage in annually alternating voting. Spain and the Netherlands each receive one permanent vote in their respective Districts (#5 and #6, respectively).

ECB Governing Council: District #1 (Germany) and the Executive Board would not be able to achieve a majority in the Council and would have to obtain the help of at least one other district to conduct strong anti-inflationary monetary policies.

Scenario # 5: An EU-15 with 5 ECB Districts and 16 ECB Governing Council Votes

Each district=2 vote; France, Italy, U.K., Spain have a permanent vote; Netherlands has a full vote every other year, others rotate; ECB (6-member) Executive Board=6 votes; Total ECB Governing Council votes=16

District NO.	Member nations	Pop. in %	GDP in %	Pop + GDP in %	ECB Gov. Council Votes (% votes)
#1	Germany	22.1	25.9	24.0	2 (12.5%)
#2	France, Benelux	22.5	26.9	24.7	2 (12.5%)
#3	Italy, Austria, Ireland	18.5	17.6	18.1	2 (12.5%)
#4	U.K., Sweden, Denmark, Finland	20.9	20.7	20.8	2 (12.5%)
#5	Spain, Portugal, Greece	16.0	9.0	12.5	2 (12.5%)
ECB EXEC (6-member) BOARD	-	-	-	-	6 (37.5%)
TOTAL	-	100%	100%	100%	16

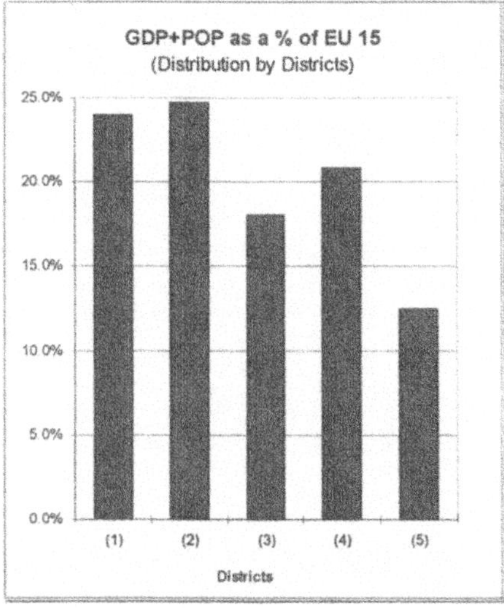

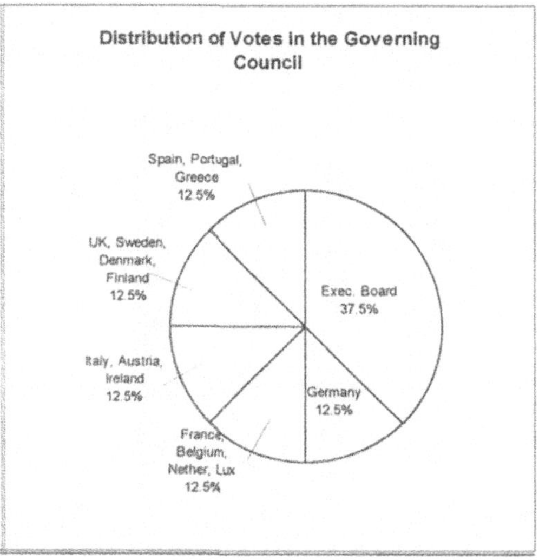

There would be five districts and each district would receive two votes while Germany receives its own district. The other nations could either have one representative in their joint district or engage in annually alternating voting. France, Italy, the U.K. and Spain each receive one permanent vote in their respective Districts (#2, #3, #4 and #5, respectively). The Netherlands receives a full vote every other year.

ECB Governing Council: District #1 (Germany) and the Executive Board represent 50% of the votes in the Council and would thus require the votes of another district or one other country with a permanent vote to ensure tough anti-inflationary monetary policies.

Scenario # 6: An EU-15 with 4 ECB Districts and 14 ECB Governing Council Votes

Each district=2 vote; France, U.K. and Spain have a permanent vote; Netherlands has a permanent vote every other year, others rotate; ECB (6-member) Executive Board=6 votes; Total ECB Governing Council votes=14

District NO.	Member nations	Pop. in %	GDP in %	Pop + GDP in %	ECB Gov. Council Votes (% votes)
#1	Germany, Austria	24.2	28.6	26.4	2 (14.3%)
#2	France, Benelux	22.5	26.9	24.7	2 (14.3%)
#3	U.K., Ireland, Sweden, Denmark, Finland	21.9	21.4	21.7	2 (14.3%)
#4	Italy, Spain, Portugal, Greece	31.4	23.2	27.3	2 (14.3%)
ECB (6-member) Exec Board	-	-	-	-	6 (42.9%)
TOTAL	-	100%	100%	100%	14

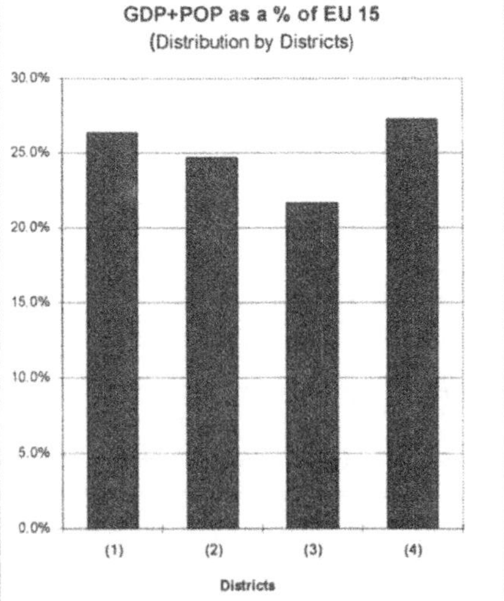

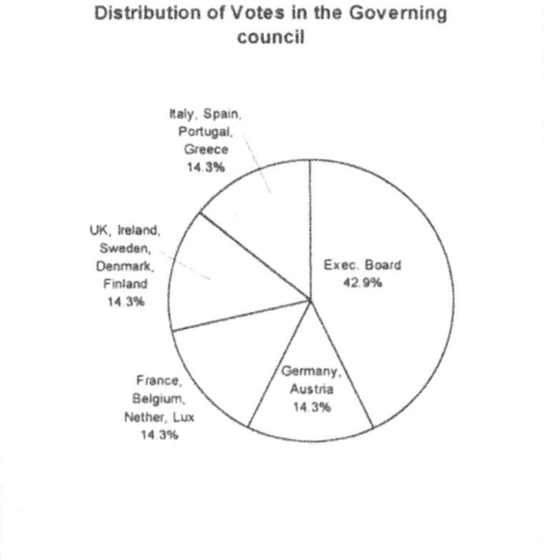

There would be four districts with two votes each. Nations could either have one representative in their joint district or engage in annually alternating voting. Germany, France, Italy, the U.K. and Spain each receives one permanent vote in their respective Districts (#1, #2, #3, #4 and #5, respectively) while the Netherlands and Austria receive a full vote every other year.

ECB Governing Council: District #1 (Germany and Austria) and the Executive Board would obtain a clear majority of 57.2% in the Council. This would ensure the pursuit of strong anti-inflationary policies.

Scenario # 7: An EU-14 (U.K. opt-out) with 6 ECB Districts and 18 ECB Governing Council Votes

Each district=2 vote; Spain has 1 permanent vote; Netherlands has a full vote every other year, others rotate; ECB (6-member) Executive Board=6 votes; Total ECB Governing Council votes=18

District NO.	Member nations	Pop. in %	GDP in %	Pop + GDP in %	ECB Gov. Council Votes (% votes)
#1	Germany	26.2	30.3	28.3	2 (11.1%)
#2	France	18.6	21.9	20.3	2 (11.1%)
#3	Italy	18.2	16.5	17.4	2 (11.1%)
#4	Spain, Portugal, Greece,	19.0	10.6	14.8	2 (11.1%)
#5	Netherlands Sweden, Finland, Ireland	10.3	11.3	10.8	2 (11.1%)
#6	Belgium, Luxembourg, Austria, Denmark	7.5	9.4	8.5	2 (11.1%)
ECB (6-member) Exec Board	-	-	-	-	6 (33.3%)
TOTAL	-	100%	100%	100%	18

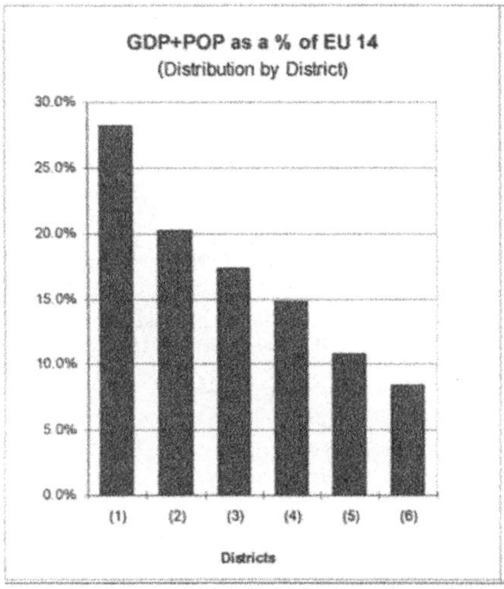

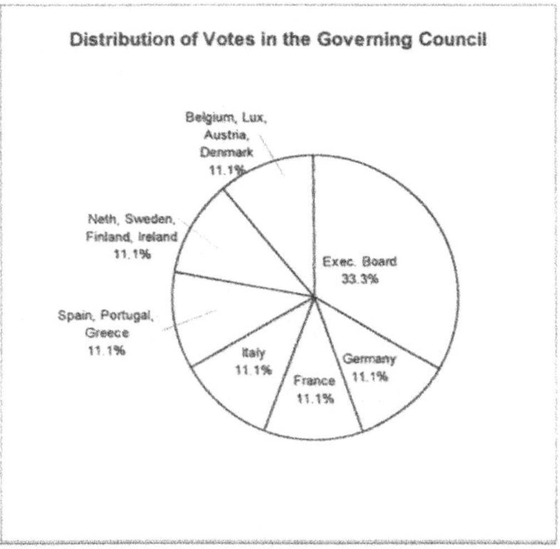

This assumes that the U.K. has opted out of the last stage of the EMU. There would be six districts with two votes each. The three largest economies, Germany, France, and Italy, receive their own districts. The other nations could either have one representative in their joint district or engage in annually alternating voting. Spain receives one permanent vote within its District (#4) and the Netherlands would receive a full a vote every other year.

ECB Governing Council: District #1 (Germany) and the Executive Board represent less than a majority in the Council (44.4%) and would, thus require the votes of another district to ensure tough anti-inflationary monetary policies.

Scenario # 8: An EU-14 (U.K. opt-out) with 5 ECB Districts and 16 ECB Governing Council Votes

Each district=2 votes; Spain has a permanent vote, Netherlands has a full vote every other year, others rotate, ECB (6-member) Executive Board=6 votes; Total ECB Governing Council votes=16

District NO.	Member nations	Pop. in %	GDP in %	Pop + GDP in %	ECB Gov. Council Votes (% votes)
#1	Germany	26.2	30.3	28.3	2 (12.5%)
#2	France	18.5	21.9	20.2	2 (12.5%)
#3	Italy, Belgium, Austria	23.9	23.3	23.6	2 (12.5%)
#4	Netherlands, Sweden, Denmark, Finland, Luxembourg	11.1	13.1	12.1	2 (12.5%)
#5	Spain, Portugal, Greece, Ireland	20.1	11.4	15.8	2 (12.5%)
ECB (6-member) Exec Board	-	-	-	-	6 (37.5%)
TOTAL	-	100%	100%	100%	16

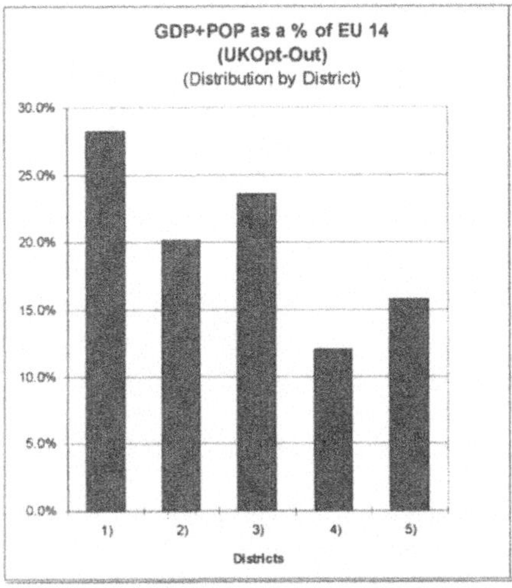

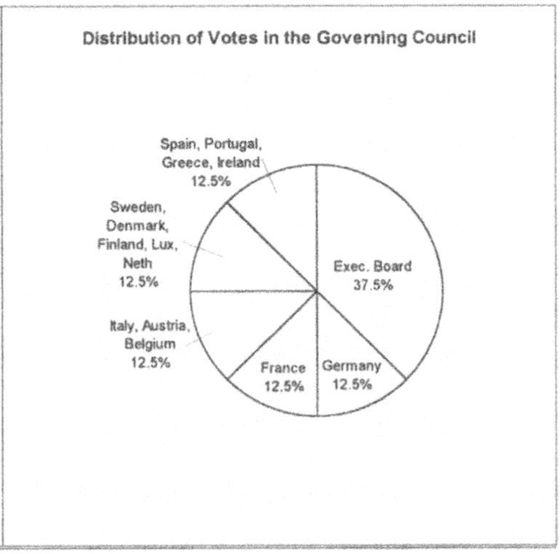

This assumes that the U.K. has opted out of the last stage of the EMU. There would be five districts with two votes each. The two largest economies, Germany and France, have their own districts. The other nations could either have one representative in their joint district or engage in annually alternating voting. Italy and Spain receive one permanent vote within their District (#3 and #4, respectively) and the Netherlands receives a full vote every other year.

ECB Governing Council: District #1 (Germany) and the Executive Board make up 50% of the votes in the Council. Although it is less than a majority and would thus, need the vote of another district, or one other country with a permanent vote to ensure strong anti-inflationary monetary policies, it could, however, stop any undesirable action by the Council.

Scenario # 9: An EU-13 (U.K. & Denmark opt-out) with 6 ECB Districts and 18 ECB Gov. Council Votes

Each district=2 votes; Spain and Netherlands has a permanent vote, others rotate; ECB (6-member) Executive Board=6 votes; Total ECB Governing Council votes=18

District NO.	Member nations	Pop. in %	GDP in %	Pop + GDP in %	ECB Gov. Council Votes (% votes)
#1	Germany	26.6	31.0	28.8	2 (11.1%)
#2	France	18.9	22.5	20.7	2 (11.1%)
#3	Italy	18.6	16.9	17.8	2 (11.1%)
#4	Spain, Portugal, Greece	19.4	10.9	15.2	2 (11.1%)
#5	Netherlands, Sweden, Finland	9.5	10.6	10.1	2 (11.1%)
#6	Belgium, Luxembourg, Austria, Ireland	7.2	8.1	7.7	2 (11.1%)
ECB (6-member) Exec Board	-	-	-	-	6 (33.3%)
TOTAL	-	100%	100%	100%	18

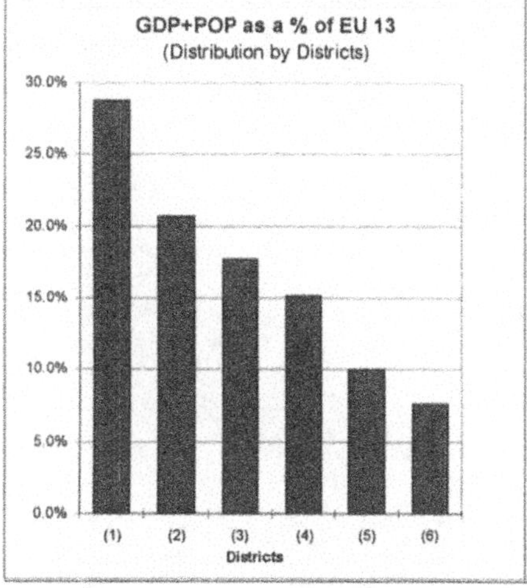

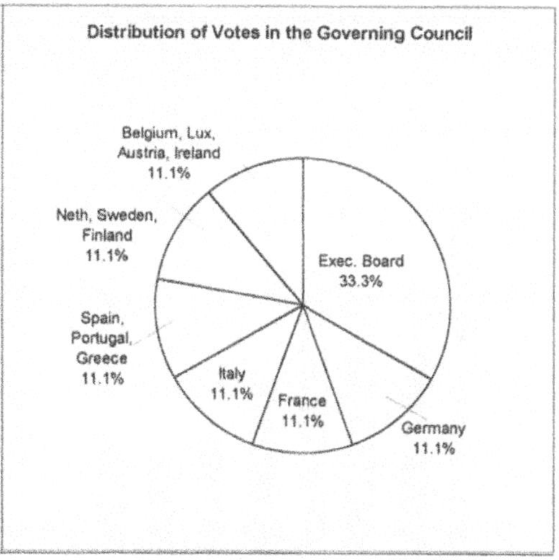

This assumes that the U.K. and Denmark have opted out of the last stage of the EMU. There would be six districts with two votes each. The three largest economies, Germany, France, and Italy, obtain their own districts. The other nations could either have one representative in their joint district or engage in annually alternating voting. Spain and the Netherlands each receive one permanent vote within their District (#4 and #5, respectively).

ECB Governing Council: District #1 (Germany) and the Executive Board make up less than a majority with 44.4% of the Council votes and would thus, need the votes of another district to assure tough anti-inflationary monetary policies.

<u>Scenario # 10:</u> An EU-17 with 8 ECB Districts and 14 ECB Governing Council Votes

Each district=1 vote; the Netherlands has a full vote every other year, others rotate; Italy, U.K., and Spain each have a veto power (within their districts); ECB (6-member) Executive Board=6 votes; Total ECB Governing Council votes=14

District NO.	Member nations	Pop. in %	GDP in %	Pop + GDP in %	ECB Gov. Council Votes (% votes)
#1	Germany	21.4	24.6	23.0	1 (7.1%)
#2	Italy, Greece	17.6	14.5	16.1	1 (7.1%)
#3	U.K., Ireland	16.2	14.4	15.3	1 (7.1%)
#4	France	15.2	17.8	16.5	1 (7.1%)
#5	Spain, Portugal	12.8	7.6	10.2	1 (7.1%)
#6	Benelux	6.8	7.6	7.2	1 (7.1%)
#7	Sweden, Denmark, Finland,	5.0	6.0	5.5	1 (7.1%)
#8	Austria, Switzerland, Norway	5.0	7.5	6.3	1 (7.1%)
ECB (6-member) Exec Board	-	-	-	-	6 (42.9%)
TOTAL	-	100%	100%	100%	14

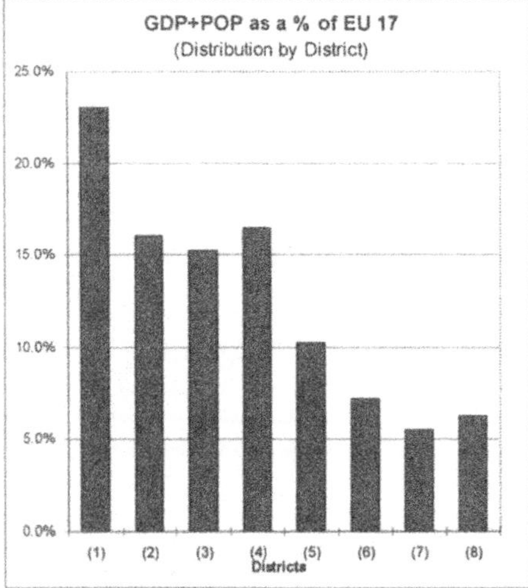

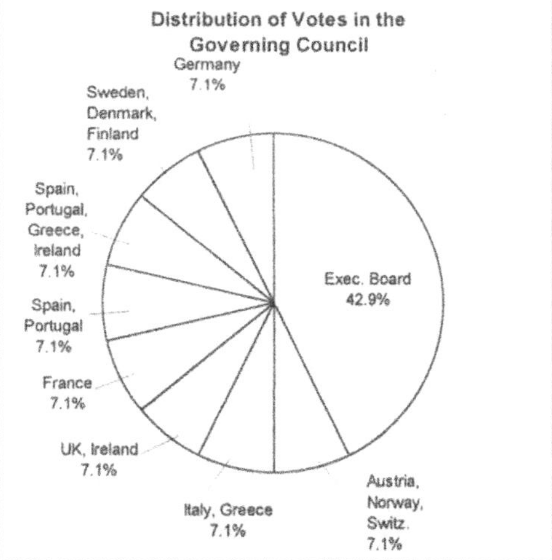

This assumes that Switzerland and Norway have joined the EU and are full participants of the EMU. There would be eight districts with each receiving one vote. The two largest economies, Germany and France, obtain their own districts. The other nations could either have one representative in their joint district or engage in annually alternating voting. The Netherlands has a full vote every other year. Italy, U.K., and Spain each have a majority vote (i.e. veto power) within their District (#2, #3 and #5, respectively).

ECB Governing Council: District #1 (Germany) and the Executive Board make up 50% of the vote in the Council. Although it is less than a majority and would thus, need the vote of another district to assure tough anti-inflationary monetary policies, it could, however, stop any undesirable action by the Council.

Scenario # 11: An EU-32 with 10 ECB Districts and 16 ECB Governing Council Votes

Each district=1 vote; the Netherlands has a full vote every other year, others rotate; Italy, U.K., and Spain each have a veto power (within their districts); ECB (6-member) Executive Board=6 votes; Total ECB Governing Council votes=13

District NO.	Member nations	Pop. in %	ECB Gov. Council Votes (% votes)
#1	Germany	15.9	1 (6.25%)
#2	Italy, Greece	13.1	1 (6.25%)
#3	U.K., Ireland	12.0	1 (6.25%)
#4	France	11.2	1 (6.25%)
#5	Spain, Portugal	9.5	1 (6.25%)
#6	Benelux	5.0	1 (6.25%)
#7	Sweden, Denmark, Finland, Norway, Latvia, Lithuania, Estonia	6.1	1 (6.25%)
#8	Austria, Switzerland, Hungary, Slovenia, Croatia	6.2	1 (6.25%)
#9	Poland, Czech Republic, Slovak Republic	10.6	1 (6.25%)
#10	Romania, Bulgaria, Serbia, Albania, Bosnia, Macedonia	10.3	1 (6.25%)
ECB (6-member) Exec Board	-	-	6 (37.5%)
TOTAL	-	100%	16

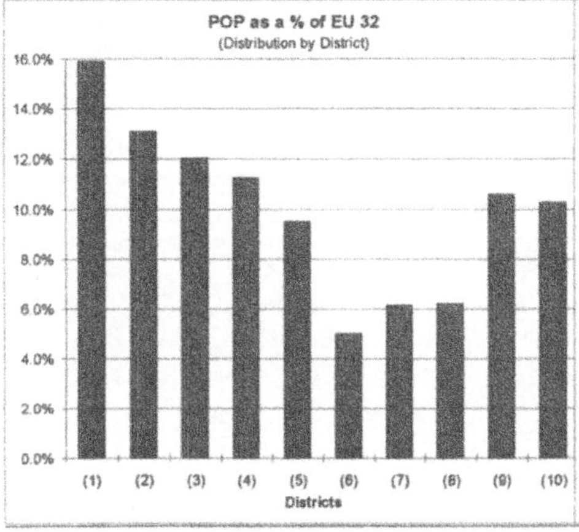

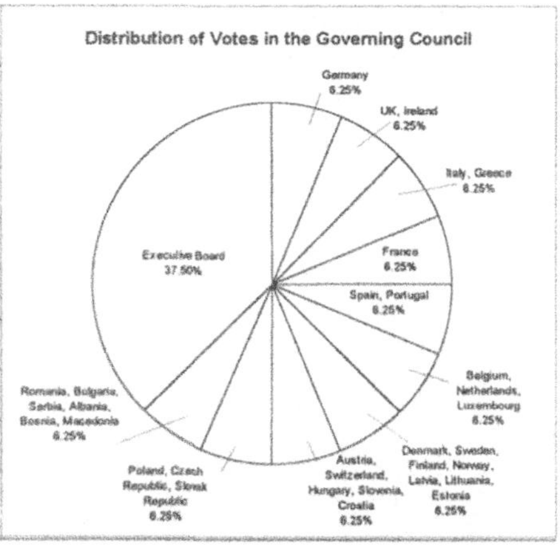

This assumes a significantly enlarged EU with all the above listed countries participating in the EMU. There would be ten districts with each receiving one vote. The two largest economies, Germany and France, obtain their own districts. The other nations could either have one representative in their joint district or engage in annually alternating voting. The Netherlands has a full vote every other year. Italy, U.K., and Spain each have a majority vote (i.e. veto power) within their District (#2, #3 and #5, respectively).

ECB Governing Council: District #1 (Germany) and the Executive Board do not represent a majority with only 43.75% of the vote in the Council and would thus, need the votes of two other districts to assure tough anti-inflationary monetary policies. But the assumed 17 additional new member countries can not obtain a majority on the Council.

Scenario # 12: An EU-34 with 10 ECB Districts and 16 ECB Governing Council Votes

Each district=1 vote; the Netherlands and Spain have a full vote every other year, others rotate; the U.K. and Italy each have a veto power (within their districts); ECB (6-member) Executive Board=6 votes; Total ECB Governing Council votes=13

District NO.	Member nations	Pop. in %	ECB Gov. Council Votes (% votes)
#1	Germany	14.2	1 (6.25%)
#2	Italy, Greece	11.7	1 (6.25%)
#3	U.K., Ireland	10.7	1 (6.25%)
#4	France	10.0	1 (6.25%)
#5	Spain, Portugal, Malta	8.5	1 (6.25%)
#6	Benelux	4.5	1 (6.25%)
#7	Sweden, Denmark, Finland, Norway, Latvia, Lithuania, Estonia	5.5	1 (6.25%)
#8	Austria, Switzerland, Hungary, Slovenia, Croatia, Romania, Macedonia	9.9	1 (6.25%)
#9	Poland, Czech Republic, Slovak Republic, Serbia	11.3	1 (6.25%)
#10	Turkey, Bulgaria, Albania, Bosnia	13.7	1 (6.25%)
ECB (6-member) Exec Board	-	-	6 (37.5%)
TOTAL	-	100%	16

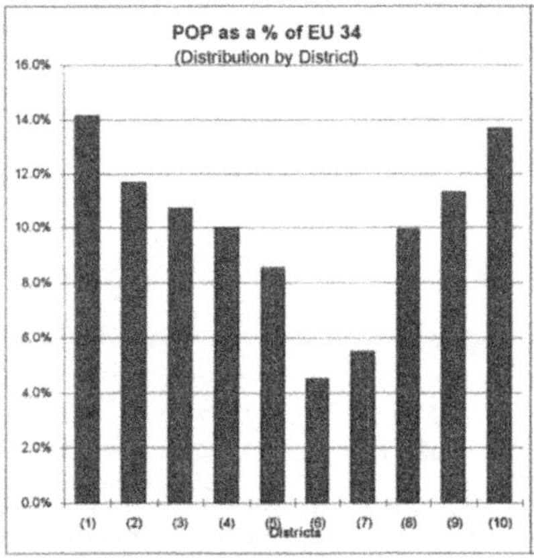

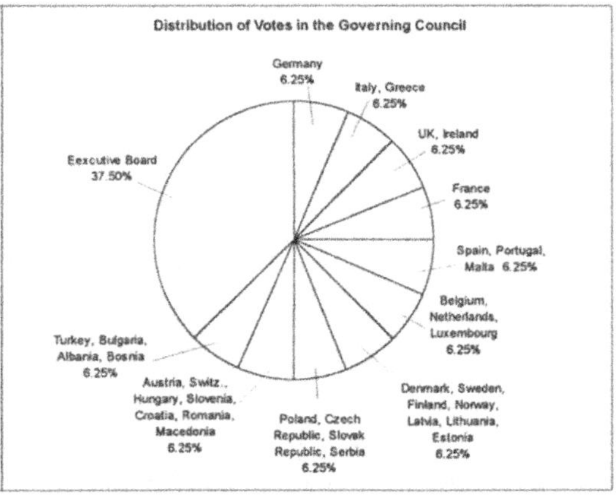

This assumes an even larger EU than Scenario #11 with the addition of Turkey and Malta participating in the EMU. There would be ten districts with each receiving one vote. The two largest economies, Germany and France, obtain their own districts. The other nations could either have one representative in their joint district or engage in annually alternating voting. The Netherlands and Spain have a full vote every other year. The U.K. and Italy each have a majority vote (i.e. veto power) within their District (#2, and #3, respectively).

ECB Governing Council: District #1 (Germany) and the Executive Board make up less than a majority in the Council. Although it is less than a majority and would thus, require the votes of three other districts to assure tough anti-inflationary monetary policies, it could, however, stop any undesirable action by the Council with the help of two other districts as they would have 50% of the vote. But the assumed 19 additional new member countries can not obtain a majority on the Council.

III FISCAL POLICY AND THE EMU

One of the critical issues involved in the continued integration of the EU is the fiscal policy implication of the EMU. The following discussion explores the relationship between fiscal policies and the economic and monetary integration process. Although the economic union and monetary union are two separate entities, in accordance with the Delors Report[1], the Maastricht Treaty called for a simultaneous pursuit of both.

The creation of an economic union is not a new idea. It was the premise on which the European Economic Community (EEC) was built in 1957. The EEC aimed at creating a common market providing for the eventual free movement of goods, services, capital and labor.[2]

An economic union is defined in the Delors Report as follows:

> *(1) the single market within which persons, goods, services and capital can move freely;*
> *(2) competition policy and other measures aimed at strengthening market mechanisms;*
> *(3) common policies aimed at structural change and regional development; and*
> *(4) macroeconomic policy coordination including binding rules for*

---

[1] The Committee for the Study of EMU. Report on Economic and Monetary Union in the European Community, Luxembourg: Office for Official Publications of the European Communities, 1989, paragraph 25. Also known as the Delors Report.

[2] These objectives are gradually achieved under the "Single Market," albeit with some ongoing limitations, in particular as they relate to the free movement of labor.

> *budgetary policies.*[3]

According to the Delors Report, a monetary union constitutes

> *a currency area in which policies are managed jointly with a view to attaining common macroeconomic objectives...there are three necessary conditions for a monetary union:*
> *(1) the assurance of total and irreversible convertibility of currencies;*
> *(2) the complete liberalization of capital transactions and full integration of banking and other financial markets; and*
> *(3) the elimination of margins of fluctuation and the irrevocable locking of exchange rate parities.*[4]

To date, it appears that EU member nations have embraced the monetary concept of the EMU. The national monetary policies pursued support this conclusion. Governments strive to sustain low levels of inflation amid slower economic growth and rising unemployment. In contrast, fiscal coordination as called for by the Treaty is not yet agreed to,[5] although it can be argued that it is fiscal policies that are critical to the realization and sustainability of the EMU. But budgetary and tax policies, unlike monetary policy, are far more politicized, and thus considerably more complex. The goals of monetary policy are better defined as, for example, keeping inflation within a predetermined range. Its policy tools are fewer and the scope of its functions is finite. In contrast, fiscal policies are more intricate, as they tend to be considerably more discretionary. There are, for example, many ways to manage resource allocations.

The Maastricht Treaty includes the Delors Reports definition of an economic union, as given at the beginning of this chapter. There is little disagreement concerning items (1) and (2) of this definition. Evidence suggests that the creation of an integrated market is beneficial to a regional economic bloc, as it introduces and enforces competitive conditions throughout the region. However, the full benefits of competition are obtained only if there is free movement of goods, services, capital and labor. Currently, the "Single Market" does not meet such requirements. Not only is labor mobility limited, but politically sensitive legislation is needed to ensure more integration, among others of the EU, taxation and common external economic policies.

Although EMU enthusiasts argue that elements (3) and (4) of the economic union definition are neither controversial nor particularly significant, they do raise problems. The third element, referring to common structural changes and regional

---

[3] The Delors Report, 1989, paragraph 25.

[4] The Delors Report, 1989, paragraph 22.

[5] To date, the only agreements on fiscal matters concern the Maastricht Treaty's two fiscal convergence criteria needed to enter Stage III of the EMU and the 1996 post-EMU fiscal "stability and growth pact" sanctions to be imposed for non-compliance.

development policies, is controversial. The purpose of the changes and of the development policies is to promote equity (i.e., more equal income distribution) as opposed to efficiency, and thus such policies are associated with "fiscal federalism"[6] and/or "fiscal shock absorbers."[7] The fourth element, calling for non-voluntary, binding and coordinated national budgetary policies,[8] is politically the most controversial part of the economic union as envisioned in the Delors Report and stated in the Maastricht Treaty.

It is not clear whether economic and monetary integration should be pursued in parallel, and whether under the EMU fiscal policy should be managed in the same manner as monetary policy. It is generally accepted that the irrevocable locking of exchange rates and, ultimately, the introduction of the single currency, require an institutional framework for the conduct of a common monetary policy. However, there is considerable debate about the need for a similar institutional framework to manage national fiscal policies.

The Delors Report emphasizes that "economic and monetary union form two integral parts of a single whole and would therefore have to be implemented in parallel."[9] This recommendation was the result of a political compromise, as are most major EU decisions. The call for parallelism in the EMU implies not only that the benefits of economic and monetary integration are mutually supportive but also that, through synergy, they generate more economic benefits. However, there is not much discussion of how to pursue and, in particular, how to measure and compare, the extent of monetary versus economic integration so as to judge parallelism. Given the political and economic realities of the EU and the interdependence of monetary and fiscal policies, the two kinds of processes cannot be separated and sustained independently.

In addition to the difficulties of designing fiscal systems, one of the problems of regional economic integration is the division of functions among supranational and national institutions. This is particularly true for fiscal restraints (i.e., binding budgetary guidelines) and/or fiscal federalism, both of which the authors of the Maastricht Treaty have identified as essential to the smooth functioning of the EMU. Fiscal restraints such as binding budgetary constraints are represented by the Treaty's two fiscal convergence criteria (or reference values) which are prerequisites to taking the third and final step toward the EMU. The upper limit of the budget deficit/GDP ratio is set at 3 percent and that of the debt/GDP ratio at 60 percent. It should be noted that the Treaty makes

---

[6] The philosophy of fiscal federalism maintains that economic efficiency plays only a partial role in the provision of public goods and services.

[7] Fiscal shock absorbers are common mechanisms to help national governments weather the impact of country-specific shocks in the absence of monetary and exchange rate policy tools.

[8] The term fiscal and/or budgetary policy coordination refers to larger, more general activities, while binding budgetary and/or fiscal policies (also known as fiscal restraints) refer specifically to the public debt and budget deficit convergence criteria (also known as reference values) of the Maastricht Treaty.

[9] Delors Report, 1989, paragraph 42.

inadequate provisions for fiscal federalism, owing to its politically controversial impact on income redistribution throughout the EU.

As mentioned before, the philosophy of fiscal federalism maintains that economic efficiency is only partially important in the provision of public goods and services. According to the spirit of the EMU, the promotion of overall welfare is not only a national or regional (the subsidiarity principle) but also a common consideration. But fiscal systems are primarily justified by political considerations and often tend to be as diverse as they are complex. Under the EMU, national monetary policies will be transformed into a common monetary policy managed by the European Central Bank (ECB). But what is uncertain, and more controversial, are the EMU's implications for fiscal policies. The Maastricht Treaty is important not only in terms of what it says about such policy, but also in terms of what it does not say. Yet, what matters in the end is whether the omissions are fatal flaws or political necessities and why they occurred. Table 3.1 shows the fiscal and public finance effects of the EMU as summarized in the 1990 EU Commission study, "One Market, One Money."[10]

Table 3.1
Summary of the Fiscal and Public Finance Effects of EMU

		Monetary Union (I)	Economic Union (II)	Aggregate Effect In The Medium Term (I+II)
1.	**FISCAL POLICY**			
a)	Need for autonomy	increases	decreases	increases
b)	Need for discipline	increases	neutral	increases
c)	Incentives to discipline*	+/-	+/-	+/-
d)	Need for coordination	increases	increases	increases
2.	**GOVERNMENT INCOME AND EXPENDITURE**			
(a)	Seigniorage revenues	decreases	decreases	decreases
(b)	Debt service	decreases	+/-	decreases
(c)	Tax revenue**	neutral	decreases	decreases
(d)	Provision of public goods**	neutral	decreases	decreases
	GOVERNMENT BALANCE (a+c-b-d)****	increases	+/-	+/-

KEY = * = Without specific community budgetary rules.
** = Without coordination.
*** = Increase means increased budget surplus.

Source: "One Money, One Market : An Evolution of the Potential Benefits and Costs of Forming an Economic and Monetary Union." European Economy, No.44, Commission of the European Communities Directorate-General for Economic and Financial Affairs, October 1990, p.101.

[10] "One Market, One Money : An Evolution of the Potential Benefits and Costs of Forming an Economic and Monetary Union." European Economy, No.44, Commission of the European Communities Directorate-General for Economic and Financial Affairs, October 1990.

FISCAL COORDINATION AND BINDING CONSTRAINTS

The Need for Fiscal Coordination[11]

Ever since the formation of the EEC, the economic rationale for fiscal coordination has been a source of debate, yet to date fiscal policy coordination per se has not been a topic of concern among the EU nations.[12] It has been discussed only with respect to the containment of budget deficits and public debt. Yet, fiscal policy coordination is an idea whose time has come. Since the signing of the Maastricht Treaty a series of events such as the 1995 dollar crisis has led the G-7 to the conclusion that stronger fiscal policy coordination and surveillance is desirable. In the past, the domestic budgetary policies of industrialized countries have been influenced only in a limited fashion by external factors such as the movement of currency exchange and interest rates under flexible and/or semi-pegged exchange rate systems. However, recently the financial markets have started to pay more attention to national budgetary policies as one of the key factors affecting exchange rate movements, rather than the other way around.

But reliance on the financial markets to enforce fiscal discipline is not sufficient. Therefore, EMU supporters have taken the position that fiscal and monetary policies must be coordinated. Such coordination can take many forms, and may be informal and implicit or formal and negotiated. In the case of the EMU, the Maastricht Treaty authors have concluded that both monetary and fiscal coordination should be formal and negotiated. Inflation and interest rate convergence criteria, as well as fiscal restraints such as binding budgetary guidelines, must be established.

Although there is little opposition to monetary coordination, there is significant resistance to fiscal coordination through restraints. Opponents of fiscal restraints argue that once independent monetary policy is given up under the EMU, fiscal policies will become more important. Fiscal flexibility is necessary to compensate for the loss of monetary policy autonomy, because EMU member nations will continue to experience differing macroeconomic imbalances. However, as pragmatic as these arguments are, there are equally, if not more, convincing arguments supporting coordinated fiscal policies. This view, supported by Brussels and incorporated into the Maastricht Treaty, maintains that to ensure the smooth functioning of the monetary union, fiscal policies must be harmonized. EMU member nations have to protect themselves against spill-over effects and require a cushion against internal and external shocks. If some EMU member nations incur large budget deficits, this would distort

---

[11] This section is based on the EC Commission publication "One Market, One Money, 1990."

[12] The ERM/EMS is viewed as a mechanism for monetary and exchange rate coordination only as it was set up to promote inflation and interest rate convergence.

intra-EMU real exchange rates, place upward pressure on interest rates and subvert the ECB's commitment to price stability. Hence, the Maastricht Treaty convergence criteria call for reference values that specify quantitative standards against which fiscal performance can be judged.

The Treaty gives both existing and yet-to-be-created common institutions the responsibility to monitor the fiscal policies of member states, to recommend adjustments and sanction on governments that do not heed the recommendations. Whether such provisions are necessary and sufficient to ensure appropriate fiscal policies has emerged as a contentious issue in the debate over the EMU. But fiscal coordination itself is no longer debated: it is viewed as mandatory because certain key EU nations such as Germany would not join the EMU without common fiscal restraints, let alone some form of overall fiscal coordination. In the view of the large nations, the EMU could promote fiscal laxity and allow weaker economies to "free-ride" on the stronger economies. The lack of fiscal restraints could also make the financial markets skeptical about the EMU's ability to sustain the required ECB policy of not "bailing out" high public debt nations -- especially if they happen to be politically influential member countries. This is specifically true given the rigid labor markets of the EU.

Spill-over Effects

The Maastricht Treaty requires monetary policy coordination through mandated rules and procedures, discusses the role of national fiscal policies and emphasizes the need for their coordination to mitigate potential spill-over effects. The magnitude of the impact of fiscal spill-overs are uncertain. Spill-overs could be positive, especially with the completion of the "Single Market." An increase in public spending by an EU nation could spur consumption of both domestic and foreign goods. The negative effect of such spill-overs might be higher domestic spending and consumption which could raise domestic and eventually foreign interest rates. The two outcomes are to some degree offsetting, but it is debatable to what extent this is the case. Whether the EMU would create a bias toward excessive deficits, monetization and inflation depends on its institutional and market structure.

EMU's cross-country spill-overs may manifest themselves: (i) in goods and capital market integration; (ii) common monetary policy which would eliminate "beggar-thy-neighbor" monetary and exchange rate policies but might increase spill-over effects that affect the common interest rate; and (iii) in common exchange rate policies against other currencies, which could be affected by the budgetary policy of any country.[13]

[13] With little or no coordination, the EU current account would become a "public good" for the member nations and would not be influenced by national economic policies.

Fiscal spill-overs can be assessed through (i) the short-term effects; (ii) the effects on the common EU current account and exchange rate; and (iii) the long-term changes in fiscal positions following the adjustment of relative prices. The short-term to medium-term (up to five years) impact is primarily related to aggregate demand -- that is, to growth and inflation.

The key spill-over effects are twofold: income and price effects caused by trade flows, and interest rate effects on demand. They can be analyzed using the Mundell-Fleming model, which assumes that economies characterized by sticky prices and unemployment are linked by goods and capital markets.[14] The more integrated national product markets are, the larger the spill-over effects of both demand and relative prices. Capital market liberalization under a fixed exchange rate regime (which increases capital mobility and asset substitutability) augments the effectiveness of domestic fiscal policies as access to global capital markets diminishes crowding-out effects.[15] But the same process reduces the "locomotive" function of fiscal policy abroad. Thus, under this model of free capital markets and high capital mobility, the domestic impact of fiscal policies on output under a fully flexible exchange rate system is minimized while under a fixed exchange rate system it is maximized.

Under a pure currency float with capital mobility, demand and competitiveness are affected. Fiscal expansion appreciates the currency which, in turn, increases the competitiveness of neighboring nations. However, under the asymmetric EMS/ERM, expansionary fiscal policies on the part of the anchor country, Germany, could result in "beggar-thy-neighbor" effects, because the income of the other member nations would be affected by German interest and exchange rate policies.[16] It has been argued that fiscal expansion in a non-anchor currency ERM member nation could serve as a "locomotive" for economic growth because it does not directly affect interest rates. However, past experience indicates that spill-over effects under the EMS/ERM system have tended to be unpredictable and ambivalent in their nature, magnitude and direction (i.e. sign). Germany's post-reunification fiscal experience illustrates this point. From a more-or-less balanced budget in 1989 (0.5 percent deficit/GDP ratio), the country's fiscal position shifted to a 3.3 percent deficit/GDP ratio in 1991 and 3.9 percent in 1996. As a result, other EU member nations have experienced an approximately 30 billion Ecu (US$36.9 billion) increase in import demand; this represented almost 1 percent of the combined GDP, exclusive of Germany.[17] To restrain the resulting inflationary pressures, Germany

---

[14] Although this model represents a standard framework for cross-country spill-over analysis, its simplified assumptions with regard to price and exchange rate determination have been modified over the years.

[15] For a small country, the crowding-out effects are more or less eliminated.

[16] Whether the overall spill-over effects of German expansion would be negative or positive is difficult to assess. However, the financial markets seem to assume that it would be mostly negative.

[17] Gros, Daniel and Niels Thygesen. European Monetary Integration : From the European Monetary System to European Monetary Union, London: Longman Group UK Ltd, 1992, p.273.

increased its interest rate. Through the ERM, this reduced demand in the other nations, leading to a recession which resulted in the 1992 and 1993 ERM currency crises. Thus, in the long run, Germany's expansionary fiscal policies may not have benefited the other EU nations.

Under the EMU, more emphasis is put on fiscal policies as domestic stabilization tools. The resulting impact on income, interest rates and the prevailing exchange rate regime determines the nature of the EMU spill-over effects. Because of the price stability objective of the EMU plan, the (+/-) signs of the fiscal policy spill-over effects are theoretically ambiguous; the monetary effect is about equal to the economic effect. However, despite the theoretical ambiguity, it is likely that under the EMU, as opposed to the EMS/ERM, German expansionary fiscal policies would be less "beggar-thy-neighbor" in their effect. Similarly, expansionary fiscal policies in non-anchor nations would perform less of a "locomotive" function. Table 3.2 shows the short-term spill-over effects of a bond-financed fiscal expansion under alternative exchange rate regimes.

Table 3.2
Short-Term Spill-Over Effects of a Bond-Financed Fiscal Expansion under Alternative Exchange Rate Regimes

Exchange Rate Regime	**Origin of Policy Move**	
	EMS/ERM anchor country	Other member countries
Float	+	+
EMS	+/- to -	++
EMU	+/-	+/-

Note: The signs refer to the impact of spill-over effects on the GDP of other member countries. In all regimes, full capital mobility is assumed and the currencies are supposed to float with respect to non-EU currencies. Monetary policy is assumed to be focused on price stability.
Source: Adopted from "One Market, One Money," 1990, p.115.

Simulation programs such as the IMF's "Multimod and Quest" have shown that in the EMU short-term fiscal policy spill-over effects would be generally modest, because they could be offset by changes in import growth as well as an increase in interest and exchange rates. For example, under the EMU as opposed to the EMS/ERM, a bond-driven fiscal expansion in Germany would result in greater domestic expansion and less external contraction because the common monetary policies would respond to the common economic conditions and not to only those in Germany.

Box 3.1 illustrates the IMF's "Multimod and Quest" model's simulation of the short-run fiscal policy spill-over effects. The results imply that because national fiscal policies have minimal spill-over effects, short-term and/or daily fiscal coordination is not required. However, not only is the IMF model biased by the assumption that full capital mobility exists and that fiscal growth under a clean floating exchange rate system would result in an exchange rate appreciation, but it is also affected by the assumption that no common monetary response would be made to the fiscal policies of individual countries.

Box 3.1
Shorter-Run Fiscal Policy Spill-over Effects

Model simulations can help to assess the sensitivity of spill-over effects to different exchange rate regimes. However, only some of the linkages are sensitive to the exchange rate regime. Demand effects in goods market caused by a bond-financed fiscal expansion are quite independent of the exchange rate regime. In contrast, interest rate and exchange rate linkages are a function of the exchange rate regime.

Table A
Spill-Over Effects of an Increase of Government Expenditures by 2% of GDP, (Multimod Simulation)

	Germany				France			
	Float	EMS	AEMU	EMU	Float	EMS	AEMU	EMU
GDP (first year effect)								
Germany	1.1	1.06	1.04	1.6	0.12	0.14	0.18	-0.16
France	0.06	-0.24	0.34	0	1.18	1.62	1.74	1.6
Italy	0.12	-0.24	-0.36	0	0.1	0.10	0.1	-0.08
United Kingdom	-0.02	-0.26	-0.32	-0.02	0.04	0.06	0.06	-0.1
Short-term interest rate (first year effect)								
Germany	0.2	0.26	0.26	0.18	0.12	0.12	0.1	0.14
France	0.18	0.4	0.26	0.18	0.28	-0.12	0.1	0.14
Italy	0.26	0.42	0.26	0.18	0.18	0.18	0.1	0.14
United Kingdom	0.26	0.42	0.26	0.18	0.14	0.14	0.1	0.14
Dollar exchange rate (first year effect)								
Germany	-2.2	-2.26	-2.28	-0.9	-0.44	-0.42	-0.3	-1.22
France	-0.48	-1.9	-2.28	-0.9	-3.26	-1.30	-0.3	-1.22
Italy	-0.38	-1.88	-2.28	-0.9	-0.28	-0.46	-0.3	-1.22
United Kingdom	-0.44	-1.84	-2.28	-0.9	-0.28	-0.42	-0.3	-1.22
Absorption deflator (fifth year effect)								
Germany	1.3	1.24	1.2	2.0	0.26	0.34	0.26	0.0
France	0.4	-0.34	-0.62	0.16	2.06	3.48	3.4	3.66
Italy	0.52	-0.44	-0.76	0.1	0.34	0.34	0.18	-0.34
United Kingdom	0.4	-0.22	-0.36	0.1	0.28	0.24	0.16	-0.14

KEY: Multimod simulations by the Commission services. Standard monetary policy. A decrease in the dollar exchange rate means appreciation. AEMU: asymmetric EMU.

Since the EMS/ERM is asymmetric, it is necessary to consider both the effects of a fiscal expansion in Germany and in another ERM member country, in this case, France. The asymmetry between the two countries is apparent in both the EMS/ERM and the asymmetric EMU, because a fiscal expansion in France has much smaller effects on the interest rate and the exchange rate than a fiscal expansion in Germany.

In a pure float regime, most of the effects of expansion are experienced by the country expanding, which experiences a rise in interest rates and an appreciation of its currency. Spill-over effects are mainly positive, but small.

In the EMS/ERM, a fiscal expansion in Germany is "beggar-thy-neighbor" in character and provokes disinflation in the other nations because interest rates increase in al of the ERM countries (although the fluctuation bands of the ERM allow for some offsetting of this effect). In contrast, French fiscal policy has a 'locomotive' character and has an inflationary effect in the other ERM countries because trade linkage effects dominate.

.....Box 3.1 continued on next page.....

.....Box 3.1 continued.....

The hypothetical "asymmetric EMU" is in between the EMS/ERM and the EMU. Since monetary policy is entirely set by Germany (without the flexibility that bands allow) the fiscal policy multiplier is higher than under any other regime in France. In contrast, the "beggar-thy-neighbor" effects of the German fiscal expansion are amplified. In the ERM/EMS price effects are also amplified.

In the EMU, the effects of a fiscal policy are qualitatively the same for Germany and France, since in both countries the reaction of the monetary authorities is identical. In the case of German expansion trade and interest rate linkages to offset each other almost entirely. In the French case, "beggar-thy-neighbor" effects dominate, but inflation spill-overs are small.

The spill-over effects conform to the results which can be obtained from an analysis using the standard Mundell-Fleming model. However, the results could be model-specific since the sign of the spill-over effects depends on the relative intensity of trade and financial linkages. Therefore, a Quest based simulation has also been carried out to determine the spill-over effects of a German fiscal expansion under an EMU regime setting the exogenous value of interest rates and exchange rates at levels consistent with the monetary policy reaction function and the open interest rate parity condition (Table B). With the same kind of monetary policy assumptions and exchange rates, the results confirm the small size of fiscal policy spill-over effects under the EMU.

Table B
Spill-over Effects of an Increase in German Fiscal Expenditures by 2% of GDP under the EMU
(Quest Simulation)

	GDP	Interest rate	Dollar exchange rate	Absorption* deflator
Germany	2.10	1.5	-2.7	4.5
France	0.14	1.5	-2.7	-1.5
Italy	0.18	1.5	-2.7	-0.9
United Kingdom	0.34	1.5	-2.7	-1.7

* First-year effect for GDP, interest rates and exchange rate. Fifth-year effects for absorption deflator. Interest rate and exchange rate effects are exogenous.
Source: Quest simulation by the Commission services.

Source: Adopted from "One Market, One Money," 1990, pp.116-17.

Under the EMU, member nations not only share a single currency but also have a common current account balance.[18] As long as this balance remains within acceptable ranges, there is no reason to promote fiscal coordination. However, when the current account deficit reaches undesirable levels, common monetary policies cannot correct the problem because of their opposite effects on foreign trade volumes and on currency appreciation. Thus, coordinated fiscal action becomes necessary. The fiscal

[18] Under the EMS/ERM, due to lack of fiscal coordination, there was a tendency toward a deflationary bias in nations with limited capital mobility or current account imbalances. Under the EMU, the common current account balance would diminish the influence of individual country current account balances on fiscal coordination.

policy adjustments by individual nations would be beneficial to the EU as a whole, but the costs of such actions would be borne by the individual nations. The Maastricht Treaty's fiscal convergence criteria cannot substitute for fiscal coordination. Nonetheless, they are better than the absence of any fiscal discipline that would lead to eventual coordination only in the event of severe symmetric or asymmetric shocks. Fiscal coordination measures must be in place before shocks occur not only to ensure a quick response to the crisis, but also to provide a sense of predictability so as to maintain stability in the financial markets.

In the short-run, fiscal spill-overs such as economic growth, unemployment and inflation are important. However, in the long run, persistent fiscal problems and their impacts on real interest rates and on the terms of trade are more relevant. For example, a nation's continual budget deficits can lead to higher real interest rates. Without a nominal exchange rate as an adjustment tool, the appreciation of the real interest rate in the deficit country will spill-over to its neighbors, worsening their terms of trade and supporting the argument for fiscal convergence criteria. The single currency generates similar changes in the terms of trade because of its changing value in relation to third country currencies such as the U.S. dollar. This requires intra-EU terms of trade adjustments through price changes rather than exchange rate adjustments.

In summary, establishing a proper policy mix under the EMU is imperative as national fiscal policies (national demand management) would have spill-over effects on other member nations. The nature, magnitude and direction (i.e., "sign") of such effects is unpredictable. Thus the need for a proper policy mix is reinforced, because past experience has shown that in absolute terms the effects are small and frequently negative. Their magnitude depends on the combination of domestic and external shocks with political circumstances. Table 3.3 shows the spill-over effects of a 2 percent of GDP rise in government expenditures, originating in either Germany or France.

Fiscal policy spill-over effects can also have an impact on the monetary union dimension of the EMU. The single currency can change the demand elasticity of intra-EU exports or the wage-price relationship. These arguments suggest that strict common fiscal constraints and procedures are appropriate for the sake of erring on the side of caution, as any instability, regardless of its origins, would shatter the credibility of the EMU.

Table 3.3
Spill-Over Effect of a 2 percent of GDP Rise in Government Expenditure in Germany or France

	Country originating the policy:	
	GERMANY	**FRANCE**
GDP:		
Germany	1.6	-0.16
France	0	1.6
Italy	0	- 0.08
U.K.	-0.02	0.1
Inflation:		
Germany	2.0	0
France	0.16	3.66
Italy	0.1	-0.34
U.K.	0.1	-0.14

Source: Gros, Daniel and Niels Thygesen. European Monetary Integration, London: Longman Group UK Ltd, 1992, p.274.

Budgetary Coordination

The coordination of short to medium-term budgetary policies under EMU does not require close, day-to-day supervision of national fiscal policies. The spill-overs do not substantially change prevailing economic conditions as long as the common exchange rate and current account are not subject to major external influences. If and when adjustments are required, they have to be coordinated efficiently. Any laxity would create serious spill-over effects, as it would deter some member nations from taking the required corrective actions, necessary for the common good, such as reducing expenditures.

But fiscal coordination is also needed to achieve and sustain an appropriate common policy mix, as the economic and political importance of national budgets far outweighs that of the relatively small EU common budget. The absence of fiscal coordination would force the ECB to develop an appropriate common policy mix, which in all probability would cause political disagreements concerning the ECB's role as an independent central bank with a mandate to maintain price stability.

Although day-to-day fiscal coordination is neither required nor desirable, a common action plan is needed to deal with external events. Prior agreements are necessary as external developments such as exchange rate movements may require immediate responses. The action plan affects national fiscal autonomy only to the extent that it calls for a change in common budgetary policies. Other changes depend on a nation's macroeconomic performance and its impact on the achievement of common economic objectives. The nations most affected would be those with undisciplined fiscal policies or strong economies.

Whether the lack of coordination in the EMU fosters short-term fiscal laxity and whether the repercussions of such laxity are of the "beggar-thy-neighbor" type, is an important issue. The answers are not obvious, especially in the short-term.[19] In the medium- to long-term, a prolonged deficit[20] used to sustain full domestic employment could cause spill-over effects in terms of higher real interest rates and worsening terms of trade. If there is no coordination and surveillance, such negative spill-over effects, assuming that they are not too large, could be overlooked.

In summary, although day-to-day fiscal coordination is neither required nor desired under the EMU, surveillance and coordination is needed to safeguard an appropriate common external policy mix in relation to the rest of the world (i.e., in relation to the common exchange rate and current account). Such coordination is also needed to reduce the likelihood of some nations "free-riding" on the corrective measures of others designed to curtail budget deficits in the medium-term.

Although it is widely accepted that the international coordination of macroeconomic policies is beneficial to the participating nations, the question of exactly what those gains are and what their extent is, continues to be controversial. Full coordination of exchange rate policies is desirable because under the EMU exchange rates are not available as policy instruments. Yet, even full coordination may be less beneficial than individual exchange rate adjustments. Such coordination is more beneficial under a flexible, and, to a lesser degree, under a semi-pegged exchange rate system. Thus, any EMU cost-benefit trade-off analysis must compare the cost of losing adjustment flexibility against the gains obtained from coordination. Prior to 1992, the EMS/ERM system, while it mandated cooperative exchange rate adjustments from the viewpoint of non-anchor nations, was also asymmetric and suboptimal whenever internal or external shocks had to be responded to.

Opponents of fiscal coordination argue that EMU's fixed exchange rate regime or single currency entails the loss of national monetary and exchange rate policies. Consequently, fiscal policies become the most important economic and political tools to respond to, particularly country-specific shocks. The opponents also point out that fiscal intervention by common institutions is unnecessary because the financial markets provide restraints on national budgets and thus eliminate the need for binding fiscal constraints. In contrast, supporters of fiscal coordination emphasize that historically financial markets have failed to enforce fiscal discipline.[21] To this, the

[19] Under a flexible or even a semi-pegged (i.e., ERM) system member nations pursuing employment and output gains by way of "real depreciation" create "beggar-thy-neighbor" conditions in the short-term.

[20] This assumes a protracted but not permanent deficit financed through higher taxes.

[21] For a detailed discussion of the influence of financial markets, see the section on "Fiscal

opponents of fiscal coordination respond that such coordination by Brussels is not like coordination at the national level because the EU budget represents only a little over 1 percent of the common GDP. They also argue that budgetary coordination by Brussels is of little significance when compared with the impact of the policies of large member nations[22] and claim that fiscal experience to date shows that agreements concerning the common budget are influenced by the composition of national budgets. In response, proponents of fiscal coordination emphasize that it is precisely because of this that there must be policy coordination among member nations so as to achieve a correct mix of monetary and fiscal policy pursued.

Apart from safeguarding against spill-over effects and providing a cushion against internal and external shocks, it is questionable whether policy coordination results in other gains. The welfare benefits of fiscal policy coordination are still unclear at best, and the absence of centralized budgets does not always result in policy mix imbalances. During much of the 1980s the United States ran a sizable federal deficit while the budgets of the 50 states were in an, albeit small surplus. Centralization of fiscal policies does not always provide the desired results.

The Need for Fiscal Discipline

The argument in favor of fiscal discipline rests on the use of intertemporal budget constraints -- that is, on the ability of national governments to sustain public debts over time to ensure solvency. Unsustainable budget deficits and public debt directly affect monetary policy because in the long run there is a great deal of interdependence between the two. This is best illustrated by a scenario in which continuous deficits, especially in the larger EMU nations, result in an erosion of the financial markets' confidence that places pressure on the single currency and on the ECB, which would be forced to consider either monetary policy adjustments or a "bail-out" scheme. At the extreme, the continuous deficits could result in unsustainable debts that would have to be monetized, bailed-out or defaulted. If this happened in an EMU member country lacking fiscal discipline, the result would be a challenge to the credibility of the ECB.

Insolvency problems of an EMU nation could have serious implications for the ECB and for the other member nations. In all probability, the ECB would "soften" its monetary policies, as any restrictions would exacerbate the budgetary problems, because an economic slowdown reduces tax revenues. Regardless of the degree of central bank independence, the mere fact that monetary tightening could result in a financial crisis is a de facto constraint on such independence. Monetary tightening brings with it a liquidity risk if the public debt includes short-term maturity or floating

---

Discipline in the EMU."

[22] Federal governments are relatively relaxed about regional/state budgetary policies because typically the federal budgets are 20 to 30 percent of GDP; this provides adequate policy leverage.

interest rate debt instruments. Under such conditions the financial markets may believe that the ECB will resort to inflation to alleviate the budgetary problem. This would immediately affect interest rates and the central bank's credibility. Thus, the budget deficits of one nation could affect the economies of the other EMU member nations.

Assuming that the ECB enforces a tight monetary policy regardless of budgetary implications, the country with the insolvency problem could resort to debt monetization or default or withdrawal from the EMU. Because no debt bail-outs are permitted, if the debt is denominated in the national rather than the single currency, withdrawal is more likely. This could create a credibility crisis for the EMU. Once the single currency is adopted as the sole legal tender, the EMU's credibility problem is magnified tenfold. Then debt monetization is no longer possible and either option mentioned above could lead to chaos in the financial markets.

The spill-over effects of an EMU member nation's economic policies could raise concerns about financial solidarity. Despite the repeated assertions of a "no bail-out" policy, there could be strong pressures to provide assistance. It could be disguised by the ECB by providing a loan that includes disproportionate share of the public bonds of the insolvent country. However, this would not only impair the credibility of the ECB's "no bail-out" policy but inadvertently increase the risk of insolvency in the other EMU nations. They could pursue undisciplined fiscal policies and pass on the burden to the stronger EMU member economies.

All of this reinforces the need for fiscal discipline in the EMU, in particular with respect to the management of public debt. The question is whether to achieve such discipline through the financial markets or through binding rules. But because national budget deficits arise out of different situations, no single set of rules may be appropriate. What might be an unacceptably high deficit or public debt for the EU as a whole, may be sustainable by an individual nation. For example, if the large current account deficit of an EMU member is caused by a lack of domestic savings and the ECB does not accommodate this shortfall, the common interest rate has to increase. This affects the exchange rate of the single currency or of the irrevocably locked national currencies against the dollar and the yen, and could increase the common current account deficit. Therefore, even if the deficit of the nation in question is sustainable, it has to be reduced for the common good. Similarly, a member nation's tight fiscal policies that generate large current account surpluses, not only at the country but also at the common level could result in unwanted exchange rate consequences. Thus, the definition of "sustainable fiscal deficits" continues to be a matter of judgment. This calls for continuous policy coordination and surveillance.

Although the public debt ratios of the EU member nations are high or increasing,[23] the sustainability of their budgetary policies is unclear. It depends on future tax revenues, government spending and other macroeconomic variables such as

[23] For example, Italy and Greece.

growth and the movement of real interest rates. In general, a nation's fiscal position is considered sustainable if the debt/GDP ratio is stable or decreasing.[24]

Fiscal Discipline in the EMU

Ever since the creation of the EEC in 1958, the enforcement of fiscal discipline was left to the national governments. However, under the EMU lack of fiscal discipline on the part of any member nation could affect all other nations. Thus, the Maastricht Treaty calls for fiscal constraints. The economic rationale and the effects of the constraints continue to be the subject of extended debates.

There are several arguments in favor of establishing binding budgetary constraints. The larger, wealthier economies such as Germany will commit themselves to the EMU only if they receive assurances that the common monetary policy and the single currency will not be derailed by the undisciplined fiscal policies of some other member nations. Thus, constraints for membership are the only prudent option for safeguarding the political and economic future of the EMU.

Fiscal coordination in general and the application of binding budgetary constraints in particular is an extremely difficult undertaking because it results in a loss of sovereignty and it affects domestic politics. Nonetheless, it is generally recognized that a good aggregate policy mix is beneficial to the EU as a whole. The common budget is a small percentage of the common GDP when compared with the share of the country budgets in the country GDPs. In other words, the common budget cannot make a contribution to an effective policy mix. Thus, while the Maastricht Treaty's binding budgetary constraints that impose upper limits on budget deficits and the public debt are necessary, it is difficult to rationalize the need for more fiscal symmetry at the common budget level in the name of pursuing an appropriate policy mix.

The management of monetary policies in tandem with fiscal policies is not only necessary at the domestic level but in today's integrated and interdependent global economy, is also required at the international level. Thus, coordinated monetary and fiscal policies are necessary regardless of the relevant rules of the Maastricht Treaty. Under flexible exchange rates, a country's budget deficit puts an upward pressure on interest and thus on exchange rates.[25] This crowds out private investments and if budget financing relies on foreign capital inflow, this could put additional upward pressures on the currency. If sustained over a period of time, this leads to trade imbalances. Thus, governments do not want to sustain large budget deficits; higher interest rates result in higher exchange rates, lower output and worsening trade balances. Not to mention the

---

[24] For a more detailed discussion of debt sustainability in the EU, see "One Market, One Money," 1990, pp.108-110.

[25] If the financial markets fear debt monetization, there could be downward pressures on the exchange rate. However, the interest rate would be subject to even greater upward pressures.

negative long-term impact on international competitiveness.[26]

The EMU could generate fiscal laxity in individual nations. There are those who argue that binding budgetary constraints are necessary to prevent this from happening. They point out that as long as national monetary policy still exists, coupled with irrevocably locked exchange rates, higher interest rates could limit the transmission of fiscal expansion. However, with fixed exchange rates or a single currency with common monetary policies (which would generate lower common interest rates), some of the budget constraints would be removed. This could make it easier for member nations to generate large deficits without a negative effect on their currencies or interest rates. Deficit countries could be encouraged to continue spending and borrowing as the cost of capital would be lower than if interest rates were domestically controlled. Because the effects would be disseminated, the negative impact on exchange rates, trade balances and output could be minimized. This is the argument that justifies fiscal discipline based on binding budgetary constraints to deter "free-riding" nations.

If governments come under strong political pressure to reduce fiscal deficits during difficult economic times, they might turn to monetizing their debt, preferring currency depreciation to debt consolidation. Under such circumstances the risk premium of monetizing the debt is reflected in high interest rates. But in a flexible exchange rate system the risk premium is absorbed mostly by the country affected. Under a fixed exchange rate or a single currency, the risk premium is spread across all nations – thus, in some sense rewarding fiscal laxity.

Lax aggregate fiscal policies over the long-run could negatively affect the EU's relations with the rest of the world. For example, there could be a downward pressure on the fixed exchange rate or single currency against other currencies such as the U.S. dollar or yen. Interest rates could be higher than those in other major industrialized economies and the EU's global trade balance could be negatively affected. In addition, the international competitiveness of EU industries could be reduced, particularly when compared with that of U.S. or Japanese industries.

When a common interest rate is introduced, countries with sound fiscal positions are penalized as they have to endure higher rates due to the fiscal laxities of other nations. It can, thus, be argued that under the EMU the impact of interest rates on national budgetary policies is augmented and that this calls for binding budgetary constraints.

To monitor potentially "free-riding" member nations, the EMU needs a centralized authority. Supervision by such an authority would be much less burdensome

---

[26] Borrowing in the capital markets to sustain interest payments on government debt leaves less capital for productive investments.

if binding budgetary constraints are imposed from the beginning,[27] particularly since the lessons of the 1992-93 ERM crises indicate that fixed exchange rates are difficult to sustain under strong political pressures generated by unsustainable budget deficits. These crises showed that narrow currency bands, let alone irrevocably fixed exchange rates, cannot be maintained under extreme pressures emanating from the financial markets. As budget deficits are a political reality, it is difficult to envision an unquestionable commitment to irrevocable exchange rates.

To date, the establishment and enforcement of fiscal discipline has been the responsibility of national politicians. However, under the EMU such responsibility will be transferred to common institutions. This is necessary, because the lack of fiscal discipline in one member nation, if unchecked, could affect all other nations. Hence, the EMU requires a set of binding budgetary constraints. What is debatable is the nature of such constraints.

Financial market liberalization has increased concerns about the ability of the markets to correctly evaluate default risk premiums and to properly respond to government borrowing. But there is no disagreement about the markets' ability to distinguish among sovereign borrowers. Yet, it is unclear whether, and to what extent, this makes a difference in sovereign borrowing ability. While it can be argued that higher debt burdens increase the cost of borrowing because of the increased credit risk, governments with high debt are not necessarily shut out of the markets. Past Eurobond financing experience suggests that there is no strong correlation between the maturity yields of identical public bonds and a borrower's budgetary position.[28]

The financial markets are also unable to assess and forecast the degree of government default risk. Cases in point are the Latin American debt crisis in the early 1980s, the 1987 world stock market crash, the 1990, Japanese financial problems, the 1992 pound sterling crisis, and the Mexican debacle of 1994-95. A partial explanation for the inability of the markets to assess and forecast the degree of risk is the inherent difficulty of assessing sovereign and institutional risk that is due to random shocks. Other explanations include the absence of prior experience, the difficulty in obtaining full and timely information, the possibility of a "bail-out" and the unreliability or inadequacy of the public borrowers' policy measures, such as the use of taxation to service the debt. It can, of course, be argued that under the EMU capital markets will be more integrated and will become more similar, which might make risk assessment easier. But even then the markets may not be able to exert fiscal discipline, because of expectations of assistance and/or inadequate responses by governments to market signals.

---

[27] To date, the budgetary imbalances of the smaller EU nations have been much more tolerated than those of the large countries. This, will not be the case in the EMU.

[28] For more details on this correlation, see the discussion of the case of Italian government bonds in "One Market, One Money," 1990, p.112.

The small size of the public debt of large EU countries in relation to the common GDP could also reduce the discipline exerted by financial markets. Moreover, there is little evidence to suggest that changes in credit ratings would cause governments to behave like private borrowers. In fact, experience shows that in most cases an increase in the cost of borrowing does not provoke the required fiscal adjustment, as public debt is a function not only of rational economic but also of political considerations and social consciousness.

Financial market discipline under the EMU will be influenced by the rules governing the behavior of the ECB and other common institutions. Implicit in these rules is adherence to the Maastricht fiscal convergence criteria such as the binding budgetary constraints,[29] efforts to avoid debt monetization, and a policy of not bailing out governments with high debts. It is, however, unclear whether Brussels would assist member nations experiencing acute country-specific shocks and, if so, to what extent this would weaken the EMU's fiscal discipline and credibility. There could be a system of temporal transfers with conditionality provisions so as to minimize the risk of moral hazard.[30]

For the financial markets to play a role in exerting fiscal discipline and in determining the sustainability of national debts, several conditions must exist. First, the role of national governments in relation to common institutions such as the ECB and the budget authorities has to be clearly defined. The common institutions should be financially independent; the structure, design, credibility and goals of the independent ECB should be observed without any conflicts and/or other influences. National debt maturities should be medium- to long-term and government regulators should refrain from exerting pressure on private agents to hold government securities or proclaim them to be risk free. Moreover, the financial markets should receive information about the public finances of all nations.

If the sustainability of national debt is questioned, the default risk should be reflected in a downgrading of government credit ratings, thus increasing the marginal cost of borrowing, which could result in a change of fiscal policies. But common fiscal rules, procedures and surveillance would still be indispensable, because member nations on the brink of default would not only affect other nations but could undermine the credibility of the EMU. Thus, there is a rationale for "bailing out" insolvent nations. But, the financial markets believe that the "no bail-out" rule is necessary to reinforce the negative image of undisciplined governments which, in turn, helps to preserve the credibility of the EMU. This prevents the financial markets from interpreting the EMU as a mechanism to upgrade the creditworthiness of weaker nations. Yet, political reality mandates some assistance in the classic situation of "you're damned if you do and

---

[29] Wyplosz, Charles. "Monetary Union and Fiscal Policy Discipline," European Economy, October 1990. The author argues that the EMU will make the budgetary constraints even tougher than the manner in which they are spelled out in the Treaty.

[30] For more details see "One Market, One Money," 1990, pp.136-77.

damned if you don't."

The EMU nations cannot use devaluations and inflation as a mechanism to reduce the real value of public debt. In the past, they could finance deficits at below-market interest rates by requiring high reserve levels on bank deposits and a minimum holding of government bonds. With such privileges gone, financial markets are in a better position to evaluate the creditworthiness of national governments. Those with increasing debts could face rising borrowing costs and some rationing of credit, probably combined with lower credit ratings.

It is, however, difficult to predict whether the constraints provided under the EMU would affect national budgets. The experiences of large federal nations such as those of the United States, have shown that reduced country credit ratings are not a strong budgetary restraint. Moreover, there are numerous international debt crises which showed that global capital markets are not always reliable arbitrators of credit risks. Usually, there is a narrow interest rate spread between good and bad loans until a certain critical threshold is reached, at which point excessive discipline is imposed. Studies[31] have pointed out that a slight contraction of credit could develop into protracted credit rationing resulting in a liquidity crunch. If the ECB, which is politically committed to the "no bail-out" rule, faces such conditions it is unlikely that it would refuse temporary financing. Thus, it is better to have binding budgetary guidelines as a precondition to EMU membership.

It is not clear whether financial markets would apply gradual[32] constraints on the EMU nations so that the weaker economies could benefit from an improvement of creditworthiness over time. Studies[33] have shown that interest rate differentials among the current EU member nations are not large enough to reflect the risk associated with debt burdens. It is therefore possible that under the EMU there would be insufficient market pressure to restrain deficit spending, as it is politically very difficult to foresee the enforcement of the "no bail-out" rule without exceptions. This may be a convincing rationale for even more stringent guidelines, such as a requirement for budgetary discipline over a period of three years.

Studies[34] have also indicated that independent central banks can achieve relatively low levels of inflation despite fiscal laxity on the part of their governments.

---

[31] Stiglitz, Joseph and Andrew Weiss. "Credit Rationing in Markets with Imperfect Information," American Economic Review, Vol.71, No.3, June 1981, pp.393-410.

[32] Historically, it has been very difficult for financial markets to apply gradual disciplinary pressure. Usually, when a problem occurs it is already too late and the markets generate a liquidity crises.

[33] Bishop, Graham. *"The EC's Public Debt Disease: Discipline with Credit Spreads and Cure with Price Stability,"* London: Salomon Brothers, May 1991.

[34] Grilli, Vittorio, Donato Masciandro and Guido Tabellini. "Political and Monetary Institutions and Public Financial Policies in Industrial Countries," Economic Policy, October 13, 1991, pp.342-92.

However, it is unclear to what extent this task is made more arduous by excessive fiscal deficits, since the inflationary impact of large public debts can only be mitigated but not eliminated.

In the absence of coordination, national economic agendas determine fiscal policies without consideration for the spill-over effects on neighboring nations. Owing to economies of scale, excessive public debt in one country can have a negative impact on the growth rate of neighboring nations, because the financing of such debt could decrease domestic savings needed for investments, thus reducing domestic growth rates. Therefore, EMU member nations need to be concerned about sustained and excessively high debts in other member countries. Coordination and surveillance could correct excessive budget deficits in the medium-term so that interest rate effects would not spill-over. This means interference with the budgetary policies of nations on economic grounds.

Experience underscores the need for explicit commitments to fiscal restraints such as the Maastricht convergence criteria. Thus, the Treaty is well designed and farsighted. It prudently addresses both public debt and budget deficits. Limits on public debt promote sustainability in the medium-term and allow for short-term political flexibility in dealing with economic shocks. Budgetary limits are necessary (despite some resulting loss of short-term flexibility), because they give an early warning of spill-over effects to neighboring states. But, the use of such binding guidelines also raises problems, and so the debate continues.

As a result of the loss of monetary and exchange rate policies, it is possible that under the EMU the fiscal policies of member nations will differ. Such policies are likely to be used more often and may become the main tool to combat not only major internal but also external shocks. Because under severe economic pressure national governments may be tempted to deviate from the EMU guidelines, rules are needed, and these rules should be set aside only under extreme conditions through a consensus. But events of the 1990s have shown that political circumstances are difficult to predict. Thus, if major internal or external shocks occur, it is almost certain that at some point exceptions will be made to the Maastricht Treaty rules. It can also be argued that, although central bankers and other non-elected officials may define what is beneficial for the economy in the medium to long- term, it is the politicians who best represent public wishes and who therefore should be involved in the process of setting objectives. But the voting public, which is usually not well informed about monetary and fiscal issues, should be responsible for its own actions. Thus, the notion that "only a select few know what is best for the public" could, in the extreme, lead to an Orwellian EMU. It is also important to combine national and common policies in a balanced manner. It is perhaps best to centralize monetary policies while fiscal policies remain decentralized and monitored through budgetary constraints, as stated in the Maastricht Treaty.

It needs to pointed out that currently there is no concrete evidence that the EMU would significantly increase fiscal laxity, although it could provide member nations with easier and wider access to external financing. But, this does not necessarily change the perception of sovereign creditworthiness as long as the public debt is sustainable. Sustainability is not inverse to budgetary laxity, although it is not clear whether the EMU would create an environment in which the binding fiscal constraints could be relaxed. It is also unclear whether weakened fiscal restraints would increase sovereign default risk. As long as the savings-investment balance is sustainable, external equilibrium is possible despite high public debt or budget deficits. A case in point is Italy, where the deficit and the debt are high but so are private savings. Consequently, with or without restraints, it is the sustainability and not the extent of the public debt that is the major determinant of perceived default risk.

The binding budgetary constraints have to be asymmetrical as they apply only to excessive deficits. Yet an appropriate policy mix must deal not only with excessive budget deficits but also with restrictive budgets, because they could create undesirable domestic results or internationally unacceptable conditions. For example, if restrictive budgets generate either sustained current-account surpluses or balanced accounts for the EMU nations, the international response would be negative. If restrictive policies leading to a current-account surplus place upward pressures on individual currencies or the single currency, this would hinder monetary expansion and run counter to long-term price stability. Such distortions were part of the ERM's mid-1980s experience as member nations pursued budgetary consolidation while their money supplies grew. Asymmetric fiscal policy rules could also raise other concerns. While most EMU member nations will probably have deficits, certain nations such as Germany could generate and maintain surpluses. If they are large and prolonged, it could underscore the need for symmetric fiscal rules. But placing limits on budgetary surpluses is politically impossible.

It is difficult to rationalize across-the-board proportional adjustments of budgetary balances in the name of pursuing an appropriate policy mix. The prevailing economic and political differences are too great to pursue effective common monetary, let alone fiscal, policies. It would be far more realistic and effective to pursue coordinated fiscal policies among member nations with similar fiscal conditions. But if this is done, some nations may not be able to participate in the EMU within the foreseeable future. Thus, a multi-speed EMU is necessary.

Economic outcomes are uncertain; therefore, it is not clear whether countries could meet the EMU fiscal criteria during the transitory Stage II. It is also an open question whether centralized fiscal policies could be effective even if countries met the convergence criteria and to what extent once a nation becomes an EMU member, the threat of sanctions[35] would be enough to prevent fiscal irresponsibility.

---

[35] According to the Maastricht Treaty rules, sanctions imposed on a country for not effectively implementing the ECOFIN Council's recommendations require the submission of a fiscal adjustment program accompanied by an explicit timetable. If this does not result in an improvement, the ECOFIN Council can restrict the issue of bonds and securities and can open discussions with the European Investment Bank (EIB) to reconsider its lending policy to the nation involved. The ECOFIN Council may also impose fines on the member state and/or require it to

It is also difficult to determine in advance whether large internal shocks in a couple of nations or external shocks could be evenly distributed and whether the common policy mix would be adequate to handle such disturbances. Coupled with domestic political cycles, such uncertainty is bound to create anxiety in the financial markets, at least in the early stages of the EMU. Given the differing fiscal conditions in the various nations and the reasons for the varying economic developments, it is unlikely that the economies could converge any time in the foreseeable future. Thus, if an effective policy mix is pursued, fiscal policy convergence through only binding budget rules may be inadequate or even inappropriate. Nonetheless, the EU nations agreed to a post-EMU "Stability and Growth Pact" in 1996. But it only contained near-automatic fines for exceeding the Maastricht deficit convergence criteria which ultimately are at the political discretion of the ECOFIN Council. See Chapter VI for a discussion of the 1996 "Stability and Growth Pact".

Thus, although the loss of exchange rate and monetary policies turns fiscal policies into critical tools to deal with economic shocks, there is evidence that relying on the financial markets to enforce fiscal discipline is not enough. Fiscal coordination must be combined with monetary policies to obtain an appropriate policy mix. A strong case can be made for binding budgetary guidelines so as to err on the side of caution. Any instability, regardless of its origins, would shatter the EMU's credibility.

The Implementation of Binding Constraints

As discussed in the previous sections, it is unlikely that the financial markets will discipline budgetary policies to prevent fiscal laxity. Consequently, common oversight policies must be established. The authors of the Maastricht Treaty put a ceiling on budget deficits (3 percent) and public debt (60 percent) as a share of GDP as proposed in the Delors Report. Although these limits are relatively easy to administer, like most simple proposals they are too crude to be implemented uniformly because they ignore important considerations such as the impact of the savings-investment balances. The Delors Report authors were aware of these limitations and pointed out that "....the situation of each country might have to be taken into consideration."[36] Opponents of binding budgetary constraints have often compared the budgetary concerns of the EMU member nations to those generated in the U.S. federal system where no federally imposed constraints on state deficits exist. However, what they ignore is that many U.S. states have adopted balanced budget amendments which are a variation on deficit ceilings.[37] Moreover, the fiscal differences among the EU nations

maintain non-interest-bearing deposits with the EU. This policy towards sanctions was further refined under the post-EMU fiscal "Stability and Growth Pact" of 1996 agreed to at the Dublin European Council Summit. See Chapter VI for details on the "pact".

[36] The Delors Report, 1989, paragraph 30.

[37] The emphasis on legal provisions has been questioned by some as, for example, by Jürgen

are far greater than those among the U.S. states. The public debt/GDP ratios, for example, ranged from 56 percent in France to 131 percent in Belgium in 1996. The net costs of servicing these debts is equally diverse. Furthermore, although the U.S. Gramm-Rudman-Hollings Act of 1985 strives to reduce federal deficits, the U.S. Administration and the Congress have continued to generate deficits through the early 1990s. At the same time, the states have generally balanced their budgets over the medium-term. In contrast, in the EU the common deficit and debt limits are stated in the Maastricht Treaty, yet member nations routinely produce excessive national deficits.[38]

There are other ways than those spelled out in the Maastricht Treaty to implement binding constraints. The primary deficits (deficits net of interest payments) relative to GDP could be limited by a fixed ceiling which determines the permissible debt/GDP ratio.[39] This could accommodate differences in the level of interest payments, past economic policies and the size of the debts. But it would not take into account other important factors such as the sustainability of debts or the occurrence of internal shocks. At the extreme, this proposal calls for balanced budgets (i.e., zero primary deficits). Due to economic and political considerations, such expectations are unrealistic.[40]

Another approach could involve the use of long-run deficit sustainability as a constraint. The standard could be the primary deficit that would be determined by the difference between the increase in interest rates and the GDP growth rate. Although this is an attractive approach in that it accommodates country differences, it involves certain problems. It could be plagued by uncertainty and differing interpretations. For example, the definitions of net public and gross government debt could vary, as could the competition of actual long-term market interest rates with projected real interest rates and the interpretation of the magnitude of the fiscal adjustment necessary to realize a sustainable fiscal position. Differences could also exist in the past reporting of deficits and the actual level of public debt/GDP ratios. Table 3.4 shows the discrepancy between reported deficits and actual changes in EU debt levels between 1981 and 1989. In most cases the official fiscal statistics are of little value. Over a period of ten years, Belgium's public debt/GDP ratio , for example, increased by more than 50 percent (5.2

Von Hagen in "Fiscal Arrangements in a Monetary Union: Evidence from the U.S.", discussion Paper #58, Center for Global Business, Indiana University, May 1991. Von Hagen found a weak correlation among government deficits, public debts and the nature of formal legal constraints.

[38] Although the first stage of the EMU has the same characteristics as that of the U.S. federal system had had with its original 13 states, following 1789 the new U.S. federal government absorbed a major share of the state debt which had been incurred jointly during the Revolutionary War.

[39] It is assumed that in this case countries would not engage in monetary financing and that member nations' nominal interest rates would roughly correspond to growth in nominal incomes. Thus the primary deficit to GDP ratio would reflect the public debt to GDP ratio.

[40] During the early transition stages to the EMU it is possible that even with a zero primary deficit the large debtor member nations' debt/income ratios would rise, as they would still have to pay a premium on any outstanding debt which would not be offset by more rapid growth in their nominal GDPs.

multiplied by 10 years) and the discrepancy was more than 30 percent (3.2 multiplied by 10 years). It is apparent that an unbiased indicator of sustainability would be very difficult to find, except in extreme cases.

Table 3.4
Discrepancies between Reported Deficits and Changes in Debt Levels, 1981-89

	Averages over 1981-1989:		
	Reported (theoretical) change in debt/GDP	Actual change in debt/GDP	Discrepancy *
Belgium	2.0	5.2	3.2
Denmark	-2.0	2.4	4.4
Germany	0.1	1.1	1.0
Greece	3.6	6.1	2.5
Spain	0.3	2.7	2.4
France	-0.1	1.2	1.3
Ireland	0.3	2.5	2.2
Italy	2.5	4.2	1.7
Netherlands	3.2	3.2	-0.0
UK	-2.9	-1.1	1.8

* = Difference between actual reported changes in debt levels and the change in debt that would have resulted from the reported deficits.

Source: Gros, Daniel and Niels Thygesen. European Monetary Integration, New York: St. Martin's Press, 1992, p.283.

The problem is magnified by the different interpretations of the measures even by international institutions, let alone by the EU institutions and governments. For example, even the most basic measure, the debt/GDP ratio, is reported differently by the EU Commission and by the OECD. The Commission estimates that in the case of Denmark and Germany, the ratio is 40 and 21 percent higher, respectively, than the ratios reported by the OECD. In part, this is explained by the fact that the EU uses gross whereas the OECD uses net debt figures.

Table 3.5 illustrates the differences between the fiscal data reported by the OECD and The EU for the year 1990. The table also shows the magnitude of the needed fiscal adjustments. It should be noted that the OECD's uses of growth rates and actual long-term interest rates, whereas the EU Commission assumes that for most member nations, in the long-run, real interest rates exceed real growth rates by 2 percent.

Table 3.5
Discrepancies Between OECD and EU Fiscal Data and the Need for Fiscal Adjustments, 1990

	debt/GDP[(a)]	interest rate minus growth rate[(b)]	Adjustment in Fiscal Deficit Needed to: achieve primary balance	stabilize debt/GDP	achieve convergence in debt/GDP in 10 years
Belgium	6.1	-1.2	-1.8	0.45	0.21
Denmark	40.4	-4.4	0.9	-1.11	2.08
Germany	21.1	0.0	0.2	0.22	1.48
Greece	7.2	-0.4	-4.3	4.13	4.00
Spain	14.5	-1.9	-2.5	2.16	2.76
France	8.1	-1.7	-0.2	-0.03	0.13
Ireland	-17.7	-2.6	1.9	-5.35	-7.97
Italy	4.6	-2.2	-1.2	-0.81	-1.20
Netherlands	21.2	-0.9	1.3	-1.39	-0.12
U.K.	11.40	-2.5	1.9	-2.49	-2.20

(a) = shows the discrepancies between OECD and EU debt/GDP calculation results.
(b) = shows the discrepancies between OECD and EU interest rate minus growth rate calculations results.
Note: The positive/negative signs reflect the percentage increase/decrease of EU over OECD estimates. There are no entries for Luxembourg and Portugal because they are not included in the OECD data.
Source: Gros, Daniel and Niels Thygesen. European Monetary Integration, 1992, p.282.

Finally, binding constraints could be implemented through the so-called "golden rule" which requires that public deficits not exceed investment expenditures. This is similar to the concept of current receipts (taxes and social security contributions) matching current expenditures as used in the German fiscal model. Such an approach is meritorious because it distinguishes between government deficits created by public investments and deficits resulting from excessive public consumption and transfer payments. Thus, a distinction is made between current expenditures, such as salaries to civil servants and social security transfers, and public investments, as, for example, infrastructure developments and capital transfers. But the definitions of current and capital expenditures are arbitrary. Furthermore, the quality of public spending is ignored, as not all public investments (for example, environmental projects) increase future tax revenues. Hence, the "golden rule" may not be a useful policy tool at all.

THE EU COMMON BUDGET AND THE EMU

Revenues and Expenditures

The EU common budget is small compared with the national budgets of the larger economies. It amounted to Ecu 86,573 million[41] (US$107,264 million) in 1996, representing approximately 1.197 percent of the combined GDP and 4.0 percent of total

[41] This is adjusted data and thus differs slightly from Table 3.6.

public spending of the EU in 1996. The budget has features not commonly found in other budgeting systems. For example, the role of the EU Parliament in the budgeting pressures is very limited. Moreover, it is divided into compulsory and non-compulsory expenditures but only the latter can be controlled through traditional methods. In addition, all major taxes are imposed and collected at the national level. Finally, according to Article 199 of the "Financial Provision of the Treaty Establishing the EEC" (Title II of part 5), the budget has to balance. Thus, if expenditures exceed revenues, additional revenues must be generated, borrowing is not permitted. Table 3.6 presents a breakdown of the 1996 common budget's revenues and expenditures, Table 3.7 presents the member nations' contributions to and reimbursements from the EU common budget in 1993 and 1994, while Table 3.8 presents a comparison of member nation contributions in 1986 and 1995. Table 3.9 shows the increase in spending during the 1970-96 period.

Table 3.6
EU Common Budget Revenues and Expenditures, 1996

Budgetary Category	million Ecu	% of budget
EXPENDITURES:		
agriculture policy	40,797.00	47.1
structural operations	29,131.00	33.7
internal policy	5,266.98	6.2
external policy	5,157.33	6.1
administrative outlays	4,075.13	4.8
reserves	1,152.00	1.33
compensation	701.00	0.81
TOTAL	86,280.44	100.00
(percent of EU GNP)	(1.197%)	
compulsory	43,385.42	50.28
non-compulsory	42,895.02	49.71
REVENUES:		
value-added tax	34,591.30	42.20
GNP-levy	31,971.70	39.00
customs duties	12,852.90	15.70
agriculture & sugar levies	1,935.50	2.40
miscellaneous	573.50	0.70
TOTAL	81,927.90	100.00

Source: "EU Commission Preliminary Draft General Budget of the EU for the Financial Year 1996," Brussels: EU Commission, May 1995.

Table 3.7
EU Common Budget Net Contributions and Receipts
(1993 and 1994)

	GDP per capita 1994*	1993 Ecu million
NET CONTRIBUTORS:		
Germany	115.5	11,830
U.K.	99.8	3,125
Italy	104.5	1,525
Netherlands	100.3	1,327
France	109.5	1,020
NET RECIPIENTS:		
Greece	48.5	4,135
Spain	75.4	3,090
Portugal	60.5	2,508
Ireland	80.0	2,372
Denmark	108.6	377
Luxembourg	133.8	190
Belgium	106.3	60
EU	** 100.0	-

* = GDP per capita at current prices and current PPS (EU 12=100).

** = Not all expenditure and income are included.

Source: Barnes, Ian and Pamela M. Barnes. The Enlarged European Union, London: Longman Group U.K. Ltd., 1995, p.156.

Table 3.8
A Comparison of Member Nations Contributions to the EU Budget in 1986 and 1995

	1995				1986		
	Net Contribution			GDP per head as % of EU average*	Net Contribution		
	Total Ecu (mil.)	per head			Total Ecu (mil.)	per head	
		Ecu	Rank			Ecu	Rank
Germany	13431	164.6	(1)	106.7	3742	61.3	(2)
Britain	4720	80.7	(6)	98.2	1438	25.3	(4)
Netherlands	2005	129.7	(2)	100.4	-217	-14.9	(8)
France	1727	29.6	(9)	107.2	561	10.1	(5)
Sweden	937	105.5	(5)	95.3	-	-	-
Austria	905	112.9	(3)	109.3	-	-	-
Italy	614	10.7	(10)	101.7	195	3.4	(6)
Belgium	311	30.6	(8)	110.4	284	28.7	(3)
Finland	165	32.3	(7)	92.5	-	-	-
Luxembourg	45	110.6	(4)	128.2	59	160.3	(1)
Denmark	-306	-58.6	(11)	112	-421	-82.2	(10)
Ireland	-1887	-527	(15)	85.3	-1230	-374	(12)
Portugal	-2381	-242	(13)	67.9	-219	-22.1	(9)
Greece	-3489	-333	(14)	60	-1273	-128	(11)
Spain	-7218	-184	(12)	76.1	-95	-2.5	(7)

* = Based on PPP.

Source: "European Union; Who pays for it ?", The Economist, November 23 1996, p.57.

Table 3.9
EU Budget Spending Increase, 1970-96

	Spending (in Ecu million)	per capita spending (in Ecu)	% of public spending in member nations	Annual rate of growth of spending (%)	Spending as % of member nation GDP
1970	3,576	19	1.90	-	0.74
1980	16,455	63	1.70	-	0.80
1988	42,495	131	2.30	16.90	1.05
1990	45,608	139	2.00	7.90	0.96
1991	55,156	160	2.20	20.90	1.07
1992	60,501	174	2.20	9.70	1.12
1993	69,233	199	2.40	14.40	1.19
1994	72,304	207	2.40	4.40	1.24
1995	79,846	n/a	n/a	10.43	n/a
1996	86,280	n/a	n/a	8.06	1.197
Average 1988-96				11.59	

Source: Barnes, Ian and Pamela M. Barnes. The Enlarged European Union, London: Longman Group U.K. Ltd., 1995, p.150; and "EU Commission Preliminary Draft General Budget of the EU for the Financial Year 1996", 1995.

Revenues

The common budget revenues are comprised of customs duties, agriculture levies, 1 percent of the national VATs and 1.2 percent of national GNPs[42]. The VAT accounts for approximately 51.6 percent, variable GNP contributions for 27.3 percent, tariffs and customs duties for 18.2 percent, while agricultural and sugar levies for 2.9 percent.[43]

Table 3.10 shows the revenue sources of the EU common budget in 1993 and 1994. The budget is provided with a steady stream of revenues, but all major taxes are imposed and collected at the national level. Taxes that are directly collected, are either eroding or are volatile in nature.

---

[42] Since the rule changes of 1988, the budget contribution of each nation is almost a linear function of GNP. Following the admission of Spain and Portugal in 1986, the contribution increased from 1 percent of GNP in 1988 to 1.2 percent in 1992. Contributions are determined as follows: 2.9 + 0.91*GNP with R square = 0.99 .

[43] The percentages are based on the 1994 common budget. They tend to slightly vary from year to year.

Table 3.10
Common Budget Revenue Sources, 1993 and 1994
(Ecu millions)

	1993	%	1994	%
Agriculture & sugar levies	2,239	3.4%	2,039	2.9%
Customs duties	13,118	20.0%	12,619	18.2%
VAT	35,677	54.5%	35,850	51.6%
GNP levy	14,030	21.4%	18,989	27.3%
Miscellaneous	456	0.7%	0	0.0%
TOTAL	65,523	100%	69,498	100%
% of EU-GDP	1.19%		1.24%	

Source: Barnes, Ian and Pamela Barnes. The Enlarged European Union, 1995, p.148; and EU Commission data, 1995.

The common budget is at the mercy of the member states. Because the taxing power of Brussels is limited, revenues cannot be increased through higher taxes. This is particularly true for direct i.e., personal and corporate income taxes and such indirect taxes as transaction, sales, customs, excise, tariff, and stock transfer taxes as well as green levies, to name only a few. Customs duties are a limited source of revenue because of the elimination of such duties in the "Single Market." Agricultural levies, which are set by the Council of Ministers, are based on such considerations as the exchange rate of the U.S. dollar and the output response of farmers to Common Agricultural Policy (CAP) measures.

The common authorities exercise de facto fiscal coordination to promote regional economic and social cohesion within the EU. Vertical fiscal equalization[44] within the common budget follows the German model[45] of revenue sharing and subsidiarity, while horizontal fiscal coordination and equalization is more in line with the Swiss approach.[46]

The prohibition on debt financing makes the implementation of long-term

---

[44] Tax theory provides two distinct concepts of fairness: horizontal equity and vertical equity. "A tax system is said to be horizontally equitable if individuals who are the same in all relevant respects are treated equally. While the principle of horizontal equity says that individuals who are essentially identical should be treated the same, the principle of vertical equity says that some individuals are in a position to pay higher taxes than others, and that these individuals should do so." Stiglitz, Joseph. Economics of the Public Sector, London: W.W. Norton & Company, 1986, p.333-37.

[45] For a detailed description of the German tax system and vertical equalization, see Spahn, Paul Bernd. The Community Budget for an Economic and Monetary Union, London: The Macmillan Press Ltd., 1993, pp.54-67.

[46] For a detailed discussion of the Swiss tax system and horizontal equalization, see Spahn, Paul Bernard. The Community Budget for an Economic and Monetary Union, 1993, pp.45-54.

projects difficult. The activities of the European Investment Bank (EIB) which operates independently of the common budget, reduces the difficulties only to some extent. Other measures to deal with the problem include supplemental and amended budgets, intergovernmental advance disbursements, "negative reserve" entries and liberal interpretations of budgetary regulations. However, such measures are inadequate; major crises, such as those of the 1980s, were resolved through political pressure put on governments rather than through attempts at flexibility.

As mentioned before, all taxes are imposed and collected at the country level. Moreover, although the VAT revenue flows to Brussels, the common budget has to reimburse member nations for the cost of collecting such taxes. This, coupled with the inability to borrow and the vulnerability of the CAP revenues, makes the common budget dependent on national revenues transferred by governments, thereby reinforcing the principle of subsidiarity.

Expenditures

Compulsory, primarily CAP budget expenditures account for a little over half of all payments. They are ongoing as long as the underlying activities are sound and are regulated through: (i) market reactions such as farmers' output decisions; (ii) The Council of Ministers' ad hoc decisions, particularly as they relate to intervention prices; (iii) world market prices of agricultural goods, common levies and movements of the US dollar; and (iv) procedures (regarding formula flexibility and adjustment), that were introduced by the Council of Ministers in 1988.[47]

The redistribution capacity of the common budget is limited because it depends on the member nations' contributions, the importance of the agricultural sectors, and on the impact of Structural Funds interventions, which are geographically determined. There are plans to gradually replace the guaranteed CAP payments with direct income subsidies, yet the common budget disbursement is still overshadowed by common policies that guarantee farm prices.[48]

Although the EU Commission proposal known as the Delors I Package of 1988 instituted some budgetary reforms as, for example, extending the budgetary cycle from one to five years, it was not until 1992 that new integration promoting funding measures were introduced. The so-called Delors II Package of 1992 was a special, one-time, seven-year budget through 1999, calling for an increase in contributions from 1.2 to 1.37 per cent of GDP and the creation of a Cohesion Fund. The package was passed in a modified form at the Edinburgh European Council Summit in December 1992. The contribution rate was raised to only 1.27 percent but the Cohesion Fund was established, albeit, with only US$18 billion for the 1993-97 period. Table 3.11 shows

[47] Spahn, Paul Bernard. The Community Budget for an Economic and Monetary Union, 1993.
[48] These outlays have been decreasing since the 1988 Delors budget reform.

the common budget expenditures for the 1993-1999 period.

Table 3.11
EU Common Budget Expenditures, 1993-99
(1992 prices in millions of ECUs)

	1993	1994	1995	1996	1997	1998	1999
1. Agricultural guideline	35,230	35,095	35,722	36,364	37,023	37,697	38,389
2. Structural actions	21,277	21,885	23,480	24,990	26,526	28,240	30,000
- Cohesion Fund	1,500	1,750	2,000	2,250	2,500	2,550	2,600
- Structural Funds & other operations	19,777	20,135	21,480	22,740	24,026	25,690	27,400
3. Internal polices	3,940	4,084	4,323	4,520	4,710	4,910	5,100
4. External action	3,950	4,000	4,280	4,560	4,830	5,180	5,600
5. Administrative expenditure	3,280	3,380	3,580	3,690	3,800	3,850	3,900
6. Reserves	1,500	1,500	1,100	1,100	1,100	1,100	1,100
- Monetary Reserve	1,000	1,000	500	500	500	500	500
- External Action							
= emergency aid	200	200	300	300	300	300	300
= loan guarantees	300	300	300	300	300	300	300
Total appropriations for commitments	69,177	69,944	72,485	75,224	77,989	80,977	84,089
Appropriations for payments required	65,908	67,036	69,150	71,290	94,491	77,249	80,114
Appropriations for payments (% GNP)	1.20	1.19	1.20	1.21	1.23	1.25	1.26
Margin for unforeseen expenditure (% GNP)		0.01	0.01	0.01	0.01	0.01	0.01
Own resources ceiling (% GNP)	1.20	1.20	1.21	1.22	1.24	1.26	1.27
Total external expenditure	4,450	4,500	4,880	5,160	5,430	5,780	6,200

Note: The inflation rate applied is 4.3 percent. Thus, the data presented here differ slightly from that shown in previous tables.
Source: Nicoll, William and Trevor C. Salmon. Understanding the New European Community, New York: Harvester Wheatsheaf, 1994, p.106.

The Common Budget and the EMU

Economic and monetary integration is likely to affect the common budget in a number of ways. The most important of these is the potential impact of the EMU on national fiscal policies and conditions -- which could directly affect the common budget because of its dependence on the member nations' contributions. Due to the loss of monetary and exchange rate policies, the EMU not only puts new demands on national fiscal policies but also encroaches on such policies through the binding budgetary guidelines of the Maastricht Treaty. The EMU also promotes fiscal federalism to equalize economic and social disparities through the Cohesion Fund. Therefore, it requires the close coordination of monetary and budgetary policies, with particular emphasis on unsustainable national deficits. Converging inflation and interest rates as well as public borrowing could also affect the common budget, as could taxation, and the Cohesion and other Funds. The European Central Bank's (ECB) collection of seigniorage revenues and the opt-out rights of nations (such as those of the U.K.) are also relevant considerations.

Among the numerous EMU effects on the common budget, two issues stand out in relation to fiscal federalism: (i) the size of the seigniorage revenues of the European System of Central Bank's (ESCB)[49]; and (ii) access to private capital markets to finance common budget deficits.

Seigniorage Revenues

Central banks obtain seigniorage revenues through their monopoly on the issuance of currencies. More specifically, such revenues are generated through the distribution of non-interest or low-interest-bearing debt, which is held by the public in the form of currency or by the commercial banks as required reserves.[50] If governments stay away from monetizing debt,[51] seigniorage privileges can be beneficial in providing a steady source of revenues. Seigniorage can also be viewed as an inflation tax, because most taxes are based on nominal income as opposed to real income. However, as a share of GDP, such revenues are relatively small. Under the EMU, they would be reduced even more because there could be a convergence toward not only lower interest rates but also toward lower official bank reserves.[52] Because seigniorage is a major source of government revenues in nations with high inflation, under the EMU such nations would face a permanent reduction of revenues that would have to be made up through higher taxes or reduced expenditures.

Because the primary mandate of the ECB is price stability, its monetary policies may eventually reduce inflation in nations experiencing above average inflation rates. Thus, in the long run, such policies reduce and converge the seigniorage revenues obtained by these countries. Table 3.12 presents a comparison between the 1990 actual and the 1997 projected seigniorage revenue streams accruing to the EU member nations.

---

[49] The ESCB includes the 15 national central banks plus the ECB.

[50] It is for this reason that even with steady inflation rates neutrality with respect to public financing cannot be achieved.

[51] Most governments, to some extent, monetize debt (i.e., issue new money). However, if the monetization of the budget deficit is substantial, inflation ensues.

[52] According to the ESCB Statute, Articles 32 and 33, seigniorage revenues will be redistributed to member nations through the ECB in proportion to the paid-up shares of the ECB's capital.

Table 3.12
Reserve Requirements as a Percentage of Demand Deposits, Average Inflation Rates and Seigniorage Revenues Measured Implicitly as a Percentage of GDP in 1990, 1997 & After (1990 estimates in parentheses)

EU member nation	Reserve requirements, mid-1988	Inflation rate 1980-1990 (%)	Seigniorage revenues, 1990	Steady-nation seigniorage, 1997 and after
Belgium	0	4.5	0.75 (0.30)	0.46
Denmark	0	5.8	0.46 (0.50)	0.22
France	5	6.3	0.55 (0.76)	0.28
Germany	6.6 to 12.1	2.9	0.86 (0.40)	0.39
Greece	7.5	18.5	2.33 (2.69)	0.67
Ireland	10	7.8	0.58 (1.17)	0.34
Italy	25	8.7	1.29 (1.84)	0.36
Luxembourg	0	4.8	0.11 (0.35)	0.16
Netherlands	15	2.0	0.79 (0.48)	0.46
Portugal	15	18.4	3.57 (2.95)	0.50
Spain	18.5	9.6	1.88 (1.75)	0.54
U.K.	0.5	6.2	0.34 (0.58)	0.23

Note: The seigniorage revenue data estimates were reported in an April 16, 1991 internal EU document authored by M. Vanheukelen who computed "implicit measures." Calculation of the "steady-state values for 1997 and after" used the following assumptions: "cash holdings relative to GNP are constant; interest rates decline in a linear progression to a common 5 percent in 1997; commercial bank reserves converge to 2 percent of a broad money aggregate; remuneration of reserves is zero by 1997; nominal GDP growth rates converge to 5 percent by 1997; ratio of representative broad aggregate to GDP as constant."

KEY: Regression results:

	Intercept	Reserve Requirement	Avg. inflation rate
Coefficients =	-0.358	0.0365	0.1460
Standard deviation =	(0.450)	(0.017)	(0.027)

R^2=0.83

Source: Spahn, Paul Bernard. The Community Budget for an Economic and Monetary Union, 1993, p.154.

Seigniorage revenues under the EMU would be affected not only by just price stability but also by other factors such as a decrease in money circulation as a percentage of nominal GNP, the erosion of cash holdings due to technological developments, the general reduction of central bank monopoly powers and the competitive reduction of reserve requirements. For example, a reduction of 1.5 percent in reserve requirements could lead to a reduction of money stock by 22 percent in France and by 62 percent in Italy, with corresponding seigniorage losses.

Seigniorage revenue under the EMU could be increased by the idle foreign exchange reserves held by the ESCB, which would in all probability be lower than similar types of reserve levels held by central banks. This would affect the international reserve holdings of the non-EU nations' central banks and of the private sector. By reducing their U.S. dollar and yen holdings, they could benefit the single currency. Seigniorage revenues could also go up owing to the EU-wide open market operations by the ECB, which could reduce the volume of low-interest-bearing assets i.e., paper accepted at the discount windows. As a result of establishing the EMU, international competition for reserves could be reduced, as a tripolar currency system dominated by the Euro, the U.S. dollar and the yen would allow easier monetary policy coordination, thereby increasing seigniorage revenues worldwide. The ECB's monetary policy and international trade activities could also affect such revenues.

Thus, it is difficult to predict how the EMU will affect seigniorage revenues. In all probability, they will be reduced. The calculations shown previously in Table 3.12 imply that the seigniorage revenue share of the common budget could average 0.4 percent of the member nations' GDPs. Following the introduction of the single currency, it would be much more efficient to simply pool the ESCB's seigniorage revenues, because intra-EU distribution of ESCB liabilities would be extremely arduous and, in the case of cash holdings, impossible. The redistribution of the ESCB's revenues generated by money market interventions such as the selling and buying of financial assets or the reevaluation of ESCB assets into national accounts would also be difficult to redistribute.

The argument calling for the pooling of seigniorage revenues is convincing. However, the use of such revenues raises questions. They could be transferred to the common budget, used to pay the Maastricht Treaty bills, service public debts or could be redistributed to member nations on the basis of an equalizing, horizontal or asymmetrical apportionment formula similar to that used for the redistribution of the VAT. Such revenues could also be redistributed in proportion to GNP. Redistribution based on the proportion of current national seigniorage revenues would reward the high inflation economies and take into consideration "policy induced factors" such as the size of reserve requirements. Distribution on a per capita basis would create regional equity problems, particularly if ESCB seigniorage revenues were high and led to negative outcomes during monetary contraction or currency devaluation. Allocation on an ad hoc basis would be very erratic.

The Maastricht Treaty's Articles 32 and 33 lay down the following simple rules for the redistribution of the ESCB's monetary income among the member nations:

> ...the monetary income shall be allocated at the end of each financial year...the amount of each national central bank's monetary income shall be equal to its annual income derived from its assets held against notes in circulation and deposit liabilities to credit institutions. ...The sum of the national central banks' monetary income shall be allocated to the national central banks in proportion to their paid-up shares in the capital of the ECB...the net profit of the

> ECB shall be transferred in the following order: (a) an amount to be determined by the Governing Council, which may not exceed 20% of the net profits, shall be transferred to the general reserve fund subject to a limit equal to 100% of the capital; (b) the remaining net profit shall be distributed to the shareholders of the ECB in proportion to their paid-up shares. In the event of a loss incurred by the ECB, the shortfall may be offset against the general reserve fund of the ECB and, if necessary, following a decision by the Governing Council, against the monetary income of the relevant financial year in proportion and up to the amounts allocated to the national central banks...in proportion to their paid-up shares in the capital of the ECB.[53]

Capital Market Financing

Financing the common budget deficit by private capital markets is restricted by law, for example, long-term public investment projects are possible only if and when borrowing against the fixed capital formation plans. Member nations not only fear fiscal irresponsibility on part of the common institutions but are also concerned about the lack of a consensus concerning the nature of sound fiscal policies and procedures. The restriction has come under criticism on the grounds that more than half of the common budget's expenditures are not subject to parliamentary oversight and that such (compulsory) expenditures are affected, in part, by external market conditions.

The common budget must be flexible enough to provide for the financing of public investments by private capital markets, however limited access to such markets may be. The German and Swiss model of providing access is more appropriate than the U.S. model, which is based on negotiation between the Administration and Congress rather than on any constitutional requirement. Other non-U.S. models limit government deficit financing through a cap set by investment outlays.[54]

Caps may be appropriate for the common budget under the EMU. Theoretically, there could be a legal limit on the financing of investments. But, governments have been known to circumvent such limits. Other constraints could also be imposed – the financing of investments could be limited to the cash flow earmarked for the servicing of loans. This would require a capital budget within the common budget and would reflect the debt amortization and interest costs of investment projects.

---

[53] The Maastricht Treaty, Article 32 and 33, 1992.

[54] Some countries, such as Germany, have managed to create off-balance funds to bypass the institutional constraints, but this is usually done only under extraordinary circumstances such as German reunification. It typically requires a consensus involving all major political parties.

Budget Reform

As part of the EMU budget reform process, the role of the EU Parliament could be strengthened. This would enhance the fiscal responsibility of politicians. Other changes could include an increase in the taxing authority of the EU Commission with respect to energy, ecotaxes and corporate cash flows while limiting the Commission's access to national tax bases. All such changes would have to be harmonized with national tax regimes.

Compulsory and non-compulsory expenditures could also be separated. To date, approximately a little over half of the EU budget is comprised of compulsory expenditures. This is particularly true for the Common Agricultural Policy (CAP) which still represents more than 50 percent of the common budget. But this would require three decision-making changes. First, the role of the Parliament would have to be enhanced. Second, the Council of Ministers would have to coordinate common expenditures through a process that included all ministers, particularly the Ministers of Finance. Third, a joint decision-making mechanism would have to be set up involving the EU Commission, Parliament and the national governments to determine tax sharing, redistribution, grant and horizontal fiscal equalization policies and the corresponding regional payment mechanisms. Such a joint decision-making mechanism could be supplemented by an independent advisory body similar to the Australian Grants Commission.

Additional reforms could entail a more comprehensive common budget which would not only include the various funds currently outside the budget, but also encompass new categories such as capital expenditures. This is not to suggest that the funds could not function outside the common budget but to point out that they require oversight.

By its nature the EMU encroaches on national fiscal policies and affects intergovernmental fiscal relations -- that is, the common budget. Yet, there is little doubt that national budgetary and tax processes will remain decentralized. The Maastricht Treaty's fiscal convergence criteria, such as the budget and debt constraints, however, place quantitative limits on national budgets and in the name of fiscal federalism, foster broader common fiscal policies to equalize economic and social conditions. Thus, it is likely that the VAT will continue to serve as the primary vehicle to remedy the vertical imbalances in the common budget's revenue sources and that no major national tax is likely to become a common tax. As origin-based value-added taxation becomes more homogeneous, so national tax autonomy could become even more important, specially in the domain of direct taxation.

There will, however, be a need for more efficient reporting, payment and clearing systems at the EMU level. Greater economic cohesion and fiscal integration would increase the scope of tax-sharing schemes such as the VAT. However, such developments could be slow and arduous at best, owing to the political sensitivity of these issues. It is possible that direct income taxes will remain the cornerstone of national autonomy while indirect taxation will be more harmonized at the EU level. Taxes that would be easy to harmonize include mineral and oil, energy and transportation levies. Even ecotaxes such as the carbon tax stand a good chance of becoming uniform. But the harmonization of excise taxes, of taxes on "demerit goods" such as alcohol and cigarettes, or of wealth taxes, is unlikely.

Corporate taxation also remains a difficult topic although the "Single Market" requires the reduction of national tax differences. There are strong arguments for a common, origin-based corporate cash flow tax which could be used to develop regions and which would not breach any double-taxation agreements. As discussed before, an additional, albeit small, common budget revenue source could be the ESCB's seigniorage revenues under the EMU. While the eventual collection and pooling of these revenues is uncontested, their redistribution remains a matter of debate despite in Maastricht Treaty's Articles 32 and 33.[55]

The United States provides a good example of the complexities of centralizing fiscal activities, particularly taxation. In addition to the federal tax, each of the 50 states has individually tailored direct (income, corporate, property[56]) and indirect (sales) taxes. The states do not want to transfer fiscal authority to the federal government and consider such intentions as an infringement on their sovereignty. It is only recently that they have become more receptive to the idea of coordinated tax revenue sharing with Washington DC. It is an understatement to say that the European situation in which 15 sovereign countries are involved in the debate, is more complex than that in the United States. Yet, it is difficult to envision any substantive economic, social or monetary integration without increased fiscal harmonization, especially of income and corporate taxes.

Fiscal Federalism under the EMU

The common budget's ability to promote gradual integration is an important issue. The idea of cohesion has been used to promote North-South bargaining to bring about the EMU. As a result, during the Edinburgh Summit in December 1992, the European Council set aside Ecu 15 billion (US$18.6 billion) for a Cohesion Fund.[57] The Fund is merely a prelude to future financing demands by the less developed member nations. Table 3.13 gives the annual distribution of the Cohesion Fund's Ecu

---

[55] Currently, redistribution is determined by the member nation's paid-up ECB capital share.

[56] There is an ongoing debate as to whether the property tax is a direct or an indirect tax.

[57] The Cohesion Fund was set up in 1993. It provides Ecu 15 billion over seven years to finance key environmental and transportation infrastructure projects in the four least developed EU nations of Ireland, Greece, Portugal and Spain. The Structural Funds, representing 30% of all Common Budget outlays, include the European Regional Development Fund, the European Social Fund, the European Agricultural Guidance and Guarantee Fund and the Financial Instrument for Fisheries Guidance.

15 billion over the 1993-99 period while Table 3.14 shows the assistance provided by the Cohesion Fund in 1993 alone. The key differences between the Cohesion Fund and the Structural Funds are shown in Table 3.15.

Table 3.13
Annual Distribution of the Cohesion Fund's Ecu 15 billion over the 1993-99 Period

Amounts available:

1993: Ecu 1,50 billion (Ecu 1,565 billion at 1993 prices)
1994: Ecu 1,75 billion (Ecu 1,853 billion at 1994 prices)
1995: Ecu 2,00 billion (Ecu 2,152 billion at 1995 prices)
1996: Ecu 2,25 billion (Ecu 2,421 billion at 1995 prices)
1997: Ecu 2,50 billion (Ecu 2,690 billion at 1995 prices)
1998: Ecu 2,55 billion (Ecu 2,744 billion at 1995 prices)
1999: Ecu 2,60 billion (Ecu 2,798 billion at 1995 prices)

Total: Ecu 15,1 billion (more than Ecu 16,223 billion in adjusted prices)

Source: "The European Union's Cohesion Fund". European Commission: Directorate-General for Information, Communication, Culture, Audiovisual, Luxembourg: Office of Official Publications of the EC, 1994, p.7.

Table 3.14
1993 Cohesion Fund Expenditures in Ecu

	Total	Environment	Transport
Spain	858,450,703 (54.9%)	252,083,242 (29%)	606,367,461 (71%)
Portugal	283,568,700 (18.1%)	122,794,100 (43%)	160,774,600 (57%)
Greece	280,364,000 (17.9%)	175,222,400 (62%)	105,141,600 (38%)
Ireland	141,887,100 (9.1%)	55,917,250 (39%)	85,969,850 (61%)
Technical Assistance	374,125 (0.02%)	-	-
Total	1,564,644,628 (100%)	606,016,992 (38.7%)	958,253,511 (61.3)

Source: "The European Union's Cohesion Fund," European Commission, 1994, p.8.

Table 3.15
Differences Between the Cohesion Fund and the Structural Funds

	Cohesion Fund	Structural Funds
Aims	To reduce economic disparities among member states	To reduce regional disparities
Parties involved	The Commission and member states concerned	While the member states bear the main responsibility, the regional authorities and the promoters play a prominent role
Conditions	Strict compliance with the convergence programs is a condition of funding	No conditions
Geographical coverage limits	Spain, Portugal, Greece & Ireland	Objectives 1,2 and 5b regions.* No regional objectives
Areas	Environment and transport infrastructures only	In principle, all sectors
Procedures	Funding is granted on a project-by-project basis	Most of the funding is granted for programs
Funding available	Ecu 16,223 million between 1993 and 1999	Ecu 172,506 million between 1993 and 1999

* = Objective 1= to promote the development and adjustment of those regions that are lagging (per capita GDP less than 75 percent of the EU average); Objective 2= specifically targets industrial decline (based on an above average unemployment rate); and Objective 5b= promotes the development of rural areas. The Structural Fund has five major objectives. The other objectives include the combating of long-term unemployment (Objective 3), the assistance of youth unemployment purposes (Objective 4), and the adjustment of agriculture structures (Objective 5a).
Source: "The European Union's Cohesion Fund," European Commission, 1994, p.4.

The source of new Cohesion Fund financial resources is an open question because it is unlikely that the richer nations are ready to make additional contributions for the sake of greater cohesion, even if this aids the establishment of the EMU. To date, the new member nations have not contributed adequate new resources. Early predictions in the 1990s estimated the net contributions of Austria, Sweden and Finland to the EU budget to be Ecu 3 billion (US$3.7 billion). But, more recent (1994) estimates imply that the net contributions of the three new member nations would reach only Ecu 1.7 billion by 1999 -- half of what had been predicted.[58] Table 3.16 shows the rebates to Austria, Sweden and Finland.

[58] Is Bigger Better? The Economics of EC Enlargement. CEPR, 1992, p.72, and Ian Barnes and Pamela Barnes, The Enlarged European Union, 1990, p.159.

Table 3.16
Rebates to New EU Member Nations of Austria, Sweden and Finland (in Ecu million)

	1995	1996	1997	1998
Austria	583	106	71	35
Finland	476	163	63	33
Sweden	201	128	52	26

Source: Barnes, Ian and Pamela Barnes. The Enlarged European Union, 1995, p.160.

Attempts to obtain additional financial resources by changing existing tax-sharing schemes, such as the VAT, agricultural levies, and customs duties or introducing new tax-sharing schemes, as for example, cash flow corporate taxes, is politically difficult. The opt-out countries create additional complications.

It is unlikely that under the current common budget structure large-scale regional equalization policies could be developed. Economic integration schemes such as the EMU promote centralist tendencies as, for example, common trade policies and foreign exchange operations. Consequently, the common budget will have additional functions, including Cohesion Fund disbursements and the promotion of macroeconomic stabilization in the case of asymmetrical shocks. To sustain the EMU, it will be necessary to reform the common budget and to consider fiscal harmonization (and fiscal federalism) a policy priority, not only for the common institutions but also for the member states. The Maastricht Treaty does not provide for fiscal federalism and, considering the political and economic circumstances prevailing, it is unlikely that any relevant decisions will be reached within the foreseeable future.

The EU's 1995 common budget represented only a little over 1 percent of the common GNP. The relatively small size of the budget in conjunction with the absence of any reform makes it difficult to envision the common budget as a fiscal redistribution mechanism with capabilities similar to the budgets used in other large monetary unions, as for example, the United States or Canada. Most monetary unions counterbalance the loss of internal exchange rates as adjustment tools in the case of asymmetrical shocks with large interregional fiscal transfers or fiscal "shock absorbers". The Maastricht Treaty's failure to address the issue of fiscal federalism, coupled with the small relative size of the common budget and the Treaty's monetary and fiscal constraints, leaves the EMU in a vulnerable position because it does not provide member nations with sufficient options to deal with macroeconomic shocks. It is quite possible that, at least until the year 2000, the common budget will not exceed 2-2.5 percent of the combined GDP of the EU nations and that national governments will be able to retain fiscal policy as an adjustment tool. The debate about the inability of the fiscal mechanisms to redistribute income is irrelevant because of the relatively small size of the common budget. In the same vein, the debate over fiscal federalism that is the management of, for example, labor markets by both the common institutions and national governments also becomes irrelevant.

THE ROLE OF NATIONAL FISCAL POLICIES IN THE EMU

Monetary union brings with it a certain degree of fiscal laxity, because it provides easier and wider access to external financing. Simultaneously, it restraints long-term national budget plans because it eliminates the option of monetizing the public debt. Even disciplined national budgets could be misaligned with common fiscal policies, underscoring the importance of fiscal coordination and surveillance.

The evidence supporting the desirability of autonomous national fiscal policies in a monetary union is convincing. But, what is less clear is the extent to which such policies should become a common concern. Thus, the appropriate mix of fiscal autonomy, enforced discipline and coordination is an important policy consideration in the EMU.

The Need for Budgetary Policy Autonomy

Budgetary Policy as a Stabilization Tool

When in a monetary union, monetary policies are lost as macroeconomic adjustment tools, the role of national fiscal policies is enhanced. There is a consensus that the best substitute for nominal exchange rates is wage-price flexibility as opposed to fiscal policies. But because the wage-price system is not flexible, exchange rates, fiscal policy or budgetary adjustments may be used to allay the medium-term temporal, country-specific imbalances or permanent shocks.[59]

If a demand shock such as a temporary increase in household consumption or a fall in the savings rate is experienced by a national economy together with inflation, the demand for domestic output could increase. In a floating exchange rate system monetary policies would respond to this with an increase in interest rates, which reduces domestic demand and raises the exchange rate. Both outcomes reduce the inflationary effects of the shock. But in the EMU, monetary policies will be directed by the ECB at the common economic issues. Consequently, the response to country-specific shocks could, at least, only be potential. Under such circumstances the burden of stabilization rests on price and wage adjustments.[60] However, in imperfectly integrated markets, wage-price adjustments could take time. This is why fiscal policies need to be used to

---

[59] The use of budgetary adjustments to address permanent shocks in the medium-term is not specific to the EMU. For further details and evidence, see "One Market, One Money," 1990, pp.103-4.

[60] An equilibrium in the goods market still mandates a real exchange rate appreciation, as this market would still not be perfectly integrated.

offset the impact of an increase in domestic demand. If fiscal expenditures are curtailed in time, prices increase to a lesser degree. Following a resumption of savings, this could limit output and employment losses.

Despite the increased effectiveness of fiscal policies under the EMU,[61] budgetary policies could be applied only in the medium-term and could not be used to fine-tune in the short-term. Nor could effective fiscal policies alleviate the risk of higher budget deficits. Thus, fiscal stabilization policies under the EMU could result in a trade-off of short-term stabilization for a more difficult adjustment in the long-run.

Although conditions could be right to maximize fiscal effectiveness, EMU member nations do not have to adopt fiscal fine-tuning methods. According to the Mundell-Fleming model,[62] such effectiveness depends on fixed exchange rates and free capital movements which would minimize the interest cost of fiscal policies. The pre-1993 ERM environment, which was characterized by such conditions, did not result in budgetary management because only severe country-specific shocks justify such an action. Thus, the use of common fiscal "shock-absorber" mechanisms reduces the need for short-term stabilization efforts at the national level.

The Budget as an Adjustment Tool

If a nation encounters a permanent shock as, for example, an ongoing rather than a temporary fall in the savings rate, it is reasonable to assume that the medium-term repercussions are similar regardless of the exchange rate regime. Real currency appreciation takes place and an external deficit develops. However, the response to such a deficit is influenced by the type of exchange rate system that is used. In a floating system, real appreciation is reflected in a rise in the nominal exchange rate, whereas under the EMU, the real appreciation takes place primarily through a rise in domestic prices.

Regardless of the exchange rate system, external balance must eventually be achieved. There are three possible adjustment mechanisms to do this. The first is the raising of external debt to the point where wealth and disposable income through inflation deteriorate, which reduces consumption. This mechanism is independent of the exchange rate system and can be effectively used only in the long run, because it requires the private sector to build up net foreign debt or assets and allowing inflation to

---

[61] According to the Mundell-Fleming model, the most effective fiscal policies require an environment that includes (i) fixed exchange rates and (ii) free capital movements which would minimize the interest rate cost of fiscal policies. "A Reply: Capital Mobility and Size." Canadian Journal of Economics and Political Science, 30 August 1964, pp.421-31. (It should be noted that this is the original reference for the two-country Mundell-Fleming model and its two-country version.)

[62] "A Reply: Capital Mobility and Size," 1964, pp.421-31; and Dornbusch, Rudiger. Open Economy Macroeconomic, New York: Basic Books Inc., 1980.

diminish wealth.

The reduction of wealth through the erosion of the real value of money balances through inflation is a second possible adjustment mechanism. This approach also uses nominal exchange rates to offset inflationary consequences. However, under the EMU this cannot be done except when the EU is treated as a whole in relation to the rest of the world. Nor is this mechanism a very powerful or desirable approach, as it violates the price stability goal of the EMU. Thus, it is preferable to place more reliance on the third adjustment mechanism, fiscal policy, because this would raise the aggregate nominal savings rates by permanently decreasing budget deficits. If the need in the EMU arises to change real exchange rates because of a buildup of undesirable external imbalances, the only available macroeconomic tool is fiscal policy.

Whether the EMU enhances or diminishes the role of fiscal policies as an adjustment tool depends on the equilibrium between surpluses and deficits caused by free capital movements and the elimination of exchange rate risks. The use of fiscal policies to adjust real exchange rates and the external account also matters. EMU optimists claim that, on balance, the need for fiscal policy adjustments would decrease. Others, however, believe that national fiscal surpluses and deficits would not converge in the medium-term. Current national budget deficits or surpluses are a function of social safety nets such as social security or pension systems, differing future demographic needs, varying magnitudes and modes of public investment financing and/or varying sizes of capital stock. This is why "fiscal shock absorbers" are necessary.

Under the EMU, fiscal policy is important not only as a stabilization tool but also as an adjustment mechanism. The establishment of external balances requires such policies, as does the stabilization effort in the case of country-specific shocks. But this can be done only over the medium-term. National budgets are likely to differ in their medium-term targets, thus fiscal autonomy is warranted. Yet, this increases the need for fiscal discipline.

The Use of Fiscal "Shock Absorbers"

National fiscal policy instruments become critical under the EMU because they are the only tools available to governments to react to external shocks, particularly if these shocks are accompanied by unemployment in low labor mobility environments. If the shocks are transient, depending on the size of outstanding national debts, governments may finance temporary deficits through the international capital markets. Thus, it may be necessary to develop common assistance mechanisms to help governments "weather the storm."

Advocates of common fiscal "shock absorbers" concede that they should not be used as a mechanism to balance income levels but should rather be employed to provide insurance against country-specific shocks. They should be automatic and invisible, because of moral hazard problems. Already several such fiscal "shock absorbers" have been proposed. One is based on the U.S. federal reinsurance model.[63] It call for Brussels to partially finance national unemployment insurance schemes through an automatic transfer of funds from countries with below average to those with above average unemployment rates. Supporters of this scheme argue that it is needed because labor mobility in the EU is limited and therefore economic shocks cannot be dispersed. However, under present political and budgetary conditions, this argument is unrealistic. Moreover, even in the United States unemployment insurance is financed and provided mostly at the state level.

Another set of common fiscal "shock absorbers," discussed in the MacDougall Report,[64] call for a federal structure to partially offset regional income differences by way of income redistribution through the budget. The report uses the United States as an example, quoting studies[65] which have shown that the federal budget offsets 30 to 40 percent of the differences in per capita income across states. Poor states contribute less in income taxes but receive higher social security payments. However, other studies[66] not only question but contradict such findings, and argue that the U.S. tax and social security system has a limited role as an automatic fiscal equalizer. A federal fiscal system cannot ensure against shocks such as changes in income -- it can only react to them. Thus, it is difficult to justify fiscal "shock absorbers" using the U.S. as an example.

When financial market efficiency is considered, such propositions become even more questionable. Yet the fact that the international capital markets do not always finance transient economic shocks is a good argument for the introduction of fiscal "shock absorbers". It is important, however, to distinguish between transitory and permanent shocks, as the latter cannot be financed forever and would therefore require adjustments in real wages and/or labor mobility. It should also be kept in mind that it is not clear whether Brussels could provide insurance against permanent country-specific shocks without addressing the issue of income redistribution.

---

63 Eichengreen, Barry. "One Money for Europe? Lessons from the US Currency Union," Economic Policy, No. 10, April 1990, pp.117-87.

64 MacDougall, Sir Donald, Dieter Bciche, Arthur Brown, Francesco Forte, Yves Fréville, Martin O'Donoghue and Theo Peters. "Public Finance in European Integration," Commission of the European Communities, Brussels, 1977.

65 Sachs, Jeffery and Xavier Sali-i-Martin. "Federal Fiscal Policy and Optimum Currency Areas." Working Paper, Harvard University, 1989. Also, MacDougall, Sir Donald et al. "Public Finance in European Integration." Commission of the European Communities, Brussels, 1977.

66 Von Hagen, Jürgen. "Fiscal Arrangements in a Monetary Union," May 1991. Also, Gros, Daniel and Erik Jones. "Fiscal Shock Absorbers in the US," Manuscript, Center for European Policy Studies, Brussels, July 1991.

The EMU's Impact on Government Budgets

Under the EMU, governments lose income. As inflation rates converge, they cannot use high inflation rates through either seigniorage, or in the short run, through the non-indexation of tax brackets and rates to generate revenues. But the EMU also affects interest rates and public debt service which, in turn, shapes government expenditures. In the most inflationary nations the nominal exchange rate is reduced and the public debt and, therefore the recorded deficits, shrink. Finally, the EMU affects taxation and the provision of public goods. While the first and second effects are direct consequences of the EMU, the third involves the broader issues of taxation and spending convergence.

Seigniorage Revenue Losses

Seigniorage revenue losses in a low-inflation economic and monetary union have negative effects on welfare in the weaker economies with higher inflation, such as the Southern EU nations. These countries would have to either increase taxes or lower public spending. But the welfare cost of higher taxes has to be weighed against the welfare gains of lower inflation and its impact on the debt-service burden. All in all, the welfare cost of seigniorage losses under the EMU may be relatively small. While some countries view seigniorage losses as a gross public finance loss to the extent that a reduction in such revenues mitigates inflation and fiscal laxity, seigniorage losses could also be seen as a source of welfare gains. Therefore, it is important to weigh the economic costs and benefits of resorting to seigniorage as opposed to taxation-based financing.

Government revenues are also affected by inflation in a variety of other ways such as tax collection delays, the VAT, and lags in the determination of income tax brackets and/or social security benefits. In other words, inflation can either increase or decrease government revenues. But even if in a low-inflationary EMU taxes could be increased to compensate for the loss of government revenues, it is highly debatable whether this would reduce welfare. Figure 3.1 illustrates the seigniorage revenue incomes of the EU governments in 1988.[67]

---

[67] 1988 data are used because this section is based on the EU study "One Market, One Money," 1990, pp.121-22.

Figure 3.1
Seigniorage Revenues in the European Union, 1988
(as a % of GDP)

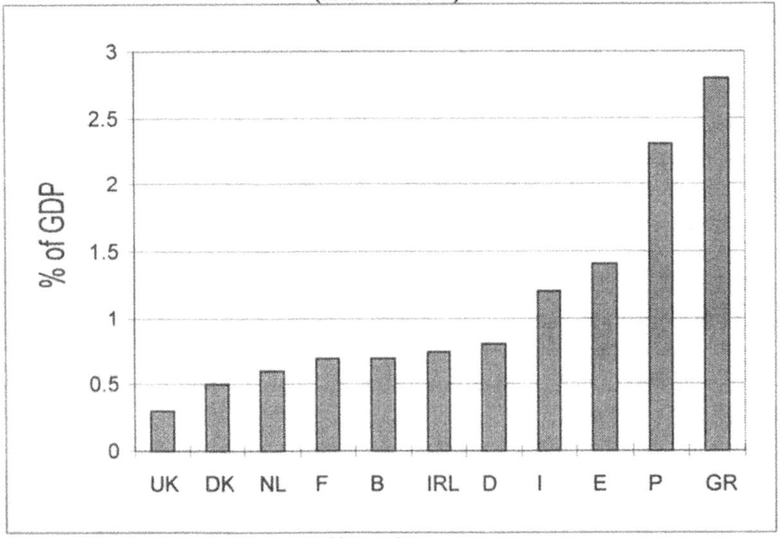

Source: "One Market, One Money," 1990, p.121.

Table 3.17 shows the potential gross seigniorage revenue effects of the EMU on four EU nations (Greece, Portugal, Spain and Italy) whose seigniorage revenues were above 1 percent of GDP in 1988. The 1993 scenario not only assumes the full effects of the "Single Market," the convergence of reserve ratios to 2 percent and the elimination of interest payments on reserves, but also the decline in the use of cash owing to technology developments. But no convergence of inflation rates is assumed. The EMU scenario assumes all of the conditions in the 1993 scenario as well as the convergence of inflation rates at 2 percent per annum.

Table 3.17
Potential Gross Seigniorage Revenue Effects of the EMU

	1982-84 (1)	1985-87 (2)	1988 (3)	1993 (4)	EMU (5)	Single market effect (6)=(4)-(3)	EMU effect (7)=(5)-(4)
Greece	2.46	2.34	2.75	1.84	0.71	0.91	1.13
Portugal	4.39	2.85	2.23	1.62	0.71	0.61	0.91
Spain	1.93	1.03	1.36	1.20	0.86	0.16	0.34
Italy	2.23	1.21	1.13	0.72	0.51	0.41	0.21

Source: "One Market, One Money," 1990, p.122.

Impact on Interest Rates and Public Debt Service

The EMU will affect member country public debt in direct relation to its impact on interest rates. The average public debt interest payment of the EU member nations is approximately 5 percent of GDP. But some nations, such as Italy, Belgium, Ireland and Greece have interest payments of 10 percent or higher, amounting to more than 20 percent of all government expenditures. If the EMU becomes a low-inflationary and low-interest rate area, the budget deficits could be pruned but the real depreciation of the public debts would slow down.[68] Other repercussions would also take place. The analysis of long-term nominal interest rate and of inflation trends in the EU show a direct correlation between higher inflation and higher long-term interest rates. Thus, inflation-prone nations experience a higher interest burden on their public debt.[69] However, if ex post (or realized) real long-term interest rates and inflation are observed over the same period it is difficult to establish such a correlation because other factors such as the role of capital controls also have to be taken into consideration.

The EMU's impact on real interest rate differentials will be significant in that it permanently affects the absence of exchange rate premiums, which is, however, not relevant as regards interest rates. This holds true for identical assets only. It is an entirely different matter when the identity of the borrower is taken into consideration. Then, government bond yields differ because of the varying degrees of credit worthiness and private financial portfolio movements. Under the EMS/ERM, the financial markets generally expect low default risk within the EU, as any sign of unsustainability is seen as leading to debt monetization rather than default, and, consequently, as depreciating the relevant national currencies. If, however, the ECB remains true to its "no bail-out" policy, debt monetization will not be possible in the EMU and thus in the high debt nations the risk premiums would increase which raises the cost of public borrowing for these nations. For example, German "Euro" (single currency) bonds will in all probability be graded as AAA while the Italian "Euro" bond could be AA, thus, the German "Euro" bonds would have a higher value. This would affect non-EU nations as well. Yet, it is not likely that ECB policy will not be affected by a large nation's unsustainable debt. Consequently, financial markets continue to assume that debt monetization will take place rather than default.

Financial portfolio structures may affect public bond rates if the debt is mostly held domestically. Public bond rates increase if private portfolio holders, depending on yields, are reluctant to increase their share of the public debt. Thus, in the EMU, high debt/risk member nations benefit because they would have access to a wider capital market and could thus obtain lower borrowing costs.[70] This is based on the assumption

---

[68] High inflation generates high interest rates which increase the interest payments on the public debt. This is counterbalanced by the real depreciation of the debt.

[69] This is basically a nominal phenomenon.

[70] This assumes that private financial portfolios will be similar within the EU and that the portfolios consist largely of domestic financial assets. The latter assumption is more plausible because within the EU, a very large proportion of public debt is held domestically. For example, the 1986 Italian budget deficit was held primarily by households (53 percent) and banks (30 percent),

that public bonds of the same maturity and risk are perfect substitutes and thus generate similar yields, regardless of which government issued them. It is not clear to what extent the increase in the risk premiums, and thus the cost of public borrowing in the high-debt nations would offset the increased availability of funds in the wider capital market, thereby reducing the potential cost of public borrowing. Nonetheless, it is reasonable to assume that EMU member nations with a high but stable public debt will experience the greatest benefit.

High-debt nations might be reluctant to join the EMU because of the public finance cost of price convergence. Downward convergence limits seigniorage revenues and initially increases real interest rates, which could result in debt monetization. Such disinflation could cause temporary complications for nations with long-term debt rather than long-term, fixed-interest bonds, because of an increase of the real yields. But debt stabilization may not only reduce the cost of disinflation but also reduce the risk of debt monetization. Additionally, medium-term budgetary savings could offset seigniorage revenue losses for the high-inflation and high-debt nations. For high inflation nations, because of the sustainability of such an approach, a middle of the road solution is better than the extremes of rapid fiscal convergence and immediate commitment to irrevocably fixed exchange rates. Although ex ante real interest rate reductions could aid investment and growth in the medium-term, a too early commitment to the EMU might result in unsustainable negative side-effects owing to an excessive drop in real interest rates. Yet, a too early commitment to exchange rate stability could make disinflation slow and more painful in the more inflation-prone countries such as Italy, where firms have access to foreign borrowing.

Impact on Taxation

Several EU Commission studies[71] have concluded that there is little need for overall convergence requirements in fiscal matters such as social security contributions[72] or taxation.[73] However, different tax systems coupled with labor mobility could complicate such matters as tax redistribution and mobile taxes, while negative revenue spill-overs such as high taxes could reduce consumption. The limited mobility of unskilled workers and the economies of scale in the provision of public goods add complications and strengthen the case for harmonization.

Studies have shown that in the "Single Market," and in the EMU, certain categories of taxes (for example, social security and income taxes) which are a large part of government revenues, do not have to be harmonized. Some harmonization and convergence, however, is desirable for direct taxes as, for example, capital income or

---

while foreign borrowing amounted to only 3 percent of the total outstanding debt.

[71] For example, "One Market, One Money," 1990.

[72] Such contributions must be accompanied by differences in real wages.

[73] As long as labor mobility is factored in. Labor mobility is expected to remain low, especially due to language barriers.

withholding taxes and indirect taxes such as the VAT. But VAT rates have to be changed only insofar as cross-border differences can be reduced.

Corporate tax harmonization is necessary in an economic union while income tax harmonization is essential in a monetary union. The former not only needs a harmonized tax base but also a common minimum rate. The largest overall impact on taxes will come from the completion of the "Single Market" and not from the establishment of the EMU, because inflation convergence, tighter constraints on fiscal deficits and the loss of exchange rates as policy tools do not promote tax convergence. Inflation convergence could lead to slightly higher taxes because of seigniorage losses in the high inflation nations. Tighter constraints on fiscal deficits could lead to tax increases in some countries -- but with little or no ramification for tax convergence in the EMU. Tax differentiation due to tax autonomy will put additional pressures on the financial markets and public sector efficiency.

SUSTAINING THE MAASTRICHT TREATY FISCAL CONVERGENCE CRITERIA

Since it is unlikely that financial markets will provide the discipline needed to pursue budgetary coordination, it will be necessary to establish common oversight of national budgetary policies. To prevent fiscal laxity, the Maastricht Treaty has charged member nations with achieving the EMU through adherence to two quantitative convergence criteria, termed "reference values," which are prerequisites for taking the third and final step toward the EMU. These "reference values" must be met during the Stage II transition period. They consist of an upper limit of 3 percent on the budget deficit/GDP and a 60 percent limit on the public debt/GDP ratio. The key post-Maastricht Treaty question is how to implement and enforce such limits.[74]

Budget deficits are not only major national economic problems but are also the single most important block on the road to meeting the Maastricht convergence criteria. This is a result of the struggle between the budget "hardliners," such as the Bundesbank, and others who see political advantages in a flexible approach to deficit reduction. The first EMI Report on the subject, "Progress Towards Convergence,"[75] published in November 1995, found that only four countries -- Ireland, Luxembourg, Denmark and Germany – met the 3 percent deficit/GDP ratio requirement in 1995; the Netherlands was a close fifth. The second EMI "Progress Towards Convergence" report[76] published in November 1996, found that only three countries -- Ireland,

[74] The Maastricht Treaty's provisions for fiscal federalism are deficient.

[75] "Progress Towards Convergence." European Monetary Institute, Frankfurt am Main, November 1995.

[76] "Progress Towards Convergence 1996." European Monetary Institute, Frankfurt am Main, November 1996.

Luxembourg and the Netherlands -- met the 3 percent deficit/GDP ratio requirement in 1996, with Finland and Belgium begin quite close.

The 1995 EMI Report pointed out that the majority of EU member nations exceeded the 60 debt/GDP percent limit, with two countries (Belgium and Italy, members of the original EEC) scoring more than 50 percent above the limit. Only four countries (Germany, France, U.K. and Luxembourg) met the 60 percent/GDP debt criterion. In 1996, the EMI found that debt performance was mixed among the member nations and had not improved very much as only three countries (France, Luxembourg and the United Kingdom) met the criterion, with Germany and Finland slightly above the 60% limit. Although the majority of nations will probably satisfy the deficit and debt criteria by 1998, Belgium, Italy, Ireland and especially Greece may not be able to do so.[77] Table 3.18 shows general government borrowing and gross debt as a percentage of GDP of all EU member nations in 1995 and 1996.

Table 3.18
Budgetary Convergence in 1995 and 1996
(as a percentage of GDP)

	Deficit % of GDP 1995[(a)]	Debt % of GDP 1995[(a)]	Change In Debt 1993-1995[(a)]	Deficit % of GDP 1996[(b)]	Debt % of GDP 1996[(b)]
Reference Value	***-3.0***	***60***		***-3.0***	***60***
Belgium	-4.5	134.4	-3.1	-3.3	130.6
Denmark	-2.0	73.6	-6.7	-1.4	70.2
Germany	-2.9	58.8	10.6	-4.0	60.8
Greece	-9.3	114.4	-0.1	-7.9	110.6
Spain	-5.9	64.8	4.4	-4.4	67.8
France	-5.0	51.5	6.2	-4.0	56.4
Ireland	-2.7	85.9	-11.5	-1.6	74.7
Italy	-7.4	124.9	5.5	-6.6	123.4
Luxembourg	+0.4	6.3	0.0	+0.9	7.8
Netherlands	-3.1	78.4	-2.9	-2.6	78.7
Austria	-5.5	68.0	5.0	-4.3	71.7
Portugal	-5.4	70.5	3.3	-4.0	71.7
Finland	-5.4	63.2	5.9	-3.3	61.3
Sweden	-7.0	81.4	5.2	-3.9	78.1
U.K.	-5.1	52.5	3.9	-4.6	56.3

(a) = data from "Progress Towards Convergence," EMI, 1995.
(b) = data from "Progress Towards Convergence," EMI, 1996.
Source: "Progress Towards Convergence," EMI: Frankfurt am Main, November 1995, p.21 and "Progress Towards Convergence 1996," EMI: Frankfurt am Main, November 1996, p.IV.

---

[77] Due to political reasons, Belgium is likely to join the EMU through the looser interpretation of the convergence criteria. Ireland's high public debt ratio is falling, thus her chances to participate are good. See Chapter VI for additional information on the potential EMU entrants.

The relatively high interest rates and moderate growth rates during 1995-96 did not improve the debt situation. There is growing political pressure on Italy, Ireland and Belgium, which meet most other convergence criteria, to curtail their debt so as to be able to join the EMU.[78] But there is no concern about Greece, the economic delinquent of the EU, even though the Maastricht Treaty makes some exceptions concerning the meeting of the deficit and debt criteria by individual nations. For example, the deficit criterion can be relaxed if the ratio has declined substantially and continuously toward the 3 percent limit or if the deficit is exceptional and temporary. However, in both instances the ratio must be close to the 3 percent requirement. Debt ratio requirement exceptions can be made only if the ratio is diminishing and approaching the reference value at an acceptable rate. It was Jacques Delors who enabled the Commission to apply the Treaty requirements in such a discretionary manner.

The process of defining excessive deficits and taking action against member nations with such deficits is technically and politically complex. It is the ECOFIN Council that determines whether a country has a deficit excessive enough to prevent it from entering the EMU. However, according to Article 104c, para.5 of the Maastricht Treaty, the Council's decision must be based on the recommendation of the Commission. Thus, it is in fact the Commission that decides whether a country's deficit is excessive or not. If the Commission does not have an opinion, the Council of Ministers has no basis for deciding whether a country violates the criterion. Thus, the Council of Ministers could not block a country's membership. But it is unlikely that the Commission could or would act without reaching an understanding with the national governments, the EMI, the ECOFIN and the European Council. It needs to be emphasized that the EMI "Progress Towards Convergence" reports which provide the raw data for evaluating national performance in meeting the convergence criteria are a product of cooperation between the EMI and the national central banks.

Policy formulators keen on the early establishment of the EMU are trying to ease the political, social and economic costs of meeting the fiscal convergence criteria. For example, in 1996 they have suggested that Belgium's privatization revenues should be counted toward deficit reduction, although this is not permissible under the Maastricht Treaty. Others have suggested even more liberal interpretations of the deficit and debt criteria by emphasizing overall directions and trends as opposed to the mechanical application of the requirements. However, it is these types of suggestions and proposals that could bring strong responses from the deficit hardliners such as Germany, specifically the Bundesbank and the German Constitutional Court which has pledged to uphold the letter of the law with regard to the convergence criteria. At some point, German Finance Minister Theo Waigel has even insisted that nations wanting to join by 1999 submit to an additional set of strict fiscal rules beyond the convergence criteria.[79]

---

[78] In 1996 and 1997 many of the member nations applied one-time revenue generating schemes and engaged in fiscal fudging to augment their budgets. See Chapter VI for a detailed discussion.

[79] During 1995, Minister Waigel argued that budget deficits should be limited to less than 1

Under such circumstances, the role of the EMI, the ECOFIN and the Commission is quite complicated as taking a hard line with deficit offenders might arrest the momentum toward the EMU by emphasizing the extent to which nations are not meeting the requirements. But "going soft" would upset the most important and influential future EMU member nation -- Germany. With this in mind, and in view of the French government's domestic social problems (unemployment and the strikes caused by budget cuts), it would seem that any substantial budget cuts in the short-term may be politically difficult. Nonetheless, a strong political determination to meet the 1999 deadline may override such differences. Chapter VI discusses this subject in more detail.

The Transition Stage

There is considerable debate about whether binding budgetary constraints are necessary during the transitional Stage II, in which nations are still in control of their national currencies and their central banks are aware of the inflationary consequences of debt monetization. Proponents of binding budgetary constraints argue that the constraints would identify the desirable EMU participants (i.e., the fiscally disciplined nations), while opponents claim that governments could manipulate the quantitative criteria requirements to make their budget balances look artificially strong as it happened during 1996-1997. Current expenditures can, for example, be adjusted using zero coupon bonds to deal with outstanding obligations so as to suspend debt service payments in the short-run. This, in turn, could reduce government interest charges and lead to more positive budget balances. Numerous other schemes, such as, new one-time taxes and privatization profits can also been used. Opponents of binding constraints argue that the convergence criteria or reference values are soft because the language of the Maastricht Treaty allows political considerations.[80] They claim that unpredictable shocks to national income might distort the various nations' economic credibility, making it difficult to distinguish fiscally disciplined from undisciplined governments. In contrast, supporters of binding budgetary constraints point out that, owing to the financial markets' concern about the EMU and its consequences, it is better to have the formal budgetary constraints prior to Stage III so as to instill confidence and take budget measures that are similar to those of the highly credible Bundesbank. This is the most convincing argument for binding budgetary constraints during Stage II.

It has also been argued that binding budgetary constraints would not be necessary in Stage III if the ECB is seen as unwavering in fighting inflation. The Maastricht Treaty mandates price stability as the ECB's primary policy objective, but has restricted it from providing credit to both the common institutions and member

---

percent of national GDPs. This, of course, proved politically unacceptable by the other EU nations.

[80] The Treaty allows arbitrary exemptions if fiscal deficits exceeding the reference values are "only exceptional and temporary" or if member nations' excessive deficits are decreasing "at a satisfactory pace" toward the reference value.

nations through the "no bail-out" rule which prevents the ECB from acquiring the debt of nations undergoing fiscal crises. Yet it is not too difficult to conceive of circumstances under which the ECB reneges on its commitment not to monetize budget deficits, albeit, in a discrete manner. Thus, excessive deficit restrictions are seen as a necessary precaution.

In the event of excessive deficits and/or debt accumulation during the transitional Stage II, the Commission, after taking into account the share of the deficit accounted for by capital expenditures and considering other relevant issues such as the long-term budgetary and economic position of a country, may declare that an excessive deficit and debt exists and report its findings to the Council of Ministers. The ECB's predecessor, the EMI, has to collaborate with the Commission in filing such reports with the Council.

Following an explanation by the government incurring the excessive deficit and debt, the ECOFIN Council uses a qualified decision-making process to decide whether to ratify the Commission's ruling. If the Council concurs with the Commission, it makes confidential recommendations to the nation affected on how to resolve the deficit/debt problems. If the ECOFIN Council subsequently determines that the country did not comply with the recommendations, the Council may make the recommendations public, implying that the country does not qualify for entry into Stage III of the EMU. The ECOFIN Council must also set up guidelines through which it can determine whether the nation could sustain an irrevocably fixed exchange rate (during the early phases of Stage III) without monetary financing. The guidelines have to be clear and transparent with little room for interpretation so as to limit political pressure for exceptions and to enable the ECOFIN Council to use the guidelines as a basis for sanctions.

According to the Maastricht Treaty, through a qualified majority vote, the European Council must decide by early 1998 as to which member states satisfy all five conditions of EMU participation. Following this, Stage III may begin on January 1, 1999.

The Post-EMU Stage

Following the establishment of the EMU, the ECOFIN Council will continue as the oversight institution and will not only coordinate economic policies but also formulate broad policy guidelines. Once nations have joined the EMU, the Treaty prohibits excessive deficits and debt in both Stage II[81] and Stage III. Just as in Stage II, the ECOFIN Council, on the basis of the Commission's recommendation, may make appropriate policy recommendations to countries generating extreme deficits and/or

[81] Although the EMU membership decision will be made in early 1988, Stage III will not begin until January 1, 1999. Thus, it is important that the EMU member countries sustain the Maastricht fiscal convergence criteria until the start of Stage III.

debt. If they fail to take corrective action, the Council may publish the recommendations. This raises a dilemma. While non-EMU member nations can be pressured to follow appropriate policies, the Maastricht Treaty has no provisions to penalize and/or expel EMU members for noncompliance.

If an EMU member nation fails to make progress on the ECOFIN Council's recommendations, the Council may require it to submit a program of fiscal adjustment accompanied by an explicit timetable. If it fails to do so, the Council can institute procedures through a qualified majority decision to (i) restrict the nation's ability to issue bonds and securities; (ii) open discussions with the European Investment Bank to reconsider its lending policy; and (iii) impose fines on and/or require the offending nation to maintain non-interest-bearing deposits with the EU. But the effectiveness of such sanctions is questionable. If oversight is left to national governments, in a self-regulatory setting, politicians will always find some political, economic or social rationale to incur deficits. Thus, for political reasons, there are no provisions in the Maastricht Treaty to expel EMU members nations for non-compliance. This could foster uncertainty and affect the credibility of the EMU. However, on German insistence, member nations agreed to a post-EMU fiscal “Stability and Growth Pact” during the Dublin European Council Summit in December 1996. But this agreement was watered-down resulting in only semi-automatic fines which are determined politically. (See Chapter VI for a detailed discussion of the 1996 post-EMU fiscal “Stability and Growth Pact”.)

Yet, it is probable that even with the excessive deficit and debt criteria, the "no bail-out" rule and the post-EMU fiscal “Stability and Growth Pact”, the ECB will decide in a discretionary, subjective and/or discriminatory manner when it comes to the EMU “core” as opposed to the smaller economies. It is possible that it will relax the rules for the large, and, in the long-run, fiscally more "trustworthy" economies such as Germany. Thus, the EMU is like George Orwell's world where "all animals are equal but some are more equal than others."[82]

[82] Orwell, George. Animal Farm, New York: Harcourt Brace Publishing, 1946, p.112.

IV THE SINGLE CURRENCY (THE EURO): COSTS AND BENEFITS

TOWARDS THE "EURO"

Political, economic and financial market forces have prompted the EU member nations to seek ever closer economic, monetary and political integration at the end of the century -- by way of the single currency. The 1989 Delors Report, the ratification of the Maastricht Treaty in 1993 and the European Council Summits held in Madrid in 1995 and Dublin in 1996, were major milestones on the road towards this objective.[1] The Euro has been chosen as the new single currency, to be introduced in 1999 on a non-cash basis and in 2002 as the sole legal tender of the EMU member nations. Box 4.1 provides a brief historical overview of the evolution of the single currency, which is not an entirely new idea in Europe.

---

[1] In part, based on the success of the Ecu in the private capital markets, the Delors Report promoted the introduction of a European single currency.

Box 4.1
A Brief History of Europe's Single Currency

The road toward a single European currency had begun a long time ago:

Middle Ages:	Feudal rulers frequently tried to unify coins with their trading partners.
1865-1927:	The Latin Coin Union was created among France, Belgium, Italy, Switzerland and Greece (undermined by policy quarrels).
1957:	The Treaty of Rome provided for coordination of economic and monetary policies.
1970:	The Werner Plan sought a monetary union by 1980 (derailed by the fall of Bretton Woods and the international oil crisis).
1972:	The EC nations had linked their currencies within the confinements of the currency bands of the "Snake."
1979:	The creation of the European monetary system (EMS) and its exchange rate mechanism (ERM) in 1979, which mandated +/-2.25 percent currency bands.
1987:	The Single European Act addresses the issue of a monetary union in a treaty for the first time.
1989:	The Delors Report outlined a three-stage plan for an economic and monetary union (EMU).
1991:	The EU heads of state agreed to the Maastricht Treaty (signed in 1992) to create an EMU, at the earliest in 1997 or at the latest by 1999. Fiscal, monetary and exchange rate convergence criteria are created for entrance requirements into the EMU.
1992:	An ERM crisis leads to the pound sterling and Italian lira dropping out of the system.
1993:	An ERM crisis occurred during which the speculative attack on the French franc almost led to the ruin of the ERM, whose bands were widened to +/-15 percent. The Maastricht Treaty is ratified.
1994:	The European Monetary Institute (EMI), the forerunner of the European Central Bank (ECB) was created as stipulated by the Maastricht Treaty.
1995:	The May 1995 EMI Green Report presented a revised, extended deadline for Stage III of the EMU. The December 1995 European Council Madrid Summit adopted the name "Euro" for the European single currency and also adopted the EMI recommendations on the new deadline for introducing the single currency.
1996:	The December 1996 European Council Dublin Summit unveiled the "Euro" and the new "ERM II" is agreed to begin January 1, 1999. The Italian lira rejoins the ERM.
1997:	EMI's "Progress Towards Convergence" report provides the official statistics on member nations meeting the Maastricht convergence criteria in 1997.
1998:	Using 1997 data, the EU is scheduled to decide which member nations meet the Maastricht convergence criteria and thus, can participate in EMU.
1999:	The EMU members' currency parities are supposed to be irrevocably fixed and new "ERM II" is to begin. Post-EMU fiscal "Stability and Growth Pact" becomes active for EMU participants. The ECB is to come into existence and to conduct a common EU monetary policy. The Euro is to be introduced on a non-cash basis and is to be utilized for EU monetary policy and central banking.
Jan-July 2002:	Notes and coins of the Euro are to be issued to the public.
July 1, 2002:	EMU participants' national currencies are to be abolished and the Euro is to become the sole legal tender.

Source: Adopted from Financial Times, March 26-27, 1996.

Single Currency Types

The single currency proposals developed over time fall into two categories depending on the manner in which such currencies are introduced into a monetary and economic system: (i) the market-led, competing or parallel currency approach; and the (ii) institution-led approach.

Market-Led Approach

The market-led approach involves a new or redefined currency which is introduced through competition. Although it is usually assumed that governments would issue money, at the extreme, this can mean the free, private issue of currencies. The public would then chose the best i.e. the one that offers the most stable purchasing power. The introduction of such a currency requires little in the way of official action as it is introduced and used in parallel with the existing currency (ies.) In time such a currency can become the single currency by gradually crowding out the other currency (ies) through competition without fixing exchange rates and converging national economic and monetary policies.

Until the 1980s little had been written about the nature of the parallel currency in general and its introduction into an economic and monetary system in particular. However, with the gradual evolution of the EMU plan in the EU, including the agreement on the single currency, the parallel currency and its introduction process became the focus of attention.

Other studies[2] have explored the circumstances under which a parallel currency could be used under conditions of moderate exchange rate flexibility. They do not assume capital controls or legal restrictions on the use of a particular currency but do predicate national financial markets and payments systems that are in the process of integration while still maintaining some national characteristics -- a scenario approximating that of the EU. The studies agree that a parallel currency is desirable only if it has substantial advantages over national currencies.

A single currency must fulfill the classic functions of money: it must serve as a unit of account, as a store of value and as a transaction medium. However, a parallel currency's marginal advantage in only one of these functions is not a sufficient reason to adopt it as the single currency.

The concept of a parallel currency becomes meaningful and its existence

[2] Gros, Daniel and Niels Thygesen. Concrete Steps Towards Monetary Union, Brussels: Center for European Policy Studies (CEPS), 1989 and Triffin, Robert. "The Intermixture of Politics and Economics in the World Monetary Scandal," American Economist, 1989.

relevant only during the intermediate stage of a monetary union, when the different currencies are not substituted for one another because of transaction costs and/or exchange rate expectations.[3] But, because of high transaction costs, a parallel currency is unlikely to emerge as the single currency if national currencies and the parallel currency are not perfect substitutes for one another. Therefore, a parallel currency can be widely used only in a setting of a high degree of monetary integration. But it is not clear whether this also increases the demand for a parallel currency.

Factors that influence the use of a parallel currency in a monetary union characterized by less than perfect exchange rates and less than perfectly integrated financial markets and payment systems, include: (i) the remaining degree of exchange rate variability; (ii) the predictable or expected exchange rate fluctuations of the parallel currency against the other currencies; (iii) the bid-ask spreads; and (iv) the legal tender status of the parallel currency.

The literature addresses these issues only in a limited fashion. There is a need for more sophisticated analyses and discussions of the parallel currency approach, not only to fill in the theoretical gaps but also to better understand the practical implications.

Institution-Led Approach

In contrast to the parallel currency approach, the institution-led approach involves a currency that is introduced by a common authority, a government(s) and is used as legal tender within a sovereign region. Such an approach can involve an existing national or institutionalized currency, as, for example, the redefined Ecu, or a new single currency, the Euro. The institutionalized currency performs the three classical functions of money, but it is not privately issued. It is issued by a common authority or government. For the Euro to become the legal tender in the EMU nations, it has to be officially declared the single currency by amending the Treaties of Rome.

European Single Currency Proposals

Concurrent with the 1989 Delors Report, which recommended the adoption of the new, redefined Ecu as the single currency, several other currency proposals were also considered. They had been developed by individuals and the U.K. government, and had been the subject of discussions during the late 1980s and early 1990s. The following three proposals were the most widely considered: the European Commodity Money (ECOM), the European Parallel Currency (EPC), and the "Hard" Ecu. Other proposals such as a "hard" EMS/ERM i.e., fixed exchanged rates, or the transformation

---

[3] Gros, Daniel. "Paradigms for the Monetary Union of Europe," Journal of Common Market Studies, 1989.

of a strong national currency such as the Deutsche mark into the single currency were discarded early during the discussions because of economic efficiency considerations and political concerns.

The European Commodity Money (ECOM)

The European Commodity Money (ECOM)[4] was proposed by Sir Alan Walters[5]. Based on a commodity basket, the ECOM would have existed as a parallel currency alongside the current EU currencies and the Ecu basket. Sir Alan believed that the people of Europe should be free to use the currency of their choice and emphasized that currency competition preserves not only individual choice but also the reliability of the currency as a unit of account. The ECOM would have been issued by a newly created European Investment Bank (EIB).

The ECOM would not have involved bimetallism. It would not have been based on gold stocks or on silver because a fixed mint-ratio of precious metals generally falls victim to Gresham's Law - bad money drives out good money. Nor did it call for a "basket" of the two metals - an obvious way to circumvent the Gresham effect.

The ECOM would have been indexed to goods that are produced rather than those that are consumed: thus the currency would not have been protected against changes in the terms of trade. Therefore, the retail price index would have been a much more appropriate unit of value standardization.

The advantage of a convertible basket of commodities as proposed by Sir Alan is the avoidance of the "idiosyncrasies of gold or silver supplies and of all the political problems associated with gold producers or owners."[6] Moreover, in a monetary system based on such a basket, "velocity adjusts endogenously, whatever happens to the demand for [base] money, to keep the price level constant."[7] Although the commodity basket is redeemable in convertible currencies of equivalent value, "the commodities must be readily storable and of identified uniform quality, in the same way that, under the gold standard, the gold content is of a given purity."[8] Such a basket, however, has to be large enough to accommodate the normal lot of wholesale trade. This requires the monetary authorities to engage in commodity dealing.

Most politicians would hesitate to use large stocks of commodities as a basis for their nation's monetary system. However, the ECOM did not necessarily require

---

[4] Alan Walters, Sterling in Danger: The Economic Consequences of Pegged Exchange Rates, London: Fontana/Collins, 1990, p.117.

[5] Sir Alan Walters was Prime Minister Margaret Thatcher's chief economic adviser. Currently, he is the Vice-Chairman of the American International Group (AIG).

[6] Walters, Alan. Sterling in Danger, 1990, p.117.

[7] Walters, Alan. Sterling in Danger, 1990, p.117.

[8] Walters, Alan. Sterling in Danger, 1990, p.118.

commodities as reserve assets. It could have been redeemed for financial assets (i.e., existing convertible currencies), which would have provided holders with sufficient resources to buy the commodities. But the problem of insuring the uniform quality of commodities would not have been so easily resolved. Moreover, commodity indexes and exchanges would have had to be modified and harmonized to ensure ECOM standards that would have kept the currency in line with the weighted average of retail price indices. While the ECOM system could have provided protection against government interference by eliminating incentives to distort national indices, such indices are usually not calculated frequently enough for this to be effective.

The European Parallel Currency (EPC)

The European Parallel Currency (EPC) was proposed by Roland Vaubel[9] as a floating, indexed, parallel (competing) currency based on the money supply (M1 or M2) index.[10] In 1978 and again in 1990,[11] Vaubel argued in favor of the parallel as opposed to the institution-led approach of introducing the single currency, because the former entails a discovery process that allows the identification of the currency's strengths and weaknesses. Vaubel advocated free competition among existing national currencies, adding that competition was the only empirical way of finding out whether a currency union could be efficient. Over time, competition could determine not only which currency is efficient and who is its most efficient supplier, but also what the optimal money supply rules are. But Vaubel cautioned that such rules would vary over time. Thus, he recommended that national governments take a neutral position on currency competition and leave the decision on currency preferences to private users. To this end, he emphasized that the EPC would have had to be used as a means of tax payments and government expenditures. Moreover, legal tender laws would have had to be adjusted so that the EPC could not have been discriminated against.

Vaubel argued that if free competition among all currency union member nations is not politically feasible, the use of a parallel currency is the second best solution. He suggested the use of the indexed Ecu currency basket, as recommended in the 1975 "All Saints' Day Manifesto for European Monetary Union,"[12] and ruled out the use of a simple basket comprised of the EU currencies because some of these were highly inflationary. Moreover, he argued against the linking of currencies to the

---

[9] Roland Vaubel is a Professor at the University of Mannheim, Germany.

[10] Vaubel, Roland. Strategies for Currency Unification: The Economics of Currency Competition and the Case for a European Parallel Currency, No. 156, Germany: J.C.B. Mohr (Paul Siebeck) Tübingen, 1978; and Vaubel, Roland and Emil-Mann Claassen, eds. International and European Monetary Systems, "Currency Unification, Currency Competition, and the Private ECU: Second Thoughts," New York, 1990, p.181.

[11] Vaubel, Roland. Strategies for Currency Unification, 1978; and Vaubel, Roland, "Currency Competition and the European Monetary Integration," The Economic Journal, London: Royal Economic Society, 100, No.402, September 1990, pp.936-46.

[12] "The All Saints' Day Manifesto for European Monetary Union: A Currency for Europe." The Economist, November 1, 1975.

strongest currency (a "hardened" EMS/ERM) because this would create inflationary pressures. He added that the EPC would have had to be consistently anti-inflationary, because anything less than a stable EPC could not have overcome the entry barriers that new currencies face and thus the EPC would not have been able to compete on an equal footing with the established national currencies.

Vaubel's parallel currency would have been based on a weighted floating basket analogous to the present-day Ecu basket. However, unlike the Ecu basket Vaubel would have permitted member nation currencies to respond "permanently to the currency preferences of European money holders. In the simplest case, the EPC currency weights would have been equal to the share that each member currency occupied in the EU money supply at market exchange rates."[13] In other words, the basket weights of EU member currencies could have been increased by the same percentage as the decline in a national currency's purchasing power, measured by the consumer price index.

Such an approach would have involved using the monetary aggregate that yielded the smallest rate of overall inflation since March 1979. The weights would have been adjusted automatically at regular (annual) intervals, on the basis of a moving average. "To the extent that a national member currency was displaced by the EPC, its weight in the EPC would diminish."[14] As the EPC would have probably displaced the weakest (high inflation) currencies, the weight adjustments would have strengthened the EPC. "Even if all member currencies that are weaker than the EPC basket [were to drop] out completely, the weight adjustments would ensure that the EPC basket is always stronger than at least one of the remaining member currencies. Only if the EPC...displaced all but the strongest member currency [i.e., if it ceased to be a basket] would the process of currency substitution have come to an end."[15] Hence, in this final phase the EPC would have been as strong as the strongest national currency.

According to Vaubel, his indexed basket would have minimized inflation and real exchange rate risks but he cautioned that the EPC would not have minimized nominal exchange rate risks, exchange rate information costs, or the deviation from the money-holding optimum. He also pointed out that exchange rate costs would have been relatively small, because nominal exchange rate risks are relevant only in the short-run. Moreover, because seigniorage could have been eliminated through interest payments on all types of money except currency in circulation, an EPC, defined as an indexed basket of all currencies, would probably have offered the highest benefits.

---

[13] Vaubel, Roland and Emil Mann Claassen, eds. International and European Monetary Systems, 1990, p.181.
[14] Vaubel, Roland and Emil Mann Claassen, eds. International and European Monetary Systems, 1990, p.181.
[15] Vaubel, Roland and Emil Mann Claassen, eds. International and European Monetary Systems, 1990, p.181.

Vaubel believed that the parallel currency approach i.e. currency competition, would not have been accepted by governments. They would have rather opted for an exchange rate union because such an arrangement would leave some discretion to politicians and their central banks in dealing with electoral concerns. Nevertheless, he realized that an exchange rate union would not eliminate currency conversion costs, risk of parity changes and exchange controls. Lack of credibility would be another major weakness because it would make the reduction of inflation difficult.

The "Hard" Ecu

The U.K. government proposed the introduction of a thirteenth currency, the "Hard" Ecu,[16] to exist together with (i.e., in parallel) the other 12 EC member nation currencies. The proposal was vague, calling for the "Hard" Ecu to be a new floating currency that, unlike the Ecu, would not have been based on a basket.[17] This new currency would have been managed by a European Monetary Fund (EMF) whose statutes would have been written into law through amendments or additions to the Treaties of Rome.

The "Hard" Ecu would have been placed in the narrow band (+/-2.25 percent) of the original ERM, and its exchange rate would have been free to vary within the band against the other national currencies. However, this currency would never have been allowed to depreciate. Thus, if and when realignments would have been required, the "Hard" Ecu would have been at least as strong as the strongest national currency, the Deutsche mark. This unique feature would not have been automatic. It would have been the EMF's responsibility to ensure that a devaluation of the "Hard" Ecu would have never occurred.[18]

The U.K. proposal was vague as to details in order to leave the development and refinement of the plan to the Intergovernmental Conferences (IGCs) managed by the European Council. The U.K. plan envisioned that the EMF would have managed the currency. For example, it would have issued notes and coins denominated in the "Hard" Ecu, provided clearing functions and it would have been active in money markets to sustain "Hard" Ecu interest rates. The EMF's balance sheet would have maintained two main monetary liabilities: (i) interest-bearing deposits denominated in the "Hard" Ecu, and (ii) "Hard" Ecu notes and coins issued in accordance with transaction demand. The liabilities, especially the above-mentioned interest-bearing deposits, would have constituted most of the "Hard" Ecu money stock (monetary base) during the early stages of development.

---

[16] Grice, Joe. "The U.K. Proposals for a European Monetary Fund and a "Hard Ecu:" Making Progress Towards Economic and Monetary Union," Bank of England -- Monetary Policy Division, November 1990, and Bishop, Graham. The Creation of an EC "Hard Money, Salomon Brothers, London: European Business Analysis, July 1990.

[17] The content or index of this currency has yet to be disclosed by the British Government.

[18] Grice, Joe. Bank of England, 1990, p.2.

The EMF would have been required to control inflationary pressures. Thus, it could not have expanded its balance sheet by adding to the aggregate money supply and could have issued only liabilities (interest-bearing deposits and notes and coins) in exchange for national currencies. This would have meant that the increased use and issuance of the "Hard" Ecu would have been accompanied by an equivalent reduction in national currency supplies.

Through a repurchase requirement the EMF would have limited inflationary pressures, which parallel currencies are prone to generate if not properly restrained. The main liabilities would have been "Hard" Ecu deposits, and the main assets would have been national currencies which could have been used to purchase such deposits. However, had the EMF held these national currencies indefinitely, a "potentially dangerous loophole in monetary discipline would be created."[19] For example, as a result of loose monetary policies and excessive currency supplies, exchange rates could have experienced downward pressures. However, had the EMF bought unlimited amounts of the "Hard" Ecu, the downward pressures would have been reduced, as the currency would have had a safety net.

The "Hard" Ecu proposal received little support from the other governments, which were concerned that the introduction of "an additional source of money creation without a precise linkage to economic activity could jeopardize price stability."[20]

The Selection of the Euro[21]

The ratification of the Maastricht Treaty in November 1993[22] and the subsequent agreements have ended both the official and unofficial discussions of the single currency alternatives and of the ways in which such a currency should be introduced.[23] It has been decided that the start of the third and final stage of the process toward the EMU will entail the irrevocable locking of exchange rate parities of the qualifying member nations[24] on January 1, 1999. As originally proposed by the 1989 Delors Report, following this stage the present-day European currency unit (the Ecu) will become a free floating single currency in its own right also on January 1, 1999 and at the same time, the Ecu will be renamed the Euro,[25] the ECB begins its operations and

---

[19] Grice, Joe. Bank of England, 1990, p.4.

[20] Delors Report, 1989.

[21] The following discussion of the Euro is a summary of the May 1995 EU Commission "Green Paper," the two EMI "Progress Towards Convergence," reports of November 1995 and 1996, and the 1995 Madrid and 1996 Dublin European Council Summits, as stated in Chapter I.

[22] The Maastricht Treaty was agreed on at the December 1991 European Council Summit, signed in February 1992 and ratified in November 1993.

[23] The Euro "sales campaign" was launched at a conference hosted by the EU Commission in Brussels on January 22, 1996. It was attended by businessmen, financiers, media representatives and politicians.

[24] Qualification will be determined by meeting the Maastricht convergence criteria.

[25] It should be noted that in the Delors Report and The Maastricht Treaty the single currency

common monetary policies will be introduced.

From January 1, 1999 to December 31, 2001,[26] the first phase of Stage III, private economic agents may but will not be required to use the Euro. However, the ECB and its national central bank affiliates (the ESCB) will have to use the new currency for all monetary policy and exchange rate transactions. All new traded public debt issues will also have to be denominated in the Euro, in particular securities actively traded in the financial markets, so as to create a "critical mass" that will foster its use and augment the liquidity and depth of the financial markets. Commercial banks will have the option of taking deposits and opening accounts in the Euro ahead of the mandatory changeover deadline of July 1, 2002. However non-traded debt may still be denominated in national currencies. It is not yet clear when existing stocks of public debt will have to be converted into the Euro.

To aid the smaller banks during the transition, conversion facilities will be established which will go out of business once national currencies are discontinued as legal tender. These facilities will be provided by the central banks "to enable those counter-parties to deal with the national central banks in the national monetary units for all payments, in particular for all monetary policy operations. These facilities will allow them to send payment orders or other information to national central banks expressed in national monetary units."[27] EMU member nations with a large number of small banks will experience large conversion costs in moving toward the Euro.

When the first phase of Stage III is completed by December 31, 2001, it will be succeeded by the second and final phase, which will begin on January 1, 2002, and will last through July 1, 2002. During this stage the Euro will for the first time be physically introduced and will become the sole legal tender of the EMU nations. It should be borne in mind, however, that due to potential logistical difficulties the introduction of the new banknotes and coins cannot be done overnight. Time will be needed to mint a sufficient number of new coins and to modify existing automated teller machines. Therefore, the introductory period will extend over six months -- a short enough period to avoid prolonged problems arising from what will amount to a dual currency system in each member nation. On July 1, 2002, the changeover to the Euro will be completed "for all operations and all agents"[28] as national banknotes and coins will be withdrawn from circulation and the Euro will become the sole legal tender. All monetary liabilities will de jure be redeemable only in the Euro and the banking and finance industries will no longer be permitted to transact in national currencies. Thus,

---

was referred to as the "Ecu." The name was changed to the "Euro" at the December 1995 European Summit in Madrid.

[26] All EU national currencies will remain in circulation. On January 1 1999, the exchange rates of the chosen EMU member nations' currencies will be permanently fixed through predetermined "conversion rates."

[27] "Progress Towards Convergence." EMI, November 1995.

[28] "Progress Towards Convergence." EMI, November 1995.

on July 1, 2002, the process of implementing the EMU will end.[29] For a more detailed discussion on unanswered Euro questions and the impact on the financial markets see Chapter VI.

However, while all of these dates are set, the protracted discussions of the political and economic costs as well as of the benefits of the single currency continue unabated. Among the issues still to be resolved is the sensitive question of the relationship between the "inner core" of Euro users and those who either fail to qualify for the EMU (the "outer core") or wish to opt out of the same. To date, the new "ERM II", set to begin on January 1, 1999, is designed to provide the link between the "inner core" and "outer core" currencies and serve as a transition mechanism towards the Euro.

The Determinants of Exchange Rate Regimes

The international monetary system is characterized by a wide range of exchange rate arrangements. The Bretton Woods system was based on fixed exchange rates tied to gold through the U.S. dollar. This was followed by a system in which the U.S. dollar functioned as an anchor to which other national currencies were pegged. In 1973 a number of countries adopted freely floating exchange rates which were legitimized through the Jamaica Agreement in 1976. Since then some countries have chosen to maintain fixed exchange rates, others use the adjustable peg approach while still others use managed floating (or flexible) rates.[30]

Perfectly fixed or pegged exchange rates are similar to the gold standard in that currencies are fixed to every other currency. Under such a system each country has to follow the monetary policies of the anchor currency country to obtain the same inflation rate and to keep the exchange rate fixed or within the established currency bands.

In a flexible regime, exchange rates are determined by market forces. When demand for a currency increases, the currency appreciates and when demand falls, it depreciates. A major advantage of flexible rates is that each country can follow domestic macroeconomic policies independent of other countries also using such rates.

To maintain fixed or pegged exchange rates, countries have to have similar inflation levels -- a requirement that creates problems. If the anchor currency country experiences inflation pressures, this could lead to a depreciation of its currency. Thus, due to accumulated tensions, the initially fixed rates may need adjustment. The anticipation of such changes causes speculative capital movements; thus, in the end, parities change, but in the worst and most costly way. The same holds true for semi-

[29] Due to the complexity of this undertaking, the timetable could be extended.

[30] "Floating" and "flexible" exchange rates are interchangeable terms.

pegged exchange rate systems such as the ERM of the EMS, only to a lesser degree.

Monetary policies differ from country to country. Fixed exchange rates, however, make it difficult for countries to carry out monetary policies suited only to their domestic stabilization needs. Under flexible exchange rates they can choose desired levels of inflation and the financial markets will adjust the exchange rate. Thus, flexible exchange rates permit smoother adjustments without inflating or deflating economies, as might be necessary under fixed rates.

In fixed and semi-pegged exchange rate regimes, central banks must maintain large reserves to intervene in the exchange markets to sustain parities whenever necessary. Such interventions are sterilized to offset the adverse impact on the domestic money supply. Under flexible exchange rates, central banks do not have to intervene and thus do not need to maintain the large reserves that are required when an inappropriate exchange rate[31] is defended over an extended period of time.

Flexible exchange rates, however, remove the external discipline imposed on monetary and fiscal policies. The lack of such pressure renders the floating exchange rates inherently inflationary unless strict internal monetary discipline is applied, as is the case in Germany. The volatility of flexible exchange rates also increases uncertainty which, in turn, might lead to a reduction in international trade and the lowering of global living standards. In contrast, fixed exchange rates provide an anchor for countries with high inflation levels and variability. They can tie their inflation levels to that of the anchor nation by maintaining a fixed exchange rate with the anchor currency. This forces countries to follow the policies set in the anchor currency country and keeps the overall inflation level and variability relatively low as long as the anchor currency remains strong.

Under flexible exchange rates, destabilizing speculation in foreign exchange markets may take place. Speculators can cause exchange rate fluctuations through transactions in the US$8 trillion daily foreign exchange and capital markets. When they expect a currency to depreciate, they take short positions. This increases the downward pressures on the currency's exchange rate. As a result, if an economic or political shock occurs, exchange rates overshoot their equilibrium level more than they would have in the absence of speculation. Such misaligned rates which do not reflect economic fundamentals can lead to inefficient resource allocation which might create temporary unemployment and/or results in wasted production capacities.

A flexible exchange rate regime creates uncertainty. Economic units can minimize the resulting risk through hedging in the forward and future markets. But hedging is costly. Moreover, small countries do not have efficient forward and futures markets to enable firms to offset such risks. This creates a bias against trade and an

---

[31] An inappropriate exchange rate exists when, for example, a currency's value is not in line with economic fundamentals.

incentive for foreign direct investment.

Countries with fixed exchange rate regimes as opposed to countries with floating exchange rate regimes exhibit systemic differences and generate different costs and benefits. In the smaller and more open economies that depend on international trade, the price of tradable goods affects the overall national price index which increases the impact of the exchange rate on prices. Accordingly, fixed exchange rates are preferable in open economies because their effect on competitiveness is minimal.

Countries that prefer high inflation rates to generate an increase in short-term employment or to reduce real government debt will have difficulties maintaining fixed exchange rates. Nations that conduct most of their trade with one other country may fix their currency to such a country's currency and thus achieve a degree of price stability. But, countries with diversified trading partners may find fixed exchange rates less beneficial.

The exchange rate regime affects economic stability to varying degrees. If the goal is to minimize unexpected domestic price level fluctuations, an exchange rate system that will do this should be chosen. If, for example, the prices of foreign goods fluctuate more than domestic prices, then floating rates would be more appropriate since they help to insulate the domestic economy against international price effects. If domestic money supply fluctuations are large, fixed rates are better because they will reduce the domestic price impact of the fluctuations. The excess money supply can be contained through floating exchange rates but this is reflected in higher domestic price levels and depreciating currencies.

Monetary and Fiscal Policies under Fixed, Flexible and Managed Exchange Rates

Under the proposed EMU, the EU wants to establish permanently fixed exchange rates and, eventually, introduce the single currency, the Euro. However, such a monetary system must still function in relation to the other currencies of the rest of the world.

Standard monetary and fiscal policy tools allow governments to control economic activity within a country or region. Such tools, however, have a different impact on an open as opposed to a closed economy. In the open economies of the EU nations the effectiveness of fiscal and monetary policies depends to a large extent on exchange rate flexibility and the international mobility of capital.

Fiscal policies influence the allocation of resources in complex ways. They determine the share of the resources absorbed by the public and private sectors and influence resource allocation and use within each sector. They can do so through the imposition of taxes or the granting of their counterpart, subsidies, that may make some products relatively more expensive than others. Fiscal policies also influence the distribution of income among different groups of individuals or regions within a country.

Fiscal policies also have a Keynesian impact. The balance between government revenues and expenditures and the manner in which a deficit is financed can influence the level of aggregate demand and thus affect the level of output, employment and prices. In other words, fiscal policies play a crucial role in macroeconomic policy formulation. The monetarists, however, reject this proposition.

International capital movements involve the flow of funds for the purpose of buying and selling financial assets across national boundaries. Thus, they can be understood as a response to the differing rates of return in various countries. Capital mobility is high if a change in the relative interest rates across countries generates large flows. In contrast, capital mobility is low if such changes generate small flows. Capital mobility is "perfect" if the slightest difference between domestic and foreign interest rates generates such massive flows that the difference immediately disappears. But this can happen only if investors view domestic and foreign assets as perfect substitutes.

Monetary Policies under Fixed Exchange Rates

Monetary policies involve the expansion or contraction of the domestic credit component of a country's money base. An expansion in the domestic credit component causes a corresponding increase in the money supply.[32] This places downward pressures on interest rates which increases investments and aggregate demand, thus raising output and employment. However, with high capital mobility a decline in interest rates could result in a rapid capital outflow that could lead to a balance of payments deficit. To keep a currency from depreciating under such circumstances, the monetary authorities intervene in the foreign exchange markets through the purchase of the currency. But a contraction in the overall money supply acts against the initial expansion which was intended to stimulate the economy. Thus, under fixed exchange rates, monetary policies are weakened if capital is internationally mobile.

In the extreme case of perfect capital mobility among countries, the downward pressure on interest rates could result in a huge outflow of capital that would offset the initial monetary expansion. Hence, there is no net expansion in the money supply and stimulation of economic activity. Under conditions of perfect capital mobility and rigidly fixed exchange rates, monetary policies could be ineffective in a small country. A larger country has a better chance of applying effective monetary policies under the same conditions.

---

[32] A contraction in the domestic credit component of the money base could result in opposite reactions following exactly the same sequence of events as in the case of an expansion in the domestic credit component.

Capital outflows that contract the money supply can be constrained through official limits on such outflows. The resulting foreign exchange market interventions cause the money supply to contract and this reduces the balance of payments deficit. Capital outflows can also be limited through the less rigid pegging of the currency exchange rate. If a nation is willing to accept a slight depreciation of its currency, it can reduce the extent of foreign exchange intervention and can thus minimize the reduction in its money supply.

Fiscal Policies under Fixed Exchange Rates[33]

Fiscal policies are concerned with the level and structure of revenues and expenditures. They may involve changes in government spending patterns and/or in taxation. The causal sequence of fiscal policies (assuming that there is a change only in government spending while tax rates and the money supply are held constant) shows that in the case of expansionary fiscal policies government spending will rise, thereby causing a direct increase in the level of aggregate demand, which raises the level of output and employment. This, in turn, increases the public's demand for money. Assuming high capital mobility, the resulting higher interest rates could lead to a rapid capital inflow, generating a capital account surplus. Simultaneously, the increase in output and employment could increase imports which could push the trade account into a deficit. Hence, the overall effect of expansionary fiscal policies on the balance of payments depends on whether the trade account deficit or the capital account surplus is larger. Since capital is highly mobile, the capital account surplus may outweigh the trade account deficit, resulting in an overall balance of payments surplus.

If the balance of payments is in surplus and the government is committed to fixed exchange rates, it will sell its currency to keep it from appreciating. This results in an expansion of the international reserve component of the money base which generates an expansion in the overall money supply. Thus, the higher the international mobility of capital, the greater the effectiveness of fiscal policies under a fixed exchange rate.

Monetary Policies under Flexible Exchange Rates

A government may wish to increase income levels through expansionary monetary policies. As before, an increase in the domestic credit component of the money base results in a corresponding increase in the money supply. This causes interest rates to decline which, in turn, stimulates investments and aggregate demand. Because capital is highly mobile, there is a rapid outflow of capital, which creates a deficit in the capital account of the balance of payments, depreciating the currency.

---

[33] This discussion is based on Keynes, John M. General Theory of Employment, Interest and Money, New York: Harcourt, Brace, & World, 1936.

However, because exchange rates are flexible, there is no need to intervene in the foreign exchange markets. Currency depreciation stimulates exports and curtails imports until, under perfectly flexible exchange rates, the trade account is in balance or surplus. If there is a surplus, it is equal to the capital account deficit which keeps the overall balance of payments in balance. But the trade account surplus adds to the aggregate demand for domestic goods, reinforcing the expansionary effects of the reduction in interest rates. This supports the initial attempt by the monetary authorities to expand output and employment.

Capital outflows keep domestic interest rates from declining, which weakens the interest rate induced stimulation of investments and aggregate demand. However, an increase in external trade demand can make up the difference. If capital is perfectly mobile, all the increase in aggregate demand can be generated through a trade account surplus.

Monetary policies are effective under flexible exchange rates because of the capital outflow and its effect on the exchange rate and the trade account. In contrast, under fixed exchange rates monetary policies are hampered by the capital outflow and its impact on the balance of payments and on foreign exchange interventions.

Fiscal Policies under Flexible Exchange Rates

Expansionary fiscal policies under flexible exchange rates result in the same outcome as under fixed exchange rates, until a capital account surplus and an increase in imports occur. The difference lies in their effect on the trade balance. A capital account surplus causes the currency to appreciate, and this, in conjunction with an income growth induced increase in imports, pushes the trade account into a deficit. As imports increase and exports decrease, aggregate demand declines, which offsets any rise in such demand caused by an increase in government spending. Hence, in an open economy with high capital mobility and flexible exchange rates, attempts to increase output and employment through expansionary fiscal policies are not fully effective.

If capital is perfectly mobile, the trade deficit offsets an increase in government spending. This renders fiscal policies ineffective until the trade deficit rises sufficiently to offset the increase in government expenditures. Thus, aggregate demand and therefore output and income could be above their original levels, as could be the demand for money. As long as this is the case, capital continues to flow in, the currency continues to appreciate and the trade deficit increases. This process comes to a halt only when the trade deficit matches the increase in government spending. Then aggregate demand reaches its original level, as do output, income and employment. Under perfect capital mobility the process could work so rapidly that the trade deficit could rise more or less in tandem with government spending, in which case the temporary increase in income would be limited. Hence, under freely fluctuating exchange rates and perfect international capital mobility, fiscal policies are ineffective.

For a summary of the impact of monetary and fiscal policies under fixed as opposed to flexible exchange rates, see Table 4.1.

Table 4.1
Summary of the Impact of Monetary and Fiscal Policies under Fixed versus Flexible Exchange Rates

Under Fixed Exchange Rates *
Expansionary Monetary Policies: Expansion of the money supply will be reversed by subsequent foreign exchange market intervention. Since actual monetary expansion will be smaller than originally intended, the increase in output and income will not be as great as anticipated. In the case of perfect international capital mobility, the monetary authorities will be contracting the international reserves component of the monetary base just as rapidly as they are expanding the domestic credit component, so that the money supply itself remains unchanged. Output and income, therefore, will not rise permanently.
Expansionary Fiscal Policies: There is no initial expansion of the domestic credit component of the money base to accompany the increase in government spending. However, the international reserves component is expanded as the monetary authorities intervene in the foreign exchange markets to keep their currency from appreciating. This provides the necessary monetary support for an expansion in income and output.
Under Flexible Exchange Rates*
Expansionary Monetary Policies: In this case expansion of the domestic credit component of the money base is not offset by foreign exchange market intervention, as exchange rates are free to fluctuate. The larger money stock will support a higher level of output.
Expansionary Fiscal Policies: There is no expansion of the domestic credit component of the money base to accommodate government spending, nor is there a subsequent expansion of the international reserve component owing to foreign exchange intervention. Thus, there is no expansion of the money stock to support any permanent increase in income and output.
* Exactly the opposite would occur, in the same sequence, under a contractionary monetary and fiscal policy.

Source: Hodgson, John S. and Mark G. Herands. International Economic Relations, New York: Prentice Hall, 1983, p.153.

Monetary and Fiscal Policies under a Managed Float

To a large extent foreign exchange markets are characterized by managed floats. This has several important policy implications.[34] If, for example, a government decides to implement monetary policies in an open economy with high international capital mobility, it can enhance the effectiveness of such policies by limiting foreign exchange market interventions through the free-floating of exchange rates. This minimizes changes in the international reserves component of the money base that might offset the deliberate changes in domestic credit.

If the objective is to keep exchange rates stable and to implement a given set of monetary policies, then capital inflows and outflows may have to be controlled to achieve and maintain the intended effects. But governments have to accept the costs of imposing such controls such as the misallocation of capital and, ultimately, of real resources.

If a government wishes to conduct fiscal policies without changes in the domestic credit component of the money base, it can increase the effectiveness of such policies by stepping up its foreign exchange interventions to keep interest rates stable. This, however, changes the international reserve component of the money base that supports fiscal policies.

By generating different costs and benefits, flexible as opposed to fixed exchange rates have differing economic impacts. For a summary of the effects of monetary and fiscal policies in an open economy with high international capital mobility, see Table 4.2. For a more detailed discussion of inflation and unemployment generated by monetary and fiscal policies under fixed and flexible exchange rates, see **Annex 4.1** at the end of this chapter.

[34] In each case, under conditions of high international capital mobility.

Table 4.2
Summary of the Effectiveness of Monetary and Fiscal Policy in an Open Economy with High International Capital Mobility

Home Macroeconomic Policy	Domestic Exchange Rate Policy	Effect on Domestic Money Supply	Effectiveness on Domestic Macroeconomic Policy
Monetary Policy	Fixed exchange rates	Attempt to change domestic credit component of money base offset by change in international reserves component of money base	Monetary policy weakened
	Freely fluctuating exchange rates	Attempt to change domestic credit component of money base not offset by change in international reserves component of money base	Monetary policy remains effective
Pure Fiscal Policy	Fixed exchange rates	International reserves component of money base changes so as to support fiscal policy	Pure fiscal policy strengthened
	Freely fluctuating exchange rates	No change in either domestic credit component or international reserves component of money base	Pure fiscal policy ineffective

Source: Hodgson, John S. and Mark G. Herands. International Economic Relations, 1983, p.154.

Nations do not function in a void and are effected by the spill-over effects generated by other nations' monetary and fiscal policies. This is especially true under conditions of high international capital mobility. See Table 4.3 for a summary of the effects of foreign monetary and fiscal policies on the domestic economy under conditions of high international capital mobility.

Table 4.3
Summary of the Effects of Foreign Monetary and Fiscal Policy on the Domestic Economy under High International Capital Mobility

Foreign Macroeconomic Policy	Domestic Exchange Rate Policy	Effect on Domestic Economy
Expansionary (contractionary) Monetary Policy	Fixed exchange rates	Inflation (deflation and unemployment)
	Freely fluctuating exchange rates	Little or no change in price level or overall level of economic activity
Expansionary (contractionary) Fiscal Policy	Fixed exchange rates	Deflation or unemployment (inflation)
	Freely fluctuating exchange rates	Little or no change in price level or overall level of economic activity

Source: Hodgson, John S. and Mark G. Herands. International Economic Relations, 1983, p.161.

Irrevocably Fixed Exchange Rates and the Single Currency

A monetary union with irrevocably fixed exchange rates has three main macroeconomic implications. First, with perfect capital mobility nominal interest rates across the member economies are equalized. Second, since exchange rates are fixed and interest rates are equalized, the national currencies become almost perfect substitutes. However, as long as national currencies continue to exist, they will be used to quote prices and they will continue to be traded. But even with irrevocably fixed exchange rates, such trade involves transaction costs through the bid-ask spreads. These costs and the ever-present possibility of exchange rate adjustments prevent national currencies from becoming perfect substitutes. In addition, doubts about the maintenance of fixed exchange rates could generate interest rate differentials in the member nations. Thus, it is the credibility of the irrevocable exchange rate commitment that determines the extent of interest rate equalization. Yet even if exchange rates are irrevocably fixed, interest rate differentials could still exist.

The third macroeconomic implication is that to maintain the credibility of irrevocably fixed exchange rates, the unlimited conversion of any currency at a fixed exchange rate must be guaranteed within the union. But such a multilateral guarantee requires the implementation of monetary policies by a common institution. In the absence of this, any money supply increase by a country's central bank could affect the entire union, thus creating incentives for countries to pursue domestic goals at the expense of other member nations.

The single currency of the EMU, the Euro, will provide additional benefits beyond those provided by fixed exchange rates. International business within the EMU will become domestic business, thus, transaction costs will be limited. Using the Euro as a common unit of account, a store of value and as a means of payment will improve the efficiency and profitability of business activities. Furthermore, through the pooling of currency reserves the Euro will help eliminate speculative capital flows, promote the enlargement of foreign exchange markets and the provision of more financial depth with less volatility.

The benefits of the Euro will be offset by the loss of monetary policies and to some extent exchange rate policies as adjustment tools, leaving fiscal policies as the only effective adjustment mechanism. There is also the risk that following the abolition of national currencies it may be difficult to provide for monetary stability. It is uncertain whether the Euro could provide the same or a better level of stability than does the ERM with the Deutsche mark as the anchor.[35] Indeed, the reaction of those in Germany who fear that their stable national currency will not only be abolished but will also be replaced by an unknown and unproved single currency exemplifies such a risk. The switch from national currencies to the Euro also generate switching costs. Moreover,

---

[35] Prior to 1992.

while a commitment to the Euro increases its chance to succeed, it can also generate costs if currency linkages have to be dissolved at a later date.

The Optimum Currency Area (OCA) and the EU

The costs and benefits of monetary integration with emphasis on a single currency are addressed by the theory of Optimum Currency Areas (OCAs), developed by Robert Mundell in 1961.[36] The theory explores the relative desirability of fixed as opposed to flexible exchange rates in general and the costs and benefits of a single currency in particular.

Mundell identified the characteristics of an optimal geographic area in which a monetary union can be established either through the adoption of a single currency or through the use of different currencies, involving the following arrangements: (i) fully convertible currencies at irrevocably fixed exchange rates; (ii) the absence of bands around currency parities; and (iii) the complete integration of financial markets.[37]

Mundell defines an OCA as "an economic unit composed of regions affected symmetrically by disturbances and between which labor and other factors of production flow freely."[38] His criteria for a functioning OCA are as follows.

1. *Labor and Capital Mobility:* The existence of labor and capital mobility across countries reduces the necessity for using exchange rates as adjustment tools to restore competitiveness and to eliminate imbalances. If labor can move from high to low unemployment regions, wages and other costs can converge. Financial market integration lessens the need for changes in relative costs and prices among countries via exchange rate adjustments, since capital movements can finance inter-regional imbalances. If labor and capital are immobile, relative price changes are the only means of restoring equilibrium. In such a case, flexible exchange rates are more effective than fixed exchange rates and a currency union.

2. *The Openness and Size of the Economy:* The more open and the smaller an economy, the more effective fixed exchange rates are and the more inclined a country is to join a currency union.

3. *Price and Wage Flexibility:* In the case of price and wage flexibility, adjustments can take place through market forces, thereby reducing

[36] Mundell, Robert. "A Theory of Optimum Currency Areas," American Economic Review, 51, 1961, pp.657-65.

[37] Tavlas, George S. "The Theory of Optimum Currency Areas Revised," Finance & Development, June 1993, pp.32-35.

[38] Mundell, Robert. "A Theory of Optimum Currency Areas," 1961, p.657-65.

the need for exchange rate adjustments.

4. *The Integration of Goods Markets:* Countries with similar production structures are affected in the same way by external shocks, which diminishes the effectiveness of exchange rates as adjustment tools.

5. *Fiscal Integration:* If fiscal integration among member countries exists, shocks can be offset through fiscal transfers.

Mundell also addresses the major cost of an OCA -- the loss of monetary policies as adjustment tools. When a country joins a currency union, monetary policies are no longer formulated at the national but at the union level. This eliminates the short-term political option of easing monetary policies during domestic economic downturns. It also limits the flexibility needed to achieve a desired short-term policy mix of inflation, economic growth and unemployment.

The possible symmetrical nature of disturbances and the accompanying high degree of factor mobility may turn the abandonment of nominal exchange rates into an optimal outcome. The adoption of a single currency may also reduce transaction costs which adds to the benefits. Yet, the experience of the EU shows that asymmetrical shocks in its member countries are an economic reality and that labor mobility is quite restricted thus, the benefits of an OCA in the EU may be limited.

The development of the OCA theory in the 1960s was the result of the debate over the usefulness of fixed as opposed to flexible exchange rates. Recently the debate has shifted to a discussion of stabilization policies that disregard the microeconomics of factor reallocation. Newer studies[39] involve (i) real exchange rate variability; (ii) the types of disturbances that affect regions symmetrically (i.e., the co-movement of securities prices; and (iii) the degree of labor mobility.

Exchange rate adjustments are desirable in order to facilitate adjustments among regions experiencing large changes in relative prices, assuming that wages and other nominally denominated costs are slow to adapt. Germany and France are a case in point. An increase in relative productivity in Germany or a shift in demand from French to German goods requires a decrease in relative French costs and prices, otherwise unemployment will result. A failure to respond (i.e., to coordinate) increases the cost of adjustment. However, if the French franc is devalued, the problem is bypassed, which makes rapid progress toward a more stable economy possible. In other words, the more variable real exchange rates are, the stronger the case is for exchange rate flexibility.

As far as regional equity price differentials are concerned, the price of equities, in theory, should reflect the present value of current and expected returns. If

---

[39] Eichengreen, Barry. Is Europe an Optimum Currency Area?, No.478, Discussion Paper Series, London: Center for Economic Policy Research, November 1990.

shocks are symmetrical, returns will rise in one region relative to the others. Thus, the more closely real share prices move across regions, the more symmetrical the disturbances are and the more quickly factors of production will be reallocated from regions experiencing negative to regions experiencing positive shocks.

Finally, the more mobile labor is within a region, the more likely it is that, ceteris paribus, a region may constitute an OCA. Again using Germany and France as an example, if labor productivity in France declines relative to Germany or if demand shifts from the products of French firms to those of their German competitors, assuming that French labor costs do not decline and that there is no change in the nominal exchange rate, French labor should move to Germany where an excess demand for labor exists. Only in this manner can unemployment be prevented.

The OCA literature implies that if most disturbances are external to the EU's ERM zone, and if they affect the member countries symmetrically, a fixed exchange rate is desirable.[40] However, if most disturbances are country-specific, with sticky prices and wages, a flexible exchange rate is preferable. This is an empirical issue that is complicated by the fact that both expected and past disturbances must be considered. The EU is relatively closed to the rest of the world and more open to its members states, thus the most significant disturbances are likely to be originating within the EU. Consequently, country-specific rather than EU-wide shocks will occur. This implies that the ERM is not an optimum exchange rate arrangement for a currency area.

There is no simple answer to the question of whether the EU is an OCA. Given the realization of the "Single Market", it is unfortunate that the OCA literature does not provide insight for the resolution of this issue. Nevertheless, there are some standards that can be applied. They include real exchange rate variability, symmetrical regional disturbances and the degree of labor mobility.

The establishment of a currency union in the EU is likely to be associated with "non-negligible" regional problems. This makes it all the more essential to develop the political and economic conditions necessary for the smooth operation of an OCA. Of the above-mentioned three standards of evaluation, the most important is the degree of labor mobility which is very limited within the EU and will probably remain so for a long time to come. It is important to bear in mind that the elimination of legal restrictions, although necessary, is not a sufficient condition for a high degree of labor mobility. Thus, by all criteria, the current ERM of the EU does not represent an OCA.

[40] This argument is based on the literature on fixed versus flexible exchange rates (i.e. it treats factor [mainly labor] immobility as a given and focuses on the distributions in the channels of transmission).

The EMU as an OCA

The EMU plans have raised questions about whether it could satisfy the criteria of an OCA. A comparison of nominal wage rate flexibility, of labor and of capital mobility in the EMU nations as opposed to the United States may provide insights, but no conclusive answers.

Recent studies[41] on the rigidities of nominal and real wages show that various EU countries suffer from considerable real but little nominal wage rigidity. In contrast the US experiences more nominal but much less real-wage rigidity. This makes it unlikely that wage flexibility could play a significant adjustment role in dealing with asymmetrical shocks in the EMU.

Views concerning the effects of the EMU on future wage flexibility are mixed.[42] The optimists believe that abandoning exchange rate adjustments will force workers and unions to be more flexible in wage negotiations. The pessimists point out that the increased transparency in nominal wage differences following the adoption of the Euro is likely to lead to less flexibility. This view is supported by the unification experience of Germany where nominal wage parity between the eastern and western parts of the country has increased in spite of large productivity differences.

The studies[43] also show that labor mobility in the EU nations is lower than in the United States. Migration rates are relatively low not only among nations but also within countries. Americans move from state to state three times more frequently than do the French and Germans within their countries. If EU citizens do not move among the depressed regions of their countries, they can hardly be expected to move among countries with differing cultural characteristics and languages. Thus, the level of labor mobility is much lower than the level that is required to reduce the need for flexible exchange rates as adjustment tools.

The Delors Report called for the free movement of capital through the deregulation of the financial markets. Research on whether the EU financial markets have become more integrated, is inconclusive.[44] It is possible that capital mobility may increase the economic differences among the EU regions if integration efforts attract more capital to the successful regions rather than to the less successful areas. Therefore, it is not clear whether capital mobility could be an efficient alternative to exchange rate

[41] Layard, Richard, Stephen Nickell and Richard Jackman. Unemployment: Macroeconomic Performance and the Labour Market, Oxford: Oxford University Press, 1991; and Dreze, Jacques H. and Charles R. Bean. Europe's Employment Problem, Cambridge, Mass.: MIT Press, 1990; and Bini-Smaghi, Lorenzo and Silvia Vori, "Currency Substitution, Monetary Stability and European Monetary Unification," in Giacomo Vaciago ed., Europe 1992 and Monetary Union, Milano: Vita e Pensiero, 1991.

[42] "One Market, One Money," 1990, pp.170-74.

[43] Eichengreen, Barry. "One Money for Europe? Lessons from the U.S. currency union," Economic Policy, no. 10, April, 1990 and "One Market, One Money," 1990, pp.170-74.

[44] Fraser, Robert and Robert MacDonald, 1993.

adjustments.

Owing to the removal of intra-regional trade barriers, the EU countries have become more open. Yet, the trade volumes are high in the Benelux countries, but low in the U.K. Thus, the monetary union is less favored by the U.K than the Benelux countries.

A more important problem is inflation variability among member countries. Inflation levels differ because of varying policy preferences. Because the Phillips curve trade-off is no longer accepted, governments have little choice but to target price stability. This speaks in favor of the EMU.

Overall, the arguments for and against the EMU as an OCA are inconclusive. In any case, the debate has switched from this issue to the ability of the EU member countries to meet the Maastricht Treaty convergence criteria. The suspension of several currencies from the ERM and its realignment have increased the importance of the nature of EMU membership.

Overall, EU countries probably do not meet the requirements of an OCA. As a result, an EMU involving all member countries is not economically sound. But a subset[45] of the EU nations such as Germany, the Benelux nations, and France, could form an effective EMU/OCA.

COSTS AND BENEFITS OF THE EMU

The highest level of economic integration is represented by an economic union. A monetary union is part of such a union and must be achieved in parallel to eventually create an economic and monetary union. However, whether an integrated market such as the "Single Market" necessarily leads to an economic and monetary union is not clear. Some of the major benefits that the EMU could generate are microeconomic efficiencies, macroeconomic stability and increased equity among countries and regions. The single currency, the Euro, and the economic union complement and enhance the "Single Market" and this generates micro-economic efficiency. Macroeconomic stability would be derived from better overall price stability achieved through low average inflation and variability but this is feasible only if the ECB can implement and sustain credible monetary policies. The EMU could generate additional gains in the real economy as well such as lesser fluctuations in output and employment. The least-developed regions of the EMU could be given an opportunity to "catch up" rapidly. These are the positive aspects of the EMU.

But an EMU involves considerable loss of sovereignty as it requires a high degree of integration not only of production but also of macroeconomic factors -- in

---

[45] De Grauwe, Paul. "The Political Economy of Monetary Union in Europe," The World Economy, vol.16, no.6, November 1993, pp.653-61.

particular, of monetary and fiscal policies. Under the EMU, member nations cease to function as independent economic entities, thus their political structures also have to be integrated as member nations can no longer determine their own monetary policies such as inflation levels, foreign exchange or economic growth targets. In connection with this, some argue that,[46] a political union would automatically follow an economic and monetary union.[47] Table 4.4 provides an overview of the major effects of the EMU.

Table 4.4
Major Categories of EMU Effects

	Nature of the final impact	**Main channels of actions**	
		Direct	***Indirect***
Microeconomic Efficiency	Steady state level of output and income in the EU	Savings in transition and hedging costs. Disappearance of exchange rate uncertainty and instability	Strengthening of the internal market. Integration of goods and capital markets. Effects of lower uncertainty on the riskiness of investment. Induced dynamic effects. Seigniorage revenue losses for some member nations. Effects on taxation and provision of public goods
Macroeconomic Stability	Steady state rate of inflation. Variability of output and inflation, with associated consequences for welfare	Loss of an adjustment instrument for asymmetric shocks. Disappearance of non-cooperative exchange rate policies. Greater availability of external financing	Price stability as a consequence of ECB policy. Sound, coordinated fiscal policies
Regional Equity	Distributional effects among member nations and regions	Spatial distribution of direct micro and macro gains	Differentiated impacts of EMU depending on initial macroeconomic conditions and economic policy strategies
External Effects	Both micro and macro effects for the EU	Additional savings on transaction costs, revenues from international seigniorage and reduction in the need for exchange reserves	Better coordination internationally. Changes in the international monetary system.
Transitional Effects	Changes in the macroeconomic transition path towards EMU	Dis-inflation costs. Costs of fiscal adjustments	Drop in real interest rates. Effects on the dollar/Ecu [Euro] exchange rate

Source: "One Market, One Money," 1990, p.50.

---

[46] El-Agraa, Ali M. Economics of the European Community, 3rd ed. New York: Philip Alan, 1990, p.1.

[47] The broad categories of regional integration arrangements, in descending order of integration, are: (i) preferential trade area (PTA), (ii) free trade area (FTA), (iii) customs union, (iv) common market, and (v) economic and monetary union.

The Economic Union

Although economic integration is motivated primarily by political reasons, there are several economic arguments in favor of integrating "geographically discriminating groups." They include:

1. The enhancement of efficiency through an increase in specialization;
2. increase in market sizes which allow for economies of scale that lead to higher production levels;
3. improved international bargaining positions which result in better terms of trade;
4. enhanced competition ;
5. technological advances that improve the quality of factor inputs.

Additional gains are:

1. Cross-border factor mobility;
2. monetary and fiscal policy coordination;
3. the unification of higher economic growth rates, the attainment of nearly full employment and better income distribution.[48]

The necessary but politically sensitive issue of cross-border factor mobility can have both beneficial and harmful effects. Although such mobility may enhance efficiency through a more rational allocation of resources, it could worsen conditions in depressed areas and thus create or aggravate regional problems and imbalances. Monetary and fiscal policy coordination (monetary integration) could ease imbalances, thereby, creating more stable economic conditions. In particular, fiscal harmonization could increase efficiency by eliminating non-tariff barriers and distortions. There is, however, a need for all elements of an economic union to be realized simultaneously such as trade creation, the elimination of market distortions and the establishment of economies of scale conditions.

Harmonizing or removing all labor and capital mobility restrictions encourages such factors to be more mobile. Labor moves to those areas in which it can reap the greatest rewards. However, this does not necessarily mean that high wages increase mobility, because there are socio-political factors that keep labor from moving. In contrast, if the returns on capital are not equalized i.e. if differences in marginal productivity continue, capital moves until the differences are eliminated.

---

[48] El-Agraa, Ali M. Economics of the European Community, 1990, pp.79-80.

The Monetary Union

A monetary union is part of an economic union. To achieve it, countries must commit themselves to two monetary policies. First, currencies must be completely convertible.[49] Second, currency exchange rates must be irrevocably fixed allowing only small fluctuations while the currencies of the individual member countries float against the currencies of the rest of the world. Such an arrangement is the relationship between the U.K. and the Scottish pound. The best way to realize the features of a monetary union is to switch to a single currency. An example is the use of the pound sterling in England, Wales and Northern Ireland.

The requirements of a monetary union have far-reaching implications for the participating nations. The most important of these is the common management of the money supply. The price of a currency (i.e., its exchange rate) is subject to the laws of demand and supply, like any other commodity. For example, if the amount of French francs increases in relation to the amount of the Deutsche mark and if demand is constant, then a fixed exchange rate between the two currencies is no longer possible. Such a rate could, however, be achieved in either of two ways: first, through very close cooperation and coordination among the central banks, or through the creation of a common central bank. The second alternative, although more controversial, is more effective. Common money supply management has important ramifications for governments as they are no longer able to finance budget deficits by official central bank borrowing i.e. creating new money and thereby increasing their money supply. In a monetary union with common control over the money supply, national budget deficits can be financed only through private capital market borrowing and not by creating new money.

It is important to emphasize the need for careful and explicit policy coordination and cooperation in a monetary union. For example, if member nations conduct their own monetary policies, they can create as much domestic credit as they wish. As a result, surplus countries are financing deficit nations, with no incentives for the deficit countries to restore equilibrium. If a country runs a large fiscal deficit, the common exchange rate depreciates, although some member nations' economies could be generating fiscal surpluses. Furthermore, if wages are rising at different rates at the same time that productivity growth does not offset the effects of relative prices, nations with lower inflation rates could be permanently financing other countries.

In a monetary union the international exchange rates of the national currencies must be jointly managed. This involves the establishment of a common pool of reserves by a common authority. Thus, a monetary union implies the loss of national sovereignty with regard to two crucially important economic policy tools: control over the domestic money supply and over exchange rate policies.

---

[49] This refers to capital transactions as well as to the purchase and sale of physical goods, financial assets and services.

Some economists[50] have concluded that the potential gains from a monetary union are larger than those derived from a customs union[51] in that the increased specialization and economies of scale in a customs union are unlikely to be fully exploited as long as exchange rates are flexible. Moreover, intra-customs union investments involve exchange rate risks that do not exist in a domestic environment such as the creation of new or the imposition of existing restrictions on currency convertibility.

A monetary union provides its member states with fixed exchange rates and full currency convertibility. No foreign exchange reserves are required to finance balance of payments deficits with other member nations because domestic currencies can be used to settle debts. Reserves are needed only to maintain exchange rates in relation to the currencies of the rest of the world. This could lessen the role of international reserve currencies such as the U.S. dollar. A single currency could also become a major international currency competing on equal terms with the other major currencies.

The growth rate of an economy is frequently restrained by balance of payment problems. This cannot happen in a monetary union, because member nations are using the same currency and thus, growth rates tend to be less constrained by such problems. The costs of financial transactions can also be reduced because monetary integration enables such costs to be spread. In addition, certain foreign exchange activities might be discontinued, which could result in more savings .

Irrevocably locked exchange rates or a single currency can encourage capital to move into activities that generate higher profits, thereby promoting the movement of labor to regions where the rewards are high. This does not imply that all labor and capital is mobile, but that sufficient movement may take place to benefit an economy.

The integration of financial markets in a monetary union has additional advantages. If a country generates a deficit, it can borrow in the markets of other member countries or raise interest rates to attract capital. Even more important, integrated economic policies can ensure that deficit nations receive capital through a common central bank.

The common fiscal authority present in a monetary union with its own budget can also generate benefits. The larger the budget, the greater the degree of fiscal harmonization. This, in turn, promotes regional development through the common authority, and also provides for the consolidation of social security payments obtained through progressive tax contributions, which helps stabilize the monetary union.

---

[50] Nevin, Edward. The Economics of Europe, London: Macmillan Education Ltd., 1990, p.258.
[51] A customs union is a trading bloc in which member nations maintain only common external tariffs.

The benefits of a monetary union are relatively clear and are seldom disputed. But the costs of a such a union are subject to a great deal of arguments. Economists point out that although a monetary union involves the irrevocable fixing of exchange rates among the member states resulting in the adoption of a single currency, such a currency still fluctuates against the currencies of the rest of the world, generating transaction costs.[52] Other costs of a monetary union are temporary and result from the reallocation of resources and the enforcement of national standards, which can be a considerable stumbling block on the road toward a monetary union. The loss of national control over monetary policy (money stock) is yet another significant cost. This could be a fatal flaw. Other costs include increasing regional imbalances and public transfers.

Recent studies[53] have raised concerns about borrowed central bank credibility. In particular these studies address the case of the Bundesbank lending its reputation to other EU central banks, first through the ERM and now through the EMI and the future ECB. The studies have raised the question as to why countries cannot achieve economic credibility through the reform of national institutions or policies as, for example, the indexation of public debt. The reality is that such instruments are rarely issued because large disturbances for which unanticipated inflation would be an appropriate policy response, do not occur frequently. This can be used as an argument against the EMU and in favor of adjustable exchange rates.

The EU-EMU Costs and Benefits[54]

Efficiency and Growth

EMU efficiency gains arise from the elimination of exchange rate uncertainty[55] and of transaction costs,[56] and from financial refinements in the "Single Market" generated by the establishment of the economic and monetary union. The EU's single currency, the Euro, if credible, could improve the risk-adjusted rate of return on capital. It can also improve the general business climate, which could increase investments and promote growth.

---

[52] Fleming, John M. "On Exchange Rate Unification," Economic Journal, 1971, p. 81.

[53] For example, De Cecco, Marcello, and Alberto Giovannini. A European Central Bank: Perspectives on Monetary Unification after Ten Years of the EMS, "A Discussion by Charles Wyplosz," Center for Economic Policy Research, Cambridge, Cambridge University Press, 1989, p.213.

[54] The following discussion of the costs and benefits of the EMU and of the Euro pertains primarily to the EMU member nations and to a lesser extent the non-EMU EU countries.

[55] The EMU eliminates exchange rate variability. Prior to 1992 such variability averaged 7 percent/month for the ERM currencies and 1.9 percent for the non-ERM currencies.

[56] Annual transaction costs amount up to approximately 1-2 percent of GDP for the EU as a whole and up to 1 percent for small EU member nations. The transaction cost savings that will be generated by the introduction of the single currency have been estimated to reach approximately 3-4 percent of the combined GDP (Ecu 13-19 billion or US$ 19-23.5 billion). "One Market, One Money," 1990, pp.63-68.

Price Stability

The EMU central bank's, the ECB's, structure, management and principal objective -- sustaining price stability -- are similar to those of the Bundesbank. It is building its reputation and that of the EMU by initially borrowing the credibility of those member countries that have a record of sustained low inflationary growth and have managed to establish internationally credible central banks such as the Bundesbank. If the ECB sustains price stability, the Euro will enjoy the confidence of the international financial markets as long as the ECB achieves such stability at a low cost and can sustain it.

Public Finances

The Maastricht Treaty fiscal convergence criteria provide a framework within which autonomy (a country-specific response to problems) is possible, discipline (refraining from excess deficits) is emphasized and coordination (maintaining an appropriate overall EU policy mix) is fostered. When inflation and exchange rate premiums are abolished, national budgets can benefit from the reduction of interest rates. These benefits are expected to outweigh the loss of seigniorage revenues.[57]

Adjustment to Economic Shocks

The principal cost of the EMU to the individual member nations is the loss of monetary and exchange rate policies as tools of economic adjustment. Proponents of the EMU believe that the loss of the exchange rate policy adjustment mechanism is not substantial, since the ERM has already limited the use of the nominal exchange rate instrument.[58] Moreover, the Euro's exchange rate in relation to the currencies of the rest of the world remains flexible, subject to adjustments. The EMU will reduce the incidence of country-specific shocks and the EU will be able to absorb such shocks with fewer inflationary disruptions. Relative real labor costs can still change and national and EU budgetary polices will be able to absorb the shocks and assist with the necessary adjustments, while external current account constraints will fade.

International Implications

If the Euro becomes a major international currency, this will benefit not only the EU banking industry and internationally involved enterprises, but also the ECB and

---

[57] The most inflationary member nations will lose approximately 1 percent of GDP in seigniorage revenue. However, seigniorage gains arise from the use of Euro notes in non-EU nations. This could add up to a one-time gain of approximately US$35 billion.

[58] Except perhaps for Germany.

national monetary authorities, as they will be able to scale down foreign exchange reserves such as their U.S. dollar and yen holdings, and realize international seigniorage gains. A strong Euro will also provide the EU with a strengthened bargaining position in the G-7, other international organizations and within the TRIAD.[59]

Table 4.5 provides a summary overview of the main economic benefits and costs generated by the EMU.

Table 4.5
Economic Mechanisms Generating Costs and Benefits, by Stages of EMU (as in the Delors Report)

	Stage I	Stage III(a) Fixed Exchange Rates	Stage III(b) Single Currency
EFFICIENCY AND GROWTH:			
1. Exchange rate variability and uncertainty	+	++	++
2. Exchange transaction costs	*	+	++
3. Extending 1992 to economic union	*	+	+
4. Dynamic gains	*	+	++
PRICE STABILITY:			
5. Price discipline	+	++	++
6. Institutions conducive to stability-oriented monetary policy	*	+	++
7. Transitional costs of dis-inflation	--	-	-
PUBLIC FINANCE:			
8. Autonomy, discipline and coordination	-/+	-/+	-/+
9. Lower interest-rate costs (less seigniorage losses)	-/+	+	++
10. Public sector efficiency	+	+	+
ADJUSTMENT WITHOUT EXCHANGE RATE CHANGES:			
11. Loss of nominal exchange rate instruments	-	--	--
12. Adjustment of real wage levels	-/+	-/+	-/+
13. Lesser country-specific shocks	+	++	++
14. Removal of external constraints	*	+	++
INTERNATIONAL SYSTEM:			
15. Euro as international currency	*	+	++
16. Improved international coordination	*	+	++

KEY : + = benefit;
- = costs
* = insignificant or uncertain

Note: The comparisons are between the stages and a baseline case that assumes completion of the single market and membership of the EMS exchange rate mechanism.
Source: "One Market, One Money," 1990, p.26.

[59] The TRIAD is comprised of the EU, United States and Japan.

Other Costs and Benefits

The Costs and Benefits of Transition: The EMU transition costs are generated by the processes of dis-inflation, the reduction of budget deficits and of public debts, the restructuring of financial markets and of central banks, and by the corresponding impact on fiscal policy. The key ingredient of the EMU's and Euro's success is political will. However, such will usually falters in the face of prolonged, high economic and social costs and national elections.

The primary costs of the EMU and of the Euro appear during the transitional Stage II, while the benefits such as the elimination of exchange rate uncertainty and of transaction costs, are only realized when Stage III is completed and the Euro is introduced. Therefore, it would be politically expedient to make the transitional stage as short as possible.

Impact on the Regions: It is difficult to predict the relative gains and losses generated by the EMU in regions that are implementing clear-cut policy objectives such as those of the "Single Market." But it can be argued that, in general, the effects are positive in that they upgrade the less favored regional economies, although substantial economic, social and thus political costs are also incurred, -- at least in the short-run.

Convergence: The convergence of inflation, long-term interest rates and budget deficits is not only beneficial for the EU but is also a condition for moving toward the EMU, characterized by the irrevocable locking of exchange rates. Some of the EU member nations -- Germany, Benelux, France, Austria and too a lesser extent Ireland and Finland -- are more or less ready to embark on the EMU. The U.K., Denmark, Spain, Italy and Sweden still have some political, economic policy and structural adjustments to make, but their membership is possible within two years of the commencement of the EMU. Greece and Portugal, however, face serious political, structural and economic policy adjustment problems that may keep these countries out of the EMU for some time to come.

COSTS AND BENEFITS OF THE EURO

As discussed previously, the introduction of the Euro can generate both benefits and costs for the EU as a whole as well as for its individual member nations. Given the nature of these costs and benefits, it is difficult to assess the net impact of the new single currency. One of the measurable benefits is the reduction in transaction costs -- often cited as one of the most important gains. For all EU nations, such savings could amount to approximately 0.4 percent of the common GDP. In contrast, the one-time Euro conversion costs are estimated to be around Ecu7-8 billion (approximately US$9-

10 billion).[60]

The Euro, Irrevocable Exchange Rates and Other Alternative Exchange Rate Systems

The irrevocable locking of exchange rates during the last phase of transitional Stage II eliminates exchange rate variability. But in a monetary union a single currency is preferable to a system of irrevocably locked exchange rates because it eliminates the high transaction costs. Nations could also have difficulties maintaining a long-term commitment to fixed exchange rates, and this could result in a lack of credibility.

The Euro can yield significant benefits generated by the following five sources: (i) the elimination of transaction costs; (ii) elimination of information costs and price discrimination; (iii) additional dynamic efficiency gains in the marginal productivity of capital;[61] (iv) increased savings through lower official international reserves; and (v) a stronger EU presence in the international monetary system, in the global financial markets and in the international policy fora such as the Bank of International Settlements (BIS) and the Group of Seven (G-7).[62] Additional benefits could include the transparency of prices, economies of scale and visibility. See Box 4.2 for the six major differences between a monetary union with a single currency as compared to a system of irrevocably locked exchange rates.

---

[60] Crawford, Malcolm. One Money for Europe, London: The MacMillan Press Ltd, 1993, p.167.

[61] This, in turn, should increase investments and, over a period of time, result in a larger capital stock. With an unchanging labor stock, a larger capital stock results in greater output. It has been estimated that the overall increase in output generated by the introduction of the Euro, after sufficient time has elapsed to allow the capital stock to adjust, could be approximately 0.50 percent - 0.67 percent of the common GDP. Source: Gros, Daniel and Niels Thygesen. European Monetary Integration: From the European Monetary System to European Monetary Union, London: Longman Group UK Ltd., 1992, p.252.

[62] Gros, Daniel and Niels Thygesen. European Monetary Integration, 1992, pp.249-56.

Box 4.2
Monetary Union with the Single Currency (the Euro) versus Irrevocably Fixed Exchange Rates

1. **Transaction Costs**: The single currency, [the Euro], would eliminate all the costs arising to firms and individuals from conversions from one EU currency into another.
2. **Transparency of Prices**: As goods and services would be priced in the same currency, the Euro, this would further strengthen the pro-competitive effect of the single market and reduce information costs and price discrimination.
3. **Economies of Scale**: [The Euro] would lead markets in the same categories of financial instruments to merge, yielding benefits in terms of market depth and efficiency. The single currency would increase the marginal productivity of capital and savings through lower official international reserves.
4. **Credibility**: [The Euro] would give from the outset, maximum credibility to monetary union.
5. **Visibility**: The single currency would be for all EU agents a visible sign of the creation of the EMU and would make those agents more conscious of the associated wage and price discipline.
6. **External Benefits**: Only with the single currency can the EMU lead to a recasting of international currencies and to a more balanced international monetary regime. This would result in a stronger EU presence in the international monetary system, in global financial markets and in international policy forums such as the Bank of International Settlements (BIS) and the Group of Seven (G-7).

Source: One Market, One Money, 1990, p.36.

To determine the costs and benefits of the EMU, it should be compared not only to the "Single Market" and the EMS/ERM but also to other exchange rate regimes. Table 4.6 provides such a comparison.

Table 4.6
The Costs and Benefits of Other Exchange Rate Regimes

	Financial Autarky*	**Free Float**	**EMU**
MICROECONOMIC:	Low	Medium	High
MACROECONOMIC:			
(a) In the Presence of Shocks:			
- Asymmetric shocks	Low	High	Low
- Symmetric shocks	Medium	Low	High
- Exchange rate instability	High	Low	High
(b) Resulting from Policy Discipline:			
- Monetary credibility	Medium	Country-dependent	High
- Fiscal discipline	Country-dependent	Medium	Medium
EXTERNAL INFLUENCE:	Low	Low	High

* = Autarky is the theoretical assumption that a nation is self-sufficient and conducts no trade.
Source: One Market, One Money, 1990, p.56.

The following is a more detailed discussion of some of the major costs and benefits of the Euro, once introduced under the EMU.

Impact on Transaction Costs

Replacing national currencies with the Euro eliminates all exchange rate conversion costs on intra-EU transactions.[63] Numerous studies[64] have tried to estimate such costs. One study conducted by the EU Commission in 1990[65] used the assumption that an individual citizen takes a tour of the 12 member nations, converting money to national currencies in each country. He/she starts the trip in Germany with DM1,000 and concludes it in Germany, with DM340 remaining of the original amount -- a 60 percent (or DM660) reduction that is due to conversion costs. Although this example is somewhat oversimplified, it illustrates the potential gains that can be achieved through the elimination of intra-EU transaction costs.

Currency conversion costs can be analyzed through two different approaches. First, through the tracking of financial transaction costs that firms and individuals incur in the form of foreign exchange commissions expressed as the difference between the bid (buying) and ask (selling) rates; and, second through an analysis of the in-house costs[66] of businesses that arise from allocating resources to foreign exchange management activities.

Financial Transaction Costs[67]

The financial transaction costs that firms and individuals incur depend on the currency involved, the transaction volume and the foreign exchange instrument used. Switching in and out of weaker currencies such as the Portuguese escudo or the Greek drachma is more costly than converting into or out of currencies such as the Deutsche mark or French franc. As the transaction volume increases, bid-ask spreads decrease; thus, transaction costs are subject to economies of scale. Costs also depend on whether the transactions occur in the spot or the futures market, and whether they involve a swap or an option contract. Hedging by means of forward contracts is more costly than spot market transactions. For example, a forward contract transaction involving Ecu10,000 (US$12,390), costs about 0.2 to 0.3 percentage points more than a similar spot deal.

---

63 Referring to EMU member nations.

64 For example, Bureau Européan des Unions de Consommateurs (BEUC), "Holiday Money," July 1988.

65 "One Market, One Money," 1990, pp.65-67.

66 Costs that are internal to the non-financial corporate sector.

67 This section is based on "One Market, One Money: An Evaluation of the Potential Benefits and Costs of Forming an Economic and Monetary Union," European Economy, no.44, Brussels: European Commission, October 1990, pp.63-86 and 251-68.

There are four major sources of transaction costs. The first is the bid-ask spread on the interbank market. On the average, the implicit cost of a bank obtaining foreign currency in the spot market amounts to approximately half of the bid-ask spread. Exchange rate spreads among EU currencies vary depending on the international strength of the currency. However, it is estimated that on the average, spreads are approximately 0.05 to 0.1 percent of the transactions. The spread of internationally fully traded currencies, such as the Deutsche mark or the pound sterling is approximately one-third that of the currencies that are traded in a more limited fashion such as the Portuguese escudo and the Greek drachma.

The second source of financial transaction costs are the commissions and fees charged for the use of Eurocheques and/or credit cards. Eurocheques can be used at almost no cost if they are denominated in the domestic currency. If they are denominated in a foreign currency, a commission fee of about 1.6 percent is charged in addition to the exchange margin, which can be as high as 1 percent. Similarly, when credit cards are used there is a fixed fee of approximately 1 percent in addition to the conversion cost.

The third and largest source of transaction costs are the charges on the use of cash and traveler's checks. Although the cost of traveler's check transactions differs from country to country, on the average an Ecu100 (US$123.90) instrument draws an Ecu5 to Ecu7 charge. The cost of converting foreign banknotes also fluctuates, depending on the currency and on the country in which the transaction takes place. Cash transaction bid-ask spreads range from 3 to 5 percent, on the average. The highest charges apply when the conversion is made from a weaker into a stronger currency.

The fourth source of transaction costs, cross-border bank transfers, involve service fees and lengthy delays. A cross-border transfer of Ecu100 (US$123.90), on the average, incurs a 12 percent charge based on the transaction value. Such relatively high costs and the associated delays in processing cross-border payments are due mainly to technical reasons. The Euro could reduce such costs by simplifying the banks' treasury and accounting operations.

Estimates of exchange transaction cost savings differ from country to country, depending on the strength of the currency, the depth of the financial sector and the types of traders involved. Less frequently traded currencies generate greater savings under the single currency system because of their higher transaction costs. Nations that have unstable currencies and inefficient foreign exchange services will also gain from the use of the Euro, as will nations with large trading volumes. Thus, transaction cost savings will be unevenly spread among the EMU member countries. For the smaller and less developed economies, the savings could be as high as 0.9 percent of GDP, whereas for the larger nations such as Germany and France they may range from approximately 0.1 percent to 0.2 percent. The overall gains are estimated to range from 0.17 percent to 0.27 percent of the common GDP.

The introduction of the Euro will affect the financial sector in other ways as well. Foreign exchange dealing in EU currencies will be eliminated as will exchange rate-related fees charged by banks engaged in intra-EU trade. All of the exchange rate-related savings will be achieved at the expense of bank revenues. But banks will have a larger market in which to engage in different types of financial transactions. The Euro could also generate lending risks that are lower than those that are incurred when lending is carried out in national currencies. What is not clear, however, is whether the net savings less the banks' loss of revenue and associated taxes, will outweigh the economic and political costs of the Euro.

In-house Costs[68]

Non-financial EU companies that use multiple currencies can obtain in-house benefits from switching to the Euro. Some of these benefits will be immediately obtainable whereas others will materialize only over time as firms restructure their activities.

There are four major sources of in-house gains. First, working with multiple currencies requires large staffs and resources to oversee the multitude of spot, forward, and swap transactions. The Euro eliminates such activities and/or reduces the resources needed to perform these tasks. Foreign exchange activities in non-EU currencies, however, are going to continue, thus, the net savings may be somewhat limited. Doing business in multiple countries also forces firms and their subsidiaries to maintain cash balances in different currencies. This may lead to less efficient corporate cash flow and capital budgeting management. In contrast, with the use of the Euro, cash management can be more efficient. It should be noted that although firms that transact in multiple currencies may benefit from arbitrage opportunities whenever interest rates differ, such benefits are limited.

The second source of in-house gains is the absence of cash management inefficiencies which generate interest costs on debit positions in multiple currency settings. The third source of gains is the fact that the new single currency also eliminates foreign exchange exposure risks, thus, eliminating the source of opportunity costs. The fourth and final source of in-house gains is the reduction of the time period between debiting and crediting bank accounts in the Euro rather than multiple currencies. However, in most cases such delays are not due to the nature of the currency used but are the result of the extent of financial market integration, the efficiency of clearing systems and of the type of technology used. Thus, the Euro may not eliminate the long delays in less sophisticated financial markets where modern technology and efficient clearing systems are not available.

---

[68] In-house costs are costs that are internal to the non-financial corporate sector.

As a common unit of account of intra-EU transactions,[69] the Euro will also provide transparency. It will facilitate the monitoring of business operations as well as the analysis of intra-EMU corporate business activities. The resulting simplifications and increased accuracy will enhance the efficiency of the decision-making process in multinational companies.

Predicting the amount of in-house savings with any degree of accuracy is difficult since the gains are not very explicit and most of the savings will materialize only over time. Various studies[70] estimate that the in-house costs of EU multinational companies currently amount to approximately 0.1 percent of the common GDP, thus any reduction of such costs could be very beneficial to the business sector.

The financial transaction and in-house costs incurred by exchange rate-related conversion activities in the EU range from 0.3 percent to 0.4 percent of the common GDP, or approximately Ecu13-19 billion per annum.[71] But there are also one-time costs of switching to the Euro which are estimated to be around Ecu7-8 billion. These costs are associated with the recall of the national banknotes and coins that have to be reissued in Euros; the renegotiation of the existing contracts denominated in national currencies; the need to modify the foreign exchange operating systems in firms and banks, which includes the restructuring of departments and the retraining of staff as well as the modification of automated vending and teller machines.

The EU public will also have to adjust to the Euro-based financial system which will be a costly and time-consuming process. Therefore, initially the transition to the Euro will be disruptive for businesses and individuals. The multinational companies involved in international trade can offset the conversion costs through the transaction costs savings. Companies with limited involvement in foreign exchange transactions will not obtain any compensatory benefits nor will individuals.

Elimination of Exchange Rate Uncertainty

The elimination of exchange rate uncertainty is one of the most frequently cited benefits that the Euro will generate. Exchange rate stability will enhance free trade in goods and services and will increase capital flows throughout the "Single Market."

Past discussions focused on the question of whether irrevocably fixed exchange rates or a single currency are required to achieve the level of integration that by now already exists in the EU's "Single Market." The success of the ERM in reducing

---

[69] This generally pertains to EMU member nations.

[70] Ernst and Young, the National Institute of Economic and Social Research and the Association for the Monetary Union of Europe. A Strategy for the ECU, London: Kogan Page Ltd., 1990.

[71] "One Market, One Money," 1990, p.68.

exchange rate uncertainty has provided some answers. Yet, the recent crises involving the mechanism have resurrected old fears concerning linked or shared currencies, particularly as they affect countries with strong international currencies such as Germany.

Exchange Rate Variability

Under a floating exchange rate systems a reduction in the variability of nominal exchange rates is equal to the reduction in real exchange rate variability, because price levels move much more slowly than exchange rates. The EMU and the Euro eliminate exchange rate movements and thus uncertainty about intra-EU exchange rates, providing a more favorable environment for trade and investments. But a monetary union eliminates only nominal and not real exchange rate variability.[72] Thus, long-term real exchange rate movements can still occur in the EMU. However such movements are more or less expected, therefore, they will not have an adverse effect on trade and capital flows, unlike unexpected short-term real exchange rate variations i.e. exchange rate uncertainty. But the welfare gains generated by the use of a the Euro are difficult to measure, as the relationship between exchange rate uncertainty and trade or investment is tenuous at best.

If exchange rate adjustments represent efficient responses to market developments such as productivity and investment trends, the repression of the adjustment mechanism through the introduction of irrevocably fixed exchange rates might lead to a decrease in welfare. However, caution must be exercised in claiming a correlation between exchange rate variability and economic welfare, as such correlation is tenuous and, if analyzed, "must be based on the assumption that existing exchange rate variability is not warranted by variability in underlying economic conditions."[73] To date, there is very little evidence supporting a causal relationship between exchange rate, productivity or investment variations in a free floating exchange rate system. In a semi-pegged exchange rate system such as the ERM, currency fluctuations are caused mainly by differing national monetary policies and not by real economic factors such as productivity trends and comparative advantages which determine investment and trade. Thus, the elimination of exchange rate variability, either through irrevocably fixed exchange rates or through the Euro, does not suppress any economic fundamentals.[74] But this does not imply that the EMU does not generate economic costs. Such costs may have to be incurred because adjustments in the labor and goods markets, for example, are slower than in the foreign exchange markets.

An EU Commission study[75] has shown that global exchange rate variability is greater than the average variability of the EU currencies which, however, is greater than

---

[72] It is now believed that both nominal and real exchange rates are relevant.

[73] "One Market, One Money," 1990, p.69.

[74] "One Market, One Money," 1990, p.69.

[75] "One Market, One Money," 1990, pp.70-71.

the average exchange rate variability experienced by the ERM currencies prior to 1993. The Euro can eliminate exchange rate variability only among EMU member nations but not in relation to third country currencies such as the U.S. dollar or the Japanese yen. Of course, irrevocably fixed exchange rates could accomplish the same at less of an economic and political cost. It should also be noted that either of the two approaches would cause the non-EMU member nations of the EU to experience some reduction in real exchange rate variability. But the low exchange rate variability benefits which generate trade and investment benefits for all the EU nations must be weighed against the effects of the variability of the Euro vis-à-vis the major non-EU currencies such as the U.S. dollar and yen. The potential benefits of the Euro will be reduced if the replacement of national currencies and the elimination of exchange rate variability increase variability against these currencies. Replacing a very strong international currency such as the Deutsche mark with a new currency can easily alter the international monetary balances and create turmoil that could be destructive not only to the EU but also to international trade and investment patterns. It should also be borne in mind that the currencies of the non-EMU nations will still be subject to internal variations within the EU as well as to external variations against third country currencies.

The average monthly variation in EU currencies is approximately 0.8 percent which will be reduced to zero by the Euro. But this figure masks large differences in member country currency variations. For example, pound sterling variations can reach 1.6 percent while the Belgian franc and the Irish pound vary by only about 0.6 percent to 0.7 percent. This implies that countries with unstable currencies, such as Spain or Portugal, and those that have more trade with the rest of the world will benefit from the elimination of exchange rate uncertainty. However, these nations must still meet the Maastricht Treaty convergence criteria before participating in Stage III of the EMU. Thus, the real gains may not be as large as expected, because the EMU may eventually consist of only those nations that already have strong and stable currencies.

Exchange Rate Variability and Trade

The strongest argument against the use of multiple national currencies is the effect of foreign exchange exposure on international trade transactions. Usually, there is a time lag between the signing of the contract and the completion of the transaction. During this interval either the exporter or the importer is exposed to exchange rate risks. The only way to eliminate such risks is to hedge in the futures, forward or option markets.

The futures and forward markets of the EU have expanded rapidly in recent years. Although there is no consensus on whether such markets are deep and wide enough to eliminate foreign exchange risk at low costs, in most cases they provide efficient hedging mechanisms for the major EU currencies (most of which are likely to participate in the EMU). Thus, the currency markets may be sufficiently deep and sophisticated to minimize foreign exchange exposure risks. The Euro will be able to provide unlimited and free hedging opportunities for all types of trades and capital movements.

The impact of exchange rate variability on the volume of international trade is far from clear. Recent studies[76] have shown that the negative effects are quite small in that even doubling the standard deviation of the real exchange rate variability reduces the trade volume by only 0.7 percent. Nor did a 1984 IMF study[77] find a systematic link between short-term exchange rate variability and international trade volumes. As a result, it is not possible to estimate the real effects of the Euro on trade among the EU countries.

It has been argued by Euro opponents that the creation of an integrated market for goods and services such as the "Single Market" does not require a monetary union because any additional benefits are minimal. Moreover, they claim, while an integrated market can benefit from the use of multiple currencies, a single currency such as the Euro might actually reduce internal trade. This could happen because an integrated market encourages nations to specialize in certain industries. Such specialization makes national economies more vulnerable to industry-specific shocks, because monetary policy is no longer available as an adjustment tool. This also prevents countries from devaluing their currencies to improve the short-term competitiveness of industries. Thus, the introduction of the Euro, may reduce any potential gains from trade.

Exchange Rate Variability and Capital Flows

The elimination of exchange rate variability will affect not only international trade but also long and short-term international capital flows. Since the expected life of foreign direct investment assets exceeds the maturity dates of hedging instruments, exchange rate uncertainty has a larger effect on foreign direct investments than on trade.

Empirical studies[78] have found evidence concerning the adverse impact of exchange rate variability on intra-EU foreign direct investment. But major investments are usually made for the long-term; consequently, the importance of short-term variations should not be overstated. Yet, the EMU's ability to stimulate long-term intra-EU investments is open to question because the Euro is expected to reduce short-term rather than long-term exchange rate variability. With the elimination of capital controls in all member countries, the allocation of investments will be similar to that under the fixed exchange rate system.

---

[76] For example, Frankel, Jeffrey A. and Steven Phillips. "The European Monetary System: credible at last?," Oxford Economic Papers, v.44, October 1992, pp.791-816.

[77] International Monetary Fund (IMF). "Exchange Rate Variability and World Trade." Occasional Paper no.28, 1984.

[78] Molle, Willem and R. Morsink. "Direct Investments and Monetary Integration," European Economy : The Economics of EMU, Special Issue, 1991.

The impact of the Euro on short-term capital flows is difficult to estimate. If capital flows are caused by exchange rate variability, the Euro will reduce such flows among the EMU member nations. In addition, if the Euro increases the variability of returns to securities denominated in the EMU nation currencies, capital allocated to such securities may be reallocated to foreign currency denominated securities. But if the Euro increases the risk of portfolio investment abroad, intra-EU investments may be increased. Therefore, it is difficult to reach a conclusion about the impact of the Euro on short-term capital flows.

Commitment and Competitiveness

As discussed in the previous sections, there is no clear relationship between exchange rate variability and international trade and capital movements. To the extent that there is such a relationship, the effectiveness of the ERM in reducing exchange rate variability raises doubts about the necessity of the Euro. The ERM has effectively stabilized the exchange rate movements of the different national currencies within the mechanism.

An alternative to the Euro would be irrevocably locked exchange rates based on a strong commitment to maintain such intra-EU rates. If the commitment is credible, capital flows could be enhanced and speculation reduced. But regardless of the irrevocable locking of rates, and the commitment to the exchange rates, adjustments are always possible. Political pressures such as elections, changes in governments or in economic policies can cause currencies to break away from a rate. This is the key difference between the irrevocable locking of exchange rates and the Euro. The Euro is not subject to short-term political pressures. If an EMU nation decides to revert back to its domestic currency, such a decision cannot be made easily because of the resulting short-term political implications. Thus, the elimination of national institutions and the sunk cost of the single currency are important factors in preventing an escape from the Euro.

A system of irrevocably fixed exchange rates differs from that of a monetary union with a single currency. While national currencies with irrevocably fixed exchange rates may become perfect substitutes for each other, to function in this way they have to be reliable units of account, stores of value and transaction mediums. This requires interest rate equalization. However, as long as currencies continue to exist, prices will continue to be quoted in these currencies because translating prices from one currency into another is inconvenient. As previously discussed, exchange rate fluctuations cannot be ruled out even with a very strong commitment to the irrevocable locking of exchange rates. Therefore, achieving and maintaining interest rate equalization over a long period of time is not feasible without a single currency. Finally, as long as national currencies exist, they have to be converted; which means that transaction costs will have to be incurred even with irrevocably fixed exchange rates. Thus, regardless of the strength of commitment, in an irrevocably fixed exchange rate system, national currencies do not function as perfect substitutes.

However, achieving a monetary union based on a single currency such as the Euro is an equally difficult proposition. In addition to the economic costs, political problems complicate the task. Currencies are a symbol of national identity as are institutions such as central banks. Thus, politically, a monetary union based on a single currency is more difficult to accomplish than a union with irrevocably locked exchange rates. But once the political difficulties are overcome, maintaining a monetary union with a single currency is easier. In contrast, a monetary union with irrevocably locked exchange rates is subject to continuous pressures by speculators, and thus the future prospects of such a union are open to question.

Price Stability

One of the main goals of the EMU is to maintain price stability through the ECB. However, the pursuit of such a goal to the exclusion of all others will cause short-term political and economic problems in nations with historically high inflation rates.

The cost of inflation depends on the nature of its causes and on the structure of the economy in which it is experienced. Anticipated inflation manifests itself as a steady rate of price increases over long periods of time. Yet, inflation levels do not stay constant and are not always predictable. Economic theory suggests that unanticipated inflation has a more adverse effect on an economy. It is harmful as it creates economic instability, ruins government credibility and eventually wipes out even the inherent inflation tax benefits.

For years, the long-term Phillips curve has provided an incentive to governments to pursue inflationary policies to boost growth and employment. However, research has shown that the long-term Phillips curve does not exist in reality. Thus, politicians are now focusing on dis-inflationary policies. The Euro, backed by an ECB dedicated to price stability, will bring additional discipline to the economic policies of the EMU nations that want to achieve low and stable inflation levels.

Anticipated Inflation

As mentioned above, until recently, the long-term Phillips curve trade-off shaped the economic policies of most nations. The economic theories of the 1960s and 1970s maintained that inflation was necessary for growth. Moreover, they assumed that inflation and unemployment levels were inversely related and that governments could achieve acceptable levels of unemployment by choosing the proper inflation rate. In other words, it was believed that lower levels of unemployment could be achieved through higher rates of inflation.

However, a multitude of empirical studies conducted during the 1980s and data gathered by the OECD in its member countries show that there is no relationship between inflation levels and growth rates. Nor did an analysis of the average inflation and unemployment rates in OECD countries over the 1970-85 period yield a direct long-run relationship between the two.[79] The analysis, however, has indicated that low inflation levels encourage economic growth by providing a stable investment environment. Studies[80] have also shown a very strong negative relationship between inflation and income. Although this does not prove the adverse effect of inflation on economic growth and efficiency, it suggests that countries with high levels of inflation, on the average, do not perform better than countries with lower levels of inflation.

The inflation-unemployment and inflation-growth trade-offs suggested by the Phillips curve were used in the past to justify high inflation in rapidly growing developing countries. However, in view of the above mentioned empirical findings, the less developed EU nations such as Greece cannot justify inflationary policies in the name of long-term macroeconomic gains.

Anticipated inflation also has microeconomic effects. An inflation rate higher than the optimal level reduces cash holdings by encouraging the substitution of consumption goods or interest-bearing near-money assets for money. Depending on the nature of the substitutes, the opportunity cost of holding money in an inflationary environment is equal to the inflation or interest rate. Since the private cost of holding money is greater than zero, welfare losses are inevitable. Studies[81] have calculated the cost of inflation using the monetary base. For example, an average 5 percent inflation in the EU could cause a reduction of 0.03 percent of the common GDP. If M1 is used instead of the monetary base as a measure of money, the loss increases to 0.09 percent.

Anticipated inflation affects price lists, because it causes economic agents to change prices. However, on the average, such changes are not very costly.

Inflation generates revenues. But such revenues decrease when inflation levels are achieved through dis-inflationary policies. The revenue decreases may be small for countries that already have very low inflation rates, but they reach about 1 percent of GDP in countries that have lived with high inflation for a long time -- as, for example, Greece and Portugal.

---

[79] "One Market, One Money," 1990, p.90 and OECD data, 1970-1988.

[80] For example, "One Market, One Money," 1990.

[81] For example, Lucas, Robert E. Studies in Business Cycle Theory. Cambridge: MIT Press, 1981.

Effects of Unanticipated Inflation

The welfare losses generated by unanticipated inflation are larger than those caused by anticipated inflation. Empirical evidence[82] shows that inflation levels and variability are positively correlated. Data gathered from the OECD countries for the period of 1955-1985 yield a strong relationship between average inflation levels and its variability as measured by the standard deviation. As inflation variability increases, inflation levels go up.

Macroeconomic theory suggests that in the short run the Phillips curve effect may exist; thus, there may be a relationship between growth, employment and inflation. In other words, unanticipated inflation can temporarily increase growth and employment. Similarly, lower than anticipated inflation can reduce growth and cause output losses, thus increasing unemployment. This short-term relationship encourages governments to use unanticipated inflation to increase output and to create new jobs while reducing the real value of the public debt, particularly prior to elections. But, such policies harm the credibility of governments and create public expectations of similar actions in the future. Thus, in the long run, such policies do not yield any benefits but rather increase inflation levels and variability.

Inflation variability is also caused by dis-inflationary policies that are not fully implemented. This happens when governments try to reduce inflation through tight monetary and fiscal policies. Because such policies often generate public criticism and cannot be maintained over long periods of time, a dis-inflation/inflation cycle is created. This implies that, on the average, high inflation levels are associated with periods of dis-inflation. Thus, inflation keeps output and employment levels in a continuous disequilibrium and destabilizes the economy.

The inflation tax generated by unanticipated inflation is greater than that generated by anticipated inflation. The base of the unanticipated inflation tax is the entire public debt, while the base of an anticipated inflation tax is the monetary base. An unanticipated increase in inflation reduces real interest rates on public debt, thus helping governments to service such debt. Since the total debt of the EU is greater than its total monetary base, unanticipated inflation creates higher revenues than anticipated inflation. However, using unanticipated inflation to generate revenues reduces government credibility. Moreover, in response to such government actions, financial markets quickly increase interest rates to include an inflation risk premium. Thus, in the long run short-term gains may be eliminated and governments lose credibility.

---

[82] For example, Cukierman, Alex. "Interest Rates during the Cycle, Inventories and Monetary Policy: A Theoretical Analysis," Carnegie-Rochester Conference Series on Public Policy 15, 1981, pp.87-144.

Dis-inflationary Policies

Despite the costs of inflation, dis-inflationary policies cannot always be implemented or maintained because of political problems and economic costs. Reducing inflation requires the implementation of credible programs by fully committed governments because such policies may reduce output. If wages are rigid, any decrease in inflation levels may not be reflected;, unchanged nominal wages will increase real wages. Such a rise in real wages results in lower output, reduces the demand for labor and increases unemployment.

The lack of credible dis-inflationary policies may also reduce output. Even if governments succeed in reducing inflation, if financial markets anticipate future inflation, the decrease may not be reflected in the nominal interest rates. Reduced inflation without accompanying reductions in nominal interest rates increases real interest rates. This, in turn, not only raises the debt service burden but also discourages investments.

The success of dis-inflationary policies depends on the exchange rate commitment. In the absence of such a commitment, dis-inflationary policies might not be credible since exchange rate adjustments will always be available as an escape route. In contrast, a strong exchange rate commitment through irrevocably locked exchange rates or a single currency, such as the Euro, does not offer escape provisions.

Irrevocably locked exchange rates or a single currency as, for example, the Euro, while strengthening the effectiveness of dis-inflationary policies, can also generate costs. The degree of capital market integration and real interest rate convergence is important in this respect. With a high degree of capital mobility, irrevocably locked exchange rates imply the equalization of interest rates. However, if nations have different inflation levels, those with higher levels will have lower real interest rates. Such rates stimulate domestic investment and increase output but may also cause budget deficits. While less external financing will be needed as inflation levels converge, countries may accumulate a considerable amount of external debt by the time convergence takes place. This increases the debt burden and reduces the standard of living, which could make it more difficult for certain EMU member nations to sustain the Maastricht Treaty convergence criteria.

Nominal Exchange Rates and Economic Shocks

As internal and external economic variables change, nations are forced to adjust export prices. This can be done through a revision of exchange rates. With independent national currencies this is possible without requiring corresponding changes in domestic price levels. However, with the introduction of the Euro (while abolishing national currencies) real exchange rates will no longer be available as adjustment tools. Thus, the necessary price changes have to be achieved by other means such as domestic wage and/or price adjustments generated through labor mobility. But this is not always possible and may not be as effective as exchange rate adjustments. Large variations in real or nominal macroeconomic factors such as output and inflation are generally considered to be welfare-reducing. If it is assumed that nominal exchange rates are affecting macroeconomic variability, they could have welfare implications.

Proponents of the EMU claim that the loss of the nominal exchange rates as a policy tool is not particularly significant for a number of reasons. First, even if intra-EU exchange rates are irrevocably locked among the EMU member nations, the exchange rates with respect to the rest of the world can still be adjusted. Moreover, changes in real exchange rates can still occur through relative price movements. Second, until 1992 the original ERM member nations' nominal exchange rates had not significantly changed. Thus, the costs of irrevocably locking exchange rates had already been incurred, without the benefits of the EMU. Third, the short-run rigidity of wages and prices allows nominal exchange rates to affect real exchange rates only temporarily. Although this may stifle output fluctuations, it may amplify inflation trends. In the long run, nominal exchange rates at best, may "accommodate inflation differentials without having a lasting impact on real exchange rates."[83] Fourth, since the sustainability of EU growth differentials in the long is affected by a multitude of factors, the contribution of the real exchange rate is limited. Fifth, the deeper the integration is, the less is the likelihood of region or country-specific shocks.[84] Enhanced competition in the "Single Market" will ensure that part of the price adjustment burden is carried by businesses through lower profit margins. But it is difficult to foresee any real increase in wage discipline in the EMU, owing to its multifarious nature.

Economic Shocks

Economic shocks are unanticipated external events that affect an economy. They may consist of drastic raw material price changes (for example, the oil price increases of the 1970s) or rapid productivity growth as experienced in Japan between the 1960s and the 1980s. If such events have a simultaneous impact on a number of countries, they are considered common shocks, whereas if they affect only one country, they are referred to as country-specific shocks.

Economic shocks can be further differentiated as symmetrical or asymmetrical. If the impact of a shock on countries is comparable, it is called a symmetrical shock. If it is not, it is referred to as an asymmetrical shock.

Country-specific shocks are by definition asymmetrical since they affect only one nation. Common shocks may be asymmetrical depending on certain conditions. For

---

[83] "One Market, One Money," 1990, p.136.

[84] Because product differentiation overshadows product specialization, this is amplified.

example, if product market integration is characterized by inter-industry specialization, a common shock specific to an industry will affect primarily the countries that specializes in that industry. But removal of trade barriers and the establishment of the "Single Market" decreases the asymmetrical impact of common shocks by stimulating intra-industry specialization.

As a result of different economic structures common shocks can also be strongly asymmetrical. The differences may include production factors, consumption and/or trade patterns. An energy crisis, for example, affects the U.K. less than Germany or France because the U.K. is an oil producer. Differences in wage structures can also lead to diverse effects. Nations that use a more limited form of wage indexation experience lower unemployment following inflationary shocks. In contrast, nations that practice broader wage indexation may not be able to adjust wages in times of dis-inflation. This keeps real wages high, decreases the demand for labor and increases unemployment.

Economic Shocks and the EMU

An economic shock can cause a change in export demand or in the international competitiveness of industries, either of which could bring the current account into disequilibrium. A devaluation, a nominal exchange rate adjustment that strengthens the competitiveness of a country and increases import prices, could improve a country's trade balance and re-establish equilibrium. However, after a while, increasing import prices will be reflected in higher domestic prices and wages. This cancels out part of the improved competitiveness obtained through the nominal exchange rate adjustment. Thus, the slower the wage increase is, the higher the benefits obtained from exchange rate adjustments. However, domestic price increases could also stimulate inflationary expectations and thereby create an inflationary cost as well. Thus, adjustments in nominal exchange rates are helpful only to the extent to which they affect real exchange rates.

Empirical studies[85] have shown that during the period 1979-89 the rate of increase in the EU nations' nominal exchange rates was positively correlated with the rate of increase in real exchange rates during the same quarter. The correlations ranged from 0.75 to almost 1.00, depending on the country. Such high correlations imply that nominal exchange rate adjustments are similar to real exchange rate changes. Therefore, exchange rate adjustments are an effective tool for dealing with economic shocks. Simulation results confirm this.[86] In the case of an adverse shock to exports, currency devaluations cushion the size of output losses by improving competitiveness. Greater output losses are observed when exchange rates are kept fixed. The simulations also showed that devaluations can have inflationary effects and that wage increases can

---

[85] For example, "One Market, One Money," 1990, p.138.
[86] "One Market, One Money," 1990, pp.138-40.

restrain domestic output levels from reaching equilibrium levels.

It may be argued that the above discussion is not relevant to the EMU, as it is the nature of the shocks that matters. The most harmful shocks are temporary and asymmetrical in nature.[87] An adverse temporary shock can produce a budget deficit while preventing the implementation of proper fiscal adjustments because of the shock's temporary nature. An asymmetrical shock can create an incentive to take measures that might be against the interests of other EMU member countries. But if the countries face permanent symmetrical shocks, they can implement common fiscal and monetary policies, since the effects of both the shocks and the remedies will be comparable.

Supporters of the EMU claim that asymmetrical shocks, although present in the EU during 1970-1980, may diminish as financial markets are integrated and economic structures converge. The converging rates of inflation and domestic demand and supply shocks are all symmetrical in their impact.[88] The completion of the "Single Market" is also expected to reduce the occurrence of asymmetrical sector-specific shocks and/or will make them more symmetrical. This may be the case, but real wages and unemployment rates are dominated by asymmetrical behavior, and to date there is a significant divergence among EU member nations in this respect. Even with the eventual completion of the "Single Market," wage rate convergence and the free movement of labor is not certain.

Overall, nominal exchange rate changes have proven quite effective in establishing equilibria. With the introduction of the Euro, the exchange rate mechanism, however, will no longer be available as an adjustment tool. It is also not clear to what extent future integration will eliminate asymmetrical shocks. Both Italy and the U.K. had left the ERM in September 1992 and subsequently devalued their currencies so as to improve their competitiveness, which had worsened owing to inflation differentials. The devaluation has worked and both countries have significantly improved their economic performance. Thus, the cost of losing the exchange rate adjustment mechanism is still controversial.

Alternative Adjustment Tools for Asymmetrical Shocks

Several tools other than exchange rate adjustments have been proposed to deal with asymmetrical shocks. They include wage flexibility, labor mobility, external financing and budgetary policies. There is no consensus on the effectiveness of any of these alternatives.

---

[87] Charles Wyplosz and Cohen, D. "The European Monetary Union: An Agnostic Evaluation," in Bryant, Ralph C., David A. Currie, Jacob A. Frenkel, Paul R. Masson, Richard Portes, eds. Macroeconomic Policies in an Interdependent World, International Monetary Fund, Washington, DC, 1989, pp.331-37.

[88] Weber, Axel A. "Asymmetries and Adjustment Problems: Some Empirical Evidence," European Economy, 1990.

Wage Flexibility: Flexible exchange rates are effective because they reduce export prices even though domestic prices remain the same. The same result can be achieved through a decrease of domestic prices generated through wage reductions resulting from unemployment. This improves competitiveness without any change in the exchange rates.

Wages in the EU nations are not flexible enough to use such an approach. However, a credible commitment to the Euro may force economic agents to be more flexible when setting wages, since exchange rate changes will no longer be available as adjustment tools. But social considerations could constrain such effects to increase wage differentials. In particular, the minimum wage may restrict downward movements and could aggravate unemployment.

The effectiveness of wages as an adjustment tool depends largely on the actions of labor unions and employers. Thus, wage flexibility is far from a reliable alternative to exchange rate adjustments.

Labor Mobility: In the case of asymmetrical shocks, labor mobility can be effective as an adjustment mechanism if unemployed workers migrate to other regions. Empirical studies[89] have shown that there are major differences in unemployment rates among the EU regions. This implies that despite legislation providing for the free movement of people and the mutual recognition of professional qualifications, labor is not mobile. Mobility is still limited owing mainly to political but also to cultural and other socio-economic barriers such as different social security systems. Since these barriers are not likely to be reduced in the near future, labor mobility may not be available as an adjustment tool to deal with asymmetrical shocks.

External Financing: External financing can be used as an adjustment mechanism in the absence of exchange rate adjustments. Nations facing asymmetrical shocks can borrow externally to maintain output and consumption levels as well as to provide for investments that can offset the adverse effects of shocks.

Although in the short-term external borrowing partly compensates for the loss of exchange rate adjustment capability, it can cause an accumulation of foreign debt and lead to current account problems. If the EU does not restrict external financing, nations could be faced with moral hazard problems, because with integration through higher interest rates the burden of national debts could spill-over to other nations, which, thus, will assume some of the costs of borrowing from abroad.

An accumulation of external debt could easily create solvency problems, in which case nations have to restrict the issue of new liabilities to service such debt.

---

[89] Eichengreen, Barry. "One Money for Europe? Lessons from the US Currency Union," Economic Policy, No.1, April 1990, pp.117-87.

External financing may not be available on an ongoing basis; thus, such financing is a poor substitute for exchange rate adjustments.

Budgetary Policies: Budgetary policies are also proposed as temporary alternatives to compensate for the loss of exchange rate adjustments. Government spending could cushion the adverse effects of shocks until the short-term labor market equilibrium is restored through wage reductions. However, there are two arguments against such measures. First, as discussed in the previous section, wages in the EU are not sufficiently flexible to ensure wage reductions that could help offset the impact of asymmetrical shocks. Second, there is the moral hazard problem. As government spending increases, debt goes up, which puts upward pressures on interest rates. Higher interest rates spill-over to other nations and reduce their output levels.

Therefore, government spending, although effective in the short term, cannot be a substitute for exchange rate adjustments. As long as fiscal policies are not coordinated at the EU level, fiscal expansion in one nation will cause problems in the other nations.

Macroeconomic Stability in the EMU

Economic shocks affect output, employment and inflation equilibria and increase variability. Under the EMU, the variability of some economic factors is expected to increase since no effective substitutes for exchange rate adjustments are available. Such an outcome may not only be welfare reducing but could generate additional welfare costs.

Germany has a major role in influencing EU monetary policies. The costs and benefits of the Bundesbank's moves are transferred to other member nations through the ERM. But the loss of monetary policy independence does not leave the other nations sufficient room to counteract severe asymmetrical shocks, and thus output variability has increased. Yet, the discipline and credibility of the Bundesbank has led to significant reductions in inflation levels and variability in a number of nations.

The introduction of the Euro will dilute German monetary policy influence. Although the ECB must maintain price stability, its commitment to stable, low levels of inflation will not be as strict as that of the Bundesbank. Moreover, because exchange rate adjustments will no longer be available, low or stable inflation levels will become even more difficult to maintain. Thus, following the introduction of the Euro, inflation variability will depend on the ability of the ECB to resist pressures from national governments.

The EMU could constrain sub-optimal monetary policies. When a common shock occurs, adjustments are easier at the common level. This eliminates sub-optimal country policies and reduces economic variability. However, as discussed before, in the absence of exchange rate adjustments, asymmetrical shocks are likely to increase variability. The Euro could reduce the variations in real exchange rates and import prices by reducing the frequency of unpredictable exchange rate fluctuations.

The EMU will have mixed effects on macroeconomic stability. It may increase the stability of certain economic variables such as exchange rates, but it could also result in higher output variability owing to the absence of stabilizing monetary policy instruments at the national level. The overall net welfare effect depends on the nature of the shocks as well as on the reactions to them. Therefore, the impact of the EMU on economic welfare is far from certain.

THE EURO'S NATIONAL AND REGIONAL IMPACT

The EMU has been characterized as a positive as opposed to a zero-sum situation despite the fact that the costs and benefits to different countries vary. Nations that are currently more converged within the ERM, have already "undergone the major adjustment costs of EMU, but have not reaped all the benefits."[90] Countries that have converged to a lesser degree, will experience greater gains from the EMU but will also face higher transitional costs. The greatest benefits of the EMU will be obtained by those EU nations that have small, open economies (such as Belgium) and that have currencies that are infrequently used internationally (high transaction costs). Countries with less than credible national institutions and less than sound monetary and budgetary policies will also gain by participating in the EMU whereas nations with highly credible institutions and monetary and budgetary policies (such as Germany) will have little to gain from it. Alternatively, EU member nations that are heavily involved in intra-EU trade as, for example, Germany, the largest intra-EU exporter of goods and services, will obtain significant gains from the expected increase in price and monetary stability and transparency generated by the EMU within the EU.

The debate over the specific costs and benefits of the Euro to EU member nations is dominated by those who believe that economic and monetary integration will exacerbate national and regional differences and problems, especially in the peripheral regions[91] and those that believe that integration will result in convergence. One study found that:

> [The] reduction of regional disparities coincides with periods of rapid growth whereas the problems of poorer and disadvantaged regions are accentuated in periods of recession. Also convergence occurs more spontaneously among countries and regions that have already reached a relatively mature stage of economic development.[92]

[90] "One Market, One Money," 1990, p.235.

[91] The peripheral regions are classified as consisting of those EU member nations that would not be among the first group of EMU participants.

[92] "One Market, One Money," 1990, p.212.

Other studies[93] have analyzed the relationship between integration-specific variables such as trade flows, migration and foreign investment on the one hand and the convergence performance of nations on the other hand. Although the findings do not show a steady relationship in all of the EU nations over time, one conclusion could be drawn: "Convergence tends to dominate in periods of strong growth, and to recede in periods of stagnation."[94]

Most of the studies analyzing the impact of the Euro on the different nations and on different regions have provided ambiguous results. For the most part, the costs and benefits of the Euro will probably depend on the combination of individual country and EU policies. For example, policies that are aimed at achieving economic and social cohesion among the EU member nations will increase the benefits of using the Euro, though the overall costs and benefits are also dependent on the initial conditions existing in the nations and regions. They involve public spending rates, infrastructure, human capital development, GDP per capita trends and political attitudes.[95] Others involve transportation costs, the scale and agglomeration of economies and structural disadvantages which hamper competitiveness, particularly in the lagging EU nations and regions.[96]

The Costs and Benefits of the Euro

The EU economies are dissimilar in their economic structures, per capita income, unemployment levels, trading behavior, regional development and degree of financial market sophistication. This implies an uneven distribution of the benefits and costs of the Euro; thus, the net impact of the Euro on any member nation is difficult to predict. Nevertheless, two indicators may be used to assess the most important costs and benefits that nations may incur or obtain.[97] The benefits can best be assessed through the level of transaction cost savings. The most important of these savings is generated by intra-EU trade. Therefore, trade as a percentage of a nation's GDP provides a rough estimate of the potential transaction cost savings i.e. benefits.

The costs can best be estimated by observing the variation in national economic structures[98] as compared with the average EU structure, defined by the EU

[93] For example, Vanhove, Norbert and Leo H. Klaassen, Regional Policy: A European Approach, London: Saxon House, 1980.

[94] "One Market, One Money," 1990, p.212.

[95] Intra-industry specialization is expected to be high under the EMU, as it is expected to decrease the likelihood of asymmetric shocks and, thus, to reduce adjustment problems.

[96] Other considerations include, the "interaction between economies of scale and transportation and transaction costs, imperfectly competitive market structures, large welfare (static) benefits for small nations, and the multipolar structure of the world economy." "One Market, One Money," 1990, p.215.

[97] This section draws on Gros, Daniel and Niels Thygesen. European Monetary Integration. London: Longman Group U.K. Ltd., 1992, pp.229-68.

[98] National economic structures are measured by "the distribution of value added of over 30

Commission's statistical indicator. This indicator measures the costs incurred as a result of the loss of exchange rate policies as an adjustment tool. Since it measures a cost, it is reported as a negative value. The more negative the value is, the more dissimilar the economic structure of a nation when compared with the average EU structure and the higher the cost. The more this is the case, the greater the likelihood that a nation may be exposed to asymmetrical shocks. Hence, the greater the cost of loosing exchange rate policy as an adjustment tool. Table 4.7 illustrates the Euro's major benefit defined as transaction cost savings within intra-EU trade and cost defined as the loss of the exchange rate adjustment mechanisms.

Table 4.7
Euro Benefits and Costs [(a)]

	Benefits Intra-EU [(b)] trade as a % of GDP	**Costs [(c)]** $(R^2-1)*100$	**Net Gain/Loss**
Belgium/Luxembourg	44.50	- 1.39[(d)]	43.11
Denmark	13.65	- 6.47	7.18
Germany	14.35	- 1.81	12.54
Greece	13.25	-14.01	-0.76
Spain	8.95	- 2.07	6.88
France	12.95	- 0.71	12.24
Ireland	38.85	- 8.48	30.37
Italy	9.7	- 2.02	7.68
Netherlands	34.2	- 5.14	29.06
Portugal	24.55	-10.31	14.24
United Kingdom	10.70	- 8.40	2.3

(a) = Costs = The measure used is the adjusted correlation coefficient of the national values and of the EU averages of the shares of about 30 economic sectors in total value added. The table reports the value of this coefficient minus one.

(b) = Intra-EU trade = (exports + imports)/2.

(c) = R = a regression of each nation's economic structure as a weighted EU average (using Ecu weights). European Commission data.
(d) = Data on the industrial structure for Luxembourg were not available.

Source: Adopted from Gros, Daniel and Niels Thygesen, European Monetary Integration, 1992, pp.257-58.

---

different branches of the economy." Gros, Daniel and Niels Thygesen, European Monetary Integration, 1992, p.257.

The major benefit i.e. transaction costs savings is obtained by nations with the highest level of intra-EU trade/GDP ratio. Belgium/Luxembourg represent more than 40 percent of such trade, thus they gain the most They are followed by Ireland and the Netherlands with approximately 40 and 35 percent trade shares, respectively. The smallest intra-EU trade gains accrue to Spain, Italy and the U.K. Thus, in terms of transaction cost savings, the Benelux nations and Ireland will benefit the most from introduction of the Euro.

The major cost shown in Table 4.7, is defined as the loss of the exchange rate as an adjustment tool. The least developed countries such as Greece and Portugal incur the highest costs. A relative comparison shows Greece with the lowest score, at -14.01, followed by Portugal, Ireland and the U.K. at -10.31, -8.48 and -8.40, respectively. The wealthy economies such as France, Belgium/Luxembourg and Germany incur the lowest costs, at -0.71, -1.39 and -1.81, respectively. Belgium and the Netherlands are very open economies with economic structures similar to the average EU structure.

When the overall benefits and costs of introducing the Euro are compared, the results are not similar. The Benelux nations and Ireland have the best overall score, which explains their support and enthusiasm for the single currency. In the case of Germany, Portugal, Italy, France, Denmark and Spain, the Euro is promising, although the net impact is not as positive as in the case of the above mentioned nations. The U.K. and Greece have the poorest overall score. The U.K.'s different industrial structure as well as lower trade volume with the other EU member nations explains its reluctance to adopt the Euro.[99]

The introduction of the Euro and the elimination of national currencies is a controversial proposition. In addition to the loss of what are national sovereignty symbols, the potential risks are high. The evidence concerning the potential net benefits of the single currency, is inconclusive. Thus, the introduction of the Euro is a precarious undertaking -- especially in light of the enormous uncertainties and risks surrounding such a move. The uneven distribution of costs and benefits together with the limited number of nations that are likely to satisfy the Maastricht Treaty convergence criteria, reduces the potential benefits even further.

Yet, the less quantifiable benefits of the introduction of the Euro may be more important than the reduction of transaction costs. They are generated by the integration of the financial markets. This, however, raises the question of whether the Euro, which implies the elimination of national monetary and exchange rate policies, is really necessary for the completion of the integration process as already established by the "Single Market." If the Euro is necessary, then the risks and costs are justified; if this is not the case, then the benefits of the "Single Market" could be captured without abandoning national monetary and exchange rate policies.

---

[99] The U.K.'s political reluctance to pursue the Euro is based on the issue of loss of sovereignty.

The Euro and Lagging Regions

Lagging regions contain not only a higher proportion of sensitive economic sectors but also more small and marginally efficient firms. These sensitive sectors and small firms are usually among the first to be affected by recessions, which further depresses the entire region. Because such regions are the most responsive to economic policies, they receive a relatively high proportion of new public and private investment.[100] As a matter of fact, some regional disparities have already been reduced through financial transfers and the mobility of the factors of production.

The problems that the lagging regions face are exacerbated under the EMU and by the Euro. This is a burden that such regions have to carry in addition to the high costs of adjusting to the "Single Market." Thus, they need not only additional financial support from the EU but also more policy coordination aimed at reducing location disadvantages and enhancing market efficiencies. The small and open economies with lagging regions can increase welfare benefits only through external trade, because their intra-EU trade patterns are dependent on industry structures. But intra-industry trade among the less developed EU nations is limited.

Lagging regions are trying to achieve,

(i) a spatially balanced distribution of population and economic activities -- in order to avoid negative externalities and long-run social and environmental problems;[101]
(ii) an adequate level of provision and accessibility of public goods and local services to all the populations;
(iii) equalization of levels of GDP per capita;
(iv) equalization of levels of personal disposable income, or per capita consumption, or welfare -- not the same as the previous due, inter alia, to taxes, transfers and price changes affecting the consumer surplus.[102]

It is difficult to predict the impact of the Euro[103] on these regions. They are more severely affected by the loss of nominal exchange rates and by the elimination of hidden forms of taxation than wealthier regions. They also have less developed financial markets. Table 4.8 illustrates the disparities in GDP per capita of the EU

---

[100] As opposed to replacement investment.
[101] Additional considerations are economies of scale, transportation costs and the size of the manufacturing sector.
[102] "One Market, One Money," 1990, p.213.
[103] The intensity of regional problems is difficult to measure. The definition of regions, the lack of reliable data and results sensitive the measure of dispersion, are some of the reasons for this.

nations between 1980 to 1987.

Table 4.8
Disparities in Per Capita GDP in the EU, 1980-87 (Theil coefficient)

	1980	1981	1982	1983	1984	1985	1986	1987	1988
Average 10 weakest regions	47	46	46	45	45	45	45	45	45
Average 10 strongest regions	145	146	147	149	149	150	151	151	151
Weighted coefficient of variation	26.1	26.5	26.8	27	27.2	27.2	27.9	27.5	27.5

Source: "One Market, One Money," 1990, p.215.

These differences are significant and will probably not be reduced, at least for some time to come.

ANNEX IV.1
THE IMPACT OF FIXED, FLEXIBLE AND MANAGED EXCHANGE RATES ON INFLATION

Under the conditions discussed in the section on "The Impact of Monetary and Fiscal Policies Under Fixed and Flexible Exchange Rates" in this chapter, prices are held constant. However, if they are not, monetary expansion could result in an upward pressure on prices as well as on income and output. The conclusions drawn earlier in the chapter under the flexible exchange rate regime hold only if increases in the nominal money supply are related to increases in money income.

Irving Fisher in his book The Purchasing Power of Money (1911),[104] provided the connection between an increase in the quantity of money and the ensuing price increases. This so-called "missing link," which maintains the monetary equilibrium, is known as the "real-balance" effect. Fisher based his explanation on "Walras' Law,"[105] according to which demand is simply another way of looking at supply. This led Fisher to conclude that at the existing price levels more money creates an excess supply of money balances in individual hands. This disturbs the optimal relation between individual cash balances and expenditures. Thus, individuals seek to reduce their excess money balances by increasing expenditures. If output remains unchanged, the increased money demand pushes up prices in proportion to the increase in the money supply. In this way, a new equilibrium is reached and maintained because the individual money balances have returned to their optimal level.

It should be pointed out that Fisher did not demonstrate how an increase in money could raise output through lower interest rates (i.e., how excess money could be used to purchase securities, thus, pushing up their prices while holding down interest rates). Instead, he turned to the interrelationship between inflation, interest rates, expectations and the holding of real-cash balances. In his The Theory of Interest[106], Fisher argued that there is a mechanism through which inflation could be self-perpetuating. Higher rates of monetary expansion could lead to initially lower nominal interest rates because of the increase in the supply of loanable funds. But eventually, through inflationary expectations, higher prices lead to an increase in the nominal rate and inflation. This "Fisher effect" is "a stock-in-trade" analytical tool of modern-day monetarists.

In 1936 the Swedish economist Knut Wicksell, filled in the gap in Fisher's real-balance effect by emphasizing the relationship between savings and investments in his aggregate-supply versus aggregate-demand analysis. Wicksell's work[107] has substantially advanced the cause of neoclassical monetary theory.

Milton Friedman of the University of Chicago clarified and expanded the theory of demand for money. In a set of 1956 essays, Studies in the Quantity Theory of Money,[108] Friedman expanded the money-demand function to include income and nominal interest rates. In fact, when the Fisher effect is combined with Friedman's concept of money demand, a lucid explanation of inflation emerges. Although monetary expansion initially lowers the nominal interest rate, inflation and the "Fisher effect" eventually take over and cause nominal interest rates to rise. The only way to depress such rates is to keep increasing the

---

[104] Fisher, Irving. The Purchasing Power of Money, New York: A. M. Kelly, Publishers, 1963 [1911].

[105] Walras, Leon. Elements of Pure Economics. (William Jaffe [trans.]). Illinois: Irwin; 1954 [1874].

[106] Fisher, Irving. Theory of Interest as Determined by Impatience to Spend Income and Opportunity to Invest It., New York: The Macmillan Company, 1930.

[107] Wicksell, Knut. Interest and Prices. (R. F. [trans.]). London: Macmillan, 1936.

[108] Friedman, Milton. Studies in the Quantity Theory of Money. Chicago: University of Chicago Press, 1956.

money supply in the long run. In his empirical study, coauthored with Anna J. Schwartz in 1963, A Monetary History of the United States, 1867-1960,[109] Friedman argued that inflation is a monetary phenomenon. He pointed out that the earlier versions of the quantity theory of money that were used to explain inflation were erroneous in that they explained the cause of inflation as a result of an increase in velocity (reduced money-demand growth), reduced income growth, and/or an increase of monetary expansion. He and other contemporary monetarists have pointed out that not only is the increase in velocity limited, but growth in income and employment is determined by real factors in the long-run. Because, through the process of elimination, the only other remaining variable is monetary expansion, Friedman concluded that it is the erratic discretionary changes in money supply growth that produce inflation.

In the discussion of the causal sequence of monetary and fiscal policies, it was assumed that the velocity of money is constant. However, an increase in velocity could produce effects similar to those of an increase in the money supply, and vice versa. It is also possible that an increase in the money supply could be accompanied by a slight decrease in velocity, which would partially offset the monetary expansion. But, as most modern monetarists believe, any decrease in velocity that occurs as a reaction to an increase in the money stock cannot fully offset the effects of monetary expansion.

Although modern-day monetarists relate the problem of inflation to that of employment and income growth, the idea can be traced back to 1958, when the British economist A. W. Phillips discussed the relationship between unemployment and inflation in his "The Relation Between Unemployment Rate and the Rate of Change of Money Wage Rates in the United Kingdom, 1861-1957."[110] The resulting "Phillips curve" predicates an inverse relationship between unemployment and inflation rates so that increasing inflation rates are required to decrease unemployment rates.

Phillips' propositions were challenged by such economic events as stagflation, which could not be adequately explained. It was Milton Friedman who in his 1968 presidential address to the American Economic Association provided the needed insight.[111] He argued that in the long-run, rates of monetary expansion and inflation have little, if anything, to do with the natural unemployment rate and concluded that the Phillips curve was vertical at some "natural rate of unemployment."

---

[109] Friedman, Milton and Anna J. Schwartz. A Monetary History of the United States, 1867-1960. Princeton, New Jersey: Princeton University Press, 1963.

[110] Phillips, Alban W. "The Relation Between Unemployment Rate and the Rate of Change of Money Wage Rates in the United Kingdom, 1861-1957," Economica, vol.25, November 1958, pp.283-99.

[111] Later published as an article: Friedman, Milton. "The Role of Monetary Policy," American Economic Review, 58; March 1968, pp.1-17.

V THE EUROPEAN CENTRAL BANK

The European Economic and Monetary Union (EMU) is not yet a reality but the process of economic and monetary integration has already had an impact on the global financial markets and the international monetary system. Hence, it is important to understand the nature of the EMU and of the institutions that will coordinate and administer its activities. Yet, while most member nations support the idea of a single currency and of common monetary policies, there are serious problems with the technical aspects of the transition process, the convergence criteria, and the design of the EMU institutions as well as the EMU's membership.

This chapter provides a discussion of the principles that govern the EMU and of the issues involved in designing its key policy formulating institutions. The structure and functions of the current EMI, the forerunner of the European Central Bank (ECB), and the European System of Central Banks (ESCB)[1] are examined. In addition, the chapter offers an exploration of the future impact of these institutions on the independence of country central banks and of the ways in which the controversies surrounding the implementation of the Maastricht Treaty could be overcome.

THE EUROPEAN MONETARY INSTITUTE (EMI)

The main purpose of the transitional Stage II of the EMU is to create the necessary environment for the final Stage III. This involves the establishment of the EMI which is based in the "Eurotower," in Frankfurt, Germany. It took over the functions of the Committee of Central Bank Governors, the EU's monetary policy coordination body on January 1, 1994.

---

[1] The ESCB will be made up of the member nations' central banks and the ECB.

Organizational Structure and Role of the EMI

Organizational Structure

As an official institution of the EU, the EMI was established under the Maastricht Treaty, with its membership made up of the central bankers of the member states. Figure 5.1 shows the EMI's organizational structure.

Figure 5.1
The European Monetary Institute

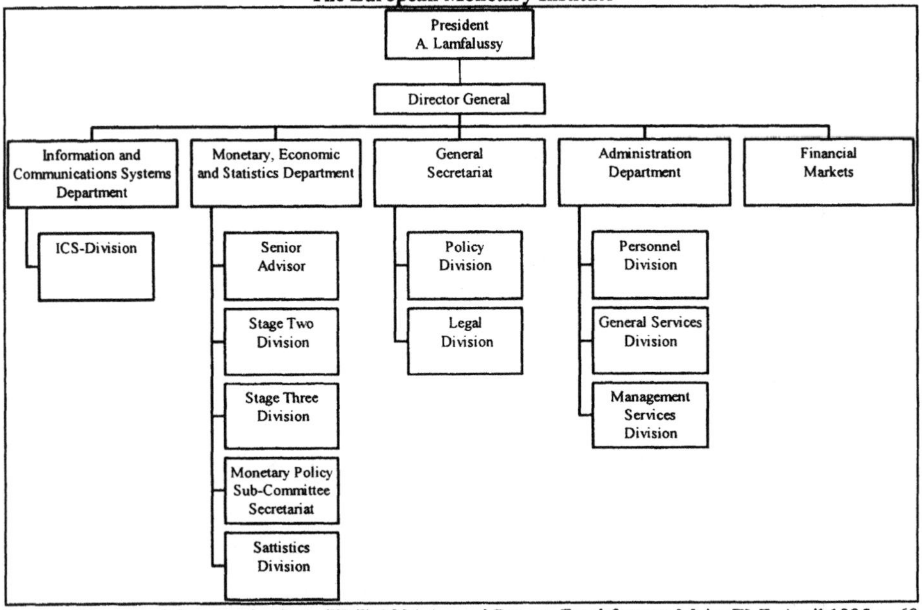

Source: European Monetary Institute (EMI) 1994 Annual Report, Frankfurt am Main: EMI, April 1995, p.68.

The EMI Council: The EMI Council is the decision-making body which directs and manages the Institute. It is comprised of the President and of the member nations' central bank governors. (See Annex V.1 for a list of the EMI Council members). One of the governors serves as the Vice-President. As in the case of the ESCB Council, a member of the EU Commission and the president of the European Council may attend its confidential meetings, which must be held at least ten times a year. The President of the EMI is appointed for a three-year term by common accord of the European Council on a recommendation by the Committee of Governors or the EMI Council, following consultations with the EU Parliament and the European Council. The President prepares and chairs the Council meetings, represents the institution to the outside world and is responsible for its day-to-day management. In the absence of the President, the duties are assumed by the Vice-President who also serves a three-year term.

In exercising their authority, members of the EMI Council act on their own accord. They may not seek or take any instructions from other common institutions, bodies or national governments, which are all expected to respect the institution's independence. Each member of the EMI Council has one vote and decisions are reached by a simple majority. However, under special circumstances a qualified majority or even unanimity may be required. A qualified majority of two-thirds is required for recommendations relating to monetary or foreign exchange policies, for decisions concerning the EMI's financial resources or for the establishment of guidelines necessary for the ESCB to perform its tasks. Unanimity is required for decisions concerning the design of the ESCB's regulatory, organizational and logistical structure, for publishing opinions and recommendations or for granting the monetary authorities of third countries the status of "Other Holder" of the Euro, the single currency.

The EMI Management: The management group of the EMI is comprised of the President, the Director General and the four Heads of Departments. (See Annex V.2 for a list of the names of the EMI management group members). The Director General assists the President in his tasks, in particular in the day-to-day management of the EMI. The four departments include the General Secretariat, the Monetary, Economic and Statistics Department, the Administration Department and the Information and Communications Systems Department.

The General Secretariat itself consists of two divisions: the Policy Division and the Legal Division.

The Policy Division is responsible for:

- preparing [EMI] Council meetings, maintaining inter-institutional relations, supporting the production and distribution of EMI reports and maintaining the archives;
- overseeing the ECU Clearing and Settlement System, monitoring member states' payment systems and preparing for the EU-wide payment systems in Stage III;
- supporting the activities of the Monitoring and Concentration Groups, monitoring the functioning of the EMS, facilitating the use of the Ecu and overseeing its development, carrying out EMS
- related operations and preparing the foreign exchange market operations of the ESCB in Stage III;
- conducting analyses of issues affecting the stability of financial institutions and markets; and
- coordinating the preparatory work for Stage III as well as

monitoring, evaluating and reporting on progress made against the timetable of the Maastricht Treaty.[2]

The Legal Division is responsible for the interpretation of the Maastricht Treaty as it affects the EMI. In addition, the Legal Division helps prepare EMI opinions or recommendations whenever the European Council or national governments request such assistance concerning drafts of EU or national legislation falling within its jurisdiction. The division also provides legal guidance on administrative matters to EMI's management.

The Monetary, Economic and Statistics Department provides administrative support to the Monetary Policy Sub-Committee. The department consists of three divisions and one department. The so-called Stage II Division provides economic analyses concerning the strengthening of monetary cooperation among central banks and the coordination of monetary policies with a view to promoting price stability. It also assists the EMI Council in formulating opinions and recommendations on macroeconomic policies, including those related to the convergence criteria. Finally, it provides analyses on issues regarding financial markets. The Stage III Division is responsible for providing analyses of the concepts, framework and rules relating to the common monetary policies in Stage III. This involves the definition of the instruments, the setting and management of intermediate common monetary policy objectives and the implementation of foreign exchange policies.

The Statistics Division is responsible for generating the data essential for the coordination of monetary policies during Stage II and the harmonization of the regulatory environment to facilitate the ESCB's tasks. The division also provides the statistical data required by the EMI.

The Information and Communications Systems Department is responsible for the design and implementation of the information and communications systems of the institution and of the future ESCB.

Staff: On January 1, 1994, the EMI started out with 28 staff members in the Secretariat of the Committee of Governors. By the end of the year their number had increased to 126 and, by the end of 1995, to about 200. All staff members are appointed for three-year terms.

The EMI Committees, Sub-Committees and Working Groups: The EMI Council is assisted by several committees and working groups. Figure 5.2 shows the place within the organization of these committees, sub-committees and working groups.

---

[2] European Monetary Institute (EMI) 1994 Annual Report, Frankfurt am Main, April 1995, p.66.

Figure 5.2
The EMI's Committees, Sub-Committees and Working Groups

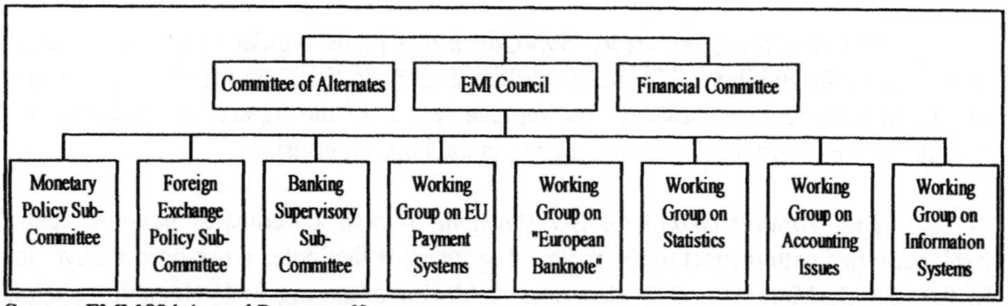

Source: EMI 1994 Annual Report, p.69.

The Committee of Alternates is comprised of senior central bankers appointed by the respective national central bank governors as their representatives to the EMI Council. The committee is chaired by the Director General of the EMI and is responsible for the preparation of meetings.

The Financial Committee is made up of two of the most senior members of the EMI Council serving on a rotational basis for one year. It is chaired by the EMI Vice-President and is responsible for the analysis of the annual budget on behalf of the EMI Council and for proposals concerning the annual accounts as well as the periodic expense statements incurred by the EMI. It delivers its opinion directly to the EMI Council.

In addition, there are three sub-committees and five working groups. They are comprised of experts delegated by the central banks and are under the authority of the Committee of Governors and the EMI Council. The chairmen of the sub-committees and working groups are appointed for three-year terms.

The Monetary Policy Sub-Committee is responsible for assisting the EMI Council in strengthening common monetary policy coordination. Its major objective is to examine the monetary policy goals and strategies of the member states and to assess their impact on price stability throughout the EU. The committee participates in the periodic consultations on the monitoring of national monetary policies. It also analyzes the methods and organizational conditions required by the ESCB to prepare the instruments and methods of common monetary policies as applied in Stage III.

The Foreign Exchange Policy Sub-Committee conducts discussions on exchange rate developments, the functioning of the EMS and the use of the Ecu in private transactions. It interacts with non-EU central banks through the so-called "concentration procedure" in which representatives of the central banks of 19 industrialized countries participate. This interaction generates information on market developments, interventions and other official foreign exchange transactions. In addition, the Sub-Committee is responsible for assisting the EMI in the preparation of the ESCB's future foreign exchange activities.

The Banking Supervisory Sub-Committee holds regular meetings on issues important to the stability of financial markets and institutions. Its membership consists of central bank representatives or the representatives of the supervisory authorities of nations whose central banks do not engage in banking supervision.

The Working Group on EU Payment Systems coordinates national central bank activities with respect to the payment systems. It facilitates cross-border payments in the "Single Market" and is also responsible for preparing EMI Council decisions concerning the Euro Clearing and Settlement System.

The Working Group on Printing and Issuing a European Banknote assists the EMI in supervising the technical preparations needed for the introduction of Euro bank notes. This involves the analysis of various design and production options and the issuing, distribution, sorting and handling of the notes.

The Working Group on Statistics is responsible for the continuous improvement of statistical data needed for promoting the harmonization of monetary policies in Stage II and for the conduct of common monetary policies in Stage III.

The Working Group on Accounting Issues develops the accounting system used by the EMI. It is responsible for the harmonization of accounting rules and standards used by the ESCB.

The Working Group on Information Systems is in charge of devising and implementing the EMI and ESCB information and communications systems.

Objectives, Tasks and Functions of the EMI

Article 109.f of the Maastricht Treaty and of the Protocol on the Statute of the EMI[3] defines the EMI's tasks, objectives and functions. The EMI is in charge of achieving the EMU by establishing the transition process leading to Stage III. Within this general mission, the EMI is responsible for five primary functions.

(i) The first of the primary functions of the EMI is to strengthen central bank cooperation and monetary policy coordination so as to promote convergence and to ensure price stability, the later being the primary objective of monetary policy: To this end, the EMI formulates opinions and/or recommendations concerning the overall direction of national monetary and exchange rate policies as well as associated

---

[3] It should be noted that the Protocol on the Statute of the EMI is part of the Maastricht Treaty.

activities conducted by the member states. The EMI submits such opinions and recommendations to national governments and to the Council of Ministers. The EMI also has an important role in assessing the relationship between monetary and fiscal policies; it closely follows the public finance developments and, as in the spring of 1994, may express its concerns about the status of public finances in the various countries to the Council of Ministers. Moreover, it reports annually to the Council of Ministers on the progress made by the member states in meeting their obligations under the EMU. As this process falls under the jurisdiction of central banking and affects the stability of financial institutions and markets, consultation with national central banks and their respective governments is mandatory. The EMI provides a forum for consultations and the exchange of information and views on policy options available to the national authorities during the transitional Stage II of the EMU, during which the ultimate responsibility for monetary policies is still with the national authorities.

When it drafts proposed EU legislation, the EMI must consult the Council of Ministers and national authorities. If necessary, it may also have to consult the European Council.[4] It is also required to perform advisory activities for the ECB prior to its establishment.[5] Finally, the EMI facilitates the use of the Ecu, oversees the development and smooth functioning of the EU clearing system and monitors the exchange rate mechanism (ERM). It also administers the ERM's Very-Short-Term Facility (VSTF) and Short-Term Monetary Support instruments which serve as a basis for foreign exchange market interventions by the central banks within the +/-15 percent ERM bands. To facilitate exchange rate policy cooperation, the EMI holds and manages foreign exchange reserves as an agent of national central banks.

(ii) Another primary responsibility of the EMI is to prepare for Stage III of the EMU which calls for the establishment of the ESCB, the management of common monetary policies, and the creation of a single currency in the final phase of Stage III: Article 4.2 of the EMI protocol states that "...at the latest by December 1996,[6] the EMI shall specify the regulatory, organizational and logistical framework necessary for the ESCB to perform its tasks in the Third Stage." This involves the following objectives:

- the definition of the concepts and framework for conducting common monetary policies and the preparation of the ESCB's operational rules and procedures;
- the implementation of common foreign exchange policies;
- the promotion of efficient cross-border payments;
- the collection and harmonization, where necessary, of reliable and timely statistics to support the conduct of common monetary policies;

[4] Article 109.f.6 of the Maastricht Treaty, 1992.
[5] Article 109.f.8-9 of the Maastricht Treaty, 1992.
[6] Owing to the complex nature of this task, this date will probably be delayed.

- the supervision of the planning, printing and issuing of European banknotes; and
- the harmonization of accounting rules and standards of the national central banks and the setting-up of adequate information systems for the ESCB.[7]

Monetary Policy Coordination: Although the Maastricht Treaty clearly designates price stability as the EMI's primary objective, it provides only general principles concerning the management of common monetary policies. These principles include the maintenance of open and competitive markets, the ban on central bank financing of budget deficits and the possible decentralization of the ESCB's operations so that national central banks can be used as implementors of ECB policies "to the extent deemed possible and appropriate."[8] The vagueness of the Treaty, coupled with the fact that national monetary policies vary in both structure and institutional arrangements, complicates the development of such policies. See Table 5.1 for an illustration of the differing monetary policy instruments and procedures used by EU member nations.

The governors of the 15 European central banks sitting on the EMI's Governing Council represent different views on monetary union and policies. As each central bank favors its own methods and wants to retain them for as long as possible, the EMI must give careful consideration to the need for harmonization. For example, although most EU central banks are relatively independent, some, like the Banque de France, Banco de España and Banca d'Italia were given their independence only in 1995 and 1996. Others, like the Bank of England, are still required to coordinate their activities with the government. The admission of Austria, Finland and Sweden on January 1, 1995 has added to the diversity of arrangements. See Annex V.3 for the differences in monetary transmission processes among the EU member nations.

[7] EMI 1994 Annual Report, p.63.
[8] Article 12 , ESCB and ECB Protocol, Maastricht Treaty, 1992.

Table 5.1
EU Member Nations' Monetary Policy Instruments and Procedures

Item	Belgium	Denmark	Germany	Greece	Spain	France	Ireland	Italy	Netherlands	Portugal	U.K.
A. Reserve requirements for monetary policy	no	no	yes	yes	yes	yes	yes	yes	no	yes	no
1. Size(% of GDP)*	-	-	2.7	3.9	2.0	.1	1.8	8.0	-	16.1	-
2. Remuneration	-	-	no	partly	no	no	below market rates	partly	-	partly	-
B. Standing facilities**											
1. Lending facilities at below or close to market rate(s)	L (below market)	-	M	-	-	-	-	M (close to market)	H (below market)	-	-
2. Deposit facilities	L	L	-	-	-	-	M	-	-	-	-
3. Marginal refinancing	L	-	L	M	L	L	M	M	L	L	M
C. Open market operations											
1. Types**											
*-Outright transactions****	L	H	L	M	-	M	-	M	L	H	H
-Reserved transactions in domestic securities	H	H	H	L	H	H	H	H	H	M	M
-Foreign currency swap transactions	M	L	L	L	L	-	H	M	L	L	-
2. Frequency of operations****	H	M	L	M	M	M	H	M	L	M	H
3. Auction procedures**											
-Volume tender	H	H	L	-	L	-	-	H	M	-	-
-Interest rate tender	L	-	H	L	H	H	H	H	-	M	H

* = amount outstanding at the end of 1992.
** = importance in providing(or withdrawing) liquidity to(or from) the market: L Low; M Medium; H High
*** = these include issues of certificates of deposit by the central bank in the cases of Denmark and Portugal; and unsecured overnight loans in the case of Greece.
**** = L = about once a week; M = Several times a week; H = More than once a day.

Source: "Strategy and Tactics of Monetary Policy: Examples from Europe and the Antipodes," Goodhart, Charles A.E. and Jose Vinals, in Fuhrer, Jeffrey C., ed., Goals, Guidelines and Constraints Facing Monetary Policymakers. Federal Reserve Bank of Boston, June 1994, p.171.

The choice between money supply targets and price stability is likely to generate major controversy. The ECB could use the money supply as an intermediate target (the growth of M3, for example), as is the case in Germany and some other nations.[9] Monetary aggregates could be used as an information variable and the ECB could focus on price stability as in New Zealand, where inflation is at 0-2 percent. Some economists[10] have argued that "...to the extent that fluctuations in money growth contain useful information about subsequent movements of income prices, the central bank should exploit that information." However, these economists also refer to the need to consider other variables:

> We have seen all sorts of definitions of money from narrow to broad credit, from M1 to MX, but none of them offers any real hold. This is due to the broad range of substitutes which have come to function as money in our modern times, a development which has attended financial innovation, deregulation and the emergence of an array of entirely new financial instruments. If...the concept of money cannot be defined with any degree of precision, regulating the money stock becomes...highly problematic.[11]

In fact, some central banks are already tracking money supply aggregates while taking other factors into account. For example, Germany, Spain and France are using M3 in combination with an exchange rate target.[12] Such an approach provides valuable information concerning economic growth, while taking other factors into account as well.

The most important consideration in designing and using monetary policies is not limited to the achievement of the objectives but also includes the impact of such policies on economic factors. This requires a high degree of transparency and credibility. Regardless of the choice between direct and indirect targets and among a variety of intermediate targets, the ECB has to monitor other indicators which could signal current and future monetary, economic and financial conditions. In light of this, the EMI has identified three indicators: exchange rate, monetary aggregate and inflation targeting.[13] Of these, the EMI favors monetary aggregate and inflation targeting as

---

[9] Denmark, Germany, Spain and France have been using M3 and Italy has been using M2 as monetary targets.

[10] Friedman, Benjamin M. "Intermediate Targets Versus Information Variables as Operating Guides for Monetary Policy," in Wijnholds, J Onno de Beaufort, Sylvester C. W. Eijffinger and Lex H. Hoogduin, eds., A Framework for Monetary Stability, in Financial and Monetary Policy Studies, London: Kluwer Academic Publishers, 1994.

[11] Friedman, Benjamin M. "Intermediate Targets Versus Information Variables as Operating Guides for Monetary Policy," unpublished paper presented at an International Conference of De Nederlandsche Bank and Tilburg University on "A Framework for Monetary Stability," Amsterdam, October 1993.

[12] EMI 1994 Annual Report, p.128.

[13] "Progress Towards Convergence, " European Monetary Institute (EMI), Frankfurt am

policy choices for the ECB. It believes that exchange rate targeting is suitable for smaller nations whose exchange rates have a larger impact on inflation. Commitment to price stability is the most important feature in this design, but, as has been mentioned, it is the EMI's monetary policy strategy that has the greatest influence on economic factors.

In its 1994 Annual Report the EMI emphasizes that "...in the day-to-day implementation of monetary policy, the ESCB will focus on one or several short-term interest rates. In influencing this rate (or these rates) it will convey information to market participants."[14] This statement sends clear monetary policy signals to market participants. But such signals are effective only if harmonized interbank markets, payments systems, monetary policy instruments and management exist. To achieve these ends, the ESCB must pursue its targets efficiently. To this end the monetary policy signals of the ESCB must be uniform and consistent; that is, the following conditions must be present:

- conformity with market principles: monetary policy implementation should be "in accordance with the principle of an open market economy with free competition, favoring an efficient allocation of resources" (Maastricht Treaty, Article 105);

- equal treatment: the ESCB must treat all groups of financial institutions that have access to its facilities equally and regardless of their country of origin;

- simplicity and transparency: the monetary policy and procedures must be simple and be employed with clarity, so as to contribute towards meeting the criteria of equal treatment and conformity with market principles in a decentralized central banking system;

- decentralization: the ESCB must have recourse to the national central banks to carry out operations "to the extent deemed possible and appropriate" (Article 12 of the ESCB Statute). The fulfillment of this principle may be of practical relevance, in that the ECB can take advantage of national central banks' experience and knowledge of local markets;

- continuity: the transition to the new operational framework at the beginning of Stage Three can be facilitated by relying as much as possible on the initial infrastructure and employing instruments that can be adapted to the changing environment.[15]

Main, November 1995, p.70.

[14] EMI 1994 Annual Report, p.74.

[15] EMI 1994 Annual Report, pp.74-75.

The EU central banks not only differ with respect to monetary policy choices and structures but also with respect to the financial instruments used to conduct monetary policies. The choice of instruments depends on the breadth of national financial markets. Thus, it is essential that the ECB adopt flexible policy instruments and an efficient operational structure. It must assess the relative impact of instruments on the targeted variables under the differing operating conditions of the EU financial centers.[16]

There are variations among national monetary policy instruments which are reflected not only in the choice of instruments, but also in the frequency and application of the same. As shown previously in Table 5.1, the various nations have different combinations of reserve requirements, standing facilities and open market operations, although some of these features have converged during 1994 and 1995. The EMI's assessment shows that, for example, the use of open market operations and repurchase agreements has increased and that the Bank of England, as well as of Greece and Austria have introduced repurchase agreements. Reserve requirements among member nations, excluding Greece, have converged. Moreover, in line with other EU member nations, the Bank of France will soon issue its own debt paper to reduce liquidity.[17]

The EMI favors open market operations[18] and expects the ECB to introduce reversed transactions (repos) in the Euro, outright transactions, foreign currency swap transactions and central bank paper issues. Repos are currently the most popular financial instrument applied by central banks and it is likely that the ECB will use them to implement monetary policies. This will provide the ECB with flexibility in designing the timing, frequency and nature of its activities. While outright transactions and foreign currency swaps are not as flexible as repos, they may be useful in setting up the ECB's long-term position in relation to the commercial banking sector.

It is difficult to harmonize EU-wide standing facilities and reserve requirements because such instruments have not been implemented as widely as open market operations. Standing facilities might be useful to central banks to set up positions when acting as agents for the fiscal authorities. In its November 1995 EMU report, "Progress Towards Convergence,"[19] the EMI suggests that the decisions on the use of reserve requirements be left to the ESCB, because reserve requirements can have a strong impact on the competitiveness of the banking industry. However, before setting reserve requirements, it is important to asses the financial markets and economic structures at the beginning of Stage III.

---

[16] The assessment of the impact of different monetary policy instruments on targeted variables requires a working gross settlement system, which the ECB will apply.

[17] "Progress Towards Convergence," EMI, 1995, p.72. Also see Tables 5.1 and 5.3.

[18] See "Progress Towards Convergence," EMI, 1995, for a detailed explanation.

[19] "Progress Towards Convergence," EMI, 1995.

Establishment of the ESCB:[20] The EMI is in charge of making all the necessary preparations for Stage III. This involves the development of common monetary policy instruments and procedures such as the standardized accounting and reporting rules for the national central banks within the ESCB. In addition, the EMI must harmonize the collection and distribution of statistics, promote the efficiency of cross-border payment systems and supervise the technical preparation of Euro bank notes. By December 31, 1996, the EMI must also have set up the policy framework of the ESCB[21] so that it can function effectively at the start of Stage III. This gives the EMI a high profile and great influence.

The EMI is also developing the ECB's organizational structure. This raises several questions. Will the ECB have a role in banking supervision? How and what level of reserves will be required? How will monetary stability (or price stability) be measured? How and where will open market operations be performed? The answers to these questions will have to be drawn out of the vague descriptions of the ECB's activities contained in the Maastricht Treaty. To do this, the EMI needs a basic premise agreed to by all member states.

A common accounting system is a prerequisite of common monetary policies. The EMI has already begun the harmonization of accounting rules and standards to develop a consolidated balance sheet for the ESCB to be used at the start of Stage III. This involves the formation of assets valuation and liability principles and of procedures for the recognition of income, a chart of accounts, capitalization and depreciation rules, accounting techniques and control mechanisms.

Foreign Exchange Policies:[22] With the start of Stage III of the EMU, the foreign exchange reserve assets of the national central banks will be transferred to the ECB, which will be responsible for the management of the common ECB reserves. In addition, the ECB will be responsible for the implementation of foreign exchange policies while the actual decision-making authority will rest with the ECOFIN Council. As a result, foreign exchange management procedures must be established before the start of Stage III, including technical constraints, classifications of the role of nations with derogations[23] and of the role of non-EU currencies.

The EMI will develop a decentralized and a centralized approach within which the ECB can make the necessary intervention decisions.[24] Thus, the ECB may choose to act either by itself or through national central banks. The decentralized approach provides more operational flexibility and efficiency, but this could create conflicts with non-EMU member central banks, and thus the use of such an approach

---

[20] EMI 1994 Annual Report, p.80.
[21] Under Article 109.f.3 of the Maastricht Treaty, 1992.
[22] EMI 1994 Annual Report, pp.75-76.
[23] EU member nations that have opted out of the EMU.
[24] "Progress Towards Convergence," EMI, 1995.

should be carefully evaluated.

The design of the new intervention system involves three areas: operations, telecommunications and common dealings. These have to be harmonized. Communications networks and dealing systems must also be integrated and upgraded. Moreover, market participants will have to be identified. This is an important task, because the choices will have an impact on financial institutions and possibly on financial centers.

Payments Systems:[25] One of the main tasks of the EMI is to design a sound cross-border payments system which the ECB and the financial markets can start using at the beginning of Stage III. To date, the EMI has focused on large-value payments -- the core of payments systems in modern economies. It has paid less attention to retail payments and securities settlement systems.

Current EU payment systems are based on correspondent banking. However, such systems are not efficient enough to facilitate the large-value interbank payments of the future as well as the payments resulting from the monetary policy operations of the ESCB. There must be a system through which high-value central bank payments can be made with high standards of security, speed and efficiency to minimize possible risks. In addition, such a system must be able to transmit the impact of policies effectively to all market participants. Thus, the system's structure and operation calls for a high degree of coordination among national central banks, the EMI and financial market participants.

In its 1994 Annual Report, the EMI identified three basic principles that the so-called Trans-European Automated Real-Time Gross Settlement Express Transfer (TARGET) system has to meet: efficiency, market-orientation and decentralization. The TARGET, however, will process only transactions related to monetary policy actions. It will offer a Real-Time Gross Settlement (RTGS) system in each EMU participant nation and will provide a connecting web to all nations and to the ECB's payments system to process cross-border payments as if they were domestic transactions. The system will also provide settlement procedures among central banks and between the ECB and central banks, and also for the ECB's own settlement activities. Other retail and large-value payment systems may also be used, provided that they meet safety standards similar to those of the TARGET system.

Payment System Cooperation among Central Banks:[26] Cooperation among central banks involves three major areas: (i) the cooperative oversight of payment systems; (ii) minimum common requirements in domestic payments systems; and (iii) prepaid cards.

---

[25] EMI 1994 Annual Report, pp.77-79.
[26] EMI 1994 Annual Report, pp.87-94.

Cooperative oversight is needed to ensure the smooth functioning of payments systems and to insulate the financial sector from the so-called "domino effect." This effect takes place when market participants face credit or liquidity problems in their domestic interbank markets and payments systems.

Cooperative oversight of cross-border participation by domestic payments systems was established by the member nations' central banks in 1988 in response to the Second Banking Coordination Directive. This Directive places the primary responsibility for the supervision of credit institution branches operating in EU nations with the "home country" authorities. The "host country" has only limited authority.

Cooperative arrangements among the various national authorities were established by the Committee of Governors in 1993. Cross-border information exchanges take place among central banks or bank supervisors only. The EMI, which will establish the EU Payment Systems, is going to reinforce this cooperative oversight arrangement. A monitoring group, created in September 1994, collects and dispatches information and keeps up-to-date records on the rules of national interbank fund transfer systems. It also monitors non-EU interbank fund transfer arrangements.

There is a need for cooperation in establishing the minimum common features of the domestic payment systems. The "Report on the Payment Systems in EC Member States,"[27] the so-called "Blue Book," issued by the Committee of Central Bank Governors in November 1992, reveals significant differences among national high-value funds transfer systems, including differing risk control measures, legal and technical dimensions, access conditions, pricing policies and business hours. Such differences can negatively affect cross-border payment processes and competitiveness. Differing national cost structures may result in shifts to the less efficient and less costly systems which could affect the efficiency of the large EU-wide system.

To reduce risks, domestic interbank fund transfer systems must share certain minimum standards. Member nations have already upgraded and redesigned their RTGS systems which may be in place before the EMU membership decisions are completed. France, Luxembourg and Portugal are designing new RTGS systems while other EU nations are upgrading their existing systems. RTGS are currently also used in Denmark, Germany, Sweden and Finland. For an overview of the implementation of the RTGS system in the EU nations see Table 5.2.

---

[27] "Report on the Payment Systems in EC Member States," Committee of Central Bank Governors, 1992.

Table 5.2
Overview of the Implementation of the RTGS System in the EU Nations

COUNTRY	B	DK	D	SP	GR	F	IE	I	NL	P	UK	O	S	FIN
Name of the system	ELLIPS	DNF	EIL-ZV/AZV	SLBE	HERMES	TBF	IRIS	BIREL	TOP	SPGT	CHAPS	EBK	RIX	BOF
System already in operation*	No	Yes	Yes	No	No	No	No	No	No	No	No	No	Yes	Yes
Date of starting		1981	1988										1990	1991
Start of work	Mar 1992	1980	1985	Dec 1992	Sep 1993	Dec 1990	Dec 1993	Dec 1992	1991	Mar 1993	1989	Dec 1993	1988	1989
General specifications	Jun 1993	1981	1986	Jun 1993	Dec 1993	Dec 1994	Jan 1995	Sep 1994	1992	Jun 1993	1992	Dec 1993	1989	1989
Detailed specifications	Sep 1994	1981	1986	Sep 1994	Apr 1995	Sep 1995	Sep 1995	Mar 1995	1993	Dec 1993	1993	Jun 1995	1990	1989
Implementation of project	Jan 1995	1981	1987	Jan 1995	1996	1996	1996	Sep 1995	1994	Jun 1994	1994	1996	1990	1990
System fully in operation	Jun 1996	1981	1988	Jun 1997	Dec 1996	Dec 1996	Dec 1996	Jun 1997	Jun 1996	Dec 1995	Jun 1996	Dec 1997	1990	Mar 1991

Key: B: Belgium; DK: Denmark; D: Germany; SP: Spain; GR: Greece; F: France; IE: Ireland; I: Italy; NL: The Netherlands; P: Portugal; UK:United Kingdom; O: Austria; S: Sweden; FIN: Finland.

* = Real-time book entries on a gross basis are already possible in Austria (via the EBK system which has been available since 1989), Italy (via the BISS, which has been available since 1989) and the Netherlands. However, these systems will be transformed or completely redesigned.

Source: "Progress Towards Convergence," EMI, November 1995, p. 83.

Prepaid Cards are multi-purpose plastic cards (or "electronic purses") which provide "purchasing power for which the customer has paid in advance."[28] In May 1994 the EMI, along with the EU central banks, released a report on these cards to the EU banking community. The report concluded that in order to protect customers and the integrity of the retail payment system, prepaid cards should be issued only by credit institutions. They should be used to facilitate monetary policies and enhance competition. The EMI is continuing to investigate the potential of this payment system.

(iii) The third function of the EMI is to facilitate the use of the present-day Ecu basket, oversee the Ecu Clearing and Settlement System and manage the transition to the new single currency, the Euro:[29] There is a consensus among the EU institutions and most member governments that the growing use of the Ecu in private transactions (as opposed to national currencies or other hard non-EU currencies) reflects the market participants' trust in the future single currency.[30] Thus the EMI is expected to promote the present-day Ecu. In January 1994 it assumed the Ecu clearing and settlement system oversight function, previously exercised by the Committee of EU Central Bank Governors. It is expected that this system will be transformed into the Euro clearing and settlement system. To this end the EMI must ensure that: (i) the clearing operations do not pose unacceptable systemic risks either to the Ecu market or to the domestic financial markets; and (ii) the risks assumed by the participating banks are under control. To reduce the systemic risk, the EMI coordinates with the Ecu Banking Association (EBA), which manages the system, as well as with the member nations' central banks. It receives and analyzes Ecu transaction operation information on a regular basis. To date, the Ecu clearing and settlement system may continue to operate as a private net settlement system, as long as it complies with minimum safety standards.

Articles 109.g and 109.l of the Maastricht Treaty address the issue of the present-day Ecu basket and its transition to the single currency, the Euro. The EU Commission published three documents in April 1994 to reassure the financial markets on the current and future legal status of the present-day Ecu-denominated contracts. The Commission proposed the consolidation of the existing legislation concerning the currency composition of the Ecu basket. Subsequently, the Council of Ministers adopted the proposal. Other recommendations included a Commission proposal on the legal treatment of the Ecu and of the contracts denominated in Ecus, as well as a Commission "Explanatory Note" on the new clauses in bond issue prospects, ensuring legal continuity between the Ecu and the future single currency, the Euro.

---

[28] EMI 1994 Annual Report, p.90.

[29] EMI 1994 Annual Report, pp.81-84.

[30] In the course of 1993 and 1994, the use of Ecu in private transactions was influenced mainly by the political and economic environment of the EU. Tensions in the ERM in the first half of 1993 created uncertainty with respect to the interest and exchange rates of the currencies included in the Ecu basket. The widening of the ERM bands to +/-15 percent in August 1993 increased the markets' awareness of these risks. Eventually, the monetary authorities managed to keep most of the currencies within their former band limits which reassured the financial markets.

The EMI is expected to promote the smooth adoption of the Euro and to oversee its development.[31] This involves the evaluation of the legal environment in the member states to determine the possible obstacles to the Euro's private use. While the EMI is expected to eliminate legal obstacles, it must not emphasize the role of the Euro to such an extent that it poses a threat to national sovereignty as it relates to national monetary policies and currencies. The EMI must also cooperate with the EU Commission and conduct an annual review to promote the financial and non-financial use of the Euro. In addition, on its own initiative or at the request of other institutions or member states, the EMI must ensure a smooth transition to the single currency introduced in Stage III and the continued use of Euro-denominated contracts and instruments.

(iv) The fourth function of the EMI is to monitor the compliance of members states with the Maastricht Treaty, specifically in the realm of central bank financing and privileged access to financial institutions:[32] Article 169 of the Maastricht Treaty entrusts the task of ensuring compliance with the Treaty by the member nations to the EU Commission. At the same time, Articles 109.f (9) and 180 (d) of the Treaty authorize the EMI to monitor the central banks' compliance with the same. At a later date, the fiscal prohibitions were further specified in legislation issued by the Council of Ministers' Regulations No. 3603/93 and No. 3604/93, dated December 13, 1993. The limitations, based on past experience,[33] are necessary because monetary policy geared to price stability might be jeopardized by the central banks' financing of government deficits. Therefore, prohibiting the public sector from receiving monetary financing and/or from having privileged access to financial institutions is a central element of the EMU, beginning with Stage II on January 1, 1994.[34]

The legislation abolishes overdraft facilities and other types of credit facilities available to the public sector and does away with the direct purchase of public sector debt instruments by the central banks. It also abolishes central bank financing of the transaction services the banks perform for the public sector[35] and prohibits privileged access by the public sector to financial institutions for the purpose of obtaining public sector liabilities. Indirect measures which do not comply with the principles of a market economy such as the granting of tax benefits that could benefit only financial

---

[31] Article 4, EMI Protocol, Maastricht Treaty, 1992.

[32] Adopted from the EMI's 1994, Annual Report, pp.107-10.

[33] For a detailed discussion of the subject, see Alesina, Alberto, and Lawrence H. Summers. "Central Bank Independence and Macroeconomic Performance: Some Comparative Evidence," Journal of Money, Credit and Banking, May 1993, pp.151-162; and Cottarelli, Carlo. "Limiting Central Bank Credit to the Government: Theory and Practice," IMF Occasional Paper, NO: 110, Washington, DC: IMF, 1993.

[34] Article 104, Maastricht Treaty, 1992.

[35] In the case of Italy, in its 1994 Annual Report the EMI combines the national Foreign Exchange Office (Ufficio Italiano di Cambi) with the Banca d'Italia.

institutions are prohibited as are the benefits that encourage the acquisition or holding of such liabilities.

Compliance with the Prohibition of Central Bank Credit to the Public Sector: Most EU nations adapted their legislation before the beginning of Stage II to comply with the prohibition on public sector financing. However, in its 1994 Annual Report the EMI points out that minor adjustments are still required. The Council of Ministers' regulation provides exceptions, permitting, within certain limits or under certain conditions, intra-day credits and credits arising from the collection of checks on behalf of and from central banks resulting from the holdings of officially issued coins. Such exceptions are granted because a complete prohibition of claims arising out of such practices is unnecessary and might prove very costly to implement.[36]

The Council of Ministers' regulation allows public debt stock to be held by central banks as long it was acquired prior to January 1, 1994. The debt, however, must be of a fixed maturity (irrespective of the date of maturity) and the claims must be fulfilled at a market rate. In most EU nations the majority of outstanding debt has been converted into fixed-term assets, although in a few countries residual claims of the central banks against the public sector remain to be converted.

Since with 1994, the prohibition on public sector overdraft facilities provided by central banks has generally been observed. However, occasional overdrafts resulting from the transition to new arrangements or from delayed payments by third parties, are still granted. But such overdrafts do not reflect structural problems and do not have an impact on monetary policies. Moreover, the Maastricht Treaty does not prohibit primary market purchases of debt instruments issued by the public sector in the secondary markets. Thus, a few central banks purchased significant amounts of government debt in the secondary markets in 1994. The Council of Ministers and the EMI have declared such purchases as compatible with the prohibition on the direct purchase of public debt instruments.

The Prohibition against Granting Privileged Access to Financial Institutions: Even before the ratification of the Maastricht Treaty, most EU nations had abolished measures which could provide privileged access to financial institutions. This was done in accordance with the "Directive on the Liberalization of Capital Movements," which in most countries had entered into force on July 1, 1990. According to the 1994 EMI Annual Report, as a result of increased competition and deregulation in the financial markets, public sectors increasingly borrow at market rates.

The nature of the reserve requirements has also changed. Central banks may accept Treasury bills as assets to meet such requirements. Although this does not

---

[36] The financing by central banks of obligations of the public sector to the IMF or of obligations resulting from the implementation of the medium-term financial assistance facility of the EU, is also unconditionally exempted.

involve directly buying public debt, it can facilitate debt purchases. Central banks that accepted public debt instruments as eligible reserve assets in the past have stopped such practices.

(v) The EMI's fifth function is the assessment of the Maastricht Treaty's convergence criteria: The Maastricht Treaty requires countries that want to join the EMU to fulfill in advance the economic and monetary conditions essential to the introduction of the single currency, the Euro, Article 109j (1) requires that the EMI and the EU Commission must each prepare a report to the Council of Ministers on the fulfillment of the convergence criteria by reference to the following:

- the achievement of a high degree of price stability; this is measured by a rate of inflation which must be close to that of the three best-performing member states;

- the sustainability of the government financial position; this is measured by the size of excessive deficits;

- the position of currencies in relation to the "normal"[37] ERM fluctuation margins without devaluations against other ERM currencies in the mechanism for at least two years; and

- the sustainability of convergence achieved by member states as well as the quality of their participation in the ERM as reflected by long-term interest rates.

The Commission and the EMI reports must also include an evaluation of the Ecu, of the market integration process, of the current account and unit labor cost trends as well as of the trends of other price indices. In addition, under Article 7 of its Statute, the EMI once a year must provide a report to the Council of Ministers which, among other items, includes an assessment of the convergence process. The Annual Report also fulfills this requirement by providing a convergence review. In November 1995 the EMI published its first Article 7 convergence report as an independent document -- the "Progress Towards Convergence" report. This was followed by a second report in November 1996. Note that it is the 1997 EMI "Progress Towards Convergence" report that is critical as it will contain the official economic data as it pertains to the Maastricht convergence criteria and be instrumental in deciding EMU membership .

[37] "Normal" fluctuation margins originally pertained to the +/- 2.25 percent currency bands of the ERM. It should be noted that in the aftermath of the ERM crisis and the subsequent widening of the currency bands to +/-15 percent, what was "normal" was debatable (among EU member nations) for a long time. However, to date, the EU's official position is that the +/- 15 percent currency band is "normal."

The Transitional Role of the EMI

The transitional role of the EMI is critical. It not only lays the foundations of the ECB but also plays an important role in the pre-EMU monetary policy formulation through the publication of its policy views, to persuade and inform the financial markets of its future strategies and goals. It must also convince the public of the importance of central bank independence and of its firm commitment to price stability. Only such policies can minimize concerns in the financial markets and maintain public support for the EMU.

The EMI must also begin to operate as a central bank during the transitional stage so as to discover the flaws in the new common monetary policies prior to the creation of the ECB. As laid out by the Maastricht Treaty, the path to the EMU calls for a difficult transitional Stage II. (Subsequent agreements delayed the more difficult parts of the transition period which now begins on January 1, 1999 as part of Stage III.) Central bankers favored a more conservative approach but their governments endorsed continued integration. The resulting political compromise reflected in the Treaty did not provide the EMI with the authority to establish common monetary policy objectives; thus, it must coordinate such policies within the framework of national monetary targets. The central banks, in particular the Bundesbank, insisted on a long transitional period to Stage III without the transfer of any national monetary policy authority to a common institution.[38]

It should be noted that the authority and management process of the EMI and subsequently of the ECB is still unclear and will continue to remain so until EMU's membership is determined. Yet under the Maastricht Treaty there are no strict and precise rules for membership. It is important to point out that the central banks of Germany, the Netherlands, Belgium, Luxembourg and France are reluctant to relinquish their hard-earned price stability credibility in an EMU that might include less credible central banks. Thus, until the issue of membership is resolved the central banks of these nations will not give up their monetary authority. They also prefer an EMU in which the cost of termination is low i.e., an EMU in which national monetary objectives are observed, operations are decentralized, multiple currencies are used and market integration is limited. Thus, in terms of expected welfare gains, the likely EMU arrangements are inefficient. Only restricted membership could create an efficient EMU.

---

[38] According to the EU Commission's May 1995 "Green Paper" and the subsequent November 15 EMI "Progress Towards Convergence" report, Stage III is divided into three parts, Phase A, B and C. During the earlier phases, in addition to the Euro being introduced on a non-cash basis and the irrevocable locking of EMU participants exchange rates, the EU still maintains the 12 currencies; during the latter phase the Euro is introduced on a cash basis and eventually evolves into the sole legal tender of EMU participants.

The restriction on membership as in a multi-speed EMU, although a workable solution for the "credible" central bank group (i.e., Germany, the Netherlands, Belgium, Luxembourg and France), is undesirable to the peripheral nations with less credible central banks. These latter nations have trepidations about becoming second-class EU members with diminishing bargaining strength vis-à-vis the core group of nations. Moreover, the peripheral nations believe that a multi-speed EMU would allow the core nations to pursue low inflationary policies without considering the consequences on their economies. This would probably delay their entry into the EMU, although the institutional structure of the ECB's General Council and the EMI statute require that all 15 EU member nations participate.[39] Because the Council includes central bankers, it could be the venue of political disagreements between representatives of the core members and peripheral nations.

Nonetheless, the ECB, just like the EMI, will promote low-inflation oriented policies. This raises the question of what type of political compromise will be required for this purpose. Since the current EMI Council consists of all 15 EU nations, it is unlikely that the core group could readily pave their way towards a multi-speed EMU without additional concessions or assurances to the peripheral nations as the EMI decisions are based on a simple majority vote. A politically acceptable outcome has to include the medium- to long-term goal of creating a 15-member EMU. Such an arrangement, however, is politically inconceivable anytime in the near future. In view of this, the 15-member EMI Council faces a complex task in negotiating proposals concerning the future EMU technical details, such as functioning and management of the ERM II and the ECB's future role and management as long as all 15 EU nations have equal votes in the EMI Council.

The admission of the three new member nations of Austria, Finland and Sweden in 1995, changed the required EMU decision-making majority from seven of twelve to eight of 15 votes. The three new EU members have a much better chance of being in the first wave of EMU participants (if they so choose) than nations that have been members for a longer period of time. Thus, it is not surprising that the peripheral nations have a negative reaction to the EU "widening" plans and demand monetary compensation in return for a pro-enlargement vote through the Cohesion Fund.[40] It should be noted that the three new member countries are net contributors to the common budget and that the major recipients of this increased largesse are Spain, Portugal, Italy, Ireland and Greece.[41] If the U.K. and/or Denmark opt-out of the EMU,

---

[39] However, the ECB General Council has no voting authority. It is the Governing Council, comprised of the ECB President and the EMU-participating central bank governors, that is the voting power in the ECB.

[40] This compromise was formalized at the December 1992 Edinburgh IGC Summit. The agreement also increased the ratio of the EU budget to the common GDP by 12 percent beginning in 1995.

[41] Austria, Finland and Sweden are net contributors to the common budget, as they have above-EU-average per capita incomes, high levels of agricultural protection and no serious regional problems.

it would change not only the nature of the ECB Governing and General Council but also EMU.

A multi-speed EMU (and a two-tired EU) is the only realistic political and economic solution. In terms of expected welfare gains it would be the most efficient and it would also provide the periphery nations time and resources to achieve a degree of fiscal and monetary stability. By the time most of them would be eligible to join the EMU, the core members could have already gained enough practical experience to manage the common monetary policies. However, there is a danger that the core group might prolong the exclusion of the periphery nations and thus leave the EMU incomplete for some time. To safeguard against such an eventuality, it is the EMI's responsibility to make the Maastricht convergence criteria more explicit and less subject to discretion. The ECB's General Council mandate which requires all 15 EU members to participate in the EMU, may also reduce the probability of "flexible" interpretations.

It should be noted that regardless of a multi-speed EMU, most EU members, including the Bonn Government, have misgivings about such an outcome because in their view such an EMU could develop into a "Europe a la carte" with varying obligations. The U.K. and Denmark are prime examples of this, as the former has opted out of the EMU and the Social Charter and the latter declines to participate in the EMU and to adopt the common defense, interior and legal policies. Although such opt-outs are politically necessary because they facilitate integration, if they create inefficiencies they could imperil the same.

The EMI's Credibility

The EMI's Charter includes the following limitations that may affect its credibility and constrain its progress toward the EMU:

- The opinions and/or recommendations of the EMI are not binding;[42]

- The EMI may make suggestions only through a two-thirds majority vote[43] but its recommendations require a unanimous vote;[44]

- The EMI may not hold reserves, but it can hold and manage foreign exchange reserves as an agent of the central banks, if requested to do so. However, it cannot use such reserves in ways that would damage

[42] Article 15.2, EMI Protocol, Maastricht Treaty, 1992.

[43] Article 109.f.4., Maastricht Treaty, 1992.

[44] As a result, the EMI is bound to operate in a consultative manner and will have to function prudently to be effective in convincing the national and common authorities of the validity of its actions. Article 109.f.5, Maastricht Treaty, 1992.

> the monetary and exchange rate policies of any national monetary authority.[45]

Many important decisions are not made by the EMI but by the ECOFIN Council (EU Council of Economic and Finance Ministers). Although the former Commission President Jacques Delors and the current President Jacques Santer have called for a "hardened" EMI, particularly in relation to monitoring the convergence criteria, the Bundesbank does not favor an increase in the institution's power. An influential EMI could be a threat to its autonomy and could limit its control of monetary policies. It could also decrease the Bundesbank's influence on the monetary integration process and promote the centralization of power in the EMI. Past proposals providing a more influential role for the EMI included the linking of the Deutsche mark to the French and Benelux francs and the creation of a fund backed by these currencies through which the EMI could intervene in the financial markets whenever necessary. Neither came to pass.

The EMI is justified in arguing for anti-inflationary policy objectives. It needs to lessen the fears of the German public, which is concerned that the Stage III process would degrade its currency. The EMI and the ECB also need to maintain the goodwill of financial institutions during the process of converting to the Euro, because the process will be costly and painful. If the EMI can develop the rules independently and prudently, the ECB will be able to effectively manage the process. Thus, the EMI must have an efficient structure as well as room to maneuver. This could help the ECB to establish its own credibility by showing the public and the financial markets that it is ready to fight inflation and that it can formulate policies free of political influence.

The trade-off between price stability and other economic factors such as unemployment will be a matter of controversy. For example, the U.K., together with high inflation/high unemployment nations such as Spain, Italy, Portugal and Greece, does not want a strident commitment to price stability -- a notion that the Bundesbank and the future ECB cannot accept. Eddie George, Governor of the Bank of England, expressed the U.K.'s position as follows:

> Key stability...is price stability...We have learned that monetary management...can't be a matter of pumping up demand until we reach full employment without regard to the supply capacity of the economy or the implications for inflation. But, equally, we are not mindlessly seeking to drive prices down regardless of the effect on the level of activity and employment -- falling prices can be as

---

[45] France, Belgium, Italy and Spain want the EMI to help manage their currency reserves and develop a common money supply aggregate that would replace national monetary measures. Article 6.4, EMI Protocol, Maastricht Treaty, 1992

damaging as rising prices in terms of what we are trying to do.[46]

In the past, EU central bankers and finance ministers of the 15 member nations, Jacques Santer, the president of the EU Commission and Alexandre Lamfalussy of the EMI, all participated in not only formal but informal meetings of the ECOFIN Council. Most of the discussions and the resulting press releases were dominated by the governments; the EMI seems to have little influence. Thus, it appears that calls for a strong EMI are not being heard and that the EMI's recommendations are not as effective as they need to be so as not to harm the image of its successor, the ECB.

The EMI and the Convergence Criteria

Price stability

To manage the price and wage levels as well as productivity trends and thus to coordinate macroeconomic policies, an EU policy consensus is needed. Fiscal policy coordination must be conducted in parallel with monetary policy coordination, otherwise economic recovery may negatively affect price stability. Stage II is an early test of how committed member nations are to such an objective and how well fiscal and monetary policies are coordinated. The EMI's activities and monetary policies alone are not sufficient to ensure sustainable growth with price stability. For a detailed discussion of the price level convergence criteria and the role of the EMI, see Annex V.4.

Sustainability of Fiscal Positions

The Maastricht Treaty requires a regular examination of the budgetary policies of member nations by the Council of Ministers during Stage II. It also provides for sanctions against member states with excessive deficits in Stage III. In 1996, these sanctions were formalized into actual fines through the post-EMU fiscal "Stability and Growth Pact".

The existing stock of debt and its trend over time are important issues in assessing whether the debt ratio is approaching the reference value at a satisfactory pace. However, the relationship between deficit and debt trends leads to the realization that a deficit cap of around 3 percent of GDP may not be an appropriate requirement for all nations. See Annex V.5 for a detailed discussion of the fiscal convergence criteria and the role of the EMI.

---

[46] Speech by the Governor of the Bank of England Eddie George on the occasion of the CBI West Midlands Region 1994 Manufacturing Dinner at the International Convention Center in Birmingham, October 27, 1994; in *BIS Review* No. 204, November 1994.

Exchange Rate Stability

The uncertainty concerning EMU membership has been an important factor influencing exchange rate movements in the EU. While economic fundamentals affecting price stability are important issues, past experience with the original ERM has kept the financial markets cautious about speculative tendencies. Member nations need to coordinate their macroeconomic policies to convince the markets that overall macroeconomic policies are geared to price stability. See Annex V.6 for a detailed discussion of the exchange rate convergence criteria and the role of the EMI, and for the evolution of real effective exchange rates in the EU.

Convergence of Long-term Interest Rates

The Maastricht Treaty provides reference values based on the long-term interest rates of countries with the lowest levels of inflation. However, the lowest inflation levels are not associated with the lowest long-term interest rates. For example, in 1994 the best performer in terms of inflation was France, but its average long-term interest rate of 7.2 percent exceeded those of Luxembourg (6.4 percent), the Netherlands (6.9 percent) and Germany (7.0 percent).

Moreover, average annual values could hide an increase in the gap in interest rate differentials between the best-performing countries and other member nations. This justifies the financial markets' concern over national fiscal positions in the context of long-term exchange rate and price stability. Cross-country differences leading to a widening of bond yields over the course of 1994 indicate that the overall convergence progress must be improved. See Annex V.7 for a detailed discussion of the long-term interest rate convergence criteria and the role of the EMI.

THE EUROPEAN CENTRAL BANK

The success or failure of the EMU will partly depend on the performance of the ESCB, which will be a federal-style system made up of the EMU member nations' central banks and the ECB. Particularly important in this respect is the structure of the ECB, the degree of its independence, the nature of its primary and secondary tasks and the nature and effectiveness of its monetary instruments.

Organizational Structure and Management

The Committee of Central Bank Governors published the first draft of the ESCB/ECB Statute in November 1990. The draft shows that the proposed ESCB/ECB structure is similar to that of the Bundesbank and closely follows the recommendations of the Delors Report. The ESCB is envisioned as a federal system comprised of the national central banks and the European Central Bank (ECB) to which the national central banks are attached as branches. The ESCB is to be governed by the ECB's decision-making bodies -- its Governing Council and Executive Board. The ECB will serve as the common central bank for EMU participants and will be the decision-making authority for the common European monetary policy. The central banks of the EMU nations will remain in existence but will loose their national autonomy and function as district branches of the ECB under the ESCB federal structure (similar to the Bundesbank and U.S. Federal Reserve system). Each national central bank will be responsible for its own national district/territory and for carrying out the ECB policies. The ECB is expected to be independent and it will focus on price stability so as to obtain the credibility of the Bundesbank.

Decision-making Bodies

The ECB will be governed by two decision-making bodies: the Executive Board and the Governing Council. An additional non-decision making body is the General Council.

The Executive Board: The *Executive Board,* with six members, is comprised of a President, a Vice-President and four other members jointly appointed by the governments of the member nations on the recommendations of the Council of Ministers, following consultations with the European Parliament and the Governing Council.[47] The appointments are for nonrenewable eight-year terms.

The Governing Council: The Governing Council is comprised of the members of the Executive Board along with the governors of the central banks of the EMU member nations, each with one vote. The Council members serve for five years and are expected to meet at least ten times a year. The President of the Council of Ministers and a member of the EU Commission may attend the Governing Council's meetings but they do not vote. Member nations with derogations may not participate in the decision-making processes because their votes are suspended.[48]

The General Council: If there are member states with derogations,[49] the Statute of the ESCB also provides for a General Council. The General Council is comprised of the President and the Vice-President of the ECB, and the governors of the national central banks, including those with derogations. But the General Council is not a decision-making body. It deals with administrative matters and does not participate in

[47] Article 11.2, ESCB Statute, Maastricht Treaty, 1992.
[48] Article 109.a, Maastricht Treaty and Article 10, ESCB Statute, Maastricht Treaty, 1992.
[49] Countries with derogations are defined as either not having met the EMU convergence criteria or having opted out of the EMU.

the formulation or implementation of monetary policies.[50]

Nations with derogation are still subject to the Treaty requirement to establish independent central banks. According to the ESCB Statute, "the central banks shall retain their powers in the field of monetary policy according to national law,"[51] because they are an integral part of the ESCB and focus on price stability as their primary objective. They must also fulfill the convergence criteria[52] and can be taken to the EU Court of Justice if the ECB decides that they have not fulfilled their obligations under the Statute. Central banks, while independent, will also be bound by the decisions of the ESCB. Thus, if the central bank of a nation with a derogation implements decisions in the light of domestic monetary rather than common monetary concerns, controversies will be unavoidable.

The Decision-making Process

Both Executive Board and Governing Council decisions are reached through a simple majority. In the case of a tie, the President casts the deciding vote. The Governing Council requires a two-thirds quorum, but if this requirement is not met the President can convene an extraordinary meeting at which decisions may be taken without a quorum. Figure 5.3 illustrates the ESCB Council's decision-making process.

When the Governing Council deals with issues related to the ECB's capital structure, votes are weighted by the EMI subscription shares which are in proportion to populations and five-year average GDP growth rates at market prices. Executive Board members do not vote on such issues. The subscription shares may be adjusted every five years.

The Governing Council's "equal weight system" (one member/one vote) derives from the German Bundesbank's procedures. It is designed to ensure the political independence and price stability of the ECB. This, combined with extended terms of office, is expected to insure independence and prevent the larger economies and governing bodies of the EU from influencing the ESCB. It could also promote a collegial and interactive relationship on monetary policy issues among the decision-making bodies. However, such a system would not guarantee German participation or an inflation-free Euro.

---

[50] Article 45 and 47, ESCB Statute, Maastricht Treaty, 1992.
[51] Article 43.2, ESCB Statute, Maastricht Treaty, 1992.
[52] This is not mentioned explicitly, but it is derived from the provisions of Articles 2 and 3 of the Maastricht Treaty combined with Article 2 of the Statute.

Figure 5.3
Decision-making Process of the ECB Governing Council

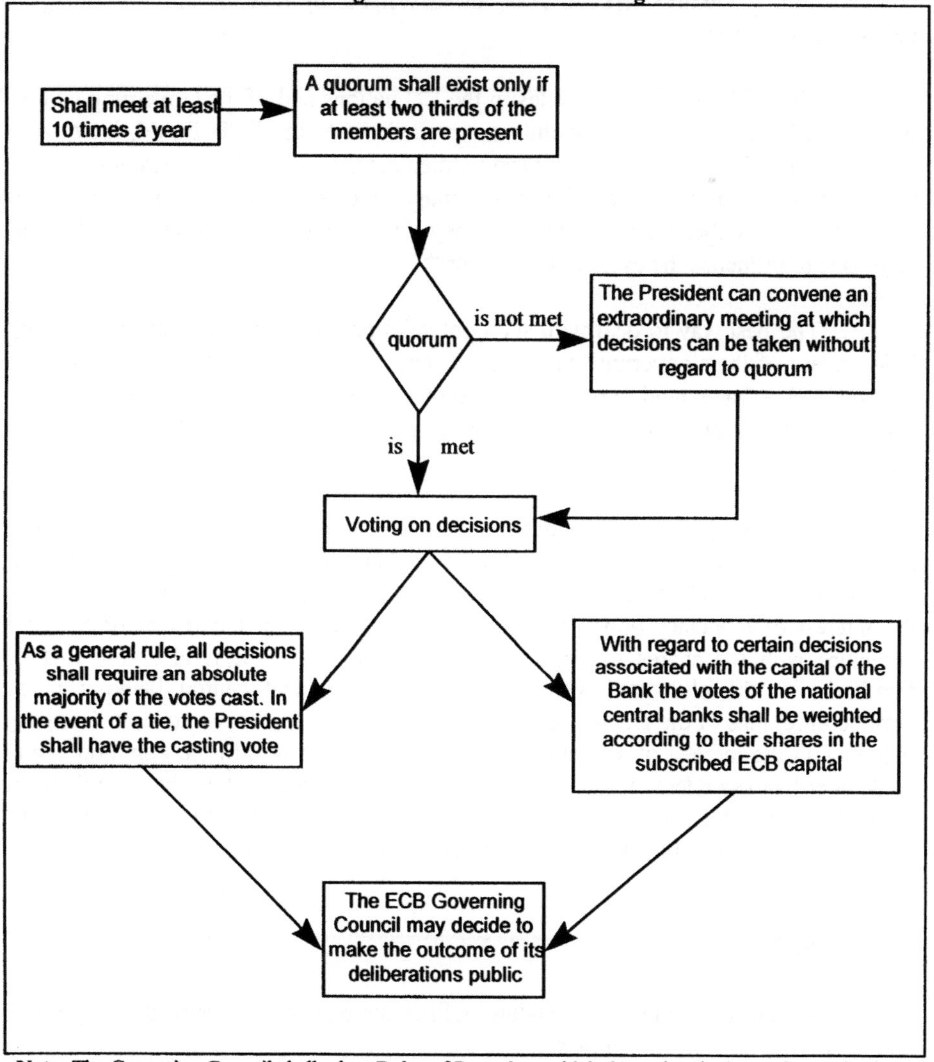

Note: The Governing Council shall adopt Rules of Procedure which determine the internal organization of the ECB and its decision- making bodies.
Source: Nolling, Wilhelm. Monetary Policy in Europe After Maastricht, New York: St. Martin's Press, Inc., 1993, p.145.

An alternative to the existing voting system could be a weighted voting system that would enhance the influence of core nations on common monetary policies, considering their national interests.[53] The votes could be weighted according to (i)

[53] However, this could reduce the confidence of the financial markets and of the EU citizens in the decision-making process.

economic performance; (ii) the extent to which nations can meet the convergence criteria; and/or (iii) current Ecu basket weights. Over the years economically weaker nations could gradually increase their voting weights by meeting and sustaining the convergence criteria.

The differing election cycles in the EU nations and of the Governing Council of the ESCB, as well as the appointment procedures to the ECB Board, have raised some concerns. It has, for example, been pointed out that "the political business cycle of the European Union will affect the disadvantaged member governments in one of two ways: they will either be less stable, or they will engage in log-rolling or offer-side payments to influence the cycle in their favor."[54]

The best way to deal with such potential problems is to render central banks independent of their governments. ECB Governing Council members could be given terms of office that extend to retirement and they could be contractually required not to accept any public or political party office for a specified time period after leaving the ECB.

The disproportionate nature of the electoral and of the ESCB Council representation system could result in monetary policies that are different from the policy expectations of the electorate. It has been asked whether it is "really necessary and in the interest of monetary policy that the division of seats on the Board of the ECB coincides with the shares of popular votes in Europe?"[55] It is also true that the familiarity of the electorate with the idea of independent central banking in the peripheral regions of the EU is not as strongly developed as, for example, in Germany. It is thus in the interest of all nations to have the composition of the common central bank board independent of political election cycles. This implies that simultaneous general parliamentary elections are of no significance. But if this is the case, limiting the impact of monetary policy decisions does not mean commitment to price stability.

Responsibilities

Article 12 of the ESCB Statute defines the responsibilities of the Governing and Executive Councils as follows:

> The Governing Council shall adopt the guidelines and take the decisions necessary to ensure the performance of the tasks entrusted to the ESCB under this Treaty and this Statute. The Governing Council shall formulate the monetary policy of the Community including, as appropriate, decisions relating to intermediate monetary objectives, key interest rates and the supply of reserves in the ESCB, and shall establish the necessary

[54] Roland Vaubel, 1994.
[55] Peter Bofinger, 1992.

guidelines for their implementation.

The Executive Board shall implement monetary policy in accordance with the guidelines and decisions laid down by the Governing Council. In doing so the Executive Board shall give the necessary instructions to national central banks. In addition the Executive Board may have certain powers delegated to it where the Governing Council so decides.

To the extent deemed possible and appropriate and without prejudice to the provisions of this Article, the ECB shall have recourse to the national central banks to carry out operations which form part of the tasks of the ESCB.[56]

The "possible and appropriate" clause in the last paragraph is not clear. It is uncertain which governing body would decide whether it is "possible and appropriate" to interfere with the decisions or actions of central banks. It is unclear whether the Governing Council sets guidelines and the Executive Board implements them, or whether the Executive Board more or less influences the national central banks within the Governing Council. In either case, the national central banks are allowed to choose methods of implementation other than those specified by the ESCB Statute, unless the Governing Council decides, through a two-thirds majority, that this interferes with the ESCB's objectives and tasks.

According to the ESCB Statute, all major decisions must be taken by the Governing Council. However, with a membership of 18 to 22, the Council could be an inefficient decision-making body. Thus, it might delegate some of its functions just as the U.S. Federal Reserve System does.[57] This could minimize the concerns of potential member nations which are not represented on the Executive Board. The ESCB could also designate the Bundesbank or the Bank of England as its trading arm, as the U.S. Federal Reserve did with the New York Federal Reserve Bank. London's "City" is the site of the largest daily volume of foreign exchange trading, and thus the delegation of certain features to it may be appropriate, although it could be politically difficult.

The ECB and the national central banks may engage in open market operations may buy and sell securities and other financial market instruments such as spot or forward contracts in Euro or other EU and non-EU currencies, may lend and borrow securities and may trade in precious metals. They may also participate in credit transactions with other banks and institutions based on adequate collateral. But while the ECB is responsible for the notes issued by the central banks, it is the Governing Council that has the exclusive right to authorize the issue. The ECB has to prepare an

---

[56] Article 12.1, ESCB Statute, Maastricht Treaty, 1992.

[57] The U.S. Federal Reserve System delegates power (monetary policy decisions) to its 12-member Federal Open Market Committee (FOMC).

annual report on all of these activities which its President presents to the Council of Ministers and the Parliament.

The ECB is subject to audits and is under the jurisdiction of the EU Court of Justice. Its President and the other members of the Executive Board may testify to the relevant committees of the EU Parliament on their own or at the request of parliamentary committees.

Monetary Policies

The Maastricht Treaty identifies the characteristics of successful common monetary policies as conducted by the ECB. But without a consent on strategic goals and an effective set of shared policy tools, it may be difficult to develop and implement such policies. This is particularly true as it is the national central banks (within the context of the ESCB) that will, in the end, implement the ECB's common monetary policies. The monetary and exchange rate policies of national central banks are ultimately influenced by their governments. However, monetary policies are not always compatible with the stability criteria laid down in the Maastricht Treaty, because monetary structures and policies and their implementation are the products of differing national political objectives and economic circumstances. Combined with the organization of each member state's governmental administration and banking structures, such differences affect the central banks' leadership, management, relationship with the banking industry and range of tasks. See Annex V.8 (Table 5.5) for a summary of the institutional features of the 15 EU central banks.

Price Stability

The ESCB's objectives are defined in Article 2 of its Maastricht Treaty Statute as follows:

> ...the primary objective of the ESCB shall be to maintain price stability. Without prejudice to the objective of price stability, it shall support the general economic policies in the Community with a view to contributing to the achievement of the objectives of the Community.... The ESCB shall act in accordance with the principle of an open market economy with free competition, favoring an efficient allocation of resources....[58]

The Statute identifies price stability as the ESCB's basic objective. It also requires it to contribute to "a harmonious and balanced development of economic activities, sustainable and non-inflationary growth...a high degree of convergence of

[58] Article 2, ESCB Statue, Maastricht Treaty, 1992.

economic performance...and economic and social cohesion...among member states."[59] These objectives do not differ from those of the U.S. Federal Reserve System, which is expected to foster monetary and credit conditions favorable to "the maintenance of a high level of employment, stable values and a rising standard of living."[60]

It is difficult to evaluate the extent to which central banks can conduct effective monetary policies that are geared to price stability. The goods and services which make up the consumer price index differ from country to country and change from year to year. The measurement of their quality is also difficult, because from year to year the quality of some products and services increases while prices may slightly overstate inflation. Thus, it would be helpful to have a "quality adjusted" price index. But price stability is not solely dependent on the ability of the central banks to take proper measures (i.e., their credibility). Price stability also depends on the actions of other decision-making bodies involved in national economic policy formulation.

The Maastricht Treaty sets specific targets for convergence, but it does not define "price stability" in any detail. Thus central bankers, for all practical purposes, may define price stability as they wish, which could lead to variations ranging from rates from 0 to 1 to 2 percent. Some economists argue that to reflect periodic improvements in the quality of goods and services a 1 to 2 percent rate of inflation is necessary.

Constitutional guarantees do not automatically ensure price stability. Although the ESCB will be independent of national governments and common institutions, its credibility will be based on public opinion. It may choose inflation targets which are possible to achieve but which may require reductions in prices or wages -- moves that the public may not want to support. If the ECB is to obtain credibility and authority, its flexibility must be used prudently.

Banking Supervision

The EU central banks operate under different national regulations with regard to banking supervision, payment transactions, refinancing of commercial banks, government access to central bank loans and foreign exchange transactions.[61]

Central banks must oversee or participate in the supervision of their financial and banking systems because a sound banking and financial structure is essential to effective monetary policies. Supervision provides the central banks with the ability to respond to financial disturbances before they lead to economic crises. It also generates valuable information which shapes judgments about conditions in the financial markets

---

[59] Article 2, Maastricht Treaty, 1992.
[60] Humphrey-Hawkins Act of 1978.
[61] See Annex V.8 (Table 5.5) for a summary of the institutional features of the various EU central banks.

and financial institutions.

The Maastricht Treaty and the ESCB/ECB Statute are not clear with respect to prudential supervision. The Treaty vaguely points out that the ESCB is "to contribute to the smooth conduct of policies pursued by the competent authorities relating to the prudential supervision of credit institutions and the stability of the financial system."[62]

The model for the ECB, the Bundesbank, does not worry about supervising banks or protecting depositors: such tasks are entrusted to the Federal Banking Office, the *Bundesaufisichtamt für das Kreditwesen*, which cooperates with the Bundesbank. The Federal Banking Office monitors the risks inherent in the banking system. But it is the Bundesbank that rejects financial innovations whenever they might undermine monetary policies.

National differences in supervisory responsibilities and reserve requirements vary considerably among the EU nations. For example, in France, liquidity and solvency ratios are laid down by the *Comité de la Reglementation Bancaire* and are applied by the Commission Bancaire, in coordination with the Banque de France. In comparison with the other EU central banks, the Bank of England is overburdened. It not only advises the government on monetary policies but also supervises the domestic banking system under the Banking Act of 1987. It manages both short-term and long-term government debt and promotes London as a financial center. Table 5.3 shows the differences in supervisory responsibilities and reserve requirements among the major EU member nations on the one hand and between the United States on the other hand.

Table 5.3
Supervisory Responsibility and Reserve Requirements in Major Countries

	Central bank	**Supervisory Responsibility (systemic risk)**	**Reserve Requirement**	**Government Funding**
Germany	Deutsche Bundesbank	Bundesaufsichtsamt für das Kreditwesen/Deutsche Bundesbank	Yes	No
France	Banque de France	Banque de France/ Commission Bancaire	Yes	No
U.K.	Bank of England	Bank of England	No	Yes
Netherlands	Nederlandsche Bank	Nederlandsche Bank	No	Yes
Spain	Bank of Spain	Bank of Spain	Yes	No
Italy	Bank of Italy	Bank of Italy	Yes	No
U.S.	U.S. Federal Reserve	Office of the Comptroller of the Currency/Federal Reserve/ State governments/Federal Deposit Insurance Corporation	Yes	No

Source: Bakker, Age, H. Boot, Gerardus L. Sleijpen, W. F. Vanthoor, eds., Monetary Stability Through International Cooperation, The Netherlands: Kluwer Academic Publishers, 1994.

[62] Article 105.5, Maastricht Treaty, 1992.

The refinancing of the commercial banking system is another important central bank function. Such funding influences money supply and credit costs as well as the interest paid on savings deposits. All the EU central banks are involved in open market operations; six of them extend credit against pledged securities as a means of safeguarding liquidity.

It is not clear whether Bundesbank rediscounting practices would be assumed by the ESCB. If not, this instrument would cease to exist as one of the effective German bank rates. It is also open to question whether a centrally set common interest rate might be enough to set interest rate levels throughout the EMU nations.

The ECB will take on the responsibility of formulating common monetary policies simultaneously with the introduction of the single currency. However, primary responsibility for prudential supervision will remain the responsibility of the national authorities. Efficient interaction between banking supervision and monetary policies is the best guarantee for the effective fulfillment of both functions. Thus, it is possible that the traditional arguments against combining prudential supervision and monetary policies may not be well founded.

Reserve Requirements

Minimum reserve requirements are an important monetary policy instrument. The ECB Governing Council may require banks and/or credit institutions to hold minimum reserves in the ECB or in the central banks to sustain monetary policy objectives. In case of non-compliance, the ECB can impose interest penalties or other sanctions.

The Bundesbank attaches great importance to minimum reserve requirements and uses them as one of the key instruments to control monetary aggregates because the German financial system is dominated by banks. The Bundesbank also uses reserves as a device to maintain tight control over the money markets. In 1994 the reserve requirement ratio was 9 percent on domestic currency liabilities and up to 100 percent on foreign currency deposits held by citizens and legal residents. These requirements and the resulting refinancing obligations reached 4.3 percent of GDP in the same year.[63]

The Bundesbank is sensitive to the efficiency of reserve requirements as a policy instrument; thus, it includes short-term bank bonds in the reserves to make it more difficult to escape from such obligations. But it supplies reserves to the banking sector whenever needed.

---

[63] EMI 1994 Annual Report.

The Banque de France also uses interest-bearing compulsory reserve requirements to control monetary aggregates. The reserve requirements were 1 percent on sight deposits and 0.5 percent on remaining eligible liabilities in 1994.[64] The Netherlands, Belgium and Denmark have no minimum reserve requirements nor does the U.K., where there is a ratio of only 0.35 percent on eligible liabilities used to raise revenue for the Bank of England.[65] In Italy, the central banking legislation of 1993 transferred the decision-making authority concerning compulsory reserve requirements to the Bank of Italy, although such requirements have been replaced almost entirely by capital adequacy measures. However, there was a reserve requirement of 15 percent in 1994.[66] Other EU member nations were using reserve requirement that ranged from 1 to 9 percent in the same year.[67]

During the structural changes prior to Stage III, minimum reserve requirements may be used as an automatic constraint on the money supply until policy instruments are harmonized. However, as minimum reserves increase, more banks may be forced to transfer their operations to reserve-free branches abroad. Such an expansion of the Eurobanking system to off-shore locations could create problems for the nations which use minimum reserve requirements. Therefore, to promote competitive financial markets, the ECB should operate without reserve requirements or should pay market interest rates on the reserves that it requires banks to maintain.[68]

Exchange Rate Policies

Article 4 of the Maastricht Treaty enables the Council of Economics and Finance Ministers, the ECOFIN, and other common institutions to consult the ESCB on issues under their jurisdiction. Thus, although the formulation of international economic policies as well as the determination of exchange rate policies, does not directly involve the ESCB, there could be ongoing conflicts between the common institutions on the one hand and the ESCB and member nation governments on the other.

When intervening, the ECB implements ECOFIN policies based on a consensus reached within its own price-stability oriented organization. But such a consensus is difficult to achieve, especially when some nations, for example, the U.K.

---

[64] EMI 1994 Annual Report.

[65] EMI 1994 Annual Report.

[66] Deane, Marjorie and Robert Pringle. The Central Banks. New York: Penguin Books, 1994; and EMI, Annual Report, 1994.

[67] EMI 1994 Annual Report.

[68] "The ESCB should then carry out its monetary policy by focusing on the level of interest rate," Ciampi, Carlo Azeglio. "An Operational Framework for an Integrated Monetary Policy in Europe" in Report on Economic and Monetary Union in the European Community (Delors Committee for the Study of Economic and Monetary Union), Luxembourg: Office for Official Publications of EEC, 1989.

and Denmark, and perhaps others, are not EMU members. It is inevitable that at some point the exchange rate policies of such nations will conflict with the ESCB's domestic targets which, in turn, will affect the relationship between the EMU and non-EMU member nations.

The management of exchange rate policies differs widely among EU countries. In Germany, the Netherlands and Denmark, policies are set by the governments in coordination with the central banks. But while the central banks have the legal authority to set exchange rates, in a flexible exchange rate system this is less important than the central banks' executive functions in the exchange markets. For example, the relationship between the Bundesbank and the Bonn Government is characterized by the responsibility of the Bank to take the advice of the government and then to decide independently. The Nederlandsche Bank and the Bank of Denmark manage the exchange rates of their currencies and decide on their own when and to what extent to intervene in the markets. The Banque de France regulates exchange rates within the policy guidelines formulated by its government. In contrast, the Bank of England acts in the foreign exchange markets only as an agent of the Treasury.[69]

The choice of interest rates as an instrument of monetary policy is the result of not using aggregate monetary targets and controls based on reserve requirements. This has been attributed to the unstable relationship between monetary aggregates and macroeconomic variables on the one hand, and between monetary aggregates and reserve requirements on the other. It has been argued that "financial innovation and liberalization appear to have eroded the stability of these relationships in most EC countries."[70]

Independence and Credibility

The debate concerning the independence of the ECB opened a new era of research on central bank independence, particularly since 1989. Some studies differentiate between political and economic independence and define the former as "the ability of a central bank to autonomously choose its economic policy objectives without constraints or influence from government."[71]

The degree of central bank independence required for the management of monetary policies geared to price stability is the core of the debate on central banking. Studies show that there is a correlation between central bank independence and

---

[69] Deane, Majorie and Robert Pringle, The Central Banks, 1994.

[70] Fry, Maxwell J. "Choosing a Money for Europe," Journal of Common Market Studies, September 1991, pp.481-504.

[71] Alesina, Alberto, and Vittorio Grilli. "The European Central Bank: Reshaping Monetary Politics in Europe," National Bureau of Economic Research, Working Paper No. 3860, 1991.

inflation.[72] Central banks with higher levels of independence have a better inflation record than less independent central banks such as those in France and New Zealand. The studies propose an analytical index based on the following considerations:

> (i) Governor not appointed by government; (ii) Governor appointed for more than 5 years; (iii) Board not appointed by government; (iv) Board appointed for more than 5 years; (v) No mandatory participation of government representative on the Board; (vi) No government approval of monetary policies; (vii) Statutes requiring the central bank to pursue monetary stability; and (viii) Priority of explicit conflicts between the central bank and the government.[73]

The studies conclude that "the ECB, according to this statute, will be as independent from national and European political institutions as the Bundesbank. In fact, the proposed statute is in many respects quite similar to that of the Bundesbank."[74]

Economic independence is defined as: "the ability to use, without restrictions, monetary policy instruments to pursue monetary policy goals. Specifically, the most important and common constraint to the daily management of monetary policy derives from the central bank's obligations to finance public deficits."[75] As before, the authors of the studies identify key considerations that can be used to determine the economic independence of central banks. They include: (i) direct credit facilities: not automatic; (ii) direct credit facilities: market interest rate; (iii) direct credit facilities: temporary; (iv) direct credit facilities: limited in amount; (v) no central bank participation in the primary market for public debt; (vi) discount rate set by central bank; (vii) no portfolio constraints in place since 1980; and (viii) no bank loan ceilings since 1980.

With regard to the ECB's economic independence they conclude that: "... its level of independence will be high and, thus, its ability to credibly pursue its objectives should be guaranteed. In fact, it is as high as the Bundesbank."[76]

Other studies have taken the concept of central bank independence one step further by introducing a distinction between "goal independence" and "instrument independence":

---

[72] For a detailed discussion of central bank independence and macroeconomic performance see Alesina, Alberto and Lawerence H. Summers, 1990; and Pollard, Patricia S. "Central Bank Independence and Economic Performance," Federal Reserve Bank of St. Louis Economic Review, July/August, 1993.

[73] Alesina and Grilli, "The European Central Bank: Reshaping Monetary Politics in Europe," 1992, p.69.

[74] Alesina and Grilli, "The European Central Bank: Reshaping Monetary Politics in Europe," 1992, p.69.

[75] Alesina and Grilli, "The European Central Bank: Reshaping Monetary Politics in Europe," 1992, p.69.

[76] Alesina and Grilli, "The European Central Bank: Reshaping Monetary Politics in Europe," 1992, p.69.

> A central bank has goal independence when it is free to set the final goals of monetary policy. Thus, a central bank with goal independence could, for instance, decide that price stability was less important than output stability and act accordingly. A central bank that has instrument independence is free to choose the means by which it seeks to achieve its goals. The Reserve Bank of New Zealand, whose goals are precisely described in a contract with the government, has no goal independence; however, it has instrument independence since it chooses the method by which it tries to achieve the pre-assigned goals.[77]

However, these studies also note that "[other studies[78]] would describe the Reserve Bank of New Zealand as having complete political independence," and then argue that clear mandates and incentives for central banks that are accountable to elected representatives would result in better management of the length and depth of recessions and the variability of inflation. It is interesting to note that they conclude that the Bundesbank has a high level of accountability similar to that of the U.S. Federal Reserve.[79]

It is not clear whether central bankers would side with a politically more accountable ECB or would prefer "controlled independence." The governors of major central banks probably would not even risk discussing such considerations. Nevertheless, to inspire a high level of commitment to price stability, the ECB may have to become the most independent and least accountable institution managing monetary policies.

The ECB's independence is guaranteed by various provisions, many based on the Bundesbank's Charter. Article 107 of the Maastricht Treaty states that:

> When exercising the powers and carrying out the tasks and duties conferred upon them by this Treaty and the Statute of the ESCB, neither the ECB, nor a national central bank, or any member of their decision making bodies shall seek or take instructions from community institutions or bodies, from any Government of a member state or from any other body. The Community institutions and bodies, and governments of the member states undertake to respect this principle and not to seek to influence the members of the decision-making bodies of the ECB or of the national central banks in the

---

[77] Debelle, Guy and Stanley Fischer. "How Independent Should a Central Bank Be?" in "Goals, Guidelines and Constraints Facing Monetary Policymakers; Proceedings of a Conference held in June 1994," Jeffrey C. Fuhrer, ed., Federal Reserve Bank of Boston, 1994.

[78] Grilli, Vittorio, Donato Masciandro and Guido E. Tabellini. "Political and Monetary Institutions and Public Financial Policies in Industrial Countries," Economic Policy, October 13, 1991, pp.342-92.

[79] Debelle, Guy and Stanley Fischer, "How Independent Should a Central Bank Be?," 1994.

performance of their tasks.[80]

The ECB and the national central banks may act as fiscal agents for public institutions but cannot grant credit facilities or buy debt instruments from them. This is the so-called "no bailout" policy. The ECB must also support common economic policies, but only if such support does not affect price stability. Yet since it is the ECB itself that determines what price stability is and how to use its policies to achieve it, the responsibilities of supporting common economic policies do not permit other public authorities to interfere. In fact, the ECB is protected by a more tightly drafted version of the same provisions that apply to the Bundesbank, whose accountability and independence can be modified only through amendments by the Bundestag.[81] To change the "Protocol on the Statute of the ESCB," consensus and ratification by all member nations is required.

The election cycles of the EU nations and that of the ESCB Governing Council may not be important in determining the effectiveness of the ESCB in pursuing independent monetary policies geared to price stability. Some observers argue that central bank governors might favor their governments because they would like to be reappointed. Members of the Executive Board might also seek new appointments from their national governments or the common institutions (as they can be reappointed under the Maastricht Treaty). But the Governing Council can reach a decision only through a two-thirds majority vote. Thus, even if a few members of the Council favored their national governments' fiscal policies and tried to influence the ESCB's monetary policies, without the support of the majority of the other Council members they could not do so.

The Bundesbank's Influence

The Bundesbank has served as a point of reference in the ECB debate mainly for two reasons. First, it is the central bank with the highest degree of autonomy, and because its federal structure involves the Länder banks, the Bundesbank districts have a major influence on decision making.[82] Second, when it was established, the Bundesbank was structured so as to obtain credibility for a new currency from the skeptical post-World War II German public. Both considerations apply to the ECB.

By law, the Bundesbank's primary objective is to secure a domestically and externally stable currency. It has to support the economic policies of the government, but only insofar as such policies do not conflict with monetary stability. The main

[80] Article 107, Maastricht Treaty, 1992.
[81] The Bundesbankgesetz of 1957 provides that "without prejudice to the performance of its functions, the Deutsche Bundesbank shall be required to support the general economic policies of the Federal Government. In exercising the powers conferred on it by this Act it shall be independent of instructions from the Federal Government."
[82] See Annex V.8 (Table 5.5) for detailed information on the Deutsche Bundesbank's structure.

decision-making body, the Central Bank Council (*Zentralbankrat*) consists of the Executive Board (including the President and the Vice-President) selected by the Federal Government as well as the presidents of the state (Länder) central banks (*Landeszentralbanken*), who are appointed by the Länder governments. Following Germany's reunification, primarily to lessen the influence of the eastern states, the Bundesbank reduced the size of the Central Bank Council by reorganizing the existing and creating new districts through the merger of several smaller districts.[83] It is possible that the smaller nations of the EU would also be disturbed by a similar attempt to reduce their influence in the ECB.

Another important issue is the management selection process. The selection process used by the Bundesbank is strongly influenced by the German government. This represents a form of indirect control. But the eight-year term of office of the President with the possibility of reappointment, the pluralistic selection process and the professional qualification requirements make any attempt to exercise direct political influence very difficult.

Concluding Remarks on the ECB

The basic goal of the Maastricht Treaty monetary policy framework is the maintenance of price stability by the ESCB. Thus, a great deal depends on how the ESCB is going to use its independence. However, such independence may be meaningless unless the right individuals are appointed to the responsible positions in which they can prudently control price levels. Thus, competition among the regions, especially among the peripheral ones, could increase. A centralized common policy-formulating institution combined with the free movement of capital and common financial and banking directives could also lead to increased financial concentration through mergers and acquisitions.

When Stage III of the EMU begins, member nation governments will have less flexibility in managing their financial sectors. Fiscal policy will be the only macroeconomic instrument available to respond to the economic expectations of citizens. However, fiscal policy might be constrained by the excessive deficit criterion and the post-EMU fiscal "Stability and Growth Pact".

Fiscal and monetary policies have a joint impact. Thus, unless such policies are interactive, sound economic convergence may not be possible, which may create two problems. First, the ECB may be regarded as the "monetary government" of the EU. Financial markets and the electorates may hold the ECB responsible for the decisions of ECOFIN, while governments would be responsible only for their regional fiscal policies. Second, regulations proposed to harmonize the EU-wide financial markets, together with economic integration, may increase the struggles among different

[83] The current Central Bank Council can have up to 17 members.

interest groups. To minimize this and to correct inefficient or inequitable financial market practices, the ECB has to formulate price stability requirements. In response, governments may try to influence monetary policies by pressuring the ECB. Thus, populist economic and fiscal policies based on political considerations could be the outcome. Consequently, the ECB may find itself in conflict with the governments rather than cooperating with them in the development of common fiscal policies.

THE MAASTRICHT TREATY STATUTORY REQUIREMENTS FOR NATIONAL CENTRAL BANKS

According to Article 108 of the Maastricht Treaty and Article 14.1 of the ESCB and ECB Protocol, the EMU member nations' national legislation, including their central bank charters, must be compatible with the Treaty and its Protocols by January 1, 1999, the date on which the ESCB and the ECB will be in place. Under Article 7 of its Protocol and Article 109j(1) of the Maastricht Treaty, by the end of 1997 the EMI, like the EU Commission, must report to the ECOFIN Council on the state of readiness[84] of the potential EMU participants.

Legislative amendments are required mainly in two areas: (i) central bank independence[85] and (ii) integration of the national central banks into the ESCB.[86] Independence is a prerequisite to participation in the ESCB. The ECB is the decision-making body in the ESCB and EMU member nations can influence ECB decisions through participation in the ECB Governing Council. The Treaty underscores the importance of the role of the national central bank governors in EU monetary policy formulation and of the national central banks in the ESCB.

While the Treaty stipulates that national legislation governing central banks must be compatible, it does not require harmonization of their respective statutes with one another or with the ECB. Thus, not only will national differences continue to exist, but central banks may continue performing functions other than those stipulated by the ESCB protocol as long as they do not interfere with the objectives and tasks of the ESCB. Therefore, it appears that the legislative changes required will only eliminate inconsistencies with the Treaty.

Mandatory Central Bank Independence under the ESCB

As has been mentioned, the ESCB is comprised of the ECB and of all EU central banks, whether or not their governments meet the Maastricht Treaty

[84] That is, their ability to meet the Maastricht Treaty convergence criteria (Article 109j, Maastricht Treaty, 1992) and the central bank independence requirement (Articles 107 and 108, and Article 14-ESCB-ECB Protocol, Maastricht Treaty, 1992).
[85] Article 107, Maastricht Treaty and Article 14, ESCB and ECB Protocol, Maastricht Treaty, 1992.
[86] Articles 12.1 and 14.3, ESCB and ECB Protocol, Maastricht Treaty, 1992.

convergence criteria and subsequently participate in Stage III of the EMU. Thus, all central banks, except those representing nations that have opted out of the EMU (the U.K. and Denmark), must adhere to the ESCB protocol. Of particular importance is the establishment and insuring of central bank independence. At the beginning of Stage III, when the ESCB and ECB begin to function, all central banks (with the exception of those of the U.K. and Denmark) must be independent. Other ESCB requirements become effective only when a nation joins the EMU, that is, when it meets the convergence criteria. Member nations with derogations may retain control over their monetary policies and participate in the ESCB on a restricted basis.[87] See Annex V.9 for the role and degree of independence of selected EU central banks.

The ESCB, managed by the ECB's Governing Council, will have the exclusive right to define and implement monetary policies for all EMU member nations. But in doing so, the ESCB and ECB must be independent of both national and common political authorities, so as to be able to pursue their statutory objective of preserving long-term price stability without being subjected to short-term political and economic pressures.

Institutional Features of the EU Central Banks, Financial Sectors and Their Adaptation to ESCB Statutes.[88]

This section describes the current institutional features of the EU member nations' central banks together with the changes needed to adapt to the Maastricht Treaty and its ESCB and ECB protocol. As previously stated Annex V.8 (Table 5.5) provides a summary of the institutional features of the various EU central banks.

Austria

The Austrian National Bank, together with the Ministry of Finance, is in charge of monetary policies. The central bank executes such policies through lending and through the issuance of bank notes. The law governing its activities states that the Bank "shall ensure...that the value of the Austrian currency is maintained." However, in doing so, the Bank takes into account the economic policies of the government.

The Bank is set up as a joint stock company and is administered by the General Meeting of Shareholders, the General Council and its Board of Executive Directors. The General Meeting elects the six members of the General Council, which

[87] As mentioned before, member nations with derogations are those that have either failed to meet the convergence criteria or have opted out of the EMU. The U.K. and Denmark have obtained special protocols that exempt them, among others, from Article 14 of the ESCB/ECB Protocol mandating central bank independence.

[88] The banking and financial sector summaries in this section are adapted from the Walden Country Reports (January 1995 updates); and "Progress Towards Convergence," EMI, 1995.

is comprised of a President, 2 Vice-Presidents and 11 additional members. The General Council's President is appointed by the President of the Republic on the recommendation of the government. The Vice-Presidents as well as the remaining five members of the Council are also appointed by the government for five-year renewable terms.

Directly or indirectly the Bank controls about 60 percent of all banking activities. The *Kreditwesengestz* (Banking Act of 1986) specifies a 4.5 percent equity ratio and defines the maximum lending amounts. A special section of the Ministry of Finance supervises the banks.

In 1991 the Banking Act of 1986 was revised to meet EU standards. It is now possible for all banks with an EU license to open subsidiaries in Austria without special permission. Other features, such as the bank secrecy law and free unlimited transferability of capital, are also attracting more foreign banks as well as investors.

In 1992 there were 1,104 banks in Austria. To meet the increased competition following EU membership, a number of new banks were established while others merged. Following these changes, only 80 savings banks remained.

Austria has a relatively small stock exchange with 111 companies listed in 1994. However, EU membership and deregulations as well as other developments are likely to increase this number.

The Central Bank Statute contains several inconsistencies with the Treaty and Statute requirements that limit the Bank's independence as, for example, the composition of the General Council and the tasks of Office of the Executive Directors. To date, the Austrian government has not notified the EMI of any impending changes.

Belgium

The Bank of Belgium is responsible for the formulation and implementation of monetary policies. The exchange rate regime is determined by the government in consultation with the Bank, which implements the same. The Bank is also responsible for the smooth functioning of the payments systems and for the management of European and international monetary cooperation activities. But the Bank's charter does not specify any particular objectives it must achieve.

The Bank is managed by the Board of Directors presided over by the Governor. The Board is assisted by the Council of Regency and supervised by the Board of Cencors. Together they form the General Council, which determines the distribution of profits. The Governor is nominated by the government and appointed by the King to a five year term, while the members of the Board of Directors are appointed for six years. The Board develops monetary policies under the oversight of the Regency Council which also sets the rates, terms of discount, advances and loans and also approves the Bank's annual report.

Belgium's banking sector is comprised of commercial banks, public credit institutions and private savings banks which operate in the same market segments. The six major banks owned by the state and the communities are undergoing restructuring. To increase efficiency, two new types of institutions with up to 49 percent of private ownership will also be established. Foreign banks are active in the non-retail sectors such as domestic money market operations, corporate and wholesale banking and Eurocurrency transactions.

There are three stock exchanges -- Antwerp, Brussels and Liège. They are relatively small owing to a tax on transactions by foreign investors. Of the three, the Brussels Stock Exchange is the most important, with a 90 percent share of all securities trading.[89] As soon as the "EU Investment Directive" is enacted, the transaction tax will be abolished.

The Bank's statute does not meet several of the Treaty and Statute requirements concerning independence. The inconsistencies include, among others, the powers of the Government Commissioner, the Council of Regency, the security of tenure of the government and members of the Board of Directors. The statute of the Bank also does not reflect the priority of maintaining price stability.

The compatibility of the Bank of Belgium's Statute with the Stage II requirements of the EMU is under consideration. A draft proposal concerning credit operations by the Bank of Belgium within the framework of the ESCB Statute, Article 18.1, was submitted to the EMI in July 1995 which delivered its opinion in August 1995 (CON/95/12).[90] In August 1996, Belgium Finance Minister Philippe Maystadt pledged to meet the timetable for transition to the single currency -- including issuing central bank and market information and conducting all interbank payments in the Euro from January 1, 1999. Pledges were also made to go beyond the Maastricht requirement and issue bonds and treasury bills in the Euro from 1999.[91]

Denmark

The Bank of Denmark is responsible for maintaining a safe and secure currency and for facilitating and regulating payment flows and credit procedures. It also manages official reserves and serves as the fiscal agent of the government.

The Bank is governed by the Board of Governors, the Board of Directors and the Committee of Directors. The Board of Governors is comprised of a Chairman and

---

[89] "1995 Guide to Developments in the World's Equity and Bond Markets," Euromoney, 1995, pp.4-5.

[90] "Progress Towards Convergence," EMI, 1995, p.102.

[91] "Belgium Urges New Debate on EMU Sanctions," Financial Times, August 9, 1996, p.1.

two Governors. The Chairman is appointed for life by the Queen and the other two members, also appointed for life, are appointed by the 25-member Board of Directors which also maintains a Committee of Directors. The Board of Governors has complete freedom to formulate and implement monetary policies.

The "National Bank of Denmark" Act gives the Minister of Economic Affairs the authority to supervise the Bank in his/her capacity as the Royal Bank Commissioner. Although the Ministers may participate in the meetings of the Committee of Directors, this has never happened.

Denmark has a relatively small stock exchange. At the end of 1994, 252 companies were listed on the Copenhagen Stock Exchange with a market value of US$54.4 billion.[92] During the first half of 1995, market capitalization reached about US$62 billion.

Although the Bank's Statute does not reflect the policy primacy of price stability, there are no plans to change the same. Denmark has opted-out of the EMU.

Finland

Even though it is an independent institution, the Bank of Finland cooperates closely with the government and operates under the oversight of the Parliamentary Supervisory Board. Its main function is to oversee and regulate the nation's financial institutions, but it is also the lender of last resort to the banking system. Moreover, it manages open-market operations and foreign exchange interventions and issues permits for international transactions. The Parliamentary Supervisory Board sets the Bank's base rate and other interest rates. The Governor of the Bank and five other members of the Board are appointed by the President of the Republic. The Statute of the Bank is inconsistent with the Treaty and the Statute requirements of Central Bank independence.

The independence of the Bank was reviewed. Finland submitted a draft legislation to the EMI in April 1996, containing the required changes. The EMI's evaluation acknowledged that the draft legislation is a step toward meeting the Treaty and Statute requirements. But it also pointed out that more needs to be done.

At the end of 1994 there were 65 companies listed on the Helsinki Stock Exchange with market capitalization of US$38.3 billion. With the removal of restrictions on foreign stock ownership, the prospects of the exchange look good.[93]

Traditionally, Finland's financial system was protected from foreign competition, but owing to the emergence of the Scandinavian financial market it is

---

[92] Euromoney "1995 Guide," pp.41-43.

[93] Euromoney "1995 Guide," pp.41-43.

becoming more open. There are proposals for a unified Nordic Stock Exchange, to increase foreign investment.[94]

France

The objective of the Bank of France is price stability. In addition, it implements exchange rate policies, manages official reserves, safeguards the payments systems and ensures European and international monetary cooperation. The Bank is managed by the Monetary Policy Council and the Governor. The Council is comprised of the Governor, two Vice-Governors and six other members. The Governor and the Vice-Governors are appointed by the government for six-year renewable terms. The other six members are appointed by the government to nine-year renewable terms.

The Ministry of Economy and Finance oversees the financial system, setting economic policies consistent with the government's overall objectives and implementing the same through general and selective fiscal and monetary measures.

Ceilings on bank credits were abolished in January 1987. The obligatory reserves on credits have been replaced by reserve requirements on deposits. The Bank regulates the money market by raising or lowering interest rates through open-market operations.

The National Credit Council advises the government on monetary and credit policies. It is managed by a Ministry of Finance representative and is comprised of the Director of the Treasury and representatives of banks, organized labor, economic sectors and regions. The representatives serve on the Credit Establishments Committee which sets capital and reserve requirements, authorizes the establishment of banking networks, enforces credit norms and accounting regulations and monitors relations between credit establishments and clients. The representatives also sit on the Banking Regulation Committee which sets capital and reserve requirements, authorizes the setting up of banking networks, ensures the observance of credit norms and accounting regulations, and also monitors relations between credit norms and accounting regulations on the one hand and between credit establishments and clients on the other hand.

The 1984 law on credit institutions abolished the traditional distinction between commercial and investments banking. In practice, however, most banking institutions are still specialized. The establishment of foreign bank branches or subsidiaries is limited by few barriers, but the approval of the Credit Establishments Committee is required for foreign banks directly entering the industry. Permission is generally given on the basis of reciprocity. Most new banks are established by foreign banks or by specialized financial institutions owned by existing banks, big corporations or insurance groups.

---

[94] EMI 1994 Annual Report, p.106.

The amendment of the Bank's Statute[95] established its monetary policy independence and prohibited the financing of public institutions by the Bank. The Bank is managed by the Conseil Général, whose members include representatives of the Conseil de la Politique Monétaire, which is in charge of the development and implementation of monetary policies. The Conseil may not seek or receive instructions from the government, although a representative of the government attends its meetings without voting or veto rights.[96]

There is a nationwide electronic equity trading system in France which has ended floor trading in the French stock exchanges. At the end of 1994, total market capitalization had reached US$451 billion.[97]

The Statute of the Bank still contains a few inconsistencies with the Treaty and the Statute, particularly as they pertain to the extension of the authority of governing bodies to all ESCB-related matters. The governor's reporting responsibility also needs to be adjusted. To date, the French government has not notified the EMI of planned changes.

Germany

The responsibility of the Bundesbank is to safeguard the currency i.e. price stability and the domestic and external payments systems. In doing so, the Bundesbank is required to support the general economic policies of the Federal Government without prejudice to its key objective, price stability. The Bundesbank is managed by the Central Bank Council which is comprised of the President, a Vice-President, other members of the directorate and the presidents of the Länder central banks. Members of the Council are appointed to eight-year renewable terms by the President of the Federal Republic on the recommendation of the government.

The country's financial sector is dominated by three types of banks: private commercial banks, savings banks and cooperative banks. There are about 350 commercial banks, involving 60 foreign bank branches.[98] The banks have strongly opposed the relaxation of secrecy laws because this would increase their already high operating costs which are generated by the large reserve requirements relative to Luxembourg and the U.K. Nevertheless, bank profits are high, particularly from foreign operations. Although not in compliance with EU regulations, the Bundesbank's tight control over monetary aggregates exerts strong control over money market investment funds. During the early 1990s the Bundesbank has seemed less concerned about such controls. It wants to promote Frankfurt as a leading international financial

---

[95] Acts 93-980 of August 4, 1993 and 93-1444 of December 31, 1993.
[96] EMI 1994 Annual Report, p.101.
[97] Euromoney "1995 Guide," pp.8-9.
[98] "A Special Sponsored Section: Commercial Banks," Institutional Investor, August 1995, p.14.

center.

There are eight stock exchanges in Germany; Frankfurt, Düsseldorf, Munich, Berlin, Hamburg, Stuttgart, Hanover and Bremen. More than half of the total volume is traded in Frankfurt. Compared with other nations such as the United States and the U.K., the number of traded companies is low (about 670). Within the EU, Germany's combined trading volume is second to that of London.

The Bank's Statute contains a few inconsistencies with the Maastricht Treaty and the Statute regulating independence, particularly as it relates to the terms of office of the members of the decision-making bodies and the government's right to defer a decision of the General Council. Moreover, the Bank's Statute does not unambiguously reflect the primacy of price stability. The German government has not yet notified the EMI that it will undertake the necessary changes.

Greece

The mandate of the Bank of Greece is to maintain monetary stability through the management of the money supply and credits. It also sets the exchange rate in consultation with the government. The Bank is governed by the General Council which consists of the Governor, Deputy Governors and nine Executive Councilors. The Governor and Deputy Governors are appointed by the President of the Republic on the recommendation of the government to renewable four-year terms. The Councilors are appointed by the General Meeting of Shareholders to renewable three-year terms.

The banking industry is closely controlled by the Bank of Greece. In early 1991 a committee was established to consider a reform of the financial system with the aim of implementing EU banking and securities directives as rapidly as possible.

The state-owned banks' market share has fallen from 80 to 70 percent, starting in 1989. At the same time, new legislation called for changes in solvency ratios and capital adequacy requirements which will force state-owned banks to modernize. These banks are already experiencing a sharp reduction in profits, owing to bad loans that politicians demanded over several decades. The private banks, two of which hold 14 percent of all deposits, are growing stronger. In addition, several new private banks have received operating licenses and are doing well.

Due to EU regulations the 22 foreign banks have increased market share in retail banking as well as in merger and acquisition activities. Foreign bank branches now also receive "national treatment."

Apart from the basic savings deposit rate, interest rates are freely set. However, the banks must still hold the equivalent of 40 percent of deposits as compulsory reserves in Treasury bills. Eventually this requirement will be lowered to 25 percent.

Over the last three years continuing liberalization has resulted in the emergence of a small but growing capital market. The Athens Stock Exchange is the only major stock exchange in Greece. As of August 1995, its capitalization reached US$18 billion.[99] There were 177 companies listed on the stock exchange and 23 in the over-the-counter markets.[100] Trading is thin, prices are volatile and easily affected by shocks. Most of the brokerage activities are managed by banking groups.

The Bank's Statute is inconsistent with the Treaty and the Statute with respect to independence. The government's right to veto the Bank's decision on legal grounds and the subordination of the Bank's monetary policy decisions to the government's macro-economic policy objectives as well as the regulations governing terms of office are cases in point.

Ireland

The primary objective of the Bank of Ireland is to safeguard the integrity of the currency i.e., to maintain price stability. Its main tasks include the formulation and implementation of independent monetary policies, the implementation of foreign exchange rate policies, the holding and management of official reserves, the management of financial markets and the oversight of the payments system.

The Bank is administered by the Board of Directors, comprised of the Governor and up to nine Directors. The Governor is appointed by the President of the Republic on the advice of the government to a renewable seven-year term. The other members of the Board of Directors are appointed by the Minister of Finance to five-year terms.

The country's banking system is made up of associated and non-associated banks, merchant and commercial, industrial and state banks. At the end of 1993 there were 28 different institutions.[101] The Bank of Ireland and the Allied Bank account for 70 percent of all banking activities and almost half of all financial services. Their combined assets amounted to £16 billion in 1993. The 16 foreign banks are mainly involved in merchant banking and the servicing of large international corporations with which they often have ties in other countries as well.

All banks must meet the requirements laid down by the Bank of Ireland. However, many foreign banks have started operations by acquiring existing banks rather than establishing new ones. Regulations affecting foreign banks have been amended to meet EU requirements.

---

[99] Euromoney "1995 Guide," pp.16-19.
[100] "Greece: Financing Foreign Operations," Economist Intelligence Unit, December 1995, p.28.
[101] Euromoney Handbook, September 1994, p.30.

The Bank's Statute contains several inconsistencies with the Treaty and the Statute as they pertain to independence. They include voting rights, the requirement that the Governor consult the Minister of Finance if requested, the dismissal procedures of the Governor and the lack of an unambiguous statement concerning the primacy of price stability as a policy goal.

The Bank of Ireland and the Department of Finance have developed a series of amendments to central bank legislation to comply with the Maastricht Treaty and submitted the same to the EMI in March 1996. The EMI issued its evaluation of the proposed changes in May of the same year and pointed out that while the changes are a step in the right direction, more needs to be done.

Italy

The Banca d'Italia supervises the banking sector and has the sole right to issue bank notes. But although the Constitution requires the Bank to protect savings, the Bank does not concern itself with price stability. In 1992, Law 82 gave the authority to determine discount rates to the Governor of the Bank. And in 1993, Law 483 gave the Bank the responsibility for setting reserve requirement limits.[102]

The Bank is administered by the Board of Directors, headed by the Governor who is appointed by the Board for an unlimited period of time. The Board also includes 13 independent members representing the Bank's branches. Monetary policies are set by the Governor.

The 1990 Amoto Banking Reform Act implemented an extensive restructuring of the industry. State-owned banks were transformed into joint stock companies so that they could raise funds on the stock exchange and take advantage of bank merger tax incentives. This facilitated the formation of large financial banking groups. However, the state still owns a minimum of 51 percent of each bank's capital. The changes were needed to restructure the fragmented and unprofitable banking industry and to increase its competitiveness in the "Single Market." The more liberalized branch banking rules introduced in March 1990 amended bank supervision and resulted in the opening of 2,563 new banking outlets during the first year following their adoption.[103]

With ten exchanges, the Italian stock exchange system is the sixth largest in Europe. Most of the stock trading is done on the Milan Stock Exchange which accounts for more than 90 percent of all transactions[104] and which, at the end of 1994, had 223 companies listed with a trading volume of US$118 billion. But market capitalization as a percentage of GDP (15 percent) is still relatively small when compared, for example,

---

[102] "Progress Towards Convergence," EMI, 1995, p.96.
[103] Walden Country Reports, Italy, 1995.
[104] Euromoney "1995 Guide," pp.25-26.

to that of France (35 percent).

The Bank's Statute and related provisions are inconsistent with the Treaty and the Statute with respect to independence. They include the authority of the Minister of the Treasury to fix certain interest rates, the Governor's responsibility to attend certain meetings and the lack of a clear-cut statement concerning the primary policy goal of price stability.

Luxembourg

Luxembourg is in a Deutsche mark based currency union with Belgium. This provides its financial institutions with a great deal of credibility. The Institute Monétaire Luxembourgeois (IML) is the nation's monetary authority, but it is the Bank of Belgium that acts as a central bank for both countries. The IML's tasks include the issuance of bank notes, the safeguarding of the currency i.e. price stability and oversight over financial markets. Monetary and exchange rate policy decisions are made by the government.

The IML is administered by a Council and a Management Group. The Management Group includes the Director General and two Directors, appointed for renewable six-year terms by the Grand Duke on the recommendation of the Council of Ministers. The Council of Ministers appoints seven members to the Council to renewable four-year terms.

Banking is an important economic activity in Luxembourg, and the financial services sector accounts for about 15 percent of GDP. There are no restrictions on foreign investments and companies are exempt from dividend, interest, and capital gains taxes. Banking secrecy is enforced and the country has double taxation agreements with most foreign nations. Consequently, it is a major tax haven.

Owing to money laundering in recent years, the other EU nations have put pressure on the Government of Luxembourg to tighten its control over the banking sector. As a result, secrecy laws not compatible with those of the other EU nations were relaxed in 1993. Banks have responded by diversifying their activities into new areas.

Although it is growing rapidly, Luxembourg's Stock Exchange is one of the smallest in the EU. Because of a new legislation requiring all investment funds to be registered and administered domestically, off-shore fund management activities are declining. In the past, investment funds could be administered from the home countries or from off-shore centers.

The EMI found various inconsistencies with the Treaty and Statute as they relate to independence. They concerned the IML's lack of control over monetary policy, the terms of appointment and dismissal of the members of the IML and the lack of an unambiguous statement identifying price-stability as the primary policy objective.

The beginning of Stage II of the EMU will end the monetary association between Belgium and Luxembourg. As a result, the IML will take over the central banking functions. To comply with the Maastricht Treaty, a draft law governing the IML was developed and submitted to the Parliament in December 1993. The law implements all Maastricht Treaty provisions concerning Stage II and specifies the establishment of a central bank structure before the beginning of Stage III. The draft law was submitted to the EMI for consultation in February 1994 and the EMI expressed its opinion in March 1994.[105]

According to proposed changes the primary objective of the IML will be to ensure price stability while its secondary objective will be to support the economic policies of the government. The draft also outlines the framework of monetary policies within which the IML will be active in accordance with the principles of a market economy. As required by Article 107 of the Maastricht Treaty, the law will prohibit the IML from receiving instructions from public authorities and from extending financial privileges to such authorities. It is noteworthy that the monetary association with Belgium remains unchanged during Stage II.[106]

The Netherlands

The Nederlandsche Bank is responsible for the overall coordination of national economic policies. Its major objective is to safeguard the value of the currency i.e. price stability through interest rate management or the revision of bank capital requirements. The Bank manages official reserves, supervises banks and other financial institutions and has complete control over the formulation and implementation of monetary policies. It may also intervene in the foreign exchange markets and is the sole issuer of bank notes. Exchange rate policies are determined by the government, but the Bank is responsible for their implementation.

The Bank is administered by the Governing and Supervisory Boards. The Governing Board is comprised of the President, a Secretary and two to five Executive Directors who are nominated by the Governing and Supervisory Boards and are appointed by the Queen to seven-year renewable terms.

The Amsterdam Stock Exchange is one of the oldest in the world; it trades in the shares of some of the world's largest companies. Market capitalization in 1994 reached US$283 billion, of which US$100 billion represented international investments.[107]

---

105 "Progress Towards Convergence," EMI, 1995, p.96.
106 EMI 1994 Annual Report, p.106.
107 Euromoney "1995 Guide," p.35-38.

The Bank's Statute is inconsistent with the Treaty and the Statute with respect to independence. The inconsistencies include the right of the Minister of Finance to issue instruction to the Bank, the supervisory role of the Royal Commissioner and the absence of a clear-cut statement concerning the primacy of the price-stability policy objective. The Bank is currently still engaged in discussions with the Ministry of Finance to eliminate the inconsistencies.

Portugal

The Banco de Portugal Law was changed in September 1995 by the Amendments to the Organic Law of the Bank. The new law was submitted to the EMI for consultation and the EMI delivered its opinion in July 1995 (CON/95/11).[108] The primary objective of the bank is now to maintain price stability while taking into account the overall economic policies of the government. The Bank has the exclusive right to issue bank notes, but exchange rate policies are determined in cooperation with the government. In this capacity, the Bank holds and manages foreign exchange reserves and also regulates, promotes and supervises the payments systems.

The Bank is administered by a Governor and Board of Directors. The Board of Directors is comprised of the Governor, one or two Deputy Governors, and three to five additional members. All are appointed by the government on the recommendation of the Ministry of Finance for renewable five-year terms. The Governor may be dismissed at any time.

Three types of institutions are authorized to operate in Portugal's financial sector: (i) commercial, savings and investment banks; (ii) non-banking credit institutions including investment, leasing and factoring companies; and (iii) institutions that do not exercise credit rating functions, including insurance companies, investment companies, pension funds, venture capital, wealth management companies and dealer companies. Legislation to prevent these types of institutions from taking public deposits is pending.

To more effectively cope with foreign competition, the banking and financial sectors are expanding and diversifying. Several measures to liberalize the financial sector have been implemented, including the privatization of state-owned banks and insurance companies; the liberalization of foreign exchange markets; the abolition of limits on bank credit growth to complete the transition from direct to indirect monetary controls; and the lifting of regulations forbidding banks from opening interest-bearing accounts at only nominal rates.

Portugal has two stock exchanges, Lisbon and Oporto. In July 1995, 182 companies were listed on the Portuguese Stock Market System, of which 86 were listed

---

[108] "Progress Towards Convergence," EMI, 1995, p.96.

on the nationwide electronic trading system.[109] There is also a secondary market and a market without quotations. As of March 1995 there were no foreign companies listed on the exchanges.[110]

Even following the changes introduced in 1995, the EMI found inconsistencies in the Bank's Statute with the Treaty and the Statute stipulations addressing independence. The inconsistencies relate primarily to the government's continuing influence over the Bank. To date, the Portuguese government has not notified the EMI that it is undertaking the necessary changes.

Spain

The primary objectives of the Banco de España are price stability and support of the government's overall economic policies. Since the early 1980s, the Bank has controlled the money supply and has engaged in the auctioning of Treasury bills through which it sets interest rates. The Bank develops and implements monetary policies, holds and manages reserves, and promotes the stability of the payments system.

The Bank is managed by a Governor, who is assisted by the Deputy Governor, the Governing Council and the Executive Commission. The Governor is appointed by the King to a non-renewable six-year term on the recommendation of the Prime Minister. The Deputy Governor is appointed by the government on the recommendation of the Governor, also to a non-renewable six-year term.

The 1994 "Act 13 On the Autonomy of the Banco de España" set price stability as the primary objective of the Bank and gave it full independence. The Bank may not take any instructions from the government or any other public institution. The Act also outlines the process of formulating and implementing monetary policies, defines the Bank's relations with the government, and outlines exchange rate policies, payment systems and the process of bank note issuance in accordance with the requirements of the Maastricht Treaty.

In the past, commercial banks were obliged to keep about half of their deposits tied up in fixed assets to serve as reserve requirements. As a trade-off for the deregulation of interest rates on deposits of up to 180 days, this requirement has been lowered. The deregulation of interest rates was part of the liberalization process that began when Spain joined the EU in 1986.

Following the establishment of the 1993 "Single Market," the government advised banks to merge to prepare them for increased competition from abroad through increased competition in financial services. There are now more than 130 commercial

---

[109] Euromoney "1995 Guide," pp.35-38.

[110] "Portugal: Financing Foreign Operations," Economist Intelligence Unit, May 1995, p.25.

and industrial banks with about 16,000 branches. They include 39 foreign banks with 114 branch offices. The large private sector banks account for more than 80 percent of commercial bank deposits and just under 50 percent of total deposits. The savings banks hold 11.3 percent of total deposits -- the fourth highest percentage in the EU.

To protect local banks with higher cost structures, the Banco de España limits the activities of foreign banks. In spite of this, and of the generally cautious business climate, foreign banks have capitalized on their experience and their low-cost structures. Several have skirted the restrictions on peseta funding and have started joint ventures to build branch networks.

There are four stock exchanges in Spain: Madrid, Barcelona, Bilbao, and Valencia. Of all listed companies, 375 are traded on the Madrid Stock Exchange.[111] However, lack of fiscal incentives and high taxes on capital gains have inhibited the markets' development.

In spite of the 1994 Act, the Bank's Statute still includes a few inconsistencies with the Treaty and Statute requirements with respect to independence. They include the voting rights of certain officers and the terms of appointments. To date, the government has not notified the EMI of any changes concerning these matters.

Sweden

The Riks Banken of Sweden is in charge of monetary and exchange rate policies as well as the management of the payments system. It issues bank notes, administers the gold and foreign exchange reserves and uses open market operations to determine the level of yields, and thus the cost of government borrowing in the domestic credit markets.

The Bank is administered by a Governing Board comprised of eight members. The Governor is elected by the other Board members to a renewable five-year term, while the seven other members are appointed by the Parliament for the duration of the legislative period. The Governor is responsible for day-to-day management.

All commercial banks and the two savings banks as well as the postal giro bank are authorized to engage in foreign exchange trading. The commercial banks have traditionally concentrated on business banking, but they now also engage in retail banking. Foreign banks have been able to open subsidiaries since 1986 and branch offices since 1990. Foreign investors may acquire Swedish banks, finance companies and stock brokerage firms with the proviso that majority ownership must be held by Swedish citizens.

---

[111] "Spain: Financing Foreign Operations," Economist Intelligence Unit, July 1995, p.29.

At the end of 1992 there were 15 commercial banks of which seven were foreign owned. In addition, there were 133 registered finance companies. The legal barriers among banks, finance houses and insurance companies were eliminated in 1991 to bring the Swedish financial markets up to date and in conformity with the markets of the other EU nations. Thus, banks and finance companies may create alliances while foreign finance companies may open branches.

The Stockholm Stock Exchange is the largest in Scandinavia with a listing of 114 companies and a US$130 billion capitalization at the end of 1994. Foreign equity trading is low in Sweden, but Swedish securities are traded in large volumes outside the country.[112]

There are several inconsistencies in the nation's Constitution and in the Bank's Statute with respect to the Treaty and the Statute. They involve the Bank's obligation to consult the Minister of Finance concerning major decisions, the appointment and dismissal of officers and the participation of members of parliament in the Governing Council. Moreover, the statute does not include a clear-cut statement with respect to the primacy of price stability as a policy goal. Legislation to deal with these issues will be prepared during 1996-97, but the required constitutional amendments cannot be implemented before January 1, 1999 due to the required endorsement by two consecutive parliaments.

The United Kingdom

The Bank of England is an agent of the government. Its objectives include safeguarding the currency and ensuring the stability of the financial system and the effectiveness of financial services. The Bank also advises on monetary policies, issues bank notes, manages the reserves, supervises the banking industry and promotes a sound and efficient payments system. Monetary policy objectives are set by the government but the Bank is required to implement such policies through the achievement of targeted price levels.

The Bank is governed by the Court of Directors, which is comprised of the Governor, the Deputy Governor and 16 Directors. These officials are appointed by the Queen on the recommendation of the Prime Minister. The Governor and the Deputy Governor share five-year renewable terms while the other members have four-year renewable terms.

The Bank of England remains central to the U.K. banking system, maintaining both a supervisory and a central banking role. With the exception of representative offices, all U.K. banking institutions are under the control of the Bank of England.

---

[112] Euromoney "1995 Guide," pp.41-43.

The financial center, "City" of London has undergone substantial regulatory reforms since 1986 and leads the world in foreign exchange transactions, fund management, insurance, and foreign security dealings. It accounts for 27 percent of global foreign exchange trading, 64 percent of cross-exchange trading in foreign currencies, 15 percent of turnover in commodity futures and options, 35 percent of activity in swaps, 40-50 percent of cross-border mergers and acquisitions, 60-70 percent of international Euroequity and 70 percent of international Eurobond issues.[113] The City combines strategic factors such as reputation, credibility, liquid assets, a skilled work force of 600,000 and the support of legal, accounting, telecommunications and computer services.

The London Stock Exchange was established in 1802. It is the third largest in the world in terms of number of companies listed, but in terms of the value of foreign equities traded, it is the largest. At the end of 1994 there were 2,534 companies listed on the exchange of which 464 were foreign.[114] The trading volume in domestic stocks reached US$928 billion, while the trading volume in foreign stocks amounted to US$1.1 trillion.[115]

The Statute of the Bank does not comply with the Treaty requirements and will have to be amended if the U.K. decides to join the EMU. The amendments would have to change the general relationship of the Bank with the government. It would also have to entail an unambiguous statement concerning the primacy of price-stability as a policy goal. To date, the U.K. government has not notified the EMI of any pending changes.

---

113 "Number One and Bringing Billions Home for Britain," Evening Standard, March 13, 1995, p.40.

114 "United Kingdom: Financing Foreign Operations," Economist Intelligence Unit, August 1995, p.34.

115 Euromoney "1995 Guide," pp.62-64.

Annex V.1
EMI Council Members

A. Lamfalussy	President of the EMI
L. Rojo	Banco de Espana and Vice-President of the EMI
A. Verplaestse	Nationale Bank van Belgie Banque Nationale de Belgique
B. Andersen	Danmarks Nationalbank
H. Tietmeyer	Deutsche Bundesbank
L. Papademos	Bank of Greece
J. C. Trichet	Banque de France
M. O'Connell	Central bank of Ireland
A. Fazio	Banca d'Italia
P. Jaans	Institut Monetaire Luxembourggeois
W. Duisenberg	De Nederlandsche Bank
K. Liebscher	Oesterreichische Nationalbank
A. de Sousa	Banco de Portugal
S. Hamalainen	Suomen Pankki
U. Backstrom	Sveriges Riksbank
E. George	Bank of England

Source: EMI 1995 Annual Report, Frankfurt am Main: EMI, April 1996, p.vi-ix.

Annex V.2

EMI Management Group Members

President and Director General

A. Lamfalussy	President
R. Raymond	Director General

Source: EMI 1995 Annual Report, p.vi-ix.

Heads of Department

H. K. Scheller	Secretary General
G. J. Hogeweg	Monetary, Economic and Statistics Dept.
P. W. Schluter	Administration Department
J. S. Etherington	Information and Communications Dept.

Source: EMI 1995 Annual Report, p.vi-ix.

Financial Committee

I. Rojo	Banco de Espana
P. Jaans	Danmarks Nationalbank
A. Fazio	De Nederlandsche Bank
A. Verplaetse	Nationale Bank van Belgie/ Banque Nationale de Belgique

Source: EMI 1995 Annual Report, pp.vi-ix.

Chairmen of the Sub-Committees and the Working Groups

J. J. Rey	Monetary Policy Sub-Committee
F. Saccomanni	Foreign Exchange Policy Sub-Committee
T. de Swan	Banking Supervisory Sub-Committee
W. Hortmann	Working Group on EU Payment Systems
A. Jarvis	Working Group on Printing & Issuing a European Banknote
K. Hanau	Working Group on Statistics
H. Heemskerk	Working Group on Accounting Issues
Y. Barroux	Working Group on Information Systems
J. Guill	Working Group of Legal Experts

Source: EMI 1995 Annual Report, pp.vi-ix.

Annex V.3
Differences in Monetary Transmission Processes[116]

A central bank, as monopoly supplier of base money, is in a position to influence strongly, if not control, money market interest rates by determining the conditions at which it provides or absorbs liquidity. The various channels through which such changes in official or key interest rates are transmitted to output and inflation together make up the monetary transmission process. Whereas there is broad similarity between these channels in EU countries, transnational differences in transmission processes imply that a given change in the interest rate will affect prices and output across Member States differently over time. In Stage Two, differences in transmission processes might become a source of policy conflicts in individual Member States if the interest rate policy needed to preserve exchange rate stability were to differ from that deemed consistent with domestic policy objectives. They will also have important implications for a future Monetary Union.

Some important areas of divergence between Member States concern the:
- relative importance of financing at long-term fixed rates versus variable or short-term rates;
- size and composition of balance-sheet positions of the non-financial sectors;
- degree of openness of the economy and the importance of the exchange rate channel;
- speed with which money market rates & changes in official interest rates feed through to lending and borrowing rates;
- differences in the wage-price mechanism.

Various problems may arise for monetary policy when there are divergences in these areas. When private sector financing at short-term or variable rates is predominant, monetary policy will have a greater impact on an economy for a given composition of private sector balance sheets. In the EU, lending at short-term rates is of relatively minor importance for both households and enterprises in Denmark, Germany, the Netherlands and Sweden, and to a lesser extent Belgium, France and Austria.

The size and composition of private sector balance-sheet positions will affect the degree to which these potential effects actually impinge on behavior. A high proportion of lending linked to short-term or variable rates (as in the United Kingdom and Ireland) contributes to a relatively rapid and pronounced pass-through of changes in official rates to aggregate spending. Even if debt is largely long-term and fixed rate, high indebtedness (as in Sweden) may have an effect on transmission.

If a large proportion of public sector debt is at variable rate or is short-term, as in Portugal, Italy and Greece, this implies that monetary contraction may relatively rapidly be offset by fiscal expansion, as long as increased interest payments on existing debt accrue to domestic residents. This effect will vary with public sector indebtedness. But in the medium term there may be a contractionary effect, as rising interest payments and the threat of a spiral in interest obligations forces the public sector to tighten fiscal policy. In this context there is a strong correlation between governments' ability to issue long-term fixed rate debt and past inflation. Moreover, a high proportion of debt in foreign currency introduces a relation from monetary policy to fiscal policy via the exchange rate.

The degree of openness of Member States determines, inter alia, the speed and magnitude of the pass-through of exchange rate changes provoked by monetary policy actions to output and inflation. Total openness, and hence sensitivity to external developments, is tending to increase in some EU countries in line with the process of integration. However, to the extent that Member States succeed in maintaining stable intra-EU exchange rates, differences in extra-EU trade flows are the best measure of the scope of difference in transmission via the exchange rate. Extra-EU openness is particularly high -- exports plus imports are over 25% of GDP -- in the BLEU and Ireland, and is significantly more important in Germany and the United Kingdom than in France and Italy.

Transmission may also differ between EU countries since the speed with which money market rates feed through into bank lending and deposit rates varies, and because differences in wage-price behavior

[116]Adopted from the EMI 1994 Annual Report, pp.36-37.

affect the degree to which changes in excess demand arising from monetary policy have an impact on output and inflation.

While it is relatively easy to detect individual differences in structure, it is less straightforward to assess the extent to which these differences, when they are aggregated to a macroeconomic level, have a significant impact on the overall transmission process. The most significant result which emerges from a comparison of simulations using macroeconomic models is that, among the four largest Member States, the pass-through of changes in official interest rates to nominal GDP is faster and stronger in the United Kingdom than in Germany, France or Italy. But structural breaks in empirical relationships, which might change or undermine the applicability of these results to the current situation, cannot be ruled out.

Some of these differences in transmission process are likely to diminish in the coming years as a consequence of the increasing convergence of inflation rates across Member States (which may, for example, encourage long-term fixed rate financing), as well as effects of growing international competition and financial integration (which may make the pass-through from money market rates to bank lending rates more uniform). In addition, there have been various institutional changes affecting financial markets and labor markets recently which may also increase convergence. But some differences in openness and in net asset positions, most notably those arising from differences in agents' preferences, are likely to persist.

Annex V.4
The Price Stability Convergence Criteria and the Role of the EMI[117]

The Criterion: The Maastricht Treaty, Article 109.j.1 requires that the price criterion be judged on the basis of the relative inflation performance, which is close to that of at most the three best-performing Member States in terms of price stability.

The Protocol (No. 6) on the convergence criteria referred to in Article 109.j (1) of the Maastricht Treaty, Article 1, stipulates that:

> The criterion on price stability referred to in the first indent of Article 109.j (1) of this Treaty shall mean that a Member State has a price performance that is sustainable and an average rate inflation, observed over a period of one year before the examination, that does not exceed [by] more than 1.5 percentage points that of, at most, the three best-performing Member States in terms of price stability. Inflation shall be measured by means of the consumer price index on a comparable basis, taking into account differences in national definitions.[118]

Calculation of the Reference Value: The wording of Protocol No. 6, Article 1, does not unambiguously define the reference value to which the inflation criterion should apply, as it refers to "at most, the three best-performing countries." There are also several technical questions, concerning the "average inflation" observed over a period of one year, and the calculation of averages inflation rates in cases where more than one country's performance is used when calculating the reference value.

With respect to calculating the averages of the best-performing countries, preference is given to unweighted, arithmetic averages, as opposed to geometric and/or weighted averages. The inflation rate is calculated on the basis of the arithmetic average of the latest available twelve monthly indices in relation to the average of the preceding twelve monthly indices. However, data available from other reference periods, including the latest available annual rate, are not excluded.

Regarding the definition of the reference value, the EMI has analyzed the range of possible options and concluded that it is not appropriate to determine under all circumstances which option should be applied. Two examples highlight the potential complications of such clarification. First, it may not be appropriate to focus on the inflation performance of the best-performing country only if for example, the rate is distorted by exceptional circumstances. Second, choosing the simple average of the three best-performing countries would not be appropriate if inflation rates among the best performers differed significantly either because of too high inflation in one country and a deflationary situation in another.

To the extent, that there are no indications of distorted price developments over the most recent period considered and if the price performance of the countries with low inflation rates is broadly similar, the average of the three best-performing countries could serve as a starting-point for the calculation of the reference value, while other reference values may also be taken into consideration.

The Harmonization of CPIs: Protocol No. 6 on the convergence criteria referred to in Article 109.j (1) of the Maastricht Treaty requires price convergence to be measured by means of the consumer price index on a comparable basis, taking into account differences in definitions. Though consumer price statistics are based on similar general principles, there are considerable differences concerning the definitions of the products/services and the prices covered. The procedures used to obtain the basic price data and the methods employed to derive the weights for the index calculation also differ. This affects the comparability of the national data.

---

[117] Adopted from "Progress Towards Convergence," EMI, Frankfurt am Main, November 1995, p.8.

[118] Article 1, Protocol on the Convergence Criteria Referred (to in Article 109.j), Maastricht Treaty, 1992.

The Council of Ministers in October 1995 adopted a Regulation concerning the Harmonized Indices of Consumer Prices. The conceptual work started in 1993 and is carried out by the European Commission (EUROSTAT) in close liaison with the National Statistical Institutes. As a key user of data the EMI is closely involved in this work.

The Council of Ministers Regulation serves as the framework for future harmonization measures. It sets out a step-by-step approach for harmonizing consumer price indices to provide both the necessary data for the analysis of convergence and for the conduct of a common monetary policy in Stage Three.

The calculation of Interim Indices of Consumer Prices (IICP) began in January 1996 to facilitate comparisons across the European Union, until fully harmonized indices can be established. The interim indices are based on existing national indices, excluding major items for which national practices differ significantly (owner-occupied housing costs, expenditures for education, health and insurance) and by including certain items which are not currently covered in all countries (alcoholic beverages and tobacco). They are not fully comparable because considerable differences remain. However, they are more comparable than currently used national indices and thus provide a better basis for assessing convergence, although the exclusion of major items is a drawback. The EMI expects that the IICPs is going to be the basis for measuring price convergence in its report prepared under Article 109j in 1996. The interim indices, however, are not substitutes for existing indices.

Beginning in January 1997, Harmonized Indices of Consumer Prices (HICP) will be calculated. They will be the basis for the report on convergence in 1997/98. Furthermore, HICPs will serve as the main indicator for consumer price developments under the common monetary policy in Stage Three. Of the harmonization issue, three will be particularly important in developing both comparable and meaningful national consumer price statistics. Because a wide coverage of private consumption expenditures is indispensable, common rules, particularly concerning the items excluded from the interim indices in 1996, must be established and, in due course, enacted. As agreed the quality of goods and services is also needed. Finally, the consistent updating of the index weights will also need to be considered.

Questions which cannot be resolved in the time before the introduction of the HICPs make further harmonization measures following January 1997 necessary. The EMI has emphasized the necessity of providing comparable data available by 1997 and to limit the number of stages and the delays in the harmonization process to a minimum to ensure sufficient data consistency and stability. Further efforts will be required from Member States, if the tight timetable set by the Treaty for the provision of comparable price convergence data is to be met.

Annex V.5
The Fiscal Convergence Criteria and the Role of the EMI

Public Finances[119]

Treaty Provisions: The Treaty establishing the European Community, Article 109j.1 requires that the government financial position be sustainable. This will be apparent from having achieved a government budgetary position without a deficit that is "excessive". Article 104(c) defines the criteria for deciding whether an excessive deficit exists, requiring the Commission to prepare a report if one or both of the following conditions are fulfilled:

(a) the ration of the planned (current year) or actual (past year) government deficit to gross domestic product exceeds a reference value (defined in the Protocol on the Excessive Deficit Procedure as 3% of GDP), unless:

- either the ratio has declined substantially and continuously and reached a level that comes close to the reference value;

- or, alternatively, the excess over the reference value is only exceptional and temporary and the ratio remains close to the reference value;

(b) the ratio of government debt to gross domestic product exceeds a reference value (defined in the Protocol on the Excessive Deficit Procedure as 60% of GDP), unless the ratio is sufficiently diminishing and approaching the reference value at a satisfactory pace.

In addition, the Commission's report must take into account "whether the government deficit exceeds government investment expenditure" and "all other relevant factors, including the medium-term economic and budgetary position of the Member State". The Commission may also prepare a report if, notwithstanding the fulfillment of the requirements, it is of the opinion that there is a risk of an excessive deficit. The Monetary Committee (or its successor in Stage Three, the Economic and Financial Committee) will evaluate the report of the Commission. Finally, on the basis of the recommendation of the Commission, the Council of Ministers shall, through a decision by qualified majority, determine whether an excessive deficit exists in a Member State.

The Application of Reference Values: The fiscal developments analyzed below show that even strong economic recoveries may not by themselves bring about fundamental improvements. Although actual deficits may decline during periods of buoyant economic activity, possibly falling to just below 3% of GDP, structural deficits persist in most nations, and, thus, in the event of an economic slowdown, increases in actual deficits must be expected. To show evidence of a reduction in debt ratios and to ensure that the ratio referred to in the Treaty is sufficiently diminishing and approaching the reference value at a satisfactory pace, in some cases high primary surpluses (that is, the balance net of interest rate payments).

Key Definitions: The Protocol on the Excessive Deficit Procedure defines "government deficit" and "investment" by reference to the European System of Integrated Economic Accounts (ESA). The ESA is a coherent and detailed set of national account tables accepted to facilitate comparative evaluations. Furthermore, the definitions of "debt" and "gross domestic product" as well as the rules and coverage of reporting by the member nations to the European Commission are laid down in a Council of Ministers Regulation. The Protocol on the Excessive Deficit Procedure assigns to the Commission the ultimate responsibility for providing the data to be used.

"Government" comprises central government, regional or local government and social security funds. It does not include public enterprises and is therefore to be distinguished from a more broadly defined

---

[119] Source: "Progress Towards Convergence," EMI, Frankfurt am Main, November 1995, p.19.

public sector. The ESA definition of government is being further clarified, in particular as far as certain pension funds are concerned.

"Government deficit" is defined as the difference between government gross savings and the sum of government investments, net capital transfers payable by government, the change in stocks and net purchases of land and intangible assets by government. Furthermore, "government debt" is defined as the sum of government liabilities classified in the ESA categories as currency and deposits, bills and bonds, and other loans. The definitions of government deficit and government debt imply that the change in government debt outstanding at the end of two consecutive years may differ substantially from the size of the government deficit for the year under consideration. For example, government debt could be reduced by privatizing public enterprises or by selling other financial assets. This, however, would not affect the deficit.

The Excessive Deficit Procedure[120]

1. In Article 104C (1), the Maastricht Treaty requires that in Stage Three of the EMU "Member States shall avoid excessive government deficits". In addition, Article 109e (4) says that "in the second stage, Member States shall endeavor to avoid excessive government deficits". The Excessive Deficit Procedure (EDP) is defined in article 104c and in an annexed Protocol to the Treaty. The Commission (Article 104c (2)) is in charge of supervising the fulfillment of this mandate, "with a view to identifying gross errors". The EDP stages are as follows:
2. The Commission monitors the development of the budgetary situation in the Member States (Article 104c (2)).
3. If the conditions are not fulfilled, the Commission prepares a report (Article 104c(3)).
4. The Monetary Committee formulates an opinion on this report (Article 104c (4)).
5. If the Commission decides that an Excessive Deficit exists, it addresses an opinion to the Council of Ministers (Article 104c (5)).
6. The Council of Ministers on a recommendation of the Commission decides by a qualified majority whether an Excessive Deficit exists (Article 104c (6)). Also, if the Excessive Deficit ceases to exist, the Council of Ministers shall abrogate the decision (Article 104c (12)).
7. If an Excessive Deficit exists, the Council of Ministers makes recommendations to the Member State, which are not made public (Article 104c (7)).
8. If no effective action is taken by the Member State, the Council of Ministers may make the recommendations public (Article 104c (8)).
9. If the Excessive Deficit is not corrected, the Council of Ministers may propose precise measures to be undertaken by the Member State, and monitors their implementation (Article 104c (9)).
10. If the Excessive Deficit persists, the Council of Ministers applies or intensifies one or more of the following measures: requiring the Member State to publish additional information before issuing bonds, inviting the European Investment Bank to reconsider its lending policy towards the Member State, requiring a non-interest bearing deposit or imposing fines of an appropriate size (Article 104c (11)).

During Stage Two of the EMU steps 9 to 10 (describing the penalties associated with the absence of compliance) do not hold. In other words, the EDP is extended once countries enter the European currency area (see also Article 109k (1) and (3)).

---

[120] Adopted from "Progress Towards Convergence, EMI, Frankfurt am Main, November 1995, p.27.

Annex V.6
The Exchange Rate Convergence Criteria and the Role of the EMI; and the Evolution of Real Effective Exchange Rates in the EU[121]

Exchange rate stability[122]

Treaty Provisions: The Maastricht Treaty, Article 109j (1) requires "the observance of the normal fluctuation margins provided for by the Exchange Rate Mechanism of the European Monetary System, for at least two years, without devaluing against the currency of any other Member State". In addition, the Protocol to the Treaty (No. 6, Art. 3) specifies that the above requirement should be fulfilled "...without severe tensions for at least the last two years before the examination. In particular, the Member State shall not have devalued its currency's bilateral central rate against any other Member State's currency on its own initiative for the same period."

The Widening of the ERM Fluctuation Bands: In 1991, when the Maastricht Treaty was developed, the "normal fluctuation margins" were +/-2.25% around bilateral central rates, whereas a +/-6% band was a derogation from the rule. In August 1993 the decision was taken to widen the fluctuation margins to +/-15%, and the interpretation of the criterion, in particular of the concept of "normal fluctuation margins", became less straightforward. The central parities, however, remained unchanged and the ERM membership requirement remains a part of the Treaty. The widening of the ERM bands created a new market environment.

Concerning the issue of the widening of the bands, a formal Opinion was put forward by the EMI Council in October 1994 (later endorsed by the ECOFIN Council; see the EMI 1994 Annual Report). The EMU stated that

> ...on 2nd August 1993 the Ministers of Finance and central bank Governors jointly took the decision to widen the ERM fluctuation bands for compulsory intervention to 15% while leaving central parities unchanged. Experience since then indicates that the wider band has helped to achieve a sustainable degree of exchange rate stability in the ERM. It has done so by deterring speculative attacks on ERM currencies, thereby preventing large exchange rate depreciation or excessive exchange market intervention and their potentially inflationary consequences. In the light of this experience and in the current circumstances, the EMI Council considers it advisable to maintain the present arrangements.

At the same time, the EMI Council recommended "that member countries should continue to aim at avoiding significant exchange rate fluctuations by gearing their policies to the achievement of price stability and the reduction of fiscal deficits, thereby contributing to fulfillment of the requirements set out in Article 109j (1) of the Treaty and the relevant Protocol."

Evolution of Real Effective Exchange Rates[123]

The Evolution of Real Effective Exchange Rates: The measurement of the competitive position of an economy is fraught with methodological problems. One widely used approach relies on estimates of the real effective exchange rate (REER) and the comparison of their current levels with a base or "reference" year.

---

121 Adopted from "Progress Towards Convergence," EMI, Frankfurt am Main, November 1995, p.40.

122 Adopted from "Progress Towards Convergence," EMI, Frankfurt am Main, November 1995, p.33.

123 Adopted from "Progress Towards Convergence," EMI, Frankfurt am Main, November 1995, p.40.

Table 5.4 summarizes the evolution of some indicators of real effective exchange rates (*vis-à-vis* twenty-six trading partners), measured with consumer prices, producer prices, unit labor costs and export prices, over the short, medium and long run. Currencies are grouped according to their overall real effective exchange rate trends; current levels (September 1995) are compared with December 1994 (a relatively quiet month, before the recent turbulence), with April 1992 (a quiet month before the 1992-93 crises), and 1987 (a period in which most EU members appeared to be broadly in both internal and external balance). The methodology underlying the construction of such measures is described in P. Turner and J. Van't dack, "Measuring international price and cost competitiveness," BIS Economic Papers No. 39, November 1993.

In the short run (between December 1994 and September 1995), due to limited inflation differentials, real effective exchange rate developments closely mirrored fluctuations in nominal effective exchange rates. During this period, all ERM currencies appreciated in real effective terms; also non-ERM currencies, with the exception of the Italian lira and the British pound appreciated. Over the medium and long run, a group of six ERM currencies (the Belgian franc, Danish krone, Deutsche Mark, French franc, Dutch guilder and Austrian schilling) may be identified, which, over time, displayed relatively consistent nominal and real appreciation and the French franc the lowest.

A second group of currencies (inside the ERM the Portuguese escudo and outside the ERM the Greek drachma) has appreciated strongly in real terms since 1987. In both cases, the real appreciation occurred in spite of a significant nominal depreciation, which was, however, smaller than the unfavorable price/cost differentials with trading partners, for the period as a whole. However, developments in the escudo's external value followed a specific trend, since its real effective exchange rate stood in 1995 at its mid-1992 level while its nominal effective rate has been stable since 1993.

A third group of currencies has strongly depreciated in real effective terms since 1987. They include the Italian lira and the Swedish krona. Their depreciation has been even more pronounced since April 1992, given their earlier real appreciation.

The Irish pound and the Finnish markka registered some gains in price and cost competitiveness over the medium and long run, though during the first three quarters of 1995 the Irish pound's real exchange rate was relatively stable.

Finally, the Spanish peseta and, to some extent, the pound sterling now exhibit real effective exchange rate indices close to their 1987 levels, suggesting that the sharp depreciations since April 1992 may be seen as a correction of previous losses in price and cost competitiveness. In the case of sterling and the peseta, the exchange rate adjustments also reflect a re-balancing of monetary and fiscal policies.

Table 5.4
Summary of Changes in Real Effective Exchange Rates of EU-15 Currencies up to Sept. 1995*
(monthly data; in percentages)

	Since 1987				Since April 1992				Since Dec. 1994			
	CPI (a)	ULC (b)	XPI (c)	PPI (d)	CPI (a)	ULC (b)	XPI (c)	PPI (d)	CPI (a)	ULC (b)	XPI (c)	PPI (d)
BEF	2.9	4.7	-6.3	0.8	6.7	8.1	-11.6	3.3	1.5	2.6	-1.3	0.6
DKK	1.8	9.9	2.5	5.9	6.3	13.6	5.2	7.5	2.7	4.9	2.5	3.1
DEM	4.9	16.2	-1.5	7.3	9.9	15.0	1.2	7.4	2.4	2.8	1.9	2.8
FRF	0.2	-2.8	13.0	1.2	5.4	4.1	9.1	5.1	2.5	2.0	3.6	2.8
NLG	0.5	-0.2	-0.2	3.3	7.9	4.9	4.0	5.2	2.4	1.8	2.4	1.4
ATS	5.1	-3.3	-12.1	0.8	7.8	4.8	-2.8	1.6	2.4	2.2	2.9	-3.8
GRD	20.3	21.3	-10.1	6.3	5.8	6.1	-14.8	1.6	2.0	6.2	2.0	-1.3
PTE	25.9	(e)	0.2	(e)	0.8	(e)	1.7	(e)	1.5	(e)	4.6	(e)
ITL	-18.3	-20.9	-6.6	-15.2	-23.5	-27.9	-10.7	-18.1	-1.7	-3.3	0.5	1.4
SEK	-7.1	-21.4	-4.6	-0.2	-18.5	-28.3	-8.4	-6.2	1.0	0.3	2.9	8.0
IEP	-7.6	-24.5	-0.8	-3.8	-2.7	-11.8	2.1	-1.3	0.7	-2.4	4.0	0.3
FIM	-8.6	-27.0	11.0	-5.3	-3.3	-17.3	11.9	3.7	4.7	2.8	11.4	5.7
ESP	3.6	-5.0	1.8	0.0	-14.3	-21.8	-10.9	-13.2	2.2	1.1	4.1	2.7
GBP	-5.1	-5.7	3.6	0.7	-16.5	-13.2	-2.9	-10.4	-3.8	-3.5	-3.4	-3.4

* = Effective exchange rates against 26 trading partners; a positive sign indicates an appreciation of the real effective exchange rate.

Key:

(a) Deflated by consumer prices.
(b) Deflated by unit labor costs.
(c) Deflated by export prices.
(d) Deflated by producer price indices.
(e) ULC and PPI indicators are not presented because of methodological problems: first, since producer prices series are not available for Portugal, the BIS uses the CPI for estimating the former; second, the ULC indicator used by the BIS tends to overstate the extent of the appreciation of this real effective exchange rate, compared with the Banco de Portugal's series.

Note: BEF: Belgium franc; DKK: Denmark krone; DEM: Deutsche mark; ESP: Spanish peseta; GRD: Greek drachma; FRF: French franc; IEP: Irish pound; ITL: Italian lira; NLG: Dutch guilder; PTE: Portuguese escudo; GBP: Pound sterling; ATS: Austrian schilling; SEK: Swedish krona; FIN: Finish markka.

Source: "Progress Towards Convergence," EMI, Frankfurt am Main, November 1995, p.41.

Annex V.7
The Long-Term Interest Rate Convergence Criteria and the Role of the EMI

Long-term interest rates[124]

Treaty Provisions: The Maastricht Treaty 109j (1) requires that the durability of convergence by the EU nations and of their participation in the Exchange Rate Mechanism of the European Monetary System be reflected in long-term interest rate levels. This criterion is defined as:

> The criterion on the convergence of interest rates referred to in the fourth indent of Article 109j (1) of this Treaty shall mean that, observed over a period of one year before the examination, a Member State has had an average nominal long-term interest rate that does not exceed by more than two percentage points that of, at most, the three best-performing Member States in terms of price stability. Interest rates shall be measured on the basis of long-term government bonds or comparable securities, taking into account differences in national definitions.

The Calculation of Reference Values: In applying the criterion, it is important to note that the Treaty provides for the use as reference values of the long-term interest rates of those three countries with the lowest inflation rates.

As the same definition is used in the Treaty for the choice of the reference values for both the price level and interest rate criteria, the same procedure must be followed in calculating the two indices. Thus choosing the average of the three best inflation performers as a starting-point in the price section (see Annex V.4) would suggest using the respective long-term interest rates as a reference value for measuring interest rate convergence. As for the price stability criterion, replace value, however, due regard should also be given to possible interest rate level outlier countries, which may be affected by the credibility of the policy mix. If a country, while having a low inflation rate, has a high long-term interest rate, its situation should be closely monitored to assess whether the long-term interest rate should determine the criterion. Furthermore, when calculating averages among best-performing countries, preference should be given to unweighted arithmetic averages, and the long-term interest rate should be calculated as a simple average over the last twelve months. However, information available from other reference periods, including the latest long-term interest rates should not be excluded.

The Long-Term Interest Rate Criterion: Protocol No. 6 on the convergence criteria referred to in Article 109j of the Treaty requires interest rate convergence to be assessed on the basis of long-term government bonds, or comparable securities, observed over a period of one year before the assessment, taking into account differences in national definitions. The Treaty provisions imply that the representative long-term interest rates should reflect as accurately as possible and changes in market sentiments with respect to the durability of the convergence and the participation in the ERM of the countries concerned. The distorting effects of other determinants should be limited.

Although the methodology for calculating the yields of bonds is similar across all countries, considerable differences may exist regarding the choice of securities, yield formulae used, maturities chosen, treatment of taxation and adjustments for coupon effects. The object of harmonization is to make recommendations, in particular with regard to these choices, which are general enough to allow for differences in national markets and flexible enough to allow for the evolution of those markets, without impairing the comparability of data.

While Article 5 of the Protocol assigns the responsibility for providing the statistical data to the Commission, conceptual assistance from the EMI with regard to defining representative long-term interest rate is welcomed, given its expertise in the area.

---

124 Adopted from "Progress Towards Convergence," EMI, Frankfurt am Main, November 1995, pp.43-44.

The harmonization principles called for the issue of bonds by the central government with close to ten years to maturity and yields measurable gross of tax. To ensure that the depth of the market is taken into account, and that no liquidity premium is carried into yields, the representative securities must be chosen on the basis of their liquidity. Countries may choose either a benchmark or a sample of bonds, using the liquidity of the market at the ten-year point as the determining factor. Special-feature bonds (e.g., embedded option, zero coupon) are excluded from the assessment. The selection of highly liquid bonds is also seen as an indirect means to minimize the effects of different coupon values. Finally, a uniform formula was chosen using existing international standards (such as the formula 6.3: "Formulae for Yield and other Calculations", issued by the International Securities Market Association). Where there is more than one bond in the sample, the liquidity of the selected bonds warrants the use of a simple average of the yields to produce the representative rate. The harmonized representative long-term interest rates defined above is being implemented by the central banks at present, and it is envisaged that provisional harmonized data will be produced by the end of 1996.

Annex V.8

Table 5.5

Summary of the Institutional Features of the Various EU Central Banks (continued...)

	NATIONAL BANK OF BELGIUM	DANMARKS NATIONALBANK	DEUTSCHE BUNDESBANK	BANK OF GREECE
PRINCIPAL STATUTORY OBJECTIVE	None, although safeguarding the currency implicit	To maintain a safe and secure currency system	To safeguard the currency	To control currency in circulation and credit
LEGAL AUTHORITY FOR:				
1 Exchange rate regime	1 Government	1 Government	1 Government	1 Government
2 Setting targets for:				
• monetary growth	2 Central bank[a]	2 Central bank[a]	2 Central bank	2 Central bank
• inflation	Central bank[a]	Central bank[a]	Central bank[a]	Central bank[a]
3 Changing key interest rates	3 Central bank	3 Central bank	3 Central bank	3 Central bank
RESPONSIBILITIES:				
1 Execution of monetary and exchange rate policy	1 Yes	1 Yes	1 Yes (2-week suspension of decisions possible at the request of Government but never been used)	1 Yes
2 Issue of banknotes	2 Yes	2 Yes	2 Yes	2 Yes
3 Payment system services	3 Yes	3 Yes	3 Yes	3 Yes
4 Bank of banks and government	4 Yes	4 Yes	4 Yes	4 No exclusive arrangement
5 Supervision of financial Institutions	5 No	5 No	5 No	5 Yes
6 Safeguard financial stability	6 Yes	6 Yes	6 Yes	6 Yes
7 Official reserve management	7 Yes	7 Yes	7 Yes	7 Yes
GOVERNING BODIES	• Governor • Board of Directors • Council of Regency • Board of Censors • General Council	• Board of Governors • Board of Directors • Committee of Directors • Royal Bank Commissioner	• Central Bank Council • Directorate • Managing Boards of Land Central Banks	• General Council • Governor • (Deputy Governors)
APPOINTMENT OF GOV'NOR By:	• Crown on proposal of the Government	• Crown on proposal of the Government	• Federal President on proposal of Federal Government after consultation of Central Bank Council	• President of the Republic on a proposal of the Government after being nominated by the Council
Term:	• 5 years (renewable)	• Life, up to the age of 70	• Normally 8 Years, minimum 2 years (renewable)	• 4 years (renewable)
RECENT AND PLANNED CHANGES	Legislation to ensure central bank independence on monetary policy decisions was adopted on 22nd March 1993.	None	None	The Bank of Greece has proposed to Government legislative changes which aim to increase its degree of independence and to make its Statute fully compatible with the Treaty on European Union.

Table 5.5
Summary of the Institutional Features of the Various EU Central Banks (continued...)

	BANCO DE ESPANA	BANQUE DE FRANCE	CENTRAL BANK OF IRELAND	BANCA D'ITALIA
PRINCIPAL STATUTORY OBJECTIVE	To ensure price stability	Ensuring price stability	To safeguard the integrity of the currency	Safeguard of price stability implicit in the Constitution
LEGAL AUTHORITY FOR:				
1 Exchange rate regime	1 Government after consulting the central bank	1 Government	1 Government	1 Government
2 Setting targets for: • monetary growth	2 Central bank[(b)]	2 Central bank	2 Central bank	2 Central bank[(a)]
• inflation	Central bank	Central bank	Central bank[(a)]	Government
3 Changing key interest rates	3 Central bank	3 Central bank	3 Central bank	3 Central bank
RESPONSIBILITIES:				
1 Execution of monetary and exchange rate policy	1 Yes	1 Yes	1 Yes	1 Yes
2 Issue of banknotes	2 Yes	2 Yes	2 Yes	2 Yes (production in agreement with the Government)
3 Payment system services	3 Yes	3 Yes	3 Yes	3 Yes
4 Bank of banks and government	4 Yes	4 Yes	4 Yes	4 Yes
5 Supervision of financial Institutions	5 Yes	5 Yes, through Commission Bancaire	5 Yes	5 Yes
6 Safeguard financial stability	6 Yes	6 Yes	6 Yes	6 Yes
7 Official reserve management	7 Yes	7 Yes	7 Yes	7 Yes (together with the Italian Exchange Office)
GOVERNING BODIES	• Governor • Deputy Governor • Governing Council • Executive Commission	• Monetary Policy Council • General Council	• Board of Directors	• Governor, Director-General, 2 Deputy Director-Generals (Directorate) • Board of Directors
APPOINTMENT OF GOV'NOR By:	• Crown on proposal of President of Government	• Council of Ministers	• President, on the advice of Government	• Board of Directors with approval of Government
Term:	• 6 years (non-renewable)	• 6 years (renewable)	• 7 years (renewable)	• Unlimited
RECENT AND PLANNED CHANGES	Law 13/1994 of 1st June 1994 on the Autonomy of the Banco de Espana introduced the provisions of the Treaty on European Union relating to central banks.	Law of 4th August 1993 & 31st December 1993 on the Statute of the Banque de France introduced the provisions of the Treaty on European Union relating to central banks.	Consideration is being given to amendments to national legislation.	None

Table 5.5
Summary of the Institutional Features of the Various EU Central Banks (continued…)

	INSTITUT MONETAIRE LUXEMBOURGEOIS	NEDERLANDSCHE BANK	OESTERREICHISCHE NATIONALBANK	BANCO DE PORTUGAL
PRINCIPAL STATUTORY OBJECTIVE	Includes the promotion of the stability of the currency	To safeguard the value of the currency	To maintain the internal and external value of the Austrian currency	To maintain price stability taking into account the general economic policy of the Government
LEGAL AUTHORITY FOR: 1 Exchange rate regime 2 Setting targets for: • monetary growth • inflation 3 Changing key interest rates	 1 Government 2 Central bank[a] Jointly with Government[a] 3 Central bank[a]	 1 Government 2 Central bank[a] Central bank[a] 3 Central bank	 1 Central bank in co-operation with Government 2 Central bank[a] Central bank[a] 3 Central bank	 1 Government after consulting the central bank 2 Central bank[a] Central bank[a] 3 Central bank
RESPONSIBILITIES: 1 Execution of monetary and exchange rate policy 2 Issue of banknotes 3 Payment system services 4 Bank of banks and government 5 Supervision of financial Institutions 6 Safeguard financial stability 7 Official reserve management	 1 Yes (partly) 2 Yes 3 Yes 4 No 5 Yes 6 Yes 7 Yes	 1 Yes (a right of instruction of Government still formally exists but has never been used) 2 Yes 3 Yes 4 Yes 5 Yes 6 Yes 7 Yes	 1 Yes 2 Yes 3 Yes 4 Yes 5 No 6 Yes 7 Yes	 1 Yes 2 Yes 3 Yes 4 Yes 5 Yes 6 Yes 7 Yes
GOVERNING BODIES	• Management • Council	• Governing Board • Supervisory Board	• General Council • Board of Executive Directors	• Governor • Board of Directors • Board of Auditors • Advisory Board
APPOINTMENT OF GOV'NOR By: Term:	 • Grand-Duke on proposal of Council of Minister • 6 years (renewable)	 • Nominated by joint meeting of Governing Board & Supervisory Board and appointed by Crown on proposal of Council of Ministers • 7 years (renewable)	 • President of the Republic on nomination by the Federal Government • 5 years (renewable)	 • Council of Ministers on proposal of Minister of Finance • 5 years (renewable)
RECENT AND PLANNED CHANGES	A bill to effect the changes in legislation required by the Treaty on European Union is pending in parliament.	Law of 9th December 1993 introduce provisions of the Treaty on European Union relating to central banks. Final adjustments in order to comply with the Treaty are under consideration.	None	Amendments to reinforce the independence of the central bank in line with Articles 109e (5) and 108 of the Treaty on European Union were adopted in September 1995.

Table 5.5
Summary of the Institutional Features of the Various EU Central Banks (...continued)

	SUOMEN PANKKI	SVERIBES RIKSBANK	BANK OF ENGLAND
PRINCIPAL STATUTORY OBJECTIVE	To maintain a stable and secure monetary system and to assist and facilitate the circulation of money in Finland	None, although safeguarding of the currency implicit	None, although safeguarding of the currency implicit
LEGAL AUTHORITY FOR: 1 Exchange rate regime 2 Setting targets for: • monetary growth • inflation 3 Changing key interest rates	1 Government on proposal of the central bank 2 Central bank[(a)] Central bank 3 Central bank[(a)]	1 Central bank 2 Central bank[(a)] Central bank 3 Central bank	1 Government 2 Government[(b)] Government 3 Government
RESPONSIBILITIES: 1 Execution of monetary and exchange rate policy 2 Issue of banknotes 3 Payment system services 4 Bank of banks and government 5 Supervision of financial Institutions 6 Safeguard financial stability 7 Official reserve management	1 Yes 2 Yes 3 Yes 4 Yes (bank of bank) No (bank of Government) 5 No 6 Yes 7 Yes	1 Yes 2 Yes 3 Yes 4 Yes 5 No 6 Yes 7 Yes	1 Yes 2 Yes 3 Yes 4 Yes 5 Yes 6 Yes 7 Yes (as agent for the Government)
GOVERNING BODIES	• Parliamentary Supervisory Council • Board	• Governing Board • Governor	• Court of Directors
APPOINTMENT OF GOV'NOR By: Term:	• President of the Republic on a proposal of the Parliamentary Supervisory Council • Indefinite	• Governing Board • 5 years (renewable)	• Crown on proposal of Prime Minister • 5 years (renewable)
RECENT AND PLANNED CHANGES	Legislation in order to comply with the requirements of the Treaty on European Union is under consideration.	Legislation in order to comply with the requirements of the Treaty will be proposed during the current legislative period.	None. Changes will be needed if the United Kingdom participates in Stage Three.

(a) = No targets set at present.
(b) = No targets set at present; only monitoring ranges/rates used.
Source: "Progress Towards Convergence," EMI, November 1995, p.134-36

Annex V.9
The Role and Degree of Independence of Selected EU Central Banks

Table 5.6
The Role and Degree of Independence of the Bank of Denmark in Monetary Policy

Role, Size, and Composition of Boards	Government's Representation in Bank Bodies	Role of Bank in Monetary and Exchange Policy	Resolution of Conflict Between Bank and Government	Monitoring of Bank Performance	Coordination of Bank and Government	Loans and Advances to Government
The policy body is the Board of Governors (the Chairman is appointed by the Crown, 2 deputies are elected by Board of Directors, in practice for life). Board of Directors meets quarterly to decide on administrative matters (25 members for five years of which 8 are members of parliament, one is an economist, one a lawyer ,15 are representative of the economy). The Committee of Directors meet at least monthly on administrative matters (7 members for one year renewable, elected from the Board of Directors).	Member of governing bodies are not subject to political directives. Minister of Economic Affairs is the Royal Bank Commissioner, and serves as Chairman of the Board of Directors, and may also attend meetings of the Committee of Directors. The Royal Bank Commissioner and Minister of Finance may participate in Governing Board meetings without voting rights.	The Board has powers over monetary policy. Board of Governors has full freedom in setting instruments and implementing policy. Exchange rate policy is set by Government in coordination with Bank. Management of exchange rate rests with the Bank.	No special provision.	The Royal Bank Commissioner supervises performance of the Bank. Accountability is provided through the composition of Board of Directors and Committee of Directors. The Bank is obliged to publish annual accounts.	Regular meetings of the Board of Governors and economic affairs ministers in which the Prime Minister may also participate. Monthly meetings (in the central bank) of the Prime Minister, Minister of Finance and of Economic Affairs (and their Permanent Secretaries).	No monetary financing of budget.

Source: Adapted from Zulu, J.B., Ian S. McCarthy, Susana Almuiña and Gabriel Sensenbrenner. Central Banking Technical Assistance to Countries in Transition. Monetary and Exchange Affairs Department, IMF, Washington DC, 1994, pp.114-129.

Table 5.7
The Role and Degree of Independence of the Banque de France in Monetary Policy

Role, Size, and Composition of Boards	Government's Representation in Bank Bodies	Role of Bank in Monetary and Exchange Policy	Resolution of Conflict Between Bank and Government	Monitoring of Bank Performance	Coordination of Bank and Government	Loans and Advances to Government
The Board ("Monetary Policy Council") is comprised of 9 members, including the Governor (chair) and 2 Vice-Governors, appointed by the Government for 6 years, renewable once. Six other members are of recognized standing in monetary, financial and economic matters, nominated by a resolution of the Council of Ministers for 9 years, non-renewable; 2 outside directors are replaced every 3 years. A quorum requires two-thirds. At least one meeting per month. The General Council is in charge of administrative matters and proposes the appropriation of profits.	The Prime Minister and Minister of Finance may participate in Board meetings and may submit proporsals, without voting right. Board members are expressly forbidden to seek or accept instructions from Government or any other person.	The Bank formulates and implements monetary policy with the aim of ensuring price stability. The Government determines exchange rate regime and parity of franc. Bank regulates exchange rate within the framework of general exchange rate policy guidelines formulated by the Government.	No special provision.	Annual report prepared by General Council and reviewed by statutory auditors; submitted to President and Parliament. Parliamentary committees may ask the Governor to explain (speech) as needed.	No special provision.	All types of credit to the Government are prohibited.

Source: Adapted from Zulu, J.B., Ian S. McCarthy, Susana Almuiña and Gabriel Sensenbrenner. Central Banking Technical Assistance to Countries in Transition. Monetary and Exchange Affairs Department, IMF, Washington DC, 1994, pp.114-129.

Table 5.8
The Role and Degree of Independence of the Bundesbank in Monetary Policy

Role, Size, and Composition of Boards	Government's Representation in Bank Bodies	Role of Bank in Monetary and Exchange Policy	Resolution of Conflict Between Bank and Government	Monitoring of Bank Performance	Coordination of Bank and Government	Loans and Advances to Government
The Bank Council (up to 17 members) sets policy; the Bank Directorate (up to 8 members) implements policy. Members of the Directorate (including President and Vice-President) are nominated by the Government on advice of the Council and appointed by the Federal President for up to 8 years. The Council comprises of the Directorate and the 9 presidents of Land Central Banks(nominated by the Bundesrat on the advice of the Council and appointed by the Federal President for up to 8 years). Majority vote; chairman has casting vote.	The Cabinet members may attend meetings of the Council without the right to vote; may propose motions. The Bank expressly "is independent of instructions from Federal Carbinet."	The Bank has statutory responsibility to determine monetary policy. Obligation to support general economic policy of the Government, "without prejudice to the performance of its functions." The Government decides on exchange regime and sets central exchange rates, in coordination with the Bank. The Government abstrains from setting directives.	Cabinet representative on Council may request a decision to be deferred up to two weeks.	The Bank Council and Directorate have "status of supreme Federal authorities." Not formally accountable to any authority. Council appoints external auditors whose report, together with comments of Federal Court of Auditors, is communicated to Finance Minister.	"Cabinet should invite President of Bank to attend deliberations of important monetary issues."	In the Bundesbank Act (1992), short-term advances to Federal and Land Governments and to Federal special funds, collateralized against treasury bills, are subject to absolute limits expressed in Deutsche mark. This provision was suspended since 1/1/1994 in compliance with Article 104 of Maastricht Treaty.

Source: Adapted from Zulu, J.B., Ian S. McCarthy, Susana Almuiña and Gabriel Sensenbrenner. Central Banking Technical Assistance to Countries in Transition. Monetary and Exchange Affairs Department, IMF, Washington DC, 1994, pp.114-129.

Table 5.9
The Role and Degree of Independence of the Bank of England in Monetary Policy

Role, Size, and Composition of Boards	Government's Representation in Bank Bodies	Role of Bank in Monetary and Exchange Policy	Resolution of Conflict Between Bank and Government	Monitoring of Bank Performance	Coordination of Bank and Government	Loans and Advances to Government
The Court of Directors consists of the Governor, Deputy Governor (5-year terms renewable), and 16 directors up to 4 with executive responsibilities in the Bank (4-year terms renewable), all are appointed by the Crown on advice of the Prime Minister. Directors are chosen to reflect a variety of financial, industrial, and commercial sectors. An executive committee chaired by the Governor is responsible for day-to-day management.	Government representatives explicitly ruled out.	Treasury determines monetary policy and Bank implements with limited discretion on timing of interest rate changes once these have been decided by Chancellor of Exchequer. In practice, there is extensive consultation between the Treasury and Bank on all aspects of monetary policy. Targets set and announced by the Government. The Bank publishes quarterly inflation reports, independently assessing prospects for inflation. The Bank only acts as an agent of the Treasury for foreign exchange activities.	Treasury has power to issue formal directives to the Bank, but has never done so.	The Annual report is the main instrument of accountability and presented to the Parliament through the Chancellor of Exchequer. Others include appearances by Governor and executive directors before select Parliamentary committees, speeches, and the Bank's quarterly bulletins and inflation reports.	Chancellor of the-Exchequer and Governor meet regularly once a month and otherwise whenever necessary. Minutes of the meetings are published.	Loans and advances to the public sector are prohibited by article 104 of Maastricht Treaty, which has been incorporated into U.K. law. The Government is, however, permitted to maintain its "ways and means" advances facility with the Bank(to bridge overnight balances) if and so long as the United Kingdom does move to Stage III of EMU.

Source: Adapted from Zulu, J.B., Ian S. McCarthy, Susana Almuiña and Gabriel Sensenbrenner. Central Banking Technical Assistance to Countries in Transition. Monetary and Exchange Affairs Department, IMF, Washington DC, 1994, pp.114-129.

Table 5.10
The Role and Degree of Independence of the Nederlandsche Bank in Monetary Policy

Role, Size, and Composition of Boards	Government's Representation in Bank Bodies	Role of Bank in Monetary and Exchange Policy	Resolution of Conflict Between Bank and Government	Monitoring of Bank Performance	Coordination of Bank and Government	Loans and Advances to Government
The Governing Board is responsible for policy decisions (President, Secretary and up to 5 Directors, are appointed by the Crown for 7 years renewable). Supervisory Board (12 members appointed by Ministry of Finance for 4 years renewable). Bank Council, an advisory body (17 members, chaired by the Royal Commissioner, meeting at least 6 times per year, including 6 members from Supervisory Board and 12 members appointed by the Crown representing finance, industry and labor.	The Royal Commissioner is appointed by the Crown and supervises the Bank and may attend meetings of other two Boards in advisory role.	No special provision. The Bank has a high degree of independence in determining monetary policy. The Guilder parity is decided by the Government upon advice of the Bank, whose opinion is later published. the Governing Board decides when and how much to intervene in the foreign exchange market.	The Finance Minister, in consultation with the Bank Council, can issue directives to the Governing Board. If in disagreement, the Board can appeal to the Crown. If the Crown sides with the Minister, both opinions are published if Crown deems them consistent with national interest. This provision has never been used and will be abolished under Stage III of European Economic and Monetary Union (EMU).	The Governing Board reports to the Supervisory Board. The President informs Council on policy matters. The Supervisory Board supervises management and adopts the annual report. The Royal Commissioner verifies compliance of financial statements with law. The Bank publishes Weekly summary balance sheets.	The Minister of Finance and Bank President meet informally once a week. Minutes are confidential.	Advances to the Government are prohibited under the Maastricht Treaty as of 1/1/94. The Bank had an obligation to grant secured and interest-free credit of up to f. 150 million. A further limited and collateralized facility was agreed yearly to bridge temporary cash needs.

Source: Adapted from Zulu, J.B., Ian S. McCarthy, Susana Almuiña and Gabriel Sensenbrenner. Central Banking Technical Assistance to Countries in Transition. Monetary and Exchange Affairs Department, IMF, Washington DC, 1994, pp.114-129.

Table 5.11
The Role and Degree of Independence of the Bank of Portugal in Monetary Policy

Role, Size, and Composition of Boards	Government's Representation in Bank Bodies	Role of Bank in Monetary and Exchange Policy	Resolution of Conflict Between Bank and Government	Monitoring of Bank Performance	Coordination of Bank and Government	Loans and Advances to Government
The Board is comprised of up-to 8 members appointed by the Council of Ministers for 5 years renewable. The Governor is the Chairman of the Board. A quorum requires majority; majority voting with no absentation; the Governor has the casting vote. At least one meeting per week. There is a Board of Auditors and an Advisory Board.	None	Formulation of monetary and exchange rate policy is decided jointly with the Government.The Bank assists the Government in the design and implementation of monetary and exchange rate policy, having due regard for the Government's economic and financial policy guidelines. Policy measures have to be signed by the Minister of Finance.	The Governor may suspend the Board decisions after informing the Government. Decisions of the Governor and Board may be appealed to the Courts in the manner provided by law.	The Audit Board is appointed by the Minister of Finance and monitors the functioning of the Bank and compliance with laws and regulations. The Governor is invited to appear before Parliamentary Committees.	No special provision.	Advances cannot exceed 10% of revenue collected in previous year. The Bank may also underwrite Treasury notes on terms agreed with Ministry. This provision was abolished to comply with Stage II of EMU.

Source: Adapted from Zulu, J.B., Ian S. McCarthy, Susana Almuiña and Gabriel Sensenbrenner. Central Banking Technical Assistance to Countries in Transition. Monetary and Exchange Affairs Department, IMF, Washington DC, 1994, pp.114-129.

VI KEY EMU PREDICAMENTS AND OUTLOOK

This final chapter identifies the key integration predicaments and provides insight into EMU's likely future. The following issues are discussed: (i) the impact of the common monetary policies on EMU participants; (ii) EU financial centers: gains and losses; (iii) the "City" of London and the EMU; (iv) EMU and the global financial markets; (v) the "ERM II"; (vi) the meeting of the Maastricht Treaty convergence criteria in 1997; (vii) the British dilemma, (viii) the German predicament; (ix) the Franco-German alliance and its impact on the EMU; (x) the 1996-97 IGC negotiations; (xi) prospective EMU impediments; and (xii) the EMU blueprint for the year 2002.

THE IMPACT OF COMMON MONETARY POLICIES

Although in most nations the interest rate is the most important monetary policy instrument, there is a great deal of divergence and complexity in its impact on the real economy, as transmission channels differ. Channels such as the ISLM[1] affect the quantity of money and interest rates, the credit channel affects the manner in which banks supply credit and the exchange rate channel influences the value of national

---

[1] The ISLM refers to the relationship between IS and LM. The IS curve represents the different combinations of income and interest that are consistent with equilibrium in the market for goods and services. In a closed economy such an equilibrium exists when investment equals savings. The LM curve represents the different combinations of income and interest rate at which the money market is in equilibrium or at which a given real money stock equals the quantity of real money balances demanded. (Definition adopted from Beth V. and Robert M. Yarbrough, in The World Economy: Trade and Finance. New York: The Dryden Press, 1988.)

currencies and indirectly affects inflation and real output. The relative importance of these channels in an economy determines the effectiveness of monetary policies.

The impact of changing money market interest rates on other interest rates and on financial and non-financial agents in the various EMU nations will have differing consequences for national income and wealth. The varying transmission channels, substitution and credit indexation practices and liquidity constraints are the reasons for this.

Monetary policy transmission channels will differ not only among the EMU member nations, let alone among the non-EMU EU countries, but also within the same country from one period to another. There are differences in the structure and regulation of the EMU member nations' financial systems, their degree of integration, system of financing and the openness of their economies. Given the variance of financial structures, the common monetary policies will have different and varying degrees of macroeconomic consequences. For example, an interest rate change by the European Central Bank (ECB) may vary in its impact on demand in the EMU countries. If this is the case, unwanted distortions may emerge and the ECB may have a difficult time converging inflation downward through common monetary policies. If this task is difficult in the EMU countries, it is almost impossible in the non-EMU member nations, particularly those that have opted out such as the U.K.[2]

Under the EMU some of the divergence in transmission channels will either fade away or will be eliminated. For example, differences in the exchange rate channels will, to some extent, disappear. This advances the efficiency and effectiveness of common monetary policies. But certain other transmission differences such as the openness of the economies or access to credit will persist for some time following the start of EMU, despite harmonization efforts which require lengthy implementation and adjustment periods. The equalization of indexation practices will probably take even longer because they are linked to national preferences. The establishment of a common view on inflation by the EMU nations, let alone by the non-EMU countries, will also be a drawn out and slow process. The financial markets' patience with and faith in this process will depend on how much credibility first the EMI and then the ECB can obtain. This, to a large extent, depends on the member nations' political commitment to the EMU.

In January 1997, the EMI issued a report on the future monetary policy options available to the countries that plan to adopt the Euro, titled "The Single Monetary Policy in Stage III: Specifications of the Operational Framework."[3] The EMI emphasized that all final policy option decisions will have to be made by the ECB when it begins operations in 1998. Thus it did not make any conclusive statements concerning

---

[2] This section draws on "ECU/Euro: Towards European References?," Ecu No.34, Ecu Activities, Brussels, 1996, p.7.

[3] "The Single Monetary Policy in Stage III: Specifications of the Operational Framework," EMI, Frankfurt am Main, January, 1997.

policy instruments and strategies such as whether to target money supply or inflation rates. It also left unresolved the question of whether the ECB should set minimum bank reserve requirements, as the Bundesbank currently does in Germany. In relation to this, EMI's President Alexander Lamfalussy has categorically denied that in preparing the report the EMI followed the Bundesbank's, or for that matter any other central bank's policy model.

In identifying strategic options, the EMI eliminated three possible alternatives (exchange rate targets, interest rate pegging and nominal income targets). It left it to the ECB to decide between money supply targets, as favored by the Bundesbank, and inflation targets as favored by the Bank of England. In doing so, the EMI emphasized that the differences between the two alternatives have narrowed in recent years.

As far as the use of monetary instruments is concerned, the EMI pointed out that they will be targeted at providing precise signals on monetary policies, basic financing, the absorption of liquidity and the influencing of links between the banks and the ECB. While the key policy instrument will be open market operations, two standing facilities (marginal overnight lending and a deposit facility) will also be established. They will provide a money market ceiling rate and a floor for overnight market rates.

All of the instruments will be operated by the central banks of the EMU member nations. In case of unexpected liquidity problems, the ECB will be able to do fine-tuning. But there will be no rediscount facility. And as mentioned above, it is uncertain whether minimum reserve requirements will be introduced.

As far as exchange rate operations are concerned, the ECB will be expected to act in support of the Euro, using assets transferred to it from the EMU nations' central banks. The details of the exchange rate links with the non-EMU member countries, however, were not discussed. But the report stressed that interventions should be used only in conjunction with fiscal and monetary policies designed to promote convergence and exchange-rate stability between the EMU and non-EMU member nations. The EMI did not address the contentious issue of access to the TARGET system; it left the final decision up to the ECB.

EU FINANCIAL CENTERS: GAINS AND LOSSES

The EMU regulatory frameworks governing central banks, the banking industry, capital mobility, the other financial sectors and their restructuring, will determine the international competitiveness of the EU financial centers. Increased integration and harmonization will make it easier for the EMI to develop a more efficient regulatory framework through which it can tackle the difficulties faced by the financial centers as they move toward the third and final stage of the EMU. It is in this stage that the Euro, the ECB and common monetary policies will be introduced. Not surprisingly, the financial markets are closely following the EMI's activities and proposals for the future so as to be able to swiftly respond. One of the activities that they are closely watching concerns the future role and functions of the ECB. Yet, overall, it is the level of financial integration that will determine the impact of the EMU on the financial centers.

Several studies have tried to measure the level of financial integration in the EU. The first of these was the Commission's 1988 Cecchini Report which estimated that the "Single Market" alone could generate Ecu22 billion (US$27.3 billion) in savings due to increased efficiency and lower costs.[4] Follow-up reports[5] examined the degree of money and capital market integration through a multitude of techniques such as covered and uncovered nominal interest rate parity, real interest rate parity and the Feldstein-Horioka condition[6]. Researchers found that between 1980 and 1989 money and capital market integration increased in several countries with the U.K., Germany, Luxembourg and the Netherlands leading the way. These nations were closely followed by Belgium, France, Denmark, Italy and Ireland. Spain, Portugal and Greece showed the least integration. It should be noted that these studies have not considered the effects of free capital movements and of the duality of banking sector supervision on integration.

Additional studies[7] have concluded that the integration of the EU financial markets is not based on a homogeneous design overseen by a central authority. Nor is such a market envisioned as a mere conglomerate of national financial markets/institutions. In arriving at such conclusions, the authors of the studies evaluated the competitiveness of financial centers, such as London, Paris, Frankfurt, Luxembourg, Zurich, Brussels, Copenhagen, Madrid and Milan. As could be expected, they found that London's "City" is ahead of all the other European financial centers and concluded that the challenge for the smaller centers is to do an effective cost-benefit analysis of the centralization process induced by the EMU, before making decisions about the future.

The studies emphasized that the factors influencing the competitiveness of the EU financial centers include: (i) factor endowments such as the availability of foreign capital, professional expertise and exclusive geographical or time zones; (ii) the environment i.e., the diversity and size of financial markets, openness, innovation and political stability; to a lesser degree, technology, economic growth, low inflation and the strength of the currency; (iii) the deregulation of money and capital markets and the absence of exchange controls; and (iv) taxation and costs. They also found that the level

[4] Cecchini, Paolo. The European Challenge, 1992: The Benefits of a Single Market. European Commission of the EC: Wildwood House Ltd., U.K., 1988.

[5] Lemmen, J.J.G. and S.C.W. Eijffinger. "The Degree of Financial Integration in the European Community," The Economist, V 141, NR 2, 1993, pp.189-213.

[6] The Feldstein-Horioka condition provides an explanation as to why savings and investments are highly correlated in open economies. The relationship exists due to low capital mobility.

[7] Abraham, Jean Paul. "Is Competitiveness a Dangerous Obsession?," in The Competitiveness of Financial Institutions and Centers in Europe, D.E. Fair and R.J. Raymond, eds. Amsterdam, The Netherlands, Kluwer Academic Publishers, 1994.

of private transaction costs and fees are more important than the level of taxes. It should be noted that most of the factors mentioned above can be created by governments over time. Moreover,

> ... competitiveness of an international financial center seems to be significantly sensitive to the impact of size. Not small but big is beautiful. We have traced sensitivity to size in 22 out of 47 criteria, in 12 of these 22 cases it was even high sensitivity... along with some reasoning, European integration is expected to have a significant, positive or negative, effect on 36 out of 47 criteria.[8]

All of the studies concluded that the EU financial markets would benefit from further clarification, tightening and harmonization of rules.

The Euro's Impact on EU Foreign Exchange, Bond, Stock and Derivatives Markets

The strength and impact of the Euro will greatly depend on EMU's membership. In turn, the currency will have an effect on the foreign exchange and capital i.e. bond, stock and derivatives markets. It will be used primarily as a means of eliminating currency risk, introducing common monetary policies, creating an EU-wide money and bond market and harmonizing rules and regulations.

Foreign Exchange Markets

The introduction of the Euro will sharply reduce the volume of foreign exchange transactions in the EU as well as the rest of the world. This will negatively affect revenues of foreign exchange traders. Investors and traders of the EMU member countries will not experience any currency risk when using the Euro to conduct intra-EMU transactions. However, they will still be exposed to such risks when doing business with non-participating EU or non-EU nations. An additional and more serious risk will be the extent of the financial markets' confidence in the Euro as compared to their confidence in the U.S. dollar or Japanese yen.

Bond Markets

The use of common monetary policy instruments may ensure more uniform money markets. Because bond market interest rate differentials are the result of dissimilar credit ratings and the liquidity of the issuers, EU nations of comparable economic strength could have their government bond yields converge due to their adherence to the Maastricht convergence criteria. But corporate and mortgage bond as well as securities markets will continue to be distinct. Eurobond yields will also depend on the ECB's credibility and on its choice of a centralized as opposed to a decentralized

---

[8] Abraham, Jean Paul, "Is Competitiveness a Dangerous Obsession?," 1994.

policy approach. Because liquid and uniform EU bond markets will attract foreign investors, medium-term foreign portfolio investments may increase. However, due to the constantly shifting timetable and uncertainty of EMU membership, for a while, there may be increased volatility in these markets. In markets that capitalize on the imbalances and inefficiencies i.e., currency risks and yield differentials, trading volumes could be substantially reduced. Markets that were previously hampered by the above mentioned imbalances and inefficiencies, could mature at a more rapid pace under the EMU.

Stock Markets

The impact of the Euro on stock markets will be less than that on the bond markets. The blue chip stocks of the EMU nations might become more attractive to investors because not only will currency risk be eliminated or reduced, but prices for international blue chip stocks in the same or related sectors may move in a parallel fashion. However, currency risks will be eliminated only for investors residing in the EMU nations. It is difficult to predict the risk for non-EMU or non-EU investors as this will largely depend on the financial markets' confidence in the Euro as opposed to their confidence in the other major international currencies.

The current organizational structure of the EU stock exchanges is not conducive to the introduction of the Euro. There are over 25 stock and 20 derivative exchanges and many different types of markets and trading systems. The standardization of trading, clearing and settlements systems not only facilitates the introduction of the Euro but also enhances transaction speed. The Euro and common monetary policies thus could be an additional catalyst[9] for convergence and globalization, at least in the money and bond markets.

EU stock exchanges have to provide market participants with decentralized access via networks and with a standardized trading system with uniform rules and monitoring standards. Such arrangements, however, will restrict the expansion of the off-exchange private trading systems, requiring a decentralized and harmonized clearing and settlement system in combination with uniform accounting standards.

From a cost and risk management point of view, the various market segments such as cash and derivatives markets should be integrated as should clearing and settlement systems. However, there is a danger that due to harmonization and uniformity, competition among the European exchanges could become limited, creating oligopolistic conditions. Smaller exchanges could find it too costly to introduce the necessary changes and thus, might be forced to cooperate with the larger exchanges. Yet, there are those who argue that this would force the exchanges to focus more on investor needs and expectations.

---

[9] Competitive forces are the other catalysts.

Derivatives Markets

The impact of the Euro on the derivatives market is likely to be similar to its impact on the bond markets. The bond futures, options and money market rates are likely to converge. The Euro will have the largest impact on the shorter-term financial derivatives. For example, the short-term interest rate contracts will be more vulnerable than the medium and long-term interest rate contracts. However, stock derivatives may be less affected while the derivatives of the new Euro-indices may become more prominent. Nonetheless, the EMU will require considerable modifications of options and futures exchanges and competition between the European exchanges will intensify. This is illustrated by Table 6.1 which shows examples of the impact of the EMU on short-term interest rate contracts and Table 6.2 which illustrates the impact of the EMU on medium and long-term interest rate contracts.

Table 6.1
Impact of EMU On Short-Term Interest Rate Products

Instrument	*Volume**		Expected Effects of EMU
	Futures	Options	
1-month D-mark (Liffe) 1-month D-mark (DTB)	18,044** 49,426***	- -	Both contracts will compete for European dominance of their sector. The possible launch by Matif of a short-term FFr product would intensify the competition.
3-month D-mark (Liffe) 3-month D-mark (DTB) 3-month FFr (Matif)	2,793,448 **** 1,019,047	451,202 - 221,842	Intense competition is expected in this sector, the most liquid area of the short end of the yield curve. It is very likely that there will be room for only one successful contract.
3-month eurolira (Liffe)	727,392	134,390	Likely to disappear if and when Italy joins EMU.
3-month Ecu (Liffe)	37,597	-	Likely to disappear as soon as 3-month D-mark or FFr becomes the benchmark for euro 3-month rates.
3-month sterling (Liffe)	1,541,634	260,118	Likely to disappear or be merged with Liffe's 3-month D-Mark if this becomes the European benchmark. (Subject to the UK joining EMU.)
3-month SwissFr (Liffe) 3-month euroyen (Liffe)	328,030 20,404	2,876 972	Unaffected by EMU.

* = Number of contract traded in November 1996.
** = Contract opened on November 21, 1996.
*** = Contract opened in mid-November 1996.
**** = Will start trading in early 1997.
Source: "Exchanges square up for a fight." Financial Times, December 17, 1996, p.2.

Table 6.2
Impact of EMU on Medium and Long-Term Bond Contracts

Instrument	*Volume** Futures	Options	Expected Effects of EMU
German LT bund (Liffe)	3,285,285	650,104	Will compete with DTB's bund contract and Matif's notional and Ecu for European dominance.
German LT bund (DTB)	1,561,739	29,697	Will compete with Liffe's bund and Matif's notional and Ecu.
German Bobl (DTB)	1,658,763	96,991	Set to become the European benchmark future on medium-term (3-5 year) bonds, unless Matif and Liffe come up with similar products.
Italian BTP (Liffe)	1,403,137	286,594	Likely to suffer fall in liquidity if and when Italy joins EMU.
Long gilt (Liffe)	1,770,742	183,006	Will compete with bund and notional for European dominance if and when the UK joins EMU.
Japanese bonds (Liffe)	94,610	-	Unaffected by EMU.
French notional (Matif) Ecu long bonds	2,500,162 40,502	650,291 -	Both of Matif's bond products will compete with Liffe's bund and DTB's bund. Matif has yet to decide whether to merge them into a single product after EMU.

* = Number of contracts traded in November 1996.
Source: "Exchanges square up for a fight." Financial Times, December 17, 1996, p.2.

The Euro's Impact on Financial Market Participants

The Euro will affect financial market participants in various ways. In the case of issuers, increased liquidity due to the consolidation of securities markets will decrease the cost of raising capital; the harmonization of disclosure standards will decrease the costs of on-time and ongoing disclosure; the increased number of potential investors will diversify and stabilize the investor base, at least regionally; and issuers will compete more fiercely for investment capital.

Investors may experience lower cross-border transaction costs which will result in more efficient capital allocation. Moreover, there could be increased demand for information and thus, an increased need for intermediation. For intermediary agents the introduction of the Euro could mean lower market access costs due to market concentration accompanied by increased competition.[10]

---

[10] This section draws on "ECU/Euro: Towards European References?," Ecu No.34, Ecu Activities, Brussels, 1996, p.40.

Unanswered Euro Questions

Although many large EU banks and businesses claim that they are preparing for the introduction of the Euro, they do not yet fully understand the technological and organizational issues involved. Businesses, labor unions and financial houses are complaining that the Euro timetable and legal provisions are vague and do not provide adequate information concerning the necessary preparations. The findings of a number of studies discussed on the following pages confirm the legitimacy of these views.

The Cost of Transition to Governments

The replacement of national currencies by the Euro will be expensive. For example, Germany alone has 2.5 billion notes in circulation and almost the same in storage. There are over 12 billion banknotes and 70 billion coins (weighing 300,000 tons) circulating in all of the EU nations.

Countries with strong currencies, such as Germany, may find public debt financing in the Euro more expensive than in the Deutsche mark. However, nations like Spain and Portugal will in all probability find the financing of such debt with the Euro less costly than in their national currencies. Germany may also experience lower domestic investments in its Euro denominated public debt whereas it is likely that Spain and Portugal will obtain increased investments in such debt due to the elimination of exchange rate risks.

The Cost of Transition to Central Banks[11]

National central bank income will also be affected. In Stage III of the EMU central bank profits will be distributed according to Articles 32 and 33 of the ECB Statue in the Maastricht Treaty. The central banks will be able to keep income from the ESCB's monetary policy operations according to a set of specific rules. However, net profits will be assigned in line with share-ownership in proportion to the paid up shares in the ECB. The share-ownership proportions will be decided on the basis of the equal weighting of a nation's share in the common EMU GDP and total EMU population. This is the same system that was used to allocate the EMI's shares, except that it was the common EU GDP and the total EU population share of individual nations that were used as the weighting factors.

Most of the central banks' income is generated through seigniorage, as discussed in Chapter III. In 1996, the 15 EU central banks earned between US$ 20-25 billion, primarily from seigniorage but also through the performance of other

---

[11] This section is based on, "The Winners and Losers from EMU", Central Banking, Vol. VII, no. 2, London: Central Banking Publications Ltd., Autumn 1996.

operations such as investing the minimum reserve requirements that commercial banks must deposit with the central banks.

While there is uncertainty as to the exact distribution of net central banking profits/losses once the ECB is established, a recently published study offers insight into the possible outcomes. Table 6.3 provides a summary of the study's conclusions.

Table 6.3
The Central Bank Winners and Losers from EMU

Central Bank	Shareholding in EMI, (in Ecu)	% of EMI shareholdings	Actual 1995 EU central bank profits, (in dollars, million)	1995 EU central bank profits if distributed by EMI shareholdings (in dollars, million)	Net gain or loss if 1995 profits distributed by EMI shareholdings, (in dollar, million)*
France	104,644,800	17	649	4,377	3,728
Italy	97,565,912	15.85	2,266	4,081	1,815
U.K.	94,488,252	15.35	2,313	3,952	1,639
Portugal	11,387,902	1.85	5	476	471
Greece	12,311,159	2	155	515	360
Finland	10,160,382	1.65	223	425	202
Luxembourg	923,360	0.15	6	39	33
Ireland	4,924,381	0.8	318	206	-112
Belgium	17,235,643	2.8	845	721	-124
Netherlands	26,161,252	4.25	1,284	1,094	-190
Austria	14,162,957	2.3	1,206	592	-614
Denmark	10,464,542	1.7	1,069	438	-631
Spain	54,476,907	8.85	3,472	2,279	-1,193
Germany	138,808,404	22.55	8,425	5,806	-2,619
Sweden	17,857,642	2.9	3,511	747	-2,764
Total	**615,573,495**	**100**	**25,747**	**25747**	**0**

* = Assuming all EU members participate in EMU and that EMI shareholdings are the same as ECB shareholdings. Both use the same key, 50% of shares reflecting share of EU GDP, 50% reflecting share of EU population (see Article 29, ESCB Protocol, Maastricht Treaty, 1992).

Note: All figures are from the profit and loss account in the 1995 central bank annual report, except for Spain which is the 1994 annual report, translated into dollars at the market exchange rate on the reporting date as given in International Financial Statistics.

Source : "The Winners and Losers from EMU," Central Banking, Vol. VII, no. 2, London: Central Banking Publications Ltd., Autumn 1996, p.7.

As can be seen in Table 6.3 the central banks of France, Italy, the U.K. (assuming that it joins the EMU), Portugal and Greece will probably obtain net profits under the new ECB system while those of Austria, Denmark, Spain, Germany and Sweden will incur net losses. This will undoubtedly raise question about the equity of the new central banking system.

The Cost of Transition to Banks

A 1995 study conducted by the European Banking Federation on the impact and cost of transition to the Euro found that the costs to the EU banking system might amount to Ecu 8-10 billion (US$10.1-12.6 billion), or approximately 2 percent of the annual operating expenses incurred over a period of three to four years. The study assumed that the Euro will be introduced quickly (the "Big Bang" approach). But this will not the case, thus it is very likely that the phased introduction of the Euro will be considerably more expensive.

Selected EU banks have also estimated the expenses of introducing the Euro. According to Barclays Bank it will cost US$200 million. The Deutsche Bank identified 3,500 separate steps which it will have to take to adjust its operations, costing US$175 million. The Bayerische Vereinsbank plans to spend US$98 million, the ING Group US$117 million, Postipankki US$32.6 million and the Creditanstalt US$93.5 million on the transition process. Private research groups consider these amounts to be very conservative and predict that the actual costs will be twice as high. Some banks have already revised their estimates. For example, both Barclays Bank and the Deutsche Bank concluded that their previous estimates were widely off the mark and that the cost of just revamping the information technology infrastructures could reach US$312 million.

Revenue losses are also beginning to loom larger than originally predicted. The EMU will eliminate foreign exchange trading in the member nations' currencies which will result in a large income loss to EU banks. It will also decrease treasury income and cut earnings from cross-boarder payments generated through correspondent banking relationships.

The financial sectors are concerned about a variety of problems involved in the transition process because they may not be able to resolve them. On the public side, domestic financial institutions are concerned about policies governing, for example, debt conversion. The EMU requires all new government debt to be issued in the Euro beginning January 1, 1999. However, the conversion of existing debt between 1999 and 2002 is under the jurisdiction of individual nations. The German government has not yet decided what to do with its stock of outstanding government bonds which expire after 1999 while the French have already announced that they will convert theirs to Euros during the first year of the EMU. The Germans have hesitated to do an early conversion because they not only fear that Euro denominated debt could be more expensive to service but are also concerned that German investors could shun such debt when given a choice of Deutsche mark, Swiss franc or even US dollar denominated debt. Consequently, German banks are pressuring their government to follow the French lead and convert in 1999. They fear that if Paris creates a pool of liquidity in the Euro before Frankfurt, this could give the French financial markets a competitive edge. EU financial houses and companies are also concerned about the possibility that, unless their governments speed up conversion preparations, they may be prevented from filing accounts and paying taxes in the Euro. If governments are not ready to accept corporate payments in the single currency by 1999, this could severely retard the adoption of the Euro by the corporate sector at the start of EMU, distorting competition. Many of the large MNCs have already indicated that they want to switch to Euro-based accounting by 1999.

On the private side, domestic financial institutions are concerned about the ability of software companies to speedily create programs that include dual currency and accounting systems. Non-financial institutions will also face the challenge of revamping their information systems. The most immediate problems are faced by the wholesale banking sector which will start using the Euro by January 1, 1999. Technical details such as resizing cash (Automated Teller Machines) and tills for the new Euro notes, reprinting brochures and the printing of separate checkbooks for the Euro accounts as well as the training of staffs, are yet to be addressed.

Most of the studies concerning the Euro's impact on banks have concluded that the major questions are related to the Euro's payment system and to the costs of sustaining the same. The other areas of concern pertain to securities quotations, fixed income trading, valuation methods, arbitrage models and the retraining of sales staffs.

A June 1996 survey[12] of 205 European banks showed that 54 percent have yet to develop a strategy to tackle the transition period problems and that only 15 percent had allocated a budget to pay for the necessary changes. A more comprehensive report by the Banking Foundation of the European Union surveying more than 100 banks in 14 countries concluded that adopting the Euro will be an "unprecedented challenge" to the banking industry. The Foundation also estimated the cost of transition to the Euro by products and functions as a percentage of total costs. Table 6.4 provides a summary overview of the results of the survey as they pertain to this issue.

---

[12] Survey conducted by Cap Gemini Sogeti, a Paris-based computer services and consulting group as reported in "Anxiety Over EMU Starts to Creep In," Financial Times, December 3, 1996.

Table 6.4
Cost of Transition to the Single Currency by Product and Functions
(% of total cost [Ecu 8-10 billion])

Function	Product									
	Notes and Coin	Automatic Teller Machine	Cards and Services	Payment Systems	Foreign Exchange Dealing & Treasury Management	Loans	Deposits	Capital Markets	Other	Total Cost
Information Technology	4%	3%	7%	15%	6%	5%	4%	5%	5%	54%
Marketing & PR	1%	1%	1%	6%	1%	2%	2%	0%	1%	15%
Legal	0%	0%	0%	1%	1%	0%	0%	1%	1%	4%
Audit and Security	2%	0%	0%	0%	0%	0%	0%	1%	0%	3%
Accounting & Management	0%	0%	0%	1%	1%	0%	1%	0%	0%	3%
Staff training	1%	1%	1%	2%	1%	1%	1%	1%	1%	10%
Stationery	1%	0%	0%	2%	0%	1%	2%	0%	0%	6%
External Reporting	0%	0%	0%	0%	0%	0%	0%	0%	0%	0%
Other	3%	1%	0%	0%	0%	1%	0%	0%	0%	5%
Total Cost	**12%**	**6%**	**9%**	**27%**	**10%**	**10%**	**10%**	**8%**	**8%**	**100%**

Source: "Counting the Cost of EMU," Balance Sheet, Vol.5, no.3, Autumn 1996, p.13.

The Cost of Transition to Businesses

A 1996 EU-wide study by the KPMG Management Consulting company concerning the transition readiness of 300 companies found that most have not yet estimated the costs of switching to the Euro. Moreover, only 1 in 12 have allocated funds to pay for the required changes.

A study conducted by the French National Credit Council in 1996 and jointly sponsored by the French Finance Ministry and the Banque de France provides a detailed account of the problems that the Euro timetable will create for EU companies and their customers. Based on extensive interviews with the executives of 20 large French firms and the employers' group the Patronat, the study found that the executives are most concerned about the three-year transition period (1999-2002) during which the Euro will co-exist with national currencies on a non-cash basis. They unanimously criticize the dual currency/accounting transition system and point out that it could create problems because the French government plans to switch the financial sector to the Euro in 1999 while the public sector and retailers will continue using francs until 2002. Customers will pay in francs while suppliers expect Euro payments. Large export companies that plan to use the Euro as soon as possible will also have to continue paying their employees in francs.

Other problems cited by the executives relate to government requirements concerning the filing of accounts and the paying of taxes in the Euro prior to 2002. The revaluation of long-term assets and liabilities denominated in foreign currencies is also viewed as a major problem because it could result in companies facing unexpected tax bills caused by exchange rate gains. Respondents emphasized that large companies and financial houses will eventually be able to cope with the dual currency/accounting system; it will be the small business/financial firms that will be damaged by the transition. A survey of more than 800 companies in North Rhein-Westphalia in Germany, resulted in similar findings.

Customers and small businesses are concerned about who will determine the Euro conversion rates of the EU and non-EU currencies; how the Euro will affect taxes and accounting systems; whether banks will accept Euro checks and charge for the use of the Euro; and how retailers and customers might cope with the changeover on January 1, 2002 - one of the busiest shopping days of the year in some countries. It is likely that the closer a business is to the customers, the more problems it will face adopting the Euro.

Legal Implications of the Euro

The legal arrangements involved in switching to the Euro are still in the planning stage. They involve the Euro's conversion rates, its impact on contracts, the enforcement methods used to promote its use and the potential implications of the "change in circumstances" legal clauses. The introduction of the Euro could be used as an excuse to ignore contractual obligations.

In addressing these matters, the EU Commission divided the relevant legal issues into two categories. Laws that apply to all EU nations will be introduced under the Maastricht Treaty's Article 235 while laws that apply to EMU countries only, will be introduced under Article 109l(4). Examples of laws that will be introduced under Article 235 and that will facilitate the transition from national currencies to the Euro, include: "(i) provisions that the Ecu will be replaced by the Euro at a rate of one to one, and with a "presumption" that this shall apply to all Ecu; (ii) the pledge that the introduction of the Euro "shall not have the effect of altering any term of a legal instrument...nor giving a party the right unilaterally to alter or terminate a legal instrument"; and (iii) the stipulation that conversion rates will be rounded "to six significant figures" so as to simplify computer system specifications.

The reactions of non-EU financial markets as, for example, those of New York, to the planned laws are not yet known. These markets could be affected by the legal proposals which fall under Article 109l(4), and are applied to EMU members only. They include: "(i) the provision that any debt between 1999 and 2002 may be paid "by the debtor either in Euro or in the national currency unit"; (ii) the pledge that member states can switch government bonds and financial markets to Euros; and (iii) confirmation that notes and coins in national currencies will remain legal tender until 2002. It should be noted that when these proposals come up for a decision, only EMU member nations will be allowed to vote.[13]

THE "CITY" OF LONDON AND THE EMU

The British Bankers' Association, the London Investment Banking Association and the Association of Payment Clearing Services published a joint report in September 1996, addressing the contentious question of whether London might loose its standing as the EU's foremost financial center if the U.K. chooses not to participate in the EMU. The report concluded that "... overall, if the U.K. participates in EMU, the "City"[14] should consolidate its position as Europe's leading financial center. In the event of non-participation, London's strong position should still endure."[15] The report further stated that the introduction of the Euro will dramatically increase competition in the bond and equity markets, but the "City" will be able to meet the challenges. But if the U.K. joins the EMU, this could seriously affect the "City's" money markets due to the close linkage between these markets and the ECB's monetary policy.

---

[13] "Brussels' Legal Proposals "Step in the Right Direction."" Financial Times, October 17, 1996.

[14] London's financial district is known as the "City".

[15] "EMU Should Improve London Financial Role." Financial Times, September 24, 1996.

At the same time, the report downplayed the possibility of discrimination against the banks of non-EMU member EU nations.[16] To deal with the potential problems, the U.K. banks began to prepare for the EMU in 1996, "…even if only the wholesale markets are likely to be directly effected."[17] Yet, the "City" still faces a precarious future as it struggles to determine how to position itself. To date, the U.K. government has not taken a definite stand on the EMU and on such issues as EU-wide financial services regulations and the Social Charter[18].

The Bank of England undertook a series of studies to assess the impact of economic and monetary integration on the "City." One of these reports titled "Practical Issues Arising from the Introduction of the Euro", was released in September 1996. It refrained from making any strong statements about the future of the "City" but its authors pointed out that the U.K. will be ready for the EMU in 1999, regardless of whether it joins or not. "Planning to develop the financial infrastructure is now well in hand to ensure that the Euro may be used in the U.K. at the wholesale level, in the payments system and across markets, by the beginning of 1999." [19]

The Bank of England, for obvious reasons, is reluctant to become involved in the political debate over EMU membership. Thus, it used the report to assure the "City" that it is engaged in the necessary preparations for the EMU and that it will safeguard British banks against discrimination if the U.K. does not join. But this has not satisfied the financial community. Its members expect a more detailed and concrete plan of action, including options. They are concerned about French and German intentions to limit the access of non-EMU nations to TARGET, the proposed European cross-boarder payment system which provides for the transfer of large sums of Euros among central banks. The U.K., just like Denmark, would like to have unlimited access to intra-day credit.

The sections of the report that refer to the preparations for the EMU are confusing. However, in fairness to the Bank, it needs to be pointed out that the issues are complicated as the "City's" financial markets are fragmented. For example, while the London International Financial Futures & Options Exchange has already started planning for the Euro the London Stock Exchange has begun to examine the legal implications of Euro listings only in 1996. Lloyd's of London has yet to consider the possibility of pricing its products in the Euro.

---

[16] For example, "even if the U.K. access to TARGET (the proposed cross-boarder payment system which would permit transfers of large sums of Euros among central banks) is restrained, there are other avenues available for achieving interbank settlement." Tim Sweeney, Director-General of the British Bankers' Association, September 23, 1996.

[17] Tim Sweeney, Director-General of the British Bankers' Association, September 23, 1996.

[18] For more details see the section on "The U.K. Dilemma" in this chapter.

[19] "Practical Issues Arising from the Introduction of the Euro." U.K.: Bank of England, September 1996.

Thus, for all practical purposes, the Bank of England's report is a checklist of issues that need to be considered such as: (i) the ability of the U.K. payments system to absorb Euros and to link up with the proposed TARGET; (ii) the capability of CHAPS (the U.K. sterling payments system) to support a parallel Euro payment system regardless of whether the U.K. joins the EMU; (iii) the establishment of a coordinating committee to harmonize financial market conventions such as bank holidays and the gilt market with other EU, U.S. and Japanese financial markets; (iv) legal, tax and accounting implications of the EMU in general and of the Euro in particular; (v) plans to issue joint recommendations with the Confederation of British Industry to increase the awareness of non-"City" financial and business institutions concerning the impact of the Euro. The U.K. financial community is right; while these are important concerns, the report does not provide any strategic guidance on how to deal with them.

In a follow-up speech to the report, Ian Plenderleith, an executive director of the Bank of England, explained why the "City" would retain its standing as the premier international financial market even if the U.K. opted out of the EMU. He emphasized that its business came from all over the world and not just from Europe. Thus, the global role of London as a financial center is not threatened. Moreover, even if the U.K. does not adopt the Euro, this would not divert business from the "City" but rather generate more business as it "is the international interface for the European zone."[20]

Preparations for the EMU were also discussed in reports published in the other EU countries. In its 1993 Annual Report the Bundesbank, for example, called for the harmonization of not only central banking operations and policies but also of the EU members' "financial cultures." In making this argument, the Bundesbank referred to the differences between Germany and the U.K. It emphasized that:

> An effort should be made to achieve the maximum harmonization of the underlying conditions in the financial sector - with the aim of promoting a convergence of the "financial culture" in Europe. From the point of view of monetary policy, it would be useful to gradually eliminate existing differences in the financial structures of EMS members in the wake of the progressive integration of the European financial markets. One outstanding example of such persisting differences is the prevalence in the U.K. of floating-rate loans as opposed to the preference in Germany for longer-term locked-in interest rates. For this reason changes in short-term interest rates that are subject to central bank influence have a comparatively large impact on disposable incomes in the U.K.

---

[20] "Central Bank Says London's Standing Will Survive." Financial Times, November 20, 1996, p.12.

> where households moreover have a relatively high level of indebtedness; this may well have implications for the development of the central bank's set of instruments, as well demonstrated by the events of the EMS crisis in 1992. Clearly, this could give rise to problems for monetary policy cooperation in the EMS and for the later single monetary policy.[21]

The Bundesbank's arguments are sound. But while there is some general variance among the continental EU financial sectors, there is a high degree of sector-specific variance between the U.K. and the other EU nations in the household financial sector, especially with respect to the use of mortgages.[22] In the U.K. approximately 80 percent of mortgages and consumer credit is issued at variable interest rates.[23] There is, however, less variance between the U.K. corporate sector and the corporate sectors of the other EU nations. For example, 40 percent[24] of U.K. corporate debt is at fixed interest rates; this is comparable to the 40 percent French and 50 percent German ratios.[25]

The high degree of mortgage interest rate variability which could increase in times of economic crisis has been cited as one of the reasons for the U.K.'s reluctance to join the EMU. Monetary tightening by the ECB would have a more severe impact in the U.K. than in the other EMU member nations. The introduction of fixed mortgage interest rates could alleviate this problem.[26]

Some differences in financial cultures are structural and deep-rooted, thus they will persist even after the introduction of the Euro. A case in point is the preference for securitization over bank loans as a means of corporate financing. In Germany, such financing is done mostly through bank loans and bonds rather than through securitization. In contrast, the U.K. uses equity financing exclusively, thus it has one of the lowest interest to corporate income ratios of all EU nations.

The U.K.'s household sector, however, carries a high interest rate burden. Thus, while the citizens of the other EU nations may find the "City's" flexibility and diversity appealing, U.K. mortgage owners would prefer the fixed interest rates

---

[21] Deutsche Bundesbank Annual Report, 1993, p.92.

[22] Miles, David. "Fixed and Floating-rate Finance in the UK and Abroad," Bank of England Quarterly Bulletin, Vol.34, February 1, 1994.

[23] In 1990, U.K. household interest payments as a proportion of household income (10.9 percent) were almost three times as high as the EU average. This fell to 6.5 percent in 1994. The pound sterling's departure from the EMS in 1992 was in part due to the pressure of high mortgage interest rates following the increase in the U.K. bank base rate to 15 percent in order to keep the pound within the ERM's +/-6 percent currency band.

[24] Approximately 35 percent is attributed to fixed rate bonds, the remaining percentage to fixed rate bank loans.

[25] The small to medium-sized EU companies must rely on bank loans, mostly at variable interest rates as it is difficult for them to issue bonds.

[26] Johnson, Christopher. <u>In with the Euro, out with the Pound</u>, London: Penguim Books, 1996.

offered on the continent, assuming that they would be lower. In other words, the differences in financial cultures are not a valid excuse for the U.K. to opt out of the EMU as cross-border competition would expand financial product choices and result in lower interest rates for both the corporate and household sectors.

According to the U.K. government, the ECB's common monetary policies will have a different effect on the various EMU nations. It argues that

> the way in which a given change in European interest rates will affect various countries is likely to differ greatly. So even if inflationary pressures were the same throughout the currency area before a change in monetary policy they could not be [the same] after.[27]

To alleviate this problem, EU financial markets should be standardized and harmonized. Or, alternatively, the central banks of EMU member nations should have some discretion in formulating common monetary policies on the basis of domestic circumstances. This would not only make such policies politically, economically and socially more acceptable but would also have the added benefit of not dampening competition.

But this would require EMU member nations to coordinate fiscal policies with the ECB's monetary policies so as to achieve a political and economic balance between growth and inflation. The ECB can pursue low interest rates only if EMU member nations keep a tight reign on fiscal policies, hence the requirements of the Maastricht Treaty fiscal convergence criteria. If the EMU nations manage to constrain their fiscal policies, the Euro may boost European economic growth by lowering interest rates and the ECB could introduce more flexible common monetary policies providing a favorable climate for investments. But if the EMU nations apply loose fiscal policies, the ECB will be forced to raise interest rates to restrain inflation thus curtailing economic growth. If the ECB uses short-term variable interest rates, the corporate and household sectors could shift toward long-term fixed interest rates. This would minimize harm to the real economy.

The "City" and the Euro

Financial and business services account for 22 percent of the U.K.'s GDP and 25 percent of its national income. They provide approximately 800,000 jobs. This is primarily the result of the financial deregulation of the 1980s that for years has promoted growth but by now has run its course. Therefore, to sustain its comparative advantage, the "City" plans to exploit the benefits of the "Single Market" by reducing

[27] Miles, David. "A Single European Currency: Options for the UK," London: Merrill Lynch Global Fixed Income Research, March 1, 1995.

bank lending rates through more cross-border financial service competition. The introduction of the Euro could enhance such competition because the differences in national regulations and the multiplicity of national currency and payments systems would be reduced. In addition, there would probably be "more competition [and], more consolidation."[28] Interest rates and lending risks could also be reduced.

The introduction of the Euro will have a momentous impact on the "City" regardless of the U.K.'s EMU status. London has a comparative advantage in financial services and generates more investment related income than the financial markets of the other EU nations. Thus, it is in a good position to assume a leading role once the Euro is introduced. The opportunities would be even greater if the U.K. joins the EMU. Although adopting the Euro and giving up the pound sterling could lead to losses in the foreign exchange and related derivative operations, such losses could be compensated for by new Euro and derivatives related activities encompassing all of the EMU financial centers. But if the U.K. "opt-out" endures, the "City" could lose the opportunity of establishing a dominant role in the Euro markets and will become an "offshore" player,[29] capturing only a limited market share. While London is without doubt the leading financial center in the EU, to date it has not managed to displace the well-protected domestic financial markets as, for example, Frankfurt and Paris. The introduction of the Euro could provide an opportunity to do so, particularly if the U.K. joins the EMU.

Opponents of U.K. participation in the EMU have equally strong arguments. They see no benefits arising from the Euro or, to put it differently, they do not believe that the EMU could enhance the "City's" role as a major financial center. They also claim that most of the potential EMU benefits could be obtained through the "Single Market" alone and that the introduction of the new single currency that is untested against the U.S. dollar and the Japanese yen could be risky. Some argue that the changeover to the Euro could bring additional costs and emphasize that the "City" has not yet shed the financial burdens of restructuring under the 1986 Financial Services Act. The Brussels capital adequacy rules, for example, hurt the U.K. banks but help German universal banks which conduct their banking and securities businesses from a single capital base.

The effort of harmonizing "financial cultures" in line with the "Single Market" requirements is well worth the cost. However, the gains generated by the introduction of the Euro and the common monetary policies are rather dubious. The harmonization of money markets and of bank reserve systems, the discarding of unique "City" features such as the "discount houses" and the loss of the Bank of England's monopoly over money market operations could have costly consequences.

---

[28] Professor John Kay, London Business School: as stated in "ECU/Euro: Towards European References?," 1996, p.44.

[29] Part of the Euro-related financial and investment business may be shifted to the financial markets of the EMU member nations.

The impact of the Euro on the "City" will vary according to market segments. The foreign exchange market will be most negatively affected. Currently, London's "City" leads the world in foreign exchange transactions, having captured approximately 30 percent of global transactions in 1995. In comparison, during the same year, New York obtained a 16 percent, Tokyo 10 percent, Singapore 7 percent, Hong Kong and Zurich 6 percent each, Frankfurt 5 percent and Paris 4 percent market shares. Thus, if the U.K. decides not to adopt the Euro to replace the pound sterling, it could lessen the negative impact of this by continuing to obtain substantial foreign exchange trading revenues.

Equity markets, even if they use the Euro, will not be much affected. They will probably continue to do business under national laws until corporate accounting systems and regulations can be harmonized. Currently, the London Stock Exchange (LSE) captures 64 percent of all cross-border transactions. If the U.K. adopts the Euro, such transactions could increase and, thus, the LSE could become a dominant player in the Euro-based stock markets.

In the end, the "City" must weigh the benefits of the common EU financial market against the benefits generated by its traditional global competitive advantages, i.e. offshore banking, self-regulation, the English language, time zones that straddle New York and Tokyo, and financial specialization and breadth.

THE EMU AND THE GLOBAL FINANCIAL MARKETS

Past integration projects such as the 1951 European Coal and Steel Community (ECSC) or the 1992 EU "Single Market" were implemented regardless of how the financial markets were likely to react to them. However, this time their responses cannot be ignored. The size and the activities of the financial markets are critical to the EMU and the Euro[30].

To date, the financial markets have adopted a "wait-and-see" stance. But as the start of the EMU and the introduction of the Euro nears, traders and investors are becoming nervous. EU governments, particularly those of France and Germany, have gone to extraordinary lengths to convince the financial markets of their commitment to the EMU and the Euro. It seems that if financial markets required it, they might even consider a modification of the Maastricht Treaty.

The markets are particularly concerned about the likelihood of obtaining the necessary "critical mass" at the start i.e. a large enough number of “core” EMU nations. If they do not believe that such a “mass” has been achieved, alternative plans

---

[30] The daily turnover of the global foreign exchange and capital markets is over US$1 trillion and US$7 trillion, respectively.

may have to be implemented. Softening the convergence criteria to admit more members would be too risky. But non-qualifying nations could be allowed to become associate members, requiring such nations to peg their currencies to the Euro and to adhere to the ECB's monetary policies.

Most EMU related research is focused on the impact of integration on the EU financial markets. However, the EMU will also affect global macro-economic policy coordination, the financial markets and international competitiveness.

The EMU, G-7 and G-10 Macro-Economic Policy Coordination

Global financial markets are so large and so integrated that it is not possible to separate the impact of a nation's interactions with such markets from the effects of its interactions with other countries. Because the G-7 and G-10[31] nations have the world's largest economies, their policies result in spill-overs which call for macro-economic policy coordination. The benefits of such coordination are substantial. The EU Commission, for example, estimated that the G-7 nations have already obtained coordination induced welfare gains of 0.5 to 1.5 percent[32] of their GDP.

Coordination is critical in today's financial markets that are characterized by a total daily foreign exchange and capital market turnover of over US$8 trillion. To maintain stability under such circumstances, central bank activities, particularly those of the G-3 (the U.S., Japan and the EU) must be coordinated. But to date, the broader yet important G-7 mechanism is used only for exchange rate crisis management and the promotion of trade-related financial measures. Moreover, current global monetary policy coordination is primarily dominated by either U.S.-Japan trade problems or the EU's exchange rate system, the original ERM. It is only recently that the G-7 have tried to address long-term issues such as fiscal policies. In doing so, the different economic policy concerns of the seven economic and trade ministers have to be met, not to mention the expectations of the seven heads of state/government who are always looking forward to the next election.

The EU's economic and monetary integration will pose new challenges to the G-7 and G-10 policy coordination process. The nature of the meetings will change. There will be more symmetry as the number of participants[33] will be reduced through the integration of the EMU economies which will have common monetary policies, a single currency, the Euro, and will maintain a high level of fiscal policy

---

[31] The G-7 includes the United States, Japan, Canada, Germany, France, Italy and the U.K. The G-10, in addition, includes Belgium, Sweden and the Netherlands.

[32] "One Market, One Money : An Evolution of the Potential Benefits and Costs of Forming an Economic and Monetary Union," European Economy, No.44, Commission of the European Communities Directorate-General for Economic and Financial Affairs, October 1990, p.190.

[33] The EU (particularly EMU participants) will strive to speak with one voice, especially on monetary issues. Thus not all of the national representatives will have to be present at the meetings.

coordination.[34] The EU as a whole will also capture the largest share of global trade and financial flows, although intra-EU trade and transactions represent a substantial part of these flows. As a result, the EU's influence on the G-7 and G-10 decision-making process may increase, particularly if the Euro will be non-inflationary.

But the EMU will have a number of characteristics that could hamper its role in the global monetary policy coordination process. The ECB will pursue price stability and the Maastricht Treaty convergence criteria will place limitations on the EMU nations' ability to act flexibly in G-7 and G-10 negotiations. The ECB's macroeconomic coordination processes with non-EMU or "opt-out" nations may raise additional complications. Moreover, the ECB will have to consider the negative effects of its common policies on EU member countries with derogations. This could pose a moral hazard for the ECB.

The EU Commission believes that the "EMU could finally be a decisive building block for a more stable multi-polar monetary regime."[35] The Commission also argues that the adoption of common monetary policies could strengthen the EU's role in the global economy which may help develop and facilitate G-7 monetary coordination. Yet, while the EMU is going to increase the EU's role in international policy coordination, its influence will depend on the extent to which fiscal and monetary policies can be harmonized, as the outlook for policy coordination among the EMU and non-EMU member nations is uncertain. The Maastricht Treaty calls for a unified EU monetary and exchange rate representation in international negotiations. But this is not possible unless common policies can be developed and sustained. A case in point are the calls for non-EMU member currencies to fluctuate in wider ERM bands that are already creating a discord. Thus, even if member nations agree on EMU monetary policies, negotiation positions may still be distorted by the non-member countries.

To further complicate matters, the Maastricht Treaty does not contain explicit rules on how the EU should be represented in the international macroeconomic policy coordination meetings. The Treaty provides only general guidelines concerning exchange rate policy decision-making processes. For example, "the EU [ECOFIN] Council [of Ministers] may, acting unanimously on a recommendation from the ECB or from the EU Commission, and after consulting the ECB in an endeavor to reach a consensus consistent with the objective of price stability, after consulting the European Parliament,...conclude formal agreements...for the ECU [Euro] in relation to non-Community currencies."[36] The Treaty does, however, contain a well defined process for managing the Euro and for setting its exchange rates against third country currencies.

---

[34] Due to the Maastricht Treaty convergence criteria surveillance system.
[35] "One Market, One Money," 1990, p.178.
[36] Article 109.1, Maastricht Treaty, 1992.

It is the ECOFIN Council that represents the EU in international exchange rate negotiations. To this end, the Council must obtain a consensus on negotiation guidelines from the European Parliament, the ECB and its own members. Except for exchange rate policies, which require unanimous decisions, the ECOFIN uses a qualified majority decision-making process to coordinate macroeconomic policy positions.

The section of the Maastricht Treaty that deals with the management of exchange rate policies and the establishment of international representation does not contain clear rules applicable to nations with derogations or opt-out status. While the ECOFIN Council sets the general exchange rate policy guidelines,[37] it is left unclear who represents the EU in such matters. It is also not clear which EU institution decides whether a policy is compatible with the ECB's price stability objective, although the Bank must be consulted in formulating policy decisions.[38]

To eventually carry out international exchange rate negotiations on behalf of the EU in general and the EMU member nations in particular, the ECOFIN Council had to obtain the concurrence of both the EMU and non-EMU EU nations concerning an intra-EU exchange rate system similar to the original ERM. following extensive negotiations an agreement was reached in December 1996 to establish an "ERM II"[39] with the Euro as its anchor currency to which non-EMU EU members can peg their currencies so as to become part of the Euro's zone of stability. Membership in the "ERM II" is not mandatory, thus EMU nations will also have to reach an agreement with non-EMU nations with derogations and opt-out arrangements when setting policies, because the EU's international representation requires unanimity.

The ECOFIN Council can effectively negotiate with the G-7 and G-10 only on the basis of coordinated Euro exchange rate policies. While the EMU nations can easily negotiate an agreement with non-member nations waiting to qualify for the EMU, they may find reaching such an understanding with EMU opt-out nations such as the U.K far more difficult.

Despite the envisioned high level of EU cooperation in fiscal and monetary policy matters at the start of Stage III, the effectiveness of international policy coordination within the G-7 and G-10 is uncertain. EMU enthusiasts argue[40] that the EU will be more actively involved in international macroeconomic policy coordination, particularly with regard to exchange rate management and that this will minimize exchange rate volatility. They claim that in the aftermath of Stage III, the

[37] Article 109.2, Maastricht Treaty, 1992.

[38] Article 109.3 of the Maastricht Treaty states that "the [ECOFIN] Council, acting by a qualified majority on a recommendation from the Commission and after consulting the ECB, shall decide the arrangements for the negotiation and for the conclusion of such agreements."

[39] Discussed in detail later in the chapter.

[40] See, for example, "International Currency Competition and the Future Role of the Single European Currency," The ECU Institute, London: Kluwer Law International, 1995.

EU's international policies and negotiation approaches will be more symmetrical. But this could generate conflicts between the EMU member nations and the other G-10 countries because of the political necessity to maintain certain Euro exchange rate ranges against non-EMU member EU currencies.

The G-7 and IMF meetings involve not only monetary authorities but also governments. Article 109.5 of the Maastricht Treaty requires that "without prejudice to Community competence and Community agreements as regards economic and monetary union, Member States may negotiate in international bodies and conclude international agreements."[41] As mentioned before, the ECOFIN Council procedures require a qualified majority to decide EU representation in international macroeconomic negotiations. Pressure exerted by the opt-out nations such as the U.K. and Denmark as well as by countries with derogations, could create major problems during the voting process.

It is possible that the Euro and the ECB will challenge the prevailing yen and U.S. dollar exchange rate arrangements because the EU, in particular the EMU nations, cannot accept international policy agreements that do not pursue price stability. This will not only limit negotiation flexibility but will also complicate G-7 coordination because the ECB Governing Council has to agree to any monetary or exchange rate arrangements. It should be noted that the ECB President will not have the same influence on the ECB Governing Council as the Chairman of the U.S. Federal Reserve System has on his governors.

The G-7 and G-10 policy coordination process has recently shifted from short-term exchange rate and debt crisis management to mid- to long-term monetary and fiscal balancing. In light of the emphasis on U.S. budget deficits and their impact on the dollar exchange rate and as a consequence of the IMF's increased fiscal surveillance, the EU might find it easier to convince the G-7 and G-10 of its own fiscal priorities and of the importance of the Maastricht Treaty convergence criteria. This may increase its influence and change the G-7's past preoccupation with United States-Japan bilateral economic relations and, more recently, with United States-German interest rate conflicts, resulting in a more balanced tri-polar relationship among the United States, Japan and the EU.[42]

The EMU and the IMF

Because EMU member nations will remain individual members of the IMF, the impact of the EMU on this international organization is uncertain.[43] It is possible

[41] Article 109.5, Maastricht Treaty, 1992.

[42] EMU member nations will have significantly more influence in the international fora such as the G-7 or G-10 than will non-EMU nations.

[43] Article 109 of the Maastricht Treaty applies to the representation of the EMU in the IMF as well.

that the ECOFIN Council will decide that EU nations, specially the EMU members should agree on a common position while continuing as individual IMF members. But neither the IMF nor the United States and Japan are keen on having a common EU position expressed through a bloc vote. EU nations with derogations and particularly those that have chosen to opt-out of the EMU are also likely to prefer the status quo of individual country representation because common EU positions would reduce their influence in global monetary matters.

The introduction of the Euro may not affect the financial quotas established with the IMF, although the composition of currency reserves and of the SDR may change. To ensure the compatibility of its surveillance system with that of the Maastricht Treaty, the IMF is closely following the application of the Treaty clauses. In its 1995 Annual Report, it stated that the "[D]irectors expressed broad agreement with the general aims of the European Union's macro-economics strategy...as well as with the need to focus on imbalances in public finance and on unemployment."[44]

The Euro as an International Currency[45]

The Euro is expected to join the ranks of major international currencies alongside the U.S. dollar and the Japanese yen around the year 2002. But it is not clear whether this will also mean that the Euro quickly develops into a major international trade, investment, and reserve currency, affecting the established global role of the US dollar and the Japanese yen. Such a status will depend on the EMU's stability as determined by its membership, the performance of the EMU nations' economies, and in particular, by the ECB's ability to ensure price stability so as to establish the financial markets' confidence in the new single currency.[46]

The Ecu's record is not an adequate gauge for the future performance of the Euro because, among other things, it has not been extensively used as a medium of exchange in business or even intra-EU governmental transactions. Furthermore, the Ecu, based on a basket of currencies, is affected by the exchange rate movements of its component currencies. In contrast, the Euro will be a new, non-basket currency and will be managed by the ECB whose key objective is price stability. Moreover, due to the Maastricht Treaty convergence criteria, the EMU member nations will coordinate their fiscal policies. Thus both in theory and in practice, the Euro will be quite different from the Ecu.

---

[44] IMF Annual Report 1995, Washington, D.C., p.43.

[45] An international currency is defined as a major international trade, investment and reserve currency.

[46] The first wave of EMU participants will in all probability include Germany, France, Austria and the Benelux nations, with Ireland a distant possibility.

The Euro as a Trade and Investment Currency

It is unrealistic to expect the Euro to become a major international trade and investment currency overnight. Claims that it will quickly supersede the U.S. dollar in international trade and financial transactions are exaggerated. See Table 6.5 for the share of exports of selected trading nations in world exports between 1975 and 1987 and Table 6.6 for the significance of the various major currencies in international trade.

Table 6.5
Shares of World Exports (%)

	1975	1980	1984	1987
United States	13.2	11.7	12.3	10.8
Japan	6.8	6.9	9.6	9.8
Germany	11.0	10.2	9.7	12.5
United Kingdom	5.3	5.8	5.3	5.6
France	6.5	6.1	5.5	6.3
Oil-Exporting Countries	7.3	15.7	9.3	5.6

Source: IMF International Financial Statistics

Table 6.6
Currency Distribution of World Trade (%)

	Exports		Imports	
	US Dollar	National Currency	US Dollar	National Currency
United States	98.0	98.0	85.0	85.0
Japan	60.9	33.8	93.0	2.0
Germany	7.2	82.3	33.1	42.8
United Kingdom	17.0	76.0	29.0	38.0
France	11.6	62.4	28.7	35.8
World Total	**54.8**	-	**54.3**	-

Note: Figures for Japan's export's are for 1982 and for Japan's and Germany's imports for 1980. Figures for the United Kingdom and France are for 1979. Figures for the United States are estimated.
Source: Black, Stanley, "The International Use of Currencies," in Suzuki, Yoshio, Junichi Miyake and Mitsuaki Okabe, The Evolution of the International Monetary System: How can efficiency and stability be attained?, University of Tokyo Press, 1990.

Tables 6.7 and 6.8 further illustrate the role of the various major currencies in international trade through the breakdown of the currency denominations of the exports and imports of major trading nations.[47]

---

[47] While this does not provide a measurement of the global trade share of these currencies, it can be used as a basis for the indirect estimation of such shares, as these nations dominate world trade.

Table 6.7
Currency Denomination of Exports (in percentages)

	Currency (1992)							
	US$	**Yen**	**DM**	**FFR**	**UK Pd.**	**It.lira**	**Guilder**	**Other**
U.S.	92.0*	1.5*	1.3	0.9*	0.9	0.4*	0.6*	2.4
Japan	46.6	40.1	3.3	0.9*	1.6*	0.4*	1.0*	6.1
Germany	7.3	0.3	77.0	3.3	3.2	2.2	0.9	5.8
France '81)	16.5	0.8*	10.4	54.6	4.1*	3.3*	1.5*	8.8
U.K.	22.0	0.7	5.0	3.5	62.0	1.7*	2.3*	2.8
Italy	18.0	0.6*	19.0	9.0	3.0*	40.0	1.3*	9.1
Netherlands	16.0	0.5*	21.7	4.8	4.8	1.8*	43.1	7.3

* = estimates.
Source: "International Currency Competition and the Future Role of the Single European Currency." The ECU Institute, London: Kluwer Law International, 1995, p.75.

Table 6.8
Currency Denomination of Imports (in percentages)

	Currency (1992)							
	US$	**Yen**	**DM**	**FFR**	**UK Pd.**	**It.lira**	**Guilder**	**Other**
U.S.	80.0*	3.0*	4.3	1.2*	1.7	0.8*	0.4*	8.6
Japan	74.5	17.0	3.6	1.3*	1.3*	0.7*	0.3*	1.3
Germany	18.4	1.7	55.9	3.1	2.2	1.7	1.3	15.7
France ('81)	23.1	1.3*	11.7	46.7	3.6*	3.2*	1.5*	8.9
U.K.	22.0	2.4	11.9	5.3	43.0	2.2*	3.2*	10.0
Italy	26.0	0.9*	16.0	7.0	3.5*	34.0	2.4*	10.2
Netherlands	21.4	2.0*	21.8	3.7	3.9	1.1	38.9	7.2

* = estimates.
Source: "International Currency Competition and the Future Role of the Single European Currency." The ECU Institute, London: Kluwer Law International, 1995, p.77.

As shown by these tables, most major nations, including all of the EU countries but not Japan, denominate international trade primarily in their own currencies. With the cash use of the Euro by July 2002, most of intra-EMU trade will be denominated by this new currency, although nations with derogations and opt-out rights will have the choice of using their own currency or other international currencies such as the US dollar. Considering the major EU nations' global trade shares, the Euro may rapidly gain in importance as an international trade currency.[48] But this does not automatically turn it into a major international investment and reserve currency.

---

[48] The EU represents about 45 percent of total global merchandise trade, including intra-EU trade.

As far as international investments are concerned, Table 6.9 shows the share of selected currencies in the international bond markets over the last decade.

Table 6.9
International Bond Market Trends

Currency	Percentages				
	1987	1991	1992	1993	1994
U.S. Dollar	36.2	31.1	37.9	38.1	38.1
Japanese yen	14.7	13.4	12.3	12.4	18.4
Deutsche mark	8.3	6.6	10.1	11.4	7.4
Swiss franc	13.4	6.5	5.4	5.6	4.7
Pound sterling	8.3	8.4	7.0	8.9	7.1
ECU	4.1	10.6	6.4	1.5	1.8
Other	14.9	23.4	20.9	22.2	22.5

Source: "International Capital Markets: Developments, Prospects, and Policy Issues," IMF, Washington DC, August 1995, p.191.

A comparison of the net bond issues placed in the United States, Japan, Germany and the U.K. financial markets shown in Table 6.10 confirms that most bonds are issued in the U.S. and Japan. The degree to which Euro-denominated bond issues will match current bond issue levels in the potential EMU member nations and the degree to which they may increase the EU's share in the global bond markets depends on the stability of the Euro and on the financial markets' confidence in the ECB. The same reasoning applies to the role and issue of bonds in the EMU nations' financial markets.

Table 6.10
Net Issue of Bonds in Selected Industrial Countries, 1980-93
(US$ billion)

	1980	1985	1990	1991	1992	1993
United States						
Government Bonds	49.0	164.8	153.6	212.9	215.2	178.3
Corporate Bonds	36.8	106.8	85.1	156.3	109.8	103.9
Japan						
Government Bonds	1.7	13.6	50.6	46.3	87.9	117.3
Corporate Bonds	20.5	14.2	93.8	92.4	71.6	92.7
Germany						
Government Bonds	32.2	14.6	-16.8	13.8	32.8	68.7
Corporate Bonds	-0.7	-0.4	-2.1	-1.3	1.7	3.1
United Kingdom						
Government Bonds	67.5	64.0	18.4	37.5	40.0	69.5
Corporate Bonds	2.5	5.4	16.4	17.7	15.9	32.5

Source: "The Emerging Asian Bond Market," The World Bank, Washington, DC: June 1995, p. 14.

The effectiveness of price stability oriented monetary policies and of fiscal policy coordination will be a major determinant of the Euro's stability and of the financial markets' confidence in this new single currency. If policies are effective, there could be a shift from bonds denominated in the non-EMU member nations' currencies to Euro-denominated bonds. But while the role of the Euro in the EMU member nations' financial centers could increase, its role in the non-EMU nations' financial centers is uncertain. The ECB must be careful when promoting the EMU nations' financial centers, because this could increase tension within the EU.

The Euro has the potential to surpass the present share of the Deutsche mark in both trade and investments if it remains non-inflationary, yet even then it would only be second in importance to the U.S. dollar. The extent to which it will be used depends, among others, on the economies of scale of transaction costs.

The Euro as a Reserve Currency

Table 6.11 shows the official foreign exchange holdings of selected countries. The U.S. dollar continues to dominate with a 55 percent share due to its large role in international trade and financial transactions. At the start of Stage III of the EMU[49], the Euro could assume a more important reserve role than the Deutsche mark or the British pound currently do, assuming that the ECB manages to obtain the Bundesbank's credibility.

Table 6.11
Official Foreign Exchange Reserve Holdings of Selected Countries
(in percentages)

All Currencies	1985	1990	1991	1992	1993	1994
U.S. dollar	55.3	49.1	50.7	55.1	56.7	57.1
Pound sterling	2.7	3.2	3.4	3.2	3.2	3.6
Deutsche mark	13.9	17.5	15.7	13.6	14.7	14.8
French franc	0.8	2.2	2.7	2.3	2.1	2.0
Swiss franc	2.1	1.3	1.2	1.1	1.3	1.1
Netherlands guilder	0.9	1.0	1.0	0.6	0.6	0.5
Japanese yen	7.3	8.2	8.7	7.9	8.3	8.1
Ecu	11.6	9.6	10.0	10.1	8.4	7.8
Unspecified currencies	5.4	7.7	6.5	6.1	4.7	4.9

Source: "Annual Report 1995," IMF, Washington, DC, 1995, p.161.

[49] Stage III is set to begin on January 1, 1999. It is the final stage of the EMU when the Euro is introduced on a non-cash basis and the ECB commences its European-wide monetary polices. It is expected to be completed by July 2002 when the Euro replaces the national currencies and becomes the sole legal tender of all EMU member nations.

EMU nations may initially keep large amounts of the Euro to manage unexpected volatility in the foreign exchange markets but such excessive holdings will eventually disappear. It should also be noted that the ECB's official Euro-reserves holdings will not be equal to the total foreign currency reserve holdings of the EMU nations because the non-Euro official reserves will be replaced by official Euro claims on EMU central banks. Euro reserves will be required only for exchange rate realignments with third country currencies such as the U.S. dollar, the Japanese yen or the currency of nations with derogations as, for example, that of the U.K..

According to an EU Commission study[50], taking into account the ratio of reserves to imports and of the intra-EU transactions to the total international transactions of the EU member nations, the establishment of the EMU could free around US$200-$230 billion of foreign exchange reserves in these countries. Other studies[51] found that the EMU could lead to a decrease in the overall reserves by around 20 to 30 percent in EU nations, with no change in the share of dollar holdings. But they also concluded that the cumulative decline in the absolute amount of U.S. dollar reserves could amount to US$90 billion.

However, such estimates do not take into account that the future global reserve role of the Euro will be determined by its stability and the ECB's credibility, coupled with effective and consistent fiscal policies in the member nations. Thus, the Euro has a 50-50 chance to eventually assume a major role in the international financial markets. Yet claims that it could replace the U.S. dollar as the most important reserve currency are exaggerated, at least, for some time to come. This is illustrated by Table 6.12 which shows the various types of exchange rate arrangements and their relative weights as a percentage of world GDP.

---

[50] "One Market, One Money," 1990, p.183.

[51] Leahy, M. P. "The Dollar as an Official Reserve Currency Under EMU," International Finance Discussion Papers, Board of the Governors of the Federal Reserve System, June 1994, Washington, DC, p. 28.

Table 6.12
Selected Exchange Rate Arrangements

Exchange Rate Arrangement	**By No. of Countries**		**Relative Weight of Share of World GDP (%)**
Pegged to:	***1975***	***1993***	***1993***
U.S. dollar	46	26	1.40
Sterling	8	0	-
French franc	13	14	0.20
Other currencies	5	17	0.02
SDR	9	3	0.06
Basket of own design	18	28	2.50
Limited flexibility	13	12	18.4
Floating	15	78	77.4
(Number of countries)	(127)	(178)	(100)

Source: "International Currency Competition and the Future Role of the Single European Currency," The ECU Institute, 1995, p.92.

As Table 6.12 shows, several nations peg their currencies to one of the EU currencies or include one or more of these monies in their currency baskets. Once the Euro is introduced, it will replace the various currencies. Nations that will peg their currencies to the new single currency, will have to maintain Euro reserves to manage exchange rates. The trade partners of the EU nations will also have to maintain such reserves for trading purposes. As illustrated by the table above, 14 nations, mostly major trading partners and former colonies of France, have pegged their currencies to the French franc in 1993. France will be an early EMU participant, thus most, if not all, of these nations are likely to peg their currencies to the Euro because the French franc will be removed from circulation.[52]

The Central and East European (CEE) nations have already indicated that they are going to formally or informally peg their currencies to the Euro, not only in anticipation of future EU membership but also because of their extensive trade with the EU, denominated mostly in Deutsche marks and U.S. dollars. The Euro could take the place of the Deutsche mark in CEE trade, thus together with its potential role in global trade could assume a larger overall international trade role than the Deutsche mark currently enjoys.

It is possible that immediately after the introduction of the Euro in 2002, many non-EU nations will increase their U.S. dollar and Japanese yen holdings because they want to gauge how the markets react to the new currency. This could result in the hedging of short-term Euro holdings as well as a hesitation on part of the financial markets to hold long-term Euro instruments, at least initially. This might

[52] It should, however, be noted that as measured by their share of global GDP, these 14 countries are relatively unimportant, thus, such a move should not have a significant impact on the foreign exchange markets.

increase the cost of using the Euro when first introduced.

The role of the EU nations' currencies in the global financial markets has increased. As shown in Table 6.13, total global portfolio investments in such currencies have grown from 13.2 percent in 1981 to 35.6 percent in 1993, a 22.4 percent increase. At the same time, the share of U.S. dollar denominated investments has declined from 67.3 percent to 44.3 percent, a 23 percent decrease. It should be noted that the EU figure includes the EMU "opt-out" U.K.'s investments which account for a significant part of the total. Nonetheless, if the ECB obtains international credibility, these trends imply that the share of Euro-denominated investments may eventually surpass that of U.S. dollar-denominated investments.

Table 6. 13
Currency Denomination of Global Investments
(in percentages)

	US $	EU Total	DM	Ecu	SFR	Yen	Other
1981	67.3	13.2	N/A	N/A	N/A	2.2	N/A
1985	65.4	18.0	9.4	2.2	8.7	4.7	3.2
1988	55.2	24.3	12.3	3.2	8.2	6.7	5.6
1989	53.9	26.7	12.0	3.2	7.2	5.9	6.3
1990	49.2	30.6	13.1	3.7	7.7	6.3	6.2
1991	45.9	34.1	13.6	5.1	7.0	6.8	6.2
1992	46.1	34.9	14.7	4.8	6.4	7.0	5.6
1993-Sept	44.3	35.6	15.0	4.2	6.1	8.0	6.0

Source: "International Currency Competition and the Future Role of the Single European Currency," The ECU Institute, 1995, p.88.

On the road to becoming a major international currency the Euro will face the first problem when it replaces the EMU member nations' currencies in 2002. The creation of a "critical mass" to support its circulation will not be an easy task. Moreover, the EU's trading partners will use the Euro only if its associated payment system performs in a satisfactory manner.

International financial markets quickly adjust to the use of a new currency. But when the Euro is introduced and the EMU member nations' currencies will be withdrawn, financial markets will lose some of the instruments used to hedge such currencies. The ECB will have new monetary policy instruments, but their efficiency will depend on the presence of strong domestic financial centers. Thus, the ECB and the EMU institutions will have to promote not only the international use of the Euro but also the international competitiveness of the EU financial centers. This is likely to be a controversial task as the financial centers will be pitted against each-other.

The introduction of the Euro will require changes in the accounting and transaction methods of the financial institutions of EMU member nations. EMU-wide payment processing and settlement arrangements will also have to be changed to become compatible with the TARGET system[53] which will also have to be used by nations formally or informally pegging their currencies to the Euro. Such upgrading of national payment systems is going to be quite expensive.

Thus, the potential impact of the Euro on the US-dollar and Japanese yen as major international trade, investment and reserve currencies will be uncertain, at least until the end of the first decade of the next century.

THE ERM II

When the "core" group of EU nations, also known as the "ins," establish the EMU, they will leave behind those EU member nations, the "outs," that have not met or have failed to make sufficient progress toward meeting the Maastricht Treaty convergence criteria or have opted-out. But the Treaty is vague with regard to the monetary policy and exchange rate relations between the "ins" and the "outs." It requires the "outs" to conduct exchange rate policies as a "matter of common interest" and emphasizes that the qualifications for EMU membership include adherence to the "normal fluctuation margins of the European exchange rate mechanism...without severe tensions for at least two years." But it should be noted, this is a contradiction, as the original ERM will "cease to exist the day the [single currency] Euro is born."[54] The Euro will replace the Deutsche mark as the anchor currency, and will also eliminate the need for the Ecu. These developments will terminate the EMS and the original ERM around the turn of the century.

Thus, a new exchange rate mechanism had to be created. At the December 13-14, 1996 European Council Summit meeting in Dublin the EU governments accepted the "ERM II" as such a mechanism to facilitate the transition to the Euro and to insure the efficient functioning of the "Single Market." The ERM II is based on the "hub and spokes" concept i.e. the Euro will be the anchor and non-EMU member nations will target their currencies at the new single currency so as to extend its zone of stability to such currencies.

The new mechanism is a modification of the original ERM structure that was set up in 1979 to minimize currency fluctuation. It will come into force on January 1, 1999, and will incorporate the following three principles: (i) flexibility, (ii) non-coercion, and (iii) reinforced convergence. According to the flexibility principle, the EMU "outs" will select a central rate for their currency vis-à-vis the Euro in consultation with the EMU members, also known as the "Euro bloc", and the European Central Bank (ECB). Although the fluctuation band is not specified, it will

[53] "Trans-European Automated Real-time Gross Settlement Express Transfer System," which, in Stage III of the EMU, will include the national "Real-time Gross Settlement Systems" and their linkages.

[54] "If EMU, then ERM II." Financial Times, June 24, 1996.

be relatively wide like the +/-15 percent band of the original ERM. However, non-EMU member currencies will be allowed to target narrower bands if they so choose.

The principle of non-coercion was adopted at the insistence of the U.K. and Sweden. It calls for a voluntary ERM II, although the non-EMU member nations (the "outs") are "expected" to join. On the insistence of the Bundesbank this principle also includes the understanding that the ECB's obligation to support weaker currencies under speculative attacks, is limited. Although marginal intervention or the support of currencies at the extremes of the wide bands is automatic, the ECB and national central banks reserve the right not to intervene if the Euro's price stability could be compromised.

The third principle of the ERM II is "reinforced convergence." This is Brussel's term for the requirement that all member nations submit their economic plans for peer review i.e. ministerial surveillance, regardless of their participation in the EMU or the ERM II. However, at the insistence of the U.K., nations whose economic plans are not consistent with those of the other countries cannot be penalized. Furthermore, the ECOFIN Council may issue "non-binding recommendations only when necessary" to avoid misalignments and excessive nominal exchange rate fluctuations.

The ERM II is based on the lessons learned from the 1992-93 ERM crises during which the U.K., Italy, Spain and France held out against realignments for political reasons. To avoid major misalignments in the future, the adjustment of ERM II central rates must be done in a "timely fashion" through confidential talks that can be initiated by any member nation or the ECB. Thus, if the ECB no longer supports a particular currency, this could result in a realignment of the currency's central rate i.e. a pre-emptive marginal intervention. But the ECB does not have any obligation to intervene or to defend non-member currencies as it pursues independent monetary policies. The right to initiate the realignment of ERM II currencies enables the ECB to change unrealistic exchange rates and, thus, to prevent possible speculative attacks. It is not surprising that the Bundesbank and other potential EMU member nations insist on the ECB's right to demand realignments. This has, to some extent, de-politicized the process.

Yet realignments are still political by nature and this raises the question of whether governments or their independent central banks should take responsibility for such moves. [55] Under the ERM II, governments have abdicated this responsibility. This is a critical issue that the designers of the new mechanism must contend with.

---

[55] In 1987, Erik Hoffmeyer, the Governor of the Danish Central Bank, convinced the other EU members of the Board of the Bank of International Settlements (BIS) that transferring the responsibility for the ERM realignments from governments to central banks would only encourage prime ministers and finance ministers to pass on the adjustment responsibility to their central bankers. As a result, currently ERM realignments are the responsibility of governments rather than of central bankers.

The ERM II will be asymmetrical with the Euro replacing the Deutsche mark as the unofficial anchor currency. The burden of adjustments will fall squarely on non-EMU nations and not on the ECB, thus the "outs" will have to follow the policies of the Euro-bloc nations. This is the result of the larger nations' insistence on more political and economic influence. As a result, the ERM II is beginning to generate concern among the smaller and the "opt-out" nations, because they are just now beginning to realize that their relations to the EMU member nations will be different in the future.

Although it is improbable that the U.K., an EMU opt-out, will link the pound sterling to the ERM II,[56] it is very likely that most of the "outs" will join not only because membership is required under the Maastricht Treaty exchange rate criterion, but also because this will enhance the credibility of their currencies in the financial markets. ERM II member nations could receive benefits such as lower interest rates which might make it easier for the "outs" to meet the fiscal deficit and national debt convergence criteria. Yet, the U.K. is against the ERM II and was adamant during the negotiations that membership should not be required of countries that remain outside the EMU. It had argued that although the "Single Market" needed real exchange rate stability from the start, the original ERM, a pegged nominal exchange rate system was neither necessary nor adequate as demonstrated by the 1992 and 1993 crises.

According to Eddie George, Governor of the Bank of England, the real issue is the maintenance of a "certain degree of convergence" between the "ins" and the "outs." He argues that while a tight link to the Euro through the ERM II may be appropriate for some countries, the same objective could be achieved by the "outs" through the pursuit of domestic inflation targets. This would address the anxiety of the "ins" about large competitive devaluations by the "outs" against the Euro. The U.K. also claims that the convergence requirement of the original ERM should be discarded because the mechanism has been changed beyond recognition.

The EMI's response to the U.K.'s arguments is ambiguous. It points out that non-EMU nations will by default tend to have weaker currencies because they do not meet the Maastricht Treaty convergence criteria. But this is not necessarily true for the two opt-out nations, the U.K. and Denmark. Amidst this controversy, at the June 21-22, 1996 European Council Summit meeting in Florence, the heads of state had agreed to suspend until mid-1997 the decision on how to apply the exchange rate convergence criterion of the original ERM.[57]

Regardless of the U.K.'s objections, the Euro will be the anchor currency of the officially asymmetrical ERM II. But what is not clear is whether the new mechanism will be able to accommodate the needs of both the "ins" and "outs." The larger EU countries have made it clear that they will pressure the lagging and smaller

---

[56] It is also possible that Denmark may not to link the krone to the ERM II.

[57] In any case, the +/-15 percent currency band will be used.

nations whenever it suits their national interests. Thus the ERM II reinstates the influence of the large economies in a widening EU that includes more and more smaller nations with a right to veto decisions.

The successful introduction of the Euro will, to a large extent, depend on the effectiveness of the ERM II as a transition mechanism. It has to provide an institutional linkage between the "ins" and "outs" so as to insure stability and efficient monetary and economic relations between the two groups of nations. Moreover, the ERM II, as stipulated by the Treaty, must also serve as a framework for the "outs" through which they will be able to demonstrate their readiness to join the EMU at a later date.

The ERM II is viewed by many, including Bundesbank President Hans Tietmeyer, as the only arrangement through which the EMU member nations can be reassured that the "outs" will not engage in competitive devaluations against the Euro. However, according to critics, the ERM II will simply re-draw the fault lines of the original exchange rate mechanism. It places intervention obligations on the ECB and on the central banks of the "outs" which could result in an inflexibility that may recreate the tensions that had led to the near-collapse of the original ERM.[58] They also claim that competitive devaluations are not a major threat to the Euro.

THE MAASTRICHT TREATY CONVERGENCE CRITERIA

The ability of the EU nations to meet the Maastricht Treaty convergence criteria, or reference values, on time[59] is critical for the EMU timetable. The criteria mandates that budget deficit and public debt ratios stay below 3 percent and 60 percent of GDP, respectively, and that inflation and long-term interest rates stay within 1.5 and 2.0 percent, respectively, of the average of the three best-performing nations.[60] Potential EMU member nations must have also kept their currencies within the "normal" bands of the original ERM for two years without any major problems.[61]

Potential EMU Membership

Table 6.14 illustrates the economic and thus political problem of determining EMU membership in 1998. It shows that if the criteria are strictly interpreted and the EMU begins as scheduled, only Luxembourg could become a

---

[58] The near collapse refers to the 1992 and 1993 crises and the subsequent enlargement of the currency bands from +/-2.25 percent to +/-15 percent.

[59] The decision on how to apply the Maastricht Treaty's ERM criterion has been delayed until mid-1997.

[60] "Best-performing" means economies with the lowest inflation and long-term interest rates.

[61] The definition of "normal" ERM bands created a great deal of controversy. It was not clear whether this referred to the old +/-2.25 percent or to the new +/-15 percent bands. Eventually it was decided that the term refers to the +/-15 percent band.

Table 6.14
Maastricht Treaty Convergence Criteria (Reference Value) Performance in 1995, 1996 and 1997

	Inflation rate*			Budget balance as % of GDP**			Debt as % of GDP			Long-term interest rate*	ERM Band
	1995	1996	1997	1995	1996	1997	1995	1996	1997	12 months to Oct 1996	
Reference value	**2.9**	**2.5**	**3.1**		**-3.0**			**60.0**		**8.8**	
Germany	1.8	1.5	1.6	-3.5	-4.0***	-3.0	58.1	60.3	61.5	6.3	+- 15%
France	1.8	2.0	1.8	-4.9	-4.1	-3.1	53.0	56.0	58.0	6.5	+- 15%
Italy	5.3	3.9	2.9	-7.3	-7.2	-4.0	125.0	124.3	121.5	10.0	+- 15%
UK	2.8	2.6	2.1	-5.8	-4.6	-3.4	54.1	55.2	54.8	7.9	free floating
Spain	4.7	3.6	3.0	-6.6	-4.8	-3.7	65.7	67.4	67.2	9.3	+- 15%
Netherlands	1.9	2.1	2.5	-4.0	-2.6	-2.3	79.7	78.8	76.2	6.2	+- 15%
Belgium	1.5	2.0	2.6	-4.1	-3.3	-2.8	133.8	130.6	127.0	6.6	+- 15%
Sweden	2.9	1.0	1.9	-8.1	-4.0	-3.0	78.7	78.7	78.7	8.4	free floating
Austria	2.2	1.8	1.8	-5.9	-4.5	-3.4	69.0	71.8	69.9	6.4	+- 15%
Denmark	2.1	2.1	2.3	-1.6	-1.8	-1.0	72.1	71.3	69.7	7.3	+- 15%
Finland	1.0	0.6	1.5	-5.6	-3.6	-2.0	59.4	63.4	63.4	7.3	+- 15%
Portugal	4.1	3.1	2.8	-4.9	-4.3	-3.2	71.5	70.7	69.1	9.1	+- 15%
Greece	9.3	8.6	7.0	9.1	-8.0	-5.7	111.8	109.3	106.6	13.4	free floating
Ireland	2.5	1.6	2.4	-2.0	-1.6	-1.6	81.6	75.7	71.6	7.5	+- 15%
Luxembourg	1.9	1.3	2.5	0.3	0.9	0.5	5.9	7.8	8.8	6.6	+- 15%
Other European Countries											
Switzerland	1.8	0.8	1.4	-1.8	-3.0	-2.6	47.9	50.1	51.2	4.2	free floating
Norway	2.5	1.3	2.5	3.5	5.0	4.7	42.0	38.6	38.2	6.8	free floating

Average inflation rate of the "best" EU countries Finland, Belgium, France (1995) : 1.4%
Average inflation rate of the "best" EU countries Finland, Sweden, Luxembourg (1996) : 1%
Average inflation rate of the "best" EU countries Finland, Germany, Austria (1997) : 1.6%
Average long-term interest rate of the "best" EU countries (Nov. 1995/Oct. 1996) : 6.8%
* = period average
** = fiscal balance on national account basis (excluding public enterprises)
*** = The final official report of the German government set the 1996 deficit/GDP at 3.9%
Source: Deutsche Bank Research, "EMU Watch", December 9, 1996 - No.23, p.11.

member. This is, of course, an unrealistic outcome. If the criteria are interpreted less strictly, as they probably will, Germany, France, the Netherlands, Belgium and Austria could also join and, thus, the EMU may become a reality on January 1, 1999.

EMU membership will depend primarily on which nation's economic performance the German public is willing to accept rather than on the strict meeting of the Maastricht convergence criteria. The stability of the Euro is of critical importance to the German public which is represented by the Bundesbank.

If the EMU begins in 1999, France and Germany will comprise the core while Austria and the Benelux nations[62] could also become members even though they may not meet the fiscal convergence criteria. Austria's projected 1997 deficit and debt to GDP ratios are 3.4 percent and 69.9 percent, respectively; Belgium's projected 1997 debt to GDP ratio is 127 percent, and that of the Netherlands is 76.2 percent. Yet, these nations could be admitted on January 1, 1999 because it is generally believed that once they meet the criteria, they are going to have the political will to sustain the required fiscal performance. More important, Austria and the Netherlands are already de facto members of the Deutsche mark zone.

Italy is not included in this first possible wave of EMU member nations. Its projected 1997 economic data indicate that it will not meet the deficit, debt and interest rate criteria. Of particular concern is its projected debt ratio of 121.5 percent to GDP. In response to this, while acknowledging the problem, the Italians are upset about the possibility of being excluded while other nations that do not meet the criterion either, such as Belgium, could become members.

The Italians are concerned about Belgium's possible membership because its current debt ratio of 130 percent to GDP is higher than their current 124 percent ratio. In addition, Belgium's projected 1997 debt ratio of 127 percent is also higher than Italy's expected 121.5 percent ratio. But Belgium's actual 1996 and projected 1997 budget deficits of 3.3 percent and 2.8 percent are lower than Italy's 7.2 and 4.0 percent deficit ratios. Moreover, in recent years, the Belgian-Luxembourg franc has been relatively stable against the Deutsche mark. The problem-free performance of this joint currency in the original ERM as well as the lower inflation levels also favor the membership of these two nations as does their small yield spread over that of Germany. In contrast, the lira's performance in the original ERM has been very erratic; in the summer of 1992 it even dropped out, only to rejoin amidst controversy at the end of 1996. Moreover, as shown in Tables 6.15 and 6.16, the differences in consumer price inflation and yield spreads on 10-year bonds are in Belgium's favor.

---

[62] Belgium, Luxembourg and the Netherlands.

Table 6.15
1992-1996 Consumer Price Inflation: A Comparison of Belgium and Italy
(in percentage; 1991=100, n.s.a.)

	Jan. 1992	Jan. 1993	Jan. 1994	Jan. 1995	Jan. 1996
Belgium	2.3%	3.8%	2.5%	1.8%	2%
Italy	6%	4.2%	4.2%	3.8%	5.5%

Note: The largest difference during the 1992-96 time period between Belgium and Italy are 1.2 percent and 5.8 percent, respectively, in mid-to-late 1995.
Source: "Comments on EMU: Will EMU Fly in 1999?," Merrill Lynch & Co., Inc. Global Securities Research & Economic Group, International Fixed Income Research, April 22, 1996.

Table 6.16
1992-1996 Yield Spreads on 10-Year Bonds:
A Comparison of Belgium and Italy (Basis Points)

	Jan. 1992	Sept 1992	May 1993	Jan. 1994	Oct. 1994	June 1995	Feb. 1996
Belgium	100	110	60	80	95	70	45
Italy	480	780	580	280	400	600	460

Source: "Comments on EMU: Will EMU Fly in 1999?," 1996.

As mentioned before, in spite of these data, the Italians raise questions about Belgium's possible admission. Thus, if Italy will not be admitted, this could generate problems because it is not only one of the largest EU economies but is also one of the original "six" nations that founded the EEC in 1957.

Yet, the reality is that "little" Belgium maybe admitted because it is not seen as a threat to the Euro's stability. But Italy's membership would raise major concerns not only with the German public but also with the financial markets. However, Italy may still make early EMU membership because of its large and influential economic size. This would be a rather ironic outcome.

Both Denmark and the U.K. have ratified the Maastricht Treaty subject to qualifications. Denmark has opted-out of the EMU, although it can join in the future if it wishes to do so. The U.K. reserves the right to reach an entry decision until the last possible moment, but if it decides to join, Denmark may reverse its opt-out stance. It is also possible that both the U.K. and Denmark will qualify for the EMU and still retain their "opt-out" status. The 1996 and projected 1997 data for both countries indicate that they have a good chance of joining on January 1, 1999, if they so choose. But Denmark plans to hold a membership referendum and the U.K. may do the same before EMU's starting date.

Ireland[63] and Finland seem ready to join the EMU. Both countries are relatively small and do not have any serious economic problems. Ireland wants to be a first round member at any cost, but there is a slight possibility that its membership may be influenced by the U.K.'s decision. Nonetheless, on the basis of the projected 1997 data, except for the 71.6 percent debt/GDP ratio, Ireland stands a good chance of joining the EMU in 1999. Finland is on the economic borderline; its projected 1997 debt/GDP ratio is 63.4 percent. But the country has not yet decided whether it wants to join the EMU at the start.

Sweden is roughly in the same situation as Ireland and Finland are. Its 1996 and 1997 economic data do not raise any serious problems, except for the projected excessive 1997 debt level of 78.7 percent. The nation, however, had reduced its deficit/GDP ratio from 8.1 percent in 1995 to 4.0 percent in 1996 and plans to meet the 3 percent requirement by 1997. Yet the Swedish government is ambivalent about early membership and did not join the original ERM in late 1996, the last date that would have enabled it to meet the two year stable ERM membership convergence requirement of the Maastricht Treaty. In contrast to the government, the country's central bank strongly supports early membership.

Despite valiant attempts to join in 1999, Spain and Portugal need more time to qualify for the EMU. Both are trying to do their best, but despite significant improvements except for the inflation criterion, they do not meet any of the other convergence requirements. But even if they manage to meet the requirements and become early members, they would not be able to withstand the economic, political and social pressures that the EMU will eventually impose on its member nations.

Greece cannot become a member in the near future. It meets none of the convergence criteria and is not changing its economic structure and policies fast enough. It also lacks the political will to do so. Allowing Mediterranean countries such as Greece to join the core group in 1999 would make it next to impossible to convince the German public and the Bundesbank of EMU's merits.

Fiscal "Fudging"

In their rush to meet the 1999 political EMU deadline, in 1996 several nations have engaged in creative accounting to meet the budget deficit criterion by 1997. They have also issued overly optimistic economic projections. It is, to some degree, understandable that nations like Italy, Spain, and Belgium have engaged in such practices. But it is alarming that countries assured a place in the EMU as, for example, France and Germany also found it necessary to manipulate their economic data for the

---

[63] The core EMU nations may apply a "softer" version of the Maastricht criteria if they need Ireland to achieve a majority. The country's admission could represent the first use of qualified majority decision-making as opposed to unanimous decision-making.

sake of starting the project on time. It is true that the EMU cannot begin without them but fiscal "fudging" could undermine the Euro. Yet, in the Fall of 1996, German Finance Minister Theo Waigel proposed a budget that had assumed a 2.5 percent GDP growth rate in 1997 while private forecasters predicted a 2 percent rate. According to critics,[64] Mr. Waigel's projected 2.5 percent budget deficit for 1997 is also too optimistic particularly if the 3.5 and 3.9 percent 1995 and 1996 budget deficits are taken in to account.

The French government projected a 3.0 percent 1997 deficit by adding one-time privatization revenues to its budget. These revenues were generated by a 1997 monetary windfall of FFr 37.5 billion (US$7.36 billion) paid by France Télécom to "cover future pensions liability for its employees - part of a deal with the unions on the company's partial privatization."[65] Although this creates a new public liability, the French government claims that such a liability is not only difficult to calculate but is not included in the current national accounts of the other EU nations administering comparable pay-as-you-go pension schemes. The EU Commission has approved this French version of creative accounting despite protests from Germany and the U.K. and regardless of the fact that privatization sales reduce the total value of public assets by an identical amount, thus, not changing the net worth of a nation. (It is only the privatization profits that add to a country's net worth.) In lowering the 1997 projected deficit, the French government also included in its budgetary calculations the public asset value gains caused by recapitalization.

Other nations engaged in similar practices. The governments of Belgium and Spain projected a 2.9 percent 1997 budget deficit and, as discussed above in the case of France, the French as well as the Italian and Portuguese governments projected a 3.0 percent budget deficit in 1997. But private forecasters predict a 3.3 percent deficit for Belgium, 3.5-4.2 percent for Spain, 3.6 percent for France, 4.5-5.5 percent for Italy and a 3.1-3.4 percent deficit for Portugal.[66] It should be noted that the presently used EU deficit definition distorts the calculations, because it is broader than the difference between current expenditures and revenues. It is viewed as the total amount a nation needs to borrow to cover the difference between changes in its total assets and liabilities.

The quick approval by the EU Commission of the France Télécom deficit reduction scheme and the use of creative accounting by other nations has angered Germany and the U.K.. Bundesbank President Tietmeyer voiced his concern in early October 1996 when he emphasized that "it is important in the selection [of EMU participants] that the member countries do not reach the criteria through a breathless short-term effort with one-off results quickly cobbled together."[67] Tietmeyer was referring to the dangers of fiscal "fudging", specially during 1996-97, which may not

---

[64] Germany's six leading economic research institutes predicted that in 1997 the deficit would be 3.5 percent and the debt approximately 61 percent of GDP.

[65] "The Magic of Maastrichtian Mathematics." Financial Times, September 19, 1996.

[66] "EMU, Lies, Damned Lies and Statistics." Financial Times, October 9, 1996.

[67] "EMU, Lies, Damned Lies and Statistics." Financial Times, October 9, 1996.

only generate a nasty shock for the 1998 budgets but could also create problems for the Euro.

There is growing concern that fiscal "fudging" will be allowed by Brussels in order to realize the EMU's politically determined timetable. Besides France, a number of other nations such as Belgium, Spain, Portugal and Italy also want to use privatization and other special revenues to reduce their budget deficits toward the required 3 percent level. The Italians have included Lira12,000 billion (US$7.9 billion) of "ambiguous treasury operation" revenues in their budget. When queried about this, the Italian Prime Minister Romano Prodi said that "if the French can get away with it, then we can show them a trick or two as well."[68] The Belgians used a BFr222 billion (US$7 billion) surplus obtained from central bank gold sales. The Spaniards have based their 1997 budget forecasts on the assumption that the economy will grow at 3 percent a far too optimistic projection.

Other "fudging" practices used include the downward adjustments of debt service payments, new taxes and government wage freezes. The Italians, for example, have introduced a one-year Euro income tax that may raise Lira 5,500 billion (US$3.6 billion) in 1997.[69] Spain has resorted to public sector wage freezes.

There is a growing sentiment on part of the smaller countries that the larger nation's "fudging" attempts are not taken seriously. Belgium wanted to use BFr20 billion ($645 million) of privatization revenues generated by the sale of the telecommunications group Belgacom but was stopped from doing so by the EU Commission. This has strengthened the view that EMU plan entails one set of rules for the large nations and another set for the small countries.

It must, however, be pointed out that the use of proper fiscal accounting methods is made difficult by the outdated and complicated procedures used by the Luxembourg based Eurostat, the statistical agency of the EU Commission. New accounting methods have been approved, but they will not be introduced before 1999. A joint EU Commission, Eurostat and EMI team is currently examining the problems this raises for the Maastricht Treaty convergence criteria performance evaluation process.

THE U.K. DILEMMA

The decision to join the EMU and to give up the pound sterling is of momentous political and economic importance to the U.K.. Yet by early 1997 neither the Conservative nor the Labor Party has taken a direct position on the issues involved. It seems that both parties have agreed not to address them until after the 1997 elections.

---

[68] "EMU, Lies, Damned Lies and Statistics." Financial Times, October 9, 1996.

[69] The Italian Euro-tax is similar to a withholding tax on 1996 income. It will be compensated for by tax rebates and the issue of privatization bonds beginning in 1999.

They have been quoted claiming that "it is too distant a prospect for us to have a firm policy...there are too many imponderables...it might not even happen...we [Tory party] will have a referendum"[70] as will the Labour's party.[71]

But most observers of British politics realize that the EMU can no longer be portrayed as a distant possibility. While the U.K.'s membership may not be a major election issue in 1997, soon after a new government is formed, a decision concerning the U.K.'s intentions will have to be made. To date, EU governments continue to maintain that the deadline for the final membership decision is the spring of 1998. If the Maastricht Treaty and its U.K. "opt-out" protocol is strictly adhered to, the incoming U.K. Prime Minister will have to make a decision by January 1998, or at the latest by June 30, 1998. There is, of course, always the possibility that France and Germany do not meet the Maastricht fiscal convergence criteria in 1997 and thus call for a technical delay of the January 1, 1999 starting date. While this could happen, the current political view of Bonn and Paris is to start the EMU on time.

It may not be easy for the U.K., as the two political parties seem to believe, to postpone the EMU decision to the last minute. The Maastricht Treaty stipulates that EMU member central banks must be independent. But it takes an act of Parliament to create an independent Bank of England. In addition, other legislative measures would also have to be considered, addressing such matters as the procedure under which the U.K. government funds its borrowing obligations and the transfer of foreign currency reserves from the Treasury to the Bank. The replacement of the pound sterling would also require a legislative act. But even under the best of circumstances the relevant legislation cannot be passed before 1999. This means that the incoming government must decide on EMU membership by the fall of 1997, at the latest. To complicate matters, the U.K. is scheduled to assume the EU presidency at the beginning of 1998.

To expedite matters, the pragmatic members of the Conservative Party's "Eurosceptics" group formed the Referendum Party. The only purpose of this party, at least initially, was to force Prime Minister Major to hold a referendum on the replacement of the pound sterling by the Euro prior to the spring 1997 general election. Led by Sir James Goldsmith and supported by, among others, former Prime Minister Margaret Thatcher, her ex-chief economic adviser Sir Alan Walters, and the former deputy chairman of the Conservative Party Lord McAlpine, party members demanded a clear government position on the Euro and the EMU. They argued that the decisions can no longer be delayed nor can they be reached through default as financial markets need to prepare for whatever the choices will be. They also pointed out that the U.K. needs a decision on EMU membership in order to define the nation's role not only in the EU decision-making process but also in world affairs. To date, the Party has only succeeded in getting the Prime Minister to agree to a referendum on the Euro, assuming that he recommends EMU membership.

---

[70] "Conspiracy of Silence." Financial Times, July 1996.

[71] The Labour Party officially announced on November 17, 1996 that it would call a referendum on EMU. Financial Times, November 18, 1996, p.8.

As mentioned before, until early 1997, neither the Tory nor the Labour Party had publicly indicated how they would vote on EMU membership and on the abolition of the pound sterling. Prime Minister John Major had adopted a "wait-and-see" policy not only to reunite the Tory Party for the spring 1997 election but also to simultaneously convince other EU member governments that the U.K. is seriously considering EMU membership. It is through this strategy that the Prime Minister wanted to retain the U.K.'s influence at the EU negotiation table. Major knew that any decision concerning the fate of the pound sterling before the election would irrevocably split his party, leading to an election defeat and a limitation of his negotiating position. He wanted to consider the use of the EMU opt-out alternative obtained through the Maastricht Treaty only after the spring 1997 elections. Moreover, as mentioned before, he intended to call for a referendum only if he decides to give up the pound sterling.

However, the Prime Minister eventually came under great pressure. The Tory "Eurosceptics" wanted him to reach either a clear "No" decision on giving up the pound sterling or close the door to EMU membership for the duration of the next parliamentary cycle. The increasingly Eurosceptic cabinet has also pressured the Prime Minister to reach a "No" decision. This was to some extent counter-balanced by the positions of pro-EU Cabinet members, in particular by the Chancellor of the Exchequer, Kenneth Clark and Deputy Prime Minister Michael Heseltine. Kenneth Clark is one of the strongest conservative supporters of the EMU, but his preference to join it in 1999 could be tempered if domestic economic conditions are not conducive to such a move

At last, in January 1997 Prime Minister Major made an official statement on Britain's participation in the EMU and the future of the pound sterling. As could be expected, he was vague, pointing out that it was "very unlikely, though not impossible" that the EMU project could begin as scheduled on January 1, 1999. But he emphasized that if the EMU begins without reliable economic convergence i.e. if it can be started only through fiscal "fudging," the pound sterling will not participate.

Major's statement was intended to regain the support of the Tory Eurosceptics and of the members of the Referendum Party by implying that if he won the election, the U.K. would probably not surrender the pound in January 1999. However, the Eurosceptics and the Referendum Party were far from satisfied and considered his statement as a continuation of the Prime Minister's previous "wait-and-see" policy. The other EU governments were not convinced either. They doubted that a re-elected conservative government would seriously participate in the EMU, thereby further eroding the U.K.'s influence. Major's statement signified a defeat for the Chancellor of the Exchequer, Kenneth Clark who had argued very strongly for joining the EMU during the next parliamentary cycle starting in 1997.

The Labour Party's Tony Blair is also in a predicament. If he wins the 1997 election and chooses to join the EMU, the decision to abandon the pound sterling would dominate domestic policies during the first two years of his government. If he decides to join and fails to do so, the Labour Party would probably not return to power for a generation. Blair remembers the political damage that the 1992 ERM crisis inflicted on his opponent. He argues for British participation but much later - possibly at the end of the next or even at the beginning of the following parliamentary cycle. If elected he would call a referendum on the issues.

Both the Tory and the Labor Party leadership is under increasing pressure not only from within its own ranks but also from industry, labor unions and the financial markets. They want both Major and Blair to take a definitive stand on the EMU prior to the 1997 elections due to the U.K.'s growing economic interdependence with the EU nations. The ongoing unwillingness of the two party leaders to do so was dubbed by the press as a "conspiracy of silence".

It should be noted that the original idea of an EMU formed initially by a small group of elite nations is no longer widely accepted. Almost all of the current EU member nations want to qualify for the EMU by 1999. Most of them are unlikely to meet the Maastricht criteria in time, but could do so a few years later. Under such circumstances, life on the periphery of the EMU could be lonely and uncomfortable for the U.K. and, possibly, Denmark. "...it has become too difficult to distinguish hard-currency sheep from soft-currency goats. So the choice is between monetary union for all or nobody. The former is what member states will choose."[72]

The U.K. would do well either inside or outside of the EU and the EMU, but it would be harmful to the country's interests to remain in the EU legally and outside of it psychologically. [73]

THE GERMAN EMU PREDICAMENT

Unlike the 1992 "Single Market," the EMU is propelled by political as opposed to economic considerations. It is the political situation in France and Germany that sets the EMU "mood." France would like to have as much influence on EU monetary policies as the Bundesbank does,[74] but it can gain such influence only through an EU institution such as the ECB[75] where it has as much of a voice as the Germans do. In contrast, Germany aims for ever closer integration with France so as to safeguard Western European security. Thus, the nucleus of the EMU is a Franco-German understanding to move in the name of progress toward a closer political and economic union which will cost the Germans the Deutsche mark and the Bundesbank. Under such

[72] "The Danger of Dithering." Financial Times, October 1, 1996.

[73] "A Qualified Yes to EMU." Financial Times, October 8, 1996.

[74] This view emerged when due to the Bundesbank's policies the Mitterand government was more or less forced under the original ERM arrangements to undergo a series of currency devaluations between 1982 and 1983.

[75] The French would like the ECB's independence to be like that of the Banque de France rather than that of the Bundesbank. The Banque de France is less distant from the French government than the Bundesbank is from the German government.

circumstances the EMU will move ahead only when the Paris-Bonn axis is again in a harmonious state. Since France needs the EMU in order to expand its political-monetary influence,[76] it is up to Germany to say "Yes" or "No". But the German perspective is complex and continually changing.

Currently approximately 60 percent of the German population is against giving up the Deutsche mark. The public is not as committed to the EMU as are the citizens of some other EU nations because it has more to lose if the venture does not turn out well. But Chancellor Kohl believes that an ever closer integration with France is fundamental to Western security and this view is shared by other senior German officials, including Bundesbank President Tietmeyer. However, jaded observers see Chancellor Kohl's ardent commitment to European integration as an attempt to reach a new political height following German reunification. They argue that he would like to win the federal election in the fall of 1998 and launch the EMU to establish an even more eminent place in history than he has already achieved.

The Importance of the Maastricht Treaty Convergence Criteria

If the driving force behind the EMU is primarily German politics, the meeting of the Maastricht convergence criteria becomes a mere formality for France and Germany. Yet, the criteria remain a necessary guardian of economic performance. But both France and Germany will face problems only if the criteria become a major concern in their respective 1998 parliamentary elections. President Chirac and Chancellor Kohl would have difficulties convincing their voters to launch EMU in 1999 if the budget deficits cannot be reduced to 3 percent of GDP. Kohl's 1998 reelection bid depends almost entirely on the political ramifications of his federal budget plan[77] and on his ability to provide some guarantees that following the establishment of the EMU, the budget deficits of the member nations will not exceed the Maastricht convergence criteria by much.

The German EMU Decision

While there are few arguments that could convince the Germans to give up the Deutsche mark for the Euro by 2002, there are three possible reasons why they may nonetheless do so.

---

[76] During the first few months of his presidency Jacques Chirac caused some confusion regarding France's role in the EMU. Since then, however, he has expressed strong support for the project.

[77] The government coalition has proposed a 1997 tax reform to cut the "solidarity tax "and to lower and simplify taxes to stimulate investments and job creation.

First, the March 2, 1996 elections in three German Länder (states)[78] gave Chancellor Kohl's conservative-liberal coalition a major mid-term boost. All three Länder delivered more votes to the conservative CDU and the liberal FDP than in previous elections. The passing of the 5 percent hurdle[79] by the FDP was particularly important because failure to do so would have created serious problems for Kohl , his coalition and the country. Germany is not likely to have another Chancellor in the near future who is as committed to the EMU as he is. Kohl has been nicknamed "Bismarck in a cardigan" by journalists because of his bold international policy initiatives and his 14 year tenure, which makes him Germany's longest-serving head of government since the "Iron Chancellor".[80] Kohl's durability, determination and vision have surprised many at home and abroad. Despite skepticism and suspicion, he achieved German reunification without any major political problems in a short period of time. Nonetheless, his coalition government needed a boost to go ahead with the EMU plan. This the 1996 elections have provided.

The second possible reason is that the opposition Social Democratic Party (SPD) failed to galvanize support for an anti-EMU vote in the 1996. The SPD used the Baden-Würtemberg parliamentary election as a trial run for its 1998 federal campaign platform which among others,[81] included an anti-EMU stance that pitted integration against domestic stability and jobs. But the SPD failed because in economic matters the voters usually place more trust in the conservative-liberal coalition. As a result, in December 1996 the SPD not only withdrew its objections to the EMU, but decided to support the project. Yet, Chancellor Kohl still faces the dilemma of whether to agree to the unpopular EMU in early 1998, just months ahead of the fall election.

The third possible reason is that Germany has softened its position on the establishment of the political union. Since the inception of the EMU plan, the German government has insisted that a Western European political union is an "indispensable compliment to the EMU." However, Kohl's strong-arm tactics created estrangement at home and abroad. A number of EU countries resented Kohl's forceful moves and argued that Germany and like-minded nations are forcing their own particular vision of Europe on the other countries. In doing so, the argument went, they were endangering the solidarity that they profess to fortify. As a result, the Kohl government had to partially abandon its original plan.[82] To illustrate the point, the Bundesbank has recently confined itself to limiting fiscal sovereignty in the EMU nations and Foreign Minister, Klaus Kinkel announced that the EMU is Germany's major EU project. This is a

---

[78] Germany has 16 Länder.

[79] The FDP passed the 5 percent threshold required to gain seats in all three Länder, thereby ending a series of defeats (the results were below 5 percent in 12 of the 13 prior Länder elections).

[80] Otto von Bismarck not only created the United German Empire (1871-1890) but was also its first Chancellor.

[81] Other SPD campaign themes included restrictions on ethnic German immigrants from the Former Soviet Union (FSU).

[82] On March 26, 1996 German Foreign Minister Klaus Kinkel announced that Germany would limit its efforts to establish the EU political union in conjunction with the EMU.

fundamental change in the German government's position. In Kinkel's words, the country has moved away from using the EMU as "the lever to force through a political union beyond EMU; instead, it now defines the EMU as a political project."[83]

Thus, it is reasonable to assume that even if the 1996-97 IGC talks yield little in the way of moving toward a political union, the Germans will not delay, let alone prevent, the start of the EMU. This was confirmed during the special European Council Summit in Dublin on October 5, 1996, when EU member nations agreed to somewhat narrow the IGC agenda to make the June 1997 deadline for the conclusion of the talks more realistic. Not only have France and Germany scaled back their ambitions for deeper EU political integration, but they have also limited and delayed their plans for an EU institutional and decision-making reform so as to be able to focus on the launching of the EMU in 1999.

These developments together with the ERM II agreement concerning the relationship between the EMU "ins and "outs" and the role of the Euro as well as the acceptance of a post-EMU fiscal "Stability and Growth Pact" to enforce post-EMU budgetary discipline have greatly increased the likelihood of a German "Yes" on the EMU.

THE IMPORTANCE OF THE FRANCO-GERMAN ALLIANCE

Pre-Spring 1996

Just as in the case of the original ERM, the EMU's success depends on the commitment to the project by the French and German governments and the Bundesbank, the principal engines of the EU and the backbone of the integration process. But the 1992-93 ERM crises precipitated by the EMU plans were the key reasons for the difficult and costly ratification process of the Maastricht Treaty and for the debate over the convergence criteria, particularly the budget deficit and public debt limits. These events together with the departure of Jacques Delors from the EU Commission and the death of François Mitterand,[84] have exposed the weaknesses in the Franco-German relationship.

Because the EU has chosen the EMU as the next indispensable step of integration, the French-German relationship is critical. Although the EMU may be economically desirable and technically feasible, politically it is quite costly. Yet, it was not the timetable that had created the problems between the two nations, rather it was the question of sovereignty that generated deep divisions. The convergence criteria can be met by only a handful of countries and the EMU and the Euro still do not have the

---

[83] "Comments on EMU: Will EMU Fly in 1999?," 1996, p.3.
[84] Mitterand died on January 8, 1996.

support of most European citizens who find both "at best, irrelevant, and, at worst, unacceptable." They see no real benefits in the revamping of the central banking and currency systems. Most of the governments also face more pressing problems such as the reduction of unemployment and the stimulation of economic growth. Thus, it appeared that forging ahead with a multi-speed EMU to the exclusion of all else, could only make it more difficult to establish strong links between France and Germany as well as among the other EU member nations, while also trying to address the problems associated with enlargement.

Without the strong leadership of Jacques Delors and with the changeover from the low-key Spanish to the more active Italian presidency of the Council of Ministers during the first half of 1996, a tight and dynamic Franco-German alliance was needed to bring the EU back on track. But in spite of the reassuring official statements and goodwill displayed on both sides, the alliance was not as strong as in the past. There were several reasons for this. The personal chemistry between Kohl and Mitterand was strong and the 10-year Commission presidency of Jacques Delors promoted the concept of the EU as an ever-closer union of nations underpinned by the Franco-German alliance. The newly elected neo-Gaullist Chirac government, however, was initially viewed by Bonn as less committed to the cause of the EU and the Franco-German relationship. At the same time, as mentioned before, the French and other EU nations began to question Chancellor Kohl's forcefulness in calling for a political union. Thus, the two nations became more frustrated and disenchanted with each other.

During 1995 and 1996 France endured waves of social unrest while pursuing restrictive public spending policies. They were given a sense of urgency by the Maastricht Treaty's convergence criteria and the EMU timetable, because German Finance Minister Theo Waigel demanded strict fiscal EMU constraints. Moreover, the German government's position on the EMU became clearer day by day; it wanted steady progress toward political union and a German-style federal Europe. To this end, Chancellor Kohl wanted to minimize the use of the national veto and boost the powers of the European Parliament. The French, however, disagreed and preferred a multi-speed EU based on cooperation. Their vision called for increasing the power of the Council of Ministers at the expense of the European Parliament. France and Germany have also disagreed over the 1995 resumption of French nuclear testing and France's opting out of the Schengen agreement calling for the free movement of people within the EU.

There are those who believe that the relationship began to change with the reunification of Germany. They argue that it subtly shifted the balance of power to a larger, more powerful Germany. Coupled with other issues such as the emergence of a cluster of post-communist nations in the East that want EU membership, reunification changed the German view of the EU. This left France in a position of uncertainty as to its role and influence not only in the realm of monetary integration but also with respect to the EU in general. The French feared that enlargement to the East could create a

German-dominated block with an undue amount of influence.[85] This, coupled with the social unrest referred to previously further estranged the two countries and France turned inward. Some observers blamed President Mitterand who, although considered "a great European," failed to grasp the changing priorities of post-Cold War Europe. Yet, the chasm in the Paris-Bonn alliance was, for the most part, not caused by Germany looking eastward and France turning inward and southward, but by both nations pursuing their national interest first. "This has left their European rhetoric sounding increasingly hollow and irrelevant."[86]

Post-Spring 1996

Integration problems have always lead to a strengthening of the Franco-German alliance. This is exactly what had happened at the spring 1996 IGC meeting in Turin. In light of the EMU plan, Chancellor Kohl and President Chirac made an effort to reestablish close relationships. This came about as Chancellor Kohl scaled back his future vision of a German-style federalist Europe to the French concept[87] of a Europe that is neither a federal union nor a limited "free-trade zone". As a consequence, other disagreements between the two nations also became less pressing. Majority decision-making, the relative power of the EU Commission and of the European Parliament and internal security, including the free movement of people, were viewed as technical disagreements or, to put it differently, as resolvable problems rather than as major political conflicts. But defense matters continued to be a source of disagreement between the two nations. The French desire for "emancipation" from the United States has always distressed the Germans.

Thus, the Paris-Bonn axis again became the backbone of the EU in general and of the EMU in particular. But in 1997 the alliance was under a lot of strain again. To put the EU and the EMU back on track, the dynamic nature of the Franco-German alliance has to be restored, albeit under different political conditions. The Presidents of France and of the EU Commission have been replaced and the forthcoming elections in Germany and the U.K. may lead to additional changes. Moreover, Spain,[88] Portugal[89] and Greece[90] are also undergoing political transformations while the new EU countries, Sweden and Finland, appear to be skeptical about integration. It is in this changing

---

[85] When the Franco-German relationship began to show signs of strain, the French entertained the idea of "cosying up" to the British. But because the U.K. was cool to further integration, the idea was quickly discarded.

[86] Moisi, Dominique. "The Ghost of a Relationship," Financial Times, January 19, 1996, p.18.

[87] A vision similar to the original EEC during the 1950s.

[88] Spain held a general election on March 3, 1996. The ruling Socialist party of Felipe Gonzalez lost the elections to Jose Maria Azńar of the conservative Popular Party.

[89] In the Portuguese elections of January 14, 1996, Mario Soares, the Socialist president since 1986, was replaced by Jorge Sampaio.

[90] Prime Minister Andreas Papandreou who had been in power from 1981 to 1996 was replaced by Costa Simitis of the Panhellenic Socialist Movement.

context that a restructured and rejuvenated German-French alliance has to be maintained without any major problems.

The emerging EU is strikingly different from the Mitterand-Kohl concept of a union. During the previous decades, Germany's role in and ties to the EU had a clear sense of direction. Today, the country has a multiplicity of ties and the establishment of the EMU is not its only goal. Yet, there are those who want a European Germany rather than a German version of Europe incorporating German demands for a political union and stringent fiscal discipline.

Initial German doubts about President Chirac were well founded. He voted "Yes" on the Maastricht Treaty only reluctantly, opposed the SEA of 1985 and contested Spanish and Portuguese membership. At first, Chirac also opposed the adoption of the single currency. But by 1996 he had joined Chancellor Kohl as one of the strongest supporters of the Euro which both characterized as an "absolute requirement for economic advance."[91] Yet, their motives differ. Kohl sees the Euro as another step toward political union while Chirac views it as a mechanism to turn the French franc into another Deutsche mark. Nonetheless, German doubts about Chirac's European commitment seem to have disappeared, and thus the "backbone" of the EMU appears strong, at least for the time being. However, the March 1998 elections in France and the October elections in Germany in the same year may again test the strength of the Franco-German axis.

THE 1996-97 IGC NEGOTIATIONS

The 1996-97 intergovernmental conference negotiations (also known as the IGCs and "Maastricht II" talks) that began in March 1996 are scheduled to end at the Amsterdam EU Summit in June 1997. In general, they were initiated to address the neglected details of the original Maastricht Treaty and to prepare for enlargement to the East. The original agenda was ambitious and, thus, unrealistic. It specifically called for deeper political integration (French and German goals), the completion of the negotiations concerning EMU membership, the fine-tuning of the post-1999 EMU and the reform of the institutional structures as well as of the decision-making processes. The agenda also envisioned the enlargement of NATO.

The U.K. proved to be the most contentious participant of the talks. It warned the EU against taking any great leap forward so as to not repeat the mistake of the Maastricht Treaty which was signed without adequate preparations. On numerous occasions Prime Minister Major quoted EU Commission President Jacques Santer who, at the beginning of his term, stressed the need "to do less, but better." The U.K. resisted giving more power to the European Parliament, harbored animosity toward the European Court of Justice and was ambivalent about the EMU. Many member nations

---

[91] "The Helmut-and-Jacques Show." The Economist, April 6, 1996, pp.49-52.

ascribed such negative views to Major's weak parliamentary position and the influence of the Conservative Party's Euroskeptics. However, if history is any indication, the U.K. will probably again be outflanked rather than out-negotiated due to its weakening influence on the Continent. The EU nations outflanked the U.K. during the 1985 European Summit at which they adopted the qualified majority voting process (QMV) for "Single Market" legislation[92] and during the 1991 conference that had resulted in the Maastricht Treaty.

Disagreements among the other EU member nations generated additional complications. For example, at the informal meeting of EU foreign ministers in Palermo in March 1996, the French joined the U.K. in vetoing the participation of the European Parliament at the IGCs. The plan of Germany, France, the Benelux countries, Italy, Spain and Greece to incorporate the Western European Union (WEU) defense treaty into the EU was opposed by the U.K., Portugal, Denmark.[93] The traditionally neutral nations of Ireland, Austria, Finland and Sweden also disagreed with such a move.

Regardless of the U.K.'s position, the other 14 EU nations believe that they can eventually negotiate an acceptable IGC outcome. Given that the concepts of "variable geometry," "multi-speed" and "opt-out" are already part of the EU negotiation and bargaining processes, the U.K., at best, may only delay the EMU timetable. To some extent, this is what had happened at the special EU Summit in Dublin on October 5, 1996 when the member nations agreed to narrow the IGC agenda to make the June 1997 deadline more realistic and to reduce an already crowded EU calendar. The main focus of the 1996-97 IGC's had been abandoned in the name of expediency - France and Germany both scaled back their ambitions for deeper EU political integration. During the first six months of 1997, the EU Council of Ministers will be presided over by the Netherlands, followed during the second half of the year by Luxembourg. It is unlikely that the Dutch will be able to develop a major treaty for signature by mid-June due to the timing of the U.K. elections which must be held by May of the same year at the latest. Thus, it may be up to Luxembourg to bring the IGC talks to a conclusion and to develop an agreement at the December 1997 European Council Summit.

Yet, as another IGC ("Maastricht III") looms on the horizon, it is unclear whether a third set of talks would be held simultaneously with or only following EU enlargement. The admission of new members would additionally complicate future negotiations.

---

[92] The British had rejected the adoption of QMV on all " Single Market" issues and had insisted on the right to veto. Exempt from the QMV are issues related to labor, movement of people, the environment, constitutional amendments and taxes which still require unanimity.

[93] Denmark has opted out of the common defense policy and the EMU.

POSSIBLE EMU IMPEDIMENTS

German Domestic Policies[94]

Despite the March 1996 outcome of the Länder parliamentary elections, Chancellor Kohl's coalition government (CDU/CSU-FDP) remains fragile. As shown in Table 6.17, his reelection is far from certain.

Table 6.17
"German Opinion Polls: Uncertain Outlook for Chancellor Kohl"

Voting Intentions	**Forsa** April 12, 1996	**Allensbach** April 17, 1996
Government:	50%	44.6%
CDU/CSU	44%	38.1%
FDP	6%	6.5%
Opposition:	45%	51.5%
SPD	32%	32.3%
Greens	9%	12.9%
PDS	4%	6.3%

Source: Forsa/Die Woche, April 12, 1996; FAZ April 17, 1996. Published in "Comments on EMU: Will EMU Fly in 1999?," Merrill Lynch & Co., Inc. Global Securities Research & Economic Group, International Fixed Income Research, April 22, 1996, p.5.

In late 1997 a series of Länder elections will precede the federal elections of 1998. If these elections do not favor the governing coalition, Chancellor Kohl may lose in 1998. Thus, there is a chance that he may try to delay the start of the EMU beyond 1999. Three major issues could put the Chancellor's narrow majority in jeopardy. First, the fate of the government coalition's 1997 tax reform proposal which includes the FDP's March 1996 Länder parliamentary elections recommendation to cut the "solidarity tax" from 7.5 to 5.5 percent by 1998.[95] The tax reform plan also contains tax simplification and growth promoting measures to create jobs. These proposals will be an important part of the ruling coalition's re-election platform and campaign in October 1998.

The tax reform aims to cut the top and bottom income tax rates from 53 and 25.9 percent to 39 and 15 percent in January 1999. The plan also calls for business tax reductions which could reduce the German corporate tax burden by approximately

[94] This section, in part, is based on "Comments on EMU: Will EMU Fly in 1999?"

[95] The March 1996 Länder parliamentary elections were favorable to the FDP mainly because of its tax-cut platform which proposed reducing the "solidarity surcharge" from 7.5 percent to 5.5 percent. The solidarity surcharge - added to income and corporation tax bills - is used to finance reunification.

DM30 billion (US$18.5 billion) in 1999, following a possible DM7.5 billion reduction of the solidarity tax in 1998. These cuts are expected to "lead to more demand, more private investment, more sustained growth and more jobs...[and] to free citizens, companies and the administration from the superfluous baggage [of Germany's complicated tax system] and put an end to the waste of intellectual and economic resources currently engaged in tax avoidance."[96]

But if the Kohl government wants to reduce the deficit to 3 percent or below, it has little room to maneuver. Thus, the 1997 tax reform plan may not be realizable and could be offset by comparable increases in indirect i.e. VAT taxes[97] which the FDP rejects. If the tax reform plan fails, the FDP may drop below the 5 percent threshold in 1998 and thus bring down the Kohl government.[98]

The Social Democrats usually do not perform well at the polls when the economy is experiencing a downturn. The SPD is more attractive to voters when the redistribution of economic wealth rather than the fighting of recessions tops the national agenda.[99] Thus, if Chancellor Kohl's government manages to improve economic conditions over the next two years, this could also impair his election chances in 1998.

The SPD's nationalistic tone in the Baden-Würtemberg state parliamentary elections gave legitimacy to the hard-core nationalists. In the March 1996 Baden-Würtemberg parliamentary elections the right-wing extremist Republican Party with more than 9 percent of the vote was reinstated in the state parliament. The EMU plan could provide hard-core nationalists with a ready-made campaign platform for the 1998 national elections that could pull votes away from the ruling coalition. In a narrow contest this could be the difference between success and failure.

Thus Chancellor Kohl could be in a political quandary in early 1998 when he has to make a decision concerning the EMU, as it will no doubt be a matter that voters will consider. The safest course of action would be to delay the EMU decision until after the elections. However, depending on the political and economic circumstances in 1998, there is always the slight possibility that Kohl may not want to end his illustrious political career on such a negative note and thus will not run. If this is the case, he has nothing to lose by committing Germany to an EMU that will begin on January 1, 1999. It would be very difficult for an incoming SPD government to derail this schedule at the last minute.

---

[96] Theo Waigel, German Finance Minister as quoted in the article "Germany to revamp taxes to boost jobs" in the Financial Times, January 24, 1997.

[97] The 1997 tax reform proposal will have to be approved by the opposition majority in the Bundesrat which, to date consistently, has blocked plans to deregulate Germany's economy.

[98] "Comments on EMU: Will EMU Fly in 1999?," 1996, p.5.

[99] The SPD came into power in 1969 during an economic boom and lost office in 1982 in the midst of a severe recession.

A Possible EU-wide Economic Slowdown

For the EMU to start on time, it has to be assumed that the relatively low 2.24 percent average EU growth rate in 1996 can be raised to at least 2.5-3.0 percent in 1997 and 1998. This is necessary to address the high average EU unemployment levels which have reached 11.2 percent in 1996. The necessary increases in growth, in part, depend on the economic situation in Germany which will play a pivotal role in the EU's overall economic performance. See Table 6.18 for the EU nations' real GDP growth rates between 1991-96.

Table 6.18
Real GDP Growth (%)

	1991	1992	1993	1994	1995	1996
Belgium	1.6	1.7	-1.4	2.3	1.9	1.4
Denmark	1.3	0.2	1.5	4.4	2.8	2.1
Germany	5.0	2.2	-1.1	2.9	1.9	1.4
Greece	3.1	0.4	-1.0	1.5	2.0	2.4
Spain	2.3	0.7	-1.2	2.1	2.8	2.1
France	0.8	1.2	-1.3	2.8	2.2	1.0
Ireland	2.6	4.6	3.7	7.3	10.7	7.8
Italy	1.1	0.6	-1.2	2.1	3.0	0.8
Luxembourg	3.1	1.9	0.0	3.3	3.4	2.3
Netherlands	2.3	2.0	0.8	3.4	2.1	2.5
Austria	2.8	2.0	0.4	3.0	1.8	1.0
Portugal	2.3	1.1	-1.2	0.8	2.3	2.5
Finland	-7.1	-3.6	-1.2	4.4	4.2	2.3
Sweden	-1.1	-1.4	-2.2	2.6	3.0	1.7
UK	-2.0	-0.5	2.2	3.8	2.4	2.3
EU average	**1.2**	**0.87**	**-0.21**	**3.11**	**3.10**	**2.24**

Source: Data from "Progress Towards Convergence 1996," EMI, Frankfurt am Main, November, 1996.

German monetary policy has been expansionary since January 1995; the money supply, the M3 (annualized six-month) growth rates were almost 3 percent in January 1995. By early 1996 the growth rate had risen to 10 percent. Similarly, the M1 six-month annualized growth rate that was approximately 2 percent in January 1995 increased to just over 14 percent in early 1996.[100] However, the expansionary German monetary policy during 1995 was offset by a strong Deutsche mark and fiscal tightening. As a result, 1996 brought an even more expansionary monetary policy coupled with a more "normal" Deutsche mark and tax cuts accumulating to 0.3 to 0.4 percent of GDP.[101]

[100] "Comments on EMU: Will EMU Fly in 1999?," 1996, p.6.
[101] Net of increases in the social security contributions.

Germany and the Fiscal Convergence Criteria

If the Maastricht Treaty fiscal convergence criteria (reference values) are interpreted loosely, several EU nations could be admitted to the EMU even if they didn't exactly meet the 3 percent deficit and 60 percent debt to GDP criteria on time. Countries that exceed the debt and deficit levels may be admitted if they are reducing the same at a satisfactory rate. But it should be noted that the position of the member nations and of the key EU institutions (EU Commission and the EMI) on the acceptable deficit as opposed to debt ratios, is different. There is less tolerance for failing to meet the 3.0 percent deficit criterion than for missing the 60 percent debt requirement. It seems that if nations meet the deficit criterion, their inability to meet the debt criterion may be forgiven, within reason.

To preserve the credibility of the EMU, of all the EU nations, Germany must achieve and maintain a 3.0 percent deficit to GDP ratio in 1997. However, this seems difficult without severe public expenditure cuts and/or creative accounting, as the deficit in 1996 was 3.9 percent. High unemployment levels make it difficult to implement the cuts but if Germany does not meet the deficit criterion this will destroy the EMU's chance to start on schedule. It should be noted that just to maintain the current employment levels, Germany has to obtain a 3 percent growth rate in 1997.

Thus, there is a great deal of uncertainty surrounding Germany's 1997 budget deficit performance. The German government in early 1997 continued to insist that the deficit will be 2.9 percent, a level just below the Maastricht Treaty maximum of 3 percent. However, the five "Wise Men," the governments economic advisory council, during the fall of 1996 predicted that it will reach 3.3 percent while private German economic research institutions estimated it to be 3.5 percent. In February 1997, the OECD announced that the deficit to GDP ratio will reach 3.4 percent. In other words, besides the German government no other authoritative institution or group of experts seems to believe that Germany can meet the fiscal deficit convergence criterion in 1997.

There are also concerns regarding the German debt. It was 58.1 percent at the end of 1995, but the 1996 budget deficit of 3.9 percent raised it to 60.3 percent in the same year. Thus, even a drop to a 3 percent budget deficit level in 1997 would result in a debt level higher than 60 percent. Preliminary calculations indicate that the 1997 debt to GDP ratio could reach 61.5 percent. Hence, it would be difficult to claim that the Germans are reducing their debt at a satisfactory rate just as high-debt Ireland and Belgium, countries that have made substantial progress in this respect.

However, a debt ratio of 61.5 percent will not exclude Germany from the EMU, because its participation is critical and its fiscal credibility is beyond doubt. But even if the German economy becomes stronger, unemployment pressures will continue. The federal government has already announced proposed tax cuts of roughly 0.3

percent of GDP in 1997.[102] Yet, if the budget deficit is to be reduced to below 3.0 percent in 1997, spending cuts may have to be made in conjunction with an increase in the value-added tax. Otherwise it would be difficult for Chancellor Kohl to move forward with the EMU. But introducing additional spending cuts and tax increases a year before the scheduled elections is not the best way to stay in office.

France and the Fiscal Convergence Criteria

There is little question that in trying to meet the fiscal convergence criteria on time, France will experience as much, if not more, trouble than Germany. Although France does not have a debt problem, it faces a deficit predicament. The 1995 and 1996 deficit was 5.2 and 4.8 percent, respectively. In 1996, through creative accounting the French government revised its 1997 deficit prediction from 3.45 percent to 3.0. However, private economic forecasting institutions predict that the deficit will be closer to 3.6 percent. If France cannot meet the deficit criterion in 1997, Kohl may call for an EMU delay because he would not want to ask the German public to informally relax the EMU membership requirements during the 1998 election year. To save himself such an embarrassment, Jacques Chirac may pre-empt Chancellor Kohl's call for an EMU delay. If political considerations will allow it, the two could make a joint announcement citing some other reason for the delay.

A Possible EU Currency Crisis

The EMU timetable cannot be observed if a major currency crisis occurs involving "core" EU nations such as France. The potential of such a crisis increases if either of the following two scenarios occurs: (i) an EU-wide economic slow-down in 1997 as a result of which the financial markets attack the French franc, believing that the government cannot meet the deficit convergence criterion because it has to fight unemployment. If the markets suspect that French support for the EMU is dwindling, even the Bundesbank's assistance might not be enough to prevent a tumble of the franc; and/or (ii) the EU economies experience strong growth by late 1997 or early 1998 and the financial markets expect the Bundesbank to raise its discount and Lombard rates while the Bank wants to delay such increases so as to not affect the establishment of the EMU. Nonetheless, the franc and other EU currencies could come under pressure. These two scenarios are unlikely, but they cannot be ruled out as financial markets tend to overreact to unanticipated economic or financial developments.

The Bundesbank and the Euro

The Bundesbank plays a special role in the economic and monetary integration process. It may indeed be its President Tietmeyer who will go down in history as the

---

[102] A reduction in the solidarity surcharge and elimination of the wealth tax.

man who made possible the realization of the EMU.[103] Chancellor Kohl cannot "sell" the EMU plan, including the replacement of the Deutsche mark by the Euro and the demise of the Bundesbank, to the German people without the public support of the Bank, particularly of its President Tietmeyer. This puts the Bundesbank in a quandary because the EMU's success thus depends on its own demise.[104] The Bank's legal and moral obligation to the German public to safeguard the value of the nation's currency, whether it is the Deutsche mark or the Euro, is also an important consideration. If the Deutsche mark is relinquished, the Bundesbank must assure the integrity of its successor, the Euro. To date, the Bank has managed to enforce the convergence criteria to limit EMU membership and to create a post-EMU fiscal "Stability and Growth Pact", but it is uncertain how much pressure it can exert after January 1, 1999, or for that matter after July 1, 2002.

Despite the Bundesbank's demise under the EMU it is unlikely that the Bank will impede economic and monetary integration. President Tietmeyer has long been a supporter of international monetary cooperation and shares Chancellor Kohl's pro-European views. He was "the German representative on the committee that drafted the 'Werner' plan for European monetary union more than 25 years ago."[105] Other members of the Bundesbank Council, such as Peter M. Schmidhuber and Olaf Sievert, are also known for their pro-EMU views. [106] Many observers have even speculated that the April 26, 1996 interest rate cut may have been the Bundesbank's way to help Germany and France meet the fiscal convergence criteria. Nonetheless, Chancellor Kohl needs a clear public statement from the Bundesbank supporting the EMU plan, the abrogating of the Deutsche mark and the introduction of the Euro. This is critical to the EMU's success and also to Kohl's reelection campaign because it would be a major political blunder to oppose the Bundesbank in an election year. To date, however, the Bundesbank has not made such a statement as it waits for more information concerning the German and French deficits and the implications of the post-EMU fiscal "Stability and Growth Pact."

The EMI Council in which Bundesbank President Tietmeyer has one vote will formally decide on EMU membership during 1998. Minority votes will be published, thus if Tietmeyer does not vote in favor of the EMU and for the inclusion/exclusion of certain EU nations, a negative reaction by the German public and the financial markets is assured. As mentioned before, it would be very difficult for Chancellor Kohl to overrule the Bundesbank's vote in the EMI during an election year. In the past Kohl has overruled the Bank on monetary issues as, for example, the East and West German monetary union, but then he had the German public's support. This is not the case with respect to the EMU. Thus the Bundesbank is damned if it does and damned if it doesn't.

---

[103] The Bundesbank Council's voting structure is disproportionately in favor of the Länder, although the Bank's President commands a great deal of influence over the Council.

[104] This may not be apparent at first, but in time the Bundesbank is certain to lose its influence in the global financial markets.

[105] "Comments on EMU: Will EMU Fly 1999?," 1996, p.8.

[106] Peter M. Schmidhuber was a former EU Commissioner.

The German Constitutional Court and the EMU

The German Constitutional Court is not a threat to the realization of the EMU in general and of the Euro in particular. Nonetheless, there is little doubt that abrogating the Deutsche mark will require a constitutional review. In its ruling on October 12, 1993, the Court had approved the ratification of the Maastricht Treaty by stating that it does not violate the German Constitution. Yet, it made clear that the establishment of the EMU does not automatically follow the ratification process. The German Parliament could vote on the EMU anew, the Maastricht Treaty convergence criteria could be strictly interpreted and the EMU timetable could become a "target corridor" rather than a formal schedule. In other words, economic and monetary convergence concerns could preempt any timetable.

It is, however, unlikely that the German Constitutional Court would assume the role of the "ultimate arbiter of European integration"[107] and rule against a political decision to establish the EMU. Yet, it cannot disregard its earlier decision concerning strict adherence to the convergence criteria, particularly to the fiscal requirements. This, coupled with the Bundesbank's aversion to excessive fiscal deficits explains why Kohl must pay close attention to the 3 percent deficit criterion.

The "Italian Insult"

The initial core group of six EMU nations will probably include Germany, France, Austria and the Benelux countries. The Germans have expressed opposition to Italy's participation in the core group. But as Belgium's debt to GDP ratio is higher than that of Italy's, the EMU can begin only if Italy agrees to Belgium's participation.[108]

Moreover, if economics will be the only consideration in deciding EMU membership, even Spain could make it ahead of Italy. Spain's economic fundamentals are much closer to meeting the Maastricht Treaty criteria than are Italy's. Its 1996 public debt to GDP ratio of 67.4 percent is considerably less than Italy's 124.3 percent ratio. At 4.8 percent in 1996 and at 3.7 percent (estimated) in 1997, Spain's budget deficit to GDP ratio is also expected to come closer to the convergence criteria than Italy's 7.2 percent in 1996 and projected 4 percent in 1997. Moreover, in early 1997, the real yield on Spain's long-term debt was only 90 basis points more than that of the German "bunds" while the Italian yields were around 150 points higher. Thus, Spain would be less of an implicit threat to the stability of the EMU and the Euro than would Italy, if admitted.

Fortunately, the current Italian government understands the difficulties that the Germans face regarding the inclusion of Italy in 1999. Thus, it may agree to wait, even though Belgium participates in the core group. If the Italians accept Belgium's

---

[107] "Comments on EMU: Will EMU Fly in 1999?," 1996, p.8.

[108] For more detail, see the section "Potential EMU Membership," in this chapter.

admission, this decision is certain to grant Italy a place in the EMU within a few years following its establishment, particularly since the ERM II is viewed by the Italians as a halfway house to the EMU. But it is unlikely that the Italians would accept being passed over in favor of Spain. There is also no guarantee that a new Italian government would be amenable to the postponement of the country's membership under any circumstance; it could demand admission in 1999. Not surprisingly, there is a sharp debate going on in Italy regarding these issues. In light of this perceived "Italian insult" the leader of the Center Right Alliance,[109] for example, has called for either a mandatory inclusion of Italy in the EMU in 1999, or a delay until the core nations acquiesce in Italy's participation.

With the assistance of other potential non-EMU member nations such as Spain, Portugal and Greece, an acrimonious Italy could muster enough support in the European Council to make the realization of the French-German agenda very difficult. Together, these nations could object to the EU membership of the Central and Eastern European countries (CEEs), and the reform of the EU budget and of the Common Agriculture Policy. If the mood in Italy turns in this direction, France and Germany would in all probability delay the EMU for two to three years. But playing a high-stakes political game of this sort does not come without risk, as probably nothing could stop France and Germany from going ahead and forming a currency union outside the EMU if the same is delayed. Austria and the Benelux nations would be eager to join such a "pre-EMU" currency union, thus, Italy could find itself isolated.

Yet, if the "Italian Insult" is not managed well by Germany and the other core nations, Italy could obstruct the EMU's timetable.

The Outcome of the 1996-97 IGC Talks

Initially, despite moderating its demands, Germany still had high expectations of the 1996-97 IGC talks. In particular, it had wanted more qualified majority voting in the Council of Ministers and the European Council. It also called for the streamlining of the decision-making processes of the other EU institutions. This is important to Germany, because it wants to promote the membership of the CEE and Mediterranean nations such as Cyprus and Malta. Other IGC issues Germany is concerned about include increased cooperation and progress on immigration, anti-crime measures and common foreign and defense policies. It should be noted that during the special European Council Summit in Dublin on October 5, 1996, the EU member governments agreed to narrow the IGC agenda so as to make the June 1997 deadline for the conclusion of the talks more realistic. Not only did France and Germany scale back their plans for further political integration but plans for EU institutional and decision-making reform were also limited and delayed so as to focus on the timely launching of the EMU in 1999. The negotiations seem to progress just enough to eventually declare them a success.

---

[109] Silvio Berlusconi, quoted in the German weekly Welt am Sonntag, April 14, 1996.

The Post-EMU Fiscal "Stability and Growth Pact"

Both Chancellor Kohl and the Bundesbank wanted a post-EMU fiscal "stability pact" as a precondition to Germany's EMU participation. Both argued that post-EMU fiscal prudence is critical to the Euro's credibility and stability. Their demand was rooted in the lingering German suspicion that following EMU's start, some member nations will not be able to abide by the fiscal discipline requirement. Such failure could increase inflationary pressures and ultimately lead to a possible breakdown of the economic and monetary integration process.

The urgency of a post-EMU fiscal "stability pact" became apparent in 1996 and was reinforced in 1997 when it was clear that not only will most EU nations fail to meet the strict interpretation of the fiscal convergence criteria[110] but some of them have used creative accounting to reduce their deficits below the 3 percent maximum. Once admitted and obtaining lower interest rates on their debt, such nations could allow the deficits to grow again. Without a stringent post-EMU "stability pact" the German public's fears of giving up the Deutsche mark could not be mitigated. Moreover, such a pact would also allow a more political i.e. relaxed interpretation of the 1997 fiscal criteria in 1998, when membership will be decided.

German Finance Minister Theo Waigel presented a post-EMU "stability pact" proposal made up of two parts during the April 12-13, 1996 ECOFIN Council meeting in Verona, Italy[111]. The proposal is summarized in Box 6.1. The first part called for a budget deficit limit of 1 and 3 percent during normal as opposed to recessionary years. The second part required the imposition of heavy automatic fines for exceeding the limits. The latter proposition was rejected by the other EU nations due to concerns about the legality of such fines under Article 104c of the Maastricht Treaty. But the September 21-22, 1996 ECOFIN Council meeting in Dublin resurrected the idea of fines and agreed on a modified version of the same. The ministers accepted the proposal that fines could be imposed on nations that run budget deficits greater than 3 percent for more than a few months. But they emphasized that the fines should be imposed only following a discussion of the reasons for the transgression.

The idea of automatic fines continued to be controversial. Critics argued that in a world of asymmetrical economic shocks such as oil crises, a uniform automatic fine is inappropriate and that fiscal corrective measures are best imposed by the financial markets or through international pressure and negotiations but not through a mechanical formula, no matter how sophisticated. Basing the "stability pact" on rigid constructs could deepen fiscal crises when they occur. The critics also pointed out that experience has shown time and again that governments are not able to continue previously implemented economic policies when confronted by large economic shocks and the resulting social and political pressures.

---

[110] The Maastricht Treaty allows a "soft" interpretation of the convergence criteria.

[111] This meeting launched the 1996-97 IGC talks.

Box 6.1
The German Stability Pact Proposal

EMU members must agree:
- to limit their budget deficit to 1 percent in normal years; - to not exceed a 3 percent deficit limit even in a recession; - to allow exceptions only with the agreement of other EMU members and in extraordinary circumstances such as natural disasters; - to pay a non-interest bearing deposit of 0.2-0.5 percent of GDP depending on the size of the deficit; - to convert the deposit into a fine that is lost for good if the deficit exceeds 3 percent for two years.

Source: Adapted from "Comments on EMU: Will EMU Fly in 1999?," p.9.

But the critics conceded that a post-EMU fiscal "stability pact" was needed, at least in the initial stages of introducing the Euro. The pact is "an important brick in the edifice"[112] of the EMU. Thus, during the December 13-14, 1996 Dublin European Council Summit, the EU nations accepted the German-inspired plan of a post-EMU "Stability and Growth Pact," renamed at the insistence of the French. The acceptance came about because Germany softened its position by agreeing to the French view that maximum political discretion should be applied during the process of setting the fines. The agreement narrows the Maastricht Treaty's definition of "exceptional and temporary circumstances" under which EMU nations could escape the penalties of running excessive deficits, yet it manages to uphold the Treaty's commitment to retain the power of discretion of the ECOFIN Council. It will, however, place undue political pressure on the European Central Bank.

EMU member nations running excessive deficits will be exempted from automatic fines if either of the following two conditions exist: (i) a natural disaster or (ii) a decline in GDP of at least 2 percent over a period of a year.[113] If the decline is between 0.75 percent and 2 percent, the ECOFIN Council, including the representative of the nation that has generated the excessive deficit, may consider such mitigating factors as the abruptness of the downturn, when setting the fines. Although not specified in the agreement, it is assumed that automatic fines will also be imposed on nations with excessive deficits that have experienced a decline of less than 0.75 percent in their annual GDP. The fines can be as high as 0.5 percent of GDP.

If this pact had been in force in 1996, only Denmark, Ireland, the Netherlands and Luxembourg would have escaped the penalties. Germany could have been fined up to DM10 billion (US$7 billion). Nonetheless, the German's were not pleased that they

---

[112] "A Pact that Could Destabilize the EU." Financial Times, September 27, 1996.
[113] The 15 EU nations have experienced severe recessions 9 times during the last 25 years.

had to give up their original demands as illustrated by the statement made by the Bundesbank's chief economist and board member Otmar Issing following the Dublin European Council Summit: "Unrestrained automaticty would not have been possible but one cannot be satisfied with a decision mechanism in which potential sinners pass judgment on actual sinners."[114] Other related issues also discussed during the Dublin Summit included currency discipline and the legal status of the Euro.

EMU's Impact on Unemployment[115]

Over the past 26 years, the EU's average unemployment rate has increased from 3 to 11 percent. By contrast, the comparable US unemployment rate of just over 5 percent in 1997 is no higher than it was in the early 1970s. Thus, there is a growing fear in the EU nations that together with the EMU, unemployment created by labor market conditions and other related factors such as the meager 1997 average growth rate of 2.2 percent, will push the jobless rate even higher. Concerns are also raised about the social implications of fulfilling the EMU criteria. Populist politicians have started to blame economic and monetary integration for the emerging social conflicts. This is illustrated by the German and French strikes that started in 1995 and continue to plague both nations. Table 6.19 shows EU unemployment trends over the 1991 - 1996 time period.

Table 6.19
EU unemployment rates (%)

	1991	1992	1993	1994	1995	1996
Austria	3.4	3.6	4.2	4.4	3.8	4.2
Belgium	6.6	7.3	8.9	10.0	9.9	9.7
Denmark	10.6	11.3	12.4	12.3	10.3	9.0
Finland	7.6	13.1	17.9	18.4	17.2	16.5
France	9.5	10.4	11.8	12.2	11.7	12.7
Germany	5.7	7.8	8.9	9.6	9.4	10.2
Greece	7.7	8.7	9.7	9.6	10.0	9.8
Ireland	15.7	16.4	16.4	15.0	13.0	11.7
Italy	10.9	10.7	10.2	11.3	12.0	12.1
Luxembourg	1.4	1.6	2.1	2.7	3.0	3.2
Netherlands	7.0	5.6	6.2	6.8	7.0	6.3
Portugal	4.1	4.1	5.5	6.8	7.2	7.2
Spain	16.3	18.4	22.7	24.2	22.9	22.4
Sweden	3.0	5.4	8.2	8.0	7.7	7.8
U.K.	8.0	9.8	10.4	9.4	8.3	7.7
EU Average	**8.6**	**9.4**	**10.9**	**11.4**	**11.1**	**11.2**

Source: Adopted from "Progress to Convergence 1996". EMI. Frankfurt am Main, November 1996; and OECD, Financial Times and Economist 1995 and 1996 data.

---

[114] "EU Warned Over Policing EMU." Financial Times, December 17, 1996, p.1.

[115] For an analytical discussion of EMU's potential impact on unemployment see, "Monetary Union and European Unemployment." CEPR Discussion Paper No. 1458, October 1996.

The EMU will affect unemployment in two ways: (i) through the budget cuts required to meet the Maastricht convergence criteria and (ii) the introduction of the Euro. It is, however, not clear which of the two events will have more of an impact. In the short-term, budget cuts will depress demand and thus increase unemployment. But, in most EU nations such cuts are necessary irrespective of the EMU because if they are made, this could reduce long-term real interest rates which results in increased investments. This, together with a higher degree of monetary and fiscal stability, should create more jobs in the medium term.

The short-run economic and thus, political costs of relinquishing monetary and exchange rate policies as adjustment tools to deal with symmetrical or asymmetrical shocks are quite high. The extent of the costs, however, depends on the relative importance of common as opposed to country-specific policy measures that determine output and employment. If unemployment is generated by common factors, the EMU and its Euro should have little impact on employment levels. However, if unemployment is determined by country-specific factors, EMU could negatively affect national employment because a strictly anti-inflationary common monetary policy could be too constraining for the individual countries.

In order for the EMU to function well and to endure, it must represent an "optimum currency area" (OCA).[116] As discussed earlier, an OCA must meet one of the following two sets of conditions: (i) an adjustment mechanism i.e. flexible wages, highly mobile labor or flexible fiscal policy; or (ii) symmetrical as opposed to asymmetrical shocks.[117] The expectation that only symmetrical shocks will occur is unrealistic, thus in order for the EMU and the Euro to prevail, either flexible wages and labor mobility or flexible fiscal policies must be available as adjustment tools. But neither of these policy option tools is available. In fact, fiscal policy is becoming less and less of an option as nations strive to meet the convergence criteria and eventually the requirements of the post-EMU fiscal "Stability and Growth Pact." It should be noted that regardless of the EMU or the Euro, the EU labor markets need restructuring as the bulk of joblessness is structural i.e. the result of centralized wage bargaining, strict job-protection laws and generous unemployment and other social benefits.

More and more EU citizens are associating the integration process with the deterioration of social conditions and the loss of jobs. Thus, the task of the common institutions is to establish a link between deeper integration and the creation of jobs and social progress while the task of national governments is to pursue social issues as vigorously as they are pursuing the Maastricht Treaty convergence criteria. This

---

[116] See Chapter IV for a more detailed discussion on the EMU as an OCA.

[117] An EMU of a few "core nations" is more likely to experience asymmetrical shocks than an EMU of 15. Coupled with rigid and low mobile labor markets this could lead to higher unemployment. Asymmetrical shocks are costly even for the "core nations" and have occurred approximately once every decade.

does not negate the governments' responsibility to exercise budgetary discipline as sound finances are necessary for sustained medium-term growth and, thus, employment. Nor does it negate the need for labor market reforms, including better targeted training, review of the tax burdens on the low-wage workers, the creation of more flexible labor costs, and the reform of the social security systems. These issues were discussed in the 1996 "Joint Competitiveness Report"[118] issued by the EU Commission's Social and Monetary Affairs Division. The report emphasized the need to maximize the contribution of small and medium-sized companies by cutting red tape and ensuring that sufficient funds are available for trans-European networks to complete any missing transport and energy links. The national governments endorsed these propositions.

THE EMU BLUEPRINT FOR 2002

The EMI Presidency and the 1997 "Progress Towards Convergence" Report

The EMI Presidency

Alexander Lamfalussy was chosen as President of the newly created European Monetary Institute (EMI) in 1994 because of his international reputation and experience as a central banker as well as the head of the Bank of International Settlements, the central bank of central banks. By all accounts, he had steered the EMI well during its formative years. However, in 1996 Lamfalussy announced that he would like to step down in mid-1997. This raised the issue of who would succeed him. The choice of the next EMI President is critical to the success of the EMU. The transition stage (1997-1999) performance record of the EMI will determine the credibility of the European Central Bank (ECB) and of the Euro.[119] The identity of the next President is important also because he could become the first President of the ECB.

At the time of Lamfalussy's announcement, the most likely replacement candidates were Jean-Claude Trichet,[120] head of the Bank of France and Wim Duisenberg, head of the Central Bank of the Netherlands. Despite Trichet's international and political presence, Duisenberg was eventually chosen to head the EMI starting in July 1997. This was not entirely unexpected. Duisenberg is well known as

---

[118] "Joint Competitiveness Report", Social and Monetary Affairs Division, European Commission, Brussels: Office of Official Publications of the European Communities, 1996.

[119] The second critical stage, 1999 to 2002, will determine the success of the Euro, which will depend on the ECB's activities.

[120] Although Jean-Claude Trichet has an international and political presence, his EMI presidency could have created problems. The financial markets may have assumed that French enthusiasm for the EMU could cloud the EMI's judgment at the critical time of discussing EMU membership, and its starting date. They could have also believed that the EMI's discipline may have been compromised by the French political goal of starting the EMU on time.

an ultra-orthodox banker who, if the EMU were a chancy undertaking, would not risk his reputation for the sake of trying to achieve it. Moreover, his close ties to the Bundesbank and his German-style monetary policy stance provide him with instant credibility in the financial markets. He was undoubtedly the unofficial German favorite. But his international and political presence is less than that of Trichet. Thus, the French and the Germans eventually may have to compromise and keep Duisenberg as the head of the EMI during the EMU's most critical phase while selecting Trichet as the first or second President of the ECB. Duisenburg's current term of office is only 18 months. But his tenure may be extended if a short, technical EMU delay takes place.

The EMI's 1997 " Progress Towards Convergence" Report

The credibility of the EMI is critical because it will be its November 1997 "Progress Towards Convergence" report and a similar follow-up 1998 report, based on 1997 data, containing final recommendations that will set the tone for the first round of EMU membership discussions. The reports will serve as an indicator as to whether the EU nations are ready to start the EMU in 1999. Even more important, they will provide the markets with an idea of how the Maastricht Treaty criteria will be interpreted in early to mid-1998. Any sign of laxity in these EMI reports could not only revive integration doubts but severely hurt the Euro's credibility at the onset of the EMU. A "soft" interpretation of the criteria, in all probability, would also raise uncertainty in the foreign exchange markets. The introduction of the ERM II could generate additional concerns at the time that the performance data are reviewed.

The findings of the November 1997 EMI report will probably show that the majority of EU nations do not meet the fiscal criteria, thus, technically, the EMU should not start in 1999. But it is possible that the early to mid-1998 definition of "sustained" or "sustainable" debts and deficits will be politically rather than economically shaded and that the EMU will start on schedule.

Possible EMU Alternatives

Table 6.20 shows the official EMU timetable to the year 2002, when national currencies will be withdrawn and the Euro will become the sole legal tender in the member countries.

Table 6.20
Official EMU Timetable to the Year 2000

End-1996	- Finland joins ERM on October 14th; Italy rejoins ERM on November 25th. Sweden and U.K. elect to remain outside of current ERM. - EMI produces its 1996 in-depth report concerning the meeting of the Maastricht criteria during 1996. - EU member nations agree on the ERM II plans to link potential EMU "ins" and outs" to each other and to a post-EMU fiscal "growth and stability pact."
1997	- ERM II groundwork and infrastructure established. - EMI finalizes blueprints of future European Systems of Central Banks, including outlines of monetary policy procedures (key instruments, inflation and money supply targets. - May; U.K. elections.
Early to Mid-1998	- EMI names EU member nations eligible for EMU in 1999. - EU Commission identifies eligible countries. - European Council officially chooses EMU participants, probably at the mid-1998 summit meeting*. - March; French parliamentary elections.
Mid-1998-Dec.31,1999	- ERM II preparations begin (after EMU participants are chosen). - October; German federal elections.
January 1, 1999	- Stage III of EMU begins with the irrevocable fixing of exchange rates. - The Euro is introduced on a non-cash bases. - European Central Bank takes over EMU participants' monetary policies. - The ERM II begins to operate. - EMU participants must issue new marketable debt in Euro. Most existing government bonds will probably be converted into Euro (not required) to assure a liquid market in government paper. - National currencies (notes and coins) remain in circulation.
January 2002	- Euro notes and coins put into circulation.
July 2002	- EMU participants national notes and coins withdrawn and the Euro becomes the sole legal tender.

* The European Council's decision is political, thus will not be influenced by either the EMI's or the EU Commission's recommendations.

The meeting of this timetable is by no means assured. As pointed out on the previous pages, a number of events could interfere with the establishment of the EMU by January 1, 1999. This could result in the following possible outcomes, all quite different from the official plan:

1. There is enough of a political momentum with more than a 50 percent chance that a core group of nations will start the last stage of the EMU in 1999. The Deutsche mark gradually "softens" against the other EU currencies and the U.S. dollar. Yield spreads converge which might benefit even non-EMU member countries. A new, officially asymmetrical but flexible ERM II links the "ins" to the

"outs."[121] The U.K. keeps the pound sterling out of the ERM II, at least initially.

2. There is a short technical delay as a decision in 1998 may not leave enough time for the central and commercial banks to prepare for the irrevocable locking of exchange rates on Jan 1, 1999. The core group of EMU participants goes ahead with the original plan by the year 2000, at the latest. The technical delay is due to France exceeding the 3 percent deficit and Germany the 60 percent debt and 3 percent deficit limit in 1997. German federal elections take place in late 1998, just a few months before the scheduled start of the EMU in 1999, and are a major influencing factor in the final decision. A technical delay provides much needed time between the French and German political elections on the one hand and the start of the EMU on the other hand.[122] It is, however, unlikely that the short technical delay affects the credibility of the EMU, nor is it likely that the financial markets see this as a political effort to delay or derail the project.[123] But a decision to delay may not be reached prior to late 1997 or early 1998.

3. A substantial delay of two or more years takes place. But this does not mean that the EMU is abandoned. It could still start around 2002. In this case, EU nations such as Italy, Sweden, Finland, Ireland, Spain and Portugal, which would probably not have been part of the EMU core in 1999, have a good chance of joining at the start.

4. The EMU does not move beyond the early phases of Stage III and the Euro remains the 16th EU currency. There is an officially asymmetrical but flexible ERM II based on the Euro as the anchor currency. The exchange rates of the core EMU currencies are irrevocably fixed while the currencies of the periphery nations or EMU "outs" are pegged to the Euro and observe flexible ERM II currency bands. The pound sterling does not participate, at least initially. The ECB becomes an EU-Group of 15 which conducts EMU-wide economic policy involving monetary, exchange rate and fiscal measures. The Maastricht Treaty convergence criteria still hold, but now the goal is to graduate from the ERM II into the EMU core group's irrevocable exchange rate system. In an increasingly widening EU made up of smaller nations with a right to veto, the asymmetrical ERM II may reinstate some of the lost influence of the large economies.

---

121 For political reasons also known as the "pre-ins."
122 "Comments on EMU: Will EMU Fly in 1999?," 1996.
123 "Comments on EMU: Will EMU Fly in 1999?," 1996.

5. After a series of delays, the EMU is abandoned. France, Germany, Austria and the Benelux nations irrevocably fix their exchange rates and a modified ERM II becomes the EU's monetary system. The asymmetrical structure of the ERM II allows the politically and economically stronger EU nations to exert their influence in a widening EU, increasingly made up of smaller nations with veto power.

Possible Outcomes in 2002 and Beyond

Despite France and Germany's inability to meet the convergence criteria in 1997 and the failure of the other nations to meet the German-inspired conditions to move to Stage III, there is a political momentum supporting the establishment of the EMU by 1999. It can be argued that there is a 50 percent probability that a limited i.e. core-based EMU will start on time or, due to technical problems, a year later. If it starts in 1999, member nations will irrevocably lock their exchange rates and the Euro will be introduced on a non-cash basis.[124] This could happen because the current political mood in the EU is one of uncompromising determination to meet the EMU timetable, regardless of the short-term employment and, thus, political repercussions. National leaders such as Chancellor Kohl have invested too much personal and political capital in the EMU to allow it to be derailed.

However, there is a difference between starting the EMU with the irrevocable locking of exchange rates together with the subsequent introduction of the Euro on a non-cash basis, and the completion of the EMU i.e. the eventual replacement of national currencies. The uncertain outcome of the 1998 German and French elections together with the five year long transition period to the year 2002 could generate instability. An economic slowdown may, for example, destroy French hopes of meeting or, more important, sustaining the fiscal convergence criteria. This could postpone the introduction of the Euro notes and coins. There could also be a dollar crisis that might upset the currency markets and lead to a speculative attack on the French franc.

Yet, due to the prevailing political momentum, there is a 50 percent chance that the Euro notes and coins will be placed into circulation on January 1, 2002, replacing national currencies as a legal tender by July 1, 2002. Once this happens, country exchange rates policies will have to be replaced by other economic policy tools. But, to date, the Maastricht Treaty architects have not explained what these policy tools

---

[124] If the EMU begins in 1999, there is a probability that the ECOFIN Council may have to modify or even waive the ERM criterion of exchange rate stability over a period of two years. Such a decision could be seen by the financial markets as an undesirable precedent leading to a soft Euro. Taylor, Christopher. "EMU: The State of Play," The World Today, Vol.51, The Royal Institute of International Affairs, April 1995.

could be, although it is generally recognized that they would have to include competitive i.e. flexible labor markets and less rigid wage policies. Yet, such policies are a "a dirty word in social-welfare Europe."[125] Nonetheless, the Maastricht Treaty designers have argued that the elimination of exchange rates coupled with low inflation and increasing fiscal responsibility will eventually force EMU member states to address the labor market rigidities.

But such an expectation is based on too many assumptions as, for example, the absence of asymmetrical shocks in the EU. Once the EMU and the "Single Market" are fully developed and economic integration is completed, this may turn out to be the case. But in the medium- to long-term, asymmetrical shocks will continue. Therefore, it is highly probable that when an EMU nation is subject to structural or cyclical economic problems greater than those of the other countries, disagreements will occur. This will be specially true if the nations involved are large and influential EMU members. Their governments will use fiscal policies to address the problems which may violate the fiscal "Stability and Growth Pact." The resulting fines may prompt the populist politicians of the affected countries to translate domestic economic difficulties into a crusade against the European Central Bank (ECB).[126] Thus, the "Stability and Growth Pact" places undue political pressure on the ECB.

There is a 50 percent chance that the EMU will not move beyond the early phases of Stage III and that the Euro will remain the official 16th currency while national currencies continue to circulate. In this case, the ECB will remain an EU-Group of 15 (G-15) that coordinates and conducts EMU-wide monetary policies, focusing on macroeconomic issues such as exchange rate, monetary and fiscal measures affecting all EU nations. In this case, the Euro would be the only currency under the direct control of the ECB. However, the ECB could still exert indirect control over the other EMU currencies as they would be irrevocably locked with the Euro. This could result in a narrow exchange rate mechanism that is similar to the original ERM and the ERM II, except that the Euro would be the anchor currency and the ECB the main monetary policy-formulator. If this happens, the French will have achieved their long-standing objective of greater influence over EU monetary policies while maintaining a Bundesbank-type credibility. The Maastricht Treaty criteria will still serve as a gauge to measure monetary and fiscal policy performance, but the goal will be to graduate from the ERM II to the EMU core's irrevocable exchange rate system. The ERM II will link the EMU "outs" with the "ins" while Germany, France, Austria and the Benelux countries agree to adopt the Euro at a later date, perhaps in January 2005.

Thus, it seems that politico-economic rather than purely economic considerations such as the Maastricht Treaty convergence criteria will decide the fate of the EU's economic and monetary integration process. The key to achieving the EMU as envisioned by its planners is to make it seem inevitable. The way to sustain it is to

---

125 "The Danger of Dithering." Financial Times, October 1, 1996.
126 "The Danger of Dithering." Financial Times, October 1, 1996.

convince all potential member nations to fully commit to long-term economic discipline. In other words, the hard decisions have yet to be made.

EU integration moves towards the EMU can be viewed in a variety of ways. A pessimistic view includes age-old national blackmail, horse-trading and posturing, while an optimistic view is based on national and supranational political and economic cooperation. Reality, as always, is somewhere in between. The EMU and its Euro are by far the most splendid yet also riskiest ventures that the EU has ever embarked on and if the venture buckles under the weight of popular protest, the resulting damage to European unity and cooperation will be enormous. The EMU must be safeguarded from the reckless.

BIBLIOGRAPHY

BOOKS

Abraham, Jean-Paul. "Is Competitiveness a Dangerous Obsession?" in Fair D. and R. Raymond, eds., The Competitiveness of Financial Institutions and Centers in Europe, The Netherlands: Kluwer Academic Publishers, 1994.

Bakker, Age, H. Boot, O. Sleijpen, W. Vanthoor, eds. Monetary Stability Through International Cooperation. Preface by Willem F. Duisenberg; Age Bakker, eds. The Netherlands: Kluwer Academic Publishers, 1994.

Barnes, Ian and Pamela Barnes. The Enlarged European Union, New York: Longman Group U.K. Ltd., 1995.

Bini-Smaghi, Lorenzo. "Europe 1992 and Monetary Union," in Vori, Silva and Lorenzo Bini-Smaghi, Toward Monetary Union in the European Community: Why and How, Trento, Italy, 1990.

Cecchini, Paolo. The European Challenge, 1992: The Benefits of a Single Market, European Commission of the EC, U.K.: Wildwood House Ltd., 1988.

Crawford, Malcolm. One Money for Europe, London: The Macmillan Press Ltd., 1993.

Deane, Margorie and Robert Pringle. The Central Banks, New York: Penguin Books, 1994.

Debelle, Guy and Stanley Fischer. "How Independent Should a Central Bank Be?" in Jeffrey C. Fuhrer, ed., Goals, Guidelines and Constraints Facing Monetary Policymakers (Conference Proceedings), Federal Reserve Bank of Boston, June 1994.

De Cecco, Marcello and Alberto Giovannini. A European Central Bank: Perspectives on Monetary Unification after Ten Years of the EMS, Center for Economic Policy Research, Cambridge: Cambridge University Press, 1989.

Dornbusch, Rudiger. Open Economy Macroeconomics, New York: Basic Books Inc., 1980.

Dornbusch, Rudiger. Two-track EMU, Now! In Britain and EMU, Center for Economic Performance in Association with Financial Markets Group, London School of Economics, 1990.

Dreze, Jacques H., Charles R. Bean, with the assistance of Jean Paul Lambert, Fati Mehta and Henri R. Sneessens, eds. Europe's Unemployment Problem, Cambridge, Massachusetts: MIT Press, 1990.

Eichengreen, Barry and Jeffry Frieden, Editors. The Political Economy of European Monetary Unification, Oxford: Westview Press, Inc., 1994.

El-Agraa, Ali M. Economics of the European Community (3rd ed.), New York: Philip Alan, 1990.

Ernst and Young, the National Institute of Economic and Social Research and the Association for the Monetary Union of Europe. A Strategy for the ECU. London: Kogan Page Ltd., 1990.

Fisher, Irving. The Purchasing Power of Money, New York: A.M. Kelly, Publishers, 1963 [1911].

Fisher, Irving. Theory of Interest as Determined by Impatience to Spend Income and Opportunity to Invest It, New York: The Macmillan Company, 1930.

Fratianni, Michele and Jurgen von Hagen. The European Monetary System and the European Monetary Union, Oxford: Westview Press, Inc., 1992.

Fratianni, Michele and Theo Peeter. One Money for Europe, New York: Praeger Publishers, 1979.

Friedman, Milton. Studies in the Quantity Theory of Money, Chicago: University of Chicago Press, 1956.

Friedman, Milton and Anna Schwartz. A Monetary History of the United States, 1967-60, Princeton, New Jersey: Princeton University Press, 1963.

Gros, Daniel and Erik Jones. Fiscal Shock Absorbers in the US, manuscript, Center for European Policy Studies, Brussels: July 1991.

Gros, Daniel, and Niels Thygesen. European Monetary Integration: From the European Monetary System to European Monetary Union, London: Longman Group UK Ltd., 1992.

Harrop, Jeffrey. The Political Economy of Integration in the European Community, London: Edward Elgar Publishing Limited, 1989.

Henning, Randall C., Eduard Hochreiter, and Gary Clyde Hufbauer. Reviving the European Union, Washington, D.C.: Institute of International Economics and the Austrian National Bank, 1994.

Hodgson, John S. and Mark G. Herands. International Economic Relations, New York: Prentice Hall, 1983.

International Currency Competition and the Future Role of the Single European Currency. The ECU Institute, London: Kluwer Law International, 1995.

Johnson, Christopher. In With The Euro, Out With The Pound, London: Penguin Books, 1996.

Keynes, John M. General Theory of Employment, Interest and Money, New York: Harcourt, Brace, & World, 1936.

Layard, Richard P.G., Stephen J. Nickell, Richard Jackman. Unemployment: Macroeconomic Performance and the Labor Market, Oxford, England; New York: Oxford University Press, 1991.

Lucas, Robert E. Studies in Business Cycle Theory, Cambridge: MIT Press, 1981.

Nevin, Edward. The Economics of Europe, London: Macmillan Education Ltd., 1990.

Nicoll, William and Trevor Solomon. Understanding the New European Community, New York: Harvester Wheatscheaf, 1994.

Nolling, Wilhelm. Monetary Policy in Europe After Maastricht, New York: St.

Martin's Press, Inc., 1993.

Orville, George. Animal Farm, New York: Harcourt Brace Publishing, 1946.

Pinder, John. European Community - The Building of a Union, London: Oxford University Press, 1991.

Spahn, Paul Bernd. The Community Budget for an Economic and Monetary Union, London: MacMillan Press Ltd., 1993.

Stiglitz, Joseph. Economics of the Public Sector, London: W.W. Norton & Company, 1986.

Temperton, Paul, ed. The European Currency Crisis, Cambridge: Probus Publishing Company, 1993.

Thygesen, Niels and Daniel Gros. Concrete Steps Towards Monetary Union, Brussels: Center for European Policy Studies (CEPS), 1989.

Vanhove, Norbert and Leo H. Regional Policy: A European Approach, London: Saxon House, 1980.

Vaubel, Roland. Strategies for Currency Unification: The Economics of Currency Competition and the Case for a European Parallel Currency, No.156. Germany: J.C.B. Mohr (Paul Siebeck) Tubingen, 1978.

Vaubel, Roland, and Emil-Mann Claassen, Editors. International and European Monetary Systems: Currency Unification, Currency Competition, and the Private ECU: Second Thoughts, New York: 1990.

Von Hagen, Jurgen and Fratianni, Michele. "The Transition to European Monetary Union and the European Monetary Institute," in Eichengreen, Barry and Jeffry Frieden, eds., The Political Economy of European Monetary Unification, Oxford: Westview Press, Inc., 1994.

Walras, Leon. Elements of Pure Economics (translated by William Jaffe), Homewood, Illinois: Irwin, 1954 [1874].

Walters, Sir Alan. Sterling in Danger: The Economic Consequences of Pegged Exchange Rates, London: Fontana/Collins, 1990.

Wicksell, Knut. Interest and Prices (translated by R.F. Kahn), London: Macmillan, 1936.

Wyplosz, Charles and D. Cohen. "The European Monetary Union: An Agnostic Evaluation," in Bryant, Ralph, David Currie, Jacob Frenkel, Paul Masson, Richard Portes, eds., Macroeconomic Policies in an Interdependent World, International Monetary Fund (IMF), Washington, D.C., 1989.

Yarbrough, Beth V. and Robert M. The World Economy: Trade and Finance, New York: Dryden Press, 1988.

SPECIAL PUBLICATIONS

[The] Bank for International Settlements (BIS) - 21st Annual Report, Basle: June 11, 1951.

[The] Bank for International Settlements (BIS) - Review No. 204, Basle: November, 1994.

Bofinger, Peter, Stefan Collighon, Christopher Johnson and Bertrand de Maigret. The EMS in Transition (a study prepared for the EU Parliament), Paris: Association for the Monetary Union of Europe, July 1993.

Ciampi, Carlo Azeglio. "An Operational Annex for an Integrated Monetary Policy in Europe," in Delors Committee for the Study of Economic and Monetary Union, Report on Economic and Monetary Union in the European Community, Luxembourg: Office for Official Publications of EEC, 1989.

Committee for the Study of Economic and Monetary Union. Report on Economic and Monetary Union in the European Community (known as the "Delors Report"), Luxembourg: Office for Official Publications of the European Communities, 1989.

Cottarelli, Carlo. "Limiting Central Bank Credit to the Government: Theory and Practice," IMF Occasional Paper, no: 110, Washington, D.C..

Deutsche Bank Research, "EMU Watch," no.23, Frankfurt, December 9, 1996.

Deutsche Bundesbank Annual Report, Frankfurt, 1993.

ECU/Euro: Towards European References? Ecu no.34; Ecu Activities, Brussels, 1996.

European Monetary Institute (EMI) 1994 Annual Report , Frankfurt am Main: EMI. April 1995.

"EU Commission Preliminary Draft General Budget of the EU for the Financial Year 1996," Brussels, EU Commission, May 1995.

"[The] European Union's Cohesion Fund," European Commission: Directorate-general for Information, Communication, Culture, Audiovisual, Luxembourg: Office of Official Publications of the EC, 1994.

"Exchange Rate Variability and World Trade," Occasional Paper no. 28, International Monetary Fund (IMF), Washington D.C., 1984.

Genscher, Hans D. "A European Currency Area and a European Central Bank," Memorandum, 1988.

Giovannini, Alberto. "Money Demand and Monetary Control in an Integrated European Economy," European Economy, Sp. Ed. no.1, Brussels/Luxembourg: Commission of the European Communities Directorate-General for Economic and Financial Affairs, 1991.

"Green Paper: On the Practical Arrangements for the Introduction of the Single Currency." EU Commission, Brussels: May 31, 1995.

Grice, Joe. "The U.K. Proposals for a European Monetary Fund and a 'Hard ECU': Making Process Towards an Economic and Monetary Union," Monetary Policy Division, Bank of England, London, November 1990.

"International Capital Markets: Developments, Prospects, and Policy Issues." International Monetary Fund (IMF), Washington, D.C., August 1995.

International Monetary Fund (IMF) Annual Report, Washington D.C., 1995.

Kenen, Peter. "Capital Controls, The EMS and EMU." Abstract taken from the actual reports of the Monetary Committee and Committee of Central Banks.

Leahy, M.P. "The Dollar as an Official Reserve Currency Under EMU," International Finance Discussion Papers, Board of the Governors of the Federal Reserve System, Washington, D.C., June 1994.

MacDougall, Sir Donald, Dieter Beiche, Arthur Brown, Francesvo Forte, Yves Freville, Martin O'Donoghue and Theo Peeters. "Public Finance in European Integration," Commission of the European Communities, Brussels, 1977.

McDougall, Sir Donald et al. Report of the Study Group on the Role of Public Finance in European Integration, Vol. I-II, Brussels: Commission of the Communities, 1977.

Molle, Willem and R. Morsink. "Direct Investments and Monetary Integration," European Economy; The Economics of EMU, Special Issue, Commission of the European Communities Directorate-General for Economic and Financial Affairs, 1991.

OECD Economic Outlook, Paris, 1991-1995.

"One Market, One Money: An Evolution of the Potential Benefits and Costs of Forming an Economic and Monetary Union." European Economy, No. 44, Commission of the European Communities Directorate-General for Economic and Financial Affairs, October 1990.

Pollard, Patricia S. "Central Bank Independence and Economic Performance," Federal Reserve Bank of St. Louis Economic Review, July/August, 1993.

"Practical Issues Arising from the Introduction of the Euro," Bank of England, London, September 1996.

"Progress Towards Convergence." European Monetary Institute (EMI), Frankfurt am Main, November 1995.

"Progress Towards Convergence 1996." European Monetary Institute (EMI), Frankfurt am Main, November 1996

Rainer, Marian. "Credit Swiss Financial Forecasts," European Commission, Brussels, 1996.

"Report on the Payment Systems in EC Member States." Committee of Central Bank Governors, 1992.

Sardelis, Christopher. "EC enlargement and the EFTA Countries," Commission of the European Communities, Economic Papers No. 100, March 1993.

"The Emerging Bond Asian Bond Market." The World Bank, Washington, D.C.: June 1995.

Tietmeyer, Hans. "The Role of an Independent central Bank in Europe" in Downes, Patrick and Reza Vaez-Zadeh, eds., The Evolving Role of Central Banks, International Monetary Fund (IMF), Washington, D.C., 1991.

Ungerer, Horst, Jouko J. Hauvonen, August Lopez-Clatos, and Thomas Mayer. European Monetary System: Developments and Perspectives, Occasional Paper no. 73, International Monetary Fund (IMF), Washington, D.C., November 1990.

[The] Union of 16, Phoenix No. 2, Association of Former Trainees of the European Union, Brussels: ADEK, Autumn 1994.

Vinals, Jose. "Building a Monetary Union in Europe" in Tomás J.T. Baliño and Carlo Cottarelli, eds. Frameworks for Monetary Stability: Policy Issues and Country Experiences, International Monetary Fund (IMF), Washington, D.C., 1994.

Weber, Axel A. "Asymmetries and Adjustment Problems: Some Empirical Evidence," European Economy, Commission of the European Communities Directorate-General for Economic and Financial Affairs, 1990.

Werner, Pierre, Baron Hubert Ansiau, Georg Brouwers, Bernard Clappier, Ugo Mosca, Jena-Baptiste Schollhorn, and Georgio Stammati. Commission of the European Communities, Report to the Council and the Commission on the Realization by Stages of Economic and Monetary Union in the Community, Luxembourg, 1970.

World Economic and Financial Surveys, "1993 International Capital Markets: Part I: Exchange Rate Management and International Capital Flows," International Monetary Fund (IMF), Washington, D.C., April 1993.

Wyplosz, Charles, in "Monetary Union and Fiscal Policy Discipline," European Economy, Special issue no.1, Commission of the European Communities Directorate-General for Economic and Financial Affairs, 1991.

ARTICLES

A Reply : "Capital Mobility and Size." Canadian Journal of Economics and Political Science, August 30, 1964.

Alesina, Alberto, and Lawrence H. Summers. "Central Bank Independence and Macroeconomic Performance: Some Comparative Evidence," Harvard Institute of Economic Research, Discussion Paper No.1496, 1990.

Alesina, Alberto, and Vittorio Grilli. "The European Central Bank: Reshaping Monetary Politics in Europe," National Bureau of Economic Research, Working Paper No.3860, 1991.

Arrowsmith, John. "Economic and Monetary Union in a multi-tier Europe," National Institute Economic Review, No. 152, May 1995.

Bishop, Graham. "Is There a Rapid Route to an EMU of the Few?" Economic and Market Analysis, London: Salomon Brothers, 1993.

Bishop, Graham. "The Creation of an EC Hard Money," Salomon Brothers, London: European Business Analysis, July 1990.

Bishop, Graham. "The EC's Public Debt Disease: Discipline with Credit Spreads and Cure with Price Stability," London: Solomon Brothers, May 1991.

Breadshaw, Jeremy. "Constitutional Reform After Maastricht," European Trends, First Quarter, 1994.

Britto, Andrew and David Mayes. "Achieving Monetary Union in Europe," U.K.: National Institute of Economic and Social Research, 1992.

"Comments in EMU: Will EMU Fly?" Merrill Lynch & Co., Inc. Global Securities Research & Economic Group, International Fixed Income Research, April 22, 1996.

"Consumer Europe," Euromonitor International, London, U.K., 1995.

Cukierman, Alex. "Interest Rates during the Cycle, Inventories and Monetary Policy: A Theoretical Analysis," Carnegie-Rochester Conference Series on Public Policy 15, 1981.

De Grauwe, Paul. "The Political Economy of Monetary Union in Europe," The World Economy, vol.16., no.6, November 1993.

Eichengreen, Barry. "One Money for Europe? Lessons from the US Currency Union," Economic Policy, No.1, April 1990.

Eichengreen, Barry. Is Europe an Optimum Currency Area?, No.478, Discussion Paper Series, London: Center for Economic Policy Research, November 1990.

Emminger, Otmar. "Capital Controls, The EMS and EMU (translated by Peter Kenen)," The Economic Journal, Royal Economic Society, London: Blackwell Publishers, January 1995.

"EMU: The State of Play," The World Today, Vol. 51, The Royal Institute of International Affairs, April 1995.

"European Marketing Data & Statistics," Euromonitor International, London, U.K., 1995.

Fleming, John M. "On Exchange Rate Unification," Economic Journal, 81, 1971.

Frankel, Jeffrey A. and Stephen Philips. " The European Monetary System: Credible at Last?," Oxford Economic Papers, v.44, October 1992.

Friedman, Milton. "The Role of Monetary Policy," American Economic Review, 58; March 1968.

Fry, Maxwell J. "Choosing a Money for Europe," Journal of Common Market Studies, September 1991.

Grilli, Vittorio, Donato Masciandro and Guido Tabellini. "Political and Monetary Institutions and Public Financial Policies in Industrial Countries," Economic Policy, October 13, 1991.

Gros, Daniel. "Paradigms for the Monetary Union of Europe," Journal of Common Market Studies, 1989.

Is Bigger Better? - The Economics of EC Enlargement. Annual Report, London: The Center for Economic Policy Research (CEPR), 1992.

Miles, David. "A Single European Currency: Options for the UK," London: Merrill Lynch Global Fixed Income Research, March 1, 1995.

Miles, David. "Fixed and Floating-rate Finance in the UK and Abroad," Bank of England Quarterly Bulletin, Vol.34, February 1, 1994.

"Monetary Union and European Unemployment," Center for Economic Policy Research (CEPR), Discussion Paper No. 1458, London, October 1996

Mundell, Robert. "A Theory of Optimum Currency Areas," American Economic Review, 51, 1961.

Phillips, Alban W. "The Relation Between Unemployment Rate and the Rate of Change of Money Wage Rates in the United Kingdom," Economica, 1961-1957, Vol.25, November 1958.

"Preparing for 1996 and a Larger European Union: Principles and Priorities." Center for European Policy Studies (CEPS), 1995.

Sachs, Jeffery and Xavier Sali-i-Martin. "Federal Fiscal Policy and Optimum Currency Areas," Working Paper, Harvard University; 1989.

Schlesinger, Helmut. "Auf Dem Weg aur Europaischen Wahrungsunion: Die Rolle des Europaischen Wahrunginstituts," Ahszuge aus Presseartikein 39, 1992.

Stiglitz, Joseph and Andrew Weiss. "Credit Rationing in Markets with Imperfect Information," American Economic Review, Vol. 71, No. 3, June 1981.

Tavlas, George S. "The Theory of Optimum Currency Areas Revised," Finance & Development, June 1993.

Triffin, Robert. "The Intermixture of Politics and Economics in the World Monetary Scandal," American Economist, 1989.

Vaubel, Roland. "Currency Competition and the European Monetary Integration," The Economic Journal, London: Royal Economic Society, 100, no.402, September 1990.

Von Hagen, Jurgen. "Fiscal Arrangements in a Monetary Union: Evidence from the U.S.," Discussion Paper #58, Center for Global Business, Indiana University, May 1991.

Williamson, John. "Fundamental Equilibrium Exchange Rates," National Institute of Economic and Social Research Review, December 1991.

NEWSPAPERS AND MAGAZINES

"A Special Sponsored Section: Commercial Banks." Institutional Investor, August 1995.

Amato, Giuliano's February 23, 1988 memorandum to the ECOFIN Council, published as "Un motore perlo SME" in the Italian newspaper *Il Sole*.

Berlusconi, Silvio. Quoted in the German weekly, Welt am Sonntag, April 14, 1996.

[The] Economist: 1994 (November 4 and 12) and 1996 (April 6).

"European Union: European Christian Democrats Adopt Skin-Deep Consensus." European Information Service - European Report, April 4, 1995.

"Euromoney: 1995 Guide to Developments in the World's Equity and Bond Markets." Euromoney, 1995.

Euromoney Handbook, September 1994.

Financial Times: 1989 (December 12), 1992 (September 22, November 5), 1993 (November 10), 1995 (March 21, November 15), 1996 (January 19, June 24, July, August 9, September 19, September 24, September 27, October 1, October 8, October 9, October 17, November 20, November 23, December 3, December 17, December 17), and 1997 (January 24).

"Greece: Financing Foreign Operations." Economist Intelligence Unit, December 1995.

"Holiday Money." Bureau Européen des Unions de Consommateurs (BEUC), July 1988.

"Kohl's Re-election Bestows Added Clout in Setting the European's Course." The Wall Street Journal, October 18, 1994.

Lemmen, J.J.G. and S.C.W. Eijffinger. "The Degree of Financial Integration in the European Community," The Economist, V141, NR2, 1993.

Lovell, Jeremy. "EU at the Crossroads, Veto Should Go, EU Socialists Say," Reuter News, Brussels, January 31, 1995.

Meares, Richard. "Britain Vows to Opt to Veto EU Constitutional Changes," Reuter News, London, January 8, 1995.

"Multispeed Europe 'Inconceivable' EP Says." Reuter Community Report, Strasbourg, September 29, 1994.

Murphy, Richard. "Britain Floats Proposal on European Integration." Reuter News, Bonn, February 20, 1995.

"Number One and Bringing Billions Home for Britain." Evening Standard, March 13, 1995.

"Portugal: Financing Foreign Operations." Economist Intelligence Unit, May 1995.

Reuters News. AL41Oreuec-rf. Brussels: EU Parliament-IGC. January 30, 1995.

"Spain: Financing Foreign Operations." Economist Intelligence Unit, July 1995.

"United Kingdom: Financing Foreign Operations." Economist Intelligence Unit, August 1995.

Walden Country Reports (January 1995 updates).

APPENDIX A:

KEY DATES IN THE HISTORY OF EUROPEAN INTEGRATION:

Appendix A provides a detailed chronological summary of the events leading to the formation of the European Union.

1946	**September:**	In Zurich speech, Winston Churchill proposes "United States of Europe" and creation of a "Council of Europe."
1947	**June:**	George Marshall, US Secretary of State, proposes program for European recovery ("Marshall Plan").
1948	**January:**	The Netherlands, Belgium, and Luxembourg create customs union ("Benelux").
	March:	Brussels Treaty: Britain, France plus Benelux states. A treaty of collective defense against Soviets (and initially Germany).
	April:	Organization for European Economic Co-operation (1960 OECD) formed by sixteen European states + US/Canada (1960).
	May:	European Congress in the Hague proposes European Union and a College of Europe.
1949	**January:**	Establishment of CMEA by seven East-bloc countries.
	April:	North Atlantic Treaty signed in Washington (10 countries).
	May:	Statute of Council of Europe signed in Strasbourg by ten states.

	August 9:	Council of Europe inaugural session. Greece and Turkey invited to join.
	August 24:	North Atlantic Treaty enters into force.
1950	**May:**	The French Foreign Minister, Robert Schuman, in a speech inspired by Jean Monnet, proposes that France, the Federal Republic of Germany and any other European country wishing to join them should pool their coal and steel resources. "Benelux" and Italy join.
	June:	UK refuses to join ECSC.
	June:	Proposals for a European army or a European Defense Community.
1951	**April:**	Belgium, France, the Federal Republic of Germany, Italy, Luxembourg, and the Netherlands (known as the Six) sign the Treaty of Paris establishing the European Coal and Steel Community (ECSC) on April 18. Parliaments ratify the Treaty in winter 1951-spring 1952; the United Kingdom declines membership.
	May:	The Treaty establishing the European Defense Community (EDC) is signed in Paris by ECSC Six.
1952	**July:**	ECSC Treaty enters into force.
1953	**January:**	First European tax: ECSC levy.
1954	**August:**	The French Parliament rejects the EDC Treaty.
	October:	Following the London Conference, agreements on a modified Brussels Treaty are signed in Paris, and the Western European Union (WEU) comes into being with the admission of FRG and Italy.
	November:	Protesting failure of EDC, Jean Monnet resigns from ECSC presidency.
1955	**June:**	The foreign ministers of the Six, meeting in Messina, decide to extend European integration to all branches of the economy.
	June:	Intergovernmental committee, headed by Belgian Paul-Henri Spaak, set up to pursue economic union and union in nuclear energy.
1956	**May:**	Spaak Report approved in Venice - talk begins of European Economic Community and atomic energy community (EURATOM). As talk of "common" policies increases, United Kingdom declines to participate and proposes European free trade area in October 1956.
1957	**March:**	The Six sign the Treaties of Rome establishing the European Economic Community (EEC), including European Investment Bank (EIB) and the European Atomic Energy Community (EURATOM) on March 25. The Treaties of Rome together with the Treaty of Paris form the Constitution of the European Community. Parliaments ratify within a few months. Stated objectives are customs union with free movement of goods, ending trade quotas and barriers; free movement of services and capital. Also, to provide common policies in international trade, agriculture, transport, and social matters. Foreign and defense policies to remain under control of member states. Jean Monnet is credited as a leading force behind the Treaties of Rome. Maudling OEEC talks between the Six and other OEEC members.
1958	**January:**	EEC and EURATOM Treaties take effect. By spring, respective Council of Ministers and Commissions are in place. Commission presidents are Walter Hallstein and Louis Armand.

	March:	EEC Council decision drawing up rules governing the Monetary Committee established by EEC Article 105. Committee to review the monetary and financial situation in the member states and Community as a whole and to review system of currency payments in the Community.
	March:	First session, in Strasbourg, of European parliamentary Assembly of the Six; Schuman is the presiding president.
	December:	West European countries restore convertibility of their currencies under IMF articles of Agreement. End of European Payments Union. Succeeded by European Monetary Agreement.
1959	**January:**	The first step is taken toward eliminating customs duties between member states and toward establishing a common external tariff.
	June-July:	Greece and Turkey apply to become associated states.
1960	**January:**	The Stockholm Convention establishing the European Free Trade Association (EFTA) is signed on the initiative of the United Kingdom.
	May:	European Free Trade Association (EFTA) is formed - Austria, Denmark, Norway, Portugal, Sweden, Switzerland, and the United Kingdom, with Finland as an associate member. Iceland joins in 1971; Denmark and the United Kingdom leave in 1972; Finland becomes full member in 1986.
	May:	Six create European Social Fund. EEC Council adopts directive to free certain capital movements in the Community.
	September:	De Gaulle proposes regular political summit meetings of Six and referendum on Europe of Nations.
	December:	OEEC becomes OECD and includes United States and Canada.
1961	**February:**	First summit of the Six meets in Paris.
	July 9:	Signature of Treaty of association of Greece with EEC.
	July 18:	Second European summit, in Bad Godesberg, proposes a Union of European States.
	July-August:	Ireland, Denmark, Norway and the United Kingdom apply for membership of EC.
	August 13:	Berlin wall erected.
	September:	First regulation on free movement of workers comes into force.
	September 30:	OECD convention enters into force.
	October:	European Social Charter (Council of Europe).
	December:	Austria, Sweden and Switzerland apply for EEC associate membership.
1962	**January:**	Common Agricultural Policy (CAP) starts. Based on single market and prices for most products; preservation of comparable living standards for agricultural workers and workers in other sectors; preferences for Community products; establishment of European Agricultural Guidance and Guarantee Fund (EAGGF) to support objectives of CAP.
	February-May:	Spain and Portugal request EC association.
	December:	Movement of capital freed within Six.
1963	**January 14:**	General de Gaulle announces at a press conference that France will veto the United Kingdom's accession to the Community.
	January 22:	Franco-German Treaty of Friendship.
	May:	EEC Council approves agreement with Associated States.
	July:	An association agreement is signed between the Community and

		eighteen African countries in Yaounde.
	September:	Turkey and EC sign association agreement.
1964	**April-May:**	Committee of Governors of Central Banks of the EEC is set up - to review credit policies and confer on monetary measures before implementation. Member states asked to consult before changing exchange rate parities. Budgetary Policy Committee is set up, as well as Medium-Term Economic Policy Committee.
	July:	The European Agricultural Guidance and Guarantee Fund (EAGGF) begins operating to implement the CAP.
1965	**April:**	A Treaty merging the executives of the three Communities is signed in Brussels. It enters into force on July 1, 1967.
	July:	France rejects the Commission's Initiative 1964, which sought to make the EC financially autonomous, extend the powers of the European Parliament, and widen the application of qualified majority voting in the Council; thereafter it boycotts Community meetings.
1966	**January:**	The 1965 crisis is solved by the Luxembourg Compromise, which states that the other EC member states will not overrule a country that opposes a piece of draft EC legislation on the ground that a vital national interest is at stake. France resumes its seat in the Council in return for retention of the unanimity requirement in such cases.
	May:	CAP rules agreed. Six decide to reach customs union by July 1, 1968.
1967	**February:**	First steps toward harmonization of turnover taxes, leading to EC VAT system in 1970.
	May:	Denmark, Ireland and the United Kingdom re-apply for Community membership.
	July:	The Treaty provisions enter into force establishing a single Council and a single Commission to administer the EEC, the ECSC, and EURATOM. Norway applies for EEC membership.
	December:	Six fail to agree on enlargement.
1968	**July:**	EC customs union is completed, 18 months ahead of the 12-year schedule in the EEC Treaty. All customs duties are eliminated in intra-Community trade and the Common External Tariff (CET) is introduced.
1969	**February:**	The Commission's memo on the coordination of economic/monetary policies -- the Barre Report -- is issued. It emphasizes the need for compatible medium-term policies. Establishes proposals for short-term monetary support and medium-term financial assistance facilities for the Community.
	July:	The Council supports much of the Barre Report, calling for increased consultations among member states before short-term policy shifts likely to affect other members considerably and approving in principle the establishment of short-term monetary support facility.
	December:	At the Hague Summit the Community's heads of state or government decide to bring the transitional period to an end by adopting definitive arrangements for the Common Agricultural Policy (CAP) and agreeing in principle to give the Community its own resources. They declare that the Community has reached the final stage provided for in the Rome Treaties; they also call for an Economic and Monetary Union, strengthened EC institutions, and closer political cooperation.

Committee is formed in March 1970, headed by Pierre Werner, Prime Minister of Luxembourg.

1970 February: Governors of EC central banks agree to system of short-term monetary support. Currently available to all EC central banks, regardless of whether currencies are participating in the EMS exchange rate mechanics.

April: A Treaty providing for the gradual introduction of an own resources (customs duties plus share of VAT) system is signed in Luxembourg. It also extends oversight powers of the European Parliament.

June: Negotiations with four prospective member states (Denmark, Ireland, Norway and the United Kingdom) open in Luxembourg.

October: Final version of Werner Report establishes a program for the creation in stages of an Economic and Monetary Union by 1980. Envisages a union with (1) a single Community currency, or de facto single currency, with member currencies at irreversibly fixed exchange rates (with gradual narrowing of margins); (2) complete liberalization of capital movements within the Community; (3) common central banking system, organized like the U.S. Federal Reserve System, involving common management of internal and external monetary policies; (4) centralized economic policy-making body politically responsible to the European Parliament; and (5) fiscal policy coordination.

1971 March: The Council adopts a resolution on the gradual achievement by 1980 of Economic And Monetary Union. Outlines steps to be taken in an initial three-year program, including narrowing the margins of fluctuation among EC currencies, and draws up plans for a European Monetary Cooperation Fund. Implementation is disrupted by the monetary crises of 1971. In May 1971, the floating of the Deutsche mark and the Netherlands guilder; in August 1971, the United States suspends convertibility of the dollar into gold, jeopardizing the Bretton Woods system.

March: Medium-term financial assistance facility is set up. Funds are to come from member states, and decisions to be taken by finance ministers.

1972 January: The Treaty on the Accession of Denmark, Ireland, Norway and the United Kingdom is signed in Brussels. Rapidly ratified by all except Norway, where Accession Treaty is defeated in referendum. Community of nine effective January 1, 1973.

March: European common margins arrangement ("snake") is instituted, a year before the final collapse of Bretton Woods system. Involves maintaining narrow margins of exchange rate fluctuations around pegged rates among EC currencies, while maintaining fixed -- but wider -- margins against the dollar. Exchange rates among snake currencies to fluctuate in a 2 1/4 percent band (the snake), while the whole group would fluctuate within a 4 1/2 percent band against the dollar (the "tunnel," established by the Smithsonian Agreement of December 1971). When superseded by the EMS in March 1979, the Deutsche mark, Netherlands guilder, Belgian-Luxembourg francs, and the Danish krone still in the snake. At various times, France, Italy, the United Kingdom, Ireland, Norway, and Sweden participate in, or associate their currencies with, the snake.

September: Norway withdraws its proposed membership following a referendum.

October: First EC summit of the "Nine," in Paris.

1973	**January:**	Denmark, Ireland and the United Kingdom become members of the EC; the Six become the Nine. Denmark and UK leave EFTA.
	March:	With the move to floating exchange rates, defined margins for EC exchange rates against the dollar (the "tunnel") end.
	October:	Oil and economic crisis in Europe (and elsewhere).
1974	**April:**	First Gymnich informal meeting of foreign ministers. European Monetary Coordination Fund is established by the Council of Ministers. Referred to as EMCF or FECOM (the French initials), it administers short-term central bank credit facilities.
	December:	At the Paris Summit the Community's heads of state of government decide to meet three times a year as the European Council, give the go-ahead for direct elections to the European Parliament and agree to set up the European Regional Development Fund (ERDF). This summit supersedes the earlier summits.
1975	**February:**	A First Convention between the Community and 46 states in Africa, the Caribbean and the Pacific is signed in Lome.
	March:	European unit of account (EUA) is introduced, based on a basket of EC currencies.
		Dublin - First European Council meeting.
	June:	"Yes" to continued membership in United Kingdom referendum; Greece applies for membership.
	July:	A Treaty giving the European Parliament wider budgetary powers and establishing a Court of Auditors is signed. It enters into force on June 1, 1977.
1976		EUA is adopted as unit of account for the European Coal and Steel Community.
	July:	EEC opens membership negotiations with Greece.
1977	**March:**	Portugal applies for Community membership.
	July:	Customs union complete between Six and Three. EEC/EFTA free trade agreements in force. Spain applies for Community membership.
1978		EUA first used for EC budgets; EUA renamed Ecu.
	July:	At the Bremen European Council, France and the Federal Republic of Germany present a scheme for closer monetary co-operation (the European Monetary System) to replace the currency "snake."
	December:	European Council adopts a resolution of establishment of the EMS.
1979	**February:**	The European Court of Justice issues the *Cassis de Dijon* decision, based on Article 30 of the Treaty of Rome, pointing the way toward member state "mutual recognition" of other member state standards.
	March:	The European Monetary System (EMS) comes into force with an agreement between the EC central banks. It has four main components: a European currency unit (Ecu), an Exchange Rate Mechanism (ERM), credit facilities, and transfer agreements. All EC countries become members of the EMS but the United Kingdom does not participate in the exchange rate mechanism (ERM). Greece as well as Spain and Portugal join the EMS in 1981 and 1986, respectively, after joining the EC, but initially do not participate in the ERM. Spain enters the ERM in June 1989, and the United Kingdom in October 1990. Creation of

		Ecu, based on same basket of currencies as EUA.
	May:	The Treaty on the Accession of Greece is signed; it becomes the tenth EC member on January 1, 1981.
	June:	First direct elections to the European Parliament are held.
	October:	A Second Convention between the Community and 58 states in Africa, the Caribbean and the Pacific (ACP) is signed in Lome.
	November:	At the Dublin European Council Summit Margaret Thatcher calls for reduction of UK contribution to EC budget.
	December:	European Parliament for first time does not approve proposed Community budget.
1980	**April:**	Luxembourg European Council Summit fails over agricultural budget and UK contribution to EC budget.
	May:	Council of Ministers agrees on two-thirds reduction of UK contribution; raises agricultural prices 5 percent.
1981	**January:**	The Ecu replaces the EUA in the Community's general budget. Greece joins the EC; the Nine becomes the Ten.
1982	**February:**	Greenland referendum: withdrawal from EEC.
1983	**June:**	Stuttgart "Solemn Declaration on European Union."
1984	**February:**	European Parliament Draft Treaty establishing the European Union.
	June:	Direct elections to the European Parliament are held for the second time. At the Fontainebleau European Council, the Ten reach an agreement on the compensation to be granted to the United Kingdom to reduce its contribution to the Community budget.
	September:	Revision of Ecu basket to include Greek drachma and to adjust weights of the other currencies.
	December:	A Third Lome Convention between the Ten and the ACP states, now numbering 66, is signed in Togo.
1985	**January 1:**	First European passports issued. Jacques Delors becomes President of the EC Commission.
	January 14:	Addressing European Parliament, Delors proposes abolition of internal frontiers by January 1, 1993.
	March:	Jacques Delors unveils the idea of the 1992 single market program for the economic revival of Europe to the European Parliament. European Council agrees on entry of Portugal and Spain.
	June:	The EC Commission submits White Paper on Completing the Internal Market (drafted under the leadership of Lord Cockfield), identifying almost 300 decisions needed to eliminate the physical, technical, and fiscal barriers preventing the formation of a complete common market and restricting EC competitiveness with the United States and Japan. Sets a timetable for decisions through the end of 1992. Milan European Council Summit accepts Commission White Paper and calls an Intergovernmental Conference (IGC).
	December:	At the Luxembourg Council the Ten agree to amend the Treaties of Rome and to revitalize the process of European integration by drawing up a "Single European Act" (SEA).
1986	**January:**	Portugal and Spain become members of the European Community; the

		Ten become the Twelve. Finland full member of EFTA.
	February:	The Single European Act is signed.
1987	**February:**	The Commission adopts a program of action for the implementation of the Single Act entitled "The Single Act: A new frontier for Europe." President Delors presents the Commission's action program to the European Parliament. The challenge is one of establishing a common economic and social area, creating the conditions for stronger economic growth, acting decisively and in concert on matters of foreign policy, adapting the common agricultural policy to changing circumstances in the world, and ensuring that the financing of the Community is placed on a sound footing.
	April:	Turkey applies for EC membership.
	July:	The Single European Act comes into force. Main objective is to complete the internal market. Also creates a streamlined decision-making process for the EC. The Act allows passage of Council decisions by qualified majority in most areas rather than unanimity and increases the role of the European Parliament.
	September:	Basle/Nyborg Agreement. Central bank governors agree on measures liberalizing the financing of intramarginal interventions and on more flexible use of interest rates and fluctuation margins in case of exchange market pressure.
	November:	The European Parliament approves the Commission's action program for implementing the Single Act.
1988		Cecchini Report.
	January:	Commission proposes Second Banking Directive, which would allow banks to operate in any member state on a single license. Also increases the range of activities banks would be permitted to engage in (including activities in securities).
	February:	The Brussels European Council endorses the Commission's program of 15 February, 1987. The agreement of the heads of state or government after scarcely one year's negotiations leaves the way clear for the "Single Market" in 1992. Ministers Balladour (France), Amato (Italy), and Genscher (Germany) call for a strengthening of the EMS and the establishment of a European Central Bank (ECB).
	June:	Council of Ministers adopts a directive stipulating the complete liberalization of capital movements within the Community by July 1990. Extended transition periods granted to Portugal, Spain, Greece, and Ireland. Final approval on June 24, 1988. On June 27 and 28, the Hanover European Council instructs a committee chaired by Commission President Jacques Delors to make proposals on concrete steps leading towards Economic and Monetary Union (EMU). The so-called "Delors Committee" is scheduled to report to EC leaders at the June 1989 Madrid Summit.
	September:	Thatcher's "Bruges Speech" at the College of Europe, favoring a Europe of the nations over supranationalism.
	November 14:	Portugal and Spain join WEU.
	December:	At the Rhodes meeting, European Council highlights remaining obstacles to completion of the internal market in the areas of indirect tax harmonization and social policy.
1989	**April:**	The EC Commission presents a revised version of the proposed Second Banking Directive. In the amended directive, which incorporates a more

liberal formulation of reciprocity, banks from third countries providing "genuine national treatment" would not be prevented from entering the EC market. Genuine national treatment is defined as including "effective market access" and "competitive opportunities" for EC banks comparable to those available to domestic banks. The Delors Committee presents its findings in a report on Economic And Monetary Union in the European Community.

May: By early May, the EC Commission submits to the Council of Ministers 232 of the 279 pieces of legislation identified in the 1985 White Paper, with final Council agreement reached on just over half of the total.

June 15-18: Direct elections are held for the 518 seats of the European Parliament. Elections hold added significance owing to the new powers granted to the Parliament over the internal market program in the Single European Act.

June 19: The EC Council of Ministers reaches agreement in principle on the Second Banking Directive to become effective at the beginning of 1993.

June 19: Spain joins Exchange Rate Mechanism of the EMS, with a +/-6 percent fluctuation band as employed by the Italian lira.

June 26-27: At meeting in Madrid the European Council adopts the first stage of the Delors Report starting July 1, 1990 and requests that the competent bodies adopt the necessary provisions to initiate the first stage and organize an intergovernmental conference to initiate preparatory work required to "lay down the subsequent stages."

July 16: Spanish peseta joins EMS.

July 17: Austria applies for EC membership.

September 21: Revision of the Ecu basket to include the Portuguese escudo and the Spanish peseta and to adjust weights of the other currencies.

October: British Chancellor of the Exchequer Nigel Lawson resigns over Premier Thatcher's refusal to allow UK to join EMS.

November 9: Berlin Wall breached.

November 18: President François Mitterand calls EC "Summit" in Paris to discuss Eastern Europe and creation of a European Development Bank (later known as the European Bank for Reconstruction and Development (EBRD).

November: The British Chancellor of the Exchequer, John Major, rejects the idea of a single European currency and advocates a system of national currencies to compete within the framework of the EMS.

December 8-9: In Strasbourg, President François Mitterand, in his capacity as President of the European Council, declares that the necessary majority exists for convening an Inter-governmental Conference under Article 236 of the EEC Treaty to draft the amendments to the Treaties needed for the final stages of Economic And Monetary Union. Moreover, eleven heads of state of government adopt the Community Charter of the Fundamental Social Rights of Workers.

December 15: The Second Banking Directive is approved unanimously by the EC Council of Ministers. Member countries are to adapt their laws and regulations to reach compliance with the directive by January 1, 1993.

December 31: Mitterand proposes European Confederation.

1990 **January 1:** France abolishes remaining restrictions on capital movements ahead of July 1 deadline.

January 8: Italy adopts narrow margins (+/-2.25 percent) within the ERM, together with a modest devaluation of the central rate of the lira.

January 31: Gorbachev clears way for German re-unification.

March 2:	Belgium and Luxembourg abolish dual currency markets for the Belgian-Luxembourg francs.
March 12:	In preparation for the Economic Monetary Union (EMU), EC finance ministers amend the decisions of 1974 and 1964, respectively, concerning economic convergence and cooperation between central banks.
March 20:	The Commission sets out detailed ideas on EMU ("Economic Monetary Union: The Economic Rationale and Design of the System").
Mar./April:	Meeting of EC finance and economic ministers (ECOFIN) and central bank governors reveals considerable agreement on the ultimate objective of an Economic And Monetary Union (EMU).
April:	The European Council at a special meeting in Dublin states that it is "satisfied with progress achieved so far towards establishing the single market without frontiers" and asks the Intergovernmental Conference (IGC) on EMU to "conclude its work rapidly with the objective of ratification (of the Treaty amendment) by member states before the end of 1992," to coincide with the envisaged completion of the internal market. The Council confirms "its commitment to Political Union" and sets in motion an examination of Treaty changes, with the aim of strengthening the democratic legitimacy of the Union, by a second IGC to work in parallel with the IGC on EMU.
May 18:	FRG/GDR Treaty On Monetary Union signed in Bonn.
May 29:	European Bank for Reconstruction and Development (EBRD) established in London.
May:	Italy abolishes remaining restrictions on capital movements ahead of July 1 deadline.
June 20:	Then-UK Chancellor of the Exchequer John Major proposes circulation of ECU (new European single currency) in EC alongside national currencies.
June 22:	French parliament ratifies creation of EBRD. EC and European Investment Bank are full members. EC countries hold 51 percent of capital and majority of seats.
June:	The Belgian Government decides to tie the value of the Belgian franc to the Deutsche mark. On June 25 and 26, the Dublin European Council decides to convene the Inter-governmental conference on Economic and Monetary Union on December 13 and the Intergovernmental Conference on Political Union on December 14, 1990. The Council also welcomes progress toward completion of the internal market and calls for further progress in the areas of public procurement, investment services and insurance, and intellectual property.
July:	Full liberalization of capital movements comes into effect in eight member states. Exceptions continue to apply until the end of 1992 in four member states -- Spain, Portugal, Greece and Ireland -- which have not progressed as far as the others along the road to financial integration. Start of Stage I of Economic And Monetary Union involving increased coordination of individual economic policies and more intensive cooperation between central banks. Cyprus and Malta apply for EC membership.
July 2:	FRG/GDR Economic And Financial Union with single currency.
October 2:	At midnight GDR ceases to exist, is absorbed by FRG and becomes part of EC. Berlin capital of new state.
October 8:	In policy reversal, Britain joins other currencies in ERM. The U.K. government adopts a margin of fluctuation of +/-6 percent and pledges to adopt the narrow margin of +/-2.25 percent after an adjustment

		period.
	October 22:	Norway links its currency, the krone, to the Ecu and will allow the currency to fluctuate within a narrow band of +/-2.25 percent of its central rate with the Ecu.
	October:	The European Commission publishes a report ("One Market, One Money") evaluating the economic costs and benefits of the EMU.
	October 27-28:	At the European Council meeting in Rome, EC countries, except the United Kingdom, agree to start Stage II toward EMU on January 1, 1994, and to establish a new monetary institution at the beginning of this stage.
	November 1:	British Deputy PM Sir Geoffrey Howe resigns to protest PM Margaret Thatcher's opposition to EMS.
	November 22:	After failing to defeat Michael Heseltine on first leadership ballot, Margaret Thatcher resigns.
	November 28:	John Major becomes UK Prime Minister.
	December 12:	WEU Council backs Chancellor Kohl and President Mitterand calls for the EC to assume defense responsibilities to promote political and economic integration. Sweden's parliament agrees to EC membership application.
	December 13-14:	The Inter-governmental Conferences on Economic and Monetary Union and Political Union open in Rome on December 13 and 14.
	December 14:	EC Rome summit welcomes new UK "tone" under John Major.
1991	**January:**	CMEA decides dissolution, proposes OIEC. Germany and Yugoslavia invited to join new market-oriented body.
	June 17:	Iceland plans currency link to Ecu.
	June 20:	Bundestag decides by 337 votes to 320 to move to Berlin.
	June 24:	EC twelve agree on gradual VAT alignment (15 percent normal minimum, 5 percent reduced rate minimum).
	June 29:	Final dissolution of CMEA.
	July 1:	Sweden applies for EC membership.
	August 19:	Coup in Moscow; Gorbachev arrested; Yeltsin urges resistance. Western solidarity with Yeltsin and Gorbachev.
	August 21:	Gorbachev returns to Moscow.
	August 24:	Ukrainian parliament declares independence, subject to referendum (December 1). Soviet government replaced. Gorbachev resigns as CP general secretary.
	September 2:	Soviet Congress of Deputies debates new constitution (political independence, economic integration) supported by all republics except Baltics, Moldova, Georgia.
	September 17:	EC decides to consider membership application of Cyprus (which does not include Turkish controlled North).
	October 22:	EC and EFTA agree 19-nation European Economic Area (EEA).
	December 1:	Almost 90 percent majority for independence in Ukraine referendum. Leonid Kravchuk elected president.
	December 10:	The work of the Inter-governmental Conferences is completed a year later, and European Council agrees on the Treaty on European Union (Maastricht Treaty) in Maastricht: completion of Economic And Monetary Union and introduction of the single European currency by 1999 at the latest. Eleven agree to harmonize social legislation without UK.
	December 12:	Russian parliament ratifies new commonwealth.
	December 14:	European Court of Justice in Luxembourg rules proposed EEA court

		incompatible with the Treaty of Rome, causing postponement of Treaty signing.
	December 25:	President Gorbachev resigns; US recognizes new independent states.
1992	**February:**	The Twelve sign the Treaty on European Union (Maastricht Treaty) transforming the Community into an European Union. Finland announces decision to apply for EC membership.
	April:	The escudo enters the EMS.
	May:	House of Commons 1st reading approves Maastricht Treaty.
	June:	Danish referendum on the Treaty on EU is a "No" by 40,000 votes; the Irish referendum is a "Yes."
	July 2:	Luxembourg parliament ratifies Treaty on EU.
	July 17:	Belgian parliament approves Treaty on EU.
	September 16:	Britain and Italy withdraw from ERM.
	September 20:	French referendum on the Maastricht Treaty is a "Yes".
	October 16:	"Special" European Council meeting in Birmingham on October 16. The Council reviews "lesson" of Treaty on EU ratification, reaffirms subsidiarity principle.
	October 28:	Italy ratifies Treaty on EU.
	November 20:	Norwegian Parliament votes to re-apply for EC membership. Peseta and escudo devalued 6 percent, stay in ERM.
	December 3:	Danish reject proposals for softening Treaty on EU.
	December 6:	By 50.3 to 49.7 percent and 16 cantons to 7, Swiss electorate rejects membership in EEA, effectively also putting hold on Switzerland's application for EC membership.
	December 11-12:	Edinburgh Summit of European Council agrees concessions to Denmark on single currency, defense and EC citizenship. EC budget compromise set. Cohesion Fund approved.
	December 31:	SEA elimination of obstacles to free movement of goods and services across EC frontiers.
1993	**January 1:**	SEA "Single Market". Treaties of European Union (12), EEA (18) and social rights (11) scheduled to enter into force. Birth of Czech Republic and Slovakia as separate states.
	May	Danish second referendum, approval of Treaty on EU.
	July	U.K. Parliament approves Treaty on EU.
	August:	Collapse of ERM as mechanism moves to +/-15 percent currency bands.
	October:	German Federal Constitution Court rules in favor of ratification of Treaty on EU.
	November 1:	The Treaty on EU (Maastricht Treaty) goes into force. Name changed to European Union (EU).
1994	**January 1:**	Creation of European Monetary Institute (EMI).
1995	**January 1:**	EC Commission's terms extended to 5 years.
	May 8:	"Green Paper" by EMI.
	November:	1st EMI "Progress Towards Convergence" Report on EMU Maastricht Treaty convergence criteria.
	December:	European Council Summit in Madrid decides on single European currency name to be the "Euro."
1996	**January 1:**	EC constitutional conference.
	April:	European Council Summit officially starts the IGC to review the

		Maastricht Treaty and EU institutional and decision-making reform. Verona, Italy ECOFIN Council discuss the creation of a new ERM II.
	June 21-22:	Florence, Italy, European Council Summit officially decide to go ahead with planning and designing ERM II, suspend decision on how to handle the Maastricht ERM convergence criteria until mid-1997.
	September:	ECOFIN Council meet in Dublin, Ireland to agree informally on the broad outline of the new ERM II and prepare report for Dublin European Council Summit in December 1996.
	November	2nd EMI "Progress Towards Convergence" Report on EMU Maastricht Treaty convergence criteria.
	December:	European Council Summit meet in Dublin. ERM II agreed upon to begin on January 1, 1999. Post-EMU fiscal "Stability and Growth Pact" agreed upon.

Future deadlines:

1997:	**November:**	3rd EMI "Progress Towards Convergence" Report on EMU Maastricht Treaty convergence criteria.
1998:		Decision on which countries participate in EMU. EU legislation establishing a central bank and introduction of the "Euro". Production of European banknotes and coins. Starts public campaign information.
	March:	French parliamentary elections.
	October:	German national elections.
1999	**January 1:**	Creation of European Central Bank (ECB), irrevocable locking of exchange rates, beginning of a common European monetary policy, and introduction of the European single Currency, the Euro, in non-cash form. New ERM II begins.
1999 - 2001:		New public debt expected to be issued in the Euro. The ECB will conduct single monetary; provide conversion facilities between national and European monetary units; support market efforts to ensure smooth functioning of a money market in the Euro; support efforts to develop a foreign exchange market in the Euro; exchange national banknotes at par value; monitor changeover developments in the banking and finance industry; co-operate with public and financial bodies in orderly changeover of both the public and private sectors. ECOFIN (in conjunction with the ECB) to conduct Euro foreign exchange policy.
2002	**January 1:**	Introduction of the Euro in notes and coins.
	July 1:	All EMU participants' national currencies obsolete. The Euro becomes the sole legal tender of EMU participants.

ABOUT THE AUTHOR

Dr. Scheherazade S. Rehman is an Assistant Professor of International Finance at the School of Business and Public Management's International Business Department of the George Washington University in Washington D.C. She is also the Director of the Joint International MBA-MA Degree Programs. Prior to joining the University, she was a foreign exchange and money market trader. Dr. Rehman has edited *Financial Crisis Management In Regional Blocs* (1997) and authored numerous articles on various aspects of international financial/business, central banking, trade and investments. She is a Senior Associate of the International Consultants Group in Washington D.C. and regularly consults with agencies such as OPIC, the World Bank and USAID. Dr. Rehman holds a Ph.D. from the George Washington University in Washington D.C.

INDEX

A

B

C

F

G

H

I

J

K

L

M

N

O

P

R

S

T

U

W